BRITAIN & JAPAN
BIOGRAPHICAL PORTRAITS
VOLUME V

Major General F.S.G. Piggott with Crown Prince Akihito and Princess Chichibu, Tokyo, 1955

BRITAIN & JAPAN

Biographical Portraits

VOLUME V

Edited by

HUGH CORTAZZI

GLOBAL
ORIENTAL

BRITAIN & JAPAN: BIOGRAPHICAL PORTRAITS
Volume V
Edited by Hugh Cortazzi

First published 2005 by
GLOBAL ORIENTAL
PO Box 219
Folkestone
Kent CT20 2WP

www.globaloriental.co.uk

© Japan Society Publications 2005

ISBN 1–901903–48–6 [Case]

British Library Cataloguing in Publication Data
A CIP entry for this book is available
from the British Library

SPECIAL THANKS
The Joint Chairmen and the Council of the Japan Society and the Editor
and Publishers of this book wish to express great thanks to the following
organizations for their support: The Anglo-Japanese History Project, The
Daiwa Anglo-Japanese Foundation and The Great Britain Sasakawa
Foundation.

Set in Bembo 11 on 11½ point
Typesetting by Bookman, Hayes, Middlesex
Printed and bound in Great Britain by Antony Rowe Ltd., Chippenham, Wilts

Table of Contents

For Jim Hoare

Acknowledgements

THE EDITOR and publisher wish to thank the following: the National Portrait Gallery for permission to use the photographs of Lord Hankey and R.A. Butler; the Archives of the Japanese Foreign Ministry for permission to use the photographs of Komura Jūtarō, Chinda Sutemi and Matsui Keishirō. They are also grateful to Oxford University Press for permission to reproduce the essay on 'Enright in Japan' by the late Russell Greenwood in *Life by Other Means: Essays on D.J. Enright*, OUP, 1990.

Introduction

HUGH CORTAZZI
Compiler & Editor

THE EDITOR and the Japan Society are very grateful to all the contributors, who have provided their essays without any recompense. We owe them a great debt of gratitude for all their efforts to research the subjects of their essays and to write these up in a suitable form for inclusion in our volume. We have once again managed to find portrait photos of the personalities in this volume, believing that even what might be considered a poor photograph adds an extra dimension to a written portrait.

The editor wishes to record his particular thanks to Professor Ian Nish who has provided no less than five of the portraits that appear here. Without his help and advice the volume might never have been produced.

Britain and Japan: Biographical Portraits, Volume V is the seventh volume in a series of publications devoted to personalities who have been active in Anglo-Japanese relations. In addition to the four other volumes of Biographical Portraits the Society published in 1991 *Britain and Japan: Themes and Personalities 1859-1991* and in 2001 *Japan Experiences; Fifty Years, One Hundred Views, 1945-2000*. This fifth volume of Portraits includes over forty British and Japanese personalities in a wide range of careers and activities whose lives and achievements in Japan and Britain are worthy of record. Some of the subjects were controversial figures and the views expressed about them, of course, are those of the individual contributors.

Japanese names in the text are in the Japanese order, i.e. surname first and given name second. The names of Japanese contributors are in the normal English order of given name followed by surname.

A short bibliography of books about British personalities and Japan was contained in *Britain and Japan: Biographical Portraits*, Volume IV, 2002, pages xiv and xv. An index of biographical portraits in books published for the Japan Society up to and including this fifth volume is contained in the preliminary pages. This index, however, does not cover the contributors to *Japan Experiences, Fifty Years, One Hundred Views: Post-War Japan*

Through British Eyes, 1945-2000, Japan Library 2001. The largely autobiographical accounts in *Japan Experiences* do, however, throw some light on British personalities who had close contacts with Japan in the post-war era and contributed to Anglo-Japanese relations in the second half of the twentieth century. The book also included extracts from the writings of a few individuals who have been covered in volumes of biographical portraits published since 2001 such as Eric Ceadel, Richard Storry, George Fraser, Dennis Enright and Hessell Tiltman, all of whom are the subject of biographical portraits in this volume.

☐

In my introduction to Volume IV I said that there was no question of our 'scraping the barrel' to find people to write about. The contents of this volume confirm that assertion and I know that there are a number of other Anglo-Japanese personalities who should be covered if the Society can find the means to produce further volumes and suitable contributors can be found to volunteer their services.

I have once again attempted to put the portraits under different headings rather than list them chronologically. It was not always easy to decide on the correct category in which to put a subject as some qualified for inclusion in more than one category. Terashima Munenori, for example, was both a politician and a diplomat as were some of the other Japanese heads of mission in London. Frank Hawley was a scholar and bibliophile as well as a journalist, but grouping the portraits may help the reader to find what interests him/her most.

This volume begins with portraits of two of the founding members of the Japan Society. The first Chairman of the Council of the Society in 1892 was Dr William Anderson who had a distinguished career in Japan and Britain as a surgeon and teacher and who was also a major collector and historian of Japanese art. His collection still forms a significant part of the British Museum's collection of Japanese paintings. One of his friends was Marcus Huish, the managing director of The Fine Art Society in New Bond Street, who was also a founding member and in his turn went on to become Chairman of the Council of the Society. These two portraits underline the Society's work over the years in the promotion of British understanding of Japanese art.[1]

Next come essays about members of the Japanese Imperial family. Dorothy Britton staunchly defends the reputation of Prince Chichibu. The Prince who spent a short time at Magdalen College, Oxford, in the inter-war years had a controversial role in Japan in the 1930s. Princess Chichibu, whose father had been Japanese Ambassador in London, was a sincere friend of Britain and supporter of both the Japan Society in London and the Japan-British Society in Japan. The present Emperor of Japan visited Britain a number of times as Crown Prince. These visits are

INTRODUCTION

the subject of the subsequent article by your editor. The most important of his visits, which was for the Coronation in 1953, was not only helpful in rehabilitating Japan's image in Britain but also reopening relations between the Imperial and Royal families.

In the section on politicians there are essays on a few of the Japanese and British personalities who were active in Anglo-Japanese relations in the century following the opening of Japan to the West. Andrew Cobbing, who wrote a biographical portrait of Mori Arinori, another Meiji leader who was Minister in London, has provided an illuminating picture of Terashima Munenori, who was not only the first Japanese Minister in London but also played an important role in Meiji diplomacy as Vice-Minister and later Minister for Foreign Affairs. Suematsu Kenchō and Kikuchi Dairoku were both Meiji era leaders who were educated at least partly in Britain. Ozaki Yukio, who is the subject of a portrait by Fujiko Hara, was the doyen of Japanese parliamentarians and was greatly influenced by British political thought and institutions. Lord Curzon was until recent years the only British Foreign Secretary who had ever made a serious visit to Japan. Ian Nish gives an interesting account of this arrogant imperialist's relationship with Japan. Antony Best in his piece on Lord Hankey and 'Rab' Butler describes their efforts in the years leading up to the Second World War to find an accommodation with Japan.

Portraits of the majority of British envoys in Japan up to 1972 have been included in previous volumes. Others as well as British 'scholar-diplomats' are covered in *British Envoys in Japan, 1859-1972* (Global Oriental, 2004), published this year. In this volume we have concentrated on the Japanese envoys to Britain who have not been the subject of portraits in other volumes. Ian Nish has added to his studies, contained in other volumes, of Japanese heads of Mission in London, accounts of the performance as Japanese Ambassador in London of Komura Jūtarō, Inoue Katsunosuke and Chinda Sutemi. Harumi Goto-Shibata has written on Hayashi Gonsuke and Tadashi Kuramatsu on Matsui Keishirō. This means that we have now covered all heads of mission from Aoki Shūzō in the 1890s to Shigemitsu Mamoru who was Japanese Ambassador at outbreak of the Second World War. Eventually, we should like to produce a parallel volume on Japanese Envoys in Britain from 1873 (Terashima Munenori) up to 1964 (Ambassador Ohno Katsumi).

The Japanese Imperial Navy had close contacts with the Royal Navy from the beginning of the Meiji period until relations deteriorated in the 1930s. It is appropriate, therefore, to include two interesting studies by John Chapman of Admirals Fisher and Pakenham and their relationships with Japan in the early years of the twentieth century. The loss of HMS *Rattler* off Cape Soya in 1868 struck me as odd and led me to investigate how this happened. The ship's captain, Commander Stephenson, was lucky to escape with a reprimand and to go on to become an Admiral.

This is in total contrast to the story told by Suzette Jarvis of Captain Oswald Tuck RN who played an important role in teaching Japanese to those involved during the war in attempting to decipher Japanese signals. Jerry Matsumura has produced an illuminating account of Takaki Kunihiro who, following training with British doctors in Japan and in England, became Surgeon-General to the Imperial Japanese Navy and did important medical research especially on beriberi.

In the last volume we covered a number of British businessmen in developing trade with Japan especially in the Meiji period. In this volume we have included pieces on important individuals who worked for three of the first Japanese firms to be established in Britain. Sadao Oba, who worked for Mitsui, tells the story of Mitsui's early attempts to develop trade. Hiroyuki Takeno explains the debt of Nippon Yusen Kaisha (NYK) to two British pioneers and their struggle to break into the world of the shipping conferences. Keiko Itoh, whose grandfather was the last head of the Yokohama Specie Bank in London, has recorded the history in London of what was Japan's first foreign exchange bank and the forerunner of the Bank of Tokyo (now merged with Mitsubishi Bank to form the Bank of Tokyo-Mistubishi). The Bank played an important role in financing the development of the pre-war Japanese economy. Edwin Green's piece on HSBC pioneers in Japan fills in a missing part from our coverage of British business interests in Meiji Japan.

British cultural relations with Japan owe a great deal to the British poets who have taught and worked in Japan. Edmund Blunden is the best known of these figures. In our last volume we included a fascinating account of the eccentric William Empson. In this volume there are descriptions of the life and work in Japan of four other British poets whose lively personalities and eccentricities made an impact on Japanese students and helped to spread understanding of English literature. George Hughes and John Hatcher, who have written lively portraits respectively of Robert Nichols and Ralph Hodgson, have been continuing the best British traditions in teaching in Japan. Eileen Fraser has contributed a portrait of her late husband, George Fraser, who succeeded Edmund Blunden in Tokyo in 1951. He was followed by Dennis Enright, about whom my late colleague Russell Greenwood wrote a piece in 1991, which with the permission of Oxford University Press is reprinted here. Japanese poets are represented by Nishiwaki Junzaburō, whom Norimasu Morita describes as a self-made Englishman.

The scholars included here are primarily British scholars of Japanese history and culture. Richard Storry, about whom Ian Nish has written a perceptive and informative essay, stands out both as a good scholar and warm personality. Eric Ceadel, who had studied Japanese under Captain Tuck at Bedford and about whom Peter Konicki has written, was the first lecturer in Japanese at Cambridge University and was responsible for building up the collection of Japanese books in the University Library. Louis Allen never held a university post in Japanese, but, as Phillida Purvis explains in her essay on this fascinating personality, his contributions to Japanese studies and to reconciliation between Britain and Japan were significant. John Corner, biologist and botanist, about whom Carmen Blacker has written a sympathetic piece, was criticized by some for doing what he could to preserve the botanical gardens and Raffles Museum in Singapore during the Japanese occupation, but dedication to science in his view transcended other considerations. Basil Robinson, formerly of the Victoria and Albert Museum, is the subject of a portrait by Yahya Abdelsamad. Robinson is known as an outstanding expert on Japanese swords. When Shakespearean scholarship is mentioned in the Japanese context we tend to think first of Tsubouchi Shōyō, about whom Brian Powell wrote an essay in *Themes and Personalities*, but as Peter Milward, who has contributed an essay on three Japanese scholars of Shakespeare, points out Japanese scholarship on Shakespeare is very much alive today.

Russell Kennedy, who is the subject of a contribution by Peter O'Connor, who wrote about some other journalists in Japan in Volume IV, is described as a spokesman for Japan and media entrepreneur. Hessell Tiltman of the *Manchester Guardian*, who is the subject of a biographical portrait by Roger Buckley, was a perceptive commentator and interpreter of Japan to western audiences. Frank Hawley is probably best known as the Tokyo correspondent of *The Times*, who tangled with General MacArthur during the allied occupation, but as Dr Manabu Yokoyama of Okayama explains he was primarily a bibliophile and Japanese scholar. Hasegawa Nyozekan, about whom Ayako Hotta-Lister has written an interesting account, was sometimes exaggeratedly enthusiastic about England and English thought.

Dr Thomas Baty and Bishop Heaslett were two totally different characters, but both spent long years in Japan. Dr Baty, legal adviser to the Japanese Foreign Ministry, was a controversial figure who was regarded, probably unfairly, by some British officials after the war as a traitor. Bishop Heaslett had a particularly difficult task as Bishop of South Tokyo in the pre-war years in trying to keep the Anglican Communion together against Japanese government pressures for the churches to accept the demands of State Shinto and was imprisoned on the outbreak of war.

To his accounts in the last volume of two judo masters, Koizumi Gunji and Trevor Leggett, Richard Bowen has added notes on three other pioneers of judo in Britain. Noboru Koyama, in addition to his essay on Kikuchi Dairoku, has drawn attention to the work of Yoshimoto Tadasu, who was himself visually impaired and who learnt much from Britain about how to help the blind in Japan.

One of the appendices (Ia) is a description and account of the development of the Commonwealth War Graves Cemetery at Hodogaya on the outskirts of Yokohama by Len Harrop who has done so much to make this cemetery a beautiful memorial to the war dead. This is followed by notes on the Yokohama Foreign General Cemetery by Geraldine Wilcox and on other British graves in Japan by Phillida Purvis.

---

1. For an account of this aspect of the Society's work please see my article in *Arts of Asia* volume 32, no 2, March–April 2002, published in Hong Kong.

Alphabetical List of Contributors to this Volume

BEST, Antony (Dr), Senior Lecturer in International History at the London School of Economics. His latest book is *British Intelligence and the Japanese Challenge in Asia 1914-1941*, Palgrave, 2002.

BLACKER, Carmen (Dr, OBE, FBA) Lecturer in Japanese at Cambridge 1958-91, author of books and articles relating to Japan.

BOWEN, Richard, Judo expert and writer.

BRITTON, Dorothy (Lady Bouchier), author, poet and composer, born in Japan, translator of classics by Bashō and Akutagawa. Has published books and articles on Japan, instrumental works with oriental themes and arrangements of Japanese folk music.

BUCKLEY, Roger, Professor at Temple University, Tokyo, historian and writer.

CHAPMAN, John W. M. (Dr), Hon. Senior Research Fellow, Scottish Centre for War Studies, University of Glasgow, historian specializing in naval, military and communications intelligence relating to Japan.

CLARK, Timothy (Dr), British Museum, curator and historian of Japanese art.

COBBING, Andrew (Dr), Professor of Japanese History at Kyushu University, author and historian specializing in Meiji Japan.

CORTAZZI, Hugh (Sir, GCMG), former British Ambassador to Japan 1980-84 and Chairman of the Japan Society 1985-95.

FRASER, Eileen, wife of the late George Fraser.

GORNALL, Martin, independent researcher and musician, preparing an account of Dr Baty's life on behalf of his family.

GOTO-SHIBATA, Harumi, Associate Professor of International History, Chiba University, historian and writer.

GREEN, Edwin, Group Chief Archivist, HSBC Holdings plc, London, author of books and articles on the history and archives of banking.

GREENWOOD, Russell (LVO) (deceased), formerly British Consul General at Osaka/Kobe.

HARA, Fujiko, President, Diplomatt Inc, Managing Director, Ozaki Yukio Memorial Foundation, Tokyo.

HARROP, Len, MBE, Lt Colonel (retired), formerly Supervisor for Japan for the ANZAC Agency of the Commonwealth War Graves Commission with responsibility for the Commonwealth War Graves cemetery at Hodogaya, Yokohama.

HATCHER, John, a Professor of English at Fukuoka University, author of *Laurence Binyon: Poet, Scholar of East and West*, Oxford, 1995.

HOTTA-LISTER, Ayako, (Ph.D from LSE), author of *The Japan-British exhibition of 1910*, researching aspects of Treaty Revision and the Anglo-Japanese Alliance

HUGHES, George, a Professor of English literature at Tokyo University; recent publications include *Reading Novels*, Vanderbilt UP, 2002 and *Hearn no wadachi no naka de*, Kenkyusha, 2002

ION, Hamish, Professor of History, Royal Military College of Canada

ITOH, Keiko, (PhD), writer, translator and interpreter, author of *The Japanese Community in Pre-War Britain: From Integration to Disintegration*, Curzon, 2001

JARVIS, Suzette, historian specializing in Japanese and Oriental history, guide and former trustee Bletchley Park

KORNICKI, Peter (Dr, FBA), Professor of Japanese history and bibliography at the University of Cambridge.

KOYAMA, Noboru, Librarian for the Japanese Collection at Cambridge University Library, historian.

KURAMATSU, Tadashi, Assistant Professor in International History, Aoyama Gakuin University, Tokyo.

MATSUMURA, Jerry. K. (MBE), formerly with the British embassy in Tokyo, Hugo Publications, and member of the board of directors of the World Trade Centre, Tokyo.

MILWARD, Peter (Father, SJ), Shakespeare scholar, writer and teacher.

MORITA, Normasu, (PhD), currently professor at the International College of Waseda University, co-author of *Marginalia: Kakureta Bungaku/Kakusareta Bungaku*, 2000.

NISH, Ian (CBE, Professor Emeritus, Dr), Professor of International History at the London School of Economics, author and historian.

NUMATA, Hideko, Curator of Yokohama Museum of Art.

OBA, Sadao, Researcher on the History of Anglo-Japanese Relations especially pre-war Japanese community in Britain, author of *The Japanese War*, Japan Library 1995

O'CONNOR, Peter, Associate Professor at Musashino Women's University, Tokyo, writer and historian, compiled (2003) *Japanese Propaganda: Selected Readings, series 1: Books 1872-1943*, in 10 Volumes and Series 2: Pamphlets

PURVIS, Phillida, Founder and Director of Links Japan, former member of HM Diplomatic Service and Deputy Director of the Daiwa Foundation.

RAWLINS, Sir John, Surgeon Vice-Admiral, KBE, FRCP, FRAeS.

RUXTON, Ian, Associate Professor, Department of Human Sciences, Kyushu Institute of Technology, author of two studies of Sir Ernest Satow.

LIST OF CONTRIBUTORS

TAKENO, Hiroyuki, joined NYK 1957, served in London 1967–71, director NYK 1988, Curator NYK Maritime Museum 1998

WILCOX, Geraldine, MBE, President of the Yokohama Foreign Cemetery Foundation 1990–97.

YAHYA ABDELSAMAD, research student at Kyoto University, working on Japanese contemporary history, son of a United Nations official and nephew of Sudanese Ambassador to Japan 1983–6.

YOKOYAMA, Manabu, Professor of Japanese History, Notre Dame Seishin University, Okayama, author of *Shomotsu ni miserareta eikokujin*, 2003, expert on the life and works of Frank Hawley.

Index of Biographical Portraits in Japan Society Publications

INDEX OF BIOGRAPHICAL PORTRAITS

PART I

Japan Society
and
Imperial Personalities

1

William Anderson, 1842-1900: Surgeon, Teacher and Art Collector

JOHN RAWLINS[1]

(with contributions from TIM CLARK, Dr SUMIO KANABE, JERRY K, MATSUMURA and HUGH CORTAZZI)

William Anderson

WILLIAM ANDERSON had a distinguished medical career in Japan and Britain. He became a scholarly collector and connoisseur of Japanese art and supported the foundation and development of the Japan Society in London of which he was the first Chairman of the Council.

EDUCATION

Anderson was born in London on 18 December 1842. He was educated at the City of London School and began the study of medicine at the University of Aberdeen, but he did not stay there long as he wanted to become an artist. He accordingly began to study at the Lambeth School of Art where he attained considerable proficiency as a draughtsman and received a medal for artistic anatomy. This may have been a factor in persuading him at the late age of twenty-two to return to the study of medicine. He began to study surgery at St Thomas's Hospital in 1864

3

under Sir John Simon and Professor Le Gros Clerk.[2] In successive years Anderson won the first College Prize, the Physical Society's Prize and the highly prestigious Cheseldon Medal. This was a remarkable achievement.

In 1867 he qualified as an MRCS (England) and in 1868 as an LRCP (London). In 1869 only five years after enrolling as a medical student Anderson passed the examinations required for a Fellow of the Royal College of Surgeons (FRCS), a qualification coveted by all British surgeons. After qualifying Anderson was for a time house surgeon at the General Infirmary in Derby but soon returned to St Thomas's where on the opening of the new hospital in 1871 he became a surgical registrar and demonstrator of anatomy. His study of artistic anatomy now proved helpful as he used anatomical drawings in teaching anatomy. His facility in producing and using such blackboard drawings evoked the admiration of successive generations of students. It was an innovation in medical teaching and unique among medical schools at that time.

AT THE NAVAL MEDICAL COLLEGE IN JAPAN

In 1873 he was selected by Terashima Munenori, then Japan's vice-minister for foreign affairs, from among various British candidates as professor of anatomy and surgery at the Imperial Naval Medical College[3] in Tokyo. He was granted a salary twice that of the senior naval doctor Totsuka Bunkai and became one of the British employees of the Japanese government (*o-yatoi gaikokujin*). The salary which he was offered by the Japanese government was sufficiently generous to enable him to marry Margaret Hall. The pair sailed for Japan to join other pioneers of Western science and medicine in that country.

At the medical college he had, to quote the obituary of him in the *Lancet*[4] 'to combine the duties of an almost universal professor'. He lectured not only on anatomy but also on physiology and surgery. At first, he was assisted by interpreters who had been students of Dr William Willis[5] who had established a medical school at Kagoshima. One of these was Takaki Kanehiro[6] who later became Surgeon General and was instrumental in eradicating beri-beri. Anderson seems to have rapidly gained a working knowledge of Japanese although English was in those days the main medium of instruction in Western sciences. He soon won the affection and respect of his pupils not least because of his mastery of the subjects which he taught.[7] The position seems to have suited Anderson whose 'unprejudiced and genial nature rapidly adapted itself to his new surroundings'.[8]

During the seven years of his appointment thirty-two students attended the college. Of these sixteen graduated.[9] There were eleven students initially when the naval medical college and hospital were first established on the site of the former Hosokawa (daimyo of Kumamoto) mansion at

Takanawa-dai[10] near Shinagawa. Students entering the college had to pass an exam in Japanese language, a foreign language, history and mathematics. At the college they had to study anatomy, physiology, internal medicine, surgery, and clinical examination. The Japanese had hoped that the first students could graduate in 1880, but the students were required to help the army in the Seinan war (the so-called Satsuma rebellion of 1877). Anderson accompanied his students to Kyushu and a field hospital was established at Fukuoka where they were engaged in measures to combat a cholera epidemic. As a result the students' graduation had to be postponed for a year.

Anderson was not only professor of anatomy and surgery, but also practised as a doctor examining and treating patients in the adjacent naval hospital. His ability as a draughtsman helped him to overcome the handicap resulting from his limited knowledge of the Japanese language. As a member of the central hygiene council he was also active in promoting examinations and preventative steps to deal with venereal diseases affecting naval personnel. According to Dr John Z. Bowers[11] the inadequate Japanese medical programmes for handling venereal disease led him to recommend, in 1876, the establishment of a special programme to train specialists in venereal diseases. His proposal was accepted by the Japanese authorities, and the men who completed the programme became effective directors of the Lock Venereal Hospital, which had heretofore been supervised by British doctors.

Anderson became medical officer to the British Legation in Tokyo.[12] He is reported to have 'lived on intimate terms with the diplomatic circle and the English colony'.[13] In this capacity and as one of the British specialist teachers in Japan Anderson must surely have come into contact with the redoubtable British Minister at that time, Sir Harry Parkes.[14]

We do not know for sure that Anderson ever met Dr William Willis,[15] who had come to Japan in 1862 as a doctor to the British Legation and stayed until 1877, but it seems likely that they may well have met when Willis spent some weeks in Tokyo in 1877 after his departure from Kagoshima. They must also have had contact through Willis's pupil Takaki Kanehiro who acted as one of Anderson's interpreters. Kagoshima, where Willis had set up a medical school, was the Satsuma capital and Satsuma was the fief from which so many of the leaders of the Japanese Imperial Navy stemmed.

Anderson, like Willis, followed the Anglo-Saxon tradition of medicine rather than the Dutch and German school which had been favoured in Japan immediately after the Meiji Restoration under the influence of Guido Fridolin Verbeck (1830-98), a Dutch Reformed Missionary from the United States. The Dutch school had been promoted by Pompe van Meerdervoort, who at the end of the Edo period had taught medicine at Nagasaki. Throughout the Edo period Dutch manuals (through the so-called *rangaku* or Dutch studies) had been the main source of information in Japan about Western medicine. Willis who had studied medicine at Edinburgh and Glasgow and been employed at the Middlesex Hospital in London stressed the importance of the relationship between the individual doctor and the patient. In principle the condition of the patient dictated the response of the physician. This was also the basic approach advocated by Anderson. The emphasis throughout was on patient care.

Both Anderson and Willis had to compete with the practitioners of *kampō* (Chinese medicine). While Chinese herbal remedies could be efficacious in some conditions there were many diseases in which such medicines could be harmful, especially if used by practitioners without adequate knowledge of anatomy and physiology. Moreover *kampō* methods were of no help in dealing with injuries and other conditions requiring surgery.

Anderson's contribution to naval medical studies was clearly outstanding. Before he left Tokyo in 1880 he was granted an audience by the Meiji Emperor who thanked him personally for his work in Japan. A silver medal bearing his name and effigy was established at the College (from subscriptions from former pupils) as an annual prize to the student who most distinguished himself in surgery and surgical anatomy. In 1886 after his return to Britain he was elected as a member of the *Se-i-kai*,[16] 'the medical society of Tokyo, in recognition of his many and arduous labours on behalf of Japan'.

MEDICAL CAREER IN BRITAIN

Anderson left Tokyo to become a senior lecturer in anatomy at St Thomas's Hospital. He was also appointed examiner in anatomy at London University and at the Royal College of Surgeons. Many Japanese students followed him to London and St Thomas's. In 1891 he was promoted from assistant to full surgeon at St Thomas's where he took much interest in skin diseases.[17] In 1891 he was also elected Professor of Anatomy at the Royal Academy of Art in succession to Professor Marshall, where as at St Thomas's he used his artistic ability to demonstrate anatomy to art students. 'His sketches on the blackboard were the wonder of his pupils. Beginning with a bold but unerring outline he would gradually fill in the details till a finished picture, more instructive than a ready–made diagram, was before the class.'[18]

INTEREST IN JAPANESE ART

Anderson's studies of art led him to develop an early interest in Japanese art. He was already an art collector when he went out to Japan. He took with him to Japan a small collection of old engravings, etchings and illustrated books of anatomy, in which he apparently took great delight.

This collection was, however, destroyed in a fire 'from which he himself, his wife and infant child escaped with little more than such clothes as they had on, and a valued microscope, the parting present of his students at St Thomas's Hospital, which was snatched from the flames by a faithful domestic'.[19]

Anderson, unlike many of his contemporaries who looked for curios, was a serious collector and student of art. While in Japan Anderson amassed an impressive collection of art especially of paintings and of prints (3,299 items[20]) and acquired a scholarly appreciation of Japanese art in general. In June 1879, selections from Anderson's collection of Japanese paintings were exhibited by the Asiatic Society of Japan at the School of Engineering in Tokyo and he lectured on them.[21] The decade of the 1870s was a time when Japanese were primarily interested in Westernization and traditional Japanese arts were neglected and Western art and culture were favoured. In particular, while the art of the Japanese print was increasingly appreciated in the West educated Japanese at that time tended to despise what was considered a vulgar art form. It was only under the influence of major Western collectors and art lovers such as Edward Morse[22] and Ernest Fenollosa[23] and as a result of the growth in demand for traditional Japanese arts and crafts abroad that there was a revival of interest in Japan in their country's traditional art forms.

Anderson must have met American and French collectors. He may well have been acquainted with Emile Guimet[24] and Louis Gonse[25] and he must have got to know later, at least after his return to Britain, Siegfried Bing.[26]

Another English employee of the Japanese government with a wide interest in Japanese arts was Josiah Conder,[27] the architect who in 1876 was appointed to teach architecture at the Engineering College in Tokyo which later became Tokyo Imperial University. Conder designed the *Rokumeikan*[28] (literally the Deer Cry Pavilion) in Hibiya. It opened in 1883 and became the main venue for Western-style dinner and dance parties. It came to symbolize the excesses of Westernization. Conder's particular interests were landscape gardening[29] and flower arrangement[30] but he also became a friend and pupil of the prolific and humorous Japanese artist Kawanabe Kyōsai[31] about whom he published a book. Anderson also seems to have met Kyōsai and commissioned from him a set of animal sketches, now in the British museum.

ART AND MEDICINE

On his return to Britain Anderson combined his duties as a practising surgeon and teacher with work on his Japanese art collection. In one paper written in 1886 on 'Art in Relation to Medical Science' he combined both skills. It is probably the best sketch on this subject in the

English language and should be required reading for all students of anatomy, medicine and the history of art. The book shows Anderson's enquiring mind, his fierce devotion to his subject, his love of art and a sparkling literary style. Anderson's opening paragraph is worth quoting in full:

> Medicine and Art had little in common except their remote antiquity; for while Art in the earliest essays to attain its ideal was making some of its noblest records, Medicine lagged behind, century after century, wasting the previous years over idle superstitions or in gnawing the dry bones of ancient dogmas: and it was not until the Sculptor, the Architect and the Painter had done their best, that the Physician began his advance along the true path of science.

Anderson pointed out that although there had been acutely observant artists since the time of the cavemen, the artist and physician never combined their powers. It was perhaps among the Egyptians that medicine took its place as a learned profession and the surgical instruments engraved on the walls of several temples are easily recognizable as the forerunners of those in use today. Yet direct observation of human anatomy was confined to the low class of professional embalmers who were in no way affiliated to the doctors. In India, on the other hand, the *Susruta* written 2,000 years earlier, stressed that the physician could only succeed in his profession by combining practical dissection with the study of books. But, Anderson added: 'the successors of these intellectual giants mistook the finger-post for the goal and stopped forever to worship at the opening of the road to knowledge'. Anderson noted that the Chinese had used diagrams and models from over 2000 years ago in teaching an entirely imaginary anatomy. Yet upon this basis they managed to develop systems of therapeutics some of which are still employed today. The Japanese in adopting Chinese medicine used drawings which they had made themselves. One Japanese painter in the twelfth century made a detailed and accurate study of a whole range of medical and surgical conditions.

Anderson noted that as dissection was forbidden in both China and Japan artists were denied the knowledge that would have enabled them to interpret surface anatomy. Nevertheless, the artists were way ahead of the physicians in their understanding of anatomy. In Anderson's view medicine of the pre-dissection era was 'a dismal combination of empiricism, superstition, and filthy charlatanism, tinged with a slight infusion of the black art'! However, the great sculptors of ancient Greece had some knowledge of superficial anatomy and physiology derived from accurate observation, tempered by pure inspiration, from which, he thought, many of us could learn today. He noted that some statues which had survived in India and Egypt as well as Buddhist statues at Nara would bear comparison with the greatest Greek and Roman sculptures. But in general he was scathing about the lack of anatomical accuracy in Japanese and Chinese art.

Anderson noted that in Europe the medical dogmas of Galen[32] had been regarded as sacrosanct, but artists had not been bound by such restrictions and Leonardo da Vinci who performed some thirty dissections in company with the physician Marcantonio della Torre, was the first great anatomist. Unfortunately Marcantonio died and almost all the drawings and observations which they made have been lost. Anderson, however, pointed out that in one of Leonardo's earlier cartoons of a man and woman engaged in sexual intercourse the anatomy was still as described by Galen.[33]

Leonardo's work, Anderson pointed out, had been followed by that of the great Belgian physician/anatomist Versalius who, having published six volumes of Galenist anatomy, took up dissection and produced his incomparable *De Humanis Corpora Fabrica* which was condemned as heresy by the Galenists. Versalius[34] was sentenced to death by the Inquisition for desecrating the human body. Undeterred other physician/anatomists, such as the French physician Charles Estienne[35] took up the challenge. An example of Estienne's studies which reflected the anatomists' style of those days showed the subject displaying his dissected anatomy to the viewer. However, the medical profession as a whole was not much influenced by such works and it was another two hundred years before John Hunter[36] established a scientific basis for medicine and surgery. Finally, the paths of art and science converged. Anderson continued in this study to trace these convergent paths giving a wealth of detail and references, interspersed with flashes of humour.

Anderson showed his artistic and anatomical abilities in a small work on *The Deformities of the Fingers and Toes*[37] published in 1886. In the same year, in conjunction with a Mr Shattock, he wrote the section on 'Malformations' which has been described[38] as 'a laborious and recondite piece of work' in the *Nomenclature of Diseases*. He[39] was also the editor of *Heath's Practical Anatomy* and *Brücke's Beauties and Defects of the Human Figure* and contributed to various medical journals including *St Thomas's Hospital Reports.*'

ANDERSON AND THE BRITISH MUSEUM

Anderson, meanwhile, pursued his interest in Japan and Japanese art. His collection of paintings[40] was acquired by the British Museum in 1881 for £3,000 with the enthusiastic support of Augustus Wollaston Franks, Keeper of British Medieval Antiquities and Ethnography, and his assistant Hercules Reid and himself a collector of Japanese paintings, ceramics, and archaeological material. According to the inventory made at the time there were 927 *kakemono*, 101 *makimono*, 27 albums, 3 screens, 5 framed pictures and 2,236 un-mounted drawings. In addition, 311 volumes on Japanese pictorial art (mainly woodblock-printed, illustrated books) were purchased for £360 in the following year for the Japanese library. Anderson was also engaged by the Trustees to prepare *A Descriptive and Historical catalogue of A Collection of Japanese and Chinese Paintings in the British Museum*, which was published in 1886. This consisted of 544 pages of artists' biographies and detailed annotations of the paintings. These are still used today, although minimally illustrated. In the same year Anderson published *The Pictorial Arts of Japan* in a much larger format and more lavishly illustrated, though dealing with, in general, only modest works.

The two publications were clearly intended to complement one another and in *Pictorial Arts*, freed of the catalogue's responsibilities, Anderson gave a more wide-ranging and analytical account of the 'characteristics' of Japanese compared to Western pictorial art. Mixed in with many pertinent observations, however, Anderson tended to criticize Japanese artists inappropriately from the standpoint of a champion of anatomical accuracy. For Anderson, Japanese artists' incomplete scientific knowledge meant that theirs was an 'art of great potentiality but incomplete development'. They were taken to task for such failures as 'caricaturing the muscles of an athlete' or 'wilfully ignoring the facts of *chiaroscuro* and the optical phenomena of perspective.' Such comments echo curiously the polemics of Japanese eighteenth century *rangaku* scholar/painters such as Hiraga Gennai (1726-79) and Satake Shōzan (1748-85) against fellow artists of other (that is, non Western-style) schools for their inability to depict the world literally, but few would take such a rigid critical stance today. On the other hand Anderson was generous in his praise of what he saw as the great strengths of Japanese painters; 'perfect appreciation of harmony and colour', 'instinctive sense of affectiveness and propriety in composition', 'unequalled command of pencil [sic]', 'ready and fertile invention' and keen and intelligent gift of observation'. Yet in urging Japanese artists 'to shake off the encumbrance of unprofitable convention' he was denying many of the unique characteristics of painting from the Edo period (1615-1868) which are valued so highly today.

Selections from Anderson's collection were exhibited in the Print and Drawing Gallery at the British Museum in 1888 and 1910 and printed gallery guides record the contents of the displays.

In 1895 Anderson published a small book entitled *Japanese Wood Engravings: Their History, Techniques and Characteristics*. In the same year he was made a companion of the Japanese Order of the Rising Sun.

THE JAPAN SOCIETY

Anderson, of 1 Harley Street, London W1, was elected as the first

Chairman of the Council of the Japan Society of London in 1892 and remained so until his sudden death[41] on 27 October 1900, due to 'a rupture of the cord of the mitral valve'.[42] The obituary of Anderson in the Japan Society's *Proceedings*[43] noted that: 'Hardly eight and forty hours previously he had presided at one of the Society's Monthly Meetings, and addressed the audience in that scholarly and genial fashion which always distinguished him, and almost up to the hour of his death he was engaged in planning the Programme for the coming Session, to which he had agreed to contribute a paper upon "The Charities of Japan".' Anderson had at first been reluctant to take on the position of Chairman as he feared that he would not have enough time to devote to the Society. In fact, he was a very conscientious chairman.[44] Apart from chairing council meetings he very often took the chair at lectures delivered to the Society. When as was often the case the subject of the lecture was related to Japanese art he was able to add scholarly comments. For instance, when on 14 July 1892 Mr W. Gowland, formerly of the Mint in Osaka, who was also an archaeologist, read a paper to the Society on 'The Naturalistic Art of Japan', Anderson, sticking to his earlier judgements (or some might say prejudices), was critical of the Okyō school[45] saying that they were truly naturalistic 'but only up to a certain point, for tradition was too strong for them. They ignored the principles of light and shade. . .' He went on to point out the influence of 'the Naturalistic School upon Industrial Art'.

CONCLUSION

The Dictionary of National Biography[46] wrote: 'Of high culture and distinguished appearance, Anderson's retiring nature alone prevented him from becoming a more prominent personality'. The *Lancet* noted that his 'geniality, and modesty made him an attractive personality' adding that 'in all professional relations' he was known for 'his sincerity and thoroughness and for the strict conscientiousness with which he fulfilled all duties devolving to him.' He 'never allowed himself to be tired till the work was done'. The Japan Society's obituary said of him: 'His urbanity towards all with whom he was brought into contact, whether English or Japanese, was a distinguishing feature of his tenure of office [as Chairman of the Council of the Society], and had much to do with the cordial relationship which has always existed between the Japanese colony and the British community.' In a tribute to him in the *Lancet*[47] Anderson was described: 'His somewhat prematurely whitened hair, worn rather long, and his full white moustache, contrasted with his darker eyes and brows. Sensitive and retiring in disposition he nevertheless had a most courteous manner and a winning smile.' He was married twice. By his first wife Margaret Hall whom he married in 1873 he had a son and a daughter. His second wife Louisa Tetley survived him.

His contribution to the study of anatomy and his work as a teacher and a surgeon in both Britain and Japan were significant. The large number of items of Japanese art which he amassed was the foundation of the British Museum's collection of Japanese paintings and his scholarship was impressive even if his judgements were sometimes biased. He was a distinguished chairman of the Japan Society from its inception in 1892 till his death in 1900.

2

Marcus Huish (1843-1921) and Japan

HIDEKO NUMATA

Marcus Huish

MARCUS BOURNE HUISH (1843-1921) had an important role in the development of Anglo-Japanese relations, especially through his efforts to introduce Japanese art to British people. He was a managing director of The Fine Art Society, a founding member of The Japan Society and an art critic and historian.

Little is known about his youth.[1] He was born on 25 November 1843, the elder son of Marcus Huish, solicitor, of Castle Donington, Leicestershire, and his wife, Margaret Bourne. He was educated at Rossall School and Trinity Hall, Cambridge, and admitted as a student of the Inner Temple in 1864, receiving his LL.B. degree in 1866. He was called to the bar on 18 November 1867. He married Catherine Sarah, eldest daughter of Thomas Ewing Winslow QC, on 16 March 1878. However, his interest in art, having been evident even as a boy, prevailed and he decided to make his career in the world of art rather than the law, which included the study of water-colour. By the 1870s he was already working as an art critic and in 1876 he became the first managing director of The Fine Art Society at an annual salary of £400, together with a percentage of the profits from the firm's sales.

MANAGING DIRECTOR OF THE FINE ART SOCIETY

The Fine Art Society (FAS) was founded in 1876 at 148 New Bond Street in London.[3] The FAS started as a seller of prints, reproducing engravings after well-known paintings by the old masters and Victorian painters. By 1890 about two hundred reproductions had been issued. In addition to publishing and selling prints, they began to issue the original etchings for sale by subscription and to publish fine-art books and exhibition catalogues. They also organized exhibitions of the works of various artists. Because of the success of these new enterprises, by the 1890s the FAS was known as 'The Best Shop in London'.

Most of the other Victorian commercial art galleries, such as the Grosvenor Gallery, Agnew's and Colnaghi, were owned and run by a family or a principal, but FAS was a limited company owned by its shareholders and was run by a board of directors. Marcus Huish was employed as the first managing director who supervised the other five or six directors (including non-executive directors) and was responsible for the daily operations of the firm. The great success of the FAS in its early years was due to his efforts and to his outstanding ability as an art critic who appreciated the new trends in art.

Under his direction various experimental projects were undertaken by the FAS. For instance, it was his idea that the firm should publish original etchings. In the nineteenth century engravings were considered primarily as a way to reproduce well-known paintings while original etchings were not so popular. In the late nineteenth century Seymour Haden and other etchers began to promote the idea of etching as an independent art form and started the 'etching revival' movement. Huish supported the movement and promoted it through the activities of the FAS. He published a catalogue of the works of Charles Meryon, the leading French exponent of the art of etching, whose exhibition was held at the Burlington Fine Arts Club in 1879. He translated the text written by Philippe Burty, a French art critic.[4] In the same year he also organized an exhibition of original etchings, 'About Etching, A Collection by the Great Masters', which consisted of Seymour Haden's own holdings of artists' prints, ranging from Old Masters such as Dürer and Rembrandt to Turner and Charles Meryon.[5] He also arranged for the following exhibitions of original etching at the FAS: Thomas Bewick's woodcuts (1880), Exhibition of Etchings, including works by Bracquemond, Herkomer, Palmer, Whistler, etc. (1880), and Exhibition of the Society of Painter-Etchers (1882).

James McNeill Whistler's 'Venice Set' was one of the most famous original series of etchings published through the FAS.[6] These etchings recall the famous quarrel between Whistler and John Ruskin. Ruskin criticized Whistler's work 'Nocturne' as 'flinging a pot of paint in the public's face'. Whistler sued Ruskin for libel and won the case, but he was only awarded a farthing damages and the costs of the action led to his bankruptcy. Huish helped Whistler by commissioning a set of original etchings and financed his stay in Venice to work on the 'set'. Huish greatly valued Whistler and appreciated his original etchings, but he also had close connections with Ruskin.[7] At the FAS he organized exhibitions of Ruskin's collection of Turner water colours in 1878 and those of Samuel Prout and William Hunt in the following year. Ruskin also wrote various texts for the FAS exhibitions catalogues in its early years including Elizabeth Thompson's Roll Call (1874). Ruskin's influence on Huish continued at least until 1886 when the last exhibition, 'St. George's Guild: A series of drawings made under the direction of Mr. Ruskin', was held. Huish helped Whistler by commissioning a series of etchings of Venice in spite of his close connections with Ruskin. As an art critic he appreciated Whistler's expressionism which Ruskin could not see.

Some of the special exhibitions which were held at the FAS were outstanding contributions to the British art scene in the final decades of the nineteenth century. These were not only of the works of Royal Academicians but also of progressive artists like Whistler or the Pre-Raphaelites. Themes ranged widely from historical, landscape, botanical, to oriental which were in fashion at that time. For each exhibition catalogues with introduction, commentaries and list of works exhibited were published. Such catalogues are common these days but in the late nineteenth century, the FAS catalogues were outstanding for their academic, documentary and educational value. Huish himself wrote the texts for some of the catalogues but his more important task was that of planning and managing these exhibitions. Although much of the work of running the ambitious exhibition programme fell to Huish's manager Ernest Brown, the success of the FAS in these innovative activities was largely due to Huish's remarkable talents as managing director.[8]

JAPONISME AND THE FINE ART SOCIETY

It is generally said that Japanese art was first introduced to the British public at the London International Exhibition of 1862. In this exhibition 623 items of Japanese art were displayed including *ukiyo-e* prints, lacquer, ceramics, and books. Most of these were from the collection of Rutherford Alcock[9] who arrived in Yokohama in 1859 as the first British Minister and Consul General in Japan. This exhibition of Japanese art particularly impressed those dissatisfied with the academic art world at that time such as Whistler and the artists of the Aesthetic Movement, Dante Gabriel Rossetti, Edward Burne-Jones and others.

In the 1870s the cult of Japonisme became fashionable in Britain not only among artists but also among ordinary people. In 1875 Arthur

Lasenby Liberty opened his shop at 218 Regent Street to sell oriental silk textiles. He later expanded into oriental curios including Japanese decorative arts and furniture.[10]

Since the FAS opened for business during the vogue for Japonisme, it was a major element in many of the company's exhibitions. Until the beginning of the twentieth century the FAS had exhibitions featuring oriental art once or twice a year. Japanese arts were especially important for them and 'Japanese art [became] a hall mark of The Fine Art Society'. The FAS's Japonisme reflected not only the fashion of the time, but also Huish's personal interest and taste in Japanese Art. Huish himself was enchanted by Japanese art and in his youth made a collection of Japanese blue and white ceramics.[11]

The FAS's Japonisme is shown symbolically on the exterior facade of the building.[12] The style of the building itself is a mixture of Renaissance, Gothic and Queen Anne, but the facade was rebuilt in 1881. The entrance and gates, designed by the famous architect and designer E. W. Godwin, were commissioned by Huish. The arch and balcony windows with grilles were apparently inspired by Japanese windows with *shōji* screens; these were often used by Godwin for his earlier Japonisme experiments in furniture design.

The FAS's enthusiasm for Japonisme was demonstrated by its close connections with Siegfried Bing, a prominent Parisian dealer in Japanese Art and a leading light in the promotion of Japonisme in Europe. From 1889-90 the FAS lent their second floor to Bing[13] who probably used it to exhibit his collection and to promote his sales of Japanese art in other European countries while also making it the base for his activities in Britain. As Bing's name was well known among the British people interested in Japonisme the display of his collection on their premises must have helped to promote FAS sales. The connection must also have helped them to collect and disseminate information about Japan and Japanese art and about the influence and spread of Japonisme in France.

Exhibitions at the FAS on Japanese themes were either of works by Japanese artists or of works by British artists influenced by Japonisme. About ten exhibitions of Japanese art were organized by the FAS up to 1920. The most important and largest exhibition was the 'Loan Exhibition of Japanese Art' held in 1888. It was opened at almost the same time as exhibitions of 'Japanese Paintings' at the British Museum and of 'Japanese Prints' at the Burlington Fine Arts Club. This was a boom year for Japonisme in Britain. In order to avoid overlap with the other two exhibitions the exhibits at the FAS were confined to decorative and applied arts, such as metal works, ceramics, enamels, lacquer, netsuke and textiles. About 1300 objects were displayed in twenty-five cases. Most items had been loaned by private collectors, including Sir Philip Cunliffe-Owen of the South Kensington Museum, Alma-Tadema, the painter,

William Alexander, patron of Whistler, and Siegfried Bing as well as Huish himself. Catalogues with detailed introductions and notes were produced for the exhibitions. Huish wrote the text for the FAS exhibition with the assistance of Kataoka Masayuki, a Japanese art dealer and art historian. Huish described the FAS exhibition as the first systematic and academic exhibition of Japanese art in Britain.[14]

In November 1890, an exhibition of a 'Collection of Drawings and Engravings by Hokusai' was organized at the FAS. With help from Siegfried Bing, over 200 *ukiyo-e* prints and drawings by Hokusai were exhibited. Huish again wrote the text for the exhibition catalogue.[15] He said that the exhibition of Japanese prints at the École des Beaux Arts in Paris in April that year had made him aware of the importance and renown of Hokusai and had induced him to plan the exhibition. Huish's text which was a general introduction to the works of Hokusai preceded Bing's 'La vie et l'oeuvre d'Hokusai (Life and Works of Hokusai)' (1896 in *La Revue Blanche*) and Edmond and Jules de Goncourt's 'Hokusai' (1896). The records of sale show that many of the exhibits were quickly sold.

In addition to these exhibitions the FAS mounted other exhibitions of Japanese art such as 'Japanese Lacquer, Metalwork, and Netsuke' (1893), 'Rare Japanese Colour Prints'(1909), 'Japanese Dolls' (1909), 'Second Exhibition of Japanese Prints'(1910), 'Old Japanese Fan Mounts and Miniature Drawings'(1911), 'Old Japanese Fan Mounts' (1914), 'Hiroshige, Engravings in Colour' (1914). These exhibitions were highly appreciated because of their unique character, high quality and the academic content of the catalogues. The texts were written by specialists on the various subjects that were the focus of the exhibitions, but their success was largely due to Huish with his wide knowledge of Japanese art and his connections with collectors.

The FAS also held exhibitions of Japanese landscapes and genre scenes painted by British artists. In 1889 the FAS commissioned Alfred East, a painter, to travel to Japan and produce landscape paintings and drawings.[16] East went to Japan with Huish's friends, Charles Holme and Mr and Mrs Lasenby Liberty and stayed there from March to September visiting Nagasaki, Yokohama, Tokyo and Nikko, and painting various landscapes in oils and water-colours. Following his return to England an exhibition entitled 'Alfred East, Pictures and Drawings of the Landscape of Japan' was held at the FAS.[17] Alfred Parsons was another artist commissioned by the FAS in 1892 to make landscapes and botanical pictures in Japan. After his return an exhibition entitled 'Alfred Parsons, RI, Water-colours and Drawings Illustrating Landscapes and Flowers in Japan'[18] was held. During their visits to Japan, both East and Parsons had contacts with Japanese painters, especially with those studying Western–style painting. East gave a paper at the conference of the Meiji Art Society (Meiji Bijutsu-kai) and spoke about European art and his impressions of Japanese art. He also encouraged Japanese artists to develop a new style while retaining a sense of traditional Japanese art. Parsons held an exhibition of his water-colours in Tokyo. Japanese painters who visited the exhibition were deeply impressed by the detailed depiction of nature and the rich expressionism of his water-colours. Japanese artists were inspired to start a movement to promote water-colour painting in Japan.[19]

Some other exhibitions of works with Japanese subjects made by British artists were organized at the FAS. These included 'Ella du Cane, Japanese water-colours' (1908), 'Warwick Goble, Water-colours Illustrating Japanese Fairy Legends' (1910) and 'Mortimer Menpes, World's Children, Water-colours' which seem to have included Japanese subjects. Menpes, who had been a pupil of Whistler, had travelled to Japan in 1887 and 1896 and depicted many Japanese scenes. The FAS also had exhibitions of other artists who had close connection with Japan, such as Brangwyn, Frederic Leighton and Lindley Sambourne, who were well know collectors of Japanese Art. Their works did not always directly reflect Japanese art, but their exhibitions demonstrated the close relationship between Huish and the exponents of Japonisme in Britain.

ART CRITIC AND JOURNALIST

In addition to working for the FAS Huish continued to be an art critic and journalist. He was editor of *The Year's Art* from 1880 to 1893, and of the The Art Journal from 1881 to 1893 and wrote articles for various art magazines. He was the author of numerous art books including two works illustrating J. M. W. Turner's prints or photogravures, *The Seine and the Loire* (1886) and *The Southern Coast of England* (1892). The following books were by him: *Japan and its Art* (1889), *Birket Foster* (1890), *Greek Terra-Cotta Statuette* (1900), *Happy England as Painted by Helen Allingham* (1903) and *British Water-Colour Art* (1904).

In his work as editor and author he demonstrated his interest in Japanese art. *The Art Journal* was one of the most authoritative art magazines in Britain. The articles in the journal covered a wide range of art from the ancient to the present day and from European art to Asian art. In the late nineteenth century many important articles about Japan were written for this magazine such as James Jackson Jarve's 'Japanese Art' (1869) and Rutherford Alcock's 'Japanese Art' (1875-78). In 1888, when Huish was its editor, a series of his own essays 'Notes on Japan and its Wares' appeared. It was based on his lecture at The Fine Art Society on the occasion of the exhibition of Japanese Art in 1888. He developed this paper into his best-known book *Japan and its Art* which was published in 1889. Huish wrote that his book 'aimed at giving an idea of the country, its history, customs, religion, and inhabitants, as we see them portrayed in

Japanese Art'.[20] The book contained separate chapters on the various genres of Japanese art such as lacquer, metal-work, sculpture in wood and ivory, porcelain and faience, prints and books. These were followed by descriptions of the climate, history and culture of Japan. Huish believed that without an accurate understanding of the cultural background it was not possible to achieve a proper appreciation of Japanese art, its iconography and form. He acknowledged the help he had received from Kataoka Masayuki, a Japanese art dealer and art historian.[21] The format of the book is small but it contains plenty of illustrations and information and was designed for readers who need to understand the scope and achievements of Japanese art.

In his article 'Is Japanese Art Extinct?' in the magazine *The Nineteenth Century : A Monthly Review* issue for March 1888,[22] on the occasion of the 1888 Exhibition of Japanese Art at the FAS, Huish criticized the Japanese Government Commission sent to Europe and America from 1886–87 to study the condition of art in Western countries.[23] The members of the Commission consisted of F. E. Fenollosa, the American scholar of Japanese art, and two other officials. The Commission concluded that Japanese art was the only living art in the world at that time and that in a comparatively few years Japan would become the acknowledged centre and leader of Fine Art in all civilized countries. Huish was sceptical of the way in which their research had been conducted and pointed out that Fenollosa was a specialist in Japanese art but not of Western art. He noted that the Commission had ignored some institutions and museums which were important for an understanding of Western art. The Commission's boundless admiration for Japanese art aroused objections even among such enthusiastic supporters of Japonisme as Frederic Leighton and William Anderson. Huish in his essay analysed the situation of Japanese art as follows: 'But thoughtful and intelligent Japanese, and foreigners who have had opportunities of forming a dispassionate judgement, believe that the arts are at the present time in a most parlous state, that this is entirely due to the altered conditions under which the Japanese artist and artisan now works, and that unless and until many of these conditions are restored to their former state no change for the better is possible.'[24] He was alarmed that Japanese art was going through a period of decadence after reaching a peak. Huish considered that this crisis was caused by the drastic changes brought about by the Meiji Restoration of 1868. The traditional class system had collapsed and there was no one to take over the traditional role as a patron of the arts which, over the centuries, the shoguns and the daimyos had fulfilled. The demand for high quality art objects decreased and the artists and craftsmen did not know how to cover their living expenses. After Japanese ports were opened to trade with Western countries in 1859, Western culture quickly invaded Japan and had an immediate impact on Japanese life-style. As the Japanese life-style became

Westernized Japanese traditional arts became less appreciated in Japan and Westerners became the main customers of Japanese traditional arts. But Westerners did not fully appreciate the traditions and craftsmanship of Japanese artists and sometimes demanded changes in design to suit Western taste. Mass production, which resulted from such purchases, and the complicated distribution structure with many commission agents, which developed as a result, forced Japanese artists and craftsmen to work hard over long hours for low wages. The traditional aesthetics of Japanese designs were distorted and a vicious circle developed leading to a deterioration in Japanese art.

Huish stressed that Western collectors should have a correct knowledge and understanding of Japan and its art. He insisted that the Japanese government should make efforts to protect Japanese art by inhibiting the export of shoddy articles and should purchase fine art objects for museums. These opinions derived from his experience as an art dealer. His apprehensions about the crisis in Japanese art were no doubt the driving force behind his efforts to educate collectors about Japanese art.

Huish was the editor of the English edition of the French magazine *Le Japon Artistique*. The French edition had been published by Siegfried Bing in 36 volumes between May 1888 and April 1891. It was a luxury magazine introducing various aspects of Japanese art with essays by specialists in Japanese art together with plenty of illustrations mainly taken from Japanese wood-block prints. The English edition was published almost at the same time as the original French edition and it greatly contributed to the spread of Japonisme in the English-speaking world. Huish himself wrote an essay for the final volume of March 1891, entitled 'L'art de collectionneur (Skill of Collection)'. In this essay he wrote about the technique of collecting high quality Japanese art objects, how to purchase, how to judge and appreciate good objects and how to conserve them in sound condition. It is a useful guide for collectors. Huish, as an art dealer, must have seen many collectors who bought and collected Japanese objects without sufficient knowledge and felt strongly the need for such a guide book. He thought that such practical information was as important as academic knowledge of art history. Since the materials of Japanese art objects, such as silk, lacquer, ivory, are difficult to look after, he feared that without adequate knowledge good Japanese objects could not be properly preserved.

THE JAPAN SOCIETY

The Japan Society of London was founded in 1891 to encourage Japanese studies and to bring together all those in the UK, and throughout the world, interested in Japanese matters.[25] Huish was a founding member of the society and a member of the first council together with his friends

Arthur Lasenby Liberty and Alfred East. Artists and collectors who had close connections with Huish, such as Charles Holme, Christopher Dresser, Alfred Parsons, Mortimer Menpes and Frederic Leighton were also founding members.[26] Siegfried Bing and Hayashi Tadamasa were elected corresponding members on the recommendation of Huish.[27]

Huish successively held various posts in the society – librarian, curator, editor, vice-chairman, and finally chairman of the council. He contributed greatly to the success of the society.[28] He was particularly instrumental in relation to the promotion of understanding in Britain of Japanese art and industry. He was the curator responsible for the planning and display of 'Japanese Arms and Armour' in 1905. He was also curator of the exhibition of Japanese objects illustrating the growth of commercial relations and friendship between Britain and Japan put together by the Japan Society for the Japan-British Exhibition of 1910.[29] He gave a number of papers at regular meetings of the Society which were printed in *The Transactions and Proceedings of The Japan Society, London*: 'The Influence of Europe on the Art of Old Japan' (1895), 'The Evolution of a Netsuke' (1897), 'A Collection of Toys' (1902-1904), 'England's Appreciation of Japanese Art (1905-1907).

CONCLUSION

Among British collectors of Japanese art and early Japanologists the name of Huish has not been as well known as those of Rutherford Alcock or William Anderson. Little attention has been paid in Japan to Huish and only his book *Japan and its Art* has been reprinted in *Japanese Art and Japonisme, part 1: Early English texts* which appeared in 1999. The Japanese commentary in the accompanying volume said that little was known about Huish.[30] Unlike Alcock and Anderson who had lived in Japan, made large collections of Japanese art and wrote books about Japan, Huish never visited Japan and his collection of Japanese art was on a relatively small scale but it was of high quality. He was listed as a lender for the exhibition of Japanese Art in 1888 and his name occurs frequently in the FAS sale records as a purchaser of items of Japanese art. However, only eleven *tsuba* (sword guards), which were donated in 1919 to the Victoria and Albert Museum, are surviving examples of his collection.[31] His books and essays were practical rather than academic and have been criticized as lacking originality. But he did not have an academic background and his experience was as a manager of an art gallery. He understood the art market and appreciated the vogue for Japonisme in Britain. He was an enthusiastic lover of Japanese art.

Japonisme is sometimes discussed as if it was an artistic style, but it was essentially a fashion which spread widely among the middle classes in Britain. Huish should be re-valued as someone who contributed to the popularization of Japonisme and tried hard to save Japanese art.

Huish died of pneumonia after a brief illness on 4 May 1921. Joseph H. Longford, then chairman of the Japan Society wrote in the *Transactions* of the Society for 1920-21 that his character was gentle, unassuming and unselfish. He was awarded the Japanese orders of the Sacred Treasure and of the Rising Sun and was a Knight of the Order of the Crown of Italy.

3

Prince and Princess Chichibu

DOROTHY BRITTON

The Prince and Princess taking tea in their villa at Gotemba.
[*Photo:* FRANCIS HAAR]

UPBRINGING

PRINCE CHICHIBU (Yasuhito),[1] loved every moment of the time he spent, brief as it was, at Magdalen College, Oxford[2] so much so, that when he had to return prematurely to Japan because of the illness of his father the Emperor Taishō in 1926, he had a study made at his palace in Tokyo which was as exact a replica as possible of his beloved study at Magdalen.[3] The Prince was only there for one term, reading history, politics and economics. But he had already been in England over a year studying English, going to the cinema, shopping, visiting Switzerland – where he climbed the Matterhorn – and thoroughly enjoying himself.

When the Prince later became an invalid just before the outbreak of World War II and was forced to spend the rest of his life a long way from Tokyo in the bracing air of the foothills of Mount Fuji, the Prince made sure that his study there was also arranged exactly like his one at Oxford. An English rose garden, too, graces the Gotemba villa, which is now open to the public.

Prince Chichibu brought several sculls back to Japan from England to remind him of happy times on the Thames and the river Cherwell. He

23

kept the boats in a shed on the beach near his Hayama villa, and as a child I used to watch him rowing out to sea past my house on halcyon days when it was sufficiently calm. My friend the young Princess Sawa, Prince Kitashirakawa's lively and spirited daughter, often kept her cousin Yasuhito company in a second scull, but Princess Chichibu just could not seem to acquire the sculling knack. 'It was such a shame', she wrote, 'as he was so eager to have me experience the exhilaration of gliding through the sparkling blue ripples the way he did.'[4]

Prince Chichibu, known as 'the sports prince', loved all sports except boxing. He was particularly fond of mountaineering[5] and skiing,[6] and he learned to like rugby football in England, although he could not take part on the field because of his need to wear glasses. He introduced the game to Japan, where it boasts a stadium of its own named after the Prince.[7] He also introduced squash, and had a court built at his palace in Tokyo; this was modelled after the squash court at the British Embassy.

When the Oxford University rugby team came to Japan in 1952 and played against Keio University in Tokyo, Prince Chichibu attended the match in spite of his poor health. After going down to the field to greet the players, the climb back up the steps to the royal box exhausted him. Four months later he was dead. In her autobiography, *The Silver Drum*, the Princess wrote: 'It was evident to me then how deep was his nostalgia for the Oxford of his interrupted studies to which he was never able to return.'[8]

The seeds of the Prince's 'Anglophile' attitude appear to have been sown early. Imperial offspring in those days were traditionally removed from their parents' care seventy days after birth, and reared in the family of a suitable nobleman until they were five. The retired admiral Count Kawamura was chosen as his foster father – or rather grandfather – for the Emperor Taishō's first three sons Hirohito, Yasuhito (Prince Chichibu) and Nobuhito (Prince Takamatsu). Chamberlain Kanroji Osanaga[9] explained that the admiral consulted the English governess employed by the former feudal Lord of Satsuma for hints on how he should go about bringing up his little Imperial charges. Miss Ethel Howard imparted her belief in the importance of fostering such things as an independent spirit, gratitude and compassion.

When the Count died before the time was up, the boys' father, Crown Prince Yoshihito (later to become the Emperor Taishō) wanted his sons nearby; so he moved them into a house he had specially built for them in his own compound, where they were tutored together with a few other selected children prior to entering the *Gakushūin* (Peers' School).

Prince Chichibu's most recent biographer, Hosaka Masayasu,[10] related that the walls of the boys' father's drawing-room were decorated with pictures of world scenes and foreign royal families – prominent among them, no doubt, being Britain's. Prince Yoshihito had never been able to travel abroad on account of poor health, and one of his greatest joys was to have his boys gather around the piano with him and sing 'The Round-the-world-tour Song' (*Sekai manyū no uta*) popular at the time.

Prince Chichibu's elder brother, Hirohito, when he had become Crown Prince on his father's accession to the throne in 1912, returned home from his official world tour in 1921 with a portrait of himself by Augustus John, and glowing accounts of life in Britain. He loved the informal atmosphere at Buckingham Palace, where King George V treated him like a son. He was impressed, too, by the amazing fellowship between the Duke of Atholl – in whose castle he stayed in Scotland – and the villagers.[11] And ever since his return, Hirohito had insisted on an English breakfast with bacon and eggs. Later, in a letter to Prince Chichibu he wrote that England had given him his first experience of personal freedom.[12] At a news conference in 1946 he stated that the happiest time in his life had been his visit to Britain.[13] (His grandson Naruhito, the present Crown Prince, said exactly the same thing to me after his return from Oxford!)

Hirohito was much taken with British democracy, and envied the freedom of Edward, Prince of Wales, to do such things as go to the theatre, eat in restaurants and mix with friends on an equal basis. On his return, in addition to his English breakfast, Hirohito apparently tried having a party – the sort which the Prince of Wales used to give – and asked his guests not to treat him like a prince. It was not a success, and his chamberlains suggested he refrain from repeating the experiment.[14]

ARMY SERVICE AND MARRIAGE

Prince Chichibu, similarly impressed with life in Britain after his Oxford experience, was able more easily to try out his egalitarian leanings on his fellow army officers at the Military Academy, and later the War College. He, too, enjoined them not to think of him as a prince, and to treat him just like any other fellow officer. He often invited them and even ordinary soldiers back to his palace for tea, and got them to tell him about their lives. Unlike his shy, introverted elder brother the Emperor Hirohito, who became a renowned marine biologist and was happier looking through a microscope at hydrozoans than attending to affairs of state, Prince Chichibu liked people and they liked him. He was naturally gregarious and enjoyed chatting with everyone with friendly ease. The following story is typical of his selfless consideration and friendliness. It was late in the evening on the day of his wedding, which had been filled from the early hours with one ceremony after another. He and his bride must have been exhausted. She wrote:

> The night was brilliant with the light of the full moon. Led by bands, groups of marchers had been coming by since early

evening . . . representatives from each group had come in
through the side gate and were lined up opposite the porte-
cochère. They probably only intended to express their
felicitations to a footman or secretary and retire, but when
the Prince heard they were there, he jumped up, motioning
me to follow, and hurried outside – in his indoor slippers! . . .
The Prince, with spontaneous ease, thanked the representatives most warmly . . . In those days, to be spoken to
personally by a member of the Imperial Family was so
unbelievable and awe-inspiring that the representatives were
rendered speechless with emotion.[15]

Matsudaira Setsuko had been spotted by the wise and perceptive Empress
Teimei, Prince Chichibu's mother, as the perfect consort for her son. But
the attractive teenager – who, born in England, had spent time there as a
baby, and later graduated from a high school in Washington DC when her
father was Japanese Ambassador there – had tried desperately to avoid
marrying into the very circumscribed world 'above the clouds' where life
was on a frighteningly different dimension and she would be virtually cut
off from her family and friends.

The Prince, however, turned out to be a very warm and caring
husband. 'It'll all take a lot of getting used to, I know,' he told her. 'But
don't worry – I'll always be there for you to lean on.'[16] It was not long
before she obviously fell in love with her prince. She wrote: 'I knew I
would do anything in the world for him, and that nothing would be too
hard.'[17]

There was no honeymoon. There was a trip to the Grand Shrine of the
Sun Goddess at Ise. But they travelled to that beautiful edifice – constantly
renewed in ancient form in its numinous forest of cryptomerias – with a
retinue, to carry out the prescribed marriage annunciation ceremony.
Ceremony followed ceremony as 1928 neared its end, culminating in the
enthronement in Kyoto of Hirohito, as the Emperor Shōwa.

One evening in the old Kyoto Palace – where the Augustus John
portrait hung – the princess came upon her husband stealing a moment to
chat with his elder brother. They sounded happy and relaxed, but she
sensed the new line of demarcation between the two now that the elder
had become a 'divine' sovereign. 'I realized anew the awesome character
of the realm into which I had married,' she wrote, 'I still remember the
qualms that assailed me at that moment.'[18] Though in England
Shakespeare wrote, 'There's such divinity doth hedge a king', in Japan
the hedge was far more constricting.

Even the Emperor's brother was not immune. His biographer, Hosaka,
maintained it was Prince Chichibu's instinctive rebelling against that
invisible wall that caused him to fill up his schedule so tightly that the
over-exertion probably contributed to his succumbing to tuberculosis in

August, 1940. Hosaka also bemoaned the fact that there was no Palace protocol at the time allowing Prince Chichibu to discuss matters with the Emperor and offer advice, a role which might well have been helpful to them both.

Prince Chichibu, who had already graduated from the Military Academy, was instructed to enter the War College on 24 December 1928, just three months after he and Setsuko were married. In addition to a schedule already crammed with official Imperial duties and public engagements, his war college studies and the resulting homework were extremely time-consuming, keeping him up most nights until the early hours. Some nights he got no sleep at all. In reply to his wife's remonstrance that he was working too hard, he replied: 'Lots of my classmates have to do the same work in cramped quarters with an infant bawling its head off. Here am I working in quiet, palatial surroundings, so I've little to complain of.'[19]

Making friends with his officers and men, the altruistic Prince became deeply concerned about the poverty, malnutrition and economic distress among the working class at that time. He was a kind and sympathetic listener, which encouraged them to air their grievances. In many of the officers' published diaries in which these conversations were mentioned, he does not seem to have said a great deal – but just nodded in wholehearted agreement to their ideas. One of his friends, Sugenami Saburō, in a magazine interview many years later, remembered how wise he was and how deeply understanding: He listened to me with such interest, and said to please do come again and tell me more. Andō and I saw the prince again several times, and we talked about things like Kita Ikki's 'General Outline for the Reorganisation of Japan.'[20] Written in 1919, the book had been banned, but was distributed secretly among the groups of young officers in favour of reform. Describing the book, Ben-Ami Shillony said: 'It advocated a coup d'état carried out "by the emperor and the people" against the privileged ruling class, after which a sweeping reform would be made. This reform would consist of granting special powers to a "reform cabinet", which would nationalize big business and large estates, ensure a high level of welfare to the poor, entitle workers to better conditions and to a share in the profits of their employer.'[21]

Prince Chichibu read Kita's book, and was interested in the ideas for ameliorating the lot of the working class. So many of the recruits he had trained came from poor homes, and he was appalled at the number of people living in wretched conditions so different from his own. But in his position, there was little in a practical way that he could actually do to help them. It was rather like Edward VIII, when Prince of Wales, who saw the plight of the Welsh miners, and famously declared, 'Something must be done!'.

The concern of the Prince of Wales may have cheered up British workers, but it very definitely heartened the young Japanese army officers to have the ear and understanding of a prince of the blood, and though unbeknownst to him – for he had no way of knowing – Prince Chichibu became an important rallying symbol.[22] In 1936 the following poem was widely circulated among the reformist officers:

> Cleaving his way
> Thro' the deep snowdrifts
> Of the far north,
> Our Sun Prince hastens
> To the Capital![23]

Prince Chichibu did in fact try to do something. Kita Ikki had written that 'the leading ideal of the Meiji Restoration was that the Emperor should be the people's Emperor and the people should be the Emperor's people'. Why could not this basic concept of 'the people's Emperor'[24] be re-activated in order to right the inequities of society? To explain this to his brother seemed to be something positive he could do. So he went and harangued the Emperor.

Their first confrontation was recorded in the diary of General Honjō Shigeru. General Honjō was not yet the Emperor's Aide de Camp, and he did not say from whom he heard the hurriedly jotted down account, or exactly when. The entry was headed Somewhere between the end of 1931 and the spring of 1932:

> A certain day – Prince Chichibu visits Palace – talks to His Majesty – keeps advocating necessity direct imperial rule – His Majesty's angry refusal to suspend Constitution – argument becomes heated – afterwards His Majesty says to chief chamberlain, 'direct rule would be insulting to my ancestors – I cannot possibly agree – must adhere to Constitution – I rule by embracing and overseeing its principles. That's all I'm supposed to do. To do something like suspending the Constitution would be to destroy what the great Emperor Meiji established, which is something I positively cannot bring myself to do. What a dreadful younger brother I have![25]

PRINCE CHICHIBU AND THE ATTEMPTED COUPS D'ÉTAT

On 15 May 1932, after two failed attempts to overthrow the government the previous year, a group of young naval officers and army cadets managed to assassinate Prime Minister Inukai. The Prince had no previous knowledge of the uprising, and naturally did not condone the killing, but he did understand the rebels' grievances. He immediately went to the Palace and tried once again to make his brother, the Emperor, understand the reasons behind the unrest, but these harangues did nothing but cause the Emperor to grimace with painful anguish, and created a temporary rift between them.[26]

When the most serious coup d'état – the 26 February 1936, incident – took place, Prince Chichibu was in Hirosaki, in the north of Japan's main island of Honshu, whence he had been posted the year before as battalion commander of the Third Regiment. It was very possibly to distance him from the radicals in view of the misgivings beginning to be entertained about him more and more by the Emperor and courtiers like Saionji and Kido.[27]

He must have been given a choice of postings, and typically chose a hard one according to the Princess who wrote: 'When most of the new recruits he trained came from poor homes, I think he wanted to experience for himself the harsh conditions of the cold north-east.' There were endurance marches, and once he had to stand on a mountain top all night in the rain.[28] He habitually drove himself mercilessly, such as remaining standing while his men rested, and assuming rigorous tasks himself instead of delegating them.

News of the rebellion did not reach Hirosaki until the afternoon, but a 7 a.m. phone call from his younger brother Prince Takamatsu informed Prince Chichibu of the coup, although his brother did not yet have all the details.

It was 9 a.m. before the regimental commander arrived at his office and the Prince went in to see him immediately to request compassionate leave to go to Tokyo. He had used up all his regular leave touring the prefecture. He was given a form to fill out, and what he put we do not know. After that, he called seven officers from his battalion into his office. Cadet Oikawa Tsuneo, in retirement, clearly remembered what he said to them:

> 'This morning, some officers took it upon themselves to lead their men in a regrettable action completely opposed to His Majesty's desires,' said the prince, and went on, 'Whatever happens, you are not to align yourselves with them.' Then raising his voice, he added emphatically, 'Don't do anything rash!'[29]

After that, he continued with the day's normal routine, taking the 1 a.m. train for Tokyo that night. A second telephone call had come through from Prince Takamatsu in the afternoon, asking him to come, but he had already decided his duty lay in supporting and assisting his elder brother.

Tokyo had just experienced one of its biggest snowfalls, clearing up only in the early hours of the 26th. When the Emperor was told of the attack on the homes of seven government leaders, killing the Finance Minister and the Lord Keeper of the Privy Seal – wise and experienced statesmen whom the Emperor valued – his rage knew no bounds.

Chamberlain Kanroji wrote: 'Never have I seen the Emperor, a peaceful man who rarely loses his temper, as angry as when he learned of the assassinations.'[30] The Emperor immediately ordered the uprising to be put down at once, but his orders, though repeated several times, were not carried out for two whole days because various people in high places – including a general were sympathetic to the rebels.

Prince Chichibu's train journey took fourteen hours. On arrival in Tokyo at 4.59 p.m. on the 27th, he went straight to the Palace, where, according to Kido's diary, he first saw Prince Takamatsu and then spent two-and-a-half hours alone with the Emperor, from six to eight-thirty, after which they dined together, joined by their mother the Empress Dowager.[31]

There is no record of their conversation, but Prince Chichibu had obviously realized it was a time of crisis for the Imperial Family and he and the Emperor pledged their determination to stand firm together. Prince Chichibu clearly had only two alternatives: to apologize for the actions of members of his former regiment and put himself at his brother's disposal, or to try again to persuade the Emperor to see the rebels' point of view. This time he unhesitatingly chose the former.[32] It was a decision he had made before getting on the train. As the Princess wrote: 'He could not condone the act of the rebel officers in using national military forces to try to further their own ideas, killing and injuring a large number of people in the process.'[33]

Prince Chichibu's support was a great relief to the Emperor. He said afterwards to Kido Kōichi, Secretary to the Lord Keeper of the Privy Seal: 'Prince Chichibu has behaved much better than he did at the time of the May Fifteenth incident.'[34]

The insurrection was not crushed until the end of the second day of negotiations and street propaganda, in the course of which the Prince's friend Andō Teruzō made a speech of unwarranted optimism at the Sannō Hotel saying: 'Prince Chichibu has returned to Tokyo. He understands our cause well and sympathizes with us. The Shōwa Restoration is soon going to be achieved.'[35]

'The young officers' movement had been destroyed, but the army used the incident as an excuse to strengthen its hold on power and bolster its imperialist ambitions.'[36] Kita Ikki, author of the manifesto, was executed, as well as the instigators of the rebellion – many of whom were the Prince's friends. He must have felt deeply concerned when he heard that while most of the others shouted the traditional cry of a Japanese soldier before death, 'Long live the Emperor!' Andō had additionally shouted 'Long live Prince Chichibu!'[37]

With the rebels invoking his name it is hardly surprising that rumours became rife that Prince Chichibu had headed the coup – and even that the rebels planned to replace the Emperor with the Prince. Hosaka deplored the 'groundless fabrications which have been circulated so extensively' and which, he said, made his blood boil with rage many times while researching the biography. Prince Chichibu, he maintained 'was not understood during his lifetime, and remains misunderstood by history'.

It may also be argued that the Emperor's position in relation to the war and his constitutional position have been misunderstood by some historians who may not be aware of the apology which he had drafted but which was never issued.[38]

LATER CAREER

In 1937, the year following the incident, Prince and Princess Chichibu went to England to represent the Emperor and Empress at the coronation of King George VI. It was a happy visit for them both. The princess wrote: 'We were always given precedence over the representatives of the other nations . . . the extraordinary friendliness expressed to us by the British Royal Family was quite remarkable . . . world feeling towards Japan was not especially cordial. . . . That the Royal Family should have treated us so warmly at such a time touched us deeply.'[39]

They both returned to Japan with remnants of the respiratory infection which had forced them to cancel part of their intended visit to Europe, and the Prince could not get rid of his persistent cough.

Promoted to Colonel, he was sent on a long tour of duty to Manchuria, which included exhausting all-night observations of battles from the bridge of a cruiser. As usual he drove himself hard in spite of continued ill health, and finally succumbed to tuberculosis, the real cause of which, his wife maintained, 'lay in the strain he constantly subjected himself to as he strove to carry out both his imperial duties and his military duties with a high degree of excellence. That desire stemmed from the humility he felt regarding his upbringing which was so vastly different from that of the poor army recruits'.[40]

The imperial duty Prince Chichibu enjoyed most was probably being honorary patron of the Japan-British Society in Tokyo. With his special affection for Britain it must have delighted him to be asked to do so in January, 1928 – the year after his return from Oxford. During his illness and later convalescence in Gotemba he was often represented by the Princess, and she took over the honorary patronage on his death in 1953.

When the war was over, and he had regained some of his strength, Prince Chichibu realized a long-time dream of living the life of an English country gentleman. The Chichibus set up a farm on their Gotemba estate along English lines to help with the food shortage. He also took up writing, contributing a series of essays entitled 'Diary of a Convalescent' to a health magazine, as well as publishing two books: *Recollections of Life in England and America* (by them both), and *Gotemba Thoughts* in which he expounded the opening up of the monarchy and aired bold opinions never before expressed by a member of the Imperial Family. He wanted . Japan to hurry up and become a modern people with a true understanding of rights and obligations. He would have rejoiced to see the many democratic reforms, internationalization and prosperity of Japan today – a far cry from the ruin he had predicted as a result of breaking off friendly relations with England and America.

PRINCESS CHICHIBU AND BRITAIN

Princess Chichibu, widowed, carried on, promoting Anglo-Japanese friendship, continuing to grace, with exceptional elegance and charm, the functions of the Japan-British Society as well as the annual October tea of the women's Elizabeth Kai. She welcomed British royalty to Japan and made five official trips to Britain: First in 1962, when she was invested with the honorary Dame Grand Cross of the Order of the British Empire, and then in 1967 to attend the 75th anniversary of the Japan Society of London. She flew to London again in 1974 and 1979, and finally in 1981 for the opening of the Great Japan Exhibition at the Royal Academy. In 1978, at the British Embassy in Tokyo, Princess Margaret, on behalf of the Queen, bestowed upon her the insignia of an honorary Dame Grand Cross of the Order of St Michael and St George. Princess Chichibu wrote with great modesty, that she considered it 'was really bestowed on the late Prince Chichibu and the Japan-British Society he had represented, and symbolized the close ties between our two countries'.[41]

4

Crown Prince Akihito in Britain

HUGH CORTAZZI

Crown Prince Akihito spent eight days at *Cragside* in 1953 as
the guest of Lord and Lady Armstrong

THE PRESENT EMPEROR of Japan (*Heisei*) visited Britain officially
and privately on a number of occasions, while he was Crown Prince. His
most important official visit was in 1953 when he attended the
Coronation of Queen Elizabeth II. He also came to Britain in 1976
with the Crown Princess at the invitation of the Queen and stayed at
Windsor Castle. He and the Crown Princess were then guests of Her
Majesty's Government and they paid visits in England, Scotland and
Wales. In 1981 they attended the wedding of the Prince and Princess of
Wales. In addition, they made a few unofficial visits in particular to see
their son, the present Crown Prince, while he was studying at Oxford
University. This essay deals primarily with the Crown Prince's visit for the
Coronation, which was his most significant visit.[1]

PREPARATIONS

The Foreign Office started to prepare for the coronation in early 1952. Monarchs do not attend the coronations of fellow monarchs and John Pilcher in a minute[2] dated 24 July 1952 suggested that it would be good if the Crown Prince were to represent the Emperor. In Tokyo Prime Minister Yoshida strongly recommended this and according to a letter from Dening[3] 'the Imperial Household were not opposed to it'. Dening was officially informed of the selection of the Crown Prince to represent the Emperor on 9 September 1952. British and Japanese alike saw the visit as a prime opportunity for restoring relations between the Royal and Imperial families and helping the normalization of relations between Britain and Japan. It was not, however, an easy decision in view of the hostility towards Japan in Britain at that time because of the Japanese maltreatment of prisoners of war and British fears of unfair competition from Japan in textiles and other products. The Japanese decided that the Crown Prince should also visit the USA and that in addition to touring important countries such as France and Germany the Crown Prince should also visit European countries with constitutional monarchies and restore relations with European royalty.

Careful and detailed plans for the tour were drawn up and a budget allocated despite Japan's then exiguous foreign exchange reserves. Experienced diplomats and palace officials were nominated to accompany the Crown Prince.[4] The head of the suite was the Grand Chamberlain Mitani Takanobu, who was assisted by Matsui Akira from the *Gaimushō* and by the Vice-Grand Master of Ceremonies Kikkawa Shigenobu.[5] Dening wisely suggested that while in Britain the Crown Prince should be accompanied by David Symon,[6] a young second secretary in the Embassy who had been a language student. David, who was an able athlete, visited the Crown Prince a number of times before departure in order to give the Prince an opportunity to practise his English[7] and learn more about Britain. They also spoke about sport in view of the Prince's interests in tennis and other sports.

The British were particularly concerned to ensure that suitable preparations were made to deal with the press, both Japanese and British. The Foreign Office thought that the Japanese Embassy in London had not done enough to cultivate the British press and were relieved when Henry Shimanouchi was appointed. He spoke fluent English even though he had never been to Britain and his main experience had been in the United States.

There was a rather bizarre debate about the dress which the Crown Prince should wear at the coronation. The Lord Chamberlain had called for visiting dignitaries to wear 'the highest form of ceremonial dress of their own country'. This would have meant the Crown Prince appearing in Japanese court costume. Fortunately for the Prince this suggestion was eventually dropped and it was agreed that he and other dignitaries should attend wearing formal evening attire (white tie, tails and decorations).[8]

The Japanese were naturally much concerned about the Security arrangements, but were told firmly by Scotland Yard that they would take good care of these and that they did not want or need hordes of Japanese security personnel to accompany the Prince. The Japanese did not press the point.

Before the Crown Prince departed the British Ambassador gave a dinner in his honour. Dick Ellingworth, another second secretary, David Symon and I were invited – perhaps to add some youth to the occasion. Not surprisingly, in view of the average age of those present and the inevitably stuffy atmosphere, the Crown Prince found it difficult to relax and we and he no doubt were relieved when it was all over.

Dening in his despatch to the Secretary of State reporting the Crown Prince's departure from Japan strongly urged that Britain should welcome him:

> Since the Crown Prince is still young and impressionable, since he can by no stretch of the imagination bear any responsibility for what Japan did in the war: and since the Japanese people set much store by him, I venture to hope that his reception in the United Kingdom will be kindly and that everything possible will be done to enable him to carry away, when he leaves the United Kingdom, the best possible memories of our country and people.[9]

ARRIVAL IN BRITAIN

As full details of the Crown Prince's programme can be found in Japan Society bulletins published in 1953 (with a rather sycophantic commentary, no doubt inspired by Major General F.S.G. Piggott[10]). I propose in this essay to concentrate on some highlights.

The Crown Prince arrived at Southampton from the USA on 27 April 1953 on board the *Queen Elizabeth*. Asakai, the Japanese Minister in London, who had met the party in New York, warned them that there was still strong anti-Japanese sentiment in Britain and British newspapers had published articles suggesting that the Prince would not be welcome.[11] He also reported that the invitation to visit Newcastle would not take place because of opposition in the City Assembly. However, when the Japanese Ambassador in London, Matsumoto Shunichi, came on board[12] to greet the Prince he looked cheerful. Overnight the attitude of the press had completely changed and the newspapers that morning carried articles welcoming the Prince; there had not been one critical article.[13] Members of the Japanese Embassy in London and members of the Japanese community[14] also came to greet the Prince. General Piggott represented the Japan Society. There were many press representatives and photographers. The Prince read a brief message in English in which he expressed his pleasure in visiting Britain and noted: 'My father[15] has told me of the happy days he spent here when he visited your country 32 years ago.' At Waterloo Station he was greeted by Lord Selkirk in his capacity as Lord-in-Waiting, as well as by Sir Robert Craigie, Chairman of the Japan Society, and Sir Edward Crowe, Chairman of the Japan Association.

On 29 April the Japanese Ambassador gave a reception at his residence at 23 Kensington Palace Gardens, 'in the presence of the Crown Prince' to celebrate the Emperor's birthday. On the following day the Prince visited the British Museum and *The Times* building, but his most important engagement was lunch at No. 10 Downing Street as guest of the Prime Minister Sir Winston Churchill.

LUNCH AT NO 10

Among those present were Clement Attlee, former Prime Minister and leader of the opposition, and other politicians. The media were represented by the press Lords Beaverbrook,[16] Kemsley and Rothermere. The Japanologists invited were Arthur Waley[17] and Sir George Sansom.[18] The Prime Minister proposed the toast to the Emperor and spoke briefly without notes.

Sir George Sansom, after obtaining clearance from the Prime Minister's private secretary Anthony Montague Brown[19] sent an account of Sir Winston's speech to the Japanese Prime Minister Yoshida Shigeru:

> I think you may be interested in a summary of the Prime Minister's speech, though no paraphrase ever does justice to his spoken words.
>
> It was a short, unprepared speech[20] which we English guests at the luncheon found very moving and which I am sure gave pleasure to H.I.H. and the Japanese guests. We heard the voice of a wise statesman speaking out of his many years of experience to a young man who one day must undertake great responsibilities in his own country.
>
> Sir Winston Churchill pointed out the diversity of political opinions represented by those present – government, parliament, trade unions, the press – and said that this was characteristic of English life. The English, he said, are a people who, while they may disagree vigorously among themselves, are united in cherishing and upholding the English way of life, 'which we will defend with all the breath in our bodies and all the blood in our veins'.
>
> We owe much of the continuity and stability of English life to our institutions, particularly to our constitutional monarchy.

The Sovereign 'reigns but does not govern'. The Sovereign can do no wrong and if statesmen make blunders they are replaced by the people and the parliament which the people elects.

Having spoken of the affection and the trust inspired in the English people by our young Queen the Prime Minister addressed the Crown Prince directly, hoping that H.I.H. would enjoy his visit to this country and would profit by the view of English life which it would afford.

He said that the Crown Prince was fortunate in that he was a young man. Those who had to look back on the past must inevitably have a memory not only of successes, but also of the errors and misfortunes which attend human affairs. Young men like H.I.H. could look forward to a life of achievement.

I think that these were the main points of the Prime Minister's speech, though he did give some entertaining reminiscences, including some memories of what his Mother[21] had seen and heard in Japan in 1894. He recalled that at that time Japan was more esteemed for her recent naval and military progress than for her age-long achievement in the arts. He wished that the nations of the world could devote more of their resources to works of art than to the construction of aircraft and battleships.

Altogether the party was most successful, the atmosphere most genial.

Montague Brown[22] noted the Prime Minister's advice to the Prince on leaving 'to ignore any local discordant notes in his welcome to this country'. This remark was much appreciated by the Japanese party.[23]

The fact that this lunch was held so soon after the Crown Prince had reached Britain at a very busy time in the run-up to the Coronation underlines the determination of the British Government to do all they could to ensure that the Prince was given a warm welcome in Britain and shown due honour. The Government were conscious of the continuing resentment against Japan and a great deal of effort was put by the government into organizing the very full and comprehensive programme arranged for the Crown Prince whose stay lasted an unprecedented five weeks. The Japanese party recognized this.[24]

After the Crown Prince had left Britain on his European tour Sir Winston Churchill wrote[25] on 25 June in reply to a message from the Prince sent on 10 June 1953:

I trust he found his stay amongst us both agreeable and profitable. Her Majesty's Government and the British people were glad and honoured to be afforded this opportunity of meeting His Imperial Highness during a visit which I feel sure will have contributed greatly to Anglo-Japanese understanding.

THE QUEEN AND THE CORONATION

The Queen received the Crown Prince on 5 May. H.I.H. accompanied by Mr Mitani attended a Royal Garden Party on 28 May. The Prince also met the Queen during his visit to Epsom on 6 June to see the Derby. Matsui Akira recorded that the attitude of British Royalty had been extremely friendly and he noted that at Epsom the Queen had invited the Crown Prince to sit with her to watch the race. At his audience to say farewell Matsui noted[26] that the Queen had said:

> I do hope that your Highness has enjoyed your visit. I do not know His Majesty the Emperor but please tell him on your return to Japan that I am most grateful that your Highness was able to attend my coronation.

The Crown Prince's attendance at the Coronation ceremony on 2 June which lasted over three hours was, of course, the main purpose of his visit. The Foreign Office despatch of 18 June 1953 about the visit recorded that the Crown prince:

> . . . was particularly thrilled to sit among members of other royal houses and representatives of other heads of state at one of the two state banquets given at Buckingham palace for official guests at the Coronation. The pomp and splendour of this occasion undoubtedly impressed him, perhaps more so than the Coronation service itself where, although he had an excellent seat, his view was obscured by his neighbours in the choir stalls.

The service certainly greatly impressed members of his suite. Matsui noted that although there were said to have been some changes in the ceremonial it reflected many centuries of tradition and was an impressive ritual accompanied by solemn music and magnificent costumes. It made him think that he was looking at a medieval picture scroll (*emakimono*). The coronation throne, the crown, the sceptre and the jewels forming the regalia all seemed to have a traditional significance and he felt the power of tradition in Britain. They had learnt in their travels in European countries that the system of holding a coronation had not been preserved in other European monarchies. He felt that rather than suggesting the divine right of kings, the coronation service emphasized that the British monarchy reflected the will of God and the consent of the people and that the royal prerogative derived from on high and not from the sovereign herself. Mitani Takanobu, the head of the suite, in his memoirs felt that the words of the service did not simply stress that this was an occasion for celebration and joy, but rather emphasized the weight of responsibility falling on her. Matsui noted that the visits, which she made to every part of Britain during coronation week, underlined the recognition by the people of the Queen as the sovereign. Matsui was impressed by the intimate and friendly way in which the Queen had behaved. In common parlance it was very democratic. He had heard so often people commenting of the Queen 'So simple and nice'. In Britain, it seemed to him that, while an ancient system of important and dignified ceremonial was maintained, daily life at court went on in a natural and ordinary way. This seemed also to be the case in other European monarchies.

The Foreign Office despatch recorded that the Crown Prince's suite declared that the Crown Prince was greatly moved by the dignity, informality and charm of the Royal family. . . 'There is no doubt that he will perpetuate that admiration for the British Royal Family, which has become traditional in the Japanese Imperial Household'.

THE JAPAN SOCIETY'S DINNER

The Japan Society's dinner in honour of the Crown Prince was held on 4 May 1953 at the Hyde Park Hotel. It was attended by over 200 members and their guests. Before the loyal toasts the poet Edmund Blunden was asked to recite the poem which he had written to mark the visit. Like so many poems written to order it sounds banal to modern readers and its rhymes forced. Those who wish to read it in full will find it on page 2 of bulletin No 10. To give its tone I quote the fourth verse (of six):

> Prince, pilgrim, envoy, dwell
> Among us happily as in your own
> Japan; you will find those here who tell
> Their love with few words, but their love is known.

The main speech was delivered by the Chairman, Sir Robert Craigie. The following paragraph from this speech is worth recalling:

> My first recollection of him is of a boy of five busily engaged on the beach at Hayama, near our house, searching in the rocky pools for those biological specimens which, even then, interested him so greatly. But he seemed also to have a second objective – namely, to escape from the large retinue by which he was surrounded, and to wade out into the deep blue sea. Believe me, the enterprise and ingenuity he displayed on these occasions and the amount of exercise he gave to his dignified companions was most impressive. I remember my wife turning to me and saying, 'That young man, with his love of freedom, will go a long way.'

After the toast the Crown Prince replied briefly stressing how honoured he felt to be attending the coronation as proxy for his father and proposed a toast to the Society. Mr David Gammans MP, Assistant Postmaster General and a member of the Society, replied. He recalled that he had lived for three years in Japan where he had been a Foreign Office language officer. As so many politicians have done and still do he spoke of the Japanese like the British being an island race. He drew attention to Japanese loyalty to the Imperial House and said (not perhaps very wisely in view of the vivid memories of many British people of Japanese behaviour towards British prisoners of war): 'All the events of the past twenty years would never change the Japanese character at heart.'

CROWN PRINCE'S TOUR

After his audience with the Queen the Crown Prince travelled by night train to Edinburgh. Apart from seeing the usual sights there (the party were guided round by David Symon who knew Edinburgh well) the Prince 'spent some time shopping'. He exchanged visits with the Lord Provost Sir James Millar. The Japan Society's account states that 'the simple and direct speech of Sir James . . . made a great appeal to the Japanese visitors.' He then went on to visit the Duke of Buccleuch at Bowhill, Selkirk, where he was shown the Duke's hounds. He stayed at the George Hotel in Edinburgh where Scottish dances were performed in the dining-room for the enjoyment of the Prince. From Pitlochry where the party stayed two nights in a hotel the Prince went on to Blair Atholl where he was greeted by the Duke of Atholl and shown the room in the castle where his father had stayed in 1921.

On 9 May the Prince returned to England to stay at Cragside, the home of Lord and Lady Armstrong, where his father had stayed in 1921. The Prince caught his first trout[27] in Britain on 10 May. A formal dinner was held in the Crown Prince's honour on 11 May.

A visit to Newcastle and the Vickers-Armstrong works there (Vickers-Maxim and sons of Barrow-in-Furness had built Admiral Togo's battleship *Mikasa* in 1896) had been planned, but[28] this was cancelled when a proposed civic reception was 'strongly opposed by the city's Labour Party, the Newcastle and District branch of the Far East Prisoner-of-War (POW) Association and local trade union branches'. The cancellation was hailed as a 'singular victory' by a POW delegation who were told the news when they called on the Lord Mayor. Five Japanese journalists who had been planning to visit the region then cancelled their plans. The *Newcastle Journal*, which carried an article under the headline 'The North has acted below its traditions' clearly thought that the city was being discourteous to such a distinguished visitor. So also apparently did the Lord Mayor, Mrs Grantham who attended the dinner wearing her full regalia. At the end of the dinner pointing to her gold chain of office she declared[29] to the

Prince: 'The POW question is no more than a plot[30] by a few people. It is highly regrettable. This gold chain round my neck is the symbol of Newcastle. When your Highness sees this it means that you have been welcomed in Newcastle.' The Japan Society's report said that she was one of the last to leave. 'Her gold chain over a white net crinoline dress made a striking and impressive figure, as she curtsied farewell to the young Prince.'

The Prince apparently enjoyed his stay at Cragside. He rode, played tennis and when it was wet billiards. He visited the local tennis club and was made an Honorary Member. He saw the lighthouse and the bird sanctuary and was present at a garden party. At the farewell dinner party they all sang 'Auld Lang Syne' and the Prince made a gracious speech expressing his sincere thanks for Lord and Lady Armstrong's hospitality and kindness.

On his way back to London the Prince visited Durham where he was conducted over the castle, now a college of the University, and the cathedral by Louis Allen.[31]

One of his first visits after his return was to Windsor Castle and Eton College. Four days had then been set aside for a visit to Oxford. This had to be cut down as the Prince developed a feverish cold. As a result he missed a visit to Stratford-on-Avon and the opening of Eights Week. He also missed among other events a tea party given by the Archbishop of Canterbury, a visit to the Victoria and Albert Museum and a visit to Lords to watch cricket. This latter had been strongly advocated by General Piggott who delivered a lecture on cricket to members of the Prince's suite!

Fortunately for the General the Prince was sufficiently recovered to 'motor to Cranleigh' on Whit Sunday but was not well enough to take part in the friendly tennis matches arranged that afternoon. Two days were then spent in a visit to Cambridge where he stayed at Trinity as the guest of Dr (later Lord) Adrian and Mrs (Lady) Adrian. There was some controversy in the press about the Cambridge visit as it was alleged erroneously that a hotel[32] in Cambridge had refused to let accommodation to the Crown prince's party. The Japan Society's report noted that the 'services of E.B.Ceadel, Lecturer in Japanese were indispensable.

On his return to London the Crown Prince visited Pinewood Film Studios. He also had dinner with Sir Robert and Lady Craigie, visited Reuters Radio Station after lunching with Sir Christopher Chancellor, the head of Reuters, and attended a garden party at Hatfield given by the Marchioness of Salisbury, a cinema performance of the *Beggar's Opera*, a garden party given by the Archbishop of Canterbury, dinner by the Prime Minister at Lancaster House, an evening reception at Buckingham Palace and another garden party at Blenheim given by the Duke and Duchess of Marlborough. The Prince also packed into his busy schedule visits to the

Houses of Parliament, to the Tower of London and to Natural History Museum.

On many occasions during his tour he was invited to plant a tree commemorating his visit.

THE MEDIA

The Japanese press assiduously followed the Prince's schedule. 'Twenty-four reporters and cameramen from thirteen news organizations accompanied the crown prince. They carefully investigated local reactions to the Crown Prince's visit. . .'[33] In Japan there was much interest in how he was received in Britain and in the role of the monarchy in Britain which might have pointers for Japan. Henry Shimanouchi[34] told Vere Redman, the Information Counsellor in the Embassy, after he returned to Japan, that he had found the Japanese press representatives had 'a tendency to look for grievances where few or none existed: their own lack of English prevented them from sharing in the full sense of the Coronation story and in consequence they were inclined to fall back on the occasional press manifestations of hostility, the difficulties in Newcastle, and the like'.

Shimanouchi found the British journalists fairly mild (his previous experience having been with Americans) but had found it rather hard going in Newcastle where they seemed to be trying to involve him in local politics. The Times[35] reported frequently and factually on the Crown Prince's tour of Britain. But for the British media the Prince was just one of many VIPs invited to the Coronation. The Prince faced a battery of cameras on his arrival and photographers followed him around (for instance they photographed him buying a hat at Locke's in St James's) but they eventually got bored and only photographed more important items in his programme such as his visit to the Derby at Epsom when many photographs were taken of the two Royal personages sitting together. These photographs were given due prominence in the press.[36]

It was inevitable that the prisoner–of–war issue which led to what Matsui described as a 'small number of unfortunate incidents'[37] would come up, but apart from the cancellation of the visit to Newcastle this issue did not overshadow the visit. The Daily Express had gone so far as to ask its readers whether in their opinion the Crown prince should see the Queen crowned.[38] However, the announcement that the Queen was to receive him and the Prime Minister's invitation to luncheon 'put an end to these indications of incipient hostility'. There were no incidents throughout the visit and Scotland Yard:

> . . . found the visit remarkably uneventful. . . The Crown Prince and his suite, therefore, only derived perhaps the salutary impression that the resentment felt by prisoners of war

is an obstacle to the improvement of Anglo-Japanese relations which the Japanese must endeavour in the long run to remove. . . . The British public's attitude might be summed up in the remark of a woman who saw the Prince driving into Buckingham Palace: 'Oh there he is! Well I suppose he can't help it . . . let's give him a cheer!'[39]

ASSESSMENT

The official despatch from the Foreign Office about the visit to Sir Esler Dening, the British Ambassador in Tokyo, was dated 18 June 1953 and signed for the Prime Minister by John Pilcher, the then head of Japan and Pacific Department (later Sir John Pilcher and Ambassador to Tokyo (1967-72),[40] declared:

> The visit was conceived as an educational one. The Crown Prince himself and members of his suite stated that the Emperor of Japan was most anxious that his son should be able to enjoy the experiences from which he had himself once derived pleasure and instruction. The programme was, therefore, a mixture of sight-seeing and the visiting of educational establishments (Eton, Durham, Oxford and Cambridge), interspersed with visits to country houses.
>
> From the point of view of the Crown Prince and his suite, the visit was a success.

Dening in his despatch to the Foreign Secretary of 21 October 1953 confirmed that this was also the view of the Shôwa Emperor who at a luncheon party for Heads of Missions in Tokyo from countries which the Crown Prince had visited had 'referred in the warmest terms to the reception which the Crown Prince had received, in particular from the Royal Family, during his visit to England'. Dening added that afterwards he had talked with the Crown Prince himself:

> I was at once struck, not only with the marked improvement in his English, but with his ease of manner and the greater confidence which he had acquired in the course of his tour . . . he now both smiles and laughs more readily and seems to take greater pleasure in conversation.

According to Matsui's report the suite also believed that the visit had been both generally enjoyable and a success. Relations with the British Royal family had been re-established. The Queen had been gracious and friendly. The British government had worked hard to provide a varied and interesting programme. The Japan Society had done its best to welcome the Prince, although the efforts of General Piggott to insinuate himself into the programme to the maximum extent possible must have grated with the Foreign Office who noted that the success of the visit was 'due to a large extent to the good advice offered both before and during the visit by Lord Hankey to the Japanese Ambassador'.[41]

The Prince, still a young man of only nineteen behaved with decorum, but displayed the warmth of his personality and charmed his hosts by his natural friendliness. Royal visits are no longer major political events, but this visit was clearly a symbol of the reacceptance of Japan in the post-war world and was as important as a state visit.

1976 OFFICIAL VISIT

During the Queen's State Visit to Japan in 1975 Her Majesty invited the Crown Prince and Princess to stay with her at Windsor in 1976 and attend the races at Ascot. The British Government decided (I was then Deputy Under-Secretary in the Foreign and Commonwealth Office (FCO)) to invite their Imperial Highnesses to stay a few days in Britain as government guests. The invitation was accepted and plans were drawn up in discussions between the FCO and the Japanese Embassy in London for a programme of visits in England, Scotland and Wales.

Their Imperial Highnesses visited Britain between 15 and 24 June 1976. They spent the nights of 16 and 17 June as guests of the Queen at Windsor Castle where the Queen hosted dinners in their honour. She also took them to Ascot as her guests at the Royal Ascot race meetings. After leaving Windsor the Crown Prince and Princess stayed at Claridges while they were in London. Unfortunately, it was an exceptionally hot June and Claridges in those days did not have air-conditioning. The imperial couple bore the heat with fortitude and appeared to enjoy their visit. I accompanied the couple on most of their visits and do not recall any unfortunate incidents or signs of resentment and hostility such as sadly left an unfortunate impression during their State Visit as Emperor and Empress in 1998.

Visits were made in England by both the Prince and Princess to Stoke Poges Church which the Crown Princess wanted to see as a result of her study of English literature and Grey's famous elegy. The Crown Prince visited the Thames water treatment plant at Beckton while the Crown Princess went to the British Red Cross. Both visited Stoke Mandeville Sports Stadium for the disabled. The Crown Prince attached particular importance to this visit as sporting activities for the disabled has been one of his life-long interests. He had been Honorary President of the Para-Olympics which had been held in Tokyo in 1964 immediately following the Tokyo Olympics that year.

Crown Prince Akihito at the Deep Navigation Coal Mine, South Wales

On 18 June after a short trip on the Thames the couple attended a dinner by the Secretary of State for Foreign Affairs and Mrs Crosland at Trinity House. On 19 June they flew to Edinburgh where the Crown Prince visited the Royal Scottish Museum and the Crown Princess Edinburgh University's School of Scottish Studies. They both visited Edinburgh Castle. Thereafter they went on to St Andrews to visit the marine laboratory of the University. They then stayed two nights at Scone Palace, the home of the Earl and Countess of Mansfield. In addition to a visit Blair Castle for lunch with the Duke of Atholl the couple made a tour by car through the Highlands. On 21 June they lunched with the Earl and Countess of Moray at Doune Park and then flew from Glasgow to Cardiff where they stayed with the Lord Lieutenant and Lady Traherne at Coedarhydglyn. In South Wales the Crown Prince visited the Deep Navigation Coal Mine where he was dressed in miner's overalls and helmet and went down to the depths of the mine. The Crown Prince coped well with the heat.[42] The Crown Princess meanwhile visited Tintern Abbey and Chepstow castle. After lunch with the Lord Mayor and Lady Mayoress of Cardiff the imperial couple viewed the Welsh Folk Museum at St Fagans Castle and went on to the United World College of the Atlantic at St Donat's castle where they met some Japanese students. That evening they attended a 'medieval banquet' in Cardiff castle, where their host was Lord Goronwy-Roberts, Minister of State in the Foreign Office. As this involved eating off gravy covered bread plates the Crown Princess must have had some difficulty in avoiding soiling the fine kimono she was wearing.

On return by train to London they visited the Natural History Museum and called on the Duke and Duchess of Gloucester at Kensington Palace. Before leaving[43] on Thursday, 24 June 1976, they visited Kew Gardens.

The visit helped to cement relations with the Royal family and underlined the growing improvement in Anglo-Japanese relations.

PART II

Politicians
and
Diplomats

5

Terashima Munenori, 1832–93: Master of Early Meiji Diplomacy

ANDREW COBBING

Terashima Munenori

ON 11 AUGUST 1872 Terashima Munenori stepped onto the quay in Liverpool. Sporting a beard like many of his peers at that time, he looked elegant in Western clothes, his slight build and correct bearing lending him a false impression of height. Ozaki Saburō, his travelling companion on the voyage from New York, was struck by his 'good-natured and sincere manner', describing him as a man of 'traditional' views with 'a tendency to be a little stubborn at times'.[1] This was Terashima's third visit to Britain. In 1862 he had been among the party of thirty-six delegates in the Tokugawa *Bakufu*'s first mission to Europe. In 1865 he had spent several months in London as an envoy for his native Satsuma domain. Now at the age of forty he was back as Japan's first resident minister to Britain on behalf of the Meiji government.

On his arrival in London a few hours later he checked into the Langham Hotel and that evening he received a visit from Sir Harry Parkes, his counterpart in Japan. The British minister, home on leave, briefed him on their plans for the following day. In the morning they were to catch a train to Portsmouth and then cross the Solent to the Isle of Wight. Their destination was Osborne House where, on behalf of the Emperor, he presented his credentials to the Queen.[2]

With his scholarly background and reserved style, Terashima's low profile belied his lasting impact on Meiji politics. Supremely confident in his abilities, he already had considerable experience in diplomatic affairs and held no qualms about confronting envoys of the treaty powers with their own vaunted principles of international law. His arrival in London in the high summer of 1872 marked the onset of a diplomatic duel with Parkes that would unfold over the course of the decade. Conducted generally with decorum, their battle of wills encapsulated the small but significant differences in the broadly cordial relations between early Meiji Japan and Victorian Britain.

'With sunny hair and a sunny smile', Parkes, the spirited champion of British merchants' interests, was a very different personality.[3] The two men had known each other for several years, and previously their interests had largely coincided as Terashima tempted the Foreign Office with assurances of Satsuma's desire for open trade. Now there was growing discord, however, over the issue that would dominate Meiji foreign affairs, the new regime's stated desire to revise the 'unequal treaties' signed under Tokugawa rule in 1858. The combative British minister had been used to getting his way, but in Terashima he found a formidable adversary who calmly refused to be browbeaten into offering concessions like the pragmatic but short-sighted *Bakufu* officials of times past. Considering the weaknesses of the fledgling Meiji State, Parkes found his insistence on invoking Japanese sovereignty whenever possible sometimes difficult to tolerate.

AN OUTSTANDING SCHOLAR OF SCIENCE

Given his family background it was hardly surprising that the young Terashima made a name for himself in the world of Dutch Studies (*rangaku*), and with his sharp intellect and passion for learning, he soon attracted notice as a precocious talent. Born in 1832 near the town of Akune on the East China Sea coast, he was adopted at the age of five by his uncle Matsuki Muneyasu (Juan), a physician with a high reputation. On the orders of the daimyo, Juan had spent several years in Nagasaki studying under Phillip von Siebold, and now he was a leading figure in introducing Dutch-style medicine to Satsuma.[4]

In 1837 Fujitarō, as Terashima was known as a boy, was taken to Nagasaki, where he grew up surrounded by specialists in science and medicine. He and his uncle lived together with Ueno Shunnojō, clockmaker, student of gunnery and father of Ueno Hikoma, later famous as Japan's first exponent of photography During the six years he spent in Nagasaki, Fujitarō received an intensive training in Dutch from Japanese interpreters employed at Dejima, in those days the focal point of interest for scholars with an interest in the West.

His first excursion into the corridors of power was in 1841 when Matsuki Juan and Ueno Shunnojō were commissioned by Satsuma to help set up a chemical laboratory in Kagoshima. When they were granted an audience on their arrival, the nine-year-old Fujitarō, too, was presented to the daimyo.[5] Two years later, when his uncle was again summoned back from Nagasaki to serve permanently in the castle-town, he enrolled at the Zōshikan, the domain's school for samurai in Kagoshima. By the time Juan died in 1845 at the age of fifty-nine, his own standing was already such that, although just thirteen years old, he inherited his position as head of the family. With head suitably shaven and his physician's status indicated by the new name of Matsuki Kōan, he then received orders to train in Dutch Studies in Edo, an honour practically unheard of as he later recalled with pride.[6]

In the shogun's capital Matsuki went on to attend several private colleges, including the Shōsendō founded by the Dutch-style physician Itō Genboku. There, just as in Satsuma, his academic talents won universal acclaim and by the age of twenty-two he was appointed head of the Shōsendō himself. It was not until his first visit to Europe the following decade, however, that he would fully realize the shortcomings of his education in Edo. Confined to applied sciences, Dutch Studies were largely silent on social disciplines like politics and law. This was why, he concluded, early Japanese overseas travellers were so perplexed by unfamiliar institutions such as parliaments and commercial companies. The experience would persuade him to concentrate more on English, for after seeing people even in Holland relying on other languages, he declared that he could no longer recommend Dutch Studies to anyone.[7]

In the summer of 1853, when the arrival of Commodore Perry's ships off the Uraga coast heralded a new era of foreign relations, Matsuki was far away from Edo visiting his sick foster mother in Akune. Shimazu Nariakira, the new daimyo, took advantage of his return to enlist his linguistic skills in the service of Satsuma. There the security threat posed by Perry prompted a concerted effort to promote scientific research, especially in the field of gunnery. Dutch texts translated by Matsuki contributed to gunpowder experiments and the construction of Japan's third reverberating furnace.[8] Following his return to Edo the next year, the plans he drafted enabled the assembly of a steam engine. This was then fitted to a ship sent up from Kagoshima to create Japan's first motorized vessel, hailed by on-looking Edo townsfolk as 'the lord of Satsuma's steamship' when she was floated down the Sumida River that summer.[9]

In 1854 Matsuki was also one of several scholars of Dutch Studies appointed by the *Bansho Shirabesho*, the *Bakufu*'s new centre for studies on Western texts. Designed literally 'for the inspection of barbarian books', this was set up to handle the increased load of diplomatic paperwork envisaged following the commercial treaties signed with the United States, the Netherlands and Britain. He spent several years there as a young teacher and translator until, in 1857, the progressive daimyo of Satsuma had need of his expertise once more.

Recalled to Kagoshima, his work on Dutch texts prepared the way for further experiments on gas lighting and telegraphy. When the *Kanrin Maru*, a *Bakufu* training vessel called in at Kagoshima in April 1858, it was Matsuki who drew the attention of the nineteen Dutch officers on board. According to the captain, Willem Kattendyke, 'among the daimyo's retinue was one most intelligent-looking individual; this was the famous doctor Mats'ki Köan, teacher and translator of Dutch. He did not speak the language at all but his writing was impeccable'.[10] Taking copious notes throughout, his torrent of prepared questions tested the visitors' knowledge, and they were astonished by a little steamboat, complete with twelve-horsepower engine, that he had constructed himself. One of them, Pompe van Meerdervoort, was so impressed by his command of both natural and applied sciences that he claimed, 'Satsuma's recent progress is in no small part due to the doctor Matsuki Koan'.[11]

After Shimazu Nariakira's untimely death soon afterwards, Matsuki quickly tired of political affairs in Satsuma without the inspiration of his revered lord, and he was given leave to return to the *Bansho Shirabesho* in Edo. From there he was dispatched to Yokohama, where he witnessed the birth of a treaty port. Assigned to the customs house, he had the unenviable task of processing the declarations submitted by incoming ships from the day imports were first admitted on 1 July 1859. As this fishing village was transformed overnight into an international port, he was well placed to observe the growing prevalence of English in commercial affairs.

A DIPLOMAT IN THE MAKING

In the last years of Tokugawa rule, Matsuki's background as a Satsuma officer trained in Nagasaki and Edo forced him to tread a fine line through a minefield of conflicting interests. In varying contexts he was suspected by *Bakufu* officials of sympathies for Satsuma, by the British of complicity in dealings with the Bakufu, and even by Satsuma compatriots of collusion with the British. Recalling an encounter with him at Satsuma's Osaka residence in 1867, Ernest Satow later admitted: 'I had some suspicion that he was not altogether to be trusted, as he was reported to have been in the Tycoon's service.'[12]

It was certainly in the pay of the *Bakufu* that Matsuki first came to the notice of the British. In 1861, like other scholars at the *Bansho Shirabesho*, he was excited by the *Bakufu*'s decision to commission a team of experts to investigate conditions abroad during its forthcoming diplomatic mission to

Europe. His selection made him the first Satsuma officer to visit Europe, and it was again evidence of his standing in Dutch Studies that he was chosen ahead of such eminent colleagues as Nishi Amane.[13]

Matsuki's packed itinerary allowed no time for rest as he set about recording all he saw during the Takenouchi mission's travels in 1862.[14] Although impressed by the power of Britain, he was not so enamoured by the lukewarm reception the mission received from the government. Their hotel in London was 'far inferior to the one in which we had stayed in Paris', and everyone in the party, he noted, compared the two capitals with Edo and Kyoto respectively. Unlike others such as Fukuzawa Yukichi who returned to Japan glowing about the material wonders of Victorian Britain, his gaze fell upon some urban problems of the industrial age, including the conspicuous number of beggars. Distracted by tipsy Londoners who sang and danced below their hotel windows day and night, he laid the blame on brandy (he probably meant gin), adding that 'they would rather beg than live in the workhouse where drinking is forbidden'.[15]

The volatile political conditions awaiting his return to Japan in 1863 next propelled him into direct negotiations with the British, this time on behalf of Satsuma. With the movement to expel foreigners in the ascendancy, the recent assassination of a British merchant by a Satsuma officer had provoked threats of military retaliation. Responding to his domain's call to arms he hurried back to Kagoshima where he was placed in command of three second-hand steamships. He was adamant that fighting was futile, and tried to sue for peace when the expected Royal Navy squadron appeared off the coast in August. As Ernest Satow observed, at the time the steamships were seized and their crews put ashore, 'no attempt was made by us [the British] to take any prisoners, but two remained on board the *Sir George Grey*, who gave their names to me as Godai [Tomoatsu] and Matsugi Kowan'.[16] Their efforts were to no avail, for it was the capture of these vessels that prompted the batteries on shore to open fire, commencing a four-hour engagement in the rain that caused damage to both sides.[17]

Matsuki and Godai were later transported to Yokohama on board HMS *Euryalus* before being released. Now viewed as traitors in the eyes of their compatriots they were forced to spend several unsettled months as fugitives in the nearby Musashi area. Godai later travelled incognito to Nagasaki where, assisted by the Scottish merchant Thomas Blake Glover, he devised an ambitious plan for an overseas expedition to Britain. In 1864 this was approved in Satsuma, for the salutary experience of the Royal Navy's firepower had since prompted the domain to pursue closer links with its erstwhile enemy. Godai was pardoned, and as the only Satsuma officer with first-hand knowledge of Europe, Matsuki, too, was summoned back to join the party of nineteen that set sail from Hashima, a fishing village not far from Akune, on board one of Glover's ships in March 1865.[18]

Following their arrival in London, most of these officers registered as students at University College, but Matsuki was there as an envoy. An introduction from Glover secured him an interview with a prominent japanophile, the Scottish MP Laurence Oliphant,[19] who in turn arranged a meeting for him in July with Sir Austin Layard, the under-secretary at the Foreign Office. The following month, in his first despatch to Sir Harry Parkes, Foreign Secretary Lord Russell expressed growing mistrust of the *Bakufu*, and in a clear reference to Matsuki, revealed sympathy for the initiatives by Satsuma and Chōshū to send 'young men to this Country for education, and Officers to enter into confidential communication with Her Majesty's Government'.[20]

In March 1866 Matsuki accompanied Oliphant to the Foreign Office and made his case in person to the new Foreign Secretary Lord Clarendon. Satsuma's agenda was to harness external pressure from Britain through diplomatic channels to wrest control over the commercial treaties from the shogun. Matsuki's strategy, formed with Oliphant's help, attacked the *Bakufu*'s monopoly on trade and called for a council of daimyo to convene in Kyoto so as to transfer signatory power to the Emperor. This articulated a unified state and an imperial restoration, achieved through peaceful means if possible. The British, with their insistence on an outward appearance of neutrality, could not be seen to support a campaign against the *Bakufu*. Matsuki nevertheless received a sympathetic response, and his overtures reinforced the growing feeling in Whitehall that British merchants' interests were increasingly in tune with the trading aspirations of domains like Satsuma and Chōshū.[21]

It was in July 1866, shortly after his return to Japan, that Matsuki first met Parkes. Although initially sceptical about Satsuma's confidential communications, information from the Foreign Office had since persuaded the new British Minister to make an exploratory visit to Kagoshima.[22] At Parkes's own suggestion he was then transferred to Yokohama where, armed with the Minister's business card, he acted as Satsuma's principal contact with the British Legation. It was also at this juncture that he changed his name to Terashima, from the small island in the bay near his family home in Akune. Having previously served the *Bakufu* as Matsuki Kōan, this name he felt was inconsistent with his new duties working against the interests of the Edo authorities.[23]

In 1867, as the centre of political activity moved to the Kyoto area during the last months of Tokugawa rule, Terashima was transferred to the imperial capital and then to the Satsuma residence in Osaka. He often met with British diplomats like Ernest Satow and Algernon Mitford, and now worked closely with Ōkubo Toshimichi, who valued his diplomatic experience in the preparations for the transfer of power. At Ōkubo's behest it was Terashima who drafted the first document proclaiming the restoration of imperial rule to the envoys of the treaty powers. Significantly, it already indicated the new regime's desire to revise the unequal treaties. [24]

THE TERASHIMA ERA OF MEIJI DIPLOMACY

In the years following the overthrow of the Tokugawa *Bakufu*, Terashima campaigned on behalf of Japan's claims to full recognition as a sovereign state. Under the Ansei Treaties (the so-called 'unequal treaties' of 1858) a semi-colonial situation still prevailed in the treaty ports in the shape of consular jurisdiction, which gave foreign nationals extraterritorial rights, and through controls on tariffs, which suppressed the prices paid for imports. Parkes, however, 'was entirely opposed to any measure of treaty revision in Japan's favour'.[25] Not only was he determined to protect British merchants' privileges in the treaty ports, but campaigned in support of their demands for access to the interior as well. In time the vagaries of the consular court system and the growing capability of Japan's modern new institutions would serve to undermine his arguments, but not before a 'long rearguard action', fought primarily against Terashima.[26]

After joining the new government's Board of Foreign Affairs in 1868, Terashima was appointed governor of Kanagawa. Based in Yokohama, his duties were to supervise the everyday business of a treaty port, from merchants' complaints to charges of smuggling, diseased silkworms and a 21-gun salute from British men-of-war in harbour on Queen Victoria's birthday.[27] The telegraph office he established there also won him a reputation in engineering circles as 'the father of Japanese telegraphy'.[28] When the Ministry of Foreign Affairs was created in 1869 he became vice-minister at the age of thirty-seven, a position that enabled him to exercise his authority over Meiji diplomacy for the next decade. It was his choice of personnel that staffed the ministry with compatriots from the Satsuma expedition to Britain and others with experience of life overseas. In 1870, for example, the first officials to be posted abroad as chargé d'affaires were two former Satsuma students: Mori Arinori, who was sent to the United States, and Sameshima Naonobu, who arrived in London with a portfolio covering Britain, France and Prussia.

In keeping with early Meiji government policy of appointing aristocratic figureheads, the first Minister of Foreign Affairs was a court noble, Sawa Nobuyoshi. He was followed by Iwakura Tomomi and then Soejima Taneomi, but significantly most of the correspondence from the British Legation in these years was also addressed to Terashima.[29] When the question of treaty revision was first broached under Sawa, Parkes stalled by insisting on specific proposals; this was one of the reasons that prompted the launch of an ambitious diplomatic mission, the Iwakura

Embassy, which sailed for the United States at the start of its grand world tour late in 1871.

In Terashima and Soejima's view, there was little realistic chance of obtaining advantageous terms so soon, and they were dismayed to hear shortly afterwards that, on the counsel of Mori in Washington, two of Iwakura's vice-ambassadors, Ōkubo and Itō Hirobumi, were hurrying back to obtain credentials from Tokyo for formal treaty negotiations. Terashima joined them on their return voyage across the Pacific, ostensibly on his way to London to take up his new appointment as resident minister to Britain. It was with some relief that, following their arrival in Washington, he heard Kido Takayoshi's admission that negotiations had since foundered and the treaty issue would have to be shelved after all. In his first letter to Soejima from London a month later, he declared that the whole episode had made Japan 'a laughing stock in the eyes of the world'.[30]

Terashima had travelled a week in advance of the embassy on his onward voyage across the Atlantic. The timing of his new portfolio was partly circumstantial but also by design. He was of sufficient rank to placate Parkes, who had taken such exception to the appointment of the twenty-five-year-old Sameshima as chargé d'affaires in London that he had been forced to relocate to Paris.[31] Terashima also conceded that he was there on behalf of the Ministry of Foreign Affairs to monitor the Iwakura Embassy's talks with the treaty powers.[32]

He soon moved out of the Langham to the less expensive South Kensington Hotel, and in September premises were found for the first Japanese legation at No 9 Upper Belgrave Street, a terraced house accommodating an office of four Japanese officials and one British clerk.[33] Now he was busy arranging clearance through the Foreign Office for the embassy's visits to factories, mines and military installations. Also taking up much of his time was the task of securing emergency funds for distressed Japanese students left penniless after the collapse of the American Joint National Bank. In the financial scandal that followed it transpired that the owners, the Bowles Brothers, had absconded with around £24,000 deposited at their head office in Charing Cross by Japanese students and also some members of the embassy.[34] Terashima met with Itō to discuss the related problem of rationalizing the large number of students left dependent on central government funds after the recent abolition of the domains. The proposals they drafted were incorporated into regulations resulting in the recall of most of them in the course of the following year.[35]

On 22 November 1872 Iwakura was granted the first of three interviews with the Foreign Secretary Lord Granville. He arrived at the Foreign Office accompanied by Sugiura Kōzō (Hatakeyama Yoshinari), a member of staff who took notes, but for subsequent visits he requested the presence of Terashima and one of the vice-ambassadors, Yamaguchi Masuka. Granville, for his part, announced that he would be joined by Parkes. The stage was set for a sharp exchange at the second meeting on 27 November. As expected, little headway was made over Japanese claims for treaty revision. Citing an experiment in Egypt where control over civil tribunals had been ceded, Granville announced that 'in all such cases the policy of the British Government was to yield the local authorities jurisdiction over British subjects in direct proportion to their advancement in enlightenment and civilization'.[36]

This was hardly an invitation to discuss terms. Iwakura, for example, could only respond to enquiries about his government's harsh treatment of Japanese Christians by voicing his 'earnest desires' for religious toleration.[37] Parkes, moreover, was unwilling to accept that the Meiji authorities were capable of managing the treaty ports themselves. He was unreceptive to an official request from Terashima for the removal of the British garrison stationed at Yokohama and pursued the demands of British subjects to be allowed access to the interior. In Terashima's view, inland travel for foreigners with extraterritorial rights was an infringement of Japanese sovereignty. Standing his ground he pointed out a host of 'difficulties' and insisted that in this case it would be necessary 'to make foreigners amenable to Japanese law'.[38]

Terashima did not remain in London for long. Plagued by ill health during the course of the winter, in 1873 he was given permission to return to Japan on leave. He set out from London on 26 August, and in the event he would never come back, for with Ōkubo now at the helm in Tokyo, he was appointed Minister of Foreign Affairs in place of Soejima, who had just resigned over the vetoed plans to invade Korea. This was one of several regional disputes that initially prevented him from embarking on any major diplomatic initiatives. Unlike those who were impatient for military intervention, he opposed the Formosa Campaign launched in 1874 in retaliation against the murder of some Ryūkyū Island natives. He also urged peaceful engagement with Korea, rather than the Perry-style gunboat diplomacy used by Kuroda Kiyotaka in forcing the 'unequal' Kangwha Treaty of 1876. More to his liking were Enomoto Takeaki's talks in Russia that resulted in the Treaty of St Petersburg in 1875, defining the countries' respective interests in the Northern Territories with Japan gaining control over the Kurile Islands in return for Sakhalin.

At home there were also tensions in the administration of the treaty ports. In 1874, frustrated by his insistence on linking access to the interior with the issue of extraterritoriality, Parkes finally lost patience and appealed directly to Iwakura and Sanjō Sanetomi, complaining of the 'unfriendly attitude' shown in recent Meiji diplomacy. Dismayed by these senior nobles' more flexible attitude, Terashima threatened to resign, and after some delay a compromise agreement was reached which provided some limited access, although categorically not for commercial activities.[39] Meanwhile, in spite of the views of R.G.Watson who was in charge of the Legation while Parkes was away, Parkes continued to resist further requests for the removal of the British garrison in Yokohama, and it was not until 1875 that he finally agreed to the troops' departure.[40]

Terashima had now been granted the use of a new inter-ministry bureau for treaty inspection, and he seemed ready at last to launch his own diplomatic agenda. The issue of extraterritoriality remained his first priority, but pressure from Ōkuma Shigenobu, the Minister of Financial Affairs, forced him to concentrate instead on the question of tariff autonomy. As far as Parkes was concerned, this was merely an exercise to raise much-needed funds at the expense of British merchants. Terashima, however, was able to exploit the friction between Parkes and the American minister John Bingham on a range of issues, notably their understandable failure to see eye-to-eye over gun laws.[41] Encouraged by Bingham's more positive response, he instructed Yoshida Kiyonari, Japan's envoy in Washington, to pursue negotiations there. Yoshida reported enthusiastically that there could even be potential for a bilateral treaty with the United States that would restore tariff autonomy in exchange for the opening of two new treaty ports.

Aware that such concessions would doubtless be claimed by the other treaty powers as well, Terashima insisted that tariff matters should be negotiated collectively. This was why the convention that Yoshida signed with US Secretary of State William Evarts in 1878 stipulated that the terms were contingent on similar arrangements being made with the other treaty powers.[42] With one precedent already set, Terashima pressed Britain, France and Germany to follow suit. Hopes were raised when the British agreed to a conference in Tokyo, and in April 1879, Ueno Kagenori, the Japanese Minister in London, even declared: 'I believe that the British Government may finally yield at all essential points if you remain firm with S. Parkes.'[43] Encouraged by the scent of victory, Terashima grandly summoned Uneo back to Japan 'in consequence of Treaty Revision at Tokio'.[44]

Parkes, however, remained deeply suspicious of the Americans' stance on tariffs.[45] Insisting that this was just a policy of self-interest at Britain's expense, he called on the Foreign Office to orchestrate collective resistance together with France and Germany. Eventually, on 15 July, he was able to deliver to Terashima a final declaration from the Foreign Secretary, the Marquis of Salisbury, confirming that 'Her Majesty's Government decline to enter into any new negotiations for the Revision of the Treaties'. The British protested that, 'as a basis for joint negotiations', they were willing to accept specific proposals on 'the amendment or modification of the existing Tariff'. The notion of following Washington's lead and surrendering control, however, was out of the question.[46] This precipitated the total collapse of Terashima's strategy on tariffs, and his abiding concern for 'joint negotiations' meant that even Yoshida's efforts had come to nothing.

His mounting problems were now compounded by clashes over extraterritorial rights. Following outbreaks of cholera in western Japan, Terashima's attempts to impose a quarantine period of ten days on incoming ships were seen by Parkes as an assault on consular jurisdiction, and both the British and German Ministers allowed merchant vessels prematurely into Yokohama. Then there was the furore over the release of John Hartley, a British chemist charged with smuggling opium, who received only a token fine from a consular court on the grounds that his consignments had been for medicinal purposes. The growing liberal rights movement was also raising public awareness of the slights on Japanese sovereignty enshrined in the Ansei Treaties, and in September 1879, facing criticism that he had neglected extraterritorial issues in favour of tariff autonomy Terashima was forced to resign.[47]

Although not spectacular, he could in fact point to incremental progress. In 1876, for example, Britain's own Law Officers had backed the Meiji government's calls to ban the *Bankoku Shimbun*, a Japanese language newspaper seen as potentially seditious, that had been issued by the British journalist John Reddie Black.[48] Moreover, Maejima Hisoka's efficient new Japanese postal service was already taking over from British and French mail ships in the treaty ports.[49] In the political climate of 1879, however, Terashima had to make way, and with his plans for treaty revision in ruins he left for the vacant post of Minister of Education. Lamenting his wild ambition, Parkes felt that a change of personality could help smooth over differences between their governments. Others may have felt this applied in equal measure to Parkes, who still had not fully grasped the reality that Terashima's stand on sovereignty would remain the benchmark of Meiji diplomacy for years to come.[50]

AN ELDER MEIJI STATESMAN

In Tokyo circles Terashima still wielded considerable influence, sufficient, for example, to warrant an impromptu visit by the Emperor to his grand home in June 1880. The following day this was the venue of a house party for three hundred guests.[51] As the Meiji government apparatus evolved in the next few years, however, he was largely confined to consultative bodies, first as chairman of the Senate (*Genrōin*) and later as vice-chairman of the new Privy Council (*Sumitsuin*). While these appointments reflected his standing as a senior statesman, they were designed to limit his influence in the central corridors of power, where his rival the younger Itō Hirobumi was consolidating control in the years leading up to the new Meiji Constitution.

59

Now that the government had responded to pressure from the liberal rights movement and promised a new constitution, debate raged over the form of the proposed new assembly. Terashima's own involvement dated back to 1873 when both he and Itō had received instructions to prepare drafts of their own. As the natural leader of the conservative Satsuma faction since Ōkubo's assassination in 1878, Terashima argued that Japan's political culture was not sufficiently developed to allow much democratic freedom. Ōkuma, however, favoured a radical solution in the manner of an English-style parliament. The more pragmatic Itō, the ascendant figure in the aftermath of Ōkubo's death, saw off both challenges in 1881 when he used a damaging corruption scandal involving Satsuma officials to drive Ōkuma and his liberal allies out of office, while manoeuvring Terashima into a venerable post in charge of the *Genrōin*.

Tired of the factional infighting in Tokyo, in 1882 Terashima volunteered for a brief spell in Washington as minister to the United States, although his real motive was to use the opportunity to conduct research on political assemblies. It was partly on his suggestion that Itō was sent on a similar mission, and in government circles this was even viewed as a joint effort, with Terashima and Itō investigating conditions in America and Europe respectively. He took to his studies with renewed energy and published an English paper entitled 'On the National Assembly', reiterating his conservative beliefs that political representation should be viewed in the context of Japan's political evolution. This perhaps echoed the cautious advice that his compatriot Mori Arinori, currently serving as minister to Britain, was receiving in London from Herbert Spencer, the celebrated Victorian pioneer of social science.[52] Now fifty-one years old, his studies, however, were impaired by illness, and in 1883 he was again forced to return to Japan where he cut a sorry figure compared with the younger Itō who was also back after his evidently more productive research in Germany.

When the new Office for the Study of the Constitution was formed in 1884, Terashima was given a remit limited to commercial law as Itō appointed men from his own inner circle to tackle the more central question of the structure for a new assembly. Having just received the title of count (*hakushaku*) in the new Meiji peerage he was still very much part of the ruling oligarchy, but he increasingly took to campaigning against the government and fiercely criticised its fiscal and foreign policies. He became a leading figure among the neo-conservative elements in power, although their challenge was effectively defused when they were transferred en masse to the new Privy Council in 1888. In his position there as vice-chairman, Terashima's continued invectives, often in print, still carried enough weight to pressure Itō, now chairman, into the conciliatory gesture of choosing Kuroda Kiyotaka as prime minister during the transitional period when the new constitution came into force.

In the field of diplomacy he also received somewhat unexpected support from the liberal rights movement for his passionate attacks on Inoue Kaoru, his successor in the Ministry of Foreign Affairs. His defence of Japanese sovereignty resonated with the new spirit of patriotism in the late 1880s as suspicions grew over Inoue's covert attempts to win confidence in Meiji justice by inviting foreign judges into Japanese courts. In 1889 he also scored a notable success when he presented a united Privy Council memorandum to the Emperor demanding a halt to similar treaty negotiations under Ōkuma. This was instrumental in bringing down the Kuroda government, although it was the terrorist attack the next day in which Ōkuma lost a leg that effectively forced the issue.[53]

Increasingly bedridden in later years, Terashima was too weak to attend the committee convened in 1892 when a new round of treaty negotiations was announced. He nevertheless summoned the energy to send a memorandum, which contributed to the diplomatic successes later in the decade. Britain's fears over Russian encroachment from the north and Japan's now eminent credentials as the first Asian state with a modern constitution had created a more favourable climate for the negotiations that produced the Anglo-Japanese commercial treaty of 1894. The only irony was that Terashima himself did not live to see the resulting end of extraterritoriality in 1899 and the final restoration of tariff autonomy in 1911.

He died on 6 June 1893 at the age of sixty-one. In the popular memory of subsequent generations he was often viewed as one of several Meiji statesmen, Inoue and Ōkuma included, who signally failed to release Japan from the subordinate status the country had endured since the days of Perry. Later diplomats such as Mutsu Munemitsu and Komura Jutarō received the accolades of the public as the Ansei Treaties were overhauled, but in many ways Terashima had laid the foundations of their success. During his term as Minister of Foreign Affairs in the 1870s, conditions in East Asia had prevented him from making significant inroads into the agreements originally signed by the Bakufu. The fledgling Meiji regime was still an unknown quantity in a region often viewed as a natural hunting ground for commercial and even colonial expansion. His uncompromising style of diplomacy, most evident in his exchanges with Parkes, nevertheless did much to raise international awareness of Japan's emergence as a modern nation state.

6

Suematsu Kenchō, 1855-1920: Statesman, Bureaucrat, Diplomat, Journalist, Poet and Scholar

IAN RUXTON

Suematsu Kenchō

SUEMATSU KENCHŌ has been described as a 'second-ranker' in the Meiji era,[1] and indeed his name is not well-known in Japan nowadays. This is partly because the front-ranking Meiji leaders were ten or twenty years his senior, partly because of his humble (non-samurai) background, and because he was born outside the four 'Restoration fiefs' of Satsuma, Chōshū, Tosa and Hizen.[2] Baron Suematsu also died relatively young, aged sixty-five, and suffered ill health including high blood pressure.[3] Nevertheless, he headed the second tier, received recognition and patronage from the Meiji genrō (elder statesmen), and made prolific and significant contributions in many areas which deserve to be remembered today.

EARLY LIFE IN JAPAN

Suematsu Kenchō was born on 30 September 1855 (20 August in the second year of Ansei by the old calendar) in the hamlet of Maeda, then part of Miyako-gun in Buzen, and still now a farming village on a fertile plain within the city of Yukuhashi, Fukuoka prefecture. His father Suematsu Shichiuemon was an important village headman (*daishōya*), and his mother's name was Nobuko. When he was a child, he was first called Senmatsu then Kenichirō and eventually settled on Kenchō, which for a while he thought should be read as Norizumi.[4]

Kenchō was the fourth son. From the age of ten in August 1865 he was sent to the nearby private school (*juku*) of the renowned scholar and poet Murakami Bussan (1810-79) called the *Suisaien* (founded in 1835) where he studied Chinese classics (*kangaku*). In 1866 the pro-shogunate Kokura clan's territory was attacked by the Chōshū army, and the Suematsu family home was burnt to the ground. Kenchō was sent to relatives in neighbouring Tagawa-gun, from where Murakami brought him back to *Suisaien*.[5]

In 1871, there being little future at home, Suematsu Kenchō went up to Tokyo at the age of seventeen. He was taken in as a house boy by the high government official Sasaki Takayuki (1830-1910) of Tosa, and while there he met and became a friend of Takahashi Korekiyo (1854-1936), the future president of the Bank of Japan, finance minister and briefly prime minister. Takahashi taught Suematsu English in exchange for lessons on the Chinese classics.

In May 1872 Suematsu was enrolled at the *Tōkyō Shihan Gakkō* (Tokyo Normal School) but soon left on Takahashi's advice because his progress in English was so rapid. This caused a rift with the Sasaki household, recorded in Takahashi's autobiography.[6] Then Suematsu and Takahashi tried selling English translations of foreign newspapers and magazines to make a living, and eventually the Nippōsha bought them.

In 1874 Suematsu joined the Nippōsha company. The chief editor, novelist and dramatist Fukuchi Gen'ichirō (1841-1906) soon recognized Suematsu's journalistic talent and added him to the editorial staff of the *Tōkyō Nichinichi Shimbun* founded that year. Apart from his real name Suematsu also used the pen name of Sasanami Hyōji. In January 1876 he was appointed a commissioner in the Central Office of the Council of State (*Seiin goyō kakari*) and accompanied the envoys Kuroda Kiyotaka (1840-1900) and Inoue Kaoru (1835-1915) to Korea after a Japanese surveying ship the *Unyō* had been fired on. There he helped in drafting the unequal Treaty of Kanghwa of 26 February 1876.

Suematsu's newspaper articles criticizing the Meiji leaders (*genrōin-hihan*) and calling for the abolition of the Ministry of Educational Affairs (*Kyōmushō-haishiron*) attracted the attention of the great Chōshū men Itō Hirobumi (1841-1909) and General Yamagata Aritomo (1838-1922) on whose staff he served as an adjutant during the Satsuma Rebellion of 1877.[7] Another article comparing rickshawmen to oxen and calling for their early replacement by trains and horses (*jinrikisha-bōkokuron*) caught the eye of educationalist Matsumoto Mannen (1815–80).

IN ENGLAND 1878–86

Having already entered the world of officialdom with his trip to Korea, on 29 January 1878 Suematsu was ordered to go to England to be apprentice first secretary at the Japanese Legation in London, with an additional order from the Office of Historiography (*Shūshikan*) on 9 February to research English and French historical methods in his spare time.[8] It was probably at the recommendation of Itō Hirobumi that he was chosen from many candidates. Suematsu left Yokohama by ship on 10 February. Sailing via the Suez canal (completed in 1869) he reached Marseilles on 26 March, and travelled overland to Calais, arriving in London's Victoria station at 6 p.m. on 1 April 1878. He soon obtained lodgings in a well-to-do English household, giving details in letters to his family.[9] He also told them about London theatre visits, an audience with Queen Victoria and the first visit of a Japanese warship to Britain in July 1878, the sloop *Seiki* built at Yokosuka.

Much more of the next eight years is revealed in the long letters written by Suematsu to his powerful patron Itō.[10] Still in his mid-twenties, Suematsu was apparently more interested in foreign travel and the chance to study in Britain than in a serious diplomatic career, and it has been suggested that he was sent to Britain by Itō partly as his informant on the political situation in Britain and Europe.[11] Indeed, Suematsu had no particular duties at the legation, which was small and not busy.

The surviving letters to Itō cover mainly the years 1878–79 and 1881–82. The first one from England is dated 24 April 1878. It begins with the Balkan conflict and the British government's budget, and moves on to report on the Japanese envoy Ueno Kagenori (1844–88) who had been

In the garden of the Japanese legation in Notting Hill, London, between April 1878 and June 1879. Suematsu is on the far right in the back row. Ueno Kagenori (Minister in London, 1874–79) is in the centre of the front row.[12]

criticized for spending too much and not reporting back to Japan often enough. Suematsu defends Ueno and concludes that he should not be replaced, though in fact he was recalled in 1879 and succeeded by Mori Arinori.[13]

In a letter dated 10 June 1879 Suematsu wrote of his hope to enter Cambridge University in the spring of 1880, but he did not do so until the following year. In 1879 Suematsu switched from training to be first secretary to the lower rank of third secretary, and was eventually discharged from the diplomatic service at his request – and presumably with Itō's blessing – in December 1880.

Suematsu matriculated at Cambridge as a non-collegiate student in October 1881. A letter of introduction by an M.A. of the university was necessary to do this, and the brilliant student Kikuchi Dairoku (1855-1917) was the only qualified Japanese at the time. When working as a journalist, Suematsu had previously got to know Kikuchi's younger brother, the zoologist Mitsukuri Kakichi (1857-1909) and arranged for him to send letters from America – the first ever letters from a foreign correspondent to a Japanese newspaper – so it was probably this connection which was used.

In those days there was no special exemption for Asian students from Latin or Greek in the Cambridge preliminary examination (called 'Little Go', and also including Mathematics) and in a letter to Itō dated 12 May 1882[14] Suematsu confessed that he found both languages very difficult and was briefly in despair, for unlike Kikuchi Dairoku who had been schooled in England (at University College School) he had never studied classics. But in June 1882 he managed to pass the examination with a second class. In the following June he passed the second part of the exam in geometry and algebra with the same result.

Suematsu was admitted to St John's College, the college of his *senpai* Kikuchi, as a pensioner in October 1883. He financed his studies partly through a loan of £300 from the London branch of Mitsui & Co. sanctioned by Itō, and partly through tutoring his fellow-student Maeda Toshitake, for which he received £16 per month, which was enough to cover his food and clothing. Suematsu sat the law tripos exam in May 1884 and passed at the head of the third class. For this he was awarded the LL.B. (Bachelor of Laws) degree in December 1884 and also later the LL.M. on payment of a modest fee in 1888. (By a quirk of the Cambridge system he also received a B.A., awarded together with his LL.B.)

Of Suematsu's life as a student we know that he was a regular speaker at the Cambridge Union from October 1882 to June 1884 when he left the university. He also carried a motion in his college debating society 'that Party Government is injurious to the best interests of the State'.[15] Here he must have polished his English and acquired the debating skills which later made him a formidable advocate of the Japanese case in the Russo-

Japanese War. That he had a lively sense of humour is illustrated by an anecdote told to the Japan Society of London on 11 January 1905 by H. J. Edwards, then Dean of Peterhouse, in a lecture entitled 'Japanese Undergraduates at Cambridge University':

> On the towing-path, among the rowing-men of his College – who wore the familiar scarlet jackets that have added the word 'blazer' to the English language – Suyematz [*sic*] appeared in a brilliant but unknown uniform. 'What club does that blazer represent?' asked the men of scarlet. The answer came, admirable and ingenious. 'Club? Suyematz Club! I invented it myself!'[16]

Edwards added that Suematsu was remembered by contemporaries as 'a man of ready speech and merry mood' with an attractive spark of originality.[17]

Suematsu was also engaged in writing while in England. In 1879, *Meiji Teppeki Shū*, a collection of Chinese poems written during the Satsuma Rebellion was published, and then his first attempt in English, *The Identity of the Great Conqueror Genghis Khan with the Japanese hero Yoshitsune* (published by W. H. and L. Collingridge, London) dealing with the Japanese legend that Genghis and Yoshitsune were the same person, a theory which fascinated Suematsu though the evidence was inconclusive. This 'historical thesis' was printed at Suematsu's own expense and translated into Japanese. Translations of the English poets Thomas Gray, Byron and Shelley followed.

Suematsu's most famous translation, however, was of part of Murasaki Shikibu's classic novel *Genji Monogatari*. This was the first English translation, predating those by Arthur Waley (6 vols. 1925-32),[18] Edward Seidensticker (1978)[19] and Royall Tyler (2002). It was published by Trübner of London in 1882 as *Genji Monogatari, the most celebrated of the classical Japanese Romances*, and is still available today in paperback (Tuttle, 2000), a testimony to its enduring value and readability. Suematsu in his introduction to the 1900 annotated edition describes the 'Romance of Genji' as a 'national treasure', and Lady Murasaki as 'one of the most talented women that Japan has ever produced'. He nevertheless felt that the thread of the story was 'diffuse and somewhat disjointed', and that the work was 'too voluminous': hence he reproduced only the first seventeen of fifty-four chapters.

On 23 April 1881 Suematsu gave a lecture in a London hotel to the Liberal Society entitled 'The Policy of the Japanese Government'. He did not hesitate to criticize the government's financial policies, or to touch on the thorny issue of treaty revision, then the top priority of Japanese diplomacy, both in his lecture and in his letters to Itō. Presciently he expressed concern about the formation of the *Kempei* ('military police') in that year, and the state (polity) being thus put in 'a state of siege'.[20] The talk was, however, not popular with his compatriots and Tomita Tetsunosuke, a former fellow-member of the legation wrote warning Suematsu that he was endangering his career prospects.[21] In a letter to Itō dated 13 September 1882 Suematsu mentions advice from Mori Arinori that he was too rash and outspoken, and that he had better abandon hopes of a political career and become a historian, which dismayed him.[22]

After graduating in June 1884 Suematsu stayed in England for almost a further two years. Between September 1884 and February 1885 an essay 'On Poetry and Music' (Kagaku-ron) appeared in several issues of the Tōkyō Nichinichi Shimbun. It was written in a private capacity, criticized officials for failing to take any interest in Japanese poetry and argued that it had suffered for almost a thousand years from 'a debilitating and well-nigh fatal loss of musical qualities'.[23] Suematsu was thus a pioneer in campaigning for reform of Japanese poetry in the Meiji period.

In any event, it is clear that Suematsu's first period in England was excellent preparation, not only for his subsequent career in Japan, but also for his time in England as Japan's special emissary to the Court of St James's, 1904-05. It gave him not only a chance to acquire Western knowledge, but also 'a new awareness of being Japanese'.[24]

IN JAPAN, 1886-1903

In March 1886 Suematsu was appointed councillor (sanjikan) at the Ministry of Educaton and returned to Japan. In April he was transferred to the Ministry of the Interior, and in March 1887 he was promoted to Head of the Prefectural Government Bureau (kenjikyokuchō). At this time Itō was Prime Minister for the first time and Yamagata was Minister of the Interior. One of Suematsu's first achievements in this role was to approach Shibusawa Eiichi (1840-1931) on behalf of a local consortium regarding finance for the construction of the port of Moji as a vital staging post between Nagasaki and Tokyo. The Moji Port Construction Co. was founded in 1889[25] and the port was completed in 1897.

On his return Suematsu also began to campaign for improvements in Japanese drama based chiefly on the London theatre.[26] He led the Drama Reform Movement and founded the Engekikairyō-kai (Theatre Reform Society) to eliminate obscene and indecent practices, and to cause the virtual abandonment of kabuki drama. 'Traditional theatre buildings and stage design, together with traditional types of play, dramatic literary styles, production methods, and acting techniques were to be replaced . . . by an uncompromisingly Western form of drama.'[27] Suematsu's iconoclastic approach to kabuki, which he regarded as shallow and showy,[28] attracted opposition from dramatists Tsubouchi Shōyō (1859-1935), Mori Ōgai (1862-1922) and Fukuzawa Yukichi (1835-1901).

The main members of the Theatre Reform Society were Fukuchi Gen'ichirō (who had campaigned for theatre reform in his newspaper[29]) and the drama critic Yoda Gakkai (1833-1909); the politicians Itō Hirobumi, Inoue Kaoru and Mori Arinori; the businessman Shibusawa Eiichi; and the actors Morita Kanya the 12th (1846-97) and Ichikawa Danjūrō the 9th (1838-1903). But in 1887 the reform campaign petered out, partly a victim of association with the unsuccessful 'Rokumeikan diplomacy' pursued by Itō and Inoue.[30] The main positive outcome was a new theatre building for Western drama, the Imperial Theatre (*Teikoku Gekijō*), which eventually opened in Marunouchi, Tokyo in 1911.

On 7 June 1888 Suematsu was among the first in Japan to be awarded a doctorate in literature[31] for his translation of *Genji Monogatari*. On 22 April 1889 he married Itō's second (adopted) daughter Ikuko. He was thirty-five; she was just twenty-two. To the criticism that a former member of the Kokura clan had married into the 'enemy' Chōshū clan, Suematsu responded with his customary wit that he had 'taken a hostage'![32] After the wedding the couple went together from Tokyo to Yamaguchi which was reported in the *Tōkyō Nichinichi Shimbun* of 3 May as the first ever Japanese honeymoon. They had two children.

In Japan's first general election in 1890 Suematsu was elected to the House of Representatives from his native Buzen, Kyushu. He resigned from the Interior Ministry, when the Diet opened in November, and continued as a member of the House until 1894. He gave an interesting talk of uncertain date on the 1890 election, based on statistical tables he had compiled from the census of 31 December 1888 and his personal impressions gathered during the campaign. He was surprisingly critical of the *genrō* who had been in power since the Restoration, many of whom were his mentors and later colleagues, writing with severity: 'As it is the custom of the world to tire of old faces, they had naturally incurred both the jealousy and hatred of certain groups of citizens.'[33] Despite this Suematsu was made a baron in 1895 and an imperial appointee to the House of Peers (*Kizokuin*) the following year.

In 1898 Suematsu was appointed Minister of Communications in Itō's third Cabinet (January-June 1898). He also began work on the compilation of the *Bō-Chō Kaiten Shi*, an important source for the history of the *bakumatsu* and Meiji Restoration centred on the Mōri family and the old Chōshū provinces of Suō (*Bōshū*) and Nagato (*Chōshū*). Suematsu was the editor-in-chief, recommended to Inoue Kaoru by Itō, with a staff of about twelve and he wrote the general preface for the first edition (1911) and the revised edition (1920).

In 1900 Suematsu was given the important post of Minister of the Interior in Itō's fourth and last Cabinet (1900-01). He also became a member of the standing committee of the *Seiyūkai*, the party formed that year by Itō, and proscribed the nascent Socialist party. When asked why he had done this he replied that Japan must suppress the troublesome party just as other countries were doing.[34] In the same year he was appointed to the Imperial Household Ministry.

SENT TO ENGLAND 1904-6

During the Russo-Japanese War Suematsu was – partly on his own recommendation[35] – sent to England to influence European opinion, combat the Kaiser's mischievous 'Yellow Peril' doctrine and plead Japan's case,[36] as Harvard-educated Kaneko Kentarō (1853-1942) was sent to America. It was, as he wrote to Itō on 9 February 1904, a mission with 'quite a few extremely delicate points.'[37]

Suematsu left Japan on 10 February, two days after war broke out, with a letter of introduction in English from Itō to Lord Lansdowne, the British Foreign Secretary. This spoke of Suematsu's revisiting England for health reasons and described 'Russia's highhanded march towards hegemony' as a 'serious menace' to the safety of weaker states.[38] Suematsu travelled via Washington where he met President Theodore Roosevelt, who sympathized with Japan and detested the Russians.[39]

In 1905 two books by Suematsu appeared: *The Risen Sun* (the title was suggested by the British publisher Archibald Constable & Co.) and *A Fantasy of Far Japan or Summer Dream Dialogues*. The former is the more important, being mainly a collection of actual speeches and essays from this period in three parts. The latter is a series of imaginary dialogues about Japan – mostly in the salons of rich and beautiful Parisian ladies – which Suematsu claimed were based on actual conversations held in the summer of 1905. In the preface to *Fantasy* he apologizes for the polemic tone and states:

> In publishing this volume I am not in the least degree actuated by a desire to exalt my country unduly, – still less to boast about her achievements. My sole aim has been to show Japan as she is. . .'

In the preface to *Risen Sun* written at Queen Anne's Mansions, Westminster in August 1905 Suematsu acknowledges six benefactors: Murakami Bussan; Dr Thomas Waraker[40] who taught him English, Roman and international law at Cambridge; Mr Ernest Schuster who taught him German law; and the three Chōshū elder statesmen Itō, Inoue and Yamagata who had 'entrusted me with many important tasks, political or otherwise'.

The postscript, added in Paris on 1 September 1905 just before the Treaty of Portsmouth (New Hampshire) was signed, claims that 'Japan has shown a great moral heroism in the cause of humanity and civilization' and that she 'has maintained her ambition of deserving the name of a civilized nation'. No longer, Suematsu continued, could Japan be 'looked down upon by many as a petty, infantile, imitative, shallow, bellicose and aggressive nation'. Japan had emphatically confirmed her joining the comity of nations and now aspired to Great Power status!

The first part of the book ('Antecedent to the War') contains a searing indictment of the 'Machiavellian' Russian diplomacy, 1895-1905, which Suematsu claims provoked the conflict. Suematsu quotes official British and Japanese sources in detail, beginning with the Russian-originated text[41] of the notorious Russo-Franco-German Triple Intervention of 1895, couched in terms of 'sincere friendship' and advising Japan to 'renounce the definitive possession of the Liao-tung' peninsula which Russia coveted. (Only three years later Russia obtained a lease of the ice-free Port Arthur and Dalny in the peninsula after Germany obtained a lease of Kiaochow in 1897.)

In July 1900 Russia submitted notes to the Powers, including Japan, in which she stated certain 'fundamental principles' designed to preserve China and prevent partition, but she was the very Power that did most to frustrate them by occupying Manchuria and its treaty port of New-chwang, and seizing the British-owned Peking-Newchwang railway. Later Russia did all she could to delay her withdrawal from Northeast China, with prevarication and demands that no other power should replace her. Russian policy and action is characterized with extreme frankness by Suematsu as devious, reckless, high-handed, cynical, even cloven-hoofed!

Russian armies were guilty of 'barbarity' and massacres of Chinese civilians, e.g. on the south bank of the river Amur opposite Blagoveshchensk in July 1900. (Japanese soldiers at Port Arthur in November 1894 had matched their cruelty,[42] though Suematsu's account begins after the Sino-Japanese war of 1894-95.) Suematsu also robustly if controversially defended Japan against the accusation of a surprise attack against Russia based on 'nineteenth century precedents, that a formal declaration is not needed to constitute a state of war'. Indeed, there was no prior declaration of war by either side.[43]

The second part of the book ('A Nation in Training') deals with such topics as the training of soldiers, education of women, hara-kiri, ethics, religions and Emperor Meiji's 'determined' but 'amiable' character.[44] On the Japanese character Suematsu says astutely that there is no shame in being a nation of imitators because civilization is 'only an accumulation of imitation'. What would Europe be without Greek culture, Roman law and the Judaeo-Christian tradition? Some of his views now seem outdated, e.g. his refusal to accept that parents could ever be cruel to their children in Japan (p.141).

The third part ('External Relations') includes a lengthy historical paper on China which he describes as essentially pacific, her 'conquests' and growth being due to the influence of her culture. Suematsu also defends the Japanese treatment of Russian prisoners-of-war at Matsuyama (Shikoku) as gentlemanly, based on Buddhism and *Bushido*,[45] and in accordance with the Geneva and Hague conventions. He expresses confidence that in the future his *bête noire*, the discredited Yellow Peril paranoia as manifested in the Triple Intervention, will be dismissed as a 'passing fantasy', whether in economic or military guise. (Perhaps fortunately he did not live long enough to witness the rise of Japanese militarism in the 1930s.)

IN JAPAN, 1906-20

Suematsu returned to Japan in time to attend a 'luncheon' (formal lunch) on 16 March 1906 of the Cambridge and Oxford Society of Japan (the *Kengyūkai*)[46] at which he sat next to Lord Redesdale (A. B. Mitford) who described him in his *Garter Mission to Japan* (Macmillan, 1906) as 'brilliant' and 'famous all over Europe' after his lectures, letters to *The Times* and other publications.

Suematsu was made a Privy Councillor (*Sūmitsuin-komonkan*) in the same year and was also in time to see Itō before his departure to become Resident-General in Korea. In 1907 he became tutor to the newly-installed Korean crown prince (Yi Eun), a member of the Imperial Academy and a viscount. When Itō was assassinated by An Chung-gun at Harbin station on 26 October 1909, Suematsu published several eulogies of his father-in-law.

From 1912 to 1920 he was in semi-retirement, though he continued to be active as a Privy Councillor, and to work on the *Bō-Chō Kaiten Shi*, while also translating classical commentaries on Roman law. Suematsu was still politically active when he died at home in Shiba, Tokyo of influenza complicated by chronic pleurisy on 5 October 1920, three days after illness struck during a Privy Council meeting.

CONCLUDING REMARKS

Suematsu Kenchō was an intellect of great versatility, ambition and patriotism whose achievements have not been properly recognized simply because of their jack-of-all-trades diversity. He made significant efforts to introduce Japanese culture to a Western audience, and to bring Western drama and literature to Japan.

As an eloquent advocate for Japan in Britain and Europe during the Russo-Japanese War which involved unprecedented manpower and technology in a full-scale East-West confrontation Suematsu was both powerful and persuasive, though assisted by the pre-existing Anglo-Japanese Alliance and his Cambridge connections.[47]

Sometimes his passionate and frank outspokenness invited criticism and imperilled his political and bureaucratic careers, but he apparently never lost the support of his indulgent patrons. Suematsu's wit, intelligence, sincerity and charm may well have been his saving graces in their eyes.

7

Kikuchi Dairoku, 1855-1917: Educational Administrator and Pioneer of Modern Mathematical Education in Japan

NOBORU KOYAMA

Kikuchi Dairoku in later life

SENT TO BRITAIN BY THE TOKUGAWA *BAKUFU*

FOLLOWING ADVICE from Sir Harry Parkes (1828-85), British Minister to Japan, the Tokugawa *Bakufu* in 1866 sent fourteen students to Britain to study Western civilization. This was the third time students had been sent abroad from Japan. Students had been sent to Holland in 1862 and to Russia in 1865, but this was the first occasion after the removal of the ban on travel abroad. Students were also sent to France in 1866. Kikuchi Dairoku (1855-1917), accompanied by his elder brother Mitsukuri Keigo (1852-71), was, at just eleven years old, the youngest among the fourteen students.

Kikuchi Dairoku was born in Tokyo (then Edo) on 3 May 1855 (17 March of Ansei 2)[1] as the second son of Mitsukuri Shūhei (1825-86), a well-known educationist and scholar of Western learning. Shūhei was the adopted son of Mitsukuri Genpo (1799-1863) who was also a famous scholar of Western – particularly Dutch – studies. Shūhei's original family name was Kikuchi. Dairoku, the second son of Shūhei, inherited his father's original family name Kikuchi so that the name should be maintained. Mitsukuri Genpo gave his grandsons names in *kanji* (Japanese characters) which indicated the order of birth.[2] For example, Kikuchi Dairoku's elder brother's name Keigo included *go* (five). Dairoku included *roku* (six).

Kikuchi was born into a family which had had close contact with the West during the last days of the Tokugawa regime. Mitsukuri Genpo, Kikuchi Dairoku's grandfather, was involved in the negotiations with E. V. Putiatin (1803-83), the Russian envoy, as an interpreter when Putiatin came to Nagasaki in 1853. Mitsukuri Shūhei, Dairoku's father, had gone to Europe as a member of the Tokugawa shogunate mission (headed by Takeuchi Yasunari) in 1862 and visited Russia in 1866. Mitsukuri Rinshō (1846-97), Dairoku's cousin, accompanied Tokugawa Akitake (1853-1910), the Tokugawa shogun's deputy, to Paris in 1867. Mitsukuri Rinshō was well known as a scholar of Western learning and the pioneer of modern legal studies in Japan. These connections suggest why Dairoku was selected as the youngest member of the group sent in 1866.

William Lloyd (1825-96), who looked after these fourteen students and taught them English during the voyage to Britain from Japan, noticed that the Mitsukuri brothers (Mitsukuri Keigo and Kikuchi Dairoku) mastered English rapidly.[3] This was not surprising: they were younger than the other students and they had already begun to learn English in Japan.

When the Tokugawa shogunate collapsed in 1868, the fourteen students had to give up their studies in London and return to Japan. During their brief stay in England, eleven had studied at University College School (UCS) in London, including Kikuchi Dairoku. This was the college where Japanese students from Satsuma had studied under the guidance of Professor Alexander Williamson (1824-1904)[4] in order to prepare for entry to university.

After the Meiji Restoration in 1869, the new government started to send large numbers of Japanese to the West to study modern science and other aspects of Western culture. The number of Japanese sent to study abroad peaked in 1871.[5] In 1870 Kikuchi was again sent to Britain as an attendant on Prince Komatsu (then Prince Higashi-Fushimi (1846-1903)). This enabled Kikuchi to return to the UCS after over two year's absence.

STUDYING IN LONDON AND CAMBRIDGE

After returning to England Kikuchi studied at the UCS for about three

Kikuchi Dairoku as
a young scholar

years. He demonstrated his academic ability at the examination of the end of his second year and was ranked second out of the 518 students at UCS in 1872.[6] According to the Japanese newspaper article, which was based on a translation of an article in an English newspaper, he was unable go on to the University of London that year because he had not yet obtained an adequate knowledge of Latin and Greek. He determined to rectify this so that he could go on to University the following year.

In 1873, Kikuchi became head boy at UCS winning various prizes. These were Case Exhibitioner (prize in sixth form Greek), Case Prizeman (prize in sixth form Latin) and Cook Prizeman (prize in sixth form mathematics).[7] He shared the last prize with Sidney White; their friendly rivalry became almost legendary in the school.[8] When Kikuchi was taking the entrance examination to the University of London and unable to attend classes, his rival White lent him his notes.[9] Kikuchi shared the Cook Prize but the difference between his and White's marks was so small, that both received the prize in that year in recognition of White's generosity.

Originally Kikuchi had intended to study at University College in the University of London. But the mathematical tripos at Cambridge University was particularly famous among students of mathematics and science. He was good at mathematics and fortuitously the religious and other obstacles which had prevented him from becoming an undergraduate at Cambridge had recently been removed. It was, therefore, natural that Kikuchi should consider going to Cambridge. Moreover, he was aware that the University of London bestowed degrees on all students who passed the examinations and that there was no requirement for students to attend any classes or reside in London. So Kikuchi applied for both Cambridge (St John's College) and the University of London. He was accepted by St John's in May 1873, and took the entrance examination (matriculation examination) of the University of London in June 1873 winning third place.[10] The first place went to Donald MacAlister (1854-1934). MacAlister later became the Principal and Vice-Chancellor of the University of Glasgow after he had taught medicine in Cambridge. He was involved in founding the Japanese Club at Cambridge (Honorary Vice President).[11] Both MacAlister and Kikuchi went to St John's College in Cambridge in 1873 and took the mathematical tripos in 1877 whilst also receiving degrees from the University of London. In later life both went on to become successful administrators in higher education. In the tripos examination at

Cambridge MacAlister became Senior Wrangler and Smith's Prizeman while Kikuchi became 19th Wrangler.[12]

The most famous of Kikuchi's classmates at St John's was Charles Parsons (1854-1931), later the inventor of the steam turbine engine and regarded as the best engineer in Britain. Parsons was 11th Wrangler. Kikuchi was the first Japanese to receive a degree from Cambridge. His position, 19th Wrangler, was not as high as MacAlister's (Senior Wrangler) but he attained a higher position than any subsequent Japanese undergraduate. At the time when Kikuchi studied mathematics in Cambridge, academic status was dominated by the results of the tripos examination, perhaps at the expense of original research. The mathematics, which he learnt, was predominately Euclidean and probably slightly out of date compared with mathematics on the continent. At that time the mathematical tripos included a large element of physics (or natural science as it was then called).

Kikuchi seems to have enjoyed undergraduate life at Cambridge. He was the secretary of the Lady Margaret Boat Club (St John's College)[13] and in 1875 he seems to have been the cox in a rival College Boat Club, set up by a number of undergraduates from Sedbergh School.[14] He proposed a controversial motion in the St John's College Debating Society: 'That the conduct of Englishmen in Japan is unworthy of their nationality'. He was able to carry the house with him.[15] Kikuchi's choice of topic shows that he already held nationalist views which were characteristic of Meiji Japan.

PROFESSOR OF MATHEMATICS

In May 1877 Kikuchi Dairoku returned to Japan. About a month earlier, Tokyo Daigaku (the University of Tokyo) was founded, combining Tokyo Kaisei Gakkō (Tokyo Kaisei School) and Tokyo Igakkō (Tokyo Medical School). Tokyo Daigaku became Teikoku Daigaku (the Imperial University) in 1886 and Tokyo Teikoku Daigaku (Tokyo Imperial University) in 1897 (After the Second World War it again became Tokyo Daigaku (the University of Tokyo)). Kikuchi was appointed as a professor of the science college at the newly-founded Tokyo Daigaku in June 1877.[16] He was just twenty-two years old. His main task was to introduce modern mathematics into Japan.

The position of mathematics in Japan following the Meiji Restoration was different from that of science, technology or medicine on account of the fact that a strong native tradition was already in place. When the new Western mathematics was introduced, it was called yōzan or yōsan (yō meaning Western and san meaning calculation), while Japanese mathematics was called wasan (wa meaning Japanese). Wasan originally came from China and was developed during the Edo period (1600-1867) becoming widespread as a hobby during the final years of the Tokugawa regime. *Wasan* had created something similar to differential and integral calculus in the West and traditional Japanese mathematicians at the beginning of the modern period thought mathematics had developed further in Japan than in the West.

When Kikuchi returned to Japan from Cambridge in 1877, the Tokyo Mathematical Society (*Sūgaku Kaisha*) was founded and Japanese who had studied or were interested in Western mathematics, such as Kikuchi Dairoku, as well as traditional native mathematicians joined the Society. The name was changed to Tokyo Mathematics and Physics Society (Tokyo *Sūgaku Butsuri Gakkai*) in 1884 on Kikuchi's advice and it became the Mathematics and Physics Society of Japan (Nihon *Sūgaku Butsuri Gakkai*) in 1919. After the Second World War it separated into two societies, the Mathematics Society of Japan (Nihon *Sūgakkai*) and the Physics Society of Japan (Nihon *Butsuri Gakkai*).

KIKUCHI'S CAREER IN EDUCATION

In early Meiji modern sciences and Western learning were generally introduced into Japanese higher education by foreign employees (*oyatoi gaikokujin*) and the teaching was in English at institutions such as Tokyo Daigaku. No foreign employee was needed for mathematics at Tokyo Daigaku because Kikuchi, who had graduated from Cambridge with high honours, was also able to teach mathematics in English. This suited the Meiji government which, because of the high cost of foreign employees, wanted to replace foreign employees with Japanese, who had studied abroad.

Kikuchi Dairoku laid the foundations of mathematical studies at the University of Tokyo. He was promoted rapidly and became head of the Faculty of Science at the University of Tokyo in 1881. As the Japanese delegate, he participated in the International Prime Meridian and Universal Time Congress held at Washington, DC, in 1884.[17] He was named *Rigaku Hakushi* (Doctor of Science) in 1888 and was appointed a member of the Imperial Academy of Japan the following year.[18] In 1890 he was made a member of the House of Peers.[19]

Kikuchi made an important contribution towards the development of mathematical education in Japan. In 1888-89 he published a textbook of elementally geometry, entitled *Shotō kikagaku kyōkasho*, which remained for many years the standard geometry textbook for secondary schools in Japan. In this textbook Kikuchi introduced Euclidean geometry and logic into Japan. The textbook reflected the influence of the British Association for the Improvement of Geometrical Teaching.[20] It was written horizontally (rather than vertically in the traditional Japanese way) in order to display mathematical signs, etc. It was one of the earliest attempts in the Meiji period to print Japanese horizontally. Kikuchi also experimented in dividing words with spaces as in English. Since written Japanese consists of *kanji* (Japanese characters) and *kana* (phonetic script) words were normally printed or written without spaces between them. The experiment did not last and in modern Japanese words continue to be written without spaces.

Kikuchi's career as an educational administrator started as the Dean of the Science College at Tokyo Daigaku in 1881. In 1897 he was appointed the Director of the Bureau of Special Education at the Ministry of Education (*Monbushō*).[21] This post was the third highest position at the Ministry. Then, in the same year, he was appointed Vice-Minister of Education. He stayed in this post until he was appointed President of Tokyo Imperial University in 1898 where he remained for about three years.[22] In 1901 he was appointed Minister of Education in the cabinet of Prime Minister Katsura Tarō (1847-1913) and remained in this post until 1903.[23] He also served as President of the Peers School (*Gakushūin*) in 1903-04.

Kikuchi was created a Baron in recognition of his contribution to education and also in acknowledgement of the role he played in the successful conclusion of the Anglo-Japanese Alliance in 1902 to which Kikuchi had contributed as minister in the cabinet.

LECTURES ON JAPANESE EDUCATION

To foreign observers the key to Japan's rapid progress in modernization, in particular her victory in the Russo-Japanese War (1904-05), seemed to be the high level of Japanese education. The University of London asked the Japan's Ministry of Education (*Monbushō*) to send to London a Japanese, who could give a series of lectures on education in Japan, at the university under the Martin White Benefaction.[24] Sawayanagi Masatarō (1865-1927), then the Director of the Bureau of Special Education at the *Monbushō*, was selected as the lecturer, but he received news on his arrival in London of his appointment as Vice-Minister of Education and returned to Japan without giving any lectures. Kikuchi was then hurriedly asked to take over Sawayanagi's task. He came over to London and delivered lectures at the University of London during the Easter and summer terms of 1907. Considering his fluency in English and his previous post as Minister of Education Kikuchi was the most suitable person for the task. His lectures were published as a book in London in 1909, entitled *Japanese education*.

In preparation for his lectures Kikuchi paid a great deal of attention to the English translation of the Imperial Rescript on Education (*kyōiku chokugo*). He started his lecture by reading his own English translation of the rescript which he considered the basis for Japanese moral education.[25]

The significance Kikuchi attached to the rescript in his lectures shows the extent to which Kikuchi's attitude reflected official Meiji attitudes to the status of the Emperor.

Kikuchi was Minister of Education when in 1902 the inspectors, one of whom was a former pupil of his, found what they considered an unsuitable question in a graduation examination paper at a private school called Tetsugakukan. The lecturer responsible was Nakajima Tokuzō (1864-1958). The Ministry of Education took away from Tetsugakukan the right to issue teacher's licences. This became known as the Tetsugakukan incident and was aimed at discrediting liberals such as Nakajima, who was amongst those involved in attempting to revise the Imperial Rescript on Education.[26] In 1903, when wide-scale bribery was discovered amongst the private companies responsible for publishing school textbooks, Kikuchi resigned as Minister of Education, although he was not directly involved. It was in response to this scandal that national textbooks (*kokutei kyōkasho*) were issued. National textbooks have been considered one of the factors responsible for hindering the development of democracy in Japan.

While Kikuchi was in Britain in 1907, he received honorary degrees from the Universities of Glasgow and Manchester. Kikuchi's classmate Donald MacAlister had become Principal of Glasgow University that year and Kikuchi was one of the first recipients of honorary degrees while MacAlister was Principal. At Manchester, he received his honorary degree because of his lectures dealing with moral education. This was also an opportunity for Kikuchi to meet his old teachers and friends including Sidney White, Kikuchi's rival at UCS in London. When Kikuchi was in London the new campus of UCS was opened at Frognal in Hampstead having moved from Gower Street on 26 July 1907. On the following day, the traditional awards ceremony was held at the new campus. As a representative of the recipients of awards from the Gower Street days Kikuchi was invited to present the awards at Frognal. This was the last of Kikuchi's four visits to Britain.[27]

LATER LIFE

Kikuchi was appointed President of Kyoto Imperial University in 1908 and President of the Imperial Academy of Japan the following year.[28] In 1910 he delivered a lecture, similar to those he had delivered in London, at the Civic Forum of New York. This was published under the title *New Japan* (*Shin Nihon*)[29] and he received an honorary degree from Rutgers College. He was made a Privy Councillor in 1912.[30] Kikuchi's social status and fame was not matched by original contributions to mathematics. Apart from his textbook, referred to above, his main contribution lay in his introduction of the development of *wasan* (Japanese mathematics) in

English and his translation from Latin into English of Gauss's papers on hyper-geometric series.[31] A few months before he died he was appointed Director of the newly-established National Physical-Chemical Institute (*Rikagaku Kenkyūjo*). He died on 19 August 1917 and his Shinto funeral was held four days later.[32]

Kikuchi was probably the most prominent member of the Mitsukuri family, which was famous for academic achievements during the Meiji period. His younger brothers, Mitsukuri Kakichi (1857-1909) and Mitsukuri Genpachi (1862-1919), were professors of Tokyo Imperial University for zoology and Western history respectively. Kikuchi Dairoku married Fukuda Tatsu (1863-?); they had three sons and five daughters. Their first daughter, Tami married Minobe Tatsukichi (1873-1948), a jurist, famous for the controversial 'Emperor-as-an-Organ of the state' theory. Their second daughter Chiyo married Hatoyama Hideo (1884-1946), a scholar of civil law, while their fourth daughter Fuyuko married Suehiro Izutarō (1888-1951), a scholar of civil law, particularly labour law. Their husbands were professors of Tokyo Imperial University. Kikuchi's third son, Kenzō (1901-?) was a Professor of Tokyo Imperial University (zoology) and his fourth son Seishi (1902-74) was an experimental physicist, famous for his discovery of the 'Kikuchi line'. Kikuchi's heir, his second son Taiji, (1893-1921) was sent in 1919 from the National Physical-Chemical Institute as its first overseas research student in order to pursue his research at the Cavendish Laboratory in Cambridge. His college, like his father's, was St John's. Sadly, Taiji died suddenly in Cambridge in 1921.[33] He was just 29 years old.

ASSESSMENT

As a child Kikuchi must have had considerable self-reliance and determination. Even though he was accompanied by his brother it would have been daunting for an eleven-year-old Japanese boy to face life in a totally alien environment as a schoolboy in Victorian London. The interruption to his studies caused by the Meiji Restoration must have been a blow to his hopes and it cannot have been easy for him to resume his studies in London. Passing examinations in Latin and Greek as well as mastering Western-style mathematics and becoming head boy at UCS were no mean achievements. His experiences as a child no doubt coloured his attitudes in later life. He had learnt a tough form of self-discipline and developed a determined will to succeed. He found that for him success lay in being a highly competent administrator rather than becoming an outstanding scholar. He lacked the spark of genius and it does not seem that he was ever infected with the English sense of humour.

His adult life spanned the Meiji period. In his attitudes to the West, to Japan, and to the Emperor, he typified the Meiji character. Always precocious, his early exposure to England and his successful education there meant that his own career anticipated and mirrored the development of Japan at the end of the nineteenth and the beginning of the twentieth century.

8

Ozaki Yukio (1858–1954) and Britain

FUJIKO HARA

Ozaki Yukio

INTRODUCTION

FOLLOWING the Meiji Restoration of 1868 the leaders of the new government sought models from Britain and continental Europe for a structure that would earn the country an honourable place in the comity of nations. The compulsory educational system established in 1872 was modelled at first after the French but was changed to that of Germany after the latter's victory over France in 1870. Universal conscription, an equally levelling institution, was introduced in the same year. The army itself was modelled after Germany's and the navy after Britain's.

The Meiji constitution was likewise a mélange of the British parliamentary and German authoritarian systems. These two schools of thought, liberal and authoritarian competed for the minds of civil and military leaders and remained a source of tension until the middle of the twentieth century. Indeed, the European competition for power over Japan had become apparent earlier when France offered financial and military assistance to the challenged shogun while Britain supported the incoming power-holders united under the young emperor Meiji. Behind the scenes, in actual fact, Britain had hedged its bet. Ozaki Yukio (1858-1954) was a student of the British school. Much younger than Itô Hirobumi (1841-1909) and Okuma Shigenobu (1838-1922), Ozaki continued to fight for democracy long after they were dead.

WHICH SHALL IT BE: BRITAIN OR GERMANY?

On 11 and 12 July 1882 (Meiji 15), the *Hōchi Shimbun*[1] carried an article written by Ozaki Yukio, a member of its editorial board. Ozaki railed against Japan abruptly switching its model for nation-building from France to Prussia following the victory of the latter in 1870:

> In the reign of Emperor Meiji patriots are invited to participate in national affairs. At a time when the peoples' rights and freedom are gaining strength by the day and a national parliament is to be convened in the not too distant future it is crucial that a right choice be made. The choice we make between Britain and Germany in building a constitutional government will mean the difference between happiness or calamity, safety or danger for our country and its people. While the intent is to buy peace by drawing on the influence of a great power, the choice we make today does not stop at buying peace and safety, for it is made with the hope of one day transcending both Britain and Germany. . . Patriots who are concerned for the future must not take their minds off this important issue even for a day.[2]

Ozaki argued that legislative and administrative rights were the front and back wheels of national advancement. One without the other would get you nowhere. What did the people want? Were they satisfied merely being granted legislative rights? If so, that was like being allowed to forge a sword, while administrative rights conferred permission to use it. Good swords in bad hands would become instruments of oppression. Naturally, the quality of the sword had to be questioned but so had those in positions to use them.[3] In the Prussian system the constitutional government granted people legislative rights. Executive powers were entrusted to ministers handpicked by the Kaiser. As long as ministers enjoyed the favour of the Kaiser they were free to go against the will of the people. They held in contempt the parliament which they regarded as a representative chamber of the ignorant masses. The parliament was functional only in name, the government remained undeveloped and the cabinet was the handmaid of the Kaiser. All this was because the people were given legislative rights without the executive powers to remove unworthy ministers.[4]

While both Prussia and Britain professed to enjoy constitutional government the Prussian people suffered under military tyranny and had no protection for their lives or property. Proletarian socialist parties were rampant throughout the country. The legislature was constantly violated by the executive branch of the government which remained an instrument of the old guard. The legislature did not have the power to check and restrain the executive branch, and the wrath of the people was directed against the Kaiser rather than his ministers who avoided taking responsibilities. In other words, they hid behind the throne to escape the anger of a disappointed people.[5]

In the British system of governance the monarch called upon the leader of the party that commanded the highest confidence of the people to organize the government. He might appear to enjoy the favour of the monarch but was not free to organize a cabinet without the agreement of parliament. In other words, while the ministers were formally appointed by the monarch, it was indirectly the people who made the choice. Ozaki explained that, under the British system, kings were above ministers but were freed from the responsibilities which cabinet ministers bore. The British system gave the people not just legislative rights but administrative rights as well. In Ozaki's analogy of sword-making, they had the right to forge and temper the sword as well as to use it.[6] Japan must adopt the British system.

Ozaki's essay on Representation System published in 1883 focused on the need to prepare the country for the opening of the parliament scheduled for seven years later. Freedom of speech and assembly must be guaranteed; likewise, habitual dependence on moral persuasion rather than use of force, respect and protection of political parties, fair competition over policy issues among the parties and non interference of civil servants in political affairs.[7]

Other articles by Ozaki on policy published in the *Hōchi Shimbun* at about the same time included one entitled 'The Way of the Loyalist' carried on 22 May 1882. On the platform of the Constitutional Progressive Party on 14 May 1882 he asserted that no nation could have real power without the civil power: 'No civil power, no national power!' He maintained that Russia and Germany had it the wrong way around. They kept their people oppressed without giving them rights so that, no matter how formidable their military power, they did not win the respect of the nations of the world.

THE MAKING OF THE MAN

Ozaki Yukio was born in 1858.[8] His father was a samurai in Sagami province (now part of Kanazawa prefecture). He was nine years old when he and his mother moved to Edo (now Tokyo) to join his father who had been appointed to a minor government post and who had been working to topple the *Bakufu*. He was sent to learn Japanese classics at Hirata *Juku*.[9]

By the time he was fifteen years old Ozaki Yukio had studied Chinese classics and was comfortable in referring to Chinese historical events and could even compose poems in Chinese.

About a year after their move to Tokyo a rebellion broke out against the new government in Jōshū (now Gunma prefecture), where people did not take kindly to orders from strangers. Yasuoka Masataka, appointed to a post equivalent to that of a modern prefectural governor, was called to the area to pacify the rebels. Ozaki's father was deputy to Yasuoka, in charge of education and judicial matters, including overseeing torture and executions. For the purpose of education he took his son Yukio and his friends to public executions which were carried out with Japanese swords.[10] These inhumane sights left such an indelible impression on Ozaki that he resolved to do all he could to protect the lives and property of ordinary people.

In Takasaki in Gunma prefecture he was sent to a school where he was introduced to the English language. Little is known about his time at this institution, to which he refers in his autobiography simply as 'an English school'.[11] His teacher, whom Ozaki was to meet again in Mie when his father and Yasuoka moved there a year later, was Koizumi Atsushi. The awakening in Yukio of the need to halt the barbaric treatment of human beings may have been helped by his mind being opened to British notions of justice and fair play through the study of the English language.

Anxious to be free from his father's authority he left Kumamoto to which city his father had been transferred and still only fifteen and went to Keiō Gijuku in Tokyo where he studied for a year-and-a-half under the tutelage of Fukuzawa Yukichi (1834-1901). There he was trained in public speaking as well as in the translation of English books. His earliest translations were a collection of essays on public speaking including Caldwell's Elocution, in two volumes.[12]

Ozaki's most astonishing accomplishment at this young age, however, was his translation of selected passages from Herbert Spencer's *Social Statics:*[13] *Conditions Essential to Human Happiness Specified and the First of Them Developed* (first published in 1851). These were published in two volumes in December 1877 and 1878. Ozaki conveyed Spencer's thoughts in fluent and convincing Japanese as if they were his own. His undiluted commitment to liberalism, equal rights including those of women and children, and the use of land as the collective heritage of man may have been inspired by Spencer's fundamental principles: 'The Law of Equal Freedom is not a natural law but a moral law' and 'Everyman is entitled to his happiness provided he infringes not the equal rights of any other man'. Ozaki's publication was read by advocates of civil rights including Ueki Emori (1857-92).[14]

Ozaki photographed with Yei Theodora and their two daughters Shinaye and Yukika

Ozaki also translated *Thoughts on the Future Civil Policy of America* (first published in 1865) by John William Draper.[15] This translation, entitled *Policy Proposition of the Federated States of America*, covered the effects of climate, the consequences of immigration, the influence of ideas on politics and the way to national development. It was published by Keiō Gijuku Press in May 1879. Ozaki liked biographies and he translated a number of them including *The Boyhood of Great Men*.[16] Ozaki also translated a biography of Lord Beaconsfield (Benjamin Disraeli).[17]

Another major work was the complete translation which he made of *On English Parliamentary Politics*[18] by Alpheus Todd written for the Canadian parliament. The task was entrusted to Ozaki by Yano Fumio (1850-1931), a writer and politician and graduate of Keiō Gijuku, who had been approached by Prince Taruhito of Arisugawa (1835-95), a member of the imperial family and army general after the Meiji restoration who headed the committee charged with drafting the constitution. Ozaki's translated works were published in eight instalments during 1882 and 1883.

After leaving Keiō Gijuku Ozaki spent some time at the Imperial College of Engineering academy, which subsequently became part of today's Tokyo University, where lectures were given exclusively in English under the de facto presidency of Dr Henry Dyer[19] from Scotland. In order to qualify for entry Ozaki received special tuition in English and mathematics from the Reverend Alexander Croft Shaw (1847-1902),[20] an Anglican missionary who had arrived in Japan in September 1873 and was staying with Fukuzawa. Shaw seems to have had a considerable impact on the young man. He was baptized Ozaki on 25 December 1874 as one of his eight converts at Yosenji temple in Reinanzaka near Tokyo's Hotel Okura. The church records show the date of his baptism and of his marriage to Miss Yei Theodora Ozaki on 14 October 1905, conducted by the Rev. King. The baptismal record has the word (expelled, or dismissed) written across it, but without a date. According to his daughter Sohma

Yukika, her father could not live with what he regarded as a contradiction – Christians praying for victory of their own country in war.

After leaving the Imperial College of Engineering he taught English history for a short while at Kyokan Gijuku at Yushima in Hongo, one of the three main private schools at the time, before Fukuzawa recommended him as editor-in-chief of the *Niigata Shimbun*, a newspaper published in the principal port on the Japan Sea. Ozaki continued to write: writing, not politics, was his profession, as he later told his daughter Yukika as she filled in a school application.

OZAKI IN BRITAIN

Ozaki made four visits to Britain. The first was in 1888 when he and two others, Hoshi Tōru, an English-educated barrister and Tokyo assembly-man, and another were banished beyond three *ri* (about twelve kilometres) from the Imperial Palace for a period of three years under the Security Ordinance[21] hurriedly passed towards the end of December 1887 to suppress the civil liberties movement and its proponents. Three hundred others received minor penalties. Ozaki was then a member of Tokyo Metropolitan Assembly, having been elected in 1885 from Nihonbashi ward. He and other members of the Progressive Party were protesting against the government for its weak-kneed response, to the 'unequal treaties' imposed by the Western Powers, in particular against Foreign Minister Inoue Kaoru's dance parties at the Rokumeikan, designed to show how Westernized and therefore how credible Japan had become. Ozaki Saburō, whose daughter Yukio was to marry later, was responsible for drafting the ordinance as director general of the cabinet legislation bureau.

The 'exile' gave Ozaki an opportunity to travel to Britain in 1888 via the USA to study at first hand the 'Mother of Parliaments'. There he confronted a sceptical friend who told him he would never succeed in establishing an English-style parliamentary system in Japan. These words cemented Ozaki's resolve to transplant the British system to his country.

During his one-year stay in London he read a great deal and industriously wrote articles as a correspondent for the *Chōya Shimbun*[22] focusing on the two main political issues of the period, the constitution and the revision of the unequal treaties. It was during this period that he also wrote his *Thoughts on the Imperial House* which was later developed as *Thesis on Constitutional Loyalty* and translated into English as *The Voice of Japanese Democracy; Being an Essay on Constitutional Loyalty* by J. E. de Becker.[23]

Shortly before heading back to Japan to stand in its first national election scheduled for 1890, having being pardoned in a general amnesty issued on the occasion of the promulgation of the Constitution on 11

February 1890, Ozaki sent an article to the *Western Times*[24] urging Britain to change its attitude and revise the unequal treaties before he headed back to Japan to stand in its first national election scheduled for 1890.

The *Western Times* introduced Ozaki to its readers as a prominent progressive correspondent of the *Chōya Shimbun* who had written to bring to the attention of the British the misconduct of foreigners residing in Japan who took advantage of the extraterritorial rights enshrined in the 'Unequal Treaties'. Readers of the article would know, the newspaper wrote in an editorial, that the author was an educated oriental and that they should know that this was an important relationship as Britain pondered whether or not to respect the laws of Japan as a state enjoying equal status and equal rights, bearing in mind that Mr Ozaki would be returning in a few days to his country expecting to be elected successfully as a candidate from the Progressive Party to occupy a seat in the Imperial Diet.

Ozaki argued his points from a perspective of moral imperative on the one hand and of national interest on the other. Could Britons imagine a situation in which eight thousand foreigners were living in their country and yet could not be brought to justice before British law no matter how disrespectfully and criminally they behaved? That was just how arrogantly some British citizens conducted themselves in Japan, as if they were representing Great Britain, Her Majesty the Queen and the government. He went on to complain that Japanese farmers were forced to pay a crippling land tax since the government had no way of imposing customs duty on imports. If farmers who made up more than half the population enjoyed lighter taxation they would in turn increase their purchasing power. Ozaki went on to point out that the United States of America had responded to Japan's demands and the precedent could well be a yardstick to distinguish between countries that harboured goodwill towards Japan and those that did not. Ozaki warned that it would be wrong for Britain to think that it could turn away a small nation like Japan, for a proud island country of forty million on the threshold of attaining a civilization unparalleled in history would never permit itself to be slighted in this way.

Ozaki made three more trips to Britain, one in 1910 as Mayor of Tokyo, an office he held from 1903 until 1912. He was one year into his second six-year term when he took six months leave to go on an around-the-world trip with his wife, Yei Theodora. They arrived in Britain on 22 June with the intention among other things of paying a visit to Theodora's mother, Bathia Catherine Morrison. On 5 July Ozaki was presented to the King by the Japanese ambassador, Katō Takaaki. Also presented were Prince Tokugawa, General Viscount Kawamura and Baron Oura.[25]

On Tuesday 10 July *The Times* carried a rather lengthy article of two full columns under the heading 'Japanese Children' written by 'Madame Y. Theodora Ozaki, the Mayoress of Tokyo'. Though not strictly entitled to the designation she had earned it by her prominence by Ozaki's side. By now she was an established author in her own right of the first of four books in English of Japanese fairy tales. That year beginning on 29 October the Japan-British Exhibition was held at the White City to honour the alliance, but by then the couple had left for Brussels where Ozaki as head of the eleven-man delegation was to attend a meeting of the International Parliamentary Union from 29 August to 1 September.[26] During the months preceding their departure from Japan in May it is clear from the tidily kept scrapbook of correspondences with ambassadors in Japan of Germany, Italy, France and Russia that Theodora was busy setting up appointments for her husband. On leaving Europe they spent ten days in the USA from October 13 to 24 after crossing the Atlantic from Southampton on board The White Star liner *Adriatic*.

In 1919 Ozaki returned with a different purpose. While a few Japanese intellectuals recognized the world had changed most were slow in awakening to the new global reality.[27] Ozaki was one of the exceptions. Just as soon as the Great War was over he travelled to Europe to see for himself the consequences of the war, fought by impoverished and wounded countries in the name of national interest. He was deeply shocked on visiting what were but recently the killing fields of Flanders. Britain had lost its power. In London he listened as orators at Hyde Park Corner freely criticized the monarchy while 'bobbies' stood quietly by. Elsewhere in Europe socialism was gaining momentum and Ozaki realized that the days of autocratic rule were numbered. He would have to prepare his countrymen for popular government. It was a watershed in the development of his political vision for Japan.

He returned with two plans: disarmament and suffrage. The war had literally reduced the world's arsenals by one half and it was time to push for universal disarmament. In a move diametrically opposed to the majority of political and military leaders, who had seen a historic opportunity to advance Japan's expansionary ambitions in China, Ozaki introduced to the Diet a resolution proposing a limitation of Japan's naval and military forces, which was overwhelmingly rejected. Convinced that this did not represent the will of the people and the purpose of representative government he took to the road, speaking on this issue before enthusiastic crowds from one end of Japan to the other. Some 92.8% of the thousands to whom he distributed postcards recorded their support of arms limitation which, Ozaki felt, vindicated his charge that the Diet did not represent the people. This was one year before the Washington Naval Disarmament Conference.

The second item on Ozaki's agenda was to push for suffrage, which culminated in the passage of a suffrage law in 1925.

His final visit to London was in 1931, but first he took their daughters Shinaye and Yukika to visit Theodora in La Jolla, California where she had been receiving treatment for cancer. An operation that year was evidently successful and her doctors had given her a good prognosis. Ozaki had therefore decided first to visit Yei with their daughters and then to continue to New York at the invitation of the Carnegie Endowment for International Peace to speak at their friendship dinner, and from there to go on to London. As it proved difficult for Yei to travel so soon after the operation she was to follow from California. Meanwhile, Ozaki rented a house with the two girls in Campden Hill Court in Kensington to await her arrival.

By the time she joined them six months had passed, but the cancer had metastasized and Yei complained of pain. Her doctors advised the family that she should enjoy life and live as normally as possible. As Ozaki had arranged at Yei's express wish, their daughters were presented to King George V and Queen Mary at a coming out party (ball) for debutantes at Buckingham Palace.[28] The Japan Society of London, to which he had given a lecture on 'Constitutional Government in Japan' put on a dinner at the Hotel Victoria for Ozaki and Theodora, where Sir John Tilley, honorary vice-president of the Society, proposed a toast to their health. In his reply, Ozaki expressed his admiration[29] for the way Britain had not compromised freedom under the present difficulties. He admired its citizens for the sensible way they had voted in the late election. He noted with regret that the Japanese had lost their heads after the brief success of Meiji and were repeating the mistakes of the late Tokugawa period.[30]

Earlier on 13 April Ozaki had given an address on 'Japan' at a luncheon given by the Individualist Bookshop Ltd. at the same hotel presided over by Mr W.W. Paine. 'Mr. Ozaki said Japan was seized with war fever; so were all nations. Economic war was raging over the whole world. . . So-called civilized nations made many praiseworthy treaties like the Covenant of the League of Nations, the Nine Power Treaty, and the Kellogg Pact; but they did not seem to be very anxious to keep and carry them out. Most of the treaties were scraps of papers even now, but the signatories were clever enough to hide these ugly facts under many kinds of curious reasoning and so managed to evade treaty obligations. This seemed to be the chief reason why the Manchuria and Shanghai affairs were not called war. As long as they were not called war, the Covenant of the League and the Kellogg Pact were not violated and their consciences were at ease.'[31]

Ozaki was much concerned about Theodora's health and about the future of his country. He began writing his last will and testament titled 'In Lieu of A Tombstone' which was published in English later as *Japan at the Crossroads*.[32] Yukio had not finished his piece when Yei received a letter from one of the princesses and yearned to return to Japan. He decided to honour his wife's wish. One of the two nurses who looked after her was asked to accompany her back to Japan, but sadly Yei died on 29 December 1932 as the family prepared for their return.

YEI THEODORA

Ozaki's greatest link with Britain was Yei Theodora (1870-1932), whom he married in 1905 after the loss of his first wife Shigeko due to tuberculosis.

O'Yei Evelyn Theodora Kate was born 20 December 1870. Yei is said to be the product of the first recorded marriage between a Japanese man and a British woman.[33] Theodora's grandfather William Mason Morrison[34] (1819-85) was a war historian who had looked after students from Japan even before the Meiji restoration, including Itō Hirobumi (1841-1909), Inoue Kaoru (1835-1915) and Mori Arinori (1847-89). Another of his students was Toda (later Ozaki, but not a relation) Saburō who was regarded as the leader of some fifty students studying abroad at the time, and to whom Morrison appears to have given special attention as he was invited to board at the Morrisons'. He was later to marry Morrison's daughter, Bathia Catherine at a church in Kensington. The couple had three daughters of whom Theodora was the first.[35]

Yei Theodora arrived in Japan on 29 May 1887[36] at the age of sixteen to look for her estranged father. She did not live with him, but with his help was given a position teaching English at Keiō Gijuku primary school (from February 1889 to September 1902) and at Shōei Joshi Gakuin in Shirogane (from February 1901 to March 1903). Taking pity on her, Mary Fraser,[37] the wife of the British Minister Hugh Fraser, invited Theodora to be her personal assistant. After the untimely death of her husband Mary took Theodora with her when she went to stay with her brother Francis Marion Crawford, a well known author in Italy. They encouraged Theodora to write and publish stories which she told to the family after dinner. Her first book, *The Japanese Fairy Book*, was published in 1903 with a foreword by Mary Crawford Fraser.[38] Yei Theodora published three more books, *Buddha's Crystal and Other Japanese Fairy Stories* (1908), *Warriors of Old Japan and Other Stories*, (1909) and *Romances of Old Japan* (1917). Theodora feared that she would be long forgotten while her husband would long be remembered.[39]

On 7 February 1904 the wife of Baron Albert d'Anethan, the Belgian Minister and Doyen of the Diplomatic Corps, wrote with great enthusiasm:

> I returned home to find that A. [her husband] had meanwhile received a hurried visit from Miss Ozaki, who had come with the exciting news that she had been appointed to accompany the war correspondent of *The Times* on the vessel specially chartered by that organ for the purpose of following the movements of the war. She will act as interpreter, among other duties. She is to be sent off at once, and she thinks she is to go first to Korea and afterwards to Wei-hai-wei. What an exciting

and adventurous life it will be! Of course she is delighted and it is indeed a chance for her. I am so sorry to have missed her, and have written her a word of farewell, as she is off tomorrow.[40]

Theodora was seasick and was forced to return without carrying out her intended duties.

Yei met Yukio by chance. As they bore the same family name, the postman had mistakenly delivered to Yukio a letter addressed to Yei, and Yukio, having carelessly opened it, took the trouble to deliver it in person and apologize.

Mary Crawford Fraser said of Yei and Yukio:

> Both have the proud delicate reserve of the aristocrat of mind and soul, and escape whenever they can from the publicity which has been forced upon them . . . the result was a marriage happy in its perfect romance and blest with the deep sympathy of tastes and interests which forms the surest foundation for married felicity.[41]

Their marriage took place at St Andrew's Church in Shiba on 14 October 1905. Wrote Baroness d'Anethan:

> Today was Miss Ozaki's wedding-day. She was married to Mr. Ozaki, the Mayor of Tokyo. He has the same name, but is no relation. Miss O'Yei Ozaki herself is half Japanese and half English, her father Baron Ozaki, being a member of the House of Peers. It was a glorious October day. . . We arrived at Shiba church in good time. Admiral Noel had provided an escort of honour of forty sailors and marines, who were drawn up on each side of the church path. They looked extremely smart, and when the bride and bridegroom issued from the church they were greeted with a ringing British cheer. The bride, who is a talented authoress, looked very charming, and it was an extremely pretty wedding. After the ceremony the bride's father, Baron Ozaki, held a reception at the Noble's Club. A. [her husband] proposed the health of the bride and bridegroom in a neat speech.[42]

A Royal Navy ship gave them a gun salute.

As Mayor of Tokyo, Ozaki with his wife Theodora welcomed a number of distinguished visitors including Mr and Mrs William Howard Taft, then US Secretary of War and later 27th US President, Field Marshal Lord Kitchener and General William Booth, the founder of the Salvation Army whose Japanese name *kyūseigun* was given him by Ozaki.

On 19 February 1906 Prince Arthur of Connaught arrived to confer on Emperor Meiji the Order of the Garter in commemoration of the Anglo-

Japanese alliance. 'On 26 February there was a grand entertainment given by the Mayor of Tokyo, Mr. Ozaki, for Prince Arthur at the Hibiya Park', wrote Baroness d'Anethan in her diary.[43] Mary Fraser described the colourful event attended by half a million people as another superb pageant:

> . . . the largest social reunion that has ever taken place in the East, and most regally was the illustrious visitor entertained. . . The crowning feature of the day was the Daimyo's procession, a mile long, which defiled before our eyes across the great lawns in the open air. For this the last survivors of the feudal epoch had been sought out and brought in from every part of Japan, old samurai who had accompanied their imperious masters in many a famous progress and had cut down all and any who had the temerity to cross their path. In joyful arrogance they came to show a degenerate world the martial splendours of their younger days, and the sight was enough to make one overlook the wrongs and dangers of the dead time and only regret that so much colour and fire had to be swept away to make room for the nation's new life.[44]

As Ozaki wrote in his autobiography, Theodora was very hurt at not being invited to the mayoral dinner when her husband would ask an imperial princess to entertain the guest of honour. Theodora might have felt a little better had she known that baroness d'Anethan was not invited either.

When the triumphant Admiral Togo returned from Port Arthur Ozaki 'welcomed the beloved old sailor back, in glory, to the county he had saved.'[45] But when the troops returned from the warfront, Tokyo homes were sprinkled thoroughly with chloride of lime to guard against any diseases the war-weary men might have brought home with them. 'Tokyo sneezed, Tokyo wept, but Tokyo had no epidemics', wrote Mary Fraser.[46]

There was great deal of excitement and indignation about the terms of the peace. Count Okuma called it 'a disastrous peace' and there were riots in the Hibiya Park noted the Baroness. The government of General Prince Katsura was not in a position to express its appreciation to the United States of America for its mediating role. Ozaki decided that he would do so, on behalf of the citizens of Tokyo. Theodora wrote a letter to Mrs Taft, now wife of the President, to tell her the Mayor wished to present Japanese flowering cherry blossoms in gratitude for American support and 'as a living symbol of friendship'.

It is easy to imagine how difficult it must have been for Theodora to live in Japan, especially as the wife of a politician. Yei could not speak Japanese, so the family spoke English at home. Ozaki had rented at a vast discount a house, rumoured to be haunted, in Kitashinagawa district of

Tokyo. Yei posted a notice to the press on the door that her husband would only receive visitors on Tuesdays and Fridays between certain hours. Ozaki was taken aback by this but let Theodora have her way. 'I seem to live in the heart of two distinct civilizations', wrote Theodora, 'those of the East and the West, but the East is my spirit's fatherland . . . my greatest happiness is in my home life, in the companionship of my baby daughter, in the few short hours that my husband can snatch from his work to devote to me. If you must write about us, tell people about Yukio – he is so good and great. I have no wish to be mentioned apart from him.' Ozaki was completely absorbed in his work. Theodora made Yukika promise not to complain that they were lonely, because her father was fighting for righteousness.

At Theodora's insistence that the climate there was better for Yukio's health the family moved to Zushi on the cost south of the capital. But it was far from Tokyo and the family was inevitably lonely. Theodora made her two daughters promise 'not to complain we are lonely because your father is fighting for righteousness.'[47] Their home in Zushi was eventually destroyed by fire along with most of their belongings including their letters. Yukika remembers that her mother used to address her father as 'dear knight' and he called his wife 'dearest Kikkyo', the name of a white or violet bell-shaped flower that Yukio loved.

Foreign wives and Japanese women alike found a friend in Theodora.[48]

Of Yei, Mary Fraser wrote in a biographical sketch dedicated to her second Japanese Fairy Book:

> . . . if I were to single out the person who, to-day, most truly apprehends the points of contact and divergence in the thought of East and West, I would name the gentle dark-eyed lady. . . For though Yei Theodora Ozaki is a daughter of the East in heart and soul and parentage, one to whom all the fine ways and thoughts of it come by nature, she is also a child of the West in training, in culture, in the intellectual justice which enables her to discern the greatnesses and smile indulgently at the littlenesses of both.

Yei and Yukio shared the same vision of the world:

> For I dipt into the future, far as human eye could see,
> Saw the Vision of the world, and all the wonders that would be;
> Till the war-drum throbb'd no longer, and the battle-flags were furl'd
> In the Parliament of man, the Federation of the World.
> There the common sense of most shall hold a fretful realm in awe,
> And the kindly earth shall slumber, lapt in universal law.[49]

Britain gave much to Ozaki, not least through Yei Theodora, inspiring the vision he tirelessly pursued of a nation, just to all its citizens and respected in a world fair to all countries and at peace.

9

Lord Curzon (1859-1925) and Japan

IAN NISH

George Nathaniel Curzon

GEORGE NATHANIEL CURZON (1859-1925) was not continuously involved with Japan throughout his long political career but had two distinct phases of contact with her. The first was during his responsibility for Britain's relations with Japan while he was parliamentary under-secretary for foreign affairs and the Foreign Office's spokesman in the House of Commons (1895-8). The second phase was when he entered the cabinet in 1916, becoming Foreign Secretary from 1919 to 1924.

Few have gained as much from their years at Oxford University as Curzon. He acquired a coterie of friends at Balliol College who rose high in the political and diplomatic world. He became after graduation Fellow of All Souls and the winner of the Arnold History Prize. He showed himself to be a fluent writer and an eloquent orator. It was no surprise, therefore, when at the general election in 1885 he became Conservative MP for Southport and was appointed assistant private secretary to Lord Salisbury. Throughout his long career in government service, he acquired the reputation of being the intellectual in politics and was one of the few experts on Asia in British government circles.[1]

YOUTHFUL WANDERINGS

As a young man Curzon was a compulsive traveller. His first journey round the world in 1887-8 took him for six months to Canada, the US, Japan, Korea and China and thereafter followed the familiar itinerary around colonial outposts of the British Empire. In 1889 he made a journey to Central Asia and wrote a book on *Russia in Central Asia* in 1889. It was, however, his second journey to the Far East which is most significant for our purposes. At the general election of August 1892 the Salisbury government, in which Curzon had a brief stint as under-secretary for India, was defeated and he was free to travel again. While he remained an MP, he was no longer a minister. He set off for New York and Asia. In Tokyo was his bosom friend, Cecil Spring-Rice, then a third secretary only recently arrived at the legation. Curzon was, thanks to Spring-Rice, able to meet influential political leaders including the prime minister, Itō Hirobumi, whom he questioned in the manner of a Balliol tutorial to the horror of local British diplomats. He asked him

> '. . . the most searching questions on man, on nature and on human life, and as to how long the constitution would last, and was parliamentary government a success in Japan etc.'[2]

Itō's replies were hardly satisfactory to the visitor who had not formed a favourable view of the parliamentary regime which had just started in Japan. But Curzon's impressions of the ordinary people, their manners and the countryside itself were favourable. On leaving, he wrote that he was 'just tearing myself away from the fascinations of Japan for the rugged embrace of Korea'.[3] Curzon embarked on an ambitious and energetic tour of Korea and China; but he was never a relaxed traveller and insisted on Victorian standards of treatment and entertainment of which the East was still lamentably ignorant. He was accompanied as far as Shanghai by the long-suffering Spring-Rice whom Curzon appreciatively described as 'the best, cheeriest, most unselfish, most amusing of travelling companions'. For nearly two months they had been together and had 'not exchanged one jarring word'.[4]

Curzon penned a series of articles in *The Times* (which presumably financed the trip to the East since it did not then have full-time correspondents there) and set out the political conclusions reached on his wanderings. It was not a great step from this to the publication of a book *Problems of the Far East: Japan-Korea-China*. This was first published by Longmans, Green in 1894; it was then reissued in 1895; and a new and revised edition was published by Archibald Constable in 1896. This work was a critical political-economic analysis rather than the travel narrative which had become increasingly fashionable. Partly its popularity was a reflection of the fact that the British reading public was moving towards an interest in the East. Partly it was the result of fortunate timing: the book appeared just as the Sino-Japanese war broke out in August 1894.[5]

Curzon had predicted a victory by Japan. This upset those who had exaggerated expectations of the immense armies of China and the potentialities of regeneration in that country. The book therefore provoked a public debate. Curzon responded sarcastically to this criticism in a later edition by saying that 'the evil odours of Peking seem, after all, to have left a correct impression upon my civilian nostrils' and convinced him that Japan would defeat China. It was, he added, surprising that the reasons for China's collapse 'should have been so long and obstinately ignored, not by Englishmen in China, but by Englishmen at home, for whom the Celestial imposture has always possessed irresistible attractions'.[6]

By way of contrast, he saluted 'the brilliancy' of Japan's military machine and pointed out that no country ever went to war so well prepared:

> Skilled topographers in disguise had mapped the high roads of China. Hydrographical surveys had acquainted the Japanese with every inlet in the Korean coast. Her mobilization proceeded with a smoothness and rapidity that excited the admiration of European military attachés. The Japanese Intelligence Department might have been engaged upon, just as it had certainly been preparing for, a campaign for years. Its spies were everywhere, in the offices and the arsenals, in the council chambers and among the ranks of the enemy. The press was manipulated and controlled with a masterly despotism that would have been impossible in Europe. Finally the strategy of Japanese generals, if not brilliant, was deliberate, scientific and successful.[7]

This passage seems to have been borrowed from a military observer with intimate knowledge of the scene. Observant as Curzon was and confidently as he wrote, it was beyond his capabilities to comment so knowledgeably on the Japanese army without the advice of intelligence specialists. The decisiveness of Japan's victory he put down to the 'debility' of the Chinese. But it did not follow that Japan 'could beat any single European Power, much less any combination of a larger number'.[8]

So Curzon, who had enjoyed his visit to Japan (the last as it was to prove) and had appreciated her beauty and culture, was not starry-eyed about Japan's politics or its future development. He ends up the 1896 edition with a section entitled 'Is Japan the enemy?' In his judgements on foreign countries he was always preoccupied by their relevance to the future of Britain and the British Empire.

WHITEHALL AND CALCUTTA

The Conservative party returned to power under Lord Salisbury in June 1895. Salisbury appointed Curzon as parliamentary under-secretary to assist him with Foreign Office business in the House of Commons, saying (quite justly) 'you are more familiar with Eastern questions than any other man'.[9] Salisbury had little enthusiasm for Japan and was content to leave Far Eastern problems to Curzon. Curzon, as we have seen, had the knowledge which comes from direct observation and approached the developing country with respect and realism.

Curzon's custodianship of events east of Suez ran into a crisis which lasted six months from December 1897. It was a China crisis in which Russia and Germany seized leases on her coastline. It was not a Japan crisis; and indeed she did not play a prominent role during the crisis. Curzon steered the British cabinet (in Salisbury's absence) towards the policy of acquiring the port of Weihaiwei midway between the German and Russian acquisitions. This decision involved Japan insofar as Japanese troops were currently in occupation of the territory. The then Prime Minister, Itō, whom Curzon had met in 1892 was accommodating enough and pulled out his forces. But he still safeguarded his position by entering into a treaty with Russia. Still it was a remarkable success for a parliamentary under-secretary, who had previously regarded himself as under-used.

This crisis caused Curzon to speculate about relations between Britain and Japan and the possibility of an alliance between them which was much talked of at the time. He told the British Minister to Japan who had a hurried audience with him on 13 October 1897 that the Japanese were untrustworthy and it was difficult to have an alliance with them. Yet he wrote to the prime minister at the end of the year:

> If European Powers are grouping themselves against us in the Far East we shall probably be driven sooner or later to act with Japan. Ten years hence she will be the greatest naval Power in those seas and the European Powers who now ignore or flout her will then be competing for her alliance.[10]

Curzon did not stay at the Foreign Office long enough to pursue these penetrating insights.

In August 1898 Curzon was appointed Viceroy of India under the title of Lord Curzon of Kedleston. He took up office in the following January and continued to serve into a second term in 1905. He had, as we have seen, visited India in 1887 and again in 1892. The vast administrative structure of the Government of India suited Curzon's hard-working temperament; and the hierarchy of the viceregal court appealed to his personality as a 'most superior person'.

Curzon had developed during the Salisbury administration an

enthusiasm for foreign affairs; and the Government of India had foreign policy concerns of its own, quite separate from those of Whitehall. India's nearest rival was Russia, which was now allied with France. Curzon often complained of Russia's continued undermining of British India's frontiers with Tibet, Afghanistan and Persia. He became by 1900 concerned, not to say obsessed, with finding ways to defend the British Empire as a whole. The simultaneous occurrence of the South African war and the Boxer Rebellion of 1900 confirmed Britain's dependence on the Indian army. Without the 1st and 3rd Sikhs, the Royal Rajputs and the Bengal Lancers, Britain could not have provided as many as 21,500 troops for the international force which ultimately relieved the Siege of Beijing in August. Curzon was aware that Britain had to depend on Indian troops for action in the East and keep on relatively good terms with the overweening viceroy.[11]

Curzon was an imperialist through and through. When his former friends in the Conservative party obtained high office in the Salisbury cabinet, which was reformed in the autumn of 1900, he sent his congratulations to one in an enlightening letter from India:

> Well, there you all are now ruling the Empire. Do it strenuously and nobly and with courage. Do not let that cursed Treasury sit upon you. You . . . have got to save this country [Great Britain] from disaster and to ensure its victory in our next big war. It is a splendid responsibility, a glorious task. All luck to you in it, old boy, from beginning to end.[12]

In a later reply from one of these friends, Lord Selborne, the First Lord of the Admiralty, shared his anxieties about Britain's over-extension so far as the Royal Navy was concerned:

> . . . this is a year of special difficulty for us; we have some dozen or more extra ships in commission to meet the emergencies in Chinese and African waters, involving crews of more than 8,000 men, and the Duke of York's tour [to Australia] to man in addition.[13]

This shortage of resources on several fronts led the imperialist group to seek an alliance with Japan which they hoped would help to keep Russia in check. So far as we know, Calcutta was not consulted in advance over this secret development. But there is little doubt that the Viceroy would have approved, Curzon describing the alliance when it came about as 'a cleverly timed and statesmanlike coup'.[14]

By the time the alliance was publicly announced, Curzon was already planning a Coronation Durbar which was to take place in Delhi on 1 January 1903. He was anxious to honour the new monarch, Edward VII, but the King could not attend because of his illnesses. In view of the alliance, it was a natural idea that Japan should be invited to send a delegation. It was, Curzon wrote, 'an auspicious opportunity for extending reciprocal knowledge of the circumstances and interests of Japan and India'. Curzon thought that Japan should see the British Empire at its proudest moment and in particular observe the manoeuvres of the troops on whom the allies would rely if ever the alliance was to be tested on an Eastern battlefront.

Interestingly, Japan interpreted the invitation as a military one and sent a prominent senior officer, Lieutenant-General Oku Yasutaka, who had commanded the 5th Division in the Sino-Japanese War and was later to command the second army in the Russo-Japanese War. Oku stayed in the Imperial Camp and attended the coronation military manoeuvres at the expense of the Government of India. He was present also when Curzon made his state entry into Delhi riding on top of the largest elephant in the sub-continent. What Lord Salisbury characterized as a typical 'Curzonization' of the event.[15]

Oku followed in the footsteps of General Fukushima Yasumasa (1852-1919) who was one of Japan's India experts and had commanded the Japanese troops in China during the Boxer Rebellion. Fukushima had visited London for the Winchester House conference in 1902 to implement the terms of the alliance and had there requested Britain to send a British army corps to Manchuria in an emergency. This was refused. It is probably for that reason that Fukushima went to India in the autumn and had direct talks with Curzon and possibly General Lord Kitchener who had only recently arrived as Commander-in-Chief. Fukushima, however, fell sick and had to stay in hospital for six months, only returning to Japan in April 1903. This link between India and Japan was confirmed when Japan declared war on Russia in February 1904 and Major-General Sir Ian Hamilton, who had served in the Indian army and in South Africa as chief of staff to General Kitchener, went to Tokyo to act as observer. Thanks to Fukushima's influence, he and his team were able to have earlier passage to the front in Manchuria and easier access to senior officers fighting the campaign than those of other nationalities.[16]

The defence of India continued to be a major worry for Curzon who never missed an opportunity to bombard the India Office with lengthy missives on the subject. London through the newly-formed Committee of Imperial Defence was also regularly investigating the issue. Eventually, India's strategic difficulties were addressed and became one of the major issues discussed during the negotiations for the second Anglo-Japanese Alliance in 1905. The draft as proposed by Britain contained a clause which laid down that

> Japan will, in the event of war, provide a force . . . which shall
> be equal to the force of British troops from time to time in
> India up to the limit of [40,000?]

This was eventually modified in the final text to read (Art.VII):

Conditions under which armed assistance shall be afforded by either Power to the other . . . will be arranged by the Naval and Military authorities of the Contracting Parties.[17]

The revised alliance was eventually signed in August 1905 at the tail-end of the Russo-Japanese War. Although Japan's commitment to India had been watered down, there was still a strong implication that the second alliance was not just an alliance between Britain and Japan but between the British Empire and the Japanese Empire.

How far Curzon was behind this specific provision is difficult to judge. Probably not. At all events he gave up the viceroyalty just as the second alliance was being signed and left India on 21 August 1905 after a quarrel with his commander-in-chief, Lord Kitchener, in which he was not supported by the government in London. In fact London's criticisms of Curzon went much deeper:

To allow the Viceroy to run his own foreign policy would be a blunder which has brought Russia to disaster and humiliation – the blunder namely of having one Foreign Minister in the Far East, and another at home, not necessarily acting in accord.[18]

Kitchener in due course reversed any suggestion that India needed Japanese military support. Paradoxically, Japan's victory in war over Russia showed up the vulnerability of European powers in Asia and was to become an unsettling factor for Curzon's successors in India. Domestic unrest was to take a higher priority than foreign affairs, which had been Curzon's priority.

BACK TO WESTMINSTER

It was not in Curzon's nature to go into retirement at the age of 46. Entering the House of Lords in 1907, he became a frequent and influential commentator on foreign and imperial affairs. But he was distrusted and he felt that for a decade he was neglected politically. He served as president of the Royal Geographical Society and as chancellor of Oxford University. But it was only during the First World War that his fortunes rallied. He became Lord Privy Seal in Asquith's coalition government in 1915 and Lord President in Lloyd George's War Cabinet in the following year.

From this point on, Curzon was frequently asked to express his views on Japan and they proved to be remarkably inconsistent. An early case was when Foreign Secretary Balfour negotiated the difficult Anglo-Japanese Secret Treaty of February 1917, promising Japan advance support over certain of her key demands at any future peace conference. In spite of

Balfour's strong recommendation, Curzon opposed this treaty, doubtless because of his suspicions over Japan.[19] Yet, in striking contrast, he was convinced that Japan should be encouraged to send her forces into Siberia as part of an anti-Bolshevik front in 1918. This suggests that he did have confidence in Japan as an armed power and the contribution she could make to the allied war effort. But it was typical of the contradictions which sometimes appeared in Curzon's thinking in high office.[20]

In 1919 it became necessary for Balfour as Foreign Secretary to accompany Lloyd George to the Paris Peace Conference in 1919. The Prime Minister asked Curzon to take charge of the Office while Balfour was away. From February till October he was acting Foreign Secretary; thereafter he was appointed in place of Balfour until he left government in January 1924. During this period Curzon was a dominant figure in British policy-making, especially in the Asian sphere. But our concern is with Japan with which relations were at a critical stage during the Curzon years.

The Alliance had dragged Britain into dealing with Japan's policy in China which was a major headache for delegates to the Paris Conference. China insisted that her province of Shantung should be surrendered to her unconditionally by the peace settlement, while Japan relied on her treaties of 1915 and 1917 to justify retaining the territory which had been occupied by her armies since 1914. Eventually, it was agreed by the Treaty of Versailles that the unexpired part of the German lease should be given to Japan. Accordingly, China refused to sign. Because time had not allowed the powers to deal adequately with the Chinese problem at Paris, it was left to post-conference diplomacy to try to unravel the knots. Curzon had to try to resolve the impasse over Shantung. At an interview with the Japanese Ambassador on 22 July, Curzon pointed out that during the war Japan had pursued a policy which aimed at securing commercial and political supremacy in China by any form of pressure and loans. These tactics were responsible for China's refusal to sign the treaty; the day had gone by when China could be cut up into spheres of influence. Chinda Sutemi, the Japanese Ambassador in London (1916-20), put up a long and almost impassioned defence of Japan's actions which he referred to his government.[21]

In a related issue the Powers under America's lead decided to create a financial consortium to channel loans to China. Japan insisted that South Manchuria, Eastern Inner Mongolia and Shantung should be excluded from the consortium. Chinda discussed this on 1 September with Curzon who admitted that Japan's claims over South Manchuria had been recognized but could not recollect any engagement of that nature as far as Eastern Mongolia was concerned. The United States was even more adamant. On 19 November Curzon declined to agree to the exclusions which Japan wanted.

On another issue, which did not surface at the Peace Conference,

Curzon had to be equally severe: Japan's conduct in her colony, Korea. In response to extreme measures taken by the Japanese garrison army, there were serious riots in Seoul which spread throughout the country on 1 March 1919, the so-called '*Mansei jihen*'. This independence movement was put down harshly by the Japanese authorities; and the numbers of casualties were fully reported in the British press. Curzon had to tell the Japanese ambassador of the deplorable effect which the publication of the barbarous methods of quelling the disturbances had had on the British public. His remarks to Chinda may have been one factor which led to General Hasegawa's recall in the summer; and a more benign regime eventually came into being under Admiral Saito Makoto as Governor-general.[22]

These complaints lingered on over the next few years. On the nitty-gritty elements of international relations like trade, the financial consortium, territorial acquisitions, there were hardly any issues on which there was cordial agreement between Britain and Japan. Curzon's conversations with Chinda seem to have been fairly explosive sessions, though the reports are couched in the form of avuncular advice from Curzon.[23] On the other hand, Chinda who eventually left London on retirement in the summer of 1920 cannot have taken it too badly since he agreed to accompany the Japanese Crown Prince during his State Visit to Britain in 1921.

This stands in marked contrast to the attitude which was being taken over the most important issue between the two countries, the renewal (or otherwise) of the Anglo-Japanese Alliance. The third alliance of 1911 had survived into the post-war period but was due to lapse in July 1921. There was always the question of compatibility between it and the covenant of the League of Nations of which both Japan and Britain were founder members. The Head of the Far Eastern Department reported that the alliance could not be continued in its present form, condemning it as 'an unnatural and artificial compact based neither on identity of interest nor on sympathy with common aims and ideals'.[24] Then the Foreign Office bureaucrats set up a specially appointed Alliance Committee which by and large accepted this incompatibility and reported that the alliance would have to be terminated. Curzon, now responsible as Foreign Secretary, thought otherwise. He was impressed that Japan had been helpful during the war; and the alliance, if continued, would be beneficial to the stability of Japan and the Pacific region. Curzon put the matter fairly to the Imperial Conference and, supported by Lloyd George and Balfour, recommended that the alliance should be continued in some form, possibly acceptable to the United States. Otherwise, he thought, 'we shall lose the advantages of the Anglo-Japanese Alliance which have been and are considerable. [I allude] to the steadying influence which the Agreement has exercised in international politics.'[25] The majority of

Dominion Prime Ministers shared his views.

On 4 July 1921 Curzon, having agreed that the alliance would continue *ad interim*, asked Hayashi Gonsuke, the new Japanese ambassador, to contemplate some changes being made in it. The situation had, he said, changed altogether from the time when it was first concluded and there was no longer any danger to India, thus implying that in Curzon's view the defence of India had been the prime purpose of the original alliance. While the two countries were generally in agreement, politicians in the United States and China were opposed to the alliance continuing. Curzon wanted to know how Japan felt about holding a Pacific Conference at which Japan, Britain and the United States (and China if she wished) would attend. At any such conference, which would be held in America at the end of the year, Japan and Britain would be joined by representatives of the British Empire.[26]

Japan did not have to respond because the American government did not endorse Curzon's ideas and instead took the initiative by itself calling the conference. After this the future of the alliance slipped out of Curzon's control. It was in fact external forces that brought about the end of the alliance, notably the strong line taken by the Republican Party, which had been in power in the United States since March 1921. It called what came to be known as 'the Washington Conference' to deal with the three large subjects: China, the Pacific and Global Naval Development. But in the early stages of the conference priority was given to the future of the alliance.

Curzon who was by virtue of all the conferences in which he had been engaged something of a 'conference expert' certainly considered the proposed conference to be ill-conceived. This was not because of the alliance but because the conference, with such a large canvas to cover, would be bound to last several months and no world statesmen could possibly attend for such a long time. But Curzon did offer that Lloyd George and he could 'run over' to the States for preliminary talks in August. He was understandably hurt when this offer was turned down by Washington.[27]

Against this background of mounting disagreement, why did Curzon not insist on going to Washington in order to try to convince the Americans? The general argument is that Lloyd George had his hands full in the autumn with Ireland and unemployment while Curzon was preoccupied with the Egyptian treaty and could not be spared. This is not wholly convincing. Oddly enough, there was some talk that the Prime Minister would visit Japan in early August for two weeks.[28] It came to nothing. But the suggestion that they were abnormally hard-pressed may have been exaggerated. Eventually, the British delegation was led by A.J.Balfour who as a bachelor was presumably able to tolerate a long absence from home. Curzon wrote to congratulate Maurice Hankey, the

secretary to the cabinet, on going, which in his view guaranteed the success of the conference – probably an indication of his diminished confidence in the administrative abilities of Balfour.[29] In spite of Curzon's prediction that the Washington Conference when it was convened in November would 'peter out in talk', it was remarkably successful. In due course the alliance was merged into the Four-power Treaty which came into effect with the exchange of ratifications in July 1923.[30]

Throughout his career, Curzon was interested in, and relatively well-disposed towards, Japan; but he was never a Japanophile. In a book published in 1923, he included an essay dealing with Kyoto whose beauty he admired:

> The town is exquisitely situated in a cup between mountain ranges, quaintly outlined, and clothed with an astonishing wealth of trees. From the eastern range, where the visitor is probably lodged, he will get a wonderful outlook, both at sunrise and at nightfall. In the early dawn the entire city is drowned in a sea of white vapour, from which only the huge hooded roofs of the temples emerge, black and solemn, like the inverted hulls of gigantic ships. Suddenly, across the mist booms the sonorous stroke of the vast temple-bell, and rolls away in melancholy vibrations.[31]

Although Curzon had the poet's eye, his prime political concerns were Britain and the British Empire. Japan was welcomed as a friendly ally insofar as she fitted in with British interests but, when in the war and post-war periods Japan pursued her own self-interest regardless of Britain's advice, Curzon was distinctly less favourable. So he wavered in his attitude later in his career, becoming more critical the stronger Japan became. From first to last there was a strong element of paternalism in his attitude towards the Japanese.

Curzon died in 1925. His final years in office were marred by overwork, illness and political disappointment. In reflecting on his life, one can discern a thread of Asia running through it. It is striking that the places he visited in his twenties – India, Persia, Japan – played a part in his later career and were still relevant to his experience as a sixty-year-old foreign secretary. Beyond the political sphere he was an admirer of Asian culture from Moghul architecture to the shrines and temples of Japan. The Japanese saw in him someone who, despite his formidable presence, was well-informed, approachable, understanding, even if loquacious.

10

Lord Hankey[1] (1877-1963), R.A. Butler[2] (1902-82) and the 'Appeasement' of Japan, 1939-41

ANTONY BEST

R. A. Butler   Lord Hankey

INTRODUCTION

IN OCTOBER 1950 a group of individuals in Britain sent a letter to the American Parole Board in Japan calling for the early release of the former Japanese Ambassador to Britain, Shigemitsu Mamoru, who had recently been sentenced to seven years imprisonment by the Tokyo War Crimes Tribunal. Among the signatories of this letter were those who might be termed the 'usual suspects' among British Japanophiles, such as Lord Sempill, Sir Robert Craigie and Major-General F.S.G. Piggott, in other words the various pillars of the post-war Japan Society. However, the man most responsible for organizing the letter, Lord Hankey, and another of the signatories, R.A. Butler, might seem more surprising names to conjure with, for both were prominent political figures who had been members of Churchill's wartime Cabinet.[3] Why should they have risked their reputations in arguing the case for a man who had been found guilty of failing to do all he could to control the excesses of the Imperial Japanese

Army? The answer lies in the period between 1939 and 1941 when Hankey and Butler were two of the most senior figures in the government arguing for a policy of reconciliation with Japan and were in regular contact with Shigemitsu, who they believed to be a sincere partner for peace.

R.A.BUTLER AT THE FOREIGN OFFICE

The more important of the two in shaping policy in these years was Richard Austen Butler, who in February 1938 was appointed the Parliamentary Under-Secretary for Foreign Affairs. This was a considerable achievement for the still young politician, because as the Foreign Secretary was Lord Halifax, Butler had the responsibility for handling foreign affairs in the House of Commons. Butler stayed in this post for the next three and a half years until in July 1941 Churchill made him the Secretary of State for Education. In retrospect, these were controversial years in his political life for, under the premiership of Neville Chamberlain, Butler was an ardent supporter of the appeasement of Germany and later in the summer of 1940, after Churchill's accession, was involved in a damaging dalliance with defeatism.[4] It is in the context of his interest in appeasing Britain's enemies that one has to analyse Butler's efforts to tilt the Foreign Office towards a more accommodating policy regarding Japan.

Before taking office Butler showed scant interest in the subject of Japan. One of the few letters of his prior to 1938 that mentions the country was one to his cousin Lord Brabourne in December 1935. In this letter he stated that at the recent naval limitation conference he had found the Japanese delegation to be very friendly, and affirmed that 'I would like to go back to the good old days of the Anglo-Japanese treaty'.[5] This yearning for the assumed certainties of the alliance period was typical of contemporary opinion in the Conservative Party and identifies Butler not necessarily as a Japanophile but rather as one being swept along by the general air of nostalgia that pervaded the Tory ranks.

On his appointment to the Foreign Office, Butler had at first very little to do with Japan. The situation only began to change in 1939. One of the main reasons for this was that Halifax was becoming increasingly uncomfortable with meeting the representatives of regimes for which he only had contempt. Accordingly, whenever possible he passed on to Butler the responsibility for meeting with the Soviet Ambassador, Ivan Maisky, and with Shigemitsu.[6] Another possible reason for Butler's higher profile in Anglo-Japanese relations was that his orthodox Tory views on Japan seem to have become apparent to the Japanophile lobby in Britain, who for years had struggled to receive a sympathetic hearing from the Foreign Office. For example, it is notable that in March 1939 he received a letter from George Sale, the British businessman with interests in Japan, who wrote to say that the Japanese were now taking a more conciliatory line towards British firms in China.[7] Shortly after Butler indicated to the officials of the Far Eastern Department that he was happy to encourage people like Sale and 'any efforts which the new Japanese Ambassador [Shigemitsu] may make to bring our countries closer together'.[8]

During the summer of 1939 and the Tientsin crisis, Butler continued to play a fairly marginal role, for Halifax stepped into the foreground in an effort to find the correct balance between ameliorating tensions and adhering to British principles. Butler's position began to change only in late August when the worst of the crisis was over. His new prominence came about in part because Halifax was now caught up again in European affairs, but perhaps just as significant was the fact that the Japanese embassy began a concerted campaign to attract his interest. The conduit for this was Arthur Edwardes, the Japanese Embassy's adviser on world affairs. Since late 1932 Edwardes had been a representative in London of the Manchukuo government and had attempted to interest British firms in investing in Manchuria. Knowing that Edwardes had valuable contacts within the British elite, the Japanese embassy had also attempted to use him to communicate its professed desire for better relations to Whitehall. However, while Edwardes had developed good contacts with those close to Chamberlain, such as Sir Warren Fisher and Sir Horace Wilson, he had always been treated as *persona non grata* by the Foreign Office. In 1939 he was able to finally get around this problem, in part because his formal link with Manchukuo was severed, but also because he had an entrée to Butler, being a distant cousin by marriage.[9]

Edwardes first used this channel on 25 August when he saw Butler in order to ascertain whether the British government would be amenable to a proposal designed to deal with one of the more intractable issues raised by the Tientsin talks. In this venture Edwardes cleverly presented himself as not merely an employee of the Japanese Embassy but also as a patriot and honest broker who wished to restore good relations between the two countries.[10] Butler duly showed enthusiasm for this proposal, but more importantly now that the first contact had been made the two men began to meet regularly and to correspond with each other. In September 1939 Edwardes stressed on a number of occasions that the opening of the European War provided an opportunity for Britain and Japan to begin again and sent Butler a long memorandum on the subject.[11]

Butler reacted enthusiastically to these overtures largely because he believed that now Britain was at war with Germany it had somehow to relieve the pressure on its interests further afield. In his own memorandum of 22 September he stated that Britain had to get closer either to the Soviet Union or to Japan, and plumped for the latter on the grounds that it, too, desired a rapprochement, that it shared the British antipathy towards communism and that it might be possible to mediate a settlement of the Sino-Japanese War.[12] Butler's views did not, however, presage any change in British policy, for his was an isolated voice. Indeed, the Chiefs of Staff contradicted his views a few days later when they observed that it was in Britain's interest for the war in China to continue as long as possible, as this tied down Japan's forces.[13]

Butler's sympathy for better relations was not, however, without its uses, for the start of the war in Europe meant that Britain now had to engage in war trade negotiations with Japan in order to regulate the latter's access to raw materials from the Empire. Clearly as Butler had developed a cordial relationship with the Japanese Embassy, he was the best placed to supervise such intricate and potentially difficult talks. For the next six months this became Butler's most important area of activity. In this he was again encouraged by the enthusiasm of Shigemitsu, whom he had come to see as a sincere 'friend' of Britain.[14] The atmosphere of optimism surrounding the talks led him to believe that progress in this field would lay the basis for a broader move towards more cordial relations.[15] For example, in April 1940 he observed to the Minister for Economic Warfare, Ronald Cross, that the war trade talks had the potential to lead to a further lowering of tensions with Japan, which could only benefit the world situation.[16] In addition, he once again toyed with the idea that Britain should make more of the common Anglo-Japanese antipathy towards the Soviet Union. When Sir Robert Craigie raised the question of whether Britain and Japan might exchange information about the Comintern, Butler enthused that 'Such an exchange could do nothing but good . . . and would have a slight diplomatic flavour of a piquant character'.[17] The idea, however, came to nothing.

After extensive preparations and a number of false starts the formal war trade talks finally opened on 10 May 1940; an inauspicious day which witnessed not only Chamberlain's resignation as Prime Minister but also the start of the German attack on the Low Countries. Against the turbulent background in Western Europe the negotiations stood no chance of success, for with every Allied defeat the Japanese became ever more intractable. Indeed by June, when the talks were called off without result, all that Butler had strived to achieve appeared to be in ruins, for Japan reacted to the fall of France by demanding that Britain close the Burma Road. While the British War Cabinet debated the delicate issue of whether to appease Japan over the Burma Road, the Japanese embassy maintained its pressure on Butler to take an optimistic view of events. In particular, Shigemitsu stressed in his frequent meetings with Butler that this was Britain's chance to come to terms with Japan and ease its strategic position. Ironically, considering the course of future events, he used the appearance of Matsuoka Yosuke as the new Japanese Foreign Minister as evidence that Japan would seek to come to mutually acceptable terms.[18]

While Butler did not share this sense of optimism, he did recognize that Britain's strategic position made it imperative to address how the tensions in the East could be resolved. Accordingly, in the aftermath of the signing of the Burma Road agreement, on 17 July he ordered the Far Eastern Department to investigate what form an Anglo-American-Japanese settlement in East Asia might take.[19] In particular, Butler felt that it was important to press the United States to say what it wanted to achieve in the Pacific, rather than merely criticizing from the side-lines, which is what it had done during the Burma Road crisis. Butler's line, which echoed the impatience that Chamberlain had always expressed in regard to American diplomacy, brought him into collision with officials in the Foreign Office, who were disinclined to do anything that might provoke Washington's disapproval. Faced with stonewalling by the American and Far Eastern Departments, an exasperated Butler minuted: 'Let me make quite plain that I do not contemplate "hectoring" methods nor do I contemplate telling them [the Americans] what to do. I simply wish an acceleration of that process of close consultation and less academic exchanges.'[20]

Butler's prompting led in early August to the Foreign Office circulating a memorandum to other interested ministries in Whitehall calling on them to consider what areas would need to be addressed in any rapprochement with Japan. Meanwhile, Butler continued to look into other possible avenues that might lead to better Anglo-Japanese relations. This involved further consultations with Edwardes, and contacts with other British figures close to the Japanese embassy, such as Sempill and Sale.[21] These activities raised eye-brows in the Foreign Office, but Butler remained unrepentant, noting at one point that 'I am sorry to keep such funny company' and at another that he refused 'to be turned into a robot by our Gestapo'.[22] These manoeuvres, however, failed to lead to any practical proposals.

By September, Butler's idea of mapping out a general settlement had led to a series of gloomy responses being returned to the Foreign Office, which seemed to suggest that there was little room for reconciliation. Given Butler's mood in July, one might have expected that he would have been angered by these further examples of bureaucratic obstructionism, but by September his own feelings towards Japan were undergoing a metamorphosis. One of the main reasons for this was that events in late July and August contradicted Shigemitsu's predictions that Matsuoka would be able to bring about a positive upturn in Anglo-Japanese relations. In particular, the arrest of over twenty British subjects in Japan and Korea on suspicion of espionage suggested that the new Konoe government was becoming even more confrontational than its predecessors had been. Accordingly, on 18 September a resigned Butler recorded:

The head of steam on which Prince Konoye [sic] is sitting, so far with comforting success, seems to me too strong for us to consider a 'settlement' at present. I do not think . . . things can be ordered this way in the Far East. Any temptation I had to think so was killed when I realized the forces under the new Govt.[23]

Over the following fortnight his outlook became even more pessimistic as Japan in rapid succession forced Vichy to allow it to station troops in north Indo-china and signed the Tripartite Pact with Germany and Italy.

Japan's new confrontational policy did not just lead to a change in Butler's thinking but also in his responsibilities, for as British policy hardened he was appointed the chairman of the Cabinet's Far Eastern sub-committee. Among other things, this new body was established to oversee the introduction of a concerted policy of economic warfare against Japan. Butler was thus ironically now in the forefront of the British struggle to contain the Japanese threat. This was not a role that made him uncomfortable. Indeed, by the end of the year he was pressing forcefully for the Royal Navy to send a squadron to Singapore in order to boost Britain's regional defences.[24]

LORD HANKEY'S INVOLVEMENT

While Butler's role was changing, so also was Shigemitsu's thinking, for in the late summer of 1940 the latter began to make approaches to two other ministers within the cabinet, Lord Lloyd, the Colonial Secretary and long-time Churchill confidant, and Lord Hankey, the Chancellor of the Duchy of Lancaster and former Cabinet Secretary. While there is little evidence of any prior contacts with Lloyd, Hankey had for some time been seen as a useful contact by the Japanese embassy. In the spring of 1938 Shigemitsu's predecessor, Yoshida Shigeru, had held a number of meetings with Hankey about the thorny question of Japan's attitude towards the 1936 naval limitation treaty.[25] On coming to London in the autumn of 1938, Shigemitsu had not initially kept up these contacts, although he had previously met Hankey at the Paris Peace Conference in 1919. However, in March 1939 a Swedish entrepreneur, Carl Sandberg, acted to bring the two men together and they began to meet occasionally to discuss political affairs. Hankey felt such meetings were useful, for from his position as Cabinet Secretary and Secretary to the Committee of Imperial Defence he realized how greatly Britain's security relied on Japan's neutrality.[26]

Shigemitsu's sense of Hankey's worth seems to have risen in the summer of 1940 largely due to the idea, originally propounded by the Japanophiles close to the Japanese Embassy, that Britain should send a mission to the celebrations in Tokyo to mark the so-called 2,600th anniversary of the founding of Japan.[27] Shigemitsu was keen that Hankey should lead any such mission, and in September he aired this proposal at two lunches that he hosted for the latter at the Savoy, with Lloyd, Piggott and Sale also in attendance. However, before anything substantial could be agreed, events interceded in the shape of the Tripartite Pact, which, as Hankey observed to Piggott, made it certain that 'there is not the smallest chance of the Government agreeing to anything of the kind'.[28] During the autumn of 1940 both Shigemitsu and Piggott continued to urge Hankey to agree to a mission which, even if it did not formally represent the Cabinet, could proceed to Japan under the auspices of the British Council of which Lloyd was president. Hankey, however, continued to try to bring a sense of reality into proceedings, noting that until Lloyd had managed to win over Halifax to the idea of a mission no further progress could be made.[29]

Meanwhile, Lloyd did his best to impress Halifax with the wisdom of dispatching a mission to Japan, citing Shigemitsu's view that there was 'still a very strong, if silent, body of pro-British opinion worth cultivating at the present time'. Halifax, however, had no time for such views and observed in a letter to Lloyd on 17 December that such a mission might be misunderstood both in Japan and the United States and that the best policy was to continue to contain the Japanese menace.[30] After this rebuff, the mission proposal was forgotten until finally it received its *coup de grâce* in February 1941 when Lloyd died.

Even this setback and the concurrent worsening of Anglo-Japanese relations in the winter of 1941 culminating in the February war scare did not, however, lead to Shigemitsu and Piggott to give up on Hankey as a channel to the heart of government. In late February Piggott asked Hankey to come to his house in Ewhurst in Surrey to meet with Shigemitsu. Little of importance was discussed at this gathering, which eventually took place on 22 March, but in its immediate aftermath Shigemitsu hit upon a new idea that could only come to fruition with Hankey's assistance. The ambassador's proposal was that he should take advantage of Matsuoka's imminent trip to Europe to meet with his Foreign Minister and, among other things, bring to his attention that German victory in Europe was by no means certain. However, in order to visit Europe in wartime, Shigemitsu needed to arrange a transit flight to Portugal from where he would proceed to Switzerland for his rendezvous with Matsuoka. This was where Hankey came in, for as this transit was needed at short notice and Shigemitsu's flight would need official sanction, it was thought that he could use his influence to square the highest authorities.[31]

Hankey believed that Shigemitsu's scheme had value and on 24 March wrote to Butler asking the Foreign Office to help facilitate the ambassador's journey.[32] Despite the tougher stance that Butler had taken over Japan since September 1940 he, too, felt that a meeting between

Shigemitsu and Matsuoka could be useful. This reflected his belief that, while Japan itself was becoming more bellicose, the former was sincere in his protestations of friendship towards Britain and had a sound belief in the likelihood of British victory. Butler's hunch did not rely just on his frequent conversations with Shigemitsu, for he also had other ways of knowing the ambassador's thoughts, namely his access to the deciphered Japanese diplomatic traffic produced by Bletchley Park. On 5 February Butler noted just prior to the first conversation that the new Foreign Secretary, Anthony Eden, had with Shigemitsu that:

> I have always followed the secret accounts of the Japanese Ambassador's reports since I have had the responsibility of seeing him for so long. We have fortunately not had reasons for qualms about his understanding of this country's spirit.[33]

Confident that Shigemitsu would communicate the right message to Matsuoka, Butler on 28 March duly informed Churchill, who was acting Foreign Secretary in Eden's absence, about the ambassador's plan.[34] The Prime Minister in turn also believed that if Shigemitsu met Matsuoka it could do some good and approved his passage to Lisbon. Unfortunately, however, the ambassador was not able to co-ordinate his movements with those of his foreign minister and therefore the plan came to naught.

With this initiative proving as abortive as those that had preceded it, there was little more that could be done to save Anglo-Japanese relations. Indeed, the vital point of contact with Japan, Shigemitsu, returned soon after to Tokyo. In his final days in Britain, the ambassador met a few more times with Butler and Hankey. On 9 June the latter gave a farewell lunch at the Savoy for Shigemitsu in which the only other guest was the Australian High Commissioner, Stanley Bruce. Hankey subsequently recorded in his diary: '. . . the ambassador was extraordinarily moved when he bade me farewell. Said he valued my opinion and friendship more than that of any man in this country.'[35]

Following Shigemitsu's departure, the ability of Butler and Hankey to influence the course of events was reduced further by the Cabinet reshuffle of July 1941. Butler was promoted, but his new post at the Department of Education could not have been more remote from foreign affairs. Hankey for his part was demoted to Paymaster-General. This was ostensibly to free his former position for a political appointment, but probably arose from his flirting with Churchill's opponents in Whitehall.[36] Butler now concentrated on pastures new, but Hankey still continued to correspond with the Japanophiles, although he held out little hope for the future. When Sempill proposed in August 1941 that Eden should send a British mission to Japan for talks, Hankey replied gloomily that 'Unfortunately we live in days of catch-words and anything of the kind you suggest would at once be dubbed "appeasement"'.[37] Hankey was right in his judgement, for when in October he wrote one last letter to Eden stating the need to do something to prevent hostilities breaking out with Japan, the Foreign Secretary minuted: 'The old appeasement again. Of course we do not want to fight Japan, but I fear that Lord H. will never learn that to be gentle with aggressors does not avoid hostilities.'[38] Rebuffed once again, in November Hankey rejected a proposal from Piggott that he should espouse the idea of King George VI writing directly to Emperor Hirohito, noting: 'Unless I have something entirely new to suggest I do not think they would listen.'[39]

ATTEMPTS TO OBTAIN CLEMENCY FOR SHIGEMITSU

For the rest of the war Hankey and Butler had little to do with Japan. Their interest only re-emerged in 1946 when the Tokyo War Crimes Tribunal laid down charges against Shigemitsu. The indictment, which largely originated with the Soviet Union, accused him of being involved in conspiracy to wage aggressive war and his failure to prevent crimes against humanity while foreign minister between 1943 and 1945. In December 1946 Shigemitsu's American counsel, George Furness, came to Britain to collect affidavits that could be used in his client's defence. Both Hankey and Butler produced material on his behalf in which they argued that, far from planning aggressive war, Shigemitsu had done all in his power to stop the conflagration. Indeed, Hankey concluded his affidavit by affirming: 'Throughout the whole series of conversations, extending over six months, I cannot find or recollect a word to cast doubt on Mr Shigemitsu's bona fides and I believe that my associates would confirm that view.'[40]

These efforts to exonerate Shigemitsu only had limited success for in November 1948 the former ambassador was sentenced to seven years imprisonment. Butler and Hankey now became involved in an effort organized by Piggott to send a telegram to General Douglas MacArthur, the Supreme Commander Allied Powers in Japan, calling for clemency. This, too, failed to have any effect. Frustrated by the British government's refusal to support this campaign, in 1949 Hankey used his position as a member of the House of Lords to raise Shigemitsu's case and enter into a more general attack on the iniquities of the Tokyo War Crimes Tribunal. Building on this, in the following year he published a book, *Politics, Trials and Errors* in which he criticized the proceedings both in Nuremburg and Tokyo by utilizing the arguments developed by the dissenting judges, and helped to organize the petition sent to the parole board in Japan.[41] While these efforts to assist Shigemitsu did not lead to any curtailment of his sentence, both the former ambassador himself and Japan in general showed their gratitude. In 1953 when Crown Prince Akihito came to Britain to represent Japan at the Queen's Coronation, he not only met Hankey at official functions but also paid a short visit to his home.[42]

CONCLUSION

How then should we assess the role played by Butler and Hankey in Anglo-Japanese relations? On the face of it they may appear to be rather naïve in their efforts to stem the descent towards war. However, it is important to see that while they attempted to use their influence to bring about a rapprochement, they did so for sound political rather than sentimental reasons. Their assessment of the situation from 1939 to 1941 was that Britain had quite enough on its plate in Europe without opening up yet another front in Asia. In this view they were not alone, for the ambassador in Tokyo, Sir Robert Craigie, felt similarly. The experiences of the late summer of 1940 steadily weaned Butler away from this interpretation of events as he began to see that the Japanese problem had to be seen from a global perspective in which American support for Britain was crucial. However, Hankey like Craigie, never really learned this lesson and thus remained interested in improving the state of Anglo-Japanese relations until the end and criticized the Churchill government for doing too little. Hankey though never entertained the same delusions as the more rabid Japanophiles such as Edwardes, Piggott and Sempill. With his vast bureaucratic experience to draw on, he retained a sense of perspective, understood the 'art of the possible' and treated the wilder schemes of the sentimentalists with disdain. Finally, therefore, while their hopes and efforts were dashed by events, it was with their honour intact that Butler and Hankey could lobby for Shigemitsu's release from 1948 onwards. Indeed, it is a testament to their common decency that they did so.

11

Komura Jūtarō (1855-1911) and Britain[1]

IAN NISH

Komura Jūtarō

INTRODUCTION

THIS IS AN ACCOUNT of one of the strong characters of the late Meiji period and one of the great Japanese statesmen of the twentieth century, Komura Jūtarō (1855-1911). It concentrates on his dealings as a diplomat with Britain and especially his years as ambassador to the Court of St James (1906-8). At one level, it is a story of success, demonstrating how someone from a comparatively humble background could be promoted to a position of leadership in Meiji Japan. At another level, the paper argues that Komura who made a success of international conference diplomacy was less at home as a diplomat at one of the major courts of Europe, London.

Komura came from a *bushi* (samurai) family in the small Obi clan in the south of Kyushu. In 1871 he received clan assistance to study in Tokyo and four years later went to Harvard University where entrance standards were less exacting in those days. He studied in the Law School and later worked in New York. In 1880 he returned to Japan via London where he met up with Kikuchi Dairoku[2] and other students studying there (*ryūgakusei*). He also visited France before sailing home from Marseilles.

Recruited into the Foreign Ministry in 1884, he became head of the translation bureau. But Komura was plucked from this backwater by

Foreign Minister Mutsu Munemitsu who probably felt some fellow-feeling for him as the product of one of the lesser clans which had found difficulty in placing their sons in the bureaucracy since the Meiji restoration. Appointed to Peking (Beijing), he became chargé d'affaires there in November 1893. When war broke out between China and Japan, he was posted to Manchuria to act as civil administrator (*minseichō chōkan*) under the commander of the first army, General Yamagata Aritomo. In this office he got to know General Katsura Taro, a contact which was to bring him preferment for the rest of his career. After brief experience in Korea, he served as deputy foreign minister from 1896 to 1898 while he was still only in his early 40s. Komura then served briefly as minister first at Washington (1898-1900) and later at St Petersburg (1900). At the end of that year he was appointed to Peking to act as Japan's representative at the Peking conference which had to resolve the China problem created by the Boxer Uprising there.

FOREIGN MINISTER

In May 1901, while he was still in Peking, Komura was invited to serve as Foreign Minister in General Katsura's first cabinet at the comparatively young age of 45. He accepted but could not take up the assignment until the Peking conference ended in September. When he took office, he found that Japan was moving ahead with overtures for an alliance with Britain but that the country's leaders were divided over the issue. He threw his weight on the side of the alliance.[3] He had to try to persuade Prince Itō Hirobumi (then in Russia) and overcome his reluctance to make an exclusive commitment to Britain. From this time onwards Komura tended to be aligned with General Katsura and those of the Yamagata group. He steered through the negotiations until the alliance came to fruition on 30 January 1902. He had not been the initiator of the alliance but had taken a positive line during the stalemate in November. The alliance might not have come into being but for his persistence which was rewarded with the title of baron (*danshaku*).[4]

The next years were years of strain for Foreign Minister Komura. After the abortive negotiations with Russia, there were the diplomatic problems thrown up by the outbreak of war. It was Komura's strategy that Japan's diplomacy towards Europe during the Russo-Japanese War should be concentrated on Stockholm and London. Komura withdrew the Japanese Minister to Russia early in February 1904 and relocated him in Stockholm. Japan's purpose was for the diplomats, in collaboration with an active military attaché, Colonel Akashi Motojiro, to subvert the Russian war effort by encouraging disaffected groups inside Russia and the Russian Empire in Europe, like Poland, Lithuania, Latvia and Estonia. But Minister Kurino and Akashi had to act alongside the Japanese

Legation in London, which was indispensable as a source of finance and reliable because of the British alliance. They therefore acted along with Minister Hayashi Tadasu and Colonel Utsunomiya Tarō, the military attaché. Between them they conducted a sophisticated intelligence operation throughout the war period.[5] It was perhaps fitting, therefore, that Japan should in the dying days of the war have put the finishing touches to the second Anglo-Japanese treaty which was signed in August 1905 and published the following month.

At the end of the war Komura had two difficult assignments: his appointment as plenipotentiary at the Portsmouth peace conference in 1905; and later his mission to Peking to conclude the Manchurian agreement with China. When Komura returned from the first of these on the *Empress of India* and landed at Yokohama, the people who did not know the circumstances greeted him coolly without even a welcoming flag. In their view he had been forced to make too many concessions in order to secure peace. He was greeted with curses and even told 'it is better you should go back to Russia than come here to Japan'. He faced a disappointed people who felt that they had not obtained at the negotiating table the reward for the sacrifices they had made in the war, notably an indemnity. His unpopularity was moreover unjust because Komura had been in favour of holding out for better terms at Portsmouth but was overruled by the Tokyo government who wanted the war to end without delay.[6]

Sir Claude MacDonald who became the first British Ambassador in Japan reflected on the thankless task which Komura had had in Portsmouth. He wrote:

> Amongst the Japanese themselves opinions are divided in regard to Count Komura's merits, some maintaining that he is weak and timid, whilst others, and these include the greater number of those who are well acquainted with the affairs of their country, strongly support him and argue that he obtained practically the best terms possible under the circumstances at Portsmouth. I was always on the best of terms with Count Komura, and certainly never found him weak or timid. There is no doubt that he signed the Portsmouth treaty at the risk of his life of which he was only too well aware.[7]

By contrast, he came back from Peking in December with terms satisfactory to the Japanese people. These Peking talks were designed to obtain China's consent to what had been agreed at Portsmouth. The Chinese had not been involved in the war; and it required much skill – what Komura's official biography calls *kangen*, a combination of leniency and toughness – to get them to agree to the terms. Eventually, by a combination of assiduity and patience and threats, he managed to obtain their approval to the treaty of Peking in December.[8]

It has to be said, however, that that success and the security which the second alliance gave to Japan after the war were little consolation to Komura for his sense of unpopularity. It is now generally accepted that the decision to conclude the peace treaty was taken in Tokyo and not by the plenipotentiaries at Portsmouth. As Admiral Yamamoto Gombei was later to explain the position in London, 'the Japanese statesmen knew that they had a good deal to lose and perhaps not much to gain by prolonging the war'; the war had been a tremendous strain on the resources of the nation and the cabinet could not contemplate holding up the peace by standing out for improved terms. Komura obfuscated the issue by claiming that 'affairs at Portsmouth' worked out exactly as he thought they would and the terms obtained were those which he had sketched out on paper before leaving Tokyo.[9] Be that as it may, there must have been a feeling on Komura's part that he had been made the scapegoat for someone else's folly and that the Japanese people had shown ingratitude for his efforts. So Komura was bitter when his house was attacked and his person threatened.

When its outstanding business had been completed, the Katsura ministry resigned in January 1906. Komura as a reward for past services was appointed to the Privy Council, which seemed an appropriate job for a senior minister of five years' standing.

AMBASSADOR TO BRITAIN

In December 1905 it had been agreed that the Japanese Legation in London should be given embassy status. It had earned this both because of Japan's new-found reputation for defeating Russia and because of the legation's undoubted efforts for the war. The first Ambassador to Britain was Hayashi Tadasu but he returned to Tokyo on leave on 20 March 1906 and at short notice took over from the Foreign Minister who had resigned unexpectedly.[10] There is reason to believe that Hayashi hoped to return to London; but his assumption of ministerial office forced him to give up such a plan. On 23 May Komura's name was approved by the Emperor for appointment as Ambassador to London at the age of 51.[11]

It is an open question as to why Komura was willing to take on the London embassy after five years of strenuous activity as the Foreign Minister which had left him exhausted. He had never been robust in health; and it was a miracle that it had stood the test in war. The strongest motive may have been a sense that the Japanese people had been ungrateful and that a period of exile would be beneficial. Perhaps he also wanted to practise his diplomatic skills again in a more relaxed, peace-time atmosphere. His experience and diplomatic skills were readily acknowledged. MacDonald reported that:

> I have always found Komura very straight, somewhat brusque in manner and in that way a marked contrast to Hayashi. . . . He is practical and very intelligent and has a wild and irritating laugh. He is not popular in his own Foreign Office.[12]

The government was ready to send Komura to the London embassy, which was then regarded as the prime posting overseas for Japanese diplomats, in order to keep him on side.

Komura left Shimbashi station for Yokohama on 20 July 1906 and sailed on the *Empress of Japan*. He was seen off by a considerable throng including Counts Inoue and Okuma and Viscount Yoshikawa. He travelled via the United States and reached London on 16 August. It was the Edwardian age when diplomatic life was supplemented by – some might say, consisted of – banquets, entertainments, bridge parties and dances. Unlike the younger members of his embassy staff, Komura was not dazzled by this kind of social life. For someone who had seen how Japan had suffered during and after the Russian war, these pastimes did not hold much appeal: life was too serious. Komura had the reputation for spending many of his evenings instead in reading and relaxation.

The image of Japan in Britain was mixed at this time. MacDonald who took leave around this period commented:

> I was very much struck last spring coming from Japan (where the alliance and we are immensely popular) by the unpopularity of the Japanese and to a certain extent of the alliance. Most certainly the alliance is much more popular in Japan than it is in England and I suppose Komura coming direct from Japan has noticed the difference and reported accordingly.[13]

While there was appreciation of the gallantry of the Japanese army and navy and the hardships which the Japanese people had endured during the war, there were political difficulties between Britain and Japan. Some of these related to emigration to the British dominions. More telling was the problem of Manchuria. It seemed that Japan, which had fought the Russian war under the banner of the Open Door in China, had in the post-war period closed the markets of Manchuria to all except Japanese goods. Komura was in the eye of the storm and had to face the criticisms of the British ministers direct.[14]

It was criticism not just from British ministers but also of the British press, which was deeply interested in the Manchurian problem. Komura had had trouble in handling the world press at the Portsmouth conference: he had fought for secrecy being maintained over the proceedings whereas his Russian counterpart, Sergei Witte, had indulged in calculated leakages.[15] Britain by and large supported the need for secret diplomacy at Portsmouth. But in the post-war period the British press sought a special relationship with Komura as ambassador, expecting that disclosures would be readily made to the Third Estate of an allied country. This was not Komura's style as ambassador. Moreover, the post-war scene in Manchuria was a subject of controversy and disagreement; and it was certainly not one on which Komura was prepared to embark on a public debate.

The British perception of reasonable communicativeness was very different. It may be seen in this private letter written by the famous Foreign Editor of *The Times* of London, Valentine Chirol, a journalist who was generally pro-Japanese in his attitudes:

> It is quite useless to talk to Komura, whom I have given up seeing, as it is impossible to get a word out of him. My relations with Hayashi, on the other hand, when he was here were exceedingly friendly and he treated me throughout with a very considerable degree of confidence, and I should like to give him fair warning that the attitude of *The Times* towards Japan may have to suffer change.[16]

Komura's facility in English was not as good as that of Hayashi. That may have been an inhibiting factor. Another insight is, however, given by MacDonald who was visiting London and described how 'Komura lunched with me to-day and, after I had poured a flask of rich Falernian into him, became somewhat communicative'.[17] This is a portrait of a more relaxed Komura.

It may be argued that sociability and communicativeness were not the prime functions of the ambassador. Indeed, Komura was supported by a strong team of gregarious young diplomats: Count Mutsu Hirokichi who had exceptional ability in English, Sakata Shujirō, Honda Kumatarō, Matsudaira Tsuneo and others. The military attaché was Major-General Shiba Gorō, the hero of the Japanese legation at Peking during the Boxer Uprising. With this team it should have been possible to cope with the social contacts which were deemed to lie at the heart of Anglo-Japanese relations.[18]

There were two ways in which Japan dealt with this unpopularity. One was the mission to London in May 1907 of Prince Fushimi. In the previous year King Edward VII had sent a distinguished mission to Tokyo in order to confer on Emperor Meiji the Order of the Garter. In accordance with protocol, Japan sent to London a reciprocal mission led by a royal prince. At a practical level, there was a good deal of important negotiation which went on in the background to the Fushimi mission, including the rudiments of a military-and-naval understanding. At the symbolic level it was an appeal to the British crown, to the ruling élite and to the people at large. It was an attempt to bring home to both peoples that an alliance could have colour and ceremonial. In spite of his reserved nature, Komura took a full part in the various ceremonies associated with the Fushimi mission.[19]

A second approach was the arrangement for the Anglo-Japanese exhibition which eventually took place in 1910. But the foundations were laid earlier during Komura's embassy. While he was in London, Komura witnessed a number of exhibitions, notably the Franco-British exhibition of 1908, which had been organized by Imre Kiralfy, an entrepreneur in this sphere. Kiralfy approached the Japanese with a similar proposition; and Komura as ambassador became one of its strongest supporters. In the view of the most recent expert in this field, he thought that the exhibition might divert Britain's attention from major points of disagreement with Japan, notably over Manchuria.[20]

The cabinet fell in Tokyo on 3 July 1908 and General Katsura was again invited to form a ministry. He immediately asked Komura to become the new Foreign Minister and obtained his acceptance. London arranged at short notice a number of ceremonies to give Komura an appropriate send-off. He had already been decorated with the GCMG and GCVO by the grateful British government. He was not just a senior ambassador going into retirement; he was the incoming Foreign Minister who would be called on to handle difficult bilateral problems. The British Foreign Secretary asked his officials whether there were any issues which should be raised in saying goodbye to him. The Office felt that 'emigration arrangements' were 'more important than all the rest put together, the possibilities being most disagreeable'. If Britain could get an assurance about numbers of Japanese seeking to go abroad, it would mollify the Canadians who claimed to be most disadvantaged by this emigration.[21]

Komura left London on 26 July 1908, being seen off by Prince Fushimi. He travelled by Vienna in order to investigate the tension in the Balkans. He then visited St Petersburg and Moscow and was feted by the Russian establishment, including Witte, his old antagonist.[22] He did not have an audience with the Tsar who was out of the capital. He travelled home in a special car of the Trans-Siberian Railway. It was 26 August before Komura reached Tokyo and took over the Foreign Ministry, an office he was to hold for almost three years.

There is naturally speculation as to why Komura left London after a period as short as two years. Though there is little evidence on this point, Komura may have felt ill at ease and unsuccessful in London. Two months after returning, he may have provided a clue. He prepared for the cabinet on 25 September a lengthy document setting out the broad lines of his thinking entitled 'Proposals for overseas policy' (*Taigai seisaku hōshin*) in which he asserted that the British alliance was at the core of Japan's policy. But in a separate memorandum on Manchuria he stated his aim as being to ensure that Japan's current stake in Manchuria should be maintained in perpetuity and to obtain the support and recognition of the world powers for Japan's 'special position' in Manchuria.[23] These had presumably been points which were central to Komura's embassy in London where he must have found the government stance uncongenial. Komura may therefore have thought that British opinion was hostile to a central theme of his policy.[24]

CONCLUSION

This is not the place to mention the important developments which took place during his remaining three years as Foreign Minister. But there were several matters which had been initiated in London which he now carried to fruition. The South Manchurian Railway Loan of six million pounds was successfully issued in London at the end of 1910. The Anglo-Japanese treaty of commerce which gave Japan the tariff autonomy she had long sought was concluded in 1911. The revised Anglo-Japanese Alliance was signed on 15 July 1911. It was favourably received by the Japanese press which saw the revision as essential in view of Japan's annexation of Korea. Komura told the British Ambassador that practically all the items on the government's programme had been carried through and that he and Katsura preferred to allow another group of statesmen to draw up a fresh programme.[25] Accordingly, Komura resigned with the Katsura cabinet on 25 August 1911, relatively content with his achievements.

Komura who had been a victim of consumption for a long time had suffered from pleurisy for some months during 1909. Indeed, it was largely due to the strength of his personality that he overcame this long-term ailment and stayed in office so long.[26] On 6 September 1911 he went for treatment for consumption to a house at Hayama, spending his time in lonely isolation. His condition deteriorated from 1 November and he finally died on 26 November at the age of fifty-six.[27]

Komura left behind him a career of remarkable achievement. He had many good bureaucratic qualities: he was efficient, conscientious and supportive of his juniors. His subordinates praised the seriousness and thoroughness of his office-work and his abnormal powers of concentration.[28] Yoshizawa Kenkichi who as head of the first political section in the Foreign Ministry had close contact with Komura, testifies to his clear-headedness and his quick brain, concentrating on the exchange of telegrams between diplomatic capitals.[29] He was an effective Foreign Minister who dominated policy-making for a decade. He was a skilled negotiator with foreign states and secured tranquillity at home by gaining consensus with the military. On the other hand, as the British ambassador wrote, Komura was 'very guarded on all occasions'.[30] He was discreet, patient and deliberately secretive. He was not good at handling the foreign press. Like most foreign ministers of the time, he found parliamentary debate and criticism very trying.

Komura was evidently happier on the Tokyo scene than in London. In this, he stands in marked contrast to his predecessor Hayashi, who after his return to Tokyo was always sighing for peaceful times in England and remembered embassy life with affection.[31] Komura was content with the hard administrative grind in Tokyo and did not put a premium on life abroad. He entered fully into embassy activities when he was required to do so but he was more at home in Tokyo.

Komura had a special confidence in the value of the Anglo-Japanese Alliance for Japan without, one feels, being a thoroughgoing Anglophile. Whereas he has the reputation of being a hard-liner in relation to policies towards China, he was at the same time the most consistent advocate of an alliance with liberal England. He had been important in steering through the first alliance in 1901 against the opposition of some of the Elder Statesmen. The 1905 revision of the alliance was equally his handiwork: it was more important for Japan because there was a real possibility of a war of revenge on the part of Russia. That did not materialize; but it was a contingency against which Komura had to provide. In the last months of his life in 1911 he devised other amendments to the alliance, which emerged weaker than before but endured longer than the earlier treaties. It was probably the alliance that brought Komura the supreme accolade of his career, the conferment of the title of *koshaku* (marquis) in April 1911. It was a remarkable achievement for the ambitious son of a small and remote southern clan.

12

Inouye Katsunosuke, 1861–1929

IAN NISH

Inouye Katsunosuke

PROFESSOR CHRISTOPHER THORNE in his outstanding book on Anglo-American relations in the Asia-Pacific war described the wartime relationship of Britain and the United States as 'Allies of a Kind'. This description is true also of the relationship between Britain and Japan during the First World War. They were allies; but there were wartime issues where the national interests of the allies clashed seriously and led to great tensions. The task of presenting Japan's case to Britain and defending Britain's position in Japan fell to Inouye Katsunosuke who was appointed Ambassador to the Court of St James's in February 1913 and had to steer Anglo-Japanese relations till 24 July 1916. These were difficult times and Inouye coped in a way which attracted the greatest respect.[1]

Inouye's connection with England went back a long way. Born in the Chōshū domain, he was orphaned at an early age and was sent to London for education at what the Japanese call the London School of Political Economy in 1871. He was therefore on the spot when the Iwakura mission visited London in the summer of 1872. It was common for the early Japanese 'students' in the capital to do errands for the great men of the mission and Inouye won the special commendation of Kido Takayoshi, one of the senior members of that mission. He stayed on for some years studying in Europe and was around when Inouye Kaoru, later to become an important statesman, visited London to study economic and fiscal policies in 1878. It was there that Inouye who had only two daughters adopted this promising youngster (*yōshishi*) as his heir.[2]

On return to Japan, he was appointed first to the Ministry of Finance but later to the Foreign Ministry where he assisted his father when he served as the minister in charge of treaty revision negotiations. It was during this period that through the mediation of Yamagata Aritomo he married Ozawa Sueko in 1883. This was followed by his appointment to the Japanese Legation in Berlin in 1886. Returning to Japan on leave in 1892, he served in the ministry and became part of the team which went to Hiroshima with the General Headquarters (*Dai Honei*) during the war with China and took part in the Shimonoseki talks, which brought that conflict to an end in 1895. He was then briefly posted to Seoul to help sort out the crisis created by the complicity of Japanese officials in the murder of the Korean queen.

ENVOY IN BERLIN

Inouye, now a full-fledged diplomat, went to Berlin as Minister Plenipotentiary in 1898 and stayed there until 1902 when he returned home on leave. It is not for us to record all his doings in these years. But Berlin was at the heart of Europe and had a great influence on Japan's thinking, especially when she was looking around for support and security from European powers. There was a division between the elder statesmen over this. The senior Inouye initially wanted to explore the possibility of some arrangement between Japan, Britain and Germany. Whether this was because his son was in charge of the Berlin legation cannot be said. At any rate, the initiative failed. Next, Inouye *père* favoured some arrangement with Russia. A rather devious scheme whereby Itō Hirobumi would be sent to St Petersburg in November 1901 to test the ground was evolved. Itō had to stop in Berlin for a week on the return journey from Russia where the initiative was again unsuccessful.[3]

After leave in Japan in 1902, Minister Inouye returned to Berlin to find his legation playing an important role in the run-up to the Russo-Japanese war. When war broke out in 1904, the Berlin legation, like all Japanese legations in Europe, became a central point for military intelligence (*yōeki no jōhō*). It was one of Japan's objectives to destabilize the Russian government by encouraging dissident movements inside Russia and in the wider Russian Empire; and the legations acted as important sources of funds and information. Germany maintained a nominal neutrality during the war; but the Kaiser and his court left the Japanese with the impression that they were pro-Russian. In particular, Inouye had to lodge complaints over the use of German ports and installations by Russian warships.

Inouye was awarded a senior Order of the Rising Sun for his services during the war and left in November 1907 as ambassador, much feted and decorated.[4]

During his tenure Inouye had the ceremonial duty of hosting Prince and Princess Arisugawa Takehito who came to Germany to attend the wedding of the German Crown Prince in the summer of 1905. Prince Arisugawa who had trained with the Royal Navy also visited Britain, the royal couple 'being received with special distinction and staying at York House as guests of the king who conferred on the prince the Order of GCB (Military Division)'.[5]

From 1908 Inouye was *en disponibilité* to quote the diplomatic jargon. He then spent a period on mainly ceremonial tasks, basically a sort of retirement and recuperation. This included a trip to South America, taking in the celebrations for the centenary of Chilean independence. When his diplomatic appointment lapsed, he was transferred to the Upper House of the Diet. Inouye Katsunosuke joined the Imperial Household Ministry for temporary service in connection with the funeral arrangements for the Meiji Emperor who died in 1912.

The political order in Japan was changing. Itō Hirobumi had been assassinated by a Korean in 1909, leaving his father, Count Inouye, as senior *genrō*. Whether this made a great difference in Inouye Katsunosuke's fortunes is not clear because Inouye Kaoru had never won the favour of the Emperor Meiji and had never served as Prime Minister. But he now became in practice the leader of the Chōshū faction opposed to Yamagata.[6]

At the end of 1912 Japan's senior diplomat, Katō Takaaki, then Ambassador to Britain, was recalled to become Foreign Minister. One of his first acts after taking up office in Kasumigaseki was to appoint Inouye Katsunosuke as his successor on 8 February. In going to the London embassy, the senior post in the Japanese diplomatic hierarchy overseas, Inouye Katsunosuke had first to resign his seat in the Upper House. He was then given a farewell banquet in Tokyo by the newly-formed Japan-British Association at which the Foreign Minister proposed his good health.[7]

Inouye Katsunosuke left Shimbashi with his wife on 20 May, seen off by a multitude estimated at 2000 people. He faced another 500 at Yokohama before proceeding to Pusan and the Siberian railway. Reaching London on 8 June, he met Sir Edward Grey, the Foreign Secretary, and presented his credentials on the following day. He was happy returning to the place of his schooling. He was comfortable also in the cordial atmosphere created by the Anglo-Japanese Alliance which had been in existence over a decade and had been renewed only two years before. On the other hand, it had to be said that it was a curious appointment for someone who had for so long been identified with

Germany, at a juncture when British public opinion was turning strongly against that country. Moreover, Inouye always cultivated the military moustache associated with the Prussian gentry.

Because of his good (*migoto*) English, Inouye was much in demand to give public speeches of the mammoth kind favoured in spacious pre-war days. Notably, he made the keynote speech at the Japan Society party (400 attended) at which Sir Claude MacDonald spoke on his retirement from the Tokyo Embassy (19 November).[8] While Inouye stressed in these speeches the benefits of the alliance to both partners, he did acknowledge how difficult it was for Britain to understand Japan's incursions into south China. He had taken over at a time when relations had plummeted because of serious commercial confrontation over south and central China. This came to the fore over railway investment. The Japanese government wanted to obtain railway concessions in central China where Britain's existing interests were predominant. Since the Japanese had excluded British rail entrepreneurs in their sphere in Manchuria, it was argued by London that it was unreasonable for Japan to expect to have access to established British areas.[9] It was an issue on which it was difficult to secure a meeting of minds and, as the two countries slid into war against Germany, it was still an unresolved issue.

One of the new members of Inouye's embassy was Shidehara Kijūrō who joined from Washington in December 1913. Shidehara, already regarded as one of the rising stars in the diplomatic firmament, came as counsellor for a short period of six months before he was promoted to be Minister to the Netherlands. In his autobiographical writings he lets us into the atmosphere of the London embassy with a cordial ambassador and his intelligent and linguistically talented wife. He was impressed by his time in London and stated his belief that the British Foreign Secretary, Sir Edward Grey, stood out as a model Foreign Minister.[10]

WARTIME TENSIONS

The fast-moving character of the early days of the European war inevitably increased the misunderstandings, already generated over China. Ambassador Inouye, like Sir Conyngham Greene, his counterpart in Tokyo, had to try to moderate relations and smooth out mutual suspicions.[11]

When the so-called '*Oshū taisen*' (as the Japanese liked to describe the European war) broke out, Inouye's father Kaoru spoke of it as 'divine aid conferred on the new Taishō era for the achievement of Japan's destiny'. To seize the opportunity, Japan decided to get involved in the war, but only at the periphery. This did not suit Britain who, having initially asked Japan for assistance, wanted her not to go the whole hog and become a belligerent, bearing in mind the sensitivities of the United States, Australia and New Zealand over any attempt by Japan to take over territory. Japan went ahead and declared war on Germany on 23 August. Her action was not required under the alliance, as Katō made clear. She entered the war in order to secure her own national interests as she was perfectly entitled to do. But Japan would not agree to Britain's repeated request to send troops to the western front. The two allies had to agree to disagree over the limits of Japan's area of involvement in the war (*senchi kyokugen*).[12]

Early in September the Japanese army began an attack against the German leased territory in China surrounding Tsingtao, a port where Japanese trade had for long been predominant. The port and fortress in the lease (*Pachtgebiet*) were expected to hold out for six months; in fact they fell to the Japanese force on 7 November in some six weeks. The campaign was a difficult but ultimately a successful one for the Japanese army. By extension it was a victory celebrated by the Entente powers. Inouye was called on to attend many congratulatory dinners, notably the Lord Mayor of London's annual banquet at the Guildhall which included speeches by Lord Kitchener and A.J. Balfour singing the praises of Japan.[13]

But Japan's popularity soon changed in the New Year because of the crisis in China. Ambassador Inouye could not fail to be at the heart of it because Britain was apprehensive about China in spite of her prime preoccupation with the European front. The crisis broke very slowly, starting with the presentation of Japan's demands to President Yuan Shikai of China on 18 January. To the Western world this is known as the 'Twenty-one Demands Crisis' with its focus on Group V of the demands; but Japanese records do not show it as a crisis so much as a tidying-up operation rendered necessary by the successes of the occupying army and the need to reach some understanding on the administration of the occupied territory. In the run-up to the crisis, Foreign Minister Katō had been overwhelmed by receiving an avalanche of memoranda from a wide range of right-wing bodies, army officers and individuals including the *Kokuryūkai* (Amur River Society), *TōA Dōshikai* and *Tai-Shi Rengōkai*. While they had been received from early in 1914 they became more numerous in the last months of the year and tended to emphasize the strong line which should be taken towards China during the emergency created by the European war.[14] It would appear that, while the presentation of the Twenty-one Demands was undoubtedly the responsibility of the Foreign Ministry, its role was to some extent that of coordinating ideas which came from a wide variety of pressure groups.

Ambassador Inouye became involved in the crisis at two levels, diplomatically and personally. Diplomatically he was under instructions to pass over confidentially to the British government the four groups of demands, which had been presented to China, as a gesture between allies.[15] Gradually, other versions of the demands came out through various leakages, mainly in the press. But Inouye gave assurances to Britain that these were not true. On 6 February, therefore, Grey went on the record, with a degree of naïveté, saying that the versions circulating were 'greatly exaggerated'. It was only four days later that Baron Katō first mentioned to London that Japan had also presented the Chinese president with '*kibō jōkō*' – 'conditions hoped for' or 'desiderata' as distinct from 'demands'. These have subsequently gone down in history as 'Group V'. In Japan's view, these were distinctly of a lower priority than the 'demands'. In other eyes they were more extreme than the 'demands', implying on the one hand an attempt to impose a kind of Japanese suzerainty over China and on the other an intention to encroach on railway rights in the Yangtse valley which Britain thought her entrepreneurs had already acquired.

It is puzzling that Baron Katō should have been so secretive to his ambassador and the international community. Katō had a very high reputation for personal integrity and diplomatic frankness in the eyes of the British government, the British press and the treaty-port press in Japan. So his assurances seemed credible in these quarters. Obviously he wanted to avoid premature leakages while negotiations were going on with China. Presumably, he withheld them from London in particular because the last thing he wanted was to provoke Britain to raise again the Yangtse valley issue which formed part of Group V. It is possible that Katō himself disapproved of many of the demands, including those which had been forced on him by right-wing lobbies. As a former ambassador in London, he knew that the commercial implications would be seriously studied there.[16]

Personally, Ambassador Inouye was understandably annoyed. He may have learnt of Group V only from the press and felt that he had been badly let down by his ministry. He had given specious assurances to Britain in good faith. It is understood that he offered his resignation because he had not been treated openly by the Foreign Ministry, which had been secretive throughout. The evidence comes from the treaty-port journalist known by his pen-name as 'Putnam Weale' who wrote:

> Count Inouye had persistently denied the existence of Group V to Viscount Grey. When it transpired that there really was such a group of which he had been kept in ignorance he telegraphed confidentially over the heads of the cabinet asking that the Emperor recall him as his honour had been compromised by Baron Katō, forcing him to prevaricate in his dealings with Viscount Grey.[17]

It is not possible to confirm this. Inouye Katsunosuke's biographers quote it as a rumour. It was not implausible because this was Inouye's last post and so recall and possible resignation and retirement would not have been a great sacrifice.

Whatever the truth, Inouye stayed on in London. But the rumour was a not unimportant one, because it truly identified the sheer anger of a senior Japanese diplomat towards Katō who had earlier been instrumental in his appointment. It was his duty thereafter to negotiate an accommodation over the Yangtse interests of Britain and Japan. But Britain emphasized that Japan's demands should be consistent with the existing Anglo-Japanese Alliance which had guaranteed the independence and territorial integrity of China.[18] Some modifications were made in the light of protests like these, and the American and other governments weighed in to get Group V dropped. When Japan sent Beijing her final ultimatum, Britain was convinced that China would not give way to such exorbitant demands and that a 'rupture' which could have a disastrous effect on the European war would ensue. Grey came close to acting as a mediator to prevent war, ultimately counselling China to give in to the more moderate terms on offer. China accepted on 9 May and signed a new treaty on 25th. It is clear that Japan's reticence was the fault of the Foreign Ministry, not Ambassador Inouye who was not taken into Tokyo's confidence. It was widely held in Japan that Katō had mishandled the crisis, forfeiting Japan's good reputation abroad and his popularity at home.

As the crisis ended, Ambassador Inouye also became involved on a personal basis because of his father. In the summer Marquis Inouye was suffering from a serious illness but was still a figure to be reckoned with. He was one of the leaders of the Elder Statesmen (*genrō*) who felt that they had not been adequately consulted during the international crisis of 1915. Foreign Minister Katō, who believed fervently in the autonomy of his Ministry, deliberately refused to circulate papers to the Elder Statesmen and acted in this instance without obtaining their prior agreement. When the crisis turned sour, he had to shoulder the blame. In mid-June Inouye Kaoru, in incandescent rage at being by-passed, wrote to the Prime Minister that Katō must be replaced. If not, he threatened to cut all political ties, call his son home from London and retire from political life.[19] Whether these were idle threats or not, they are interesting. It is unclear whether letters or telegrams passed between son and father and, if so, on what sort of scale. It suggests that Inouye, even in London, was very much implicated in Japan's domestic political scene. But it is bizarre to think of a senior and experienced diplomat being 'recalled' by his father against the wishes of the Ministry.

The issue evaporated because Marquis Inouye died on 1 September 1915 at the age of 81, leaving Count Inouye to succeed to the title of Marquis. Inouye Katsunosuke asked permission to return to Tokyo; but this was disallowed by Katō on the grounds that the international crisis was by no means resolved.[20]

We cannot go into all aspects of Inouye's conduct of diplomacy towards Britain. But the delicacy of his position is illustrated by the story of the Russo-Japanese Alliance which came into existence in July 1916. The prime aim of Inouye's embassy had always been to polish the tarnished image of the Anglo-Japanese Alliance and to make clear the special relationship between the two countries. Britain, while disillusioned with Japan, could not afford to allow the alliance to lapse during the war. But many in Japan, perhaps doubtful of Britain's capacity for achieving ultimate victory, wanted to diversify their foreign relations by concluding a separate alliance with Russia. When the idea of expanding the alliance to take in war-time collaborators like Russia was mooted, Inouye, Katō and Grey were initially opposed. But, as Russia's military position weakened, Grey withdrew his opposition. He wanted to commit Japan to Russia in such a way that Russia could safely remove her troops from Siberia without fear of Japan taking over her territory. In this way the Russo-Japanese Alliance came about in July 1916. While London superficially welcomed this development, it may in reality have been less enthusiastic. Greene from his perspective in Tokyo took a sceptical view:

> Prior to the war. . . there was a tendency to look upon Japan as a model of all international virtues. . . Today we have come to know that Japan – the real Japan – is a frankly opportunist, not to say selfish, country of very modest importance compared with the giants of the Great War, but with a very exaggerated opinion of her own role in the universe.[21]

The time came for Inouye's recall after a fairly turbulent time in London. He left after serving over three years and received such hospitality as war-time London could muster. His Japanese biographer speaks of his popularity in Britain. He certainly was honoured by King George V on 12 July 1916, the King expressing pleasure at the friendly relations just forged between Russia and Japan: 'Inouye replied that he shared H.M.'s views on the great value of the new accord between Japan and Russia in harmonious cooperation with the Anglo-Japanese Alliance.' He was admitted to the first class of the Royal Victorian Order. Both he and his wife had been popular and made the best of a difficult job. In particular the Marchioness had been active in helping the British Red Cross during the war.[22]

Inouye finally received permission to return home. His successor was appointed on 13 June 1916. The Inouyes departed on 24 July, seen off by Lord Crewe, the acting Foreign Secretary. From the vantage-point of the London embassy, he had witnessed the first phase of an unprecedented war, the phase before the United States joined in. On 22 August the Inouye family arrived in Japan having travelled via Canada. Inouye Katsunosuke was interviewed by the press on arrival and made an interesting statement:

I was deeply impressed by the universal determination [in Britain] to fight to the bitterest end. There can be no consideration of peace proposals without complete victory of the arms of the Allies. On the other hand, Germany is weakening. She will take six months to recover from her recent heavy losses in defeat in the North Sea. While Germany claims a good harvest, her supplies are diminishing and her resources are becoming more and more limited.[23]

This was a surprisingly upbeat assessment of the allied war effort at the time. His prediction in 1916 of an allied victory was in marked contrast to the view of many Japanese policy-makers who saw things differently.

END-OF-WAR MISSIONS

As Inouye Katsunosuke entered retirement, he continued to be active. He spent the next few years involved in certain state ceremonies. He was one of the hosts of the mission to Japan led by Prince Arthur of Connaught in order to present a Field-Marshal's baton to the Emperor Taishō. This was intended to be a mark of respect and friendship to the new Japanese sovereign. In view of the danger the mission faced in the Atlantic from German submarines, it was a risky war-time gesture. On 18 June 1918 Inouye welcomed them at Yokohama. They were met at Tokyo station by the Emperor himself and placed in the Kasumigaseki Palace. The baton was passed over on the following day.[24] In order to reciprocate, Prince Higashi-Fushimi was sent on a thanksgiving mission to the British sovereign. Inouye was appointed as head of the accompanying mission which consisted of ten members, including General Shiba Gorō and Admiral Oguri Kisaburō, two pro-British officers. They set off from Yokohama in the *Fushimi Maru* on 26 September, travelling via Vancouver and Halifax. They reached Plymouth safely and reciprocated by conferring a Japanese Field-marshal's sword on the British sovereign. They inspected the Grand Fleet and set off for the battlefields of the allied powers, France, Belgium and Italy, meeting Field-Marshal Sir Douglas Haig on Armistice Day, 1918. They left again via Plymouth across the Atlantic to New York, arriving back in Yokohama on 7 January 1919. This lengthy journey of over a hundred days was to give Inouye his last sight of Britain, although he later acted as head of the committee which planned the visit of the Prince of Wales (later Edward VIII) to Japan in 1922.[25]

In his retirement Inouye became engaged in charitable and educational works and was appointed to the Privy Council. In that capacity he intervened from time to time as over the Chinese policies of the Tanaka cabinet. But his health deteriorated and he died in November 1929 at the age of 69.[26]

During his time in the London Embassy, Inouye unquestionably tried to uphold the international reputation of Japan at a particularly difficult time. His tenure coincided with a crunch-time for the Anglo-Japanese Alliance, a time when the existence of the alliance was in jeopardy because of the competing interests of the two allies and especially because of Britain's suspicions of Japanese ambitions. It cannot be said that Inouye was exclusively Anglophil like his predecessors Hayashi Tadasu or Katō Takaaki for he had spent much of his career in Germany. But he was very professional, adapting himself to the environment in which he was placed. In many of his gestures he showed himself to be a man of probity and an admirer of British institutions and culture. Inouye was, however, far from happy with the actions of his home government. He must have felt that he had been let down by its secretiveness over the Twenty-one Demands and embarrassed by its refusal to allow him to return home after his father's death. But the fact that the Anglo-Japanese Alliance which was central to the interests of both countries during the war years was in the doldrums was not the fault of Inouye. He had nursed it; and it survived his departure.

13

Chinda Sutemi, 1857–1929: Ambassador in Peace and War

IAN NISH

Chinda Sutemi

HISTORIANS HAVE A PENCHANT for examining the origins of war. That is very proper because it is important to learn the art of preventing wars. But the aftermaths of war are equally worthy of study because it is there that things go wrong for the future and the decisions have often to be taken at breakneck speed in fast-moving situations. This requires adaptability, flexibility and vision on the part of decision-makers.

This was nowhere more needed than in the case of Japan and the Paris Peace Conference of 1919 which brought an end to the 'first world war'. In spite of the description, it had been primarily a European war; and Japan had kept herself on its fringes. She had grown prosperous as a result of it. Without doubt she had made a contribution to allied victory, mainly as a result of her naval actions. But she had not suffered many casualties which for many nations was to be the criterion by which their contribution to the war effort was judged. This left the Japanese with a seat at the top table at the Paris Peace Conference where the peace was negotiated – one of the members of the Council of Five Great Powers but outside the Council of Four in which many of the critical decisions were vested. Japan had advanced on to the world stage and had much to do to adjust to her new role.[1]

Chinda Sutemi as Ambassador to Britain from 1916 to 1920 was one of those who had to attend the Paris conference and address these new international problems. He had a role in the preparation of Japan's peace terms, took his share in steering through the negotiations and conducted important business during the first two years after the armistice.[2]

Born in Mutsu, Aomori-ken, Chinda graduated at an American university and joined the Foreign Ministry in 1885. After a variety of consular posts, he became minister to Russia briefly in November 1900. He then returned to the ministry as vice-minister under Komura Jūtarō in 1903 and served throughout the stressful days of the Russo-Japanese War. Because of Komura's frequent illnesses and his absences at Portsmouth, New Hampshire and Beijing, Chinda was effectively in charge at critical junctures. He had close relations with the British ambassador who reported confidentially to London in 1908: 'Chinda is considered by some to be a man of exceptional ability. The Baron speaks excellent English but is very reticent.'[3]

In June 1908 he went to his first ambassadorial post, succeeding Inouye Katsunosuke in Berlin. He then moved to Washington from November 1911 where he had a long stint of five years. He enjoyed cordial relations with the British Ambassador there, Sir Cecil Spring Rice.[4]

CHINDA IN LONDON

Chinda was appointed to the London Embassy in the middle of the First World War and arrived at his post at a critical juncture on 1 August 1916. It was a strange coincidence that he should succeed Inouye whom he had earlier replaced in Berlin in 1908. It was rumoured that he had turned down the post of foreign minister in 1915, a sign that he was approaching the pinnacle of his career. He came to London at a depressing time for the Allies before the United States joined them in April 1917. China, which was even more a matter of concern for Japan, entered the war in August of that year. While Britain was preoccupied by the changing fortunes of the fighting, Japan was looking ahead to the bargaining which would take place at the peace-table.

In October 1916 the Okuma cabinet resigned, making way for the cabinet led by General Terauchi Masatake. The foreign minister appointed was Motono Ichirō, the former Ambassador to Russia who had played a large part in formulating the Russo-Japanese Alliance which had just been concluded in July. Motono came to the post dissatisfied with the lack of clarity over Japanese policy towards the war. Basically, Japan was at war against the Central Powers of Germany and Austro-Hungary, and should cooperate with the Entente to the fullest degree. But the situation, Motono wrote, was full of uncertainties:

Peace terms should include Japan's retention of Tsingtao and occupied islands in the Pacific and acquisition of rights possessed by Germany in Shantung province. . . But, if victory does not go either to the Alliance or the Entente, it is likely that Germany will reject Japan's claims. . . If the war ends in victory for the German Alliance, it will be even more difficult to get approval for Japan's claims. . . Even if the Entente are victorious, they will probably expect the country that made the least sacrifice in the war [i.e. Japan] to be modest in its demands. . . Hence we should give the Entente countries as much help as possible in materiel, finance etc.[5]

Clearly, from Japan's perspective, all contingencies were being explored. But Motono was seeking clarification and proposing a radical shift of emphasis away from a policy which would not send troops to the Western Front and hitherto declined to send war-ships beyond Singapore. The Japanese cabinet agreed that, now that the war was finely balanced, it was desirable that Japan should more explicitly throw in her lot with Britain and her Entente partners in the hope of securing the prizes on which she had set her sights.

Such was the policy which Chinda had to apply in the months ahead. Almost as soon as he reached London, the naval situation in the Atlantic took a turn for the worse because of German submarine attacks. Britain reiterated to Chinda her appeals for naval assistance and Japan responded by requesting a number of undertakings. These included a post-war guarantee for Japan's retention of Shantung and Germany's insular possessions in the Pacific which were already occupied by Japan. Japanese naval authorities were probably itching to go beyond the confines of the China seas; and Chinda indicated that there would probably be no difficulty in securing their cooperation. On 2 February 1917 Japan agreed to make available the necessary naval assistance. The *Tsushima* and *Niitaka* were to go to Cape of Good Hope, while the *Akashi* and two flotillas of destroyers were to be despatched to the Mediterranean.[6]

The British war cabinet duly responded by confirming the necessary guarantees on 14 February. Britain agreed in rather careful language that she would support Japan's claims in regard to the disposal of Germany's rights in Shantung and possessions in the Islands North of the Equator on the occasion of a peace conference, it being understood that Japan would '. . . treat in the same spirit Britain's claims to the German islands South of Equator'. This last phrase was included in order to create the impression of parity between the two sides. But this was spurious since Britain was in this instance the mendicant, desperate to obtain Japanese naval assistance regardless. Where this formula was devised is not clear. Probably in London; but Chinda's role in this negotiation is not completely clear. He was a newcomer to the post, compared to Sir Conyngham Greene who had been Ambassador in Tokyo since 1913 and was, of course, able to lobby the naval establishment there direct.[7]

Over the next issue Chinda took a more personal interest. A telegram from Deputy Foreign Minister Alfred Zimmermann in Berlin to Mexico on 19 January 1917 had been intercepted and successfully decoded by British intelligence.[8] The thrust of the message was that 'if war broke out between Germany and the United States, Germany would offer Mexico an alliance and try to persuade her into operations against the United States, with the ancillary suggestion that the Mexican president should mediate between Germany and Japan and request Japan to take part in their alliance'. This obscure speculation was dynamite. The intercept was passed over by Britain to Washington; by President Wilson to the press; and by the newspapers to an astonished American public. Germany was on the point of starting unrestricted submarine warfare in the Atlantic and wanted to dissuade the United States from declaring war. In April, however, the Americans severed relations with Germany because of her threat to make these submarine attacks against both enemy and neutral shipping.

The air between Washington and Tokyo was already hostile; and those suspicions were greatly intensified by the inclusion of Japan's name in the Zimmermann telegram. Chinda at Washington had had the additional responsibility as envoy to Mexico and was already familiar with the problems there. Japan had sold a considerable amount of arms to Mexico; and the arms dealers were a source of constant embarrassment to the Japanese government. Chinda was able to tell Britain with considerable authority that Japan was keeping her distance from the Mexican government. She published denials that she would have had any hand in such a deal and emphasized that there was no way that Mexico of all states could persuade Japan to make peace with Germany.

On 5 May Viscount and Viscountess Chinda were invited to spend two nights at Windsor Castle as royal guests. During their visit the king spoke to them of the need for Japanese destroyers to sink German submarines because of the Battle of the Atlantic Ocean and the need for arranging convoys. At this stage Japan asked in return for the supply of special materials required for the construction of naval ships, in other words, steel. Britain had to say that she had none to spare and urged Japan to approach the United States where she was again refused.[9]

American entry to the war on the Entente side was succeeded by the decision of the government of China to follow the same path. This had long-term consequences for Japan as the Motono statement above has shown. It was now inevitable that China would send plenipotentiaries to the ultimate peace conference and dispute the major Japanese claim.

PARIS PEACE CONFERENCE

When the war ended in 1918, Chinda as Ambassador to Britain was chosen alongside Matsui Keishirō, Ambassador to France, and Ijūin Hikokichi, Ambassador to Italy, as Japanese delegates to the peace conference. The initial idea was that Japan would rely on those who had expertise from the Portsmouth Conference of 1905 which ended the Russo-Japanese War. Viscount Chinda arrived in Paris on 11 January 1919. On the 18th the main delegation led by Baron Makino Shinken, a former ambassador and foreign minister, arrived via the United States. For the critical first six weeks Makino conducted negotiations as de facto chief. Chinda was in effect second in the pecking order, slightly higher than Matsui and Ijūin. Chinda had some advantages over the other Japanese delegates: his English was superior; and he was 'robust in argument'. More importantly, he knew most of the American delegates who had been members of the Wilson administration and had had dealings with them and with the British. He was, in particular, familiar with Arthur Balfour who as Foreign Secretary was a chief British negotiator. When Prince Saionji arrived on 2 March to head the mission, not much changed since he was content to keep a low profile and be consulted behind the scenes.[10]

Nonetheless, conference diplomacy was a novel experience for which Japan as a whole was ill-prepared. The Portsmouth negotiations of 1905 had been no real preparation. Similarly, the international conference at Beijing of 1900-1 to sort out the Boxer problem, while it was truly international, dealt only with a limited and well-defined subject. This was a problem for the delegates who were to be pitied because their instructions were strictly laid down from Tokyo. They were formulated not only by the Foreign Ministry but sometimes by the *Gaikō Chōsakai*, an extra-parliamentary group of politicians with strongly-held views and without exposure to the arts of international negotiation.

That left much of the business of the delegation to be conducted by what one Japanese scholar calls the 'Makino-Chinda *kombi*'. That is, the two tended to combine as a team and lobby together on all substantial issues. Cooperation between Makino and Chinda was to be a special feature of the Japanese delegation's actions at Paris; and it worked well. They had a broad mandate from Prime Minister Hara to follow the line taken by the British and Americans. But this was not easy to implement because they found that Anglo-Saxon feeling was generally in favour of China and this was shared by conference participants as a whole.

Japan was negotiating as one of the victors. In the initial stages of the conference Japan lost out over the racial equality clause.[12] There was a fierce determination, therefore, not to give in over her most precious demand, the transfer to Japan from Germany of the former German-leased territory in Shantung province in China. This issue became an acute embarrassment to the Council of Four, all the more so as Italy had already left Paris dissatisfied and in disgust. Chinda was at his most threatening at this stage, suggesting that Japan would not join the League of Nations. On 16 April he met Balfour to see if any compromise could be worked out over Shantung. Balfour told him that the United States and France were supporting China. Chinda assumed not inaccurately that Britain, while ready to act in accordance with her agreement of 1917, was endeavouring to induce Japan to reduce her demands in order to secure a compromise acceptable to other delegations. But he would not agree. When the Versailles treaty was signed, it transferred the residue of the German lease of Shantung to Japan, in spite of China's pleas. But, in order to secure her prime demand, the Japanese delegates, not least Chinda, had to give some assurances of the vaguest kind that Japan would ultimately restore some of Germany's rights to China. That assurance was probably given in good faith but it was not publicly endorsed by the Tokyo government.

The Paris Peace Conference left a lot of loose ends. This was particularly true of the Far Eastern field and the issue of Shantung. Since it had not been possible to resolve this to the satisfaction of the powers, it was left to the Foreign Office and the State Department to pursue the issue with Japan on a bilateral basis. These were awkward days for Chinda who was summoned to meet the acting Foreign Secretary, Lord Curzon, on 18 July for this purpose. Curzon reported that he had told Chinda that:

> . . . it was unwise of Japan to insist upon the technical rights secured to her by her agreement with China in respect of Shantung. I was aware that a declaration of her intentions had been made by Japan to other Allied Powers in Paris; but this action which was to a large extent a justification of the action taken by the Powers had never been published to the world. . . The whole policy of Japan was wrapt in a mist of doubt and suspicion which was creating very general alarm.

In response, the Ambassador (as described in the flowery language of Curzon):

> . . . intervened with an almost impassioned defence of the action of his country and his Government, the fervour of which in no wise abated until our conversation lasted for nearly an hour and a half. . . Arguments were again and again reiterated with great vigour.[13]

Something of the personality of Chinda comes out in these exchanges. He was not inexperienced in diplomacy and was not prepared to be browbeaten by Curzon. Loyal to his government, he stood up to the imperious Foreign Secretary.

Chinda continued to be actively involved in the politics of Europe after the Versailles treaty. It was one of the consequences of Japan's enhanced role in international affairs that her representatives had to be involved in the various conferences held around Europe in order to implement and expand on the findings of the Versailles treaty. There were also meetings of the nascent League of Nations of which Japan was a founder member. For example, Chinda had to attend a special meeting of the League Council which was summoned for St James Palace on 14 June 1920, London acting for the time being as the headquarters of the world body. The press were calling for the highest possible representation by prominent politicians so that the League of Nations could be launched strongly. Alas, 'apart from Lord Curzon for Britain and Viscount Chinda for Japan, other representatives lacked distinction', it was reported. Chinda was punctilious in attending to these public duties. Japan wanted to be seen as cooperating in the League Council which was the prime international body of the time; and Chinda played his part.[14]

DEPARTURE: END OF THE ALLIANCE

China's term of office in London was fast coming to an end. One item of business which he wanted to resolve before he left his post was the future of the alliance, the third treaty being due to lapse on 13 July 1921. There was no doubt that Hara Kei as Prime Minister was committed to the continuation of the alliance and carried his cabinet with him. But, as in Britain, there were discordant elements outside the cabinet. Some thought that Britain was a symbol of old-style imperialism which had been further displayed in the terms of the Versailles treaty and was not to be trusted by Japan. Others in intellectual circles were broadly favourable, taking the view that the United States had become so hostile to Japan during the war that Britain was the only great power that could be relied on to be moderately sympathetic to Japan.

Apart from xenophobic distrust, which is natural to all countries, what divided the two allies in 1920 was the relation of the alliance to the newly-founded League of Nations. To the Japanese the issue was simple: the alliance was stable and tested in time, while the League was experimental and its future unpredictable. British opinion–makers looked at it differently: the world had moved on from the days of alliances towards world organizations and so the alliance would have to take second place to the covenant of the League. The London embassy found it necessary to inform Tokyo of the existence of two contrasting strands of opinion within the British Empire: those for extending the alliance (*dōmei enchō ronsha*) and those opposed to continuing it (*hikeizoku ronsha*). To the Japanese, however, it was a nonsense to think of a contradiction existing between the League and the alliance; the two would complement one another in achieving stability in East Asia. The end result was that a formula had to be found which would preserve the alliance and would see the League through its teething period.[15] That formula was approved by the cabinet and the *Gaikō Chōsakai*.

One of Chinda's last acts was to sign, along with Curzon, at the Spa conference on 8 July 1920 the following document:

> '[Our agreement of 1911] though in harmony with the spirit of the Covenant of the League of Nations, is not entirely consistent with the letter of that Covenant. [The two governments agree] that, if the said Agreement be continued after July 1921, it must be in a form which is not inconsistent with that Covenant.'

In order to get this formula through the Privy Council where opposition was expected, it was necessary for the Ministry to append lengthy explanations.[16]

Before Chinda left his London post, there were a large number of farewell functions for the retiring ambassador. Of course, he was entertained by the Japan Society of London of which he had been president. But he was widely feted by the political establishment. In spite of all the doubts and dismays in diplomatic circles, the Japanese were generally popular in Britain in 1920. The Chindas were the symbolic beneficiaries of this affection.[17]

In particular, Chinda met with Britain's leaders. On 17 August Chinda called on the British Prime Minister, Lloyd George, whom he had known well from the various post-war conferences that they had attended together. While exchanging parting greetings, they discussed first the future of Russia and later the Anglo-Japanese Alliance. Chinda, raising the alliance issue, said that Japan wanted to continue the former Anglo-Japanese relationship which was in the interest of both countries and also in that of the world. While he was due to retire, he said he would strive for that relationship to the best of his ability. Lloyd George asked how Japanese opinion thought about continuing the alliance. Chinda said he had no doubt that the majority of the responsible intellectual classes agreed to the continuation of the alliance. The Prime Minister pointed out that he believed that British public opinion also favoured continuing the alliance but he had to consider the views of dominions overseas and of the United States. In his opinion, if it were possible, there would be advantages in adding the United States to the parties to the alliance. But, considering the present difficulties of the American administration, it would be absolutely impossible to attempt to negotiate on this problem. Following this, Chinda made his farewells to Curzon and found him very cordial. On the alliance he took the same view as the Prime Minister.[18] These views were not expressed out of politeness because they were repeating views like these to their cabinet colleagues.

Chinda, accompanied by Viscountess Chinda who had played a large part in her husband's success, sailed from Tilbury on 24 August by the *Kitano-maru*. He was succeeded by Hayashi Gonsuke. This was at roughly the same time as the arrival of Sir Charles Eliot as the new ambassador in Tokyo. So there was a change of pilots in both capitals. Exhausted after four years of wartime and post-war diplomacy, which had taken their toll on his health, the departing ambassador returned to Japan early in October.

Chinda was as good as his word to the British ministers and gave his views on the alliance in a conversation in the Foreign Ministry on 15 October, explaining how he saw British opinion:

> since the alliance had been in existence so long, it would raise all sorts of important issues for it to be abrogated without very special reasons. Besides, turning to the future of the League of Nations, the whole British nation was feeling a bit disturbed. By and large, there were no obvious objections on the part of the government to continuing the alliance. But Japan must try to avoid some cases which whipped up anti-Japanese feeling like the arrest of Shaw and the issue of Shantung and Tsingtao and make her viewpoint clearer. Britain's major problem was to take into account the opinion in the United States and the Dominions.[19]

This was a broadly accurate interpretation of British thinking. Perhaps Chinda placed undue emphasis on the views of Lloyd George and Curzon which did not wholly represent those of the people at large and the Foreign Office secretariat. But he clearly identified the intense feeling of British subservience to Washington. There was not much that Japan could do for the present while the election campaign was being fought out in the States or, in the case of the British Dominions, until the imperial conference was held during the summer of 1921. Japan should, however, avoid provocative actions which would stir up a damaging press campaign against her. This was a recognition of a new truth about the power of public opinion and the media in post-Versailles foreign policy-making in Europe. Japan could well understand that the future of the alliance would not be a simple legalistic matter such as had been the case with the renewal in July 1920 but was likely to become a major issue of international affairs.

Viscount Chinda was made a Count on 7 September 1920 for services during the First World War. Whether this was a reward for his work at the London Embassy or at the Paris and other conferences is not stated. It was merely one of a number of elevations announced at the same time.[20] Chinda was appointed to the Privy Council and in 1921 joined the Imperial Household Ministry. He played an important part in promoting the notion of international cooperation through various activities of the Japan League of Nations Association [*Nippon kokusai remmei kyōkai*], a branch of the global organization set up to win support for the cause of the League.[21]

Chinda was further honoured by his appointment to accompany the Crown Prince during his state visit to Britain commencing on 9 May 1921. It was not a political mission insofar as it was designed primarily as part of Hirohito's education and coming of age. Chinda's role was not to negotiate but to instruct him on the niceties of protocol and steer him through the byzantine rituals of the British court. He is to be seen in the photographs of the visit, a diminutive figure standing protectively close to the young prince. He only surfaces in one instance where the Prince of Wales, thinking that the Crown Prince should come closer to the British people, was alleged to have proposed that he should travel on the London underground. When, however, this madcap proposal was raised, Chinda was the one that had to veto it, or rather (to avoid lèse majesté) to discourage the enterprise. Overall, the itinerary ran smoothly thanks to Chinda; and Curzon as Foreign Secretary saluted the prince's visit as 'a uniform and conspicuous success'.[22]

The culmination of Chinda's career in London has to be measured in two respects. First, as Ambassador to London. Like his predecessor, he came without early training in London or a previous London posting. By the time he left in 1920 he had been won over to Britain and, in spite of the verbal knocks he experienced at the hands of Lord Curzon, he appears to have genuinely enjoyed his last few months. *The Times* saluted him for taking his share of the heat and burden of those anxious days.[23] Second, he has to be measured against the changing face of world diplomacy. Chinda was at the centre of things at the Paris Peace Conference and in the post-war round of international conferences. Conference diplomacy required linguistic ability and political flexibility, not qualities that Japan had conspicuously shown in the past. Nonetheless Chinda, in combination with Makino, did his best at Paris in a new and difficult role. Kimura Eiichi, a Foreign Ministry official attached to the plenipotentiaries there, described Chinda as showing great fighting spirit with special reference to the Shantung question at Paris and general coolness in negotiation.[24] While Makino appealed more to foreign observers as a man of ideas ready to explore and discuss new approaches, Chinda was a more conventional bureaucrat but he emerged as a firm believer in the League of Nations. *The Times*' editorial summed up his qualities on his departure, saying that he had 'a fixed and unswerving loyalty to the immemorial traditions of his country [which went] hand in hand with a sympathetic understanding of the problems and growth of Western democracy'.[25]

14

Hayashi Gonsuke (1860-1939) and the Path to the Washington Conference

HARUMI GOTO-SHIBATA

Hayashi Gonsuke

AMBASSADOR TO BRITAIN

THE JAPANESE AMBASSADOR to Britain from May 1920 to August 1925 was Hayashi Gonsuke. He was born in 1860[1] to a samurai family in Aizu domain (now Fukushima Prefecture). In early 1868, when Hayashi was still a child, both his father and grandfather died in the battle of Toba-Fushimi near Kyoto, one of the major conflicts fought between pro-emperor and pro-shogun forces during the Meiji Restoration. About eight months later, he experienced the siege of Aizu Castle by forces from the domains demanding the restoration of power to the emperor. Having been defeated, the Aizu samurai who were considered to be supporters of the Tokugawa *Bakufu* were punished by being expelled to northerly and infertile parts of Japan. Hayashi and his mother were among them. He later left the area to escape the hardships of life there.[2]

Hayashi was fortunate enough to come to Tokyo while still very young. In Tokyo he was looked after by a former Satsuma retainer who had known his grandfather through the Toba-Fushimi battle. This man was not a wealthy patron but was from the winning side in the struggles

146

leading up to the Meiji restoration. Hayashi, who received financial support from several other people, graduated from Tokyo Imperial University. In 1887 he entered the Foreign Ministry. This was seven years before the examination system for admission began. Among those recruited in the same year, was Uchida Yasuya, who later became the Foreign Minister at the time of the Paris Peace Conference of 1919 and the Washington Conference of 1921-22.

By the time Hayashi became Japanese Ambassador to Britain in 1920, he had served in various overseas posts. From 1893 to 1898, he had worked in London as consul and then first secretary, and had the opportunity of observing how the British reacted to the Sino-Japanese War.[3] He then spent nine years in Korea from 1899 as Minister. This was a crucial period that led to Japan's colonization of Korea in 1910. When the Great War broke out, he was in Italy. He was also appointed as Minister to China (1916-18) and the Governor of the Guandong Leased Territory (1919-20). In these last two posts he was at odds with the military and bitterly opposed to the activities of Nishihara Kamezō (a businessman known for the Nishihara Loans to the Chinese government) and his associates. He did not enjoy these posts at all,[4] while some Japanese did not rate highly the line he took.[5]

Hayashi was a sociable person and was considered favourably by the diplomats of other countries. For example, Daniel Varé, an Italian diplomat who in 1920 attended the early meetings of the League of Nations with Hayashi, wrote that Hayashi was his 'old friend from Peking'.[6] S.P.P Waterlow, a member of the Far Eastern Department of the British Foreign Office, described Hayashi as 'a sensible and moderate man, not afraid of disagreeing with his Government'.[7] Sir John Tilley, British Ambassador at Tokyo from 1926 to 1931, in a despatch of 1927 wrote of him:

> [Hayashi] has the reputation of being a clever and able diplomatist, and was popular during his stay in England. He is friendly to foreigners and pro-English in sympathies. He speaks English well.[8]

FUTURE OF THE ANGLO-JAPANESE ALLIANCE

While Hayashi was Japanese Ambassador in London, the most significant issue for Britain and Japan was the Anglo-Japanese Alliance. In this section I propose to concentrate on Hayashi's performance between the autumn of 1920 and the summer of 1921.

As soon as Hayashi arrived in Britain, he noted that some people in the government were denouncing Japan and the alliance.[9] He thought that one of the reasons was their disapproval of Japanese policies, especially her policy towards China over the previous few years, and that hence the renewal of the alliance depended on the conduct of Japan's policy in China.

As early as 29 September 1920, he wrote to the Foreign Ministry in Tokyo and suggested that the Japanese government should take steps to solve the 'misunderstandings' held by Britain and the United States. He wrote that Japan should, first of all, abolish military rule in Qingdao which she had occupied since 1914 and withdraw troops from Jinan.[10]

Later, he wrote to Foreign Minister Uchida, repeatedly suggesting the necessity of changing Japan's China policy.[11] Although Hayashi and Uchida had entered the Foreign Ministry in the same year, Hayashi was older. He did not hesitate to express straightforward opinions to a person of higher rank.

Hayashi was not the only one in the Japanese diplomatic service who disapproved of the country's China policy. For example, Makino Nobuaki, Japan's representative at the Paris Peace Conference, stated at a meeting held by *Gaikō Chōsakai* [Advisory Council on Foreign Relations] on 8 December 1918:

> Although Japan has always claimed that her stance is fair and just, and that she adheres to the policies of open door, non-intervention into China and Sino-Japanese friendship, her actual policies have been inconsistent with what she has claimed, with the result that the powers have come to regard Japan as untrustworthy.[12]

This observation is accurate and reasonable, and seems to have received some support in the Foreign Ministry.

However, this view was not acceptable to the people who were at the centre of Japan's foreign policy-making. Itō Miyoji, one of the Privy Councillors, demanded that Makino should explain why he thought Japan was regarded as unreliable. Both Itō and another senior politician Inukai Tsuyoshi strongly insisted that it was necessary for Japan to possess more territory. Following their remarks, Terauchi Masatake, the Prime Minister from 1916 to 1918, claimed that Japan had never been unfair and unjust.[13] The *Gaikō Chōsakai* did not endorse Makino's opinion.

The views, which Hayashi sent from London, were not even discussed at the *Gaikō Chōsakai* meetings. Neither Uchida nor the Asian Department of the Foreign Ministry could accept the idea of abandoning Japan's existing interests without negotiations merely to fend off British criticisms.[14] Although Hayashi continued to express similar opinions, the Ministry was determined to ignore them.

In the meantime, Britain had been busy considering the views of the Dominions as well as those of the United States. She failed to take account of the sensitive feelings of her ally during the summer of 1921, when two issues made Japan doubtful whether Britain was a trustworthy partner or not. The first issue was the argument on how to interpret the Anglo-Japanese joint announcement of July 1920 and the other was Britain's suggestion that China should be invited to the Pacific Conference. Mutual distrust of the allies grew considerably.

On 9 May 1921, the British Foreign Secretary, Lord Curzon of Kedleston, met Hayashi and proposed a three-month extension of the Anglo-Japanese Alliance, which would reach its full ten-year span on 13 July 1921. This proposal was made as a result of a very complicated situation brought about by the Anglo-Japanese joint announcement of 8 July 1920.

The creation of the League of Nations in 1919 had made it urgently necessary for the two countries to define the legal relationship between the alliance and the League Covenant. In June 1920, Britain suggested to Japan that the two governments should jointly inform the League that the alliance treaty of 1911 could only be continued after July 1921 in a form consistent with the League Covenant. Japan agreed with the idea, but argued that the announcement should state that both countries wished in principle to continue the alliance. Therefore, Curzon proposed the phrase: 'if the said Agreement *be continued* after July 1921, it must be in a form which is not inconsistent with that Covenant'.[15]

It is clear from these negotiations that Japan at this point wanted to continue the alliance. Britain was non-committal, but the decision-makers did not necessarily intend to end the alliance at this stage. However, around the time the note was signed by Hayashi's predecessor and Curzon, a legal adviser of the British Foreign Office who was asked for his views, indicated that the declaration was legally equivalent to denunciation of the alliance and that the alliance must either be modified or deemed to terminate in 1921. Curzon did not attempt to overrule this opinion, which became the official interpretation of the British Foreign Office.[16]

According to this legal adviser, the one year's notice necessary to terminate the 1911 agreement had been given in July 1920, with the result that the alliance would lapse automatically in July 1921. As Britain had to seek the views of the Dominions and as the Imperial Conference was due to assemble as late as the middle of June, Britain considered it desirable that the alliance should be extended for an interim period.[17] This was why Curzon proposed the prolongation by three months.

Hayashi advised that Japan should answer immediately without trying to scrutinize British intentions,[18] but the British suggestion understandably created a stir in Tokyo. Eleven months earlier, the Japanese Government had made it plain that Japan did not want the declaration to be treated as equivalent to a denunciation of the alliance. From Japan's point of view, Britain seemed to have suddenly begun to insist on a totally new interpretation that the alliance would end automatically. This inevitably led to doubts in Tokyo about Britain's true intentions.

In the Japanese view, the joint communication when it was made in July 1920 was not the equivalent of the one-year's notice stipulated to terminate the alliance. Furthermore, the idea that the alliance would lapse automatically without any negotiations taking place was considered to be especially unreasonable. Consequently, at a *Gaikō Chōsakai* meeting held on 28 May, the draft reply to Britain was approved with some amendments.[19] On 3 June, Hayashi sent an embassy official to the Foreign Office to seek clarification of the British view. When Sir Victor Wellesley, the head of the Far Eastern Department, was asked whether Britain's legal interpretation was adopted after Curzon's meeting with Hayashi in May, Wellesley's answer was affirmative.[20]

Hayashi's reaction to this situation was restrained. He did not show even the slightest doubt about what Curzon and the British Foreign Office were saying to him and his staff. He wrote to Uchida in his despatch sent on 6 June that to argue which legal interpretation was correct was not fruitful but only damaging to the good feelings between the two countries. According to him, if Britain intended to abrogate the treaty, it could not be maintained even if Japan's interpretation was found to be right. He was, therefore, of the opinion that Japan should agree to the prolongation and make efforts to negotiate and conclude a modified treaty successfully within three months.[21]

Curzon was less willing to back down than Hayashi. On 8 June, he gave Hayashi a formal letter, informing him that 'the communication of last year must be held to constitute the notification of termination required under article 6' of the 1911 treaty. Japan declined to accept this proposition.[22]

Curzon had not been unfavourable to the continuation of the alliance and continued to be sceptical of the opinions of his own legal expert. Professor Nish describes this British stance as follows: 'They stuck to their guns but admitted privately that there were weaknesses in the British case.'[23] To end the stalemate, Curzon suggested on 27 June that both sides should issue a second joint notification to the League so worded as to show that the agreement remained in force until October 1921.

In a letter to Uchida, Hayashi insisted that, although he fully agreed with Japan's interpretation, Japan should face the reality that the treaty might be abrogated in October. As long as the British strenuously insisted upon their own legal interpretation, Hayashi could not believe that working relations would be sustained, however well Japan made her case. If Britain wanted to terminate the alliance, he thought it more decent and respectable for Japan to accept Britain's wishes than go on nagging endlessly. He continued that, even if the treaty was not renewed, Japan should not show her disappointment. Rather, she should pronounce to the world with dignity that Anglo-Japanese relations had developed to the extent that a special alliance was no longer necessary.[24] By this stage, Hayashi seemed to have sensed that the British Foreign Office and its legal adviser strongly wanted to be rid of the alliance and were ready to use whatever excuses were available. Influenced by Hayashi, both Uchida and the Japanese Prime Minister Hara Takashi began to think that 'automatic lapse' might be inevitable.[25]

Actually, the British cabinet was much more favourable towards Japan than the Foreign Office. At a cabinet meeting convened on the morning of 30 June, the British Prime Minister David Lloyd George expressed the view that needless difficulties were being created by assuming that the communication sent to the League in July 1920 was tantamount to denouncing the alliance. The cabinet decided that Lord Birkenhead, the Lord Chancellor from 1919 to 1922, should be asked for an opinion. When the Dominion Prime Ministers met later that day in the afternoon, Lloyd George remarked that there had been no formal denunciation of the alliance. Birkenhead, who had been specially invited to attend this meeting, stated that it was 'a remarkable construction' to say that the communication to the League was to be construed as a denunciation. In effect, he endorsed the view taken by the Japanese lawyers.[26]

The Japanese government was relieved when the gist of Birkenhead's ruling was communicated to them.[27] The second joint Anglo-Japanese note was soon sent off to the League.[28] However, Japan's trust in Britain was shaken further by another issue.

On the afternoon of 4 July, Curzon called in Hayashi and asked whether his government would be prepared to join in a Pacific conference with the United States, and possibly with China. Hayashi said that he was strongly in favour of this conference and, although he could not speak authoritatively for his government, he entertained little doubt that they also would be in favour of it. From this, Curzon drew the false conclusion that Japan would welcome such a conference. Hayashi then sent a despatch to Uchida, suggesting that Japan should accept the Pacific conference proposal in principle in the first place.[29] Hayashi also suggested that Japan should not repeat the same mistakes as those committed at Paris. He was of the opinion that Japan should participate in the proposed conference in the spirit of Sino-Japanese friendship, should co-operate with Britain and the United States, and should aim at solving the powers' 'misunderstanding' about Japan.[30] Perhaps he was reflecting ideas he had acquired previously as Minister in Peking (Beijing).

As mentioned above, Hayashi's opinions concerning Japan's China policy were completely at odds with those of the Foreign Ministry and influential members of Gaikō Chōsakai back home. The Hara cabinet might not be in favour of a forward policy in China; but they were not inclined to see Japan's privileges there eroded. What Hayashi said to

Curzon was his own opinion, and his government did not endorse it. The Japanese objected to Curzon approaching China directly without clearing their approach with Japan first. The nature of the proposals and the method of their communication deeply offended the Japanese.[31]

All through July, Britain tried to convene the Pacific conference in London and to enlist Japan's support for the idea. However, the Japanese had already lost their trust in Britain and started to think that it was best for them to make a direct arrangement and cooperate with the Americans, who were simultaneously trying to hold the conference in Washington. Both London and Washington were geographically far away from Japan, and it would make no difference for the Japanese whichever place was chosen for the conference.

Curzon laid some of the blame for this discord between London and Tokyo on Hayashi.[32] However, as mentioned above, it was Hayashi who strove to solve the problem all through the difficult period in the summer of 1921. Hayashi was pro-British and never spoke ill of the ally. When the argument over the joint declaration had finally ended, Hayashi was pleased to see Curzon appearing to be genuinely relieved.[33] Furthermore, his suggestions for Japan to take initiatives in improving Sino-Japanese relations were rational. However, neither Curzon nor the Japanese Government valued the role played by Hayashi. The government did not find it necessary to ask Hayashi to travel all the way to Washington and attend the Pacific conference. Although Hayashi held the same rank as Shidehara Kijūrō, the Ambassador to the United States, he was not to play a major role during the conference.[34] This was odd considering that Shidehara was unwell at the time.

On 14 October, the instructions of the Japanese government were communicated to the conference delegates in Washington. Like Britain, Japan was prepared to give up the alliance in favour of closer ties with the United States. The alliance had been of low repute,[35] and compared with many problems relating to China on which the Japanese were less willing to make concessions, the question of how to deal with it was no longer a difficult issue for the Japanese Government. At the Washington Conference the alliance was replaced by the Four Power Pact.

Hayashi remained in London until his retirement from the diplomatic service in August 1925, and endeavoured to overcome some of the tensions which might have arisen from the break in the alliance. In 1922, he spoke at a Japan Society of London dinner insisting that the Washington conference had cleared the air: it had cut away artificial ties.[36] He certainly reacted to the end of the alliance with dignity, but most people did not know what had happened during the summer of 1921 as closely as Hayashi. There were many different reactions among the Japanese. One example is the scene described in F. S. G. Piggott's *Broken Thread*. On the day when the abrogation was discussed at Washington, he dined with his Japanese friend:

> . . . I had asked Morita to dine with us at the Racquet Club,
> and he brought with him Major Nishihara, private secretary to
> the Minister of War, who spoke English and French perfectly.
> I had not met him before the Conference, but had established
> close relations in recent weeks and considered him one of the
> most intelligent and forthcoming Japanese officers of my
> acquaintance. Morita . . . was strangely silent; Nishihara hardly
> said a word. It was a dull and gloomy evening, and we were all
> glad when the small party broke up.[37]

Some of Piggott's Japanese acquaintances felt as if they had been shell-shocked at the news of the demise of the alliance, and this feeling was to be utilized to back up an anti-British line in the late 1930s and early 1940s.

ASSESSMENT

How can we assess Hayashi as Japanese Ambassador to Britain? He had become truly internationally-minded after spending many years abroad; this is a quality that not all diplomats necessarily possess. Being sociable and outspoken, he contributed to keeping Anglo-Japanese relations as amicable as possible while he remained in London.

On the other hand, he was not in tune with the thinking of the government in Tokyo. In order to improve Anglo-Japanese relations, he placed emphasis on China, suggesting repeatedly that Japan should change her policies towards that country. Unfortunately, Japan's foreign policy was made by those who were determined to preserve existing privileges in China, and to enlarge them where possible. Hayashi's opinions concerning China were simply ignored by his government.

For Curzon and members of the British Foreign Office, Hayashi was one of the most important channels through which they could gain information on the Japanese Government, although it seems that they had lost interest in Japan by the summer of 1921. Hayashi was unwilling to be the mouthpiece of his government, and what Hayashi said sometimes lacked the backing of his government. He was remarkably independent-minded and individualistic for a Japanese diplomat, probably because he had been recruited before the examination system for admission was introduced in 1894. Hayashi's stance was fair, but he was not the best intermediary. It was probably difficult for the British who spoke only with Hayashi to realize how frustrated the politicians in Tokyo felt and had lost their trust in Britain. The blame, however, should be laid on the Japanese Government for appointing Hayashi as ambassador while pursuing policies with which he could not sympathize.

15

Matsui Keishirō, 1868–1946:
An Efficient Public Servant

TADASHI KURAMATSU

Matsui Keishirō

INTRODUCTION

MATSUI KEISHIRŌ had a distinguished diplomatic career which included the posts of Vice-Minister for Foreign Affairs, Ambassador to France, one of the chief delegates to the Paris Peace Conference, Minister for Foreign Affairs and Ambassador to Britain, which was his last post. Despite this he has been largely overlooked and there has been no biography or study of him. His autobiography was published by his son[1] thirty-seven years after his death. For students of Japanese diplomatic history he is not known for any major diplomatic achievements. Yet a closer scrutiny reveals that he was very active in the wings, being involved at numerous important turning points in the history of Japanese external relations. He was present at the Japanese Embassy in London, when the Anglo-Japanese Alliance was signed, being deputy to the Minister, Hayashi Tadasu. When the First World War broke out, he was the Vice-Minister under Katō Takaaki. Most of his long diplomatic career, which extended over nearly forty years, was spent overseas.

EARLY CAREER

Matsui was born in Osaka on 5 March 1868. After graduating from the Osaka English School (*Osaka eigo gakkō*), which was, according to Matsui, 'the only good school in the Kansai region at the time', he moved to Tokyo and studied for two years at *Daigaku yobimon*, the forerunner of the First High School (*Dai-ichi kōtō gakkō*). He studied English Law at Tokyo Imperial University, graduating in July 1889. Upon his graduation Matsui 'did not like the idea of becoming a judge or lawyer very much' and heard that there was a position at the Foreign Ministry. He therefore consulted his international law professor at his university, Hatoyama Kazuo, who also worked in the Foreign Ministry as the head of the investigation division (*torishirabe kyoku*).[2] Hatoyama told Matsui to pay a visit to Katō Takaaki,[3] who was at the time Private Secretary to Foreign Minister Ōkuma Shigenobu and the head of the political affairs section (*seimu ka*). After visiting Katō at his house in Surugadai in Tokyo, Matsui got the job.[4]

He was assigned to the political affairs section but the Foreign Ministry, being such a small-scale operation, at that time, he also worked in the translation bureau (*honyaku kyoku*). The most important issue at the time was Treaty revision. The seriousness of this issue was rammed home three months after Matsui joined the Foreign Ministry. Ōkuma was thought by nationalists to have made too many concessions to foreign powers and an attempt was made to assassinate him. In the bomb blast Ōkuma lost a leg. In December Aoki Shūzō[5] became Foreign Minister. He decided to abandon 'the multi-national approaches' and instead to concentrate on negotiating a revised treaty with Britain. The first step was to approach Hugh Fraser,[6] the British Minister in Tokyo, with 'his personal plans'.[7] According to Matsui, a legal adviser to the ministry drafted the memorandum which. Matsui had to translate it into Japanese so that Aoki could present it to the cabinet for its approval.[8] In those days Matsui was mainly dealing with Korean affairs. In November 1890 he was ordered to go to his first overseas post as the Third Secretary at the Japanese Legation in Seoul.

He spent four challenging years in the lead-up to the Sino-Japanese War. He served under no less than six Chargés d'Affaires and Ministers in Seoul. The last of these was the *genro* Inoue Kaoru with whom Matsui maintained a close relationship thereafter. In December 1894, with the war going in Japan's favour, Matsui was transferred to Washington where the Japanese Minister at the time was Kurino Shinichirō, a Harvard graduate. He left Tokyo in February 1895 and stayed in Washington for three years until the outbreak of the Spanish-American War.

FIRST ASSIGNMENT IN LONDON

Matsui was transferred to London as First Secretary in 1898, arriving there in June that year to replace Hayashi Gonsuke.[9] The Minister was Katō Takaaki. In those days there were only four members of staff under Katō, Matsui being his deputy.[10] On 27 September the Japanese Legation moved from Sussex Square to 4 Grosvenor Gardens. In the spring of 1899, Katō left London after a dispute with the Foreign Ministry, which wanted Katō to postpone his pre-arranged leave to see through the raising of a public loan on the London money market. The task fell to Matsui as Chargé d'Affaires. With help from staff sent from the Finance Ministry and the head of the Yokohama Species Bank London office, Matsui successfully organized a consortium of banks[11] and raised 10 million pounds.[12]

At the time there were two issues concerning Anglo-Japanese relations: immigration and China. Discriminatory immigration laws were being considered in Queensland (in Australia), and British Columbia (Canada). The Japanese government tried to influence the Australian and Canadian governments through London. On China Matsui was instructed to sound out the reaction of the British government to the US Secretary of State John Hay's 'Open Door' note issued in September 1899.[13] In addition, Matsui had to handle the Boxer Rebellion issue just before handing over the Embassy to Hayashi Tadasu, the new Minister.[14] Usually Matsui, as he was only a Chargé d'Affaires, saw an Assistant Under-Secretary, Francis Bertie, but on this occasion he was instructed to see the Foreign Secretary to find out what action Britain would take.[15] Matsui went to see Lord Salisbury but as he was out of London for the Whitsun holiday, he saw Bertie instead.[16] Matsui reported that, according to Bertie, it would be difficult for the British government to send a large contingent until the Boer War ended.[17] Finally Matsui met Lord Salisbury who confirmed to Matsui that because of the Boer War Britain could not send more troops at that time, but he hoped that Japan would do so.[18] On 6 July the Japanese Cabinet decided to send the 5th Division.[19] On the same date, before he learnt the decision of the Japanese government, Salisbury sent a telegram to Tokyo, pressing for more Japanese troops to be sent as 'Japan is the only Power which can act with any hope of success for the urgent purpose of saving the foreign Legations at Peking' and offered 'financial assistance which may be necessary'.[20] It was at this point that Hayashi Tadasu arrived in London on 6 July, relieving Matsui from this responsibility.

The most important event when Matsui was in London was the conclusion of the Anglo-Japanese Alliance. The negotiations leading up to it have been studied in detail elsewhere,[21] but Matsui had his share of involvement. Nearly a month before the German Chargé d'Affaires,

Eckhardstein, approached Hayashi on the subject, he had met Matsui in early February 1901 at the St James Club, suggesting an alliance between Britain, Germany and Japan.[22] Matsui was also sent to St Petersburg with a coded telegram from Prime Minister Katsura Tarō to Itō Hirobumi, explaining the situation.[23] Because he did not succeed in having a meaningful talk with Itō, who was leaving for Berlin the next day, Matsui followed Itō to Berlin. For three days Matsui tried in vain to ascertain Itō's views on the matter. In the end he called on Itō in his room on the night before his departure for London and had a frank talk lasting over three hours while they drank Rhine wine. According to Matsui, Itō was not against the idea of an alliance with Britain *per se*, but thought that due attention should be paid to Russia and Germany.[24] Matsui wrote the official report on the negotiations leading up to the signing of the alliance. He made three copies; one for the Ministry, one for the Embassy and one for Hayashi, who later published his version of the story in *Jiji shimpō*.[25]

TOKYO, PEKING, PARIS, WASHINGTON, TOKYO, PARIS

With the alliance safely negotiated, Matsui left London in July and returned to Japan in September for the first time in seven years. Matsui was given the task of reporting to the *genro* about the alliance. Just after a month in Tokyo, Matsui was sent to Peking (Beijing) to act as Chargé d'Affaires while Minister Uchida Yasuya was on winter leave. Uchida came back in April but heightening tension with Russia over Manchuria meant that Matsui had to stay on. It was only when Japan's victory looked certain that Matsui was able to come home at the end of June 1905 to cover for Yamaza Enjirō, the head of the Political Affairs Division, while the latter accompanied Foreign Minister Komura Jutarō[26] to Portsmouth (USA). One of the tasks he performed was acting as an interpreter between Prime Minister Katsura, who was acting as Foreign Minister in Komura's absence, and Sir Claude MacDonald, the British Ambassador in Tokyo,[27] the latter describing Matsui as 'a master of diplomatic English'.[28]

After another brief stay in Tokyo, he was sent to Paris as Counsellor, arriving there in May 1906. Being posted to France for the first time, Matsui's time was 'mainly devoted to the study of the language'. Again Kurino was the Ambassador in Paris.[29] The major event during his time in Paris was the signing of the Franco-Japanese Agreement of 1907.

After two years he was transferred to Washington, DC. Matsui helped Ambassador Takahira Kogorō to conclude the Root-Takahira Agreement. The agreement safely negotiated, Takahira left Washington, DC, in August 1909 and Matsui was the Chargé d'Affaires until Takahira's successor Uchida Yasuya's arrival in December 1909.[30]

Matsui arrived back in Tokyo in July 1911, starting his longest period of office work at the ministry.[31] At the end of January 1913 Katō Takaaki became Foreign Minister for the third time. He appointed Matsui to be the Vice-Minister. Although the government only lasted less than a month, Matsui stayed on in this post under the new Foreign Minister, Makino Nobuaki, in the Yamamoto cabinet. This cabinet resigned because of the Siemens scandal and Katō again became Foreign Minister in April 1914 in the new Ōkuma cabinet.

On 7 August 1914 British Ambassador Sir William Conyngham Greene[32] delivered a message from Foreign Secretary Grey requesting Japanese naval assistance against German raiders. Following the late night cabinet meeting, at which the decision was taken to go to war, Katō went to inform the emperor who was then at Nikko. It fell to Matsui to tell the British Ambassador on the following morning and to deliver Japan's ultimatum to the German Ambassador, Arthur von Rex, on 15 August.[33] As soon as Japan entered the war, preparations for the eventual peace with Germany were started in the ministry. In September 1915 a committee (*Nichi-doku seneki kōwa junbi iinkai*) was set up, its members including the Foreign, War and Navy Ministries and the Legislation Bureau. Matsui was appointed chairman. Matsui was involved in the preparation of the notorious 'Twenty-One Demands' on China. In August 1915 Katō resigned following the Interior Minister's bribery scandal and after Chinda Sutemi[34] declined to accept the offer, Ishii Kikujirō was brought back from Paris to take up the post of Foreign Minister.

Matsui was then sent to Paris to take up his first ambassadorial post. His voyage to France took two months because the ship had to go round the Cape of Good Hope. He arrived in Paris the day after the start of the battle of Verdun. During his time in Paris one of his most important assignments was to attend the various meetings of the Allied countries such as the Supreme War Council. After the armistice in November 1918, Matsui and all his family caught Spanish flu. Having recovered, he was appointed as one of the chief delegates to the Paris Peace Conference, the highlight of his diplomatic career. Matsui's main task was to sound out the French attitude. After all the other delegates had departed, Matsui was left to attend the Supreme Conference, which culminated in the signing of the peace treaties with Austria, Hungary, Bulgaria and Turkey. With the signature on 10 August 1920 of the Treaty of Sèvres, which effectively marked the end of the Ottoman Empire, Matsui decided that it was time to go home. His leave was duly granted and he set off in October. *The Times* Paris correspondent wrote a glowing report on Matsui's departure:

His departure will be regretted, for during four-and-a-half years that he has been here he has shown powers of statesmanship and tact worthy of his race.

His previous varied experience, his remarkable command of the French tongue, his personal charm and intimate knowledge of French men and affairs made him an outstanding figure in Paris very soon after his arrival, and his influence in the political world has grown every day. His work as representative of Japan at the Peace Conference and afterwards on the Supreme Council has been most fully appreciated.[35]

For his service during the war and the Peace Conference Matsui was made a baron.

It seemed that Matsui was nearing the end of his career, but he had two more assignments. In January 1924 Matsui became the Foreign Minister in the Kiyoura Cabinet. It was an unexpected appointment and the British Ambassador Sir Charles Eliot[36] explained how it came about:

> The post of Foreign Minister was originally offered to baron Fujimura, who was formerly connected with the Mitsui firm, and had no experience of service in the Japanese Foreign Office or in diplomacy. But Mr Matsudaira, Vice-Minister for Foreign Affairs, and corresponding to our Permanent Under-Secretary, protested so strongly against the appointment that Viscount Kiyoura was obliged to admit the principle that an Ambassador ought to be appointed. Baron Hayashi and Baron Ishii were mentioned, but as they are in Europe it was feared that the Cabinet might not last until their arrival. Besides Viscount Katō, who is the head of the Kenseikai party, there are two unemployed ex-Ambassadors in Tokyo, Baron Shidehara and Baron Matsui. As the former is ill, the latter was appointed by a process of elimination. He was Ambassador in Paris from 1914 to 1920, and is probably well versed in the routine work of his profession, but has not, so far as I know, any reputation for remarkable ability.[37]

The cabinet itself was not expected to last long and the British Foreign Office did not have high hopes for Matsui.[38] Following a general election, Katō Takaaki became the Prime Minister in June and Shidehara Kijurō Foreign Minister. Over six months Matsui had three issues to tackle: China, the Soviet Union and the United States. He could not make much headway on the first, but on the second he gave new impetus to the Yoshizawa-Karakhan meetings in Peking (Beijing) which led to the eventual normalization of diplomatic relations with the Soviet Union a year later. On the last issue unfortunately the Hanihara 'grave consequences' memorandum incident soured Japan-US relations although Matsui did his best to calm the situation.[39]

On the surface Matsui could not boast of any great achievements, doubtless due to the brief time he was in office. By the end of his tenure, however, Matsui impressed Eliot who stated in his memorandum reporting the change of government:

I cannot close this despatch without adding a tribute to Baron
Matsui, who now leaves the Ministry for Foreign Affairs. He
came to his post with a good reputation as an efficient public
servant but nothing more, and doubts were expressed as to
whether he had a sufficiently strong character for the high
position offered to him. He may not be a man of great
originality or determination, but he won the esteem of the
whole Corps diplomatique during the six months that he was
in office. I have never met a Japanese official who seemed so
European in speech, manners and methods of conducting
business. Not only was he much more communicative than
most of his countrymen, but he seemed genuinely anxious that
cases brought to his notice by foreign missions in Tokyo
should receive prompt and friendly attention. It is said that the
Government contemplate making considerable changes in the
Diplomatic Service before long, and that in the event of Baron
Hayashi being recalled, Baron Matsui may be sent to London.
I believe that he and Mme. Matsui would be well suited to the
post. Baron Hanihara and Baron Ishii are also mentioned as
possible candidates.[40]

Matsui was appointed to the House of Peers and it seemed to be the end
of his diplomatic career. However, the new Prime Minister Katō offered
him one more assignment before his retirement. In the summer of 1925,
while Matsui was staying at his summer cottage in Karuizawa, Katō
Takaaki came to see Matsui and asked him to become Ambassador to
Britain.

AMBASSADOR IN LONDON

Matsui left Japan in October and arrived in England in November 1925
having travelled via Canada. When he presented his credentials at
Buckingham Palace King George V enquired about the Taishō Emperor,
the regent (later the Shōwa Emperor) and the situation in China. The king
and also said that he did not like establishing diplomatic relations with the
Soviet Union but accepted his government's decision. On 19 November
Matsui paid his first visit to Foreign Secretary Austen Chamberlain at the
Foreign Office and talked about the Locarno Treaties (concluded on 1
December 1925), the tariff conference in Peking (Beijing) and Japanese
relations with Russia.[41]

Matsui and his wife were welcomed to London by the Marquess of
Salisbury, Lord Privy Seal, at the Annual Banquet of the Japan Society in
January 1926, the occasion being honoured by the presence of Prince
Chichibu.[42] Matsui's 'first considered public statement in Britain
appeared' in the *Morning Post*, in which, for a solution to the China
problem, he suggested that:

. . . China needs a strong man; no other government has been found possible in a country where distances are so vast and the conditions and peoples so diverse.

The kind of chaos we see at present has always occurred in the intervals between the emergence of strong men; yet, it is remarkable to observe that the country has, after long years of disturbance, always come out in the end as a united whole, embracing all sections of that peaceful and industrious people. How long it will be before a single man can again achieve unquestioned supremacy none can foretell; while any other solution, such as a federation of provinces, seems equally impossible of realization.[43]

After the 30 May incident in Shanghai in 1925, the boycott of British goods spread across China and the British tried to gain Japanese co-operation. The Japanese government was pursing a 'non-intervention policy' under Foreign Minister Shidehara and was not forthcoming. Matsui thought that since Japanese goods were likely eventually to become the target of a boycott, it would be wise to show some sympathy towards the British and he sent a telegram to that effect.[44] He received such a stern rebuttal that he did not pursue the issue at the time, waiting for another opportunity. With the change of government in April 1927, Tanaka Giichi became Prime Minister and served as his own Foreign Minister. The next month in conversation with the British Ambassador, Sir John Tilley,[45] Tanaka stressed the importance of Anglo-Japanese co-operation and even hinted at a revival of the alliance. Matsui thought this idea out of the question:

> Baron Matsui then observed that English friends often remarked to him that we ought to renew our old alliance. This he regarded as out of the question. He doubted whether even written understanding was desirable. Certainly Great Britain and Japan had by far the largest share of all the foreign interests in China, but America was also interested. We could not ignore that Great Power nor ought we to do anything to arouse her suspicions. He added that, whilst it was of the first consequence that these three Powers should act together, it was also important to keep unity among the Powers as a whole.[46]

Chamberlain agreed and in reply stated:

> The fullest interchange of opinion and agreement as to policy was all that I thought we should be wise to seek at the present time; possibly this might lead at a later date to some more formal agreement though not indeed to the renewal of the alliance which had been so much misunderstood in America

161

and had, therefore, proved an obstacle to the maintenance of the friendly relations with the United States which both the Japanese and ourselves wished to cultivate. For the moment I shared his view that any attempt at a written agreement was undesirable.[47]

Ashton-Gwatkin[48] of the Far Eastern Department in the Foreign Office commented on Matsui's talk of 'unity':

> Japan has done her full share in obstructing unified action by the Powers; but I do not suppose this is quite what Baron Matsui meant. He does not seem to have been very encouraging or very helpful.[49]

It was probably not fair to criticize Matsui for a lack of cooperative spirit. As we have seen he urged Tokyo to show more sympathy towards the British but never received the instructions to do so. It is interesting that when Matsui was highly praised by Eliot this was the only time he was in a position to act without instructions.

Officials in the Far Eastern Department of the Foreign Office could not agree on the real reasons for the ending of the Anglo-Japanese Alliance: some stressed American opposition, others opinion in the Dominions and still others Japan's aggressive policy in China.[50] In other words, it was a combination of factors rather than a single issue. Certainly, if there was any chance of closer Anglo-Japanese relations, even an alliance, it was from 1927 to early 1928. The Geneva Naval Conference of 1927 broke down because of Anglo-American disputes. Strong anti-American sentiments were shared by cabinet ministers.[51] While most critical of his American counterpart, the British chief delegate to the conference, First Lord of the Admiralty, William Bridgeman, reported to Chamberlain that 'one very satisfactory thing which came out of the conference was our good relationship with the Japanese'.[52] Also, during the conference Winston Churchill, the Chancellor of the Exchequer, suggested that if the United States built more, '[t]he result might be . . . to bring Japan and Great Britain closer together. . . The alternative to building ourselves would be to renew the Japanese alliance.'[53] Furthermore, the Royal and Imperial Japanese Armies both perceived a Soviet threat and there was even an exchange of intelligence information between them.[54] Indeed, the revival of the alliance with Japan was considered in the War Ministry at the beginning of 1928.[55] Tilley, who did not believe that 'an alliance was really desirable for Great Britain', thought that 'a security pact, including America and Australia, might be desirable and feasible.' However his thinking was that:

> It is also no doubt feasible to act in concert with Japan, as we are now trying to do in China, for certain particular purposes.

It has always appeared to me to be well within the bounds of possibility to act temporarily in concert with Japan for purposes of aggression, which is happily not contemplated, or defence against aggression, but not within the realm of practical policies to act with Japan in making a friendly settlement with another country, China in particular, from which we each expect to draw advantage for ourselves. Our interests are not sufficiently alike.[56]

Towards the end of 1927, Matsui received a letter from the Vice-Minister Debuchi Katsuji that his appointment was only meant to be short-term and suggested he return home.[57] Matsui was to be succeeded by Matsudaira Tsuneo.[58]

On 3 April Matsui paid a farewell call on Chamberlain, which the latter recorded as: 'Consistent to the last, he began the interview by stating that he had nothing in particular to say to me and enquiring whether there was anything of interest which I could say to him.'[59] Matsui left London in March 1928, his last diplomatic post, and arguably his most unrewarding. Ironically, a few months after Matsui's departure, the Japanese government began to try attempt to secure British co-operation in China now that the boycott targeted Japanese goods.[60]

After attending the Shōwa Emperor's coronation ceremony, Matsui retired from the diplomatic service in 1929. In his retirement Matsui became an apologist for the conduct of Japan, adding his name to open letters and articles.[61]

Matsui lived on to see the defeat of Japan. Having seen Tokyo in ruins, he spent his last year or so in bed. Matsui said to his son, 'through the Anglo-Japanese Alliance and the Paris Peace Conference, and so on, I thought I had contributed a little to Japanese diplomacy, raising the status of Japan among the Five Great Powers but in the end I wonder what it was all for'.[62] Matsui died on 4 June 1946. It was a sad end to his life not to see Japan rise once again or to see his son follow in his footsteps as the Ambassador to the United Nations and France.

PART III

Naval Officers

16

The Loss of HMS *Rattler* off Cape Soya (Hokkaido) in September 1868 – Commander (later Admiral Sir) Henry Stephenson

HUGH CORTAZZI

Henry Stephenson

SOME BRITISH SHIPS went aground both during the bombardment of Kagoshima in 1863 and of Shimonoseki in 1864 and had to be re-floated.[1] There were two basic problems. The first was the inadequacy of Admiralty charts of Japanese coastal waters. The second was the difficulty of manoeuvring wooden ships, which were partly powered by sail and partly by screw or paddle engines, in difficult weather conditions. The loss of HMS *Rattler* in September 1868 off the northern tip of Hokkaido underlined these problems.

COURT MARTIAL OF STEPHENSON AND MILLER

HMS *Rattler* was a 17-gun sloop, powered by sails and screw engine, of 952 tons, built in 1862, with a crew of 143 officers and men, under the command of Commander Henry Stephenson. According to the Admiralty records of the Court Martial held on 12 December 1868, HMS *Rattler*

. . . was wrecked in Romanson Bay [Romanzov Bay, now known as Soya *Wan*], La Perouse Straits, Yezo Island on 24 September 1868 'through want of caution on the part of Commander Stephenson and Navigating Lieutenant John Alexander Miller, in not approaching the shore at a more moderate speed, after having obtained soundings with the hand lead, and that they committed an error in judgement in the manner of reading the Directions laid down in the *China Pilot*. But taking into consideration the great and successful efforts to save the Crew and Stores under considerable difficulties, the Court only adjudged the said Commander and Navigating Lieutenant to be admonished and cautioned to be more careful in future. No blame whatever attached to the remaining Officers and Ship's Company, who were acquitted accordingly.

The career of Commander Henry Stephenson (1842-1919), who was the nephew of Admiral Sir Henry Keppel, C-in-C China Station in 1868, did not suffer as a result of the loss of his ship or the admonishment of the Court martial. He had joined the Royal Navy in 1853 and had served in the Crimean War 1854-55, the China expedition 1857, the Indian Mutiny 1857-58 and Canada 1866. After the loss of his ship he went on to become Naval ADC to Queen Victoria 1888-90. He was Equerry to the Prince of Wales from 1878-93, and Commander-in-Chief Pacific Station 1893-96. He became Principal ADC to King Edward VII 1902-04 when he retired and became Gentleman Usher of the Black Rod. He was made a KCB in 1897 and a GCVO in 1902. He was clearly very well connected.

Lieutenant Miller did not prosper, although he served at sea again as Navigating Lieutenant in a couple of ships before retiring from the Navy in 1875 after twelve years service.

THE VOYAGE OF HMS *RATTLER*

HMS *Rattler* was carrying F.O. Adams,[2] Secretary to the British Legation, and Ernest Satow, Japanese Secretary to the Legation. They had been instructed by Sir Harry Parkes, the British Minister, to investigate conditions around Hokkaido (Yezo) and in particular to report on Russian activities there and in neighbouring Japanese islands.

Adams' report to Sir Harry Parkes dated 28 September 1868 and headed 'Soya, Yezo' was not delivered until after he had returned to Yokohama. Adams wrote that HMS *Rattler* had left Hakodate on 17 September 1868. He had told Captain [sic] Stephenson that he wanted firstly to inspect the coal mines near Iwanai on the West Coast, which were being superintended by Mr Gower and secondly to visit Otarunai

[Otaru] which was 'destined to become one of the important places in Yezo and was the point of embarkation for Sakhalin'. They had made first for Iwanai and 'after encountering contrary winds' had dropped anchor off the village of Kayanoma on the evening of the 19th. Despite the rain he and Gower had visited the mines. On 21 September they left Kayanoma in rainy and windy weather and after five hours steaming reached the small village of Shakotan 'where we were obliged to anchor' as the wind was not favourable for rounding the point into Strogonoff Bay [Ishikari Bay]. As at 6 p.m. there appeared to be a lull and the rain ceased so they proceeded under sail 'trusting that it would calm by midnight. But on the contrary just about that hour the wind freshened into a gale, which blew directly off the land and precluded the possibility of our entering Strogonoff Bay. We had therefore to hold on under easy sail and during all the succeeding day the gale continued.' That night Stevenson told Adams that the ship had been so blown off course that he proposed to give up the idea of visiting Otarunai and make straight for Cape Soya at the northern tip of Hokkaido. They only had limited provisions on board and he had been unable to procure more than 8 or 9 tons of coal at Kayanoma. When the gale had ceased and they were able to change course early on the morning of 23 September they were, 'according to the reckoning, about 112 miles N.N.W of Shakotan and 145 miles from Otarunai'. They steamed in an easterly direction during 23 September and that evening passed between the islands of Rishiri and Rifunshiri (Rebunjima).

GROUNDING

Adams' report continues: Early in the morning of 24 September

> . . . the sea was perfectly calm and we were steaming slowly into Romanzov Bay [Soya Bay] with the village of Soya ahead of us. Suddenly, without any indication, either from the heaving of the lead or from any breaks in the water that we were close upon a reef, the ship bumped several times, the engines were instantly reversed, but she could not be moved. From this moment it can safely be said that every effort was made to float the ship, but all to no avail. Unfortunately, as the day wore on, a breeze sprang up and then the formidable nature of the reef was first disclosed. It extends not only along the whole portion of the Bay in which the village of Soya is situated, but several miles further to the Northward, and where in the morning there had been a dead calm, with not a single ripple on the water nothing but surf and angry breakers could be seen. The ship bumped repeatedly and heavily and towards morning, having made several feet of water, she settled down and no hope of saving her remained.

Early on the 25th Stephenson sent a Japanese messenger to Hakodate with a letter to the British Consul informing him of the wreck of his ship. Another messenger was sent to Shibetsu with a letter to Captain du Petit Thouars of the French Navy ship *Dupleix*, who had informed them at Hakodate that he intended to cruise along the East Coast while the *Rattler* was cruising along the West coast. They hoped that the letter would reach him at Shibetsu (opposite the island of Kunashiri).

During the 25th 'the sea being calm, all hands were employed in transporting provisions, luggage, furniture and gear of every description to the shore'. Satow, meanwhile, was in touch with the local Japanese officials who 'showed every disposition to afford assistance'. While large boats were sent out to the ship 'in the little village of Soya wooden houses were given over to Stephenson for the accommodation of the officers and the ship's company including Adams and Satow 'in all about 150 men'. By the evening all were ashore 'without loss of life or injury to a single man and the *Rattler* was left to the mercy of the waves'. That night a north-west gale began to blow and lasted for the greater part of the next two days. An attempt was made on the morning of the 27th to reach the ship 'but the surf was so heavy that, out of two boats each towing a large Japanese lighter, only one was able to cross the reef and bring away a number of things from the ship, which was reported to be already full of water. It was, therefore a most fortunate circumstance that everyone on board was landed on the 25th.'

RESCUE

Adams completed the story in a further report from Yokohama to Sir Harry Parkes on 17 October 1868. He began by noting that 'during the next fortnight no vessel arrived to bring us succour. Whenever the weather permitted boats were sent off to the ship and brought away guns and stores of all description.' Adams was impressed by the 'thorough order and discipline which prevailed' and with 'the heartiness manifested by every officer and man in saving all that could be saved from the wreck'.

At last, on the morning of 9 October 'a large steamer was descried on the horizon and as she came gradually into sight feeling her way cautiously into the bay' Stephenson recognized her as His Imperial Majesty's Ship (HMIS) *Dupleix*. Stephenson and Adams went out in one of the ship's boats and were received on board by Captain du Petit Thouars and Count Tascher de la Pagerie, Secretary of the French Legation who was on board. The ship had in fact been still at Hakodate when Stephenson's letter reached Eusden, the British Consul. On seeing the letter Captain du Petit Thouars who had been about to start for Nagasaki immediately decided to proceed to Romanzov Bay as soon as he could take in some coal and provisions. They left Hakodate at noon on 7 October.

Captain du Petit Thouars proposed to take on board the *Dupleix* every one who had been on the *Rattler* and convey them to Yokohama, Shanghai or even Hong Kong. The guns and other stores could be left where they were after being formally handed over to the Japanese authorities. Captain du Petit Thouars told Adams afterwards that he had urged this course on Stephenson because it would preclude the necessity of a British Ship of War coming up to this dangerous coast at the beginning of winter when the weather was likely to be bad and there could be 'days and days before the ship could even communicate with the land; nor could the embarkation of men and stores be in any event a safe operation in the month of November'. He was 'the more convinced that his advice was sound, when he discovered that the bottom was so rocky that there was really no good holding ground' for an anchor. During the night after the *Dupleix* arrived at Soya its 'anchor was continually dragging so that with a strong wind on the land a ship would stand every chance of running upon the reef'.

Stephenson was at first unwilling to leave the guns and stores without any men to guard them, but he accepted the force of Captain du Petit Thouars' arguments. Orders were accordingly given and by the evening of 9 October the entire party left Soya and went on board the *Dupleix*. The guns and other stores were mostly stowed away in a godown and delivered over to the Japanese officer who had been given passage from Hakodate at the request of the Governor to convey his sympathy to Stephenson on the loss of his ship and to offer any possible assistance.

At daylight on 10 October Stephenson attempted to have the lower masts of the *Rattler* towed ashore, but 'the violence of the breakers prevented the success of this operation'. The *Dupleix* left at 10 a.m. that day for Hakodate which they reached two days later on 12 October.

Adams immediately sent word that he, Stephenson and Satow would like to call on the governor to express their thanks for his help. En route they met the governor on horseback on his way to visit them on the ship. They then repaired to Consul Eusden's house where courtesies were exchanged and the Japanese were asked to give orders for the safe-keeping until the arrival of a British ship of War which would be sent 'either at once or early next spring'.

That same evening they set sail for Yokohama which they reached on the afternoon of 17 October.

AFTERMATH

Adams expressed his deep appreciation for all the trouble taken by Captain du Petit Thouars and his officers 'to provide for the safety and comfort of the whole of our party'. 'It was evident from the moment we came on board that there was but one sentiment pervading the ship viz to give every Englishman the warmest welcome, very much . . . at the expense of their own comfort – in a word to make us feel really and truly at home.'

Separately, Adams reported on 19 October to Parkes that although he had been unable to go around Yezo (Hokkaido) 'I think I may safely affirm that there are no Russians at the present time either on the North Coast of the island or on Kunashiri, nor do I believe there are any on Etorofu.' He also submitted a list of Russian stations in Sakhalin which he had obtained from a senior Japanese official in Hakodate.

Satow in *A Diplomat in Japan* (London, 1921), devoted only one brief paragraph to this episode. He recorded that 'From September 8 to October 17 Adams and I were absent on a wild-goose chase after the Russians who were reported to be occupying the northern coast of Yezo, in the course of which HMS *Rattler*, in which we had embarked, was wrecked in Soya Bay.' He did, however, as will be seen from the extracts from his diary (see appendix), covering the month in the autumn of 1868 in which the *Rattler* was lost, give a rather more lively account than the rather dry summary provided by Adams

Captain du Petit Thouars' story of the episode was reproduced in *Le Vice-Amiral Bergasse Du Petit-Thouars S'Après Ses Notes et sa Correspondance 1832-1890*, Paris, 1906. He reported to his superior officer, Commandant de Chaillié, on his reconnaissance of the North East Coast of Hokkaido. This had been a difficult operation and a perilous piece of navigation because of '*vent, mer, brouillard, cartes grossières et fausses, côtes semées d'écueils, . . . etc.* He had not seen any Russians and felt that he had obtained all the information he wanted about the Japanese Kuriles. He concluded that the French and English charts were so inaccurate that they could only lead to errors. On the other hand, the Japanese charts seemed much closer to the truth.

His report of the rescue of the crew of the *Rattler* confirms the account given by Adams. He noted: '*Il suffit de voir ces terres pour comprendre avec quelles difficultés un capitaine peut se trouver aux prises d'un moment à l'autre, car, en outre de ce que les instructions fort incomplètes disent des brumes, des courants et de la violence des vents, l'apparence des côtes est des plus trompeuses.*' Du Petit Thouars noted with admiration the discipline and perfect order maintained by the British crew.

On 21 October 1868 Sir Harry Parkes wrote to Admiral Sir Henry Keppel, the C-in-C, recommending that the guns and stores at Cape Soya be presented to the Japanese. In due course this recommendation was accepted.

Thomas Wright Blakiston, a British merchant in Hakodate and a persistent traveller in Hokkaido, (see Thomas Wright Blakiston (1832-91) by Hugh Cortazzi in *Biographical Portraits*, Volume III, 1999) visited Cape Soya in October 1869 to inspect, on behalf of the Japanese government, the guns, stores and material saved from HMS *Rattler*. He found them 'all as they had been left when the officers and crew were taken away by the French corvette *Dupleix*'. He recorded that 'A portion of the *Rattler* was fast on the reef to the South of the entrance into the small harbour, and the whole shore was still strewn with fragments from the wreck.' Blakiston arranged for the disposal of the stores. Near Cape Soya he met a Japanese official from Hakodate who had been in charge of the Soya station when the *Rattler* was wrecked. The latter 'was of the opinion that the vessel ought never to have been run so close to the shore, even supposing entire ignorance of the existence of reefs.'

CONCLUSION

This episode underlines the problems of navigating a wooden ship with both sails and screw in treacherous and inadequately charted waters. It also shows that there had been a huge change in the attitude of the Japanese authorities to Westerners. They did everything possible to help. Despite the rivalry and intrigues of Sir Harry Parkes, the British Minister, and Monsieur Roches, the French Minister, which had continued up to the latter's departure in 1868 good and friendly relations between the French and British naval forces, which had been manifest in the allied bombardment of Shimonoseki were maintained. The efforts of Captain du Petit Thouars to rush to the rescue of Stephenson and his crew and attend to their comforts are particularly noteworthy. Stephenson was a lucky man to emerge from the loss of his ship with an admonishment and to go on to become a full Admiral. His connections may well have helped!

17

Admiral Sir John Fisher (1841-1920) and Japan, 1894-1904

JOHN W. M. CHAPMAN[1]

Sir John Arbuthnot Fisher

INTRODUCTION

HISTORICAL DISCUSSION of the involvement of Sir John Arbuthnot Fisher[2] (1841-1920) with Japan has largely tended to focus on his role as First Sea Lord from October 1904 in the middle of the Russo-Japanese War. Even during this period, however, the extent of covert British support for Japan in its war against Imperial Russia was deliberately concealed as a result of the need to demonstrate publicly Britain's commitment to international neutrality. Britain, in reality, provided a very large range of assistance to the Japanese side, just as France also supplied favours to her Russian ally while nominally a neutral. Both Britain and Japan, however, had an agreement to conceal from all third parties the extent to which they were involved as members of the first alliance contracted by Britain since the Crimean War and the Anglo-French coalition against China in 1858.

EARLY INVOLVEMENT WITH JAPAN

In 1904, Fisher and Admiral Sir Edward Hobart Seymour[3] (1840-1929) were the two most senior officers on the Admiralty's Flag List[4] and both had served as midshipmen in these last two conflicts. Seymour had served off Sevastopol and had been involved in landing the Highland regiments which formed the 'Thin Red Line', while Fisher had been on board HMS *Highflyer* in the thick of hand-to-hand combat during attacks on forts in the Yangtse. Fisher visited Tokyo in 1859 (though no impressions of the experience seem to have survived) and subsequently served again as a flag officer from 1869 to 1872 on the China Station, where Seymour was C-in-C from 1898 to 1901. The two appear to have remained on good terms, unlike so many other relationships in Fisher's lengthy career and both played a significant role in influencing Lord Selborne,[5] First Lord of the Admiralty from 1900 to 1905, in promoting the alliance between Britain and Japan, unveiled to the public in February 1902.

TORPEDOES AND TORPEDO BOATS

While Seymour reported directly to the Admiralty about developments in the Far East from 1898 to 1901, when the area became a significant focus of international politics, Fisher's engagements at the Admiralty and in commands afloat from 1894 to 1904 appear to indicate little involvement with Japan. In fact, this was far from the case. After Fisher returned from China in 1872, much of his career was spent in developing the weapons available to the fleet: at Portsmouth, the development of the torpedo as an effective weapon of naval warfare was a significant innovation which was capped by a lengthy visit to the Whitehead works at Fiume in 1876. After numerous appointments afloat, Fisher returned in 1890 as superintendent of the Portsmouth dockyard and was Controller of the Navy (Third Sea Lord) by 1894, in overall charge of ordnance and stores. In this post, held throughout the period of the Sino-Japanese War, there is ample evidence of the information about operational developments in the Far East passing through Fisher's hands. His signature appears directly under that of the First Sea Lord, Admiral Richards,[6] on 'an intelligent and useful report' from Lieutenant Fitzherbert, the torpedo officer of HMS *Edgar* with the China Squadron off Port Arthur on 9 June 1895 on the general employment of torpedo-boats by the Japanese Navy in the engagements off Weihaiwei.[7] A more detailed report by Admiral Buller following a visit to Weihaiwei on 3 June enclosed a study supplied by Lieutenant Sir Robert Arbuthnot on the results of diving operations in the harbour to examine the wrecks of Chinese ships, which revealed the very large holes in their sides caused by the impact of exploding Schwartzkopf torpedoes. Arbuthnot recommended: 'I beg to submit that the enormous size of the holes made in all ships that have been sunk by Whitehead torpedoes is worthy of the most serious consideration.'[8]

Fitzherbert had added a note suggesting the need for 'improvements in our own system' and pointed out the lack of sufficient officers trained in the employment of torpedo weapons in the Royal Navy in the event of war: 'Under our present system the number of Lieutenants who have actually fired a torpedo during a night attack is very small.'

Both reports were ordered by Fisher to be sent to the Director of Naval Ordnance and studied by Captain Walker, in charge of the torpedo development programme at HMS *Vernon*.

That the significance of these reports was fully taken on board by Fisher can be demonstrated from the detailed accounts of his tenure of the post of C-in-C, Mediterranean from September 1899 to June 1902, a period which coincided with Britain's involvement in the South African War. The very first joint fleet manoeuvres with the Channel Fleet held off Lagos in Portugal shortly after his arrival at Malta involved an attack by torpedo craft on battleships. The umpire assigned to this exercise was Rear-Admiral Noel, Fisher's deputy, who, however, decided that the claims of the torpedo-boat commanders to have sunk several ships were not acceptable because the attackers had been spotted a long way off.[9] The joint manoeuvres also tested the effectiveness of the use of torpedo-boats to protect the fleet from attack by hostile torpedo craft and drew attention to variations in range encountered by fleet vessels equipped with the new radio equipment.[10]

A year later and undeterred by Noel's conclusions, Fisher conducted further manoeuvres in the eastern Mediterranean based on the scenario of a breakthrough of the Dardanelles by the Russian Black Sea Fleet, in conjunction with a build-up of hostile French and Russian units based on Algerian ports.[11] A test was organized for the use of wireless in the daytime to keep the six battleships of A Fleet (representing the Russian force) under surveillance by three ships of B Fleet and for instructions to be issued for launching a torpedo-boat attack on A Fleet in any anchorage to which it repaired at night. It was found that wireless contact with Fisher on his flagship, HMS *Renown*, 'saved much valuable time in keeping the Admiral informed of the progress of the manoeuvres' and that battleships without the benefit of any visibility from moonlight would be unable to spot attacking torpedo-boats or to obtain accurate ranges in order to sink these. It was therefore concluded that, as a result of the exercises, one or two battleships had been put out of action by their attackers and that 'a Battle Fleet is almost helpless at night against the attack of fast torpedo-boats or torpedo-boat-destroyers which will be following it unless a Battle Fleet has a full proportion of fast craft to chase off such boats . . . at sunset and to thoroughly search the coast line before dark sufficiently far to prevent torpedo craft hiding in the vicinity.'[12]

DANGERS IN THE MEDITERRANEAN

In the context of the South African War and the risks of French, Russian and even German intervention against Britain along lines that had been successfully pursued against Japan following the Shimonoseki Treaty in 1895, Fisher pointed to the urgent need for the expansion of the numbers of torpedo-boats at Malta because he considered it essential to employ these to launch attacks on French Mediterranean ports so that he could reach Gibraltar to join up with the Channel Fleet. Fisher warned of the possibility of a French surprise attack on Malta in 1900 and subsequently in 1901 warned of a Russo-French combined threat with the possibility of surprise attacks on Malta and Egypt. These apprehensions deepened when Fisher was told of communications between London and Malta being intercepted by the French and evidence was found of French interception of British radio communications during the joint manoeuvres off Gibraltar. To guard against hostile interception, Fisher re-routed communications with London, stressed the importance of reliance on all-British cable communications, arranged for the interception of the mail of the Russian consul at Malta, insisted on the modernization of ciphers employed by consuls and naval attachés and obtained the assistance of the Eastern Extension Telegraph Co. to supply him with cable facilities in the event of war and to relay secretly to Malta 'suspicious' cables of French and Russian origin passing through the cable station at Syra in the Levant.[13]

At first, the Admiralty refused to increase the numbers of destroyers in the Mediterranean until forced by Fisher's manipulation of Parliament, press and public opinion to concede. Lord Salisbury, the Prime Minister, who had an entrenched prejudice against the Admiralty, informed Lord Selborne: 'Adm. Fisher is subject to some of those hallucinations of which Admirals are the victims: but had hoped he was cured by this time.'[14]

This was echoed by Lord Lansdowne, the Foreign Secretary,[15] when told of Fisher's discussions with General Grenfell, the Governor of Malta, about the vulnerability of the island to surprise attack: 'since he has been in the Med. has not ceased to discover mare's nests and to hatch scares of complicated Russian designs'.

Nevertheless, by May 1901, Lansdowne was soliciting Selborne for Fisher's assistance in organizing a fleet demonstration against the Sultan in order to bring Turkey to heel and Selborne himself, following a visit to Fisher at Malta in April 1901, had succumbed to Fisher's persuasive arguments about the need for a radical shift in naval strategy in the event of embroilment in a wider war. A most important element in Fisher's argument lay in his discovery that the French fleet at Toulon had embarked on a secret voyage across the Mediterranean to Mytilene which had been unannounced and therefore unreported by foreign consuls in

France but about which Fisher had learned as a result of British interception of French fleet radio signals. Such a discovery appeared to contradict directly any charges of hallucination or mare's nests and verified the deep-seated mistrust with which Russian behaviour and intentions were viewed by military and political intelligence (i.e. the so-called 'Secret Service').

THE RUSSIAN THREAT

Fisher had visited Constantinople in person in August 1900 and was convinced that the Turks could not be relied upon to resist a Russian attempt to force the Dardanelles. He was aware of the activities of Russian agents there and the likelihood that they would bribe Turkish telegraph offices to delay the relay of warnings of Russian aggressive moves to the outside world. He knew a good deal about the Sultan's heavy financial commitment to a large body of spies throughout the Ottoman Empire, but was also convinced that the Sultan himself could be tempted by a large enough Russian bribe to permit the Russians to dispatch military and naval forces through the Bosphorus. He compared the Turkish attitude most unfavourably with the Japanese attitude to Russia. He wrote of the need for Britain to station torpedo-boats in the vicinity of the Straits and the need for 'proper armament, with batteries of Whitehead torpedoes, such are now being used by the Japanese for their coast defence, would make the Bosphorus impassable'.[16]

Initially, Fisher had taken the line that the Black Sea was the greatest point of Russian vulnerability (publicly conceded by General Kuropatkin[17]) and that it was simply necessary to restore the old Disraelian strategy of alignment with Turkey against Russia to enable the Royal Navy to go through the Straits into the Black Sea. By the summer of 1901, however, he had learned for himself that the virtual control of Turkish foreign policy had been swept away with the death of Dadian Pasha, the Sultan's foreign policy adviser, and the Turkish government's sympathies were steadily being won over by German money and political influence. Tsar Nicholas II, following a tour of Japan as Tsarevich in 1891 when he had been nearly assassinated by a Japanese fanatic, was quite firmly convinced by his advisers of the desirability of focusing on expansion into northern China after 1894 with the help of French and German finance and some of these argued that it was the Far East rather than the Black Sea that was the area of greatest Russian insecurity.[18]

The threat from the expansion of Russian naval power after 1895 was closely monitored by the Admiralty in reports from successive C-in-Cs on the China Station and the reports from Admiral Seymour to Lord Selborne were urging the necessity of standing up to the 'boundless' Russian menace, even though he privately conceded that without the presence of Russian troops in the Liaodong Peninsula in June 1900 it would have been much harder to relieve Peking. Many of the most distinguished and influential British naval officers (including Battenberg, Beatty, Custance, Jellicoe, Keyes and Lambton) served Seymour at this date and came into regular contact with officers of the Japanese fleet in the creation of the bridgehead at Taku. The First Sea Lord, Lord Walter Kerr, who himself had seen service in Japan in 1863 during the bombardment of the Kagoshima forts, unwisely tried to insinuate that Fisher was concerned only about the Mediterranean and forgot other stations and responsibilities: 'Fisher being what we know him to be, can be taken more or less seriously. If he had been in China, the Medn would not be in it.'[19]

In reality, Fisher was very well informed about the more distant stations, as can be seen from the correspondence conducted with two of his former captains sent to China, Charles Windham and Percy Scott.[20] In September 1900, he had complained bitterly to the Admiralty about the decisions to transfer three of his best-trained smaller warships from the Mediterranean to the Cape and China, arguing that the Mediterranean was 'the heart of the Empire' and deploring the dispersal of strong units at a time when he argued that his fleet was barely equal to the French forces, let alone their reinforcement by Russian units entering the Mediterranean. This was the focus of the agitation about naval strategy in the British Press with the lead being taken by Lord Charles Beresford, Fisher's deputy, but with ammunition secretly being supplied to such reporters as James Thursfield and Arnold White by Fisher himself.[21]

CHANGING NAVAL STRATEGY

Fisher's objective was nothing short of a radical reorientation in the whole of British naval strategy, particularly to create a situation of maximum readiness for wider war in time of peace, an idea echoed in the exhortations of Colonel Altham, the desk officer in the War Office responsible for Imperial defence. Fisher's strategic ideas, based on his specific experiences in the Mediterranean, were explained in detailed face-to-face discussions with Selborne at Malta in April 1901 which appears to have been the crucial turning-point in Fisher's influence over Selborne. By July 1901, Admiral Custance,[22] the Director of Naval Intelligence (DNI) conceded that Fisher's agitation had led to a 'rumpus' in the Admiralty and that Fisher's demands for strengthening his fleet had been acknowledged.[23] The main object of his criticism of Admiralty strategy was effectively Custance, who was responsible for advising Kerr, then the First Sea Lord,[24] and Selborne not only about matters of naval intelligence, but for the defence of overseas trade, planning for mobilization and for the world-wide distribution of the fleet. Fisher had already had dealings with Admiral Beaumont, Custance's predecessor as

DNI from 1894 to 1899, while Controller at the Admiralty and had not got on together. In October 1901, Fisher was joined at Malta by Prince Louis of Battenberg[25] as a cruiser commander and from Battenberg heard details of his service as Custance's deputy. This account convinced Fisher that the Admiralty's preparations for war were completely outdated and that it was essential to plan for various contingencies beyond ideas solely in Custance's head.[26]

It seems that at first Fisher was not over-impressed by Battenberg, but his connections with the Court at home and his family connections with the King of Greece, the Tsar and the Kaiser made him an invaluable informant who enhanced the network of intelligence and communications that Fisher had established 'from Brest to Perim', allegedly in the face of strenuous opposition from the Foreign Office. Effectively, Fisher established his own system of command and control with cables and wireless which was more efficient than the structure of information and communications available to the diplomats. As he observed to Admiral Wilson: 'One thing is quite certain, we shall never get information of the slightest value from our Ambassadors and Ministers, as they have no idea of what is going on more than infants in arms!'[27]

The system which Fisher had established in the Mediterranean since 1899, which Selborne saw for himself in April 1901, was one that Selborne had sufficient imagination to see extended on a worldwide basis. It was at the same moment that Selborne received information and advice from Seymour at Hong Kong in which Seymour reported that he believed Japan would 'now begin war with Russia if she thought we or Germany or America would stand by her, so strong is her feeling'. He believed that Russia would think twice if opposed firmly by Britain and pointed out that Russia was far from ready to go to war and 'must know it' because

> . . . her railway is able to carry a few passengers but not to reinforce a campaign. No sea supplies or ships could get out if she were at war with us; and hardly if at war with another power because of neutrality on our part.
> Out here we and Japan should be a match for Russia & France, but of course Japan is no use to us in Europe. . .[28]

ANGLO-JAPANESE ALLIANCE

Selborne pursued both sets of ideas within the Admiralty on his return home and had discussions with his Cabinet colleagues, Lansdowne, the Foreign Secretary and Brodrick,[29] the Secretary of State for India from 1903–05. He had already adumbrated to the Cabinet his opposition at all costs to Britain becoming embroiled in any conflict with the USA and presented his apprehensions, based on his discussions with Fisher, that the fleet was not equal to a war with Russia and France so long as the war in South Africa continued without allies. In August 1901, Selborne drafted his memorandum on the 'Balance of Naval Power in the Far East' and showed it to Lord Walter Kerr, who responded as follows:

> I have very carefully considered your Memorandum which I now return. I am not sure whether you propose to exchange views personally when we meet before sending it on its way or whether you are only waiting for my reply by letter. In the latter case I write to say that I am fully in accord with its object. The course that you propose would be from the Naval side a very great relief to us.
>
> It is true that it is a new departure in policy, but to say as I am able to form an opinion of 'high politics' it has been pressing itself upon me for some time past, that with the immense growth of Navies that is now going on and the great strides being made in all sides in creating naval power, that our hitherto beloved policy of 'splendid isolation' may no longer be possible and that great as the disadvantages in other ways may be, an understanding with other powers may be forced upon us.
>
> The proposal you make in the Memorandum shows that you also have this view, and that you propose to give practical effect to the conclusion you have arrived at, and suggests a way for doing so.
>
> I have no criticisms to offer on your draft and on the contrary am fully in agreement with its terms. The strain which is being put upon our naval resources with all our worldwide interests is, in view of the feverish developments of other nations, being subjected to a heavier strain than they can well bear, both in ships and men, especially the latter, and any relief that can in reason be obtained would be most welcome.[30]

Following the Cabinet agreement to press ahead with the negotiations for an alliance with Japan, which Salisbury himself wanted to postpone until after a peace agreement with the Boers had been concluded, the matter was passed on to Lansdowne. Consultations with Selborne, however, continued to be needed in the light of the secret naval agreement accompanying the treaty proper. This aspect, however, could be settled only after the arrival in London of Itō Hirobumi, whose activities in Russia had been the subject of anxious enquiries from London to Sir Charles Scott, then British Ambassador at St Petersburg.[31]

Before the completion of the treaty on 30 January 1902 and its public announcement on 17 February, Fisher was visited at Malta on 3 January by Sir Edward Seymour, who had lately returned home from China in the autumn. There is no indication whether Seymour and Fisher discussed the developments in the Far East, though according to a conversation between Battenberg and King-Hall on 21 January it would appear that Fisher was in favour of Seymour as his successor at Malta and this had the support of the King and the Foreign Office, but not of Kerr and Custance at the Admiralty.[32] Kerr and Custance had pressed for the appointment of Admiral Sir Cyprian Bridge[33] (a former DNI) as Seymour's successor in China and it is clear that Bridge, as well as Sir Claude MacDonald,[34] the Minister in Tokyo, had received intimations of the pending negotiations.

Bridge visited Japanese ports in the autumn of 1901 and made enquiries of MacDonald about Japanese Navy coal supplies and their latest destroyers. MacDonald recalled to Sir Thomas Sanderson, Permanent Under-Secretary at the Foreign Office, that on his transfer from Peking 'there was a very smart little R.N. officer [Ottley] here when I first came, but he was out here for a few weeks with me, and then had to hurry off and report on the navies of Italy and Russia'.[35] MacDonald regretted that in Ottley's absence he had had to rely on the advice of the US naval attaché 'who happened to be a particular friend of mine' and pressed Sanderson that 'of course, if anything comes of the alliance and we give mutual facilities in things naval we must have a naval attaché resident here'. The Admiralty reported on 16 January 1902 that such an appointment was 'in contemplation', but it was not until 25 April 1902 that the appointment of a roving naval attaché, Captain Ernest Troubridge, to Tokyo was finally confirmed.

Admiral Bridge appears not to have corresponded with Lord Selborne until more than six months after his arrival in China, but reported on 3 February 1902 that he had heard from MacDonald of the visit to Japan in December 1901 of three ships under the command of his deputy, Rear-Admiral Grenfell, which reportedly had 'an excellent effect'. However, Bridge appears to have been briefed about the alliance by Selborne only in March 1902 in a letter which focused on the strategic issues involved and in response to a cabled enquiry from Bridge about the ways in which 'it would be possible and desirable to give effect to the notes on naval reciprocity exchanged on the conclusion of the Anglo-Japanese Agreement'. The texts of the treaty and the secret annex were supplied to the Admiralty only on 28 February 1902 and were later sent to Bridge with advice from Lord Walter Kerr that 'the Japanese are aware that the above instructions have been given to him, but it may be hereafter necessary to give him additional secret instructions not known to the Japanese'. These caveats reflected Kerr's own apprehensions that the text of the secret agreement could stimulate embarrassing demands from the Japanese in peacetime and concealed from them the Admiralty's thinking on the usefulness of the treaty in permitting reductions in the force levels of the China Squadron.[36]

Such thoughts mirrored precisely the efforts of Fisher to persuade Selborne to agree to a wholesale change in the strategic and structural organization of the fleet. Embodying advice already supplied with Battenberg's assistance, Fisher wrote to Selborne on 25 February 1902 asking for his views to be circulated for consideration by all principal officers of the fleet and incorporated these in two memoranda calling for the establishment of a naval general staff to replace the NID and a centralization of command and control over the strategic redistribution of the various fleets. His main contention was that the outlying stations outside European waters were absorbing precious resources and manpower which should be concentrated at home in order to ensure command of the seas against Britain's principal opponents. If that were secured, it would then be a relatively simple matter to dispatch strong forces to the peripheral areas.[37] Some of these ideas were sent to Bridge on 12 March 1902, but Bridge's reply was essentially evasive suggesting that 'the question is purely academic', but ventured to argue that if an opponent dispatched strong forces to the Far East 'it would be indispensable for us to have an adequate force there also'.[38]

MacDonald reported the festivities attending the visit of Captain Paget of HMS *Endymion* to Japan in March 1902 and the extraordinary lengths the Japanese side went to mark the alliance in the form of an audience with the Emperor Meiji and public receptions given by Prince Komatsu, Navy Minister Yamamoto, the naval base at Yokosuka and by Admiral Ijūin, the commander of the squadron being sent to attend the Coronation Spithead Review. The importance of the last of these meetings was not lost on the Admiralty because of the plan, informally proposed in the first place by Major Utsunomiya, the Japanese military attaché in London, for Ijūin to act as the head of the naval delegation intended to negotiate the terms of the military and naval agreements for the implementation of the alliance. The Admiralty sent out circulars to all naval bases en route from Japan to Plymouth requesting special treatment for the squadron and alerted Admiral Fisher at Malta, who promised to arrange for the best berths to be allocated in Valetta Harbour and for a reception by the Governor soon after their arrival from Port Said in late May 1902.

The Battenberg papers include a copy of a letter to Fisher of 25 February 1902 drawing his attention to a report from the director of medical services in the Japanese Navy which was a precursor of the visit of the Ijūin squadron to Malta between 27 and 30 May 1902. Apart from the press reports and the log of events, there is in the British archives a note from Fisher to the Admiralty enclosing the record of interviews between Battenberg and Ijūin;[39] and there is also a long report by Ijūin composed on his arrival at Plymouth on 11 June which has survived in the archives of the Defence Agency in Tokyo.[40] Fisher noted that he had received a letter from Tokyo, presumably from MacDonald, telling him that Ijūin was 'quite one of the best officers in the Japanese Navy' and confirmed that he had had several conversations with him which verified the opinions of Battenberg, who noted that 'during the past week I have seen a good deal of Admiral Ijūin'. The memorandum to Fisher summarized Ijūin's opinions on ships' bridges, on the paint best employed on ships during operations and on the uselessness of signals in wartime and concluded:

> As the Admiral, who is a remarkably shrewd man and seemed to notice everything that came under his eye, went through the Chino-Japanese War and took part in the Battle of the Yalu, and as his selection for his present command shows him to be a man of note in his service, I thought his remarks worth reporting to you.[41]

The report was examined by Kerr and Selborne but fuller details may have been imparted in person by Fisher, who left Malta a few days later, bound for home with his staff, and already preparing to attend the Coronation and take up the post of Second Sea Lord at the Admiralty. No further British record has been traced, but the report from Ijūin to Tokyo is a much more detailed document. This indicates that Ijūin and his officers were taken all over the naval base and told by Fisher that they could ask to see anything they wanted, because there were no secrets between the British and Japanese navies. When the Japanese were shown round the signalling station at Gargur by Captain King-Hall, Fisher's chief-of-staff, they reported that the wireless equipment on board the flagship *Asama* was faulty and Fisher agreed to lend the coherer from his flagship, HMS *Renown*, to enable the Japanese vessels to make contact with British ships and shore stations. The Japanese party were shown over HMS *Caesar*, the ship on which the most up-to-date experiments in fleet wireless transmission had recently been carried out by Captain H.B. Jackson, but when they tried out the equipment on their approach to Gibraltar, they discovered that they could virtually double the range of their transmissions. Ijūin urged the need to acquire this 'excellent British-manufactured coherer' and as a result of the postponement of the Coronation until August and the lengthy stay of the squadron at Sheerness, the crew had all the time in the world to study the equipment and send detailed reports on it back home. The standard wireless equipment of the Japanese fleet was subsequently updated with the introduction of the Type-35 set which came into service from the fleet manoeuvres in spring 1903 onwards and was the principal equipment in use during the Russo-Japanese War.

The Mediterranean Fleet was trained assiduously in the use of fleet radio for operational purposes and shortly before the arrival of the Japanese squadron, Fisher had recommended to the Admiralty that scouting ships employ a coded 'Letter-Square System' of identifying ships' locations aimed at preventing any discovery of fleet operational movements by radio–listening techniques, which Captain King-Hall suggested should be applied worldwide.[42] British naval observers during the Russo-Japanese War believed that the Japanese fleet was employing a variant of the Marconi system 'improved by the Japanese', and were aware of the employment of cruisers as scouts which were able to relay their observations in code and enabled the whole of Admiral Togo's fleet to be committed to the decisive encounter off Tsushima in May 1905.[43]

There are two other accounts of Fisher's meetings with Ijūin. The first can be found in a letter from Fisher to Selborne of 31 July 1904, when he enclosed a (missing) letter he had just received from Tokyo and confirmed: 'We made great friends at Malta & he told me he should always let me know anything he thought might be of use to us.'[44] The second can be found in a handwritten note by Fisher on a letter sent to him by Ijūin of 6 May 1905 which states: 'Admiral Ijūin spent many days with me at Malta before the Japanese-Russian War broke out and we rehearsed Admiral Togo's battle of Tshushima [sic]!'[45]

In conjunction with the evidence in the Japanese archives, therefore, it would be reasonable to argue that Fisher and Ijūin withheld no secrets about new technology and the plans of operations for conduct of war at sea with Russia and that Fisher conveyed the results of his scheme for command and control to the Japanese Navy even before these were circulated more widely within the Admiralty on his return home. How far Fisher's appreciation of the significance of surprise attack employing torpedo weapons relied on evidence obtained from Japanese operational experiences and exercises is far from easy to assess, as is the question of how far Fisher's own theories of the use of surprise torpedo attack at night added much that was new to the Japanese Navy, which applied it with moderate success at Port Arthur on 8 February 1904. All that can be claimed with reasonable certainty is that the relevant information was actually exchanged in May 1902, but it established the most important basis of rapport between the Japanese and British fleets prior to the outbreak of the Russo-Japanese War.

18

Captain (later Admiral Sir) W.C. Pakenham RN (1861-1933) and the Russo-Japanese War

JOHN W.M.CHAPMAN

W.C. Pakenham RN

BACKGROUND

CAPTAIN W. C. PAKENHAM RN was the third naval attaché to the British diplomatic mission in Tokyo,[1] following the appointments of Captain C.L. Ottley[2] in 1900-1 and Captain E.C.T. Troubridge[3] from 1902 to 1904. Pakenham had seen service with the Australian, Pacific and China Squadrons during his early career and was selected by Admiral Sir Cyprian Bridge[4] as temporary captain of the battleship, HMS *Albion*, after their first meeting at Singapore, when Pakenham had been serving as commanding officer of the gunboat, HMS *Daphne*, described to his sister as a 'bug-trap', but had nevertheless figured prominently in annual prize-firing trials which were carefully assessed at the Admiralty.[5] In February 1902, Pakenham informed his sister that 'my Admiral continues as kind and friendly as can be' and, as he remained until June 1902, Pakenham would have been as aware of the developments in Anglo-Japanese naval relations as any senior officer in the China Squadron.

On his return home via the USA, Pakenham was appointed to the

Admiralty for eighteen months, submitting reports mainly on technical subjects and involving visits to the technical branches at Portsmouth. In 1903, he was moved to the Naval Intelligence Division (NID), headed from October 1902 by Prince Louis of Battenberg.[6] It is clear from his surviving drafts that Pakenham was familiar with the reports circulating in the Admiralty of the operational preparations made during Fisher's tenure of the Malta command. Given that Battenberg had been Fisher's senior captain there and that Lord Selborne's new private secretary was Captain Hugh Tyrwhitt,[7] who had served as Fisher's flag captain, there could be no doubting that the word circulating round the Navy was that Fisher's star was definitely in the ascendant and that, even before becoming First Sea Lord in October 1904, Fisher was able to twist Lord Selborne round his little finger.[8]

While there is no doubt that Fisher greatly gained in Selborne's esteem as a direct result of his successful introduction of his 'New Scheme' for a more efficient programme for manning and staffing the Navy during Fisher's tenure of the post of Second Sea Lord in 1902-3, it is clear from Selborne's personal papers that Selborne had his own clear agenda for change but had come to recognize that, for all his perceived faults, Fisher was the one admiral on the flag list with the personal drive and enthusiasm capable of winning over the younger naval officers to the radical changes which Selborne himself had drawn up as essential to the future.[9] When Fisher had been Controller of the Navy, he had in turn also been directly dependent on the First Lord of the day, Lord Spencer, to back up his efforts to get rid of the 'dead wood' in the technical departments for which he had been responsible.[10]

Pakenham had to tread quite a careful path between the bulk of the senior officers, who clearly were suspicious of or mistrusted Fisher and his methods, and the new holders of the key posts within the Admiralty, as there were many stories of how high-handedly Fisher operated even before becoming First Sea Lord. Pakenham was on close personal terms, for example, with Lady Jessica Sykes, a member of the Cavendish-Bentinck family who had married into his mother's family and who was a relation of Admiral Lord Charles Beresford[11] and it is clear that she was in regular social touch with the journalist, Arnold White,[12] who numbered both Beresford and Fisher among his informants. Fisher, who never trusted Beresford while he was his deputy at Malta, was also on bad terms with Reginald Custance,[13] Battenberg's predecessor as DNI, and his relations with Lord Walter Kerr, the current Senior Naval Lord, were equivocal to say the least. Kerr and Custance in turn were on good terms with Pakenham's patron, Admiral Bridge, the C-in-C in China who had previously served as DNI, but belonged to that category of admirals whom Kerr consistently regarded as reliable advocates of 'the Admiralty point of view', but Fisher variously denounced as 'the Methuselah Syndicate' or 'the Sanhedrin'.

Battenberg and Fisher collaborated closely together until Battenberg ceased to serve as DNI and both had conducted a vigorous mutual discussion on the role of the DNI since the end of 1901. Before appointing him DNI, Lord Selborne had written to Battenberg indicating that he was 'not satisfied' with the organization under his immediate predecessor, Custance, and wanted to encourage the recruitment of officers who showed 'special aptitude' for the work of the NID.[14] Battenberg, who had also served on the China Station, chose Pakenham in the course of 1903 and Pakenham prepared a variety of papers in connection with the Committee of Imperial Defence, founded by Prime Minister Balfour soon after replacing Salisbury.[15] As chair of the CID, the prime minister automatically became closely involved in matters of defence and national security well before Britain's serious external involvement became likely.

APPOINTMENT AS NAVAL ATTACHÉ AT TOKYO

In October 1903, it was evident in Whitehall that the situation in the Far East was boiling up to crisis point and by late December Balfour was pressing Selborne for estimates from the service intelligence departments of how the situation was likely to develop by the spring of 1904 and what the implications might be for Britain's armed forces.[16] Pakenham was employed by Battenberg to produce studies of the implications of the foundation of the CID for British national security and by the beginning of 1904 already appears to have been selected by Battenberg to replace Troubridge as British naval attaché in Japan.[17] This is evident from a letter by Pakenham to his sister dated 7 January 1904, when he thanked her for sending him the gift of a lockable correspondence holder intended for his use in Japan and he also reported that his dispatch abroad was being continuously delayed. He mentioned that several press correspondents had already left for the Far East two weeks before and confirmed:

> Our high officials continue to hope for a peaceful solution of the Russo-Japanese difficulty. The Jap. Naval attaché is in here now and says he is inclined to think war may still be averted. Let us hope for the sake of the world that it may be a long time & tho' a collision between these countries seems an eventual certainty.[18]

At the same time, however, Captain Troubridge informed Admiral Bridge at Hong Kong:

> You can readily appreciate from all I have written that war may be very near indeed. The impression here is that nothing short of a miracle can arrest it.[19]

Although Pakenham had wanted to go to Tokyo via the USA, the actual alternative was to sail there by steamer leaving Marseilles on 12 February and this was confirmed shortly beforehand by Pakenham in a note to his sister. The surprise attack on Port Arthur the previous day seemed to Pakenham to herald Japan's naval supremacy over Russia and predicted 'the eventual capture of Port Arthur to have become only a matter of time'. By now, Pakenham had been gazetted as a member of Bridge's staff on special duties until Troubridge was recalled and he expressed his satisfaction that it was infinitely preferable to be located in the Far East than waiting back home for the anticipated change.[20]

Pakenham wrote only five further letters to his sister in the course of his sojourn in Japan and Manchuria. His principal correspondent was Lady Jessica Sykes, his cousin's wife, with whom a detailed but one-sided dialogue was maintained, as only Pakenham's letters survive.[21] At Hong Kong on 11 March, Pakenham reported that at Singapore he had learned that Troubridge was serving with the Japanese fleet and that he had received instructions from Admiral Bridge to transfer to a cruiser for the last leg of his journey to Japan. Pakenham's stated preference for being left to his own devices was ignored by Bridge who was, as Pakenham claimed, 'unwilling to understand that I have not really come out to be at his disposition as to do work for the N.I.D.' Bridge, however, insisted that Pakenham accompany him to Japan in his flagship, the armoured cruiser HMS *Leviathan*, arriving there on 20 March.[22]

Pakenham found that, contrary to earlier rumours, Troubridge was still in Tokyo on his return from service on board the Japanese battleship *Asahi* and this made the handover of office a much smoother one than anticipated. Not only did Pakenham inherit Troubridge's quarters in the Hotel Metropole, but he also fell heir to the services of Troubridge's Japanese manservant, who accompanied Pakenham *en route* to the Combined Fleet at the beginning of April 1904. Pakenham had equipped himself with a typewriter to file his reports to the Legation in Tokyo and also took a camera, with which he recorded a number of scenes during his service in the Far East.

Pakenham had written apprehensively about Troubridge in private correspondence: 'he is an excellent fellow but he has done so well that he overshadows me'. When Pakenham arrived, he met the British Minister, Sir Claude MacDonald, and found that Sir Ian Hamilton,[23] the first foreign military attaché to arrive on secondment to the Japanese field forces, was staying as his guest in the Legation. Pakenham was mostly concerned about the arrangements for joining the Combined Fleet at sea as soon as possible and was dependent on MacDonald's intervention on his behalf with the Navy Minister, Admiral Yamamoto Gonbei.[24] By contrast with the Japanese Army, which kept foreign military observers waiting for many weeks and treated foreign war correspondents 'panting

189

to go to the front' even more stringently, the Japanese Navy proved to be very much more accommodating to British naval observers, who were the only foreign officers to observe the war at sea.

Consequently, Pakenham's stay in Tokyo was limited to about two weeks and he had little opportunity, unlike Hamilton, to engage in the multiplicity of diplomatic receptions at which information could be assembled and relayed to Whitehall and Simla. Pakenham abhorred the idea of being tied down in Tokyo and had initially been worried by the possibility that some other naval officer might be sent to sea while he was forced to submit reports of the kind normally expected of resident attachés.[25] Troubridge had had lengthy service in various capitals and was reported to have acquired fluency in French, Spanish and German and to have 'gained a good colloquial knowledge of Japanese'. It was a personal characteristic of Pakenham to express concern to his friends that he was making heavy weather in the promotion stakes and claiming that he would do rather better if he went into business or became a Member of Parliament rather than continue to pursue a naval career. Pakenham appears not to have been told the story, repeated by Ian Hamilton to Lord Kitchener, that Troubridge's reliability as a Japanese linguist was questionable as a result of an encounter with a young *geisha* which turned icily cool as a result of Troubridge's mistranslation of Hamilton's gallant words with the *geisha*.[26]

Sir Thomas Sanderson[27] in London expressed concern lest MacDonald's evident animus towards Troubridge could have caused Troubridge's recall, but Captain Tyrwhitt privately assured Lord Errington[28] in his Private Office that Troubridge was overdue his transfer to a sea-going command.[29] In point of fact, MacDonald was a former Army officer who had served in Egypt in the 1880s and had made a special point of insisting that Hamilton be his personal guest as a distinguished fellow Highland officer. This coincided with a period of deep factionalism and personal rivalry between senior British Army officers who had effectively been ejected from the War Office by the Esher Committee shortly before the outbreak of the Russo-Japanese War and the sparring between Generals Hamilton and Nicholson[30] greatly amused their Japanese hosts.[31]

WITH THE JAPANESE FLEET

Pakenham, before arriving in Japan, had planned to acquire enough Japanese to demonstrate a willingness to make as much of an effort as his predecessor, whose reports undoubtedly served to underline the competence of the Japanese fleet. However, when Pakenham reached the *Asahi* with his Japanese manservant, he found that the chief engineer of the ship, Commander Seki Shigetada, had served at Greenwich Naval College and became the main channel of communication with his hosts.

Seki was also a keen but more competent photographer than Pakenham and his shots of the fleet up to and during the Battle of Tsushima were subsequently published.[32]

Troubridge's reports on naval operations were limited to the first two months of war and these include interviews of first-hand witnesses of the torpedo-boat attack on Port Arthur at the opening of hostilities. News of developments, however, took some time to reach the Admiralty because of the insistence of MacDonald and the Foreign Office that reports from the fleet had to be seen to be subject to tight security precautions and were forwarded by diplomatic pouch to London. The length of time it took for Troubridge's reports to get back home meant that Troubridge himself was a regular guest at dinner to tell people such as the Prince of Wales (later King George V) and Lord Esher[33] of his personal impressions of early developments.

Subsequently, the Admiralty pressed the Foreign Office for early receipt of Pakenham's typewritten reports and copies of most of these were relayed to the King, the Prince of Wales and the Prime Minister. Among the more important revelations arose from permission being given by the Japanese Navy to Pakenham to interrogate a Russian prisoner-of-war, Captain Eggard, who served as a courier between Generals Kuropatkin and Stoessel during the siege of Port Arthur. Eggard confirmed that the Russian Army authorities were closely monitoring the reports by foreign military and naval officers at the front to their governments before these were handed over to their diplomatic missions at St Petersburg. General Gerard, the chief British Army observer in Russia, also corresponded directly with General Hamilton in Manchuria, but Hamilton already suspected the Japanese Army of intercepting his correspondence with Lord Kitchener and complained that, unlike Pakenham's, his own reports were not being transferred directly to the legation in Tokyo and then being routed by any diplomatic bag to India.[34] Pakenham certainly endeavoured to observe the maximum discretion *vis-à-vis* the Japanese naval authorities as he was most anxious to avoid the problems that had arisen as a result of the leaks associated with Troubridge.[35] He demonstrated great endurance as a member of the crew of the *Asahi*, continuously at sea for approximately seven months and taking part in the engagements with the Russian fleet off Port Arthur. From August 1904 until shortly before the fall of the fortress at the beginning of January 1905, Pakenham found it a remorselessly boring task to participate in the blockade operations. He subsequently visited the port and participated in a tour by foreign naval attachés of the front line in Manchuria during the period when the Japanese fleet was sent to home bases for refitting in anticipation of the arrival of the Russian Baltic Fleet in Far Eastern waters.[36]

For a few months, Pakenham returned to Tokyo but spent some time recuperating in the mountains, and subsequently in April 1905 rejoined the *Asahi*, while other colleagues, Captain Hutcheson and Commander Jackson, were seconded to other vessels in the Combined Fleet and composed their own separate reports for the Admiralty. Pakenham learned of the movements of the Baltic Fleet mainly from the press, but recognized that it posed a serious challenge once it sailed past Singapore in early April 1905 and set out his views for the Admiralty on Japanese preparations for further conflict before leaving for sea.

There was initially disbelief in London that the Russians would dispatch the Baltic Fleet as they did not have an adequate number of their own merchant vessels for the supply of fuel and provisions, even with the support of French territory and facilities at Djibouti, Dakar, Madagascar and Indochina. What made the operation feasible was the access provided to the supply facilities of two German shipping lines, North German and Hamburg-America Lines, which were at the core of the German Navy's *Etappendienst* or Supply Organization which had been servicing the needs of the East Asian Squadron, based at Kiaochow in North China since 1898. However, a benevolently neutral Germany was in a position to purchase anthracite and charter colliers from numerous countries in spite of the arguments put forward by Admiral Fisher, shortly before becoming First Sea Lord, that the British government could resort to the Foreign Enlistment Act of 1870 to ban such activities involving British vessels and firms. On the Japanese side, the argument that Russia's principal ally was now Germany rather than France was accepted and confirmed by reports from Japanese consular and secret agents, who pointed to the fact that the Russians were intent on continuing the dispatch of the Baltic Fleet even when it was no longer in a position to reach Port Arthur in time to prevent its fall. The Japanese archives contain reports from the Japanese Consul-General at Sydney relating information obtained by Australian journalists from a Colonel de Hardenflycht, a French officer who had served as an undercover agent in London and who confirmed the activities of the two German shipping lines west and east of Singapore. This informant confirmed the intention to supply ships of the Baltic Fleet at sea in the German Central Pacific Islands after they had left the safety of Indochinese waters and pointed to the likelihood of the Russian fleet sailing to Vladivostock via the China Sea when some of the German supply vessels made port at Woosung.[37]

Pakenham was evidently unaware of any of these circumstances or of the major complications the sailing of the Baltic Fleet posed for the Admiralty, which accepted that, on paper, the Russian forces at sea enjoyed a preponderance over the Combined Fleet, as two of its six battleships had been lost in the course of operations off Port Arthur. Although the British China Squadron had been augmented and reports were made available that fresh major warship replacements would be effected in April 1905, in fact these were ordered home by Fisher in early May 1905 in the context of secret diplomatic reports about German threats against France over Morocco many months before the first Agadir Crisis.

Pakenham left Tokyo on 13 April 1905 to rejoin the *Asahi* and wrote to Lady Sykes from Kobe the following day saying that he had no idea how the Japanese intended to handle themselves. His advice was that the Russians should not be allowed to get through to Vladivostock and set up a replay of the events at Port Arthur: 'we ought to try to wipe the floor with them outside on the open sea if possible', he argued, but recognized that it was hard to locate warships in the open sea and believed that 'we shall have to await their approach to narrow waters'. In his official letter of 17 April to Captain Ottley, Pakenham wrote strongly in favour of the most heavily armoured battleships as the core units of the fleet. He condemned the armoured cruiser (which presciently proved only too accurate when Pakenham sailed with Beatty at Jutland): 'speed to overtake is useless without power to fight, and that is what no armoured cruiser has, or can have, relatively to her contemporary battleship'. Pakenham reported that 'every new interview with Togo finds him more openly friendly and kind' and that his second-in-command, Dewa, was 'a great joker' who never failed to 'excite the most uncontrolled merriment among those present' on suggesting that Pakenham 'send in my criticisms on the Japanese Navy to the Minister of Marine'. Pakenham ended his letter by indicating the intention 'to pull off the coming knock-out somehow': 'I wish the Russians would come on! I want to know whether I am to be an admiral or an angel.'[38]

Five weeks after returning to sea, Pakenham wrote:

> It is five weeks since I left Tokio – five of the dullest weeks I ever remember. Being here full of interest and expecting to fight almost any day, the Russians have dallied in the South at a distance of 2,000 miles from Japan & at the present moment we do not even know exactly where they are. They were reported to have left the French coast on the 24th, and of course they may be coming this way, but no reports have since been received to let us know in which direction their fleet is steering. It would not be true to say this fleet is in a state of suspense. As far as outward appearances go, Russians are the last people thought of. Having made all possible preparations, everyone is calmly & confidently awaiting the meeting. That must come sooner or later.[39]

Pakenham wrote two accounts of the battle off Tsushima on 27 May 1905: the first report, written on the day of the battle was updated in November 1905 to incorporate the official Japanese reports and subsequent statements by Russian prisoners of war. The account was essentially based on observations from the *Asahi* and stressed the problems of obtaining accurate intelligence. Togo was alerted to the northward course of the Baltic Fleet by wireless reports relayed to the Combined Fleet via the land station at Takeshiki and the revised account appears to have been submitted after the visit of Admiral Noel and the China Squadron, which participated in the Imperial Fleet Review in Yokohama Bay. Noel was invited by Togo to share his bridge on the flagship *Shikishima* during the Emperor's inspection on board the *Asama*, while his cruisers and destroyers were assigned to a separate reviewing line alongside the Japanese fleet and the captured Russian warships. Tucked in at the back of the British line was the American cruiser USS *Wisconsin* – in a complete reversal of how such an event would contemporarily be staged.

END OF HIS MISSION

Pakenham remained in Tokyo for a further six months during the period when every effort was made on the Japanese side to win the peace. He found the experience of frequent diplomatic receptions and festivities very taxing and was forced to spend several weeks recuperating in the mountains once the China Fleet had left Japanese waters. Newspapers and correspondence from home during his last month in Tokyo left him dissatisfied with the criticisms of the Admiralty by Sir Cyprian Bridge and Lord Charles Beresford. In the case of Bridge, he wrote that he could not 'acquit him of sharing in the desires of most others of his standing, to find out that Sir John Fisher is wrong'. Pakenham felt the urge to write in person to Bridge to remonstrate with him, but feared to give away secrets of the service in so doing and added: 'I console myself by thinking that if the Admiralty is right, the more others that are of high standing that are wrong the better, as they may serve to mislead the foreigners.' In the case of Beresford, he received a letter containing a catalogue of complaints about Fisher and responded by imploring his relative, Lady Sykes:

> Pray do all you can to smoothe over matters between him and Fisher. Their fields are different, & with mutual toleration there is no reason they should clash. Also, Fisher is so clever. I fear C.B. will not only compromise the general rate of advance, but that he may ultimately suffer from the disagreements, which the King might not be sorry to take a hand in.

Pakenham was notified on 25 December 1905 that he would be replaced by Captain Dormer on New Year's Day, when he duly called at the Imperial Palace to say farewell and receive the Order of the Rising Sun (2nd Class) to add to his C.B. He remained in touch with Japanese officers he had known well into the 1920s and was in personal contact with Admiral Yamamoto and Captain Takarabe[40] during their visit to London in 1907, as well as with Admiral Togo during his visit to Britain in 1911. Captain Seki was a regular correspondent during World War I, when Pakenham served as commander of the 2nd Battlecruiser Squadron and succeeded Admiral Beatty in overall command of battlecruisers in the Grand Fleet. Pakenham's final command was as C-in-C of the North America and West Indies Station from 1920 to 1923. In 1927, Pakenham travelled in person to Geneva to meet Admiral Saitō Makoto,[41] the head of the Japanese naval delegation, who had been vice-minister of the Japanese Navy in 1905 and had cabled him in 1911 congratulating him on his appointment as Fourth Sea Lord, when he had worked with Lord Fisher on the equipment of the fleet with oil-fired vessels.

Pakenham's reports concentrate particularly on the weapons and tactics of the Japanese fleet and mirror the debates taking place among Japanese officers about the choices available. They provided a major focus for the Admiralty under the control of Fisher at a crucial time when Fisher was searching for the most radical of solutions to the future shape of the Royal Navy with an emphasis on the role of the battleship as a platform for the large gun at the longest viable range, which proved an asset in the subsequent naval arms race and conflict in Europe. Pakenham recommended on the basis of Admiral Togo's advice:

> I want the heaviest gun, as many of them as possible, the highest velocities, and the best gun-layers – then if each gun only lives to fire a single shot, but that shot gets home, its gun would be cheap to the country at a hundred times its possible cost. There is only one way to win ordered battles. The other fellow must be shot, and shot hard and often – oftener than yourself.[42]

This philosophy appealed strongly to Admiral Fisher and that appeal was strengthened incalculably by the overwhelming success of the battle at Tsushima, hailed as the 'Trafalgar of the East', but so overwhelmingly successful that many Japanese themselves were concerned by the threat that it was inevitably bound to pose to the established empires of the day.

19

Captain Oswald Tuck RN (1876–1950) and the Bedford Japanese School

SUE JARVIS[1]

Captain Oswald Tuck RN

CAPTAIN OSWALD T. TUCK, RN, was one of the most important people in the history of the Japanese sections of Bletchley Park, the British centre established for the reading and deciphering of enemy messages during the Second World War, even though he did not work in the Park. His war work was carried out at Bedford from early 1942 to 1945. Those to whom he taught Japanese in six-month courses had a high regard for him, both as a teacher and as a kind and helpful mentor.

NAVAL CAREER

Tuck left school at 15 and did not have a conventional academic career; this has led some to describe him as 'untrained'. Nevertheless Brigadier John Tiltman, of the Military Section of the Government Code and Cypher School (GC&CS) but popularly called 'the Govt Chess and Crossword School', turned to him in December 1941, when Japan entered the war. Tiltman realized the desperate shortage of Japanese linguists required to deal with the Japanese Armed Service messages.

Oswald Tuck was born in 1876. In 1892 he left the Greenwich Hospital School just before his sixteenth birthday to start work at the Royal Observatory. He had won the first prize and a medal at school, and the headmaster had allowed him to leave early in the summer term to take up this post. Tuck worked for four years at the Royal Observatory, and at the age of nineteen was the youngest person ever elected to membership of the Royal Astronomical Society. In 1896 he was appointed to teach astronomy and navigation on HMS *Conway*, the training ship on the Mersey. While there he applied to become a Naval Instructor and was appointed in June 1899 when he was twenty-three. Tuck was sent to the Far East, where he served first in HMS *Goliath* and later in HMS *King Alfred* between 1900 and 1909.

Oswald Tuck kept diaries of his years in the Far East[2] and these make fascinating reading. The fleet was stationed at Weihaiwei, the port in northern China used by the British Navy from 1898, but they travelled around the Far Eastern area regularly. Tuck's job was to teach astronomy and navigation to the midshipmen. In 1900, while on leave, he went with some companions to Peking during the Boxer Rebellion, when the British Legation and those of other Western countries were besieged by Chinese anti-foreign forces. Tuck and his party saw Russian soldiers shooting at the small ceramic figures on the roofs of some of the buildings at the Temple of Heaven in Peking. So they went out at night, climbed up and removed several of these figures (they were the Prince of Min, who was a villain, sitting at the end, and the various animals which were there to prevent him escaping). Tuck brought back a green bird from this expedition for which he had a proper Chinese wooden stand made[3] – and at home when his daughters were young, on every Easter Sunday the green bird laid a chocolate egg![4]

He does not write much in the diaries about teaching the midshipmen, but in June 1902, he refers to their exams. – in navigation, theoretical navigation, trigonometry, mechanics and seamanship. In the following year he noted: 'The midshipmen's exam. commenced this a.m. As the ship was rolling a fair amount in the afternoon they didn't do very well.'

LEARNING JAPANESE

Tuck began learning Japanese initially in 1901 and 1902, during two trips travelling around Japan, usually with a Japanese companion. (For example, in 1902 while on leave from 9-31 May, he travelled by train, steamer, on foot and by bicycle, from Yokohama to the Izu peninsula as far as Shimoda. Tuck continued by sea to Shikoku, and on to Beppu and other places in Kyushu – rejoining the ship at Nagasaki.) A friend called Ishida accompanied him for part of this journey. In November 1902, he took on a servant called Takego, who was on board *Goliath* with him. This was a mutual arrangement, in which Tuck practised spoken Japanese and began learning the (Chinese) characters, and in return helped Takego with his English. He was already planning to take four months' leave to study for the Interpreters' exams. At first, his letters to the Captain and the Admiral met with discouragement: he was employed to teach the midshipmen and this must continue. The Admiral later arranged for the Japanese Consul in Hong Kong to examine Tuck in Japanese, and on 24 February 1903 Tuck received a certificate from the Japanese Consul, stating that: 'he can now speak Japanese tolerably well and after one year's exclusive study there is no doubt of the possibility of his expert talking of the same. H.Kirino, Acting Consul.'[5] Tuck sent this certificate to the Admiral.

HMS *Goliath* sailed to Hong Kong, Weihaiwei, Pusan, Nagasaki, Kobe and Yokohama during the first half of 1903, and at every port Tuck took the opportunity to visit various local sights, taking Takego with him, either on long walks or travelling by train and tram. Tuck much preferred exploring areas which had escaped Western influence, and he commented: 'Takego is an excellent companion; he knows all his history, and can tell me stories of all these places, by which they naturally gain in interest.[6]

On 1 June the ship left Kobe for Yokohama, where Takego went ashore to see his father. On his return he was very silent. When Tuck remarked that this was not good for conversation practice, Takego explained that his father said he must get married, and had pointed out his wife to be. Takego had hoped to become a priest. But on 1 July 1903 Takego heard that he must serve for six months in the Army, in place of the soldier, for whom he was a reserve, as this man had just died. This ruined their plans for him to go on leave to England with Tuck. Then on 4 July, Takego said that his father had decided to retire, and leave the farm to him and his future wife. Tuck felt that Takego would never come back and he wrote that he would find it hard to fill the blank in his life on board ship. Tuck left for home leave on 5 July, arriving home on 10 September.

After two months' leave he returned to the Far East, and embarked on HMS *King Alfred* in Singapore. *King Alfred* was a large, fast cruiser which became the flagship of the Commander-in-Chief, China station, from 1906-1910. On 10 December he finished composing the 'Albemarle' march, for the men to march on to the quarterdeck each morning for prayers. One of his voluntary duties was to play the piano when required; he enjoyed this, saying that it got him out of all the whiskies that the crew drank at singsongs!

There is no diary for 1904. In 1905 Tuck only completed January and February, possibly because the Russo–Japanese War was then taking place. However, a file in the Public Record Office headed *Japanese Language Arrangements for examination of British Naval Officers* has relevant information for the period between February 1904 and August 1905.[7] The British Army authorities and J.H.Gubbins, the Japanese Secretary at the British Legation in Tokyo, had produced a two-year scheme for Japanese interpreters in the Army to study in Japan, and to take exams at the end of the first and second years. This correspondence between Admiral Noel, Commander-in-Chief of the China Squadron, Sir Claude Macdonald, the British Minister in Tokyo, and the Admiralty in London, concerns the Navy's plans for its own scheme for Japanese Interpreters. The Navy was anxious to have a shorter scheme, insisting that no more than three officers could study in Japan at any one time.

Admiral Noel's letter to the Admiralty of 23 November 1904 stated that Captain Jones and Mr Tuck, Naval Instructor, were about to proceed to Japan to study to become interpreters. This was the first mention of Tuck's official course of study. It had taken him three years to achieve. On 10 January 1905 Gubbins reported to Sir Claude Macdonald that he had given Tuck a preliminary examination, and found him to be an exceptional case, in that he had already spent nearly three years learning Japanese privately and had spent a total of about nine months in Japan itself. Gubbins considered that Tuck's progress in colloquial Japanese was such that he could take the next exam in three months, and then continue studying till just before the end of the year for which he had leave. He should then take the second exam, which would cover his ability to converse fluently and accurately, and also to have some acquaintance with the technical terms of the Japanese Navy. Gubbins believed that by the end of the year Tuck would have gained such a degree of proficiency in spoken Japanese that it might even enable him to superintend the Japanese studies of other naval officers. This report by Gubbins was sent on by Sir Claude to Admiral Noel and to the Admiralty. There is also quite a long letter in the file from Tuck dated 18 January 1905, explaining the difficulties of living ashore involving the expenses of a house and of a Japanese teacher (Gubbins had assigned a teacher called Tayama to him). He was also expected to travel to various ports to gain knowledge of the country and to make the acquaintance of Japanese naval officers, in accordance with Admiralty directions. No extra allowance above the normal pay had been made for living ashore, so Tuck requested the £100 gratuity awarded by the Navy for passing the first of the two exams, on the basis of the Gubbins report of his progress. He pointed out that Army officers on their Japanese Interpreters' course were given £200 per annum allowance in addition to their pay. Tuck's request was supported by Captain Stopford and Sir Claude Macdonald. Nevertheless, correspondence continued about whether another exam would be necessary before he could receive the gratuity. The file ends with the Admiralty scheme for Japanese Interpreters dated 24 August 1905, still a one-year course.[8]

Takego eventually reappeared in 1905 after his spell in the Japanese Army, and with his sister looked after Tuck's house. Tuck had obviously passed all the exams, because in January 1906 he was appointed Japanese Interpreter to *King Alfred*, and authorized to teach Japanese to fellow naval officers. He joined *King Alfred* with Takego on 9 March at Singapore and started his first Japanese class the next day with twenty-six students. During this year he interpreted on various occasions for the Admiral and made speeches for him at functions. He continued to travel round Japan when on leave, and in June he visited Etajima Naval College in the Inland Sea. In September he went to Manchuria, and spent two days going round Port Arthur with a naval officer who had been involved in the victorious Japanese campaign to capture this naval base during the Russo-Japanese War.

In the autumn of 1907 Tuck lived ashore again for a time. In May he had been given a confidential diary to translate for the Admiralty; this took him six months to complete. He also began the translation of the secret Japanese naval history of the Russo-Japanese War. As soon as he had settled into his house, he asked one of his Japanese friends to find him a *kugakusei* – a poor student who worked to earn his school career, because he has no money and probably no family. It was the custom in Japan for anyone, who could afford to do so, to take such a student into his house, pay his school fees, provide clothes and give him light jobs. Soon Jitsuzo, whose parents and brother had all died, was introduced to Tuck. He was nineteen, a student at Waseda University, and his previous patron had had to move away. Once again Tuck had found a Japanese companion with whom he could discuss all aspects of Japanese life, including articles in the Japanese papers, attend the theatre and exhibitions of jūjitsu and fencing. When Tuck had to leave Japan earlier than expected, he paid for Jitsuzo to complete his university course, and corresponded with him for several years. Jitsuzo eventually obtained a good job with a large firm. The name Jitsuzo is written with two Chinese characters which mean 'storehouse of truth', and Tuck found that this name was very apt. He recounted this in a lecture to the Japan Society in 1931 entitled 'Jitsuzo – a Study of a Student'.[9]

ASSISTANT NAVAL ATTACHÉ

In 1908 Tuck was appointed Assistant to the Naval Attaché in Tokyo. He continued to deliver monthly instalments of his translation to the British Embassy. The secret Japanese naval history of the Russo-Japanese War had been supplied to the Admiralty by the Japanese authorities through the Anglo-Japanese Alliance. The Russo-Japanese War of 1904-5 had put Japan on the map for the first time as a major naval power, with the capture of Port Arthur, and the famous victory over the Russian navy at the battle of Tsushima in the straits between southern Japan and Korea. In 1908 he met Admiral Togo, the victor of Tsushima, and other admirals.[10]

NAVAL INTELLIGENCE

The Admiralty recalled Tuck in 1909 to continue this translation in

London, where he became assistant to Sir Julian Corbett, who used his translation to write *Maritime Operations in the Russo-Japanese War*. This was a confidential publication in two volumes of the Intelligence Division of the Admiralty War Staff.[11] Major E.Y.Daniel, official representative of the late Sir Julian Corbett, gave a testimonial to Tuck's Japanese translation work in 1923 to the secretary of the University Extension Delegation, Oxford, in which he said the work 'called for remarkable knowledge of that difficult written language. . . Sir Julian Corbett relied entirely upon it'[12] for his study of the war. Major Daniel had himself been the translator of the Russian documents used by Corbett for his history. Incidentally, in 1909 Tuck had been asked his opinion on the founding of a school of Oriental Studies, and he thought it would not be of much use to naval officers.[13]

During the First World War Tuck served in Naval Intelligence, and was given the task of collecting documents in order to write the history of that war. After the war ended he was appointed Archivist in the Historical Section of the Admiralty, and retired in 1937 as Head of the Section. The testimonial by E.Y.Daniel, already referred to, states: 'As regards the history of the late war (i.e. the First World War), Commander Tuck . . . has been given access to all the documents, and the monographs he produces are admirable in every way and most readable.'

All through the 1920s and 1930s he was extremely busy translating, lecturing and advising on matters concerning the Japanese language. The Hydrographic Department of the Admiralty employed him to translate the Japanese Sailing Directions. This was not completed until 1942 while he was in Bedford.

His interests ranged beyond purely Japanese matters. In 1924 he wrote a history of *The Old Telegraph*.[14] He set general knowledge papers for naval officers for the Education Department of the Admiralty and gave a University of London Extension series of twelve lectures on 'Elizabethan Seamen' with forty-six questions. He also lectured at Ashridge Bonar Law College. Yet another of his activities was to read plays to unemployed people in Deptford.

THE JAPAN SOCIETY

Tuck was active in the Japan Society, serving on the Council and giving lectures on various literary subjects: 'Some Comic Medieval Plays of Japan'[15], 'A Post-war Japanese Play'[16], 'Kyogen: the Comic Drama of Japan'[17], Japanese Nightingales'[18] on Japanese poetry, with many translations by Tuck. All this shows how well versed Tuck was in so many areas of Japanese – not only the more technical language and knowledge of his work for the Admiralty, but also in the literary field.

In 1939-41 he was one of the two Press Censors in Japanese at the

Ministry of Information, where he got on extremely well with his colleague, the famous Sino-Japanese scholar Arthur Waley. But this job came to an abrupt end when the Japanese attacked Pearl Harbor. The Japanese Press Office was closed down, and the journalists were interned.

THE BEDFORD JAPANESE SCHOOL

Between the two world wars, in the Government Code and Cipher School (GC and CS) in London there was a Japanese diplomatic section staffed by Ernest Hobart-Hampden and Harold Parlett, both retired Consuls-General in Japan. But Commander Denniston, then head of the Diplomatic Section of GC & CS, applied for funding to take on four more retired service or consular officials with the necessary language qualifications, instead of people from university who had studied oriental languages. J.W.Marsden and N.K.Roscoe were taken on, and Captain Malcolm Kennedy, who had been seconded to the Imperial Japanese Army early in his career and later became Reuters Tokyo Correspondent, joined them in 1935.

This section successfully decrypted Japanese diplomatic ciphers until in February 1939 the Foreign Ministry in Tokyo introduced the machine cipher called Purple. Neither GC & CS nor the US Army Signal Intelligence Service could break the Purple cipher. The Signal Intelligence Service's small cryptographic team under William Friedman and Frank Rowlett struggled for eighteen months to solve this cipher, and the breakthrough came in September 1940, just as Japan signed the Tripartite Pact with Germany and Italy.

In August 1939 GC & CS moved to Bletchley Park, and the Japanese diplomatic section took over Elmers, a school just outside the Park. In August 1940 a conference between military representatives of the US and UK was held in London, and agreement was reached on an exchange of intelligence. As a result, a secret US deputation led by Abe Sinkov arrived at Bletchley Park in February 1941, bringing with them an analogue – a machine with the same logical structure as the Purple machine - constructed by Frank Rowlett and his team. This was an extraordinary gift; in return for which BP gave some information on British success against the German Enigma machine.

The GC & CS Japanese diplomatic section was thus enabled to read the Purple code until the end of the war, as it was never altered. They followed the increasingly warlike Japanese correspondence during the rest of 1941 leading up to Pearl Harbor, supplying Churchill with decrypts and reports, which he discussed with President Roosevelt. However, the two leaders never mentioned Pearl Harbor, thousands of miles from Japan, in their list of possible countries that might be attacked – and it was never mentioned in any of the decrypted Japanese diplomatic traffic.

Both Churchill and Captain Malcolm Kennedy of the Japanese diplomatic section – who, unusually, kept a diary during the war – heard of the attack on Pearl Harbor from the BBC's 9 o'clock news on 7 December.

The one person in Bletchley Park who immediately realized the impact of this news on its work, was John Tiltman. As head of the Military Section, and a veteran GC & CS code-breaker, he had broken the Japanese Military cipher in 1933, although he spoke very little Japanese. There were no Japanese interpreters in the Japanese Military section and few in the Japanese Naval section, which had only thirteen people including clerks, although its head Hugh Foss had learnt Japanese in childhood when his father was a missionary in Japan. The GC & CS Japanese Naval section had been working on certain Japanese naval codes, including JN25, the main fleet cypher system, in conjunction with the British Far East Combined Bureau in Singapore. Being at war with Japan meant that there would be a huge increase in the numbers of Japanese military, Army Air Force and Navy messages and a consequent need for extra staff especially interpreters.

Tiltman approached the School of Oriental and African Studies (SOAS), the only institution in Britain then teaching Japanese, and where diplomats studied, for a course to teach undergraduates enough written Japanese in six months to translate the Japanese service messages and captured documents. The School replied that teaching Japanese took five years in peacetime, but they might be able to do what was required in two years. Its staff had tried twice to get funding from the War Office to expand teaching of Japanese, Middle Eastern and South-East Asian languages. But in August 1941 the War Office replied:

> So far as can be reasonably foreseen at present, in spite of the kaleidoscopic changes which have taken place in the countries which might in the future develop into the theatres of war, we feel we are at present reasonably insured in the matter of officers knowing Oriental languages.(!)[19]

Neither this nor two years were of any use to Bletchley Park. The Foreign Office advised Tiltman that Tuck's work at the Ministry of Information had ended, and on 22 December 1941 Tiltman interviewed Tuck to find out whether the crash Japanese course he envisaged could be achieved. On 27 December, the Foreign Office offered him the job. He was then recalled by the Admiralty on full pay with the rank of Naval Captain. Although he was now sixty-five years of age, Tuck was once more a serving naval officer. He wrote in his diary of this new job: 'It sounds impossible, but it's worth a try.'

Events moved fast: on 25 and 26 January 1942 Tiltman, Tuck and a university don interviewed candidates in London for the first Japanese course. Twenty-two men and one woman were taken on, all but three of whom were Classical scholars from Oxford and Cambridge, whose names had been put forward by their Classics tutors. Their course began on 2 February in a room above the Gas showrooms at Ardour House in Bedford. They had few teaching aids – a grammar book, a book of printed Japanese characters, and three different Japanese-English dictionaries – all belonging to Captain Tuck. These were hardly ideal conditions, but they soon moved to a house in St Andrews Road and more textbooks and dictionaries arrived. Later, when two courses were running concurrently, the Bedford Japanese School moved to another house in De Parys Avenue, and in 1944 to Albany Road. At a time when most people had retired, Tuck embarked on what was probably the busiest period of his long career.

The classes ran from 9.30 a.m. to 5 p.m. Monday to Friday, and on Saturday mornings. The students learned some 1200 characters during the course, with the vocabulary which they would need for wartime translation. This first course was experimental, as no one had tried this type of short course for Japanese before, and some did not believe it could be done. It was watched with interest by GC & CS. After four months Tiltman sent two of the students to work for a short time in the Japanese Diplomatic section, which had moved to Berkeley Street in London with Commander Denniston and the rest of the GC & CS Diplomatic Section. One of these students was Jon Cohen, who said they were sent there to be tested by the long-term Japanese interpreters: 'We seemed to satisfy them.'[20]

On 16 July 1942, Tuck took Eric Ceadel[21] and Robin Gibson to a meeting at SOAS, where the staff sprang a surprise test on them. They had a quarter of an hour with a dictionary to study a text. They returned and translated the first page, and Gibson continued to translate at sight. By August the Bedford School's fame had spread. Tiltman, who had recently returned from the United States, paid a visit and said the US authorities were very interested in the teaching methods, and wanted full information. Two of the students, Robins and Alabaster, wrote a short grammar with examples and Darlow produced a Japanese dictionary on aeronautics.[22]

Despite their early scepticism SOAS set up their own Japanese short courses. They recruited candidates from grammar schools who had studied Russian or German, and in July 1942 started the Services Interrogators' Course, the Services Translators' Course, and a Translators' Short Course, which was how the Forces wanted them arranged. But in June 1944 these were amalgamated into a Services General Purposes Course. Many of these students were sent out to the Far East, where they had to do whatever was required. There was always a great demand for Japanese linguists, especially in Burma, and there were never enough.

Tuck had to live away from his home in Bromley from 1942 to 1945, and he lodged in Bedford with a Miss Hammond, who was a retired music teacher. This must have been a boon for Tuck with his musical interests, and she held open house for 'the boys' from the courses who used to visit him. His daughter Sylvia, who was working in London at the Ministry of Economic Affairs, used to come to Bedford for the weekend about once a month, and she stayed with one of Miss Hammond's friends. Mrs Tuck came occasionally, but she did not like to leave their house in Bromley empty during the bombing.

The work became even more onerous, as in 1943 Tuck had three courses which overlapped:-

> 3rd course: 28 April – 23 October
> 4th course: 5 July – 20 December
> 5th course: 30 August – 19 February 1944.

This recurred with the 6th and 7th courses, which ran from March to September 1944, and again with the 8th and 9th courses, which ran from October 1944 to April 1945. The war ended during the 10th course (April – September) and 11th course (May – November 1945).

Tuck had assistants from amongst his pupils, without whom he could not have coped with running two or three courses at once. Eric Ceadel of the first course was his assistant throughout the war. In December 1943 Hawkes became the second assistant and in March 1944 Winston became the third. Tuck taught characters i.e. the script – writing, words, meaning, pronunciation to all students; Ceadel taught grammar to all students, and Hawkes and Winston corrected the written exercises.

This was invaluable help for Tuck, but he was the head and bore the responsibility for producing trained personnel who, after a month's code-breaking course were assigned to the various Japanese sections at Bletchley Park, or to any of the Far Eastern intelligence centres linked to Bletchley. For instance, Michael Loewe[23] from the first course joined the Japanese Naval section, first at Elmers, then in Hut 7 and B Block. Christopher and Maurice Wiles (also of the first course) joined the new Japanese Military Attaché section, which Tiltman set up after he had made the first break into the JMA code in spring 1942. Christopher Wiles became head of the JMA section. One of the first messages deciphered revealed Japanese intentions to construct a Burma railway, and several months later that British prisoners-of-war would be used to build it. Maurice Wiles later moved to the Japanese Army Air Force section.

Hugh Denham of the first course was posted to the naval intelligence section of the British Eastern Fleet at Kilindini near Mombasa, and returned with them to Colombo in September 1943. This team had deciphered the message warning of the imminent Japanese attack on Ceylon in April 1942, and broke JN40, the Japanese merchant shipping code in September 1942.

In 1944, Alan Stripp of the fifth course joined the Japanese Army Air Force section to work on JAAF code 6633, which carried much information – mostly from Burma. After six months, he was sent out to continue work on this code at the Wireless Experimental Centre in Delhi, which with its three sub-stations at Bangalore, Barrackpore and Abbotabad concentrated on Japanese forces traffic from Burma.

In late 1943 the Japanese Military section and other Japanese sections were moved into F Block, a large new building in Bletchley Park, where their area became known as 'the Burma Road'. In 1943 and 1944 short courses similar to the Bedford Japanese School ones were run in the Naval Section, with students chosen from within the Park. The teacher was John Lloyd,[24] a former consular official, and the courses were designed to teach people to read Japanese Naval material. John Chadwick, who had worked on Italian codes until the Italian surrender in September 1944, was sent on this course and then assigned to the JNA Section working on the Japanese Naval Attaché code which was not broken until 1944.

Josh Cooper, head of the Air Intelligence Section, set up a course to train interpreters to listen to Japanese pilots' air–to–air and air–to–ground conversations. This intensive eleven-week course bombarded students incessantly with Japanese phonograph records, and it was directed by a phonetics expert, not a linguist. Tiltman recorded taking a US Army Japanese interpreter round, and when this officer asked the director if all the students made the grade, the reply was: 'After the fifth week, they're either carried away screaming or they're nipponified.'[25]

This was not at all Tuck's style; his courses taught the written language and, although the students had to work very hard, he tried to give them some knowledge of the country and culture and even the occasional outside lecture, as well as the vocabulary for the wartime jobs they were going to do. After the Japanese surrender in August 1945, the Tenth course ended early in September, when the students were sent to Simla to do a crash course in colloquial Japanese because of the need for interrogators. Hawkes left. Tuck and Winston completed course 11, which was naval, and the Admiralty guaranteed employment of all students of Japanese when it ended in November. Altogether 225 students graduated from the Bedford Japanese School.

It was a remarkable achievement by one man, who had also taught his assistants, without any of the facilities of a University language department. He was the pioneer who had shown that such short courses could be successful. The complete list of the students with their postings is in Bletchley Park Archives. Roughly half of his students remained in the Bletchley Japanese sections, while the rest were sent to Delhi, Colombo or Australia, two to the US and a few to Berkeley Street.

The Bedford Japanese students received an accolade in a cable from

Australia on 28 July 1945: 'Your Bedford-trained translators most highly esteemed and would like as many as we may have . . . we can never have enough.'

Frank Birch, Deputy Director of the Bletchley Park Naval Section, wrote to Captain Tuck on 7 December 1945 to thank him for his report on the Bedford Japanese School. He said:

> There are no grounds at all for thinking any of it dull. I enjoyed every bit of it. . . What you haven't said in your history (but, thank goodness, it sticks out a mile) is your tremendous triumph over wrongheaded experts, red tape, neglect and almost impossible conditions. The tremendous value of your contribution and its great significance in the total British effort in the Japanese war − that, I hope, will be recognised in the GCCS histories (it certainly will in the Naval history) now being written.[26]

Tuck was on leave after Course 11 ended, but he had not retired because in March 1946 the Admiralty employed him to teach a Japanese Naval course at Greenwich. Two of the students had been at Bletchley Park and the others at SOAS. This course ended in November, which meant that he was still in uniform at the age of seventy (his birthday being 1 September), a rare achievement of which he was very proud.

AFTER THE WAR

Tuck was living in Greenwich in 1946, but he still saw many of the former Bedford Japanese students. On 10 April Jon Cohen who had been in Ceylon for three years came to lunch. Two days later Ceadel came and Tuck showed him round the College at Greenwich, commenting: 'He was impressed with the spaciousness of the College, and quite understood my cramped and frustrated feelings when I first went to Bedford, and had so much what seemed like obstruction to fight.' Despite these difficulties, he had told the first course: 'I think my work with you has been the happiest of my life.' On 3 May he visited Ceadel at Christ's College in Cambridge, and in the evening nearly 30 of his old Bedford students came to meet him. On 26 May he went to Oxford at the invitation of Cohen and Robins, and another group of his students arrived.

By now Tuck was visiting his wife every day in a nursing home, and taking her out or home for tea when he could. He went to regular meetings of the Poetry Society and played bridge and chess with his friends. He died on 26 February 1950, aged 73.

The Japan Society, which had been suspended in 1942 and had just been revived in 1950, published his obituary in its Bulletin.[27] This mentioned that he had been a Life member since 1909 and for several years a member of the Council referring to him as 'one of the first Naval

Language Officers to be sent to Japan, and by common consent one of the foremost in proficiency'. It also referred to his translation of the secret Japanese history of the Russo-Japanese War, and to the papers he gave to the Society. The obituary ended: 'During the late War his talents were used for transmitting his own exceptional knowledge to others. At the present time the loss of a personality so versed in Japanese lore and language can ill be spared.'

After the war, some of Tuck's past students went on to teach Japanese. Eric Ceadel changed his course from Classics to Japanese in October 1945, becoming a Lecturer in Japanese at Cambridge and helped to set up the Department there. He retired as University Librarian. Geoffrey Bownas of the third course, who went to Delhi, eventually became Professor of Japanese at Sheffield. In October 1951, Eric Ceadel gave a lecture to the Japan Society on 'Impressions of Post-war Japan'.[28] Referring to past members who had made valuable contributions to the society, he said:

One of these names, that of the late Captain Oswald T. Tuck RN, who died early last year, meant much to me, for it was he who instructed me in Japanese. Over 200 of his wartime students will always treasure a clear memory of his erect and dignified figure, with white hair and beard, and of his fine qualities of mind and character. In a quiet but effective manner he drew the interest of his students, and succeeded in imparting to them not only the basis of the Japanese language, but also an understanding and appreciation of many facets of Japanese literature, art and life.

208

20

Takaki Kanehiro, 1849-1920: British-trained Medical Pioneer who became Surgeon General to the Imperial Japanese Navy

JERRY K. MATSUMURA

Takaki Kanehiro

INTRODUCTION

DR TAKAKI KANEHIRO, who studied medicine and surgery as a pupil of British doctors in Japan and at medical school in Britain, is famous for his discovery of the causes and treatment of beriberi.[1] He was also a pioneer in the study of vitamins.[2] In 1959 the UK-APC named an Antarctic point[3] after him.[4]

When he entered the Japanese navy in 1872 as a young medical officer, Takaki noticed the great havoc wrought by beriberi. At the time an extra medical officer was needed on every ship that made a long cruise because of the large number of cases of beriberi. If no cure had been found the Japanese navy would have faced great difficulties in the wars with China (1894-5) and Russia (1904-5).

Takaki's success was achieved through the statistical survey-based study method of epidemiology which developed in Britain and which he had learnt while a student at St Thomas's Hospital Medical School in London from 1875 to 1880.

In Britain Takaki had been impressed by Victorian philanthropy of which the establishment of St Thomas's Hospital as a typical example, by the whole-hearted devotion of doctors and nurses to the care of patients, by the Nightingale Nursing School attached to St Thomas's Hospital and by the cultural and spiritual background which lay behind all those activities. He felt that Japan must develop in a similar way.

Takaki, while studying in Britain, was awarded the distinguished Cheselden Medal and appointed a Fellow of the Royal College of Surgeons (F.R.C.S.). He returned to Japan in November 1880 at the age of thirty-one and was appointed Director of the Central Naval Hospital in Tokyo.[5] Within five years of his return from England, while still serving with the navy, Takaki was able to achieve many notable successes.

Takaki had a broad vision and wide sympathies. Throughout his life he was indifferent to his own comfort and was fearless in the pursuit of his ideals.

EARLY YEARS, ENCOUNTERS WITH BRITISH MEDICINE

Takaki Kanehiro was born on 15 September 1849, at Mukasa in Hyūga province (the present Miyazaki Prefecture) in Kyushu. His family had been retainers of the Shimazu family, the daimyo of Satsuma (Kagoshima prefecture). According to the family records the Takaki family came from one of the many branches of the Fujiwara family and could trace their lineage back to Fujiwara no Kaneie, regent for the Emperor Ichijo. The same family records explained that the family name had been changed to Takaki (tall tree) because one of their ancestors had been appointed to the government office at Dazaifu, where a tall tree stood at the corner of the compound, in the hope that his progeny might be as loftily-minded as the tree.

Takaki's family were low-ranking samurai, who lived in normal times in rural areas farming or making handicrafts for sale and fighting for their lord in times of strife. Their income was small but adequate for simple country life. Takaki's father, Kanetsugu, was a master carpenter. His mother, Sono, was from a nearby farming family. In childhood Takaki had two names, Tōshirō and Kanehiro; from about the age of twenty he called himself Takaki Kanehiro.

Takaki's father had strict ideas about his education and in 1856, at the age of eight, Takaki embarked on the study of the Chinese classics under Nakamura Keisuke, a nearby teacher. Takaki apparently decided at the age of twelve that he wanted to become a doctor.[6] Nakamura discussed with Mori Gōbei, who was in charge of the area for the Shimazu, the possibility of sending Kanehiro to Kagoshima to study. Mori,[7] who was to return to

Kagoshima soon on completion of his term of office, offered to take Kanehiro to Kagoshima, to give him free lodging and to pay his school fees.

Consequently, in 1866, at the age of seventeen, Takaki left for Kagoshima to study first Chinese medicine and later some rudiments of Dutch medicine at a private academy run by Ishigami Ryōsaku. Ishigami had studied Dutch medicine in Nagasaki from 1844 to 1850.[8] In Kagoshima, at the recommendation of Ishigami, Takaki also attended a Dutch language academy run by Iwasaki Shunsai, where he met three young men of his own age who later became his friends: these were Kawamura Hōshū, who also became Surgeon General to the Japanese Navy, Arishima Takeshi,[9] who joined the Ministry of Finance as a senior official, and Sonoda Kōkichi, who joined the foreign ministry, serving in the Japanese Legation in London for fifteen years from 1875 to 1890, and who on his return to Japan became President of the Yokohama Specie Bank.

In the third year of Takaki's stay in Kagoshima the Boshin Civil War of 1868/9 broke out. In early 1868 Takaki, along with Ishigami, who headed a Satsuma team of doctors accompanying the troops, joined the army as a junior doctor, and went to Kyoto where at a field hospital in Sōkokuji Temple he first saw ('over the shoulder of Ishigami who was closely watching the scene') the British Legation's doctor, William Willis,[10] treat wounded soldiers.

In the north-eastern region, to which the fighting moved, doctors from many different clans had many opportunities to meet at field hospitals, where they discussed medical treatment and collaborated in treating the wounded. Ishigami Ryōsaku was no longer with them as he had been appointed director of the imperial army hospital in Yokohama.[11]

At the time a doctor from Nagasaki, where for historical and geographical reasons Dutch medicine was most advanced, observing Takaki perform surgery burst out laughing: 'There don't seem to be any doctors worth mentioning in Satsuma.' Takaki was deeply ashamed at this affront and felt strongly that Japanese doctors must raise their standards by introducing Western medicine. However, even the Nagasaki doctor's skill could not be compared with that of Dr Willis who had studied medicine at the University of Edinburgh before coming to Japan.

In two of his reports during the civil war Dr Willis wrote:

> I may perhaps here remark, as illustrating the state of transition through which this country is passing, that I found two systems of the healing contending for mastery, one known as the Chinese and the other as the Dutch system. The latter, as the name might imply, accepts European medicine as the standard for medicine. The professors of the Chinese system deny the advantage of operations, in place of which they

employ complicated drugs and ointments, whilst the professors of the Dutch system advocate the use of the knife, which they lack the requisite skill to apply to good purpose. . . and . . . I rendered such assistance as was in my power to the wounded during my stay in Edo which extended to five days, I took frequent occasion to point out to the principal officers and doctors of the several clans with whom I came in contact the advantages that would accrue by sending their wounded to Yokohama, where European skill could always be obtained, instead of at present keeping them in Edo scattered about amongst the unwounded to the prejudice of the discipline and spirit of the men, and at the same time forming a serious burden in case of fires or fighting in Edo. . . .[12]

Takaki returned to Kagoshima in 1869. The Satsuma authorities who recognized the superiority of Western civilization after the British bombardment of Kagoshima in 1863 and the value of Western medicine during the Boshin Civil War of 1868-9 had established in 1864 a school (*Kaisei Gakkō*) to teach English and medicine (in addition to military sciences) to selected scholarship students and in 1868 a medical school (*Igakuin*). Takaki entered the former school after a brief stay in his home town, and then a year later moved to the latter school when it was reorganized to teach British medicine with the arrival of Dr William Willis in 1870 as its head. Ishigami Ryōsaku, who persuaded the Satsuma authorities, using the good offices of Saigō Takamori and Ōkubo Toshimichi, to employ Willis, went with him to assist him in running the school as its manager. Willis and Ishigami were to have great influence on Takaki's success in later years.

Dr Willis had been appointed by the new government as Head of the newly-established teaching hospital 'Tokyo Major Hospital' (*dai byōin*), which later became the University of Tokyo Faculty of Medicine. There he devoted himself to both the training of medical students and to the examination and treatment of patients. His surgical ability was outstanding: his use of chloroform as an anesthetic, the surgical methods of amputation which he used together with the application of potassium permanganate solution to wounds, the use of iron splints, etc., opened the eyes of the underdeveloped medical society in Japan. However, the government subsequently decided to adopt German rather than British medical practice and Willis had to leave the hospital after only nine months' service.

Most of Willis's time in Kagoshima was spent in teaching medicine and other relevant subjects[13] and treating patients at the hospital which he designed. As medicine was taught in English, Willis was assisted in the initial stage by Ishigami Ryōsaku and later by two star pupils, Mitamura

Hajime (who in 1901 also became Surgeon General to the Japanese Navy) and Takaki.

Ishigami Ryōsaku had to leave Kagoshima in 1870 when he was asked by the new government to go to Tokyo and help organize the military medical department. This was oriented towards Dutch medicine as most leading members there were professors of Dutch medicine. When this department was split into army and navy medical departments a year later, Ishigami was asked to head the navy medical department. In consultation with his colleague Totsuka Bunkai (who soon became the first Surgeon General to the Japanese navy) he decided that the navy should adopt British-style medicine and proposed that a British professor of medicine should be hired and that Willis's star pupils should be recruited to help. They were almost the only semi-qualified staff he could find in Japan at that time.

On 15 April 1872 Takaki, at the suggestion of Ishigami Ryōsaku, was accordingly taken on as a naval surgeon. On 6 June that year Takaki married Sewaki Tomi with Ishigami as *nakōdo* (go-between). Tomi's father, Sewaki Hisato (his original name was Tetsuka Ritsuzō) was a diplomat in the Meiji government.[14]

In the following year, 1873, Professor William Anderson[15] arrived from England as professor of anatomy and surgery to teach at the Naval Medical School, which was newly built within the premises of the naval hospital in Takanawa. In the following six years he taught the whole field of medical science from the basic subjects of anatomy, physiology, biochemistry, etc. to the clinical medical field of internal medicine and surgery. Anderson also practised as a doctor examining and treating patients in the adjacent naval hospital. In all this he was assisted by Takaki and other former star pupils of Dr Willis who were all already proficient in English.

Ishigami, having consulted Professor Anderson, proposed that Takaki be sent to England to study at St Thomas's Hospital medical school. The Japanese navy had already sent young naval cadets to study in England and the United States but had not previously sent anyone to study medicine. Takaki left for London on 13 June 1875 together with several other young naval cadets, leaving behind Tomi and their two little children, who moved to her father's home while he was away. Shortly before Takaki's departure Ishigami[16] died suddenly at the age of 55.

LONDON 1875-80

In London the Japanese Legation helped him to settle down. He and four other naval cadets, who arrived in London in July 1875, first stayed at a hotel recommended by Professor Anderson. The naval cadets were taken to the naval academy at Greenwich the following day, but Takaki's course did not open until September and he was told to stay at the Legation house until term began as 'the hotel was so expensive'.

At St Thomas's Hospital and at the medical school attached to it he got on well, not only because of his cheerful, upright character and his good command of English, but also because he was a naval officer. He kept in close touch with the Japanese Legation where the Minister, Ueno Kagenori, who was from Satsuma and had once been a professor of English at Kagoshima's 'Kaisei' school before Takaki had become a pupil there. Sonoda Kōkichi, who was in charge of commercial and economic matters in the Legation, was another Satsuma man who had been a fellow pupil at the Dutch school in Kagoshima.

The curriculum at St Thoms's Hospital medical school was a comprehensive one.[17] In addition Takaki also studied epidemiology and public hygiene through books and papers by Dr Simon[18] and by Mr E Chadwick. Takaki also learnt about Jenner's method of preventing the spread of smallpox through vaccination, the prevention of scorbutus (scurvy) through the ingestion of fruit juice by J. Lind, as well as G. Brane, and J. Snow's method of preventing the spread of cholera through improvements in water-supply. The epidemiological approach[19] which Takaki learnt from Dr Simon's books and from his former students was instrumental in enabling him to discover the cause of beriberi.

At St Thomas's Hospital Takaki served as an assistant instructor in anatomy in 1876-77, as a clinical clerk in 1877, as a surgical dresser in 1877, as an obstetric clerk in 1878, and as a duty surgeon in 1879. He was struck by the fact that quite a large number of patients received treatment free of charge. He was also greatly impressed by the nursing in the hospital and the training which the nurses received. It may be assumed that Takaki came in contact with Florence Nightingale who was still at the hospital when he was there.

Takaki's school records[20] kept at St Thomas's Hospital Medical School confirm that he was a star pupil. But he was devastated by news from home of the death in 1877-78 of his mother, of his six-year-old daughter and of his father-in-law. He and members of the Japanese Legation were also saddened by news of the Satsuma Rebellion of 1877 and the subsequent deaths of Saigō Takamori and in the following year of Ōkubo Toshimichi. Before this he had received a call from Dr Willis who was on a year's leave from Kagoshima.

In the spring of 1880 he was surprised to receive a visit from Professor Anderson whose appointment in Japan had come to an end. He was to teach at St Thomas's Hospital Medical School as a professor of anatomy while serving at the hospital as a surgeon. At Takaki's farewell reception held in the autumn of 1880 Professor Anderson gave a speech in praise of Japanese students.

Shortly after his return to Japan on 10 December 1880, Takaki was appointed Director of the Tokyo Naval Hospital. The following years until he retired from active service in the navy in 1893 were the busiest period of his life.

During his absence in England the recruitment of medical students for the navy had been ended and Professor Anderson had returned to England. It was then discovered that the newly-recruited medical officers could not understand a foreign language and were as a result unable to learn about naval and military hygiene in foreign countries or follow the progress of medical science in general. They were at a disadvantage when they went to foreign ports and could not find out about local sanitary conditions and epidemics. The foreign language used at Tokyo University in teaching medicine was German. In his view the most useful and important language for Japanese naval medical officers was English. He insisted on the re-establishment of the Naval Medical School with teaching in English. In 1881 some students were recruited.

Through this medical study group which he established Takaki sought to change the predominant German authoritarian and research-oriented style of medicine to the British style of whole-hearted devotion by doctors and nurses to the care of patients. As there were no foreign medical professors working in Japan at that time, there was a particular need for doctors to get together to brush up their knowledge, to learn about recent developments in medical practice and to gather information about the better treatment of particular diseases. Takaki undertook to give a lecture at the beginning of the Society's weekly meetings. In November 1882 he invited Dr Willis, who was about to return to Britain, to a regular meeting to give a lecture on the treatment of cholera.

ESTABLISHMENT OF PRIVATE MEDICAL SCHOOL IN 1881

Takaki established a medical school (renamed in 1887 'Tokyo Charity Hospital Medical School') to help meet the great shortage of doctors at the time when there were only very few medical schools other than that at the University of Tokyo. Takaki probably feared that the re-established naval medical school would not be sufficient to meet the rising demand in the navy. He also wanted to expand opportunities for students from less well off families to become medical doctors.

A major issue for the medical school was which foreign language should be made compulsory for its students, German or English. In explaining his choice of English to the competent Ministry of Education officials he said:

> German may be good if you are to produce doctors serving just in Japan, but it is not appropriate for doctors who travel abroad. If you teach your students English, which is an international language, it will help them to obtain far more information on developments in overseas medical practice

with the result that all mankind will benefit from our medical practices, which should be our most important goal.

Reflecting the prevailing influence of German medicine in the Japanese medical world, notably at the University of Tokyo, the number of students, who wanted to learn German, grew even at Takaki's school and some students conducted a German workshop one day without school permission. When Takaki learned of this, he was angry and dismissed them immediately. He told the students: 'Since English is a global language, you must learn it first. There is no need to learn German, because all the excellent German books are instantly translated into English.'

Because of his backing for English, students and even the professors at the school had to go to Britain or the United States when they studied abroad. One of them recollected: 'In my case, too, the order was "Go to Britain. If you want to go to Germany, do so at your own expense!"'[21]

In subsequent years, until the outbreak of the Pacific War when the government banned the teaching and use of English, the school was the only medical college in Japan which adopted English in its regular curriculum. The large number of medical doctors, who had learnt English and British medicine at the college, the college itself and its British–style hospitals helped to smooth the change-over from German medicine to Anglo-Saxon medicine after the Pacific war.

Takaki was a strict disciplinarian. When he saw a student throw away a cigarette butt on the street, for example, or a paper handkerchief on the floor of a train, he would become very annoyed: 'You should always put cigarette butts in an ash-tray, and paper handkerchiefs into a wastebasket.' He was also strict about punctuality.

ESTABLISHMENT OF TOKYO CHARITY HOSPITAL IN 1882 AND NURSING SCHOOL IN 1885

Takaki established the Tokyo Charity Hospital together with other doctors, who contributed towards the costs. The director and deputy director were Totsuka Bunkai (then Surgeon General to the Navy) and Takaki. As it provided treatment free of charge the hospital soon had to be expanded and moved to a new site. The number of patients and visitors at the hospital kept on increasing and it was recognized that the hospital could no longer depend on voluntary ad hoc support groups. On that occasion he consulted Itō Hirobumi, who arranged high level support for the new hospital. Eventually the Empress and the Imperial Household agreed to make annual grants to the hospital. In 1887 it was greatly expanded and new facilities added. It was re-started with the Empress as its President and Princess Arisugawa as Director General. Takaki was appointed the hospital director. A supporting group of ladies organized the first bazaar at the Rokumeikan to raise funds for the hospital. This was a three-day fund-raising project in support of this hospital where the wives and daughters of leading figures at the time stood at their own stalls to sell at high prices various handicrafts which they had made themselves. The event achieved a tremendous success[22] attracting more than twelve thousand visitors. It was successfully repeated in the following year, when on the first day the Empress and Empress Dowager made their appearance. The proceeds were spent on the construction of a nursing school attached to the hospital which started in 1895. The nursing school was established on the advice of and help from Oyama Sutematsu[23] (the wife of General Oyama Iwao), an active member of the support group. Miss Reade, a qualified American missionary, taught modern nursing at the school (without remuneration) for the first two years of its establishment.

Takaki himself was an outstanding physician and surgeon. There were many well-off people who wanted to consult him but who were not eligible to receive treatment at the Tokyo Charity Hospital. So he built his own private hospital 'Tokyo Hospital' in 1892, a year before his retirement from the naval service. This hospital was later donated to the Jikei University School of Medicine and combined with the Tokyo Charity Hospital.

THE ERADICATION OF BERIBERI

In the latter half of the nineteenth century, beriberi, which is characterized by impairment of the nerves and heart, was widespread throughout East Asia. In Japan, it was particularly widespread in the army and navy, and especially among sailors on lengthy sea voyages, greatly reducing the fighting strength of the navy. Beriberi patients accounted for three-quarters of all patients at the navy hospital where Takaki served until he left for England to study in 1875. So he decided that he must try to discover the cause and treatment of beriberi. Major forms of treatment adopted at the hospital until some time after his return in 1880 consisted of purgatives and digitalis for edema, palpitation, etc.; strychnine, iron, etc. for numbness and paralysis; and purgatives and venesection for acute cases. There were no firm views at that time about diet.

Takaki began his research in December 1880 (i.e. in the month after his return from England) with help from his colleagues. In his research he made full use of the study of epidemiology which he had learnt at St Thomas's. This was the first time these methods had been used in Japan. As a first step towards discovering the causes of beriberi and its cure he began to note the incidence of the disease according to localities and seasons and to examine sailors in ships, barracks, etc. He noted that beriberi occurred mostly at the end of spring and in summer, but was not limited to warm weather; it occurred sometimes during the severe cold of winter. The occurrence of the disease varied in different ships, barracks, etc. Even in the same ship it appeared in some stations and not in the others; its incidence could never be firmly predicted. The state of quarters or clothing did not seem to be relevant factors. Further investigation showed that sailors, soldiers, policemen, students, shop-boys suffered most. The upper class (including officers in the navy) rarely became affected. People living in the same place suffered unequally – that is, some suffered and others did not. Although cases occurred mostly in large cities, like Tokyo, Osaka, and Kyoto, they sometimes appeared in smaller towns.

In the summer of 1882 there was a crisis with Korea and a total of five warships were sent to Ninsen (Chemulpo) and Saibutsu Bay. They stayed there only forty days owing to a shortage of hands caused by the prevalence of beriberi among the sailors and thus the ships were unfit for battle. This caused much anxiety among those responsible for dealing with the crisis. In one of the ships 195 men out of 330 were down with beriberi. Japan's largest warship *Fuso*, which had been waiting off Shinagawa (Tokyo bay) to depart, had to send two-thirds of its crew ashore in turns for treatment of beriberi.

It was not until the autumn of 1882 that he reached the conclusion that the disease had a dietary origin. In this he was greatly helped by the science of nutrition which he had studied at St Thomas's.[24] By inspecting warships, living quarters and schools he became convinced that beriberi was caused by the food eaten by the sailors. The daily food allowance at the time for a sailor was 18 sen (or 0.18 yen) (as compared with that for officers at 40 sen). Most sailors spent only 10 sen on food and remitted the remaining 8 sen as well as their pay to their destitute families in the countryside. Their favourite meal was boiled polished rice (which is carbohydrate-rich) eaten with radish pickles.

In October 1882 Takaki submitted a proposal to the Minister of the Navy, the chief object of which was to change the old dietary system. Takaki advised the adoption of Western food, particularly bread, meat and vegetables (which contained much protein and nitrogen) and urged that the daily food allowance of sailors should be increased to 33 sen and paid in kind, not in money. When that proposal was put forward there was a great deal of opposition; moreover the sailors themselves who had long been used to a rice diet did not take kindly to the proposal.

At the meeting of the Japan Society of Hygiene on 26 September 1883, Takaki reported for the first time on the cause of beriberi. On 5 October of that year he was promoted to be Director of the Medical Bureau. He advised the Minister of the Navy to set up a special committee to investigate the causes of beriberi and again advocated that food provisions should be improved.

At this point an incident occurred which turned opinion in the navy in favour of his recommendations. The training ship, *Ryūjo*, which left

Shinagawa (Tokyo) on 19 December 1882 for New Zealand, South America and Hawaii, returned to port on 15 September 1883. Of the ship's crew of 376 a total of 169 members had come down with beriberi; 25 of them died. The *Ryūjo* had first made way under sail, but as the crew members became ill the ship had had to continue under steam. However, since the firemen also came down with beriberi, the captain and officers stoked the boilers in their place until the ship was finally able to put into Honolulu. The *Ryūjo* remained at Honolulu for about a month. During this time the crew received meat and vegetables, most of the beriberi cases recovered and the ship was able to return home.

The experience of this voyage confirmed the validity of Takaki's original assertion. His proposal to set up a special committee for research into beriberi was adopted. The first meeting of the committee was held on 12 November 1883 under the chairmanship of Admiral Maki. Takaki proposed once again that a solution could be found by an improvement in food provisions.

Takaki realized, however, that, even if the committee endorsed his view of the causes of beriberi it would take a long time before action would be taken to improve food quality. So he proposed as a first step that allowances should be paid in kind, not in money, and appealed to the Minister of the Navy, Kawamura Sumiyoshi, and to other senior members of the government of the day. Eventually, through the good offices of Itō Hirobumi, he was granted an audience[25] with the Emperor on 29 November 1883 at the Akasaka Palace. Takaki explained to the Emperor his views about the causes and prevention of beriberi, pointing out that the disease did not occur if the right type of food was provided.

To his surprise, when he returned from Akasaka Palace to his office that afternoon, Takaki found that his proposal had been accepted. Takaki then determined to carry out an experiment in order to substantiate his claim. In November 1883 he learnt of the forthcoming cruise of the training ship, *Tsukuba*, and he tried to ensure that the *Tsukuba* should follow the same route as the *Ryūjo* under as near as possible exactly the same conditions. Takaki suggested that the food provisions loaded onto the *Tsukuba* for the crew should include sufficient meat and vegetables, and exclude rice. There was much opposition to this proposal and permission could only be obtained with difficulty. Eventually, the only remaining problem was that of finance. When Matsukata Masayoshi, the Minister of Finance, learnt of the Emperor's interest in the matter the cabinet finally granted a special allowance of ¥60,000 for the project.

The *Tsukuba* set sail on 3 February 1884. Takaki despite his conviction that his experiment would succeed passed many sleepless nights worrying about the results of the voyage.[26] Having followed exactly the same route as the *Ryūjo*, the *Tsukuba* arrived back in Japan on 16 November 1884. Not one single case of beriberi had occurred. Thereafter the reform of naval provisions progressed speedily. The number of beriberi cases per 1,000 sailors amounted to 404 in 1882; 231 in 1883; 127 in 1884, the first year that Takaki's reforms were implemented, and dropped sharply to 6 in 1885, and to 0.4 in 1886.

Although the number of cases of beriberi in the navy decreased considerably (to almost half the number in the year before) and the number of deaths had decreased spectacularly as a result of the new food regulations of February 1884, the disease had not yet completely disappeared and further efforts were needed to eradicate it. On 13 February 1885 he made a new proposal that barley and rice in equal proportions should be used instead of rice alone. He also suggested that barley should be provided rather than bread to which Japanese seamen were not accustomed. Most of the seamen also disliked meat. Takaki feared that if the men, who did not understand the need to change their diet, were allowed a free choice of what they ate, cases of beriberi would continue to occur. He therefore urged that ships' officers should become involved.[27]

On 19 March 1885 he was granted a second audience with the Emperor and produced statistics proving that cases of beriberi had declined after the gradual improvement in diet dating from January 1884. He thought it probable that the disease would disappear from the navy in a few years time. At a third audience with the Emperor on 16 October 1890 he was able to confirm that beriberi had indeed been completely eradicated from the navy.

However, as Takaki could not explain the cause of beriberi, his views on the disease were criticized by scholars at the University of Tokyo and by the Army Medical Corps who adhered to the German school of medicine which argued that beriberi was caused by bacteria. This led to a considerable delay in eradicating beriberi from the Japanese army despite urgent calls for dietary improvements by the families whose sons and husbands were in the army. In the Russo-Japanese War of 1904-5 as many as 27,800 died of beriberi in the army (none in the navy) compared with a total of 47,000 soldiers killed in battle.

Although Takaki[28] did not discover vitamins, he was the first man to prevent beriberi empirically by dietary additions, in 1882, suggesting the existence of vitamins.[29] This was some twenty-six years before Funk and Suzuki discovered vitamins and fifty-one years before the structure of vitamins was determined by Williams.

SOME OTHER ACHIEVEMENTS

Takaki's practical knowledge of Western culture, his fluency in English and his skill at dancing, all of which he acquired while in England, made him extremely popular among his peers and foreigners. He was the leading light at the Rokumeikan which opened in July 1883.

Takaki, who had attended many church weddings while in England, introduced in 1887 a religious ceremony for Japanese. The first such wedding in Japan was arranged by him at Hibiya Daijingū Shrine.[30] Before then wedding rituals primarily took place at the household of the groom.[31]

Takaki encouraged the wearing of Western dress and took the initiative in holding dance parties. He was also the first private citizen to buy a car, which he took delight in driving himself.

Ability, hard work, good fortune and ambition all helped Takaki win fame as one of Japan's outstanding pioneer–innovators in medicine and public hygiene. In 1892 at the age of forty-four when he retired from the navy as Surgeon General he was appointed as a member of the House of Peers. He was granted the title of Baron in 1905 and was popularly called 'Bakuhan Danshaku' (Barley Meal Baron) because he stressed the nutritious value of barley.

TAKAKI'S SECOND TOUR ABROAD

In December 1904 Takaki visited the battlefields in the Russo-Japanese War on a tour organized by the Japanese war ministry together with military attachés from foreign countries. This seems to have prompted an invitation[32] from Columbia University in New York in 1905 to lecture on the problems of military hygiene at the time of the Russo-Japanese War. The war being over Takaki, who was now in semi-retirement at the age of fifty-six, first visited Columbia University where in January 1906 he gave a series of three lectures. He then visited Michigan, Chicago, St Louis, Pittsburgh, and Boston, and finally, Washington, D.C., where he had an audience with President Theodore Roosevelt who had been instrumental in arranging the Russo-Japanese peace treaty at Portsmouth in the previous year. He also gave lectures at Philadelphia and Jefferson Medical Colleges. He then crossed over to England, arriving in London on 8 April where he was able to meet again his old friends at St Thomas's Hospital. After quick visits to Paris, Strasbourg, Rome, Vienna, Budapest, Frankfurt, The Hague, and Brussels, he was back in London on 25 April. There on 7, 9 and 11 May he delivered lectures at St Thomas's Hospital Medical School. The gist of his lectures was published in the *Lancet* and in the *British Medical Journal*. He was then invited to give lectures at the Universities of Newcastle and Durham. At Durham he received the honorary degree of D.C.L.

He returned to Japan via America, where on 3 June he attended as an observer the General Convention of American Medical Colleges at the University of Boston, and again visited the University of Columbia, where received another honorary degree. In Canada he visited Montreal and

Toronto Medical Colleges and Hospitals. He was gratified to discover that he was already widely known in the foreign medical world.

FINAL YEARS

Takaki became much concerned about the decline in the physical strength of the Japanese people and spent much of the remainder of his life working to combat this. From 1912 he embarked on a lecture tour[33] in which he visited schools throughout Japan with the aim of improving physical education. He urged the maintenance of correct posture by children and students and emphasized the importance of bodily cleanliness, the adoption of lighter clothing and the replacement of polished rice with rice boiled with barley.

In 1917 when he was sixty-nine, he was appointed chairman of the Tokyo Metropolitan Government's Education Council. In this capacity he sent a large number of teachers overseas on study tours.[34] In the same year he was elected as a member of the Azabu Ward Assembly where he was selected as chairman. Believing firmly in the importance of local autonomy he did not consider it incongruous for a member of the House of Peers to serve concurrently as a local assemblyman.

Among the most important public projects, which he undertook in later life, was the reconstruction of the Miyazaki Shrine dedicated to the Emperor Jimmu, the legendary first emperor of Japan, on the occasion of the 2620th anniversary of his birth.[35]

Takaki in many ways sympathized with the spiritual teachings of Zen and invited prominent Zen priests to speak at his school almost on a regular basis. However, from 1915, he began to practise *Misogi*, an old Shinto style of mental, spiritual and physical training as a way of uniting oneself with the universe (the deity). He would climb mountain paths on foot, a physically demanding activity, but at the age of sixty-seven he persisted and recommended the practice to colleagues and friends although not all of them welcomed such advice.

From June 1919 Takaki was often confined to bed, suffering from nephritis and uremia. On 12 April 1920 he suffered a stroke and died in Tokyo on the following day.[36]

PART IV

Businessmen

21

Mitsui in London

SADAO OBA

Watanabe Senjirō

BEGINNINGS

MITSUI'S OFFICE in London was established to export surplus Japanese rice to Europe. In 1873 the Japanese property tax law was revised to enable farmers to pay the tax in cash instead of in rice as they had done for many centuries. Due to the underdeveloped distribution structure Japanese rice farmers had difficulty in selling rice in the market. In order to help them overcome this problem the Japanese government in the 1870s explored the possibility of exporting rice to China and Europe through foreign commercial firms based in Japan. Mitsui & Co. Ltd, which was established in 1876, was given the task by the government of managing the collection and export of rice. In 1877, the company exported 139,563 *koku* (one *koku* equals 4.96 bushels) to Europe (London and Amsterdam) and 156,097 *koku* to Hong Kong and China.[1] In Europe at that time, rice was used as starch for weaving cloth rather than for eating. Some of the exported rice was re-exported to Latin America for consumption by immigrants from Spain. Because of the long distance and time taken by sailing ships through the Indian Ocean rice for export had to be hard and a larger size. Mitsui chose rice from Kyūshū. The first shipment was made in

1877 soon after Satsuma launched its abortive Rebellion in the so-called *Seinan sensō* against the central government. Rice was loaded on board the *Niigata-maru* and the *Takasago-maru*, which belonged to Mitsubishi and was being sent to England for repair.

In April 1877, after Mitsui undertook to manage the export of rice, the company sent Robert Walker Irwin to London, who had been appointed adviser to the company by the young (twenty-nine-year-old) president of Mitsui & Co., Masuda Takashi.[2] Robert Irwin, a young and ambitious American who was said to be a descendant of Benjamin Franklin, had landed in Japan in 1866 and had acquired expertise in international trade while working in Yokohama for Walsh, Hall and Co. Irwin had established contacts with leading Japanese personalities in political and financial circles.

As soon as Irwin arrived in London he managed, thanks to an introduction from Baring Brothers, with whom Irwin had good relations, to establish business relations with Martin & Co, a leading banker. In June 1877 Irwin established Irwin & Co., as Agent of Mitsui & Co. at Crosby Square in the City of London. After the office had made a satisfactory start he handed over responsibility for the office to his elder brother Richard and returned to Japan where his Japanese wife Iki had been awaiting his return.

At the time Irwin & Co. was established there was another Japanese company in London. Okura Kihachiro, ambitious and full of entrepreneurial spirit, travelled around Britain for ten months when the Iwakura Mission visited Britain in 1872. Okura, a businessman, who had powerful connections with politicians, saw that there was an opportunity in London for profitable business. He met Kido Kōin and Okubo Toshimichi, who were the leading political members of the Embassy, and argued strongly that the life-style of the Japanese would be gradually Westernized. He advised them accordingly to promote the manufacture of woollen goods in Japan and in particular to provide woollen uniforms for the newly-established Japanese army. In 1874, after Okura returned home, Okura Gumi & Co. was opened in London.

In 1880 the London Branch of Mitsui was officially established under the management of Sasase Motoaki who had been trained in international trading business by the Irwin brothers. The branch was the fifth overseas office of the Company after Shanghai (1877), Hong Kong (1878), Paris (1878) and New York (1879).[3] As the Paris office was closed soon after the London branch was established, London was, in practical terms, the first Mitsui office in Europe. The company's staff list for 1883 records the following two members as being stationed in London:

Banto (3tou) (Clerk-third class) Sasase Motoaki
Tedai (2tou) (Shop Assistant-2nd class) Watanabe Senjiro (who had arrived on the Takasago-maru in 1877).

As *Banto* and *Tedai* were commonly used terms by shopkeepers during Tokugawa era it may seem curious that the same terms were used by a modern international trading company like Mitsui but the revolution in Japan was still in its early stages.

EARLY DEVELOPMENT OF ANGLO-JAPANESE TRADE

Since Japan had opened three ports (Kanagawa, Nagasaki and Hakodate) to ships from the USA, Britain, the Netherlands, Russia and France in 1859 Anglo-Japanese trade had been mainly handled through British trading houses such as Jardine Matheson which had offices in the Treaty ports. Japanese travelling traders, however, began to visit Britain in the early 1870s. The main export items from Japan were agricultural products such as green tea, raw silk and rice and traditional craft products such as lacquer-ware and copper-ware. Japan imported from Britain cotton yarn and cloth, woollen goods, metal products, ships, medicines, chemicals, arms and ammunition. In these early years Anglo-Japanese trade constituted a major part of Japan's external trade. Exports to Britain amounted to 50% of all Japan's exports and imports from Britain amounted to 15% of Japan's imports. For many years, Britain exported to Japan greater quantities of goods than she imported from Japan.

SONODA'S WARNING TO JAPANESE TRADERS IN BRITAIN

As happened a century later there was 'excessive competition' among those Japanese traders in Britain. Japanese traders at that time had a bad reputation because their business practices were not in accordance with the norms prevailing in Europe. Sonoda Kokichi,[4] Japanese Consul in London in 1880s, who had received many complaints from British traders on these travelling traders and fortune-seekers wrote a long essay on 'Good and Bad Points of Japanese Traders' in which he gave advice on how to do business in Britain. His main arguments were:

1. Japanese traders did not study commercial practices. Merchants had been traditionally regarded as the lowest class in Japan. Consequently, Japanese traders were, in general, neither trained nor intelligent. They relied on their obsequious attitude, prostrating themselves before their clients. Japanese traders in Britain had not studied how to conduct business in Britain and could neither speak nor write English.
2. Japanese traders were not adequately experienced in commerce. Time was money in Britain and time was very precious for British traders. Japanese traders only go down on their knees and waste time through exchanging seasonal greetings.
3. Japanese traders did not know how important honour was. The export of forged silk-worm egg pasted paper had resulted in the

Japanese product losing its reputation. Japanese traders sought only profits and were so short-sighted that they disregarded their own reputations as well as the honour of Japan. British traders were men of virtue who valued trust and esteemed honour.

4. Japanese traders lacked powers of endurance. Those who operated overseas must be prepared not to return home even when they died. Japanese traders, after only three or four years' stay overseas, got homesick and waited impatiently for the time when they could go home. Under these circumstances, success in business could not be expected. British traders overseas were, on the contrary, doing their best by bearing hardships and privations.

5. Japanese traders misunderstand what 'sample' means. There were endless complaints to the Japanese consulate over breach of contracts, such as over delivering inferior quality goods in comparison to the higher quality of samples. It was better, therefore, to do business through reliable trading houses such as Mitsui & Co. and Takata & Co.

6. Japanese traders were short of capital. Many traders could not pay for the goods which arrived from London. Those traders would fail in business.

7. Japanese traders did not understand the need for specialization in business. In Japan merchants were usually 'jacks-of-all-trades'. Japanese traders could not, therefore, compete with British traders who were specialized.[5]

Mitsui's rapid expansion and success in London was made against this background. Its ability to compete against smaller Japanese traders was undoubtedly due at least in part to official support from the Japanese consulate.

WATANABE SENJIRO

Watanabe Senjiro(1860-1916) was born in Yokohama and was a graduate of the *Shōhō Kōshūjo*, a private institute which was opened by Mori Arinori in Ginza-Owaricho, Tokyo, to teach how to do business. The institute was launched in 1875 with the support of leading financial and industrial leaders like Shibusawa Eiichi and Masuda Takashi. The institute developed to become Hitotsubashi University. Several early graduates of the college were recruited by Mitsui. Watanabe was one of them.

Watanabe stayed in London for twenty years. He is remembered as the leading figure in the early years of Mitsui in London. He was one of the founding members of the Japan Society. In April 1893 he married Mary Ann Davison, widow of Colonel Thomas Davison.[6] Mary remained long after Watanabe's death good-looking and elegant. The November 1924 issue of *the Nichi-ei Shinshi*, a local Japanese monthly, reporting her presence at the Taishō Emperor's Birthday Party at the Japanese Embassy in London wrote: 'Mrs Watanabe was beautiful and lovely. When she appeared suddenly among Japanese ladies dressed in Western or Japanese style she looked like a peacock among beautiful small birds.' Mary's charm and her social status as a widow of an Army colonel undoubtedly helped Watanabe to explore business with leading financiers and industrialists.

Watanabe's business aim was to secure the agency of leading manufacturers in order to export machinery, equipment and products for promoting the industrialization of Japan. There was much demand for cotton-spinning mills. Watanabe made contact with Platt Brothers & Co. Ltd, of Oldham, which in 1866, had exported a spinning and weaving mill to Satsuma, and Mitsui was appointed their agent for Japan. Other related manufacturers followed suit and made Mitsui their agents. His efforts extended to manufacturers in various other fields of machinery and equipment which were urgently required for the rapid expansion of industry in Japan. Up to the 1920s, Watanabe and his successors managed to sign up for the Mitsui agency for exporting to Japan and, in limited cases, to China, some of the top British engineering companies.[7]

As a result of Watanabe's efforts the total turnover of the London Branch reached 4.55 million yen which was the third largest after the turnovers of the Osaka Branch and Tokyo Head Office.[8]

A BUSY OFFICE

Mizuta Hideo, a Japanese journalist, who visited the Mitsui London office at 34 Lime Street in the City of London at the end of the nineteenth century, described how he found the office:[9]

> Mitsui occupies the whole of the second floor of a grand building. The company has six departments for coal, machinery, rice exports, railways, general merchandise and accounting. These departments are staffed by more than ten Japanese experts and nine local employees. Many are involved in book-keeping. In the Manager's room Watanabe Senjiro and Mitsui Morinosuke are working busily.

In the early stages after the head office had been established the company had difficulty in obtaining sufficient working capital in Japan, but managed to persuade the Japanese government to grant an interest-free loan of 300,000 yen to promote exports. From about 1877 this enabled Mitsui, as the first Japanese trading company, to export raw silk, coal, copper, rice, white wax, lacquer-ware, porcelain and antimony to overseas markets.

Mizuta was amazed by the skills of the staff in Mitsui's London office who competently handled many letters and documents sent not only to Japan but also to Europe, Asia and the Americas. He concluded that 'Mitsui's business was not limited only to Japan and London. The company dealt with a network of clients throughout the world.' The turnover of the London Branch, excluding ships, amounted to £884,700 in 1894, £871,800 in 1895 and £1,004,400 in 1896. The average annual turnover equalled ¥10,000,000. The average volume of products and commodities which the London office handled annually were:

Rice   30,000 tons
Coal   150,000 tons
Spinning/weaving machinery   200,000 spindles
Cotton   10,000 bales
Yarn   5,000 bales
Steel rails   More than 30,000 pieces
Locomotive and passenger cars   More than 1,000 units
Chartering of coal transportation vessels   20-30 vessels

Mizuta noted that the office also dealt with the supply of a large number of boilers. It had contracts to supply coal from the Miike mines in Kyūshū to shipping operators such as Shire Line, Glen Line, Ben Line, Norddeutsche Lloyd and China Mutual Holt. One-tenth of the total turnover of the London office came from the sale of coal. Mitsui abolished the practice of giving rebates to ship's masters and thus enhanced its reputation among ship owners.

At first Japanese rice had had to compete with Burmese rice selling at £6:10s but the office eventually managed to convince buyers to pay £10:10s per ton for better quality Japanese rice.

Sangenya Spinning and Weaving Company of Osaka, which had been founded in 1879, commissioned Mitsui to purchase spinning and weaving machinery for the mill. Mitsui concluded a special agreement with Platt Brothers and in 1895 shipped spinning machinery (188,444 spindles), silk-weaving machinery (6,870 units), weaving machinery (500 units) amounting in total to £253,800. Exports of such machinery to Japan increased in 1896 to £343,000.

Mitsui was also active in supplying heavy machinery to the Japanese army and navy arsenals as well as printing machinery for Japanese newspapers. They bought more than ten ships. Rails, locomotives and iron bridges were exported to newly-expanding railway operators such as Nippon, Sanyō, Kōbu, Osaka and Kansai Railway Companies.

Mizuta concluded that among the few Japanese traders operating in London Mitsui was the leading Japanese company.

DEVELOPMENT OF MITSUI IN LONDON

The number of Japanese expatriates working for Mitsui in London increased as the business of the office grew bigger. According to the staff directory of the company the number of Japanese expatriates was: 1883 – 2 (Sasase Motoaki and Watanabe Senjiro), 1887 – 3, 1893 – 5, 1895 – 6, 1896 – 8, 1898 – 10. These were among the 'best and brightest' employees of the company. Many were promoted to top management positions in Tokyo in later years.

The London office became the parent office of Mitsui in Europe providing staff for the offices opened in later years in other European cities. A Hamburg office was established in 1899 by a Mitsui employee sent from London. Similarly, an office was opened in Lyon in 1908. After these offices had shown that they could be profitable they were upgraded to branch status. The Hamburg office in due course became part of Mitsui & Co. Deutschland GmbH with its head office in Dusseldorf while the Lyon office became in due course Mitsui & Co. SA., Paris.

The healthy development of Mitsui's London office was due to the continuous increase in demand for equipment, machinery, materials and commodities which were needed for the very rapid industrialization of the Japanese economy which was taking place in the final decades of the nineteenth century. The office, which was located at the centre of 'The factory of the World', earned the reputation of being the most reliable Japanese trading house. Nevertheless, the office's success owed greatly to the advances in management achieved by the head office in Tokyo. For instance:

1, *The Senshū Kasisha*, the forerunner of Mitsui, had introduced Western style book-keeping before Mitsui & Co invited Vincent E. Braga, an *o-yatoi* Portuguese of the Osaka Mint and Allan Shand, an *o-yatoi* British employee of the Finance Ministry to train a wide-range of staff in the company in Western-style book-keeping.

2, Mitsui introduced its own code-books at an early stage. A simple code-book on domestic rice transactions was introduced as soon as the company began operations in 1876 and it was used until the end of the nineteenth century. A Code in English, entitled *Private Code. Mitsui Bussan Kaisha*, was compiled in 1881 and was revised in 1891. It was printed by Worall & Robey, London. It contained about 9000 code words. The code-book was mainly required for rice export business. In the days of expensive overseas telegram charges the use of these codes enabled Mitsui to increase its competitiveness.[10]

CONCLUSION

Mitsui in London, located in the centre of the largest commercial and financial centre in the world, developed steadily thanks to the high reputation of the company and also to the excellent management of Watanabe Senjiro. In the early years of the twentieth century the London Branch had the following departments:[11]

General Affairs
Camphor
Import goods
Coal & Shipping
Accountant
Lyon Representative
Marseille Representative
Hamburg Representative

There were also branch departments of major departments in the Tokyo Head Office. These were:

Machinery department
Produce and Fertilizers department
Metal department

These 'branch departments' were established by large departments in the Tokyo Head Office in order to help them to develop their global business strategy. General Managers of major Mitsui offices, such as Watanabe Senjiro in London, held concurrently the post of manager of the branch departments.

The name 'camphor department' may sound curious but the export of camphor, because of its importance in the local economy, was a monopoly of the Japanese Finance Ministry.

Watanabe was recalled to Tokyo Head Office in 1902, when Masuda Takashi, the founder of Mitsui & Co, retired. In Tokyo he assumed full responsibility for managing the company for four years from 1903. One of his accomplishments, which is still remembered, is his application for membership of Baltic Exchange in London, the world largest exchange of shipping vessels and agricultural produce. To become a member was prestigious but it was very difficult. Because of Watanabe's reputation and popularity among members of the Exchange Mitsui became in 1910 the first Japanese member of the Baltic Exchange.

Watanabe had a Western-style villa in Kamakura, which was designed by Josiah Conder, the famous English architect. He died as a result of a heart attack on 26 September 1916. His widow and son returned to England. His villa was destroyed by the great Kanto earthquake in 1923.

22

The Yokohama Specie Bank in London

KEIKO ITOH

Okubo Toshikata

INTRODUCTION

THE HISTORY of the Yokohama Specie Bank in London mirrors Japan's pre-war efforts to establish herself as a first-rate modernized empire, and gives us a glimpse of the nitty-gritty details that this entailed both in terms of the bank's financial transactions and in the efforts of the men who represented the Bank in London. The creation of the Bank, in February 1880, was in effect part of the general reaction against external threats felt in the early Meiji years. Brainchild of Fukuzawa Yukichi, and brought into being by Okuma Shigenobu, the Yokohama Specie Bank was established, with government funding and private capital, in order to enable Japan to earn foreign currency and specie through the financing of Japanese exports, a practice that hitherto had been dominated by Western bankers and merchants in Yokohama.

The Bank's presence in London was crucial from the outset because London was the financial centre of the world. Apart from financing Japan's export trade, the London branch played a primary role in furthering Japan's early imperial ambitions, first by enabling Japan to receive the Chinese indemnity payment from the Sino-Japanese War of 1894-95, and then by raising money to finance the Russo-Japanese War of 1904-05. As Japan consolidated her status on the international scene, the London branch managers came to represent Japan at a number of international conferences, including the Paris Peace Conference after the First World War, and the Board meetings of the Bank for International Settlements in Basel. However, with the outbreak of the Pacific War on 8 December 1941, the bank's operations in London came to an abrupt halt. The bank's final effort to raise money for the Japanese military and for the financial policies of Japanese-occupied territories was undertaken mainly from Shanghai, thus sparing London from being centre-stage in the final collapse of both the Japanese Empire and the Yokohama Specie Bank.

This essay recounts the story of the London Branch of the Yokohama Specie Bank primarily through the activities and personalities of its successive general managers – an attempt to draw a 'biographical portrait' of, as some may think, a dry financial institution. All institutions, however, do have certain characteristics. In the case of the Yokohama Specie Bank, there appears to have been a distinct flavour, which was created by the unique *Shōkin-jin* [Specie Bank man] trait. One former banker described it as follows:

> Given its specialized operations, and the opportunities for postings abroad, entrance was competitive. The selection was strict, and many came from an intellectual background. It was surprisingly informal within the bank, and everyone called each other So-and-so *san*, never using titles, even for superiors. The general managers were given an enormous amount of autonomy, reflecting the trust placed in them. The bank had an ethos of speaking out. It was considered better to be wrong than to be silent. Only those with opinions and originality were considered worthy. This made the bank an extremely stimulating place to work.[1]

Being one of the most important overseas postings, the general managers of the London branch had heavy doses of the *Shōkin-jin* in them. They were pioneers, not only in banking circles, but also in establishing and consolidating the small Japanese community in London with their leadership and dynamism.[2]

1881-1906

The earliest Yokohama Specie Bank bankers sent to London had to face the formidable task of building trust from scratch, at a time when Japan was barely into its modern era. The bank sent a representative to London in 1881, only a year after its inauguration, and the representative office was upgraded to a branch in 1884, at 84 Bishopsgate. Matsukata Masayoshi, Finance Minister, took great personal interest in every detail of the London operation, laying out his thoughts in an instruction document, which covered issues ranging from procedures to protocol, to bankers' attitudes. Whether the bank would be able to establish itself within the London financial markets was, for Matsukata, a matter of Japan's credibility. For the early arrivals, small events often became significant eye-openers into unfamiliar territory. The Specie Bank's main operation was to discount foreign bills of exchange for Japanese exporters, mainly silk merchants at the outset, by using paper currency lent to it by the government. The London branch would then receive the bills for the collection of the proceeds.[3] A young banker, Chō Sakio, who worked at the London branch from 1887 to 1893, learned the severity of the London banking environment when one of the Specie Bank's clients, a British merchant, dishonoured an import bill from Japan. The client's own bank simply refused to bail out the merchant because of lack of collateral, and the matter was resolved only when the merchant sold his country house to cover the dishonoured bill. Chō was also most impressed by English thrift and humour. A very wealthy lady told Chō: 'If there were a fourth class in the trains, that is what I would be taking!'[4]

Nakai Yoshigusu, who headed the foreign exchange department at the Yokohama head office, assumed the position of general manager in London at the beginning of 1891. Nakai and his wife Ryū soon became well known among the small Japanese community. Minakata Kumagusu was one who often benefited from their kindness and took many meals at their home.[5] Nakai's achievements in London are best summed up by his son, Nakai Chōsaburō, who wrote as follows:

> In London, my father was engaged in two big operations: one was to receive, manage and remit the Chinese reparation payments as the London Manager of Yokohama Specie Bank on behalf of the Bank of Japan; and the other was to raise the first 4 per cent sterling bond.
>
> The Chinese reparation payments amounted in pounds sterling to about 38 million. The money was paid in instalments between 1895 and 1898, and it was said that the amount of cheques written then was the largest in the world. A photograph of my father and a copy of a cheque even made it into *The Bankers Magazine*. It is well known that, using the reparation money, Matsukata Masayoshi brought Japan on the gold standard in 1897. My father, through his astute buying and selling of gold and silver, was able to put the Yokohama Specie Bank firmly on the London financial market scene, and contribute greatly to raising Japanese international credibility.
>
> As for the £10 million, 4 per cent, bond issue, of 1899, since there was still no representative from the Ministry of Finance or the Bank of Japan, my father was entrusted with the title of 'Attorney for the Bank of Japan' in this operation. In

order to protect secrecy, my father made all the bankers involved stay at his official residence and work day and night. One of the bankers later told me that Madame Nakai, my mother, was a very strong woman. She must have made quite an impression on the bankers. At that time, I had left the Tokyo Commercial College to join my parents in London and attend London University. I commuted to the university from my parents' house. My father liked to have Japanese dinners, and since there were no Japanese restaurants yet in London at the time, every evening, we had guests from the Japanese community. My parents had ingredients for making *tōfu* sent from Japan, but each time, the *tōfu* would never turn out quite right. My father was also very much respected by the English clerks at the bank. At the time, the chief clerk was a man by the name of Poppert, who was a fine, upright man. He and my father often had debates and discussions. Poppert said to me, 'There are many stars, but only one moon. Mr. Nakai is the moon.'

My father also kept a close eye on world developments and often included topical issues in his speeches as the Chairman of the Nihonjinkai. When it came to discussing Russo-Japanese relations, he would say that there would be a war between the two countries, and that he would be involved in issuing war bonds. With such ambitions, he returned to Japan for furlough in 1902. He never was to see his predictions come true, for he suddenly died at the end of 1902. He had damaged his health because of his great love of alcohol.[6]

The Chinese indemnity payment was a complicated operation. Because of the magnitude of the transfer, equivalent to twenty-eight per cent of the 1895 national income of Japan, Nakai and the Japanese government had to ask the Bank of England to open an account for the Specie Bank, a request that had previously been denied. The Bank of England finally agreed to open an account for the Specie Bank in October 1895 when the first instalment of the indemnity was due. This account became the first official connection between British and Japanese banking. Also, the large transfer of funds meant that any move by the London Branch carried the risk of causing undue movements in the money markets. In consultation with the head office, Nakai took great care and effort to diversify between gold, silver and pounds sterling, and carry out foreign exchange transactions in different locations such as the US, India and Shanghai in order to minimize the effect. As his son mentions, Nakai was featured, with an article and a portrait, in *The Bankers Magazine* in January 1896, and later, in the March issue of 1903, the same magazine carried an obituary of Nakai, which said:

Throughout that time [in London] he had to meet with all the difficulties which beset the path of a bank working in a city to which it was a stranger. When the office was first opened, it was treated as of little account by other Eastern exchange banks, but, by dint of the persevering labours and judicious management of its chief, the Yokohama Specie Bank worked its way into a place of prominence among those institutions having connections with Oriental countries.[7]

Nakai could not fulfil his ambition to issue war bonds for a war against Russia, which became the task for others in London and Tokyo. However, by raising the profile of the Yokohama Specie Bank in London, Nakai had laid the foundations for the important loan operations to be undertaken during the Russo-Japanese War. The main person involved in the loan issue negotiations was Takahashi Korekiyo, vice-president of the Bank of Japan, who, immediately following the outbreak of the war in February 1904, was sent to London via New York to raise foreign loans. With war, the drain of gold from Japan was so immense that the specie reserves at the Bank of Japan were rapidly diminishing. Takahashi could not afford to lose any time. Just when he thought that the government would have to take temporary measures to raise funds if the loan negotiations did not progress, Takahashi met Jacob Henry Schiff, senior partner of Kuhn, Loeb & Co. of New York, who happened to be in London. This encounter at a dinner party turned out to be crucial. The very next day, Schiff agreed to underwrite £5 million of the loan, which was half the total amount sought by the Japanese. With Schiff's intervention, a £10 million loan at six per cent and redeemable in seven years, was successfully launched on 11 May 1904, marking Japan's first ever foreign loan issue. The Yokohama Specie Bank, together with Parr's Bank (which in due course became the Westminster bank) and the Hong Kong and Shanghai Bank, participated in the loan offering. The success of this first issue made possible the second (November 1904), third (March 1905) and fourth (July 1905) issues, and in each case, Schiff underwrote half of the total sum. Pleased as he was with Schiff's decision, Takahashi did not understand Schiff's motives until much later in what became a lifelong friendship. As a prominent Jew and president of the American Jewish Association, Schiff opposed the ill-treatment of Jews in Russia, and had a particular interest in the outcome of the Russo-Japanese War. Schiff believed that Russia, if defeated, would follow a path of reform, and decided to exercise whatever influence he had for placing the weight of American resources on the side of Japan.[8]

The involvement of Schiff in the Russo-Japanese War loans had two unforeseen consequences. One was its influence on Japan's subsequent non-discrimination policy towards Jews in Japanese-occupied China. When unexpectedly in 1939 thousands of Jewish refugees arrived in

Shanghai, Japanese officials in charge, most notably Captain Inuzuka Koreshige of the Imperial Japanese Navy, were convinced that favourable treatment of the Jews under Japanese control would have a significant impact on the powerful Jews who controlled eighty per cent of America's capital and the media, and could thus avoid war. They argued that American Jews might moreover be encouraged to repeat the financial assistance rendered to Japan thirty-four years earlier by Schiff.[9] Thus, Schiff's actions were the catalyst to what later became known as the 'Fugu plan'. The other consequence of Takahashi's encounter with Schiff was related, albeit in an indirect way, to the Yokohama Specie Bank in London.

In the spring of 1906, Schiff, together with his family, was invited to Japan to be conferred with the Order of the Rising Sun (second class) from the Meiji Emperor in recognition of his contribution to Japan's victory over Russia. During their two-month stay, the Schiffs were entertained by many of the political and financial leaders of Japan, and of course by Takahashi Korekiyo and his family. Most remarkably, the Schiffs agreed to take back with them to New York Takahashi's fifteen-year old daughter, Wakiko, for whom Takahashi wanted a Western education. Accompanied by her nanny, Wakiko was sent off with the Schiffs, and initially became terribly homesick. Wakiko lived with the Schiffs for three years, during which she studied at the Briarcliff School, took piano lessons and developed into a refined young woman.[10] A few years after her return to Japan, Wakiko was to marry the eighth son of Meiji Genrō Okubo Toshimichi, Okubo Toshikata, who became the general manager of the Yokohama Specie Bank in London in 1919. In fact, Okubo had been a young banker at the London Branch from 1904 to 1911, probably witnessing on a daily basis Takahashi's frantic efforts to raise foreign loans. Little did he know that Takahashi was to become his future father-in-law and that the Russo-Japanese War loan negotiations would provide the trigger for the remarkable education of his future bride.

The general manager of the Specie Bank London branch at the time of the Russo-Japanese War loans was Yamakawa Yūki, who assumed his post in October 1903. Because Takahashi Korekiyo was the main negotiator of the loans, few records exist of Yamakawa's experience in London, except for a rather unfortunate incident that occurred during his time. Starting from 1902 and during the Russo-Japanese War, a naval paymaster officer, by the name of Takeuchi, withdrew a total of £30,000 from the Navy's account at the Specie Bank London branch and disappeared in November 1904. The government held the bank responsible for this loss because, under the agreement with the Navy, no more than £200 was to be withdrawn in any single transaction. When this embezzlement began, Nakai had already returned to Japan on leave, and the banker in charge was not aware of the £200 limit. When Yamakawa arrived as general

THE YOKOHAMA SPECIE BANK

manager, he too did not know of the limit, and continued to allow large withdrawals by Takeuchi, who claimed that the funds were needed for confidential operations in time of war. In the end, the Specie Bank paid a fine for the oversight, but the Finance Ministry reduced the penalty given the extraordinary circumstances.[11] Although this incident is hardly a reflection on Yamakawa's reputation, it provides an insight into the daily challenges of the London branch and the risks involved. Yamakawa was promoted to become general manager at the main office and left London in 1906.

1906–1927

Tatsumi Kōnojō, Yamakawa's successor, was by all accounts a giant among giants in the bank's history. He came to the London office in 1892, became the general manager in 1908 and served in that capacity until 1919. He left London in 1920. There was probably not a single Japanese who set foot in London in the late Meiji and Taishō periods who did not know of Tatsumi, and he was equally well known in the City of London where he was trusted to the highest degree. Respected by colleagues, accounts of Tatsumi abound in the records of the Yokohama Specie Bank.

Nishiyama Tsutomu, who served as Tatsumi's secretary during the last two years of the First World War, writes of his former boss:

> Tatsumi's boyhood was spent working as a messenger boy for a Chinese exchange trader in Yokohama. The Yokohama Specie Bank was on his usual rounds, and he ended up joining upon someone's introduction. He was so busy running around that he had no time for formal education. Yet, he was extremely wise and knowledgeable. He was well versed in the pure economic theory prevalent in Britain, which enabled him to make clear analyses, and take appropriate decisions. He knew all the nooks and corners of the London financial market. He was at the same time very interested in the natural sciences, and would examine plants under a microscope, and study the stars through a telescope, which was one of his prized purchases. He was gentle in appearance, and very humble. He would never flout the enormous amount of knowledge stored within him. But, when it came to observing social issues, he would jump to conclusions, and found it very difficult to present a coherent argument to win over others. In today's terms, you could call him someone very bad at PR or publicity. Part of it was because he was not a talkative man, and was not interested in being bothered about explanations. His English was impeccable, with perfect diction, extremely unusual for a Japanese.[12]

During the First World War, the Bank headquarters tended to make impossible demands on the London Branch when faced with difficult transactions. Tatsumi was adept at judging what could or could not be done, and was unwilling to expend any effort on what was not achievable. Needless to say, this caused a certain amount of friction between overbearing and arrogant headquarters, and cool and collected London. By the time Tatsumi also became a director of the Bank in 1914, he delegated all day-to-day business to his deputy, and engaged only in the most important issues. So, as his secretary, Nishiyama had an easy time. One of his few tasks was to clean out Tatsumi's desk from time to time and sort out the bits and pieces of paper. He found among the personal correspondence letters from English people, young and old, all asking Tatsumi for money for a sum anywhere between £2 and £8. Judging from the number of thank-you notes also stuffed in the drawer, Nishiyama realized that Tatsumi wrote out a cheque for each request. Tatsumi had also made a generous donation to his golf club for which he received a particularly memorable thank-you letter.

Shortly after Japan became a participant in the First World War, many Japanese who were studying or travelling on the continent came to London to seek onward passage to Japan. The counters at the Specie Bank London branch were every day swarming with Japanese customers. Seeing that the majority of them hardly had any money, Tatsumi said to his bankers: 'Try to process their requests as quickly as possible. Use the pre-war exchange rate of 1 pound for 20 marks, and give them gold or bills or whatever.' The bankers went to work following his instructions, and customers who had thought that their German paper money was worthless were extremely pleased. Tatsumi also authorized the provision of up to £50 in advance travel expenses to those stranded so long as they had a proper contact address in Japan. Despite taking such a risk, all the loans were subsequently repaid. Tatsumi's compassion and sound judgement in times of emergency made a strong impression on Yano Kanji, a banker who carried out his instructions at the time, and who later became the London branch general manager in 1922.[13]

In the autumn of 1917, the British government restricted imports of a wide range of products because it was losing many ships as a result of German submarine activity. On the restricted list was Japanese sake. Although hardly a heavy drinker, Tatsumi always enjoyed his *Kikumasamune* with the meal that his old Japanese cook prepared for him in the evenings. Tatsumi believed that the British would lift the restriction on sake if the London Japanese residents complained. But the Embassy was firmly against rocking any boats. 'At a time when Britain is fighting for its survival against the Germans, how could Japan, as an ally, request the lifting of an import ban on sake just because Mr Tatsumi wants to have a drink,' they moaned. When Tatsumi heard about the Embassy attitude, he was rather angry and said that those diplomats didn't understand true diplomacy. 'Let's solve the problem ourselves!' So, Nishiyama ended up drafting a long letter to the head of the Board of Trade, going on about the merits of sake on health and how the Japanese needed sake for their well-being. Sure enough, about three weeks later, Tatsumi received a large envelope 'On His Majesty's Service', which contained the British response: the restriction on Japanese sake imports was lifted, and could the Yokohama Specie Bank kindly inform the Japanese community to this effect.

Okada Jūkichi was another banker assigned to London from 1913 to 1919. He served as Tatsumi's assistant at the Versailles Peace Conference, and the two stayed in a quiet hotel called the Saint James for about six months in 1919. Japan, as one of the victorious countries, had an impressive delegation with five plenipotentiaries, including Saionji Kinmochi, and a large number of experts to serve on various committees. Tatsumi was a member of the reparations committee and economics committee and their sub-committees. In those days, there was no Japanese translation, so all business was conducted in either English or French. It was Okada's job to takes notes of all the proceedings. Tatsumi, whose English was impeccable, would correct his reports. Okada recalled his former boss:

> Tatsumi could look stern on the outside, but he was extremely warm-hearted. He was particularly thoughtful towards his juniors. His needs were simple, and he took care of his own every day chores, so as his assistant, there was little for me to do. During our stay in Paris, Sutton, an English clerk from London also accompanied us, and was in the same hotel. He left his wife behind in London, and as the days went on, he started showing signs of mild depression. Noticing this, Tatsumi would find opportunities for Sutton to make trips back to London and helped him in many other ways. Sutton was enormously grateful for Tatsumi's thoughtfulness, and worked even harder for the Bank. In 1937, when Sutton was invited to visit Japan in recognition for his services to the Bank, unfortunately Tatsumi had already passed away.[14]

Tatsumi became a role model for many of the élite of London's small Japanese community. He had bought a large house in Streatham as the general manager's official residence, and showed by example the way in which a general manager should live. He socialized extensively with the British, but was also very kind and supportive to the Japanese community. He was generous almost to a fault, using his own money to subsidise bank expenses, and spending all his money, mainly on other people. He was also an extremely learned man. As soon as he heard of a new book, he would get hold of it and absorb knowledge. He believed that a bank prospered when its sporting spirits were high, and so leased, as many English banks did, a sports ground with a cricket field and six tennis courts in Lower Sydenham. By the time Tatsumi left London in 1920, Japan's position in the world had risen and the bank's business had expanded. The Japanese community had also become much bigger and more established. Tatsumi had done much to instil confidence and pride in the younger generation of community leaders.[15] Having arrived in London in 1892, even before the Sino-Japanese War, Tatsumi knew what it had been like to be from a country that had little to show for itself. Later in his life, Tatsumi recalled the two most memorable events in his mind during his stay in London: one was hearing about the Japanese victory over Russia in the Battle of Tsushima over the radio; and the other was Shimizu Zenzō's accomplishments at Wimbledon. He had carefully organized all the press clippings on Shimizu's Wimbledon victories – which was totally uncharacteristic of his usual lazy self.

Succeeding Tatsumi as London general manager was Okubo Toshikata, now married to Wakiko and with children. Okubo and Wakiko were known for their elegance at official dinner parties, dressed in formal *montsuki haori hakama* on Okubo's part and Wakiko in her beautiful kimonos. It was Wakiko's poise and command of English, however, that greatly impressed the British dignitaries. Japan had by now come a long way, comfortably mixing on equal terms with the élite of the British establishment in native dress, instead of trying desperately to emulate all manners and customs of the Western world. Despite his sophistication and accomplishments, Okubo never forgot how naïve and perplexed by Western customs he had been in his youth. He would recall way into old age how, on his first voyage abroad, he had found a beautiful enamel bowl in his cabin, and carefully placed his precious Japanese *konpeitō* sweets in it, only to find out later that it was his chamber pot! In London, Wakiko tried all sorts of innovations to make Okubo's favourite Japanese food. She even pickled cucumbers and horseradish in a makeshift *nukamiso* made from mixing beer and oatmeal.[16] In 1922, Okubo was seconded as member of the Japanese delegation to the Genoa Conference, and represented Japan in the Sub-Committee on Currencies, Trust and Foreign Exchange. He was transferred back to Japan in the spring of 1923 to become general manager at the main Yokohama office.

With Okubo's departure to Genoa, Yano Kanji became the London general manager, and left an invaluable record of his experience:

> Exactly a year after my appointment came the Great Kantō Earthquake. It was a time when Japan still had a large sum of money abroad, so the earthquake did not immediately affect the Bank's business. However, as more and more resources were needed for reconstruction, there was further demand for foreign exchange. The government decided to issue 6 per

cent, 25 million pound sterling bonds in London, and 6.5 per cent 150 million dollar bonds in New York. As one of the issuers, the Bank began preparatory work. It was a very difficult time to issue non-collateral bonds in London, but fortunately, John Ley of the Westminster Bank was very favourable towards Japan, and I sought him out to discuss the situation. He agreed to the non-collateral bonds. Shortly thereafter, Mori Kengo, the Financial Attaché returned to London, and Mr Tatsumi also came to help, so the bond issue was from then on in their capable hands.

The London business was many-faceted. Following the First World War, it was a time of unrestricted foreign exchange rates, which applied to the yen. Then futures became fashionable, and the price of silver fluctuated widely, making business more complicated. In April 1925, Britain went off the gold standard and pursued a deflationary policy. I was witness to the mounting unemployment that followed, and the famous general strike of May 1926. In April 1927 came the financial crisis in Japan which brought down a number of companies including Suzuki Shōten. I had to deal with this crisis from the London end, but fortunately, the Yokohama Specie Bank had built up years of credibility in the markets, which made my work much easier. I returned to Japan at the end of 1927.[17]

1927–1942

Yano was succeeded by Nohara Daisuke. Nohara's major achievement as London general manager was to arrange for the Imperial Japanese Government Stabilisation Credit in London of £5,000,000. This was a revolving credit in favour of the Yokohama Specie Bank London, to be available for a period of twelve months to enable the lifting of the embargo on the export of gold from Japan and the restoration of the gold standard, which became effective January 1930.[18] Nohara also made numerous overseas trips in his capacity as director of the Bank for International Settlements and the International Chamber of Commerce. These trips were well remembered by his children because he would bring back little gifts for them from his travels. The family life of the Noharas was similar to many of the top Japanese banking and business élite in London. The family consisted of Daisuke, his wife Etsu, and their three children, Yuki (b.1918), Masaya (b.1922) and Katsuya (b.1923). They lived in the general manager's residence in Streatham and had a governess, two upstairs maids, a cook, a kitchen-helper, a gardener and a driver. The children went to private schools in Streatham. Katsuya recalls his childhood:

English was spoken at home as we were brought up by our governess, and we could not speak Japanese. Sometime in 1933, a teacher from Seikei University who was studying in London, came to tutor us in the Japanese language but this did not last long because we complained that this was eating into our playtime. As a result, the only Japanese words that I knew were *sayonara* and *arigatō*. My parents had parties quite frequently but I do not know who the guests were as we were packed off upstairs to bed early every night. But we were able to hear some boisterous conversations in Japanese coming from the drawing-room.

The residence was quite large and spacious in my memory as a child but I do not know how many bedrooms there were. Our governess and the help lived on the third floor. The kitchen was in the basement. There also was a billiards room on the ground floor. There was a flower garden in the front and a lawn in the back where the adults played tennis and the boys played cricket. There was a gravel path that circled the house and the gardens and this is where the boys would race their bikes with their friends. My father played golf regularly with the Palmerston Old Boys [a social gathering of Japanese general managers in London] and they used to come to our home afterwards to quench their thirst. As I mentioned earlier, the children's contact with their parents was not that frequent. My father, being 15 years older than my mother, seemed to me to be dignified and strict. He was already quite bald and had a moustache and I do not recall ever seeing him without a necktie, except when he was playing tennis. In those days, they even played golf with their neckties on.[19]

The last general manager of the London branch was Kanō Hisaakira, who served from 1934 to 1942. Kanō followed Tatsumi's example and left most of the day-to-day Bank operations to his deputies while he threw himself wholeheartedly into trying to repair Japan's reputation and international standing, which had been severely tarnished by the Manchurian Incident of 1931 followed by Japan's occupation of Manchuria, the report of the Lytton Commission and Japan's subsequent withdrawal from the League of Nations in 1933. Kanō believed that friction between Britain and Japan was mainly of an economic and commercial nature, and that the two countries could and should cooperate, especially vis-à-vis China. He spoke to business groups, wrote articles, gave press interviews and initiated the Japan Society business lunch discussions, convinced that better understanding of Japan's economic position would lead to mutual respect.[20] The outbreak of the Sino-Japanese War in July 1937 was a severe shock to Kanō, who learned of the event during a trip to Scandinavia with his daughter, Rosa. As soon

Prince Chichibu in the doorway of the London Yokohama Specie Bank with Viscount Kano Hisaakira attending

as he heard the news, he took the next boat back to London. Kanō's activities now extended to various diplomatic negotiations, which went beyond banking and business circles. Thanks to his predecessors' efforts and his own personal contacts, he had access to the highest levels within both British and Japanese banking and government circles. He used his position and connections to the full to advocate his opinions and negotiate for peace. However, the outlook was increasingly grim. In 1940, the London branch's bond-selling rights were restricted, and the Borrowing Limit Agreement was cancelled. The flow of capital between Britain and Japan and the US and Japan was also stopped. In July 1941, when the US and Britain froze Japan's assets, Kanō believed that war was inevitable. However, in November, he became party to a final round of negotiations with those within the British establishment who shared his view that war between Britain and Japan should be avoided. These efforts continued until 6 December 1941.

A few months later, Kanō wrote:

> Monday, December 8th, 1941, was a tragic day. The war broke out between Great Britain and Japan. I left Princes Gate Court [Kanō's residence which he moved from Streatham] at 7 o'clock on that morning and took No.9 Bus to the City. As soon as I arrived at my office, the London Branch of the Yokohama Specie Bank, I called in ten Japanese colleagues to

245

my room, and told each one of them the most important thing at this time were 'Health and Character'. I told all British colleagues and messengers – about 60 in all them – (about 30 were already in military service) that the extremely sad situation had developed entirely contrarily to what I had worked and wished for, and thanked them for their friendship and assistance in the past, and prayed for the early return of happy days.'[21]

On 8 December, the bank was closed for business, and in the afternoon, the police came and took nine Japanese staff for internment on the Isle of Man. Kanō, who was spared internment, continued to work with the bank's British controller to transfer all business and property under the authorization of the Board of Trade. On 23 January 1942, a chartered accountant was officially appointed as liquidator of the bank, and Kanō was relieved of his duties. In March, Kanō was arrested by Home Office officials and taken to the Isle of Man. His short internment ended when in the summer of 1942, he and the other interned bank staff and their families left for Yokohama on the *Tatsuta Maru* as a part of the exchange repatriation.

In the aftermath of the war, the Allied Occupation saw the need to dissolve the Yokohama Specie Bank for its significant role in financing the war. At the same time, it acknowledged that the experience and skills of the bank should be in some way preserved. Thus the Yokohama Specie Bank was restructured to become the Bank of Tokyo. Kanō and all other surviving London general managers were purged and banned from holding public office until 1950.

23

The Nippon Yūsen Kaisha (NYK): Two important British Managers, Albert Brown and Thomas James

H.TAKENO[1]

Thomas James   Alfred Richard Brown

IN 1864, P&O, the world's largest shipping company at that time, extended its regular UK/Far Eastern service from Shanghai to Japan, just five years after the opening of Yokohama to foreign trade. It was not until 1896, thirty-two years later, that Nippon Yusen Kaisha (NYK) inaugurated its Japan/Europe service with a cargo-passenger liner of 6,000 gross tons under the command of a British Captain, with British and Japanese Officers.

Two important British mariners, Albert R. Brown and Thomas H. James, devoted their lives to developing Japanese nautical facilities and education for the merchant marine and the navy. They also played an essential role at the inception of NYK by helping it access overseas trade using modern steamships – newly built and mainly in Scotland.

ALBERT R. BROWN

Little is known of Albert's early years except that he was born in 1839 at

Ringwood in Hampshire and that, when he was fourteen years of age, he became an ordinary seaman aboard a brig trading to the West Indies, Newfoundland, the Mediterranean, and other places. When he was eighteen years old, he was rated as an able-bodied seaman. He later became an acting fourth mate aboard a China Clipper, i.e. an East Indiaman. Brown received his second mate's certificate in 1860 and joined P&O as fourth officer in a steam-and-sail vessel on a voyage to Calcutta, where in 1864 he passed the provincial examination for his first mate's certificate. He joined the SS *Malacca* in 1865 as first officer, the last vessel of the P&O or British registry in which he would serve, and sailed from London for Bombay, thence to enter the coastal service between Hong Kong and Shanghai. P&O had started a regular mail service between Shanghai and Japan in 1864 and the company's vessels now terminated at Yokohama. In the summer of 1866 in Ringwood, he married the sister of Jim Pyne, an old shipmate. At the end of that year, the SS *Malacca* departed from her regular ferry service for her first voyage to Nagasaki and Yokohama.

The Japanese government at that time was sending young men abroad for study, and to purchase ships as well as engines and other equipment. At the same time there were attractive openings for foreign advisers and instructors to assist in the Japanese effort to make up for their long period of isolation from the outside world. At the end of 1867 when the *Malacca* arrived at Yokohama, Albert Brown met the man whose employment by the Japanese government brought his first command, and led the way to a distinguished career.

Under the terms of treaties signed between Japan and the foreign powers, lighthouses were to be erected around the coasts, lightships installed, channels buoyed, harbour works put in hand and the waters around the entire archipelago surveyed and charted. The Board of Trade in London recommended D. & T.Stevenson of Edinburgh, which had much experience in lighthouse construction, to appoint a superintendent engineer and his assistants and to supply the necessary equipment, as well as keepers to operate the lighthouses until Japanese were trained for the work. They recommended the appointment of Richard H.Brunton[2] to fill this post. Brunton reached Japan in August 1868 together with his assistants and some equipment. A lighthouse department was formed under the Japanese government and a lighthouse tender, a barque-rigged screw steamer of 374 tons, was purchased with her name changed to *Tomio Maru*.

Richard Brunton needed a qualified master and first-class navigator, capable of carrying out survey work as well as being experienced in handling heavy lifts and likely to get along with the Japanese. Brown who had already qualified for his master's certificate at Hong Kong, was offered command of the *Tomio Maru*, at $300 per month, a house at Yokohama, and paid passage for his wife and child to Yokohama. It was excellent pay, the conditions were good, and he was intrigued by the prospects of taking part in the development of the Japanese lighthouse system. So he agreed to submit his resignation to P&O and took the first available steamer back to Yokohama from Hong Kong.

Albert Brown had cause for elation and pride in his first command, the *Tomio Maru*, and was no doubt conscious of the fascinating part he would play in exploring the entire Japanese archipelago, surveying and lighting the hitherto uncharted and unmarked coasts. Afterwards, Brown drew up his own plans for what he considered the ideal lighthouse tender and survey vessel to replace the *Tomio Maru*, and in March 1870, the *Thabor*, a French paddle-steamer of 800 gross tons, was purchased from Messageries Maritimes.

In the meantime, the Japanese realized that time had come to start developing a mercantile marine for international trade. Albert Brown was appointed the first instructor of Japanese mercantile officers, training them in mathematics, navigation, seamanship, etc. This project was very much his own idea. It eventually led to the opening of the Mitsubishi Nautical School in November 1875, the forerunner of the present Tokyo Mercantile Marine College.

In November 1874, when Albert Brown was staying in England to take delivery of a new Japanese lighthouse survey vessel, SS *Meiji Maru*, embodying all that Brown had envisaged for the type of work in which she was to be engaged, he received from Tokyo a request to purchase two steam vessels, fit them out, engage officers and crew, and dispatch them to Yokohama for the Mitsubishi Mail Steamship Co.

When Brown returned to Japan in the late spring of 1875, he was immediately asked to assist in the formation of a Marine Bureau, to draw up regulations, and to take charge of all matters connected with shipbuilding and mercantile marine under the Japanese Postmaster-General. The government was delighted with the *Meiji Maru* which had arrived in March. So was Iwasaki Yatarō[3] with two new vessels, which were placed on the first overseas service between Yokohama and Shanghai. After a period of cut-throat competition, the Mitsubishi Co. bought up Pacific Mail's four vessels, as well as its land and warehouses at Kobe, Nagasaki and Shanghai. Later, P&O placed two vessels on the route, leading to such a reduction in passenger fares and freight rates that disaster threatened both firms. P&O, however, after severe competition with the Mitsubishi Co., which was protected by the Japanese government, was forced to give up serving this route.

In the spring of 1877 the Mitsubishi Co. proceeded with its plan to build new ships and requested the Postmaster-General to let Brown go to England and supervise the new building. He was busy at yards on the Clyde, the Tyne, and in London, and he was frequently asked by British shipping firms for advice on Japanese maritime affairs. He returned to Japan in 1879 and continued to manage the Marine Bureau under the Postmaster-General as 'Chief Examiner for Masters and Mates, surveyor of vessels, and Assistant Superintendent of the Mercantile Marine'.

In 1881, Albert Brown was forty-two years old. In the space of twelve years in the service of the Japanese government he had become one of its most trusted and respected advisers. Tokyo was now Brown's head-quarters and he was busily engaged in work at the bureau, at the nautical school, as examiner of masters and mates, and at the new hydro-graphic department in his capacity as assistant. This meant that he was, in effect, executive superintendent of the Marine Bureau.

Mitsubishi continued to prosper and expand, giving rise to further complaints over what were termed its unfair privileges, and claims that Japan's mercantile marine could not progress in conditions where one company held such a preponderance of shipping business. Finally, the Government agreed to sponsor the Kyōdō Transportation Company, which was formed by the merger of three companies including one organized by Mitsui & Co., Mitsubishi's rivals. Early in 1883, Brown was sent to England to place orders and supervise the construction of new vessels for Kyōdō as well as for Mitsubishi. By early 1885, Kyōdō's ships were engaged in fierce competition with Mitsubishi both in coastal trade and in the services to Shanghai and Korea. Although Mitsubishi had been well prepared from the beginning to meet the challenge from Kyōdō, the fare for a third-class passenger between Yokohama and Kobe fell from ¥5.00 to ¥0.25. Despite the fact that both companies faced the prospect of bankruptcy they continued a senseless struggle for supremacy until in January 1885 the government ordered them to conclude agreements on freights and passenger fares, schedules of services and the employment of seamen. When Iwasaki Yataro died in February 1885 there seemed to be a temporary truce between the two major shipping companies.

But in April 1885 the competition was more severe than ever. Realizing that the critical moment had now arrived, the government wisely ordered Mitsubishi and Kyōdō to conclude a merger. This resulted in October 1885, in the establishment of the Nippon Yūsen Kaisha (Japan Mail Steamship Co. or NYK). Japan's foremost shipping company was thus born with fifty-eight ships and an aggregate of 64,609 gross tons. Albert Brown was asked to take over as general manager at its head office in Tokyo.

New tonnage was, however, vital before NYK could implement its plans for expanded services. Brown left for England once again in the spring of 1887 to supervise the new building programme at shipyards on the Clyde and Tyne. During 1887 and 1888 he was fully occupied at Glasgow. Later, he decided that it would be better for him to settle there and open an office to handle all the various programmes which NYK envisaged in order to place its services on a world-wide footing. He tendered his resignation as general manager of NYK at the end of March, 1889, in order to devote all his time to the company's building programme in Britain and to give more time to his family.

In June 1896, NYK increased its capital from 8,800,000 to 22,000,000 for the purpose of building new tonnage, i.e. twelve vessels for the projected Japan/Europe service, three for the Japan/North America, and three for the Japan/Australia lines. This programme kept Brown as well as the Clyde and other shipyards busy for some time. Brown was also appointed consul for Japan at Glasgow. The SS *Shinano Maru*, built under Brown's supervision, became famous as the first ship to spot the Russian Baltic Fleet on 27 May 1905. The course and speed of the fleet was reported, thus enabling Admiral Tōgo, who had been trained at the Royal Naval College, to prepare his fleet, which had been mainly built in UK, for action in the Straits of Tsushima. This led to Japan's victory over Russia. The Anglo-Japanese Alliance was helpful to Japan in war finance, intelligence, and naval and maritime support.

In 1909 Brown was awarded the Order of the Sacred Treasure, Second Class, in recognition of his services to Japan. This was presented to him at the Japanese Embassy in London. He died at Bournemouth in 1913 at the age of 74.

NYK owes much to Brown's devotion to the operation of its ships which had been built in the UK and which in the early days had British masters.

THOMAS HENRY JAMES

Thomas Henry James was born in 1848. He joined the Royal Navy in March 1863 as master's assistant on HMS *Cossack*. In 1865 he was appointed navigating midshipman and assigned to HMS *Caradoc* in the Mediterranean. He was promoted navigating sub-lieutenant in March 1868 and navigating lieutenant in June 1875. In August of that year he retired from the Royal Navy but remained on half-pay until August 1880. In 1876 he went to Japan and was employed by the Navy Ministry as an instructor of navigation and a teacher of mathematics at the Japanese Naval College.

Henry F.Woods, who had served in Yokohama from 1863-67, who was with James on HMS *Caradoc* and who became a close friend, claims[4] that his tales of Japan induced James to 'take service under the Japanese Flag'. While serving in the Mediterranean James married Kate, the daughter of a Scottish Episcopalian Minister, then working in Constantinople as a governess.

Woods recorded that James while he was navigating instructor to the Imperial cadets 'sailed all over the Pacific in command of the Japanese training vessel with the celebrated Admiral Tōgo as one of the officers under his command. He was very much esteemed by the Japanese, as were all the members of his family, and he was trusted by them as few Europeans settled in Japan ever have been.'[5]

It is not known what James did after his six years at the Naval College, but his name appeared in a history published by the Mitsubishi Mail Steamship Co. which stated that in July 1885 he was the superintendent of navigation on the Yokohama Maru on which the Meiji Emperor was travelling by sea to Hiroshima. This was two months before the Company merged with Kyōdō and it can be assumed that James worked for the Mitsubishi Co. during the three years from 1882 to 1885.

NYK inherited all the key staff members who had worked for the Mitsubishi Co. and Kyōdō and only two months after Albert Brown had resigned from NYK in June 1889 Thomas James was appointed navigation supervisor with responsibility for the entire NYK fleet which would be operating both in coastal and overseas trades.

In terms of tonnage of ships owned and operated as well as income and profit from purely shipping business, NYK is today the world's largest shipping enterprise. But, before NYK started its first regular service between Bombay and Japan in 1893, all the distant trades of Japan had been dominated by P&O and other European and American ship-owners. In 1896 when NYK attempted to inaugurate a regular Japan/Europe cargo/passenger service with twelve new ships, of which ten were projected to be built at British shipyards, Thomas James was sent to its newly-opened London office as manager to operate the new service.

At that time, more than half of the world's merchant tonnage was flying the Red Ensign and more than 80% of the tonnage employed in the Europe/Far East trade was owned and operated by British ship-owners, including P&O, Alfred Holt & Co., and others. These companies impeded full NYK access to the major ports on the line between London and Shanghai. With the profits made during the Sino-Japanese War of 1894-5, and with the benefit of a government subsidy, NYK was able to initiate its European service, but could not sustain it in the face of the major institutional and economic barriers to entry into this British-dominated business. The most difficult barrier was the conference system, the cartel-like organization of British and other European ship-owners. The effectiveness of the Far Eastern Freight Conference (FEFC) depended on a number of exclusionary devices designed to prevent the entry of outsiders and on control measures to regulate the business of member lines.

The most important exclusionary device was the 'deferred rebate'. This rebate, usually amounting to 5 to 10% of the freight, was deferred to ensure that the shipper avoided using non-conference vessels during a period of six months. The 'loyal' shipper would receive his rebate at the end of this period. A second device was the allocation of access to ports. Most members of the FEFC had, over the years, built up their own trades around home ports, the most important being London and Liverpool in Europe, and Shanghai in the Far East. Generally, members of the FEFC were allowed to load or discharge cargo at only these designated ports. In other circumstances, an outsider seeking access to berthing facilities without the sanction of the FEFC might be subject to a rate war, or shippers aligned with it might boycott his ships. Because of the British dominance of the FEFC, control of port access was the most restrictive measure from the viewpoint of NYK.

NYK's initial strategy was to dispense with calls at London, the world's largest centre of commerce, so that it could avoid antagonizing the senior British members of the Far Eastern Freight Conference and in May 1896 NYK entered into an agreement with the FEFC on restrictive conditions. However, with the decline in its freight shipments from Middlesbrough and Southampton which were permitted under the agreement, NYK's European service was placed in a very difficult financial position. Thomas James, now the principal company negotiator with the FEFC, suggested that NYK abandon Southampton and make London its port of call on the eastbound voyage. The board approved the recommendation with the qualification: 'Since there will be fierce competition because of this move, to prevent the negative effects from spreading beyond London, implement the decision only after first negotiating with the P&O.'

Being well aware of the way of thinking of the British lines, James rejected this tactic as over-cautious, and argued that 'it is better not to negotiate with the P&O before implementing the move'. He suggested that the Company simply give notice. The directors accepted his advice and, while fully expecting strong repercussions from and severe competition with the British lines concerned, NYK made London its last port of loading on eastbound voyages and entrusted the bargaining with the FEFC and with P&O to Thomas James, who had been appointed in 1897 as the second general manager of NYK's London office after the first Japanese general manager had left London for health reasons. Several days later, as planned, James sent a withdrawal notice to the FEFC. He then started discussion with John Swire & Sons, the representative of the FEFC, who were trying to mediate between the interested lines. After tough negotiations, the principle of NYK loading at London was accepted and agreement on standard clauses was achieved fairly quickly, including the stipulation that the NYK was not to call at or carry goods for trans-shipment to Shanghai. Thus NYK became the first foreign ship-owner permitted to load cargo at London on the eastbound voyage; thanks to the subsidy granted by the Japanese government, NYK was successfully admitted to the FEFC in 1899.

While the eastbound service was profitable, NYK's westbound service was deficit ridden during the early years of the line. This was due to the different content of the trades resulting from Japan's unbalanced trade relations with Europe, and NYK's lack of privileges in Chinese ports. NYK ships bound for Europe in early 1901 were loaded only to one-fifth of capacity, and loading freight at Shanghai en route to Europe was the only way in which a financial improvement could be achieved. As negotiations bogged down in late 1901, NYK decided, as in the case of London, to act unilaterally and institute calls at Shanghai before an agreement with the FEFC had been reached. Then, after the classic response of the FEFC with a warning to shippers not to provide cargo for NYK, and owing to Thomas James's subtle negotiations with British lines, NYK was eventually permitted to load cargo at Shanghai on westbound voyages. This proved more advantageous than NYK had anticipated.

Thomas James served as general manager of NYK's London office for thirteen years from 1897 to 1910. The board established a pension plan for him in recognition of his services to the Company during the early years of the European service. This later constituted a major part of NYK's overseas business.

During the years he lived in Japan, his wife, Kate, learnt Japanese and translated many Japanese fairy tales into English. Her books, which were published in Japan in English, were read by many foreigners who visited Japan at that time and who were interested in Japanese culture. As a result she became more famous than her husband in Japan.

James died of pneumonia in 1910 and the post of General Manager of NYK's London office was assumed by R.Negishi who had been working under James in London since 1896.

24

HSBC: A Fellowship in Banking. Pioneers in Japan, 1866–1900

EDWIN GREEN

Thomas Jackson   A.M. Townsend

THE HONGKONG and Shanghai Banking Corporation [HSBC][1] has a long history of business commitment in Japan. A striking feature of that history is the way in which HSBC was a pioneer and prototype of banking and international finance in nineteenth-century Japan. It was equally important, from the point of view of the bank's own development, that the bankers who served as managers in Japan formed an especially distinguished and influential group in HSBC's early history. This essay offers a portrait of this fellowship and its role in the financial history of Japan.

THE MERCANTILE BANK

HSBC was not the first foreign bank to open in Japan. Although Japan had long-established currency and payments' systems, the first bank on the modern pattern to open an office in Japan was the Chartered Mercantile Bank of India, London and China [the Mercantile], which opened an office in Yokohama in 1863. This bank, founded in Bombay in 1853 and eventually acquired by HSBC in 1959, had already built up a network of

255

branches in the Indian sub-continent, Mauritius, the Malayan peninsular, and in Hong Kong and Shanghai. Walter Ormiston, the Mercantile's manager in Hong Kong, visited Japan in the early 1860s and reported enthusiastically to his directors on the country's prospects for banking.[2] In the aftermath of the commercial treaties between Japan and the prominent trading nations of the West in 1858, clearly there was a need for banking services in support of the changing economy of Japan. The finance of trade with treaty ports such as Yokohama was especially vital at the time of the bank's arrival.

The Mercantile's office – which issued its own bank notes at Yokohama in addition to its ordinary banking business – survived the commercial crisis of 1865-66 and appeared to have established a small but steady business. It also drew to Japan a significant newcomer, Alexander Allan Shand, who was employed mainly at the Mercantile's Yokohama office between 1866 and 1872. His contemporaries there included Takahashi Korekiyo, later a vice-president of both the Yokohama Specie Bank and the Bank of Japan.[3] Shand himself left the Mercantile in 1872 but subsequently he was a respected adviser to the Japanese government on currency and banking matters.

The London-based Mercantile, although it was the forerunner of modern banking in Japan, never devoted sufficient resources to the Yokohama office to ensure that it had a long-term presence. The office closed in September 1879 under pressure from the 1878-79 banking crisis, re-opened in May 1880 but closed again in 1885.[4] Meanwhile, other stronger competitors had appeared on the banking scene in Japan. The Oriental Bank, at that time the largest of the Eastern exchange banks, opened an office in Yokohama in 1865 and then won the contract for the Meiji government's first foreign loans in 1870 and 1873.[5] The most significant new arrival, however, came from Hong Kong.

HSBC OPENS IN JAPAN

HSBC was established in Hong Kong in March 1865, winning wide support from a local business community which was keen that Hong Kong should have its 'own' bank on the China coast and beyond. Branches were opened in Shanghai and London in the same year. Japan was also high on the list of priorities for the new bank and, as early as May 1865, the merchant firm of Macpherson and Marshall was appointed as the bank's agent in Yokohama.[6] That presence was quickly upgraded when the bank's own office was opened in Yokohama in 1866, one of only four full branches of the bank at the time. An office was rented at 62 Yamashita-cho, Yokohama, and four years later the bank acquired the property for HK$20,000.

The manager of HSBC's new office in Japan was Robert Brett,

formerly the Mercantile's manager at Yokohama. He made an early impact when in 1866 he and Septimus Short (his successor at the Mercantile) proposed a solution to the long-standing problem of different qualities of dollar currencies in Japan. Chinese compradores had been able to corner the supply of first-class coinage and force inferior currency into circulation, to the consternation of the trading community in Yokohama. Brett and Short recommended that the Japanese Custom House should only accept duty payments at par in first-rate currency, and that all the foreign banks should follow suit with their own settlements. This solution, which was approved by the Japanese authorities and by representatives of the foreign communities, provided Japan with a single, widely accepted currency standard. It was equally important from HSBC's point of view: this was the bank's first experience of advising on or influencing monetary policy in the countries where it was doing business. This was a valuable precedent for the bank's activities in Japan later in the nineteenth century.

Brett's reign in Yokohama was brief. He was dismissed in May 1867, allegedly on the grounds that he had speculated in the same currency that he had already helped to reform.[7] He was replaced as manager by John Grigor, who had the distinction of being the bank's very first employee when it had opened for business in 1865. While in Japan, Grigor was able to reinforce HSBC's presence by persuading the directors to open an agency in Hyogo in 1869, with Henry Smith as the first agent. Hyogo (later Kobe) and Osaka had only been opened to foreign trade in the previous year, and the new office soon proved to be 'very useful' to the bank's Shanghai office, especially in connection with bullion operations.[8] This office was based at 80 Kyo-machi in Kobe (this later became the Oriental Hotel), and from 1881 the bank occupied the old offices of Walsh, Hall and Co. on the Bund.

Grigor continued at Yokohama until 1871, when he was recalled to Hong Kong. The directors discovered that he had made an unauthorized loan to a European firm which had subsequently cost the bank a loss of HK$20,000. Grigor was offered the chance of a fresh start in Hong Kong but he chose to leave the service. Like Brett, Grigor had been a pathfinder but he had not been the successful pioneer that HSBC needed in Japan.

It was not until the appointment of Thomas Jackson as manager in 1871 that the bank began to enjoy longer-term success. Moreover, it was not until the 1870s that the management and staffing of HSBC branches began to settle into a distinctive pattern – a pattern which was to give character and continuity to the bank's business in Japan. Before looking at the careers of Jackson and his successors in greater detail, an explanation of this staff and management context may be helpful.

EASTERN STAFF

In the first years of the bank's existence, HSBC had recruited its senior staff from other banks in the East and from merchant houses on the China coast. Hence Brett had worked for the Mercantile and Grigor had been recruited from the Bank of Hindustan, China and Japan. Similarly, the bank borrowed from the experience and expertise of its recruits and adapted the procedures and organization of other Eastern banks.

From the late 1860s and early 1870s, in contrast, the bank recruited and trained its own 'Eastern staff'. These European staff were recruited in London and, by 1876, HSBC's directors strongly recommended that 'in future all clerks joining the service should go through the London office, save under very exceptional circumstances'.[9] Ordinarily, candidates were expected to offer experience in a British bank or in another relevant profession. New recruits served two or more years in London, learning the basics of international banking in departments such as current accounts, fixed deposits, inward and outward Bills. Those who stayed the course were then posted to Hong Kong, where they again spent a period of induction, working in the head office building and housed in the bank's bachelor mess. Both in London and in Hong Kong, these juniors formed a camaraderie and developed an understanding of the workings of the bank. They were then posted to HSBC's branches elsewhere in the East. It was a condition of service that each 'tour' continued for approximately four years, followed by a long leave of nine months. The bank's staff, in common with employees of other banks and trading 'hongs' in the East, were not permitted to marry until they had completed two tours. Depending upon their abilities (and to some extent their good fortune), members of the Eastern staff were subsequently appointed to increasingly senior positions in the branches, progressing from assistant, to accountant, acting or assistant manager, and then to manager or agent.

The first juniors who were recruited in this way 'went East' to Hong Kong in 1871 and, thereafter, the great majority of HSBC's Eastern staff followed the same path. The change in the composition of the staff was exemplified in the Japanese branches. In 1871 four of the five Eastern staff who worked in Japan during the year had all seen service with other banks or merchant houses in the East. By 1900, when ten Eastern staff were in post at Yokohama, six in Kobe (Hyogo) and two in Nagasaki (where an agency had opened in 1891), the entire group had graduated through London office and the initial period in Hong Kong.

OTHER EMPLOYEES

Clearly the history of international banking in the East is much wider in scope than the history of groups of expatriate bankers. The contribution of local staff is a large but neglected topic in banking history.[10] In the case of

HSBC in Japan, for example, the bank also employed Portuguese, Chinese and Japanese staff for banking duties. Other local staff were employed as guards, messengers and for domestic duties. In 1887, the banking staff at Yokohama consisted of seven members of the Eastern staff, four Portuguese and one Japanese clerk (S. H. Hayashi); at Hyogo there were Eastern staff and three Portuguese.[11] In each case the total number of bank employees more than doubled when messengers, guards and domestic staff at the branch and at the bank houses are included. Exact numbers have not survived in the branch records but a photograph of the entire office staff at Hyogo in 1899 shows a total of no less than 33 employees.

Important as this support was, the fortunes of the bank in Japan were tied closely to the abilities and performance of the branch managers and other senior staff. These officers, listed in Table 1, were each in post at the Japanese branches for an average period of nearly three years between 1866 and 1900.[12] There were exceptions. Rodham Home Cook, notably, worked in the Yokohama office from his arrival in the East in 1872 until 1881. Thereafter he was appointed agent at Saigon and then at Amoy but he returned to Japan as agent at Kobe (Hyogo) in 1886, from 1889 to 1892, and again from 1897 until he went on leave in 1903 (he died in the following year). Cook's total service in Japan in this way amounted to nearly 20 years. Such lengthy sojourns in the Japanese branches were rare, however, and by the 1870s it was already an accepted part of bank service that there should be a regular turnover of management and staff.

Table 1. The Hongkong and Shanghai Banking Corporation,
senior officers in Japan, 1866–1900

Date appointed	Yokohama, manager	Hyogo (Kobe), agent	Nagasaki, agent
1866	W.R. Brett		
1867	John Grigor		
1868			
1869		H.C. Smith	
1870			
1871	T. Jackson	G. Moody/W.H. Harries	
1872		W.H. Harries	
1873			
1874			
1875		J.J. Winton	
1876	J.Walter	A.M. Townsend	
1877	A.L. Turner	J. Morrison	
1878	A.M. Townsend		
1879			
1880	J. Walter		
1881		James M. Grigor	
1882		A.H.C. Haselwood	
1883			
1884	E. Morriss		
1885			
1886		R.H. Cook	
1887		J.F. Broadbent	
1888		A.Haselwood/R.H. Cook	
1889		R.H. Cook	
1890			
1891	H.M. Bevis		
1892	A. Veitch/D. Jackson	A.D. Mactavish	A.B. Anderson
1893	D. Jackson		
1894			
1895			
1896			T.S. Baker
1897	H.M. Bevis	R.H. Cook (to 1903)	
1898			
1899	D. Jackson (to 1903)		J. Maclean (to 1903)
1900			

Source: Staff lists, 1892 ff., HSBC Group Archives, S1.1; Seniority list, 1866–1891, compiled by Catherine E. King (1987), HSBC Group Archives, S1.10.

THOMAS JACKSON

Among this group of HSBC bankers, a number of individuals were able to make a longer-term impression on the bank's business in Japan and on the wider development of Japanese finance. Thomas Jackson, who succeeded Grigor in Yokohama in 1871, was already an outstanding prospect in Eastern banking. Born in 1841 at Carrigallen, County Leitrim, in Ireland, Jackson had joined the Bank of Ireland at its Belfast branch in 1860. After this apprenticeship in branch-based commercial banking, like many of his contemporaries in Irish and Scottish banking he was attracted by the openings available in overseas banking.[13] In 1864 Jackson accepted a three-year clerkship with the Agra and Masterman's Bank and was posted to the Agra's Hong Kong office. When that bank ran into difficulties in the mid-1860s, Jackson promptly sought and found a post with HSBC, where he began work in August 1866. Within a year he was accountant at the bank's Shanghai branch, already being promoted ahead of more senior members of the bank's first generation of staff, and his appointment as agent, Hankow, in 1868 was his first managerial role. Nevertheless his appointment to Yokohama in 1869 (initially as assistant manager and then as manager from 1871) was a choice which strongly influenced both the bank's business in Japan and the management succession within the bank itself.

Jackson was keenly aware of the bank's opportunities in the new Japan. In 1872 he set up facilities for Japanese merchants entering the bullion trade in connection with the Japanese Mint (which had been established at Osaka in 1869). His customers also included a variety of European and American merchant houses. Walsh, Hall and Co., trading in tea, tobacco and other commodities, was the largest of these customers in Jackson's time. Heard and Co. (trading in tea), Abegg, Borel and Co. (wine), J.M. Jacquemot (silk), Bavier and Co. (cotton, yarn and velvet), Van Oordt and Co. (copper and iron bars and plates), and the Netherlands Trading Society also banked with HSBC in Yokohama. Smaller, more domestic accounts included the Yokohama Choral Society and the Yokohama Cricket Club. At this stage it was rare for the bank to have direct banking connections with Japanese firms, as their credits and other transactions were still being handled by the foreign trading firms. However Jackson's customers in 1875 did include Senshui Kaisha, trading in rice, tea, camphor, navy cloth and straw hats.[14] His successors in the 1880s followed suit by acting as bankers for the forerunners of Furukawa, Mitsui and Mitsubishi.

A.M. Townsend, one of the first bank juniors to set out from the London office to the East, remembered meeting Jackson at this stage of his career. En route from San Francisco to Hong Kong in 1871, Townsend recalled:

. . . a fine view of Fujiyama as we approached the coast. We arrived in [Yokohama] Harbour early one morning and hastily found our way to the Bank – Thomas Jackson was the Manager. He welcomed us in his pyjamas, gave us breakfast, provided us with a guide to show us all the sights of the town, and, in the evening, got ponies and took us for a ride round Mississippi Bay . . . and then to dinner with Jackson, who dressed me up in one of his white cotton suits, which did fairly well when the trousers were turned up . . . The next morning when we returned to our steamer, we found to our surprise in our cabin, a case containing champagne and other wine, with Jackson's good wishes. This was the beginning of a life-long friendship with him . . .[15]

This snapshot of Jackson helps to explain why, in his later career, he was renowned for his view of the bank as a 'family' of shared experiences and interests. It also illustrates his enthusiasm for Japan, where he appeared to be putting down roots. He married Amelia Lydia Dare in Yokohama in 1871 and, when in 1872 he was offered the managership of the bank's prestigious Shanghai office, Jackson turned down the offer. He preferred to remain in Yokohama and develop HSBC's growing business in Japan.

Jackson remained in Yokohama until 1876, when he was recalled to Hong Kong to become chief manager of the bank. Still only thirty-four years of age, Jackson proved to be one of the outstanding bankers of his generation, facing down the banking crises of the late 1870s and then driving the growth of HSBC's business in the 1880s. When he retired in 1888, the bank's total assets had more than trebled from HK$ 34.6 million in 1875 to HK$ 114.6 million. He returned for two further terms as chief manager in 1890 and between 1893 and 1902, thereafter acting as chairman of the advisory committee in London until his death in 1915. Throughout this distinguished career, he watched over the bank's progress in Japan with special interest, particularly during negotiations over Japanese loans for which HSBC acted as the principal banker (see below). Moreover, the family connection with Japan continued. Thomas Jackson's brother David also joined the bank, going East in 1878. He also progressed to become manager in Yokohama, serving two spells between 1892 and 1897 and between 1899 and his death in service in 1903.

JOHN WALTER

Thomas Jackson was succeeded at Yokohama by John Walter, who served as manager for six months in 1876-77 before being called back to act as manager at Shanghai. His main contribution to the bank's business in Japan followed rather later, as manager at Yokohama between 1880 and 1884. Previously on the staff of the trading firm of Dent and Co. at

Shanghai, Walter had joined the bank in 1868 and he subsequently worked in Hankow and Shanghai and also deputised for Jackson in Yokohama in 1875. Like Jackson, Walter graduated from Yokohama to more senior posts in the bank, including acting chief manager in 1886, Shanghai manager in 1889-90 and, after his retirement from the East in 1891, inspector of branches and London assistant manager. He joined the London advisory committee in 1902 and continued in that influential group until 1906. 'A rather short and stocky man with . . . a twinkle in his eye',[16] Walter in this way joined the group of ex-Japan managers who were at the centre of the bank's affairs in the 1890s and early 1900s.

ALFRED TOWNSEND

Alfred Townsend, the junior who had met Jackson in Yokohama in 1871, was squarely in the same category of influential managers. Originally a clerk at the Bradford branch of the Yorkshire Banking Company, he was introduced to HSBC in 1866.[17] He then spent two years in the London office and in 1870 he was one of the first juniors to 'go East' after the standard period of induction. His periods of duty in Japan were relatively brief − he was agent in Kobe (Hyogo) in 1876-77 and manager in Yokohama in 1878-80 − but they clearly left a strong impression. Late in life, he also published valuable recollections of his career in the bank. He remembered his career in Kobe (Hyogo) as 'very pleasant and interesting':

> The old Daimio Government was being overthrown and the new Emperor installed. There was fighting in the Southern provinces and troops often passed through. A year before, when a regiment was passing through Kobe, some English sailors rudely broke through the ranks, when a young Japanese officer fired and killed one of them. For this he was condemned to death, but allowed to commit Hari-kari, which he did in the presence of his regiment (and of the British Minister), which I think was not quite right.[18]

Two years later, he was manager in Yokohama, following the death of A. L. Turner. 'Though I suffered from Malaria I managed to keep going and the business prospered'. Certainly, there was a marked growth of HSBC's activity in Japan, especially after the temporary closure of the Mercantile in 1879 and serious difficulties at the Oriental Bank. Between March and May 1879, for instance, a total of 71 new accounts were opened at the branch, increasing its deposits by HK$306,864. It was also important that Townsend followed up Brett's much earlier initiatives on the reform of the currency. In July 1879, in particular, the Japanese government deposited ¥300,000 on condition that HSBC's Yokohama branch would accept silver yen as currency. Townsend continues:

We were friendly with our Minister, Sir Harry Parkes, and I had pleasant relations with the Japanese Finance Minister, and assisted him to establish the Japanese Yen, coined at the Mint at Osaka, as currency in place of the Mexican dollar. Some of the Foreign Community were critical and thought I was forcing an inferior coinage on them; but as they were mostly debtors to the Bank, they had not a strong case, and anyhow it was not long before the yen was accepted as even a superior coin to the Mexican dollar.[19]

Townsend left Yokohama in 1880 and was then posted to New York, where he opened a new HSBC agency and oversaw the growth of the bank's American business over the next twenty years. He transferred to the London office in 1901, first as assistant manager and then as senior manager from 1905 until retirement in 1912.[20] In that role his experience and expertise in Japanese finance were vital assets to the bank. HSBC was an issuing bank for the series of Japanese government loans between 1897 and 1910, usually in partnership with Yokohama Specie Bank and Parr's Bank, London. A total of no less than £160 million was issued in this way and dedicated to industrial and infrastructural projects in Japan as well as meeting the heavy commitments incurred during Japan's war with Russia in 1904-05. In the same period HSBC also participated in Japanese railway and municipal loans for new harbours, waterworks and gasworks. The bank shared in the issue of ¥278 million of these loans between 1906 and 1912.[21] In recognition of these achievements, the Emperor of Japan awarded Townsend two Orders of the Sacred Treasure and the Order of the Rising Sun.

SETBACKS AND CASUALTIES

In common with other international enterprises in the later nineteenth century, HSBC only earned its place as a pioneer at the cost of setbacks and sacrifices. Inevitably, the bank's achievements in Japan were not an unbroken run of success. Brett and Grigor, the first two managers in Yokohama, disappointed their directors (see above). More seriously, a number of managers and staff suffered illness and death during their service in Japan. David Moncur, the first junior recruited by HSBC's London office in 1866, went East in 1871 but died in Yokohama two years later.[22] Gifford Moody, who was one of the first appointments in Hong Kong in 1865, worked as accountant in Yokohama from 1868 to 1870 and then as agent in Hyogo but was forced to retire on grounds of ill-health in 1871.

Other casualties included Edward Morriss, manager at Yokohama from 1884, who died there of exhaustion in November 1890. In April 1888 A.H.C. Haselwood, Morriss's opposite number as manager at Kobe (Hyogo) since 1882, had also died in service. In contrast to the loss of these long-serving officers in Japan, Andrew Veitch succumbed after only the briefest spell of duty. Originally with the Mercantile before joining HSBC, Veitch left the East on health grounds in 1891. Finding that the fall in silver values would not leave him with sufficient means for retirement in England, he agreed to return as manager at Yokohama in 1892. He died there only three days after his arrival, a victim of meningitis.[23]

The losses also included members of some of the banking families connected with HSBC's history in nineteenth-century Japan. H.E. Harries, the nephew of W.H. Harries, joined his uncle at the San Francisco office in 1893 and was posted to Yokohama in 1896. He died in service as a junior there in 1898. David Jackson, Thomas's younger brother, died in Yokohama in 1903 after suffering an aneurism of the heart. By then he had served nearly ten years as manager at the Yokohama branch; Charles Addis remembered him as 'an able chap and very kind-hearted'.[24] These losses are not forgotten, as their graves are marked and maintained to this day. The graves of Morriss, Veitch, Jackson and Harries are located at the Yokohama Foreign General Cemetery while Haselwood's grave lies at the Shiogahara Cemetery at Futatabi.

ACHIEVEMENTS

Similarly, the achievements of the cadre of bankers who served HSBC in its early years in Japan are not forgotten. These bankers were a remarkable and cohesive group. They were among the pioneers of modern finance in Japan, particularly on currency questions and in the development of trade finance. They also established and then maintained the importance of the Japanese offices in the first division of the bank's branches. In 1887, typically, Yokohama's net profit of HK$107,000 ranked behind only Shanghai (HK$195,000) and Hong Kong itself (HK$298,000).[25] Ten years later the managership at Yokohama – along with the same posts at Singapore, Batavia, Bombay and Calcutta – was second only to Shanghai in the hierarchy of salary scales and seniority.

In personalities such as Jackson, Walter and Townsend, this group of bankers included those who reached the topmost levels of HSBC management in Hong Kong and London. In turn their experience of (and their interest in) Japan was to be a strong influence on the bank's business in the later nineteenth and early twentieth centuries. They were especially prominent in ensuring that HSBC took a leading role in the flotation of Japanese loans in international markets in that period. That business was crucial both for Japan's financial history and for the emergence of the bank on a wider world stage. It also ensured that the bank had a clear opportunity for the later growth of its business in Japan and the basis for its continuous presence in Japan interrupted only by earthquake and war –

for nearly 140 years. HSBC is proud of that commitment and it is also proud that the archives of its connection with Japan continue to be of value to scholars in Japan and around the world.

PART V

Poets, Scholars
and
Journalists

25

Robert Nichols, 1893-1944: Poet in Japan, 1921-24

GEORGE HUGHES

Robert Nichols

ON 28 SEPTEMBER 1929 the *Daily Express* reported a coroner's inquest on the suicide of a woman in Bromley, Kent, precipitated by 'some miserable poetry broadcast on the wireless'. The poetry was by 'Robert Malise Bowyer Nichols . . . who lives at Winchelsea, is thirty-six years old, and was professor of English literature in the Imperial University, Tokyo, from 1921 to 1924'.

Robert Nichols indeed taught at the Faculty of Letters of Tokyo University in 1921-24.[1] Recruited by the critic and journalist Charles Whibley, Nichols held his post after a linguist named John Lawrence and just before Edmund Blunden. He has some claim to be considered first of the young British poets who came to teach in Japanese universities before and after the Second World War, and who have been considered so important in English literary studies in Japan.[2]

Nichols's work at Tokyo University features in even the briefest biographical sketches and he described himself as holding 'What I believe was regarded as the foremost Chair of foreign culture, as opposed to technology, in Japan'.[3]

What did Nichols do in Japan and what effect did Japan have on his writing? He can hardly be said to have made a distinguished contribution to the Japanese academic or literary world, and his first year in particular was spent in an almost hysterical rejection of the country and people. On the other hand, nobody could accuse Nichols of being dull, conventional, inactive or uncontroversial. He provides a classic case of extreme culture shock suffered by a British visitor to Japan: and he remains the only foreign teacher who has left Tokyo University to try his luck in Hollywood. Nichols moved on in 1924 to work as assistant to Douglas Fairbanks Senior.

A MAN FRESH FROM ENGLAND

When Robert Nichols first arrived in Japan in 1921, aged 27, he was not, by modern standards, well-qualified for an academic post. He had been educated for a couple of years at Winchester (until the school requested him to leave), and then briefly studied at Trinity College, Oxford (until he failed his examinations for the second time). He claimed the real reason for his dismissal was that he had thrown a mangel-wurzel at Lloyd George during the politician's visit to Oxford: the mangel-wurzel missed Lloyd George, but knocked off the Bishop of Winchester's top-hat. In any event, Nichols left without a degree in 1914 and decided to volunteer at once for service in the First World War.

It was as a First World War poet that Nichols had made his name. He started his poetic career as a poet in 1915 with an 'Invocation' ('Forward I ride. Guns must to guns. . .') and he entered the war, like Rupert Brooke, full of hope:

> The Past is Dead. A New Age now begins
> Of noble servitude to nobler laws. . .[4]

But the real experience of battle had been a shock, and in *Ardours and Endurances* (1917) it led to some powerful evocations of the horrors of warfare:

> It is midday: the deep trench glares. . . .
> A buzz and blaze of flies. . . .
> The hot wind puffs the giddy airs. . . .
> The great sun rakes the skies.
>
> No sound in all the stagnant trench
> Where forty standing men
> Endure the sweat and grit and stench,
> Like cattle in a pen.[5]

This was to be his best and most enduring poetry. After the war, he took to experiments with religious themes, Georgian lyrics and love sonnets.

He was recruited to Japan specifically as a poet and a representative of the English literary world. Professor Ichikawa Sanki[6] explained to Nichols that he was not looking for a conventional teacher. There were, he said, many foreign residents in Tokyo who would have liked the post:

> But we don't want a man who has not so long breathed his native air, who has lost touch with your literary atmosphere – in short who is neither Japanese nor English, whom, if they go back, the place will know no more. (There are many such Japanese in England!) But we want a man who, fresh from England, would be able to breathe the spirit of English Literature, who can make his influence felt in the short space of time allowed him.[7]

Nichols might well have worried that he was being treated as an exotic specimen rather than a colleague: 'I feel that we have got hold of the man we wanted all these years,' Ichikawa wrote, 'but the trouble is that the man we want to have tries to get away from us. . .' And some of the problems Nichols experienced in adjusting to Japan must surely be explained by the oddity of his university appointment. He was expected to carry round with him his cultural difference, and to preserve it intact for use by others in the 'short space of time allowed'. Ichikawa discouraged him from attempting to 'communicate in his classes; he said they would be limited to advanced students, with others 'admitted only as "hearers" like ladies'. And he need not bother to communicate to all these advanced students: 'if you can get hold of one really good man, is it not worth leaving the ninety-nine to go after him? That man will be like a grain of mustard-seed who in turn will influence his future generations.' Ichikawa explained how the seed Lafcadio Hearn had sown through his 'select pupils' was now beginning to flower in Japan and this was his model. (He seems to have conveniently forgotten that Hearn was far from being a 'fresh' foreigner when he came to work in Tokyo.)

When he later recommended himself for another academic post in Canada, Nichols said he could offer '(a) special lectures on poets (b) tuition of special pupils who want to write (c) rousing of general enthusiasm (d) a hand in the community theatre'. He added: 'I can lead. I seem to have an odd power of raising the young's enthusiasm.'[8] If this seems a rather mixed-bag of accomplishments for an academic, it should be added that he had had some lecturing experience even before coming to Japan. In 1918 he had been sent by the British Foreign Office on a tour of the United States, to 'try and show that we appreciate the American effort'.[9] His lectures had been successful enough for him to be taken up by J. B. Pinker's agency, and offered, according to his biographers, two to three thousand dollars for a ten-weeks' lecture tour.

POET AND GENTLEMAN

Nichols's Japanese colleagues welcomed him both as 'soldier poet' and representative 'English Gentleman'.[10] Perhaps Nichols encouraged this view, since Aldous Huxley said of him that he could not 'remain in any company of people for five minutes without telling them (a) that he is a poet, (b) that he is extremely successful in his profession and (c) that he knows everybody in England who is worth knowing.'[11] He had been brought up, according to Arnold Bennett in 'an atmosphere of ancient houses and connoisseurship'.[12] His father (who wrote art criticism for the *Westminster Gazette*) was last in a line of famous printers stretching back to the eighteenth century. And Ichikawa was certainly correct in thinking that he was well known in the English literary world. He had friends among the older generation of the English literary world like Thomas Hardy, John Masefield, Gilbert Murray, Robert Bridges and Edmund Gosse (Gosse found him 'distractingly violent, mercurial and excessive, but most attractive'.[13])

Nichols was also friendly with younger contemporaries such as Siegfried Sassoon, Robert Graves, Edmund Blunden, D. H. Lawrence and Aldous Huxley. He was notoriously flamboyant in public, and performed noisily at poetry-readings – like the one held at Lady Colefax's house, where Ivor Novello played ragtime in between the poems. Huxley described how 'Bob Nichols raved and screamed and hooted and moaned his filthy war poems like a Lyceum villain who hasn't learnt how to act'.[14] But there was no shortage of admirers: one reviewer saw Nichols as 'destined to become the Keats of the new century'.[15]

There were, however, darker sides to Nichols's early life which may help explain the instability and excitable temperament which became so obvious when he reached Japan. His mother had entered a mental hospital when he was fifteen, and was never to return home.[16] And his own experiences during the First World War were shadows that haunted him: 'War is suffering, intense suffering, every minute of it', he wrote to Edmund Gosse. 'Within less than a year of my proceeding to the front – at which I was for a very short time only – my whole world collapsed. Friends were killed & I was left more like an automaton than a man.'[17] Nichols experienced fighting in the trenches for only a month in September 1915 and acquitted himself bravely, but he was not physically strong, and his stay in France was cut short by what his commanding officer called 'a slight nervous breakdown': he was in hospital in France, then in England, and finally declared permanently unfit. He had also caught syphilis, which was incurable at the time, from a French prostitute (and which very likely accounts for many of his later health problems).[18]

FIRST REACTIONS TO JAPAN: THE YEAR OF HORROR

Ichikawa may have wanted a poet, but when Nichols set off for Japan on the S. S. *Kitanu Maru* in January 1921, his own principal motive was to earn money. He had fallen in love with an Englishwoman called Norah Denny, whose father objected to him on the grounds that his mother was in an asylum. Norah's money was cut off and the father was, Nichols said, 'very violent' and had 'threatened personal assault'.[19] He hoped he would be able to earn enough in Tokyo to support a wife.

It is not entirely surprising, then, that Nichols came to Japan in a state of emotional disturbance and without any strong desire to accommodate himself to Japanese culture; but it is still something of a surprise to discover how intensely alienated and unhappy he was. He wrote to friends that the people in Tokyo were so ugly he could not look at them ('I have to turn my eyes to the ground: they revolt me so'[20]). He protested that there was no privacy in Japan and that nobody would take any decisions ('persons? – they are all like eunuchs!')[21] He found the climate frightful and he called the university the 'Imperial Lunatic Asylum'.[22] He decided that the students were 'ignorant snobs' and that nobody among either students or colleagues could speak English.[23] Even when he had to admit that his colleagues had been generous to him, he quickly went on to complain: 'I have been deceived.'[24] He considered that women in Japan were treated as slaves or concubines ('they do a great deal of copulation'[25]), and when he thought about bringing Norah to the country it gave him 'the horrors'. His first year was a 'year of horror . . . climate & people & job altogether beyond my strength & from the intellectual point of view an absolute waste of time – hack–schoolmasters' work'.[26] When he went off on leave to England, he spent much of his time looking for a job so that he would not have to go back. He cannot have been an easy colleague in the department of English literature.

He arrived in April 1921, and was already demanding several months' home leave in April 1922 (he would have missed almost half a year's teaching). He went off on leave again in the summer of 1923, to the United States, before finally departing in spring 1924. He was not long in Tokyo even then: he spent the summer of 1921 in the Mampei Hotel in Karuizawa. In Tokyo he cannot have been teaching very actively, since his health was not good: he was rushed off to hospital in Yokohama in September 1922 (according to him because he had been given tubercular milk to drink), and then in early 1924 he was in hospital for an appendectomy. He later said he had 'nervous dyspepsia' twice in Japan.[27]

NICHOLS AND THE STUDENTS

Nonetheless, despite such frequent absences, and despite his 'year of horror', Nichols does seem to have become something of a cult figure among students. Yamato Moto records that after he left some of the students 'tried to preserve a Nichols-style sincerity'.[28] When he moved to the Unites States he received admiring letters from a student named Fujishima Kohei who wrote excellent English, but who sadly died in 1925. N. Irie, who said he had studied Keats and been recommended to Ichikawa by Nichols, wrote to him about the group of students he knew: Uchiyama, Inouye, Takami, Matsumoto and Nabara. Uchiyama wrote with obvious dislike of the 'cold Mr Ichikawa,' thanking Nichols for reviving the seminar at Tokyo University and telling him how dull the students found his successor, Edmund Blunden.

Nichols recounted in a broadcast of 1942 that at Tokyo University he was 'never suffered to lecture without the presence of a Japanese professor', in order to ensure that he did not 'undermine the purity of Japanese morals'.[29] It seems more likely, however, that Professor Ichikawa attended his lectures to take notes for the struggling students.[30]

Barry Webb's biography of Edmund Blunden says that Nichols 'was always elegantly dressed and travelled to his lectures by car, accompanied by his wife, from the comfort of the Imperial Hotel'.[31] This is misleading: Nichols did stay in the hotel when he first arrived, but moved out of it into the British Embassy, before going on to share a house with a lawyer named John Gadsby. When he came back to Japan after his leave in 1922, now married to Norah, they lived at '3 Hachigo, Shiba Park,' in a house with an old-fashioned Japanese bath that Norah liked very much. When she saw the house she wrote: 'I felt so happy there that tears came into my eyes. I would have a dwarf tree of plum-blossom in my sitting room; I would slide back the walls, let in the sun, seat myself on a purple cushion on that floor of golden straw. . .'[32] Norah let Robert do the public posing and take the risks, while she quietly enjoyed herself 'playing second fiddle'. She was, she said one of those people ' who know it is just as difficult, just as praiseworthy, to play second fiddle as to play first, and that one is complementary to the other.' There were days when she thought it might be 'more fun to make poetry than puddings', but after all she found she could share with Robert a 'life of high adventure on very little a year.'[33] Students who visited their house appreciated her musical talents. Nichols calmed down after his marriage, and even began to appreciate some aspects of the country.

WRITINGS FROM AND IN JAPAN

What must have seemed extremely odd to his colleagues was that Nichols had now more or less stopped writing poetry. On arrival he published a poem entitled 'Hero Song' in the *Japan Advertiser* ('Let to yourself your own self be obscure./ What is without survey. . .'), but he did not go on to publish poems about Japan. Some poems privately printed in

Hollywood in 1924, in a collection entitled *Winter Berries*, were most likely written while in Japan, but say nothing about the country. The one poem among his manuscripts which is definitely about Japan remains unpublished, and perhaps is better so, since its rather conventional evocation of the landscape around 'Asama's crater' ends with an extremely unpleasant verse on the sinister grimace' of a 'single idiot alien face' that has been watching him: 'More hideous than a cankered flower.'[34]

Anyone who had read 'At the Wars', from Nichols's 1917 collection, might have noticed that he always took much of his inspiration from the countryside in England:

> Now that I am ta'en away,
> And may not see another day,
> What is it to my eye appears?
> . . .scenes and sounds of countryside
> In far England across the tide.[35]

But Japanese admirers must surely have wondered why this man who had been chosen as a poet could no longer function as such. If Claudel could write short poems in a japonesque style about Jizō, why could not Nichols? In a country that so much enjoys occasional poems, why could Nichols produce nothing?

Nichols complained in his letters that 'the Japs provide me <u>with no art material that I can use'</u>.[36] Later on he came to appreciate some Japanese art forms: he liked the theatre and music played on the *shakuhachi*; but he seems simply to have decided that he could not find appropriate subjects for poetry in Japan. 'I have written nothing,' he told Edmund Gosse. 'I was by way of being a poet once – I am only a professor now.'[37]

WRITINGS IN TOKYO

All the same, Nichols was not idle: he wrote other things. He published a short collection of aphorisms in Tokyo in 1921 (dedicated to Professor Ichikawa), and sent off two completed manuscripts to English publishers: his play *Guilty Souls* (1922) and a collection of prose pieces, *Fantastica* (1923).[38]

Guilty Souls describes itself as the first in a series of 'Dramas for the Theatre of To-morrow': there was to be no number two. It starts with an embezzlement in an English's solicitor's office, and goes on to read like a play of ideas by George Bernard Shaw (whom Nichols much admired), or by Granville Barker (who gave advice about cutting the play to Nichols). It ends more portentously, trying to be like Paul Claudel's drama, with a crucifix, a suicide in the garden, and much agonizing over guilt and religious experience. Claudel was French ambassador while Nichols was in Tokyo, and Nichols called him 'the most sublime of all the active poets and dramatists of Europe'. He praised the climax of Claudel's *L'Otage* as 'the greatest in the modern theatre' and his first piece of journalism in Japan was a eulogy of Claudel's poetry.[39] Unfortunately, Nichols seems to have picked up the religious side of Claudel's work without grasping either his psychological depth or his new theatrical techniques: he made no attempt to imitate Claudel's famous poetic 'verset', with its base in an actor's breath group. In the long introduction to the play (written, he says, in 'this far land . . . in which I am at present residing') he explained that it was an attack on the English '*Genro*', the older generation, in the name of 'Youth' and 'Sincerity'. It was performed in 1924 at the Three Hundred Club in London and, although the actors were thought to have acquitted themselves well, it was not a great success.[40]

The volume of prose pieces that Nichols sent off from Japan, *Fantastica*, described itself as 'Romances of Idea, Volume One' (again this is over-ambitious: there was to be no volume two.) It contains a couple of previously published pieces and a new long 'philosophic *conte*, 'Golgotha & Co.' Nichols starts off by saying that for such volumes 'somebody – usually a professor – writes a Preface. I know: I'm a professor myself.' He explains that for 'Golgotha & Co.' he has left 'the world of Heartbreak House' and plunged into the 'hideous mixed world of Northcliffes, Beaverbrooks . . . and other apostles of Science-with-a-Cat-o'-nine-tails.'[41] He is writing a fable of a Second Coming, and it is dedicated, of course, to 'the occident's supreme poet and sublimest dramatist, Paul Claudel.'

The narrative starts off after a Second World War, at a meeting of 'The Brains of Power' in the palace of one Cyrus Magniferox, 'in a colossal saloon, under the radiance diffused from the fiery rose or faint azure tints ever softly-billowing within the expanses of a pearly ceiling, between lucid walls loftily panelled with representations of the Three Triumphs. . .'[42] The plot has to do with a proposal by Ulysse Mammon, a celebrated Professor of Herd-Psychology, to revive religion through making a film of the life of Christ. In a few pages it might have been amusing, but Nichols spread it over three hundred. Although he did receive some praise from contemporaries like Bertrand Russell, most seem to have found the piece 'verbose to a degree'.[43] 'Golgotha', as Anne and William Charlton in their biography of Nichols point out, suffers from the fact that it was written in Japan 'when he had no one to curb his tendency to go on and on'.[44]

Nichols also wrote regularly for the Sunday literary page of a Tokyo-based English language newspaper, the *Japan Advertiser*. His most interesting contributions are articles on 'Certain English Novelists Who Are Artists' published from 1921-22. Again, he speaks as a professor of English literature ('that is a person who is supposed to know good literature when he sees it'), rejecting best-sellers which are 'soporific', 'stimulant', 'soothing syrup', or 'aphrodisiac', and concentrating instead on E. M. Forster, D. H. Lawrence, Compton Mackenzie, Virginia Wolff [sic] and Dorothy Richardson.[45] He does a good deal of name-dropping – what Arnold Bennett has said to him 'waving a hand at Swinnerton', and what Siegfried Sassoon had suggested to him about destiny. On Forster he says: 'when I last saw him he informed me that he had two [novels] completed and ready for the press but was "biding his time". Meanwhile Mr Knopf on my recommendation has published *Howard's End* in America.'[46] (Ichikawa must have been pleased to learn how very close this fresh Englishman was to the literary world of London and the United States.)

Nichols is at his best when writing about D. H. Lawrence, who, he says, 'achieves with an extraordinary accuracy the difficult task of giving the formlessness of erotic emotion, the dream state, the furtive bitter violence of passion'.[47] He had taken Lawrence seriously since he was introduced to him in 1915, and Nichols still figures in recent biographies of Lawrence, because he insisted (wrongly) that Lawrence exaggerated the problem of police surveillance during the First World War, and because he wrote long letters describing a visit to the dying Lawrence.

The journalism in the *Japan Advertiser* continued when Nichols returned from England in 1922, with articles on Shakespeare's theatre and topics like letter-writing, science and education. He seems never to have grasped the need to cut, or stick to the point. Anne and William Charlton write that 'he had considerable talent for journalism and it is a pity that only in Japan did circumstances force him to work at it',[48] but it is difficult to find much of lasting interest.

Whatever his other deficiencies, Nichols was never short of ideas. In 1923 he was planning to write a 'Christian Noh Play' on Japan. He wanted to contact the Guest Master at Quarr Abbey in the Isle of Wight to gain advice about plain-chant music for the play ('I haven't one written yet but the <u>idea</u> gets plainer every week.')[49] Obviously, William Plomer and Benjamin Britten were not the first to attempt a combination of Noh drama and Christian church music, though there is no record that Nichols ever got down to writing the play he imagined.

NICHOLS AND THE EARTHQUAKE

Nichols was lucky enough to be on leave in the United States when the great Tokyo earthquake took place in September 1923. He arrived back in the Kansai at the end of September, and then had to wait until November before making the journey up to Tokyo, now 'an abominable rubbish heap'.[50] The earthquake led to what was perhaps his most enduring contribution to academic life in Japan: he immediately set about collecting money to replace books that had been destroyed in Tokyo University library, writing to friends in England and the United States to ask for contributions. He wrote to Gilbert Murray at Oxford, contacted the Bodleian and Oxford University Press – explaining that this was a great opportunity to get in before Cambridge. He persuaded Edmund Gosse to contribute a substantial amount. He told his father to contact Lord Curzon and the Royal Society of Antiquaries. He wrote to friends like Robert Bridges asking for autograph poems for the collection of manuscripts in the new library. According to Ichikawa, Nichols persuaded the Morgan foundation in the United States to contribute ten thousand dollars: according to the Charltons he obtained a donation of thirty thousand dollars from American friends called Lamont. He wrote a memorandum to the British Ambassador, pointing out what a good effect financial support would have on Anglo-Japanese relations. America was supplying funds for direct relief to sufferers from the earthquake, but books from England would be a more tangible and lasting contribution to rebuilding Tokyo. All this was not wasted effort; there are still many valuable books in Tokyo University library with a label indicating that they were donated after the earthquake.

Nichols's energy in collecting books and money was admirable, as was his compassion for victims of the earthquake. His colleague Saitō Takeshi wrote to Nichols's father sending cuttings from a Tokyo newspaper about the financial help his son had given to sick people in a shelter. Nichols himself felt that his colleagues had changed their attitude towards him after the earthquake and forgiven him at last for being unorthodox.

SECOND THOUGHTS

When Nichols left Japan in 1924, his feelings about the country and the university were a little different from what they once had been. According to Japanese accounts he left for health reasons. The ex-editor of the *Japan Chronicle*, A. M. Young, obviously thought politics was involved. He said that, before leaving, Nichols 'made a lonely protest' about the dismissal from Tokyo University of 'the last professor who could be suspected of harbouring a liberal thought': but Young had his own political agenda, and there is no other record of such an incident.[51]

At least we can say that, in Nichols's later letters, Tokyo University was no longer a despised lunatic asylum: he had written to Gilbert Murray explaining the intimate connection between the university, the government and the imperial household. He was hoping to help found a Union at the university on the model of Oxford: 'I have the ear of the most powerful Minister in the present cabinet & hope to effect something.'[52]

In an interview on the subject of education, given shortly before leaving, Nichols praised 'Japan's two supreme virtues: stoicism, and capacity for hard work'. He now suggested that his Japanese students were the hardest workers in the world, that many teachers were wonderfully self-sacrificing (though some were swollen-headed) and that the severest problems in Japanese universities were tuberculosis and too many examinations. Students are so much examined, he said (sounding remarkably like commentators of the twenty-first century), that when they reach university they have 'no mental kick'. He advised a bit more 'joy'.[53]

Nichols was no longer 'hilarious at getting out of Japan' as he had been in 1922. In October 1924 he wrote to H. W. Nevinson about an article in the *Baltimore Sun*, complaining 'you say that I gave up the Tokyo post because I didn't like the Japanese. That's a damned lie. On the contrary as far as it is possible to like a people as a whole I rather like the Japanese.' He went on to say that Japanese people do have their faults ('conceit and suspicion'), but that there are many beautiful things in Japan, including the bells, the fish and the seaweed soup (though he wished people would not make such a noise when eating it.) After he had left Japan, Nichols continued sending contributions back to the students' journal, *Poetica*, and he corrected the English in a translation of Chikamatsu's dramas by Miyamori Asataro in 1926.[54] In later years he was visited by Professor Ichikawa at his home in England and played him records of *shakuhachi* music in the English twilight.[55] The image of Japan mellowed, though during the war he took the opportunity to publish a few harsh thoughts on the 'relentless . . . Japanese educational machine', and he did not entirely give up referring to his time there as one of 'hated exile'.[56]

YEARS OF DECLINE

Nichols's move from Tokyo University to Hollywood does not seem quite so startling when we look at the *Japan Advertiser* of his day. Along with his articles, the paper carried a regular 'Page Devoted to Motion Pictures' – including photographs of 'the Most Famous Motion Picture Family': Mary Pickford and Douglas Fairbanks. But Hollywood did not suit Nichols any more than Tokyo; he was soon announcing that he was fed up with enslavement to the 'brainless barbaric cinema people'. His job with Douglas Fairbanks meant working from eight in the morning until six-thirty at night: he found it killing, and made his way back to England after a year.

From then on Nichols's life was a series of good ideas and false starts. He considered journalism, but Aldous Huxley tactfully told him that he was unlikely to get the job he would have liked as editor of *Vogue*. He tried to make his name in the theatre and managed to get a play produced in New York and then London: he wrote some articles for *The Times* on cinema (which the Charltons think might have made an important book.) He reviewed for newspapers: he tried to get a job at the BBC. During the war, Nichols gave talks on the BBC about Japanese psychology, and contributed to official pamphlets for servicemen. He had had, he said, 'opportunities for studying the mind and behaviour of "Young Japan"' and he thought that the Japanese belong 'By nature . . . to a type of people very different from ourselves.' He warned that they might 'turn wild-cat' in battle, and said Allied soldiers should expect 'a hardy, foxy, tenacious, resolute and extremely brave foe, who is very much and constantly in earnest about the whole matter and believes in his cause with an obsessional, fierce and burning fanaticism.'[57]

Nichols said he had 'sworn by all my gods never on any account to be a professor again', but he still angled hard to get a job teaching at Toronto University and later at Bedford College, London, though he did not get either.[58] In 1942 the British Council suggested a job as professor of English literature in Farouk University, Alexandria, but by this time his health was bad, his marriage had broken down, and things in general had gone seriously wrong for him: he had little choice but to reject it.

Nichols had money problems for much of his life, but retained his contacts in upper-class political and literary London. In later years he began to have bright ideas about inventions which he thought might interest friends in government. He sent off proposals about new communication systems to the Ministry of Information and suggested to Winston Churchill that Britain might develop a shell with a time-fuse like a giant jellyfish.[59] (Lady Churchill complained he 'has written very interesting but innumerable and copious letters to both Winston and me and we can neither of us read his writing'.[60])

He had always insisted that creative writing was his first priority – writing in 1921: 'I shall certainly chuck Norah if she comes between me and my work.'[61] But he had failed to appreciate what was happening in poetic modernism in the 1920s and 30s ('I . . . regard most of the so-called free verse of today as entirely worthless.'[62]) He had once been experimental, as in 'The Assault':

> Blindness a moment. Sick
> There the men are!
> Bayonets ready: click!
> Time goes quick;
> A stumbled prayer . . . somehow a blazing star
> In a blue night . . . where?
> Again prayer.
> The tongue trips. Start:
> How's time? Soon now. Two minutes or less.
> The gun's fury mounting higher. . .[63]

But after 1918 he lost the trick of doing things in a new way. He could not understand why 'highbrows on both sides [of the Atlantic] go on blabbing about that Museum-tea-room poet T. S. Eliot', and hoped he could 'put the kybosh on the Eliot – Pound – Wyndham Lewis group'; but things did not turn out that way.[64] His old friends like Masefield, Sassoon and Blunden, who had held on grimly to their anti-modernist views, were still alive, but had begun to look like a side-line in contemporary poetry. When the depressed woman committed suicide after listening to his poetry on the BBC in 1929, Nichols protested that his poems had been misunderstood: they were 'essentially hymns to the joy of living'. But hymns of joy hit the wrong note in the poetic landscape of the thirties. When Edward Thompson asked to include some poems in an anthology he was editing in 1931, Nichols complained that he had been 'completely forgotten by the public'.[65]

After the break-up of his marriage in the early 1930s, he had a long and complicated relationship with a woman called Vivienne Wilkinson, but he died alone in a boarding house in Cambridge in 1944. His ex-wife Norah, who had remained on friendly terms with him, made preparations to write a biography. Although she lived until 1960, she was unable to complete the project, and it was only when his papers were passed on to his niece, Anne Charlton, and her husband, that a full biography finally appeared in 2003.

WRITINGS ON JAPAN

The experience in Japan, brief and unstable though it had been, was important for Robert Nichols and, if he never was able to write poems that would have pleased his Japanese colleagues and their successors, he did try for many years to make something of Japan in literary terms. In 1924 he assured Chatto and Windus that he was definitely writing a book on Japan, in the form of an imaginary journal. He said it was to be a gentle and ironical series of essays modelled on *The Tosa Diary*. Later in the same year he had been reading Lafcadio Hearn's *Japan: An Attempt at an Interpretation*, and wrote to Gilbert Murray that, like Hearn, he wanted to base his book on the ideas of Fustel de Coulanges.[66]

Nothing came of this; but in 1929 he was talking to Chatto and Windus about a play called 'Karin' or 'Karine', based on life in Japan. It surfaced as a play called *Komuso*, performed after his death on radio in 1954, and at the Arts Theatre Club in 1955. According to the Charltons it was well received on the radio, but slated by reviewers in the theatre (though the production starred the young Paul Eddington and Honor Blackman.)

The play is set in a Japanese house – perhaps based on the one he lived in with Norah. It opens with Japanese noises ('somewhat plaintive and miauling'); there are screens and sliding doors, and there is a room where a Japanese woman has committed suicide. The main characters are foreign expatriates, including a young man who teaches English literature, 'a weedy, sandy-haired youth of twenty-two'. The plot concerns a young English woman whose husband neglects her for his work. She is driven into an affair with a visiting businessman, becomes pregnant and is then rejected by her husband. The story bears some resemblance to what happened between Robert Nicholas and Norah—in the break-up of their marriage: Nichols seems to have more or less pushed Norah into the arms of another man. But, unlike Norah, the woman in the play commits suicide.

Komuso does not live up to Nichols's own estimate of it as 'a masterpiece and one of the deepest and finest plays since the Jacobeans',[67] but it has its interest.[68] It shows English people in Japan, as Nichols had been, out of place and homesick. A character registers his confusion: 'Anything's possible in Japan'. Another says: 'I detest the Japanese.' Amongst these discontented expatriates there is also one Japanese character who is a hard-working scientist and a professor, and who proves tough and responsible at the end. Perhaps Nichols hoped finally to do justice to some of his colleagues at the Imperial University, Tokyo who had been, as even he admitted, 'considerate – more than considerate, generous'.[69]

When Nichols had left Japan in 1924, one of his ex-students, Matsumoto Hayaji wrote to him: 'I fear that Japan was not, after all, an agreeable place to you. Perhaps you will have found, with some justice, that the Land of the Rising Sun is not so full of poetry and beauty as has been described.'[70] Matsumoto was right that Nichols had not found Japan an entirely 'agreeable' place. But his years there had, all the same, proved unforgettable. And, if he had not made quite the impact that Ichikawa Sanki once hoped, he had at least initiated a line of British poet-teachers who were to play a significant role for many years in Japanese universities.

26

Ralph Hodgson, 1871–1962:
Poet and Artist

JOHN HATCHER

Ralph Hodgson in Tokyo, 1933-4[1]

INTRODUCTION

IN SOME RESPECTS, the poet and artist Ralph Hodgson was one of the most enigmatic Englishmen ever to live in Japan. A pipe-smoking, snooker-playing, dog-loving mystic, he was a walking paradox: a poet of great natural gifts who rarely wrote and even more rarely published anything, yet who took the Muse so seriously that he once refused to travel to accept an honorary degree because '*She* might come while I was away';[2] a university professor with no academic qualifications of any kind; and a fiercely private, sometimes reclusive man who was also immensely companionable, a vivid conversationalist celebrated by T.S. Eliot as the most 'delightful' of men.

Hodgson shunned fame and so enjoyed bamboozling any 'damned researchers and journalists' who came his way that establishing even the most basic facts of his early life involves traversing a minefield of disinformation. In fact, he was born in Darlington in 1871, the sixth son in a coal merchant family of seven boys and three girls. Although born in the north, he was brought up in the south, where he immersed himself in the natural world and developed the passion for birds and animals that inspired his finest poetry. Later, he supported himself by drawing illustrations and cartoons for magazines and newspapers, including a drawing of Oscar Wilde's trial for the London *Evening News* in 1895, and writing articles on outdoor life and dogs, of which he was a great lover and leading authority. He was almost certainly the only significant poet ever to be a judge at Cruft's, the world's premier dog show. Except for a period in the early 1890s when he worked as a scene designer in a theatrical troupe touring America, until 1924 he spent all his life in England. Deeply attached to English life, both London and the countryside, he was the last man anyone would have imagined uprooting himself to go and live 10,000 miles away.

INVITED TO JAPAN

The unlikely fact that he did so, and ended up living in Japan for twelve years, was due initially to the persistence and ingenuity of two young Japanese scholars of English literature destined to become leading figures in their field, Saitō Takeshi and Doi Kōchi. In 1923 both men were on sabbatical in Britain. Saitō, assistant professor at Tokyo Imperial University, had first met Hodgson in June at the London house of one of Hodgson's closest friends, Siegfried Sassoon. Saitō, who had translated one of Hodgson's poems years earlier, spent many happy hours at Hodgson's house and found him 'a master-mind of versatile knowledge . . . and an extraordinarily brilliant talker'.[3] Doi had recently been appointed professor of the newly-established Department of English at Tōhoku Imperial University in Sendai in northern Japan, and when he requested Saitō's help in finding an Englishman to invite to his university as a visiting professor, Saitō immediately suggested Hodgson.

The fact that Hodgson was already fifty-two years old, had not been to university, had no academic qualifications and had published no studies of English literature did not deter either Saitō or Doi, who both deeply admired his poetry. They believed that several of his poems, most notably 'The Bull', 'Eve' and the visionary nature lyric 'The Song of Honour' were 'the great poems of this century'.[4] They were not alone in this. Hodgson had been widely acknowledged as a major contemporary poet since the publication of *Poems* in 1917. Moreover, Saitō and Doi believed that the true value of visiting foreign professors lay not in dispensing 'information' to students, that being the task of 'academically trained Japanese scholars', but in lighting a fire inside them through their own passion for literature. 'Generally speaking,' Saitō wrote years later, 'a lecturer who will urge his students to love literary works is much more desirable than Professor Dry-as-Dust, Ph.D.' For this Hodgson seemed ideally suited, and they had 'no doubt of his great influence upon his students and intellectuals in Japan.'[5]

As Saitō had foreseen, persuading 'this lover of England and London' to come to Japan proved 'a difficult task'. He politely declined, explaining that he was not an academic, either by training or temperament. He was 'simply a poet, and for a poet a crow in the sky is more than a pile of books, which a professor ought to peruse whether he likes them or not.' Not a man to be easily deflected, however, Saitō kept on asking till Hodgson got used to the idea. The turning point came when he remembered Hodgson mentioning his interest in a breed of sledge dogs in Karafuto in the northernmost reaches of the Japanese archipelago, now Sakhalin in Russia. When he remarked that Hodgson might be able to travel there if he came to Sendai, a seed was planted. In November Hodgson introduced Saitō to his friend Edmund Blunden, and when Saitō offered Blunden a position at Tokyo Imperial University Hodgson agreed that he would accept the post at Sendai if Blunden would go to Tokyo. 'He didn't want to go without some literary companion,' Blunden recalled, 'and he just decided that we got on well.'[6] As if symbolically, his beloved bull terrier Mooster, one of the most famous literary dogs in London and emblematic of his master's rootedness in England, died a few weeks before his departure.

FIRST THREE YEARS

And so that summer Ralph Hodgson became the first, and probably last, English poet to go to Japan to see its dogs. He and his wife arrived at the end of August 1924, a few days before his fifty-third birthday. They landed at Kobe, where they were met by Doi and Blunden. Hodgson's main luggage consisted of ten boxes of books and Joseph, a crippled magpie that he had nursed back to health and could not bear to leave in England. Blunden vividly remembered this eccentric entourage 'passing in state, magpie and all, through Tokyo'.[7] Out of the welter of new impressions, the one that Hodgson remembered all his life was one that would have passed most Westerners by: the strident chirping of a *semi*, a cicada, outside Tokyo Station. He accepted this quintessential sound of Japanese summer as the country's personal welcome to him.

The Hodgsons made their way north-east up along the Pacific coast to their new home in Sendai. In 1924 Sendai was an austere, conservative castle town, which the population of 200,000 shared with soldiers both temporal and spiritual – a division of the Imperial Army and a large contingent of Western missionaries – and the teachers and students of Tōhoku Imperial University, which had been founded seventeen years earlier as the fifth Imperial University. Hodgson made an immediate impression on his new colleagues and students. 'His memory is still fresh and very dear to us', Doi recalled almost thirty years later. 'We all loved him.'[8] He had almost all the qualities that would endear him to Japanese of the pre-war era: despite his comparatively humble origins, he was an English gentleman of the old school, 'the last of the Fancy' as he described himself; he was erudite but wore his erudition lightly; modest and self-effacing; a lover of nature and mystical by temperament and inclination; and, last but by no means least, endearingly eccentric.

First impressions were of a powerful physical presence: a vigorous, muscular, ruddy-complexioned man, amiable and unaffected, given to passionate talk and emphatic gesticulation. His colleagues were entranced by his raconteurship. For Doi, 'he was a great talker, and when he talked we were all charmed just as the wedding guest who had but to listen to the Ancient Mariner like a three years' child'.[9] He talked so animatedly that strangers assumed he was intoxicated, whereas in fact he was a confirmed teetotaller. His conversation spanned a wide range of fields of human interest, many of them far removed from the usual concerns of Edwardian poets, including not only a deeply informed, as opposed to merely literary, passion for the natural world but also sports such as boxing and snooker, of which he had been an amateur champion. Something of the flavour of the man and the quirky, Dickensian richness of his conversation can be gleaned from this description by Lewis Bush, who knew him well in Japan and described him as 'one of the most interesting and humane personalities one could wish to meet':

> I can still see Ralph, always impeccably dressed, his fine teeth glistening beneath the humorous twinkle in his eyes and telling me about the man he knew who used to play a one-man band outside a London 'pub' and who also blew the horn on the London to Brighton Coach. I so well remember Ralph's reminiscences of the great fighters of the Ring, Bob Fitzsimmons, Sullivan, Jack Johnson, Jimmy Wilde, Jim Driscoll and others.

At the other extreme, Kobayashi Atsuo recalled that when he talked with Hodgson 'his topics almost always are concerned with the spiritual world, and he gave me an impression of being a mystic. Sometimes his words are very suggestive, penetrating, and enigmatic, but his manner of expression is passionate, persuasive, and eloquent.'[10]

'I had no difficulty in settling down here,' Hodgson wrote to Blunden a few months later. 'I've found excellent people here. Some of the students and others couldn't be bettered & allowing for differences of life & traditions very like many of our own.' He missed England far less than he had expected, in part because he made frequent nocturnal visits home: 'in dreams at night I find my way back very often & there are sometimes wonderful visits. . . . Dreams have always been a boon to me, but now they're at their best.'[11] Blunden often came up from Tokyo to stay with him and indulge in orgies of 'real conversation'. An inveterate smoker rarely without a pipe clamped between his teeth, the only thing Hodgson was homesick for was his strong, pungent tobacco. 'A life-time of dark shag is not to be broken without pain & I had my days of suffering,' he wryly complained to Blunden. Saitō received a telegram pleading 'For love of Heaven ask tobacconist to send some Capstan Navy Cut full strength immediately – Dying Hodgson.'[12]

During his first three years at Sendai Hodgson taught a wide range of courses in English literature. Despite his modest reluctance to don the professorial mantle, he proved a great success as a lecturer. Blunden was not exaggerating when he maintained that Hodgson was one of the best-read men in the world, 'a man of the last generation of interesting minds, and highly cultivated'.[13] He was an avid book collector and had read widely in classic and contemporary literature (he was unusual in his generation in admiring Eliot and Joyce), art history and criticism, natural history, anthropology, archaeology and a broad range of other fields. Remarkably, in the twelve years he would spend teaching in Japan he would never repeat the same course or lecture.

He overcame his lack of teaching experience by turning his thrice-weekly lectures into extensions of his informal conversations. They were, recalled Saitō, not so much lectures as 'brilliant talks full of anecdotes most vividly told'. Another author-teacher, James Joyce, had done much the same thing several years earlier in his English conversation classes in Trieste, but whereas Joyce would simply turn up and speak whatever was in his mind, Hodgson put considerable effort into preparing for his lectures. His manner of doing so, however, was uniquely his own. Unlike Blunden down in Tokyo, who wrote out all his lectures in full with an eye to later publication, Hodgson did not even make conventional notes. Using his highly developed visual sense as an artist, he spent the day before each lecture meditating on his proposed subject until it formed a vivid picture in his mind, in much the same way as he did in the creation of poems. The following day he would spend the first five minutes sketching a portrait of the day's author on the blackboard, along with the main outlines of his theme, then he would sit on the desk, his legs dangling, pipe clamped between his teeth, and speak without notes to his students as if they were friends who had dropped in for tea. He occasionally interspersed his lectures with entertaining disquisitions on birds and dogs, including a hilarious imitation of a dog meditating to illustrate his belief that animals have consciousness. 'There was nothing stiff about him,' Bush recalled. 'He radiated friendliness towards his students and at the same time, authority.' As Doi and Saitō had hoped, his effect on his students went far beyond increasing their knowledge or even their love of literature:

> He was . . . loved and respected by his students, for not only did he so cunningly instil in them an appreciation of English

literature, but at the same time by his example taught them to be gentlemen, and the amount of general knowledge which they gained through him cannot be underestimated.[14]

Doi wanted to bring in a stenographer to transcribe his lectures so they could be published, but Hodgson would have none of it.

There was, however, a darker side to Hodgson's early years in Sendai. Although everyone remarked on his vitality and perpetually youthful quality, few were aware of what he endured off-stage. For years he had suffered badly from haemorrhoids, caused by birdwatching in all seasons and weathers when he was younger ('Birds have ruined me,' he once told Doi). In Sendai it got steadily worse. 'My old bodily trouble is my master here & I've got to watch it all the time,' he wrote to Blunden.[15] Despite his fighting it 'like a bull-terrier,' it prevented him from travelling around Japan as he had wished, and at times kept him a prisoner in his house, unable to walk far or even sit upright for an hour. When he went to the university to give lectures, he packed his 'surgical paraphernalia' in his bag along with his poetry books. At home, he kept almost entirely to his bedroom, rarely coming down to the guest room to meet visitors, but instead cheerfully entertained them lying on his back in bed.

To add to his private woes, his wife Muriel, to whom he had been married for only three years, keenly missed her social life in London and found it impossible to settle down in provincial Sendai, with its muddy streets. Increasingly unhappy, she left after less than a year, never to return. This affected Hodgson all the more deeply since this was not the first time he had experienced marital trauma. He had married his first wife, Janet, back in 1896, when he was twenty-five, but she had succumbed to depression and eventually mental illness during the Great War, due largely to her husband's absence on war duty. A passionate man who needed a flesh-and-blood companion as much as he needed his Muse, he had married Muriel a year after Janet died in 1920.

The personal tragedy of his first wife's descent into insanity had combined with the infinitely greater human tragedy of the war that had precipitated it to all but rob Hodgson of his creative life. He had been at the height of his powers just before the outbreak of war. His masterpieces, 'The Bull' and 'The Song of Honour', had been published in 1912 and 1913 respectively, and in 1914 he had been awarded the Polignac Prize by the Royal Society of Literature. His experiences first in the Royal Navy, then as an officer in the Royal Garrison Artillery and the Labour Corps, combined with his wife's worsening illness, eroded his creative life until the poems slowed to a trickle, then stopped altogether.

It is possible that Hodgson went to Japan partly in the hope that travelling to the other side of the world might re-ignite his creative life, but if so he was disappointed, for the creative drought continued. Since the war, he told Doi, the 'mood was gone'.[16] The post-war world, with its world-weary cynicism, existential angst and brittle gaiety, belonged to *The Waste Land*, not 'The Song of Honour'. By temperament a natural yea-sayer, Hodgson found himself becoming increasingly gloomy about the prospects for the world. Moreover, although he threw himself whole-heartedly into his teaching, years later he would advise a young American that if he genuinely wanted to dedicate himself to poetry he should find a 'trade . . . something, like carpentering, that would tax only the hands, leaving the brain free for creativity'. Teaching, and especially teaching literature, he told him, was 'the worst profession of all for a poet'.[17]

And yet it was through teaching that deliverance came, and in a most surprising and dramatic manner. Hodgson's lectures drew large audiences, comprised not only of students and fellow professors at Tōhoku University but also teachers from colleges and schools in Sendai, including some members of the missionary community. Among these was Aurelia Bolliger, a young American teacher who greatly admired his poetry. By April 1927, barely eighteen months after Muriel's departure, they had fallen in love. Despite the disparity in their ages – Hodgson was fifty-five, Aurelia twenty-eight –, it would prove, as Hodgson described it in a letter to her, 'a great, deep and enduring love, a life-love',[18] but the path that lay in front of them was anything but smooth. When Aurelia shared her happiness with her missionary father by letter, he devastated her by writing back, more in sorrow than in anger, that the relationship was a disaster that could bring her nothing but unhappiness. She proved, however, remarkably strong-willed. When Hodgson's three-year contract came to end in July 1927 and he returned to England with Blunden, she went with them, sharing a berth on the SS *Macedoni* with Blunden's assistant and lover Hayashi Aki. They made an odd ménage a quatre, both couples blithely unaware of the other's secret and, in the eyes of the world, adulterous love.

SECOND STAY IN JAPAN

Aurelia stayed in England for a few weeks before sailing for America. Having left Sendai with a warm invitation to return the following year, reiterated in letters from Doi, Hodgson returned in September 1928, and moved into a new house the university had built for him near the campus, where he and Aurelia unobtrusively spent a great deal of time together. The house stood close to the river Hirose, with views of wooded hills across the river. Here he devoted his spare time to natural pursuits, especially bird-watching. Doi recalled his spending hours gazing 'enraptured' through field glasses at the finches, tits, tree sparrows, thrushes, bulbuls and other birds that flocked to his garden. He and Aurelia also began breeding roller canaries, which gave them endless delight. He wore a ring she had given him and in letters called her his 'darling beloved wife,' but until he was able to get a divorce everything had to be kept secret. Even Doi knew nothing about it until 1930.

Partly as a result of this and partly due to the disability that often kept him at home, Hodgson gained the reputation of living what Doi described as 'a solitary, hermit life'.[19] There were occasional visitors, such as the poets William Empson and Laurence Binyon, but Blunden was now not only back in Britain but Hodgson had unilaterally broken off contact. 'He has disappeared from my world just like a comet', Blunden complained to Saitō.[20] Their friendship had always had an edge to it. Blunden admired the older poet's forceful and vivid personality, but also found him occasionally stubborn, aggressive and cantankerous. They never met again, but years later Blunden recalled him in verse with wry, affectionate nostalgia:

> 'The Last of the Fancy!' In Sendai!
> Tales of John Roberts and C. B. Fry,
> Pictures of Cruft's; from knur and spell
> To hunting the rare book! hours sped well
> When that enchanter pointed his pipe
> At the visions of time, and enjoyed each type
> He had gathered out of the nineties, he
> The prize of them all to you and me.
> Bull-terriers, boxing and poetry
> Gallery and studio, zoology,
> 'Man's miry past,' and what will be,
> All the birds in the world, – all fantasy.
> 'The Last of the Fancy' – surely he charms
> Still a few of his kind, with dogs under their arms.[21]

Although he was often invited to speak before learned societies, Hodgson generally avoided doing so. When the English Literature Society at Tokyo University pressed him for a lecture while he was in Tokyo in September 1928, he replied that he had no interest in lecturing on literature but would be 'delighted to talk about dogs'. In fact, he delivered a talk on the younger poets he admired, which Saitō found 'illuminating, interesting and exciting', but it was this kind of thing that gave Hodgson a reputation for idiosyncrasy in English literature circles in Japan. When Stephen Spender travelled in Japan thirty years later, he found older professors still recalling him as an 'eccentric'.[22]

They may also have been remembering what transpired at the national conference of the English Literary Society of Japan, held at Kyoto Imperial University in October 1930. The previous year the Society has taken advantage of Binyon's visit to Japan to have him deliver the guest lecture at its first-ever national conference, and this year they invited Hodgson to deliver the main address. This time Hodgson did not decline, nor was there any mention of dogs, though that would have been a safer theme than the one he chose. During the 1920s he had grown increasingly dismayed by the political situation in Europe and East Asia, including Japanese expansionism in Manchuria. Hodgson, for whom the Great War had been so personally devastating, found the prospect of another war intolerable and agreed to speak at the conference because he thought it was time to speak out against the rising tide of militarism, nationalism and xenophobia. Saitō believed Hodgson sympathized with Quaker pacifism, and certainly he hated militarism of any kind, especially, according to Doi, 'Mussolini, Hitler, and the Japanese militarists'.[23]

He spent a month of his summer vacation preparing his lecture, entitled 'Christmas Bells,' and, contrary to his usual practice, wrote it out in full. Typed by Aurelia, it ran to fifty pages and took two-and-a-half hours to read. His theme was the meaning of humanism and the dangers of allowing it to be eroded, a process that he saw as having begun in the mechanized mass slaughter of the First World War. He told his audience that he feared that the world had all too soon forgotten the horrors of modern warfare and was blindly fumbling towards the precipice once more. He made his own position perfectly clear, quoting John Scott's poem 'Recruiting', which begins:

> I hate the drum's discordant sound,
> Parading round, and round, and round.

The talk 'was a serious warning to us', Saitō recalled years later, long after the war that Hodgson had foreseen and Saitō himself found 'grievous and shameful'. Doi described it as 'a warning to us against the militaristic tendency, and a cry for world peace. I often am reminded of this as the first telling of the prophetic bell, warning (of) the Second World War.'[24] Both men were profoundly impressed with the lecture and lamented the fact that what Doi described as a 'very interesting human document' never appeared it print. In other circumstances one would have expected it to appear in the English Literary Society's journal, *Studies in English Literature*, as had Binyon's talk at the 1929 conference, but given the nature of its theme it is hardly surprising that it was quietly forgotten.

Aurelia admired what she called Hodgson's 'peace lecture', but that same year their own domestic peace was shattered. Rumours about their relationship had been circulating in the missionary community for some time and things came to a head when the director of her mission school and Doi became involved (the latter brought in to mollify the former), and one of her fellow-teachers wrote to her parents urging them to call her home. Aurelia's response was to resign from the school, leave her missionary accommodation and move into a Japanese home near Hodgson.

When Hodgson's second three-year contract ended a few months later in July 1931, he returned to England, taking half the canaries with him, while Aurelia sailed for America carrying the rest. Both canaries and lovers were reunited in October, when she joined him in London.

HODGSON AND T.S.ELIOT

In December 1931 Hodgson met T.S. Eliot at the London home of Lady Ottoline Morrell. Though they belonged to different generations both chronologically and poetically – Hodgson was now 60 to Eliot's 43 – the late Victorian and the great Modernist hit it off immediately, inaugurating a close friendship that would last until their deaths in the 1960s. They shared not only a profound passion for poetry, but also a richly sardonic sense of humour and a great love for dogs and pipes (a photograph taken the following summer shows them puffing away contentedly together, accompanied by Hodgson's pit bull terrier Pickwick and Eliot's Yorkshire terrier Polly). They also shared a history of marital trauma: Hodgson was in the process of getting divorced from Muriel in order to marry Aurelia, while Eliot was enduring the death throes of his own marriage. While the friendship between the two men deepened, cemented by a symbolic exchange of walking sticks, Aurelia stayed with the Eliots at their home in Clarence Gate Gardens and grew close to the troubled Vivienne, and they often went out as a foursome.[25]

With Hodgson, Eliot could relax and reveal the lighter, more humorous side of his nature. This is richly evident in a charming Edward Lear-like poem he sent Hodgson in August 1932, illustrated with a caricature of Hodgson with his habitual double-breasted suit and pipe, and a ferocious Pickwick leaping free of his leash. The poem was later revised and published as 'Lines to Ralph Hodgson Esqre.,' which begins:

> How delightful to meet Mr. Hodgson!
> (Everyone wants to know *him*)
> With his musical sound
> And his Baskerville Hound
> Which, just at a word from his master
> Will follow you faster and faster
> And tear you limb from limb.[26]

THIRD STAY IN JAPAN

Hodgson had left Sendai with a cordial invitation to return the following year, so it became in effect another one-year sabbatical. He arrived back in Japan in September 1932 and married Aurelia in October the following year. She proved a devoted wife, companion and fellow bird-watcher, and the house on the Hirose river at last became a home. In 1934 Hodgson found another beloved companion when he acquired a rare pure-bred Akita puppy, which he named 'Towser', in addition to an abandoned Irish terrier they had adopted. The canary breeding continued. Eliot's hyperbole –

He has 999 canaries [99999999999999999 in the original poem]
And round his head finches and fairies
In jubilant rapture skim

– almost proved prophetic when at one point the house was overrun with more than sixty canaries, which Hodgson gave to a pet shop with instructions that a pair be given free to every bird lover in Sendai. In the early 1960s, many years after Hodgson had left Japan, Doi recounted this story to Emperor Hirohito. He had been awarded the signal honour of being invited to deliver a lecture to the Imperial Family, and it shows the high regard in which he held Hodgson's poetry that he chose it as the subject of his talk. Knowing that the Emperor and his eldest sons were amateur naturalists and bird-lovers, he saw it as 'a good chance for me to talk about our poet's love of birds, and his presentiment of human tragedy if we continue to violate nature and maltreat birds and other innocent animals'.[27]

In a house barking and chirping with new life, for the first time since the Great War and his first wife's illness, Hodgson's creativity began to return. Shortly after his marriage he told Doi he had dreamed of writing a poem, only to find on waking that he could recall but one line, 'Marbles bleaching in the sun'. A few months later, however, he confided in Doi, 'I had a call from my Muse last night'. From that day onwards he wrote like a man possessed, so wholly absorbed in the poetry that was flowing out of him after so long a drought that he walked to the university on winter mornings without his hat and coat. Doi persuaded him take a month off from teaching to concentrate on his writing, which emerged as a long visionary poem about dogs and men, inspired by watching Towser dreaming beneath the cherry trees beside their house. On his return, Hodgson read his still-unfinished poem to his colleagues and students, who brought him flowering bulbs in congratulation. Hearing about this, Saitō wrote from Tokyo in August 1935 expressing delight and relief: 'Japan shall not, now, be accused of stealing an extremely rare song-bird from England and making him songless.'[28] In 1936 Hodgson recited some 700 lines of his poem-in-progress at the annual conference of the English Literary Society of Japan. Although he had produced artwork sporadically since coming to Japan, during this burst of reawakened creativity he produced over 200 drawings and cartoons, mainly nature studies, sketches of friends and satirical representations of London life but also including drawings inspired by Joyce's *Ulysses* and a few with specifically Japanese subjects, such as a drawing of an Ainu chief and his son (Hodgson was interested in the Ainu and their dogs). Eliot was keen to have him to illustrate *Old Possum's Book of Practical Cats*, but Hodgson, a dog man if ever there was one, declined.

Towards the end of his third teaching stint, Hodgson was approached by the Japanese Classics Translation Committee to assist in a major project, a translation of the *Manyōshū*, the oldest anthology of early Japanese poetry. Ishii Hakuson and Obata Shigeyoshi were charged with translating 1,000 poems that experts had selected from the more than 4,500 poems in the anthology, and Hodgson, despite the fact that he had very little Japanese, was chosen to give the finishing touch to their translations. At regular intervals Ishii and Obata brought their translations to Hodgson, who pointed out defects and occasionally, though somewhat reluctantly, suggested more suitable expressions. With their intimacy with the natural world, populated by creatures of all kinds, including thirty-seven species of birds, the *Manyōshū* poems must have been congenial to Hodgson. When he completed his third teaching contract in July 1935, he remained in Sendai to teach and continue working on the translation. For his services in the translation of the *Manyōshū* he was later awarded the Order of the Rising Sun.

FINALE

Hodgson's fourth and last three-year contract ran from September 1935 to August 1938. During these years his worst fears for Japan were realized with events both at home and in China. By 1938, with stormclouds gathering and Hodgson now almost sixty-seven, well past the usual retirement age, it was time to leave for good. The Hodgsons left in July, sailing first to Britain, then to America, finally settling in a remote Ohio farmhouse, where more than twenty years later in November 1962 Hodgson died aged ninety-one, the oldest living English poet.

No one could have been more profoundly English than Ralph Hodgson, yet no one could have been less of a Little Englander. His love for England, especially the countryside and country pursuits but also the vibrancy of London and the wry eccentricities of the English people, rings through his poetry and memoirists' records of his conversation. In Japan he dressed and ate like an Englishman, never taking to Japanese food. Unlike Blunden, Plomer, Empson or even Binyon, who had spent only two months in the country, he wrote no poems about Japan. We have no record of his encounters with Noh, kabuki, the tea ceremony or Zen poetry (although one of his successors at Sendai, James Kirkup, suggested that some of the terse, one-line poems Hodgson wrote after he left Japan – such as 'Who shall paraphrase a tear?' – are reminiscent of *senryū* or Zen kōans).[29] The things that moved him most – birds, dogs, the personalities of individual Japanese, the colleagues, students and townsfolk he grew to love – were things he could have found anywhere, things endemic to nature and human nature. But in this he was perhaps a true internationalist, unbeguiled by the exoticism that had lured so many Western artists and writers to Japan. In 1929 he had suggested to Saitō that Japanese universities needed professorships of 'International Discourse.' 'I love England; I keep her customs,' he told him, 'but I'll be happy if I am a mere man and belong to no nation. . . . I hope there'll be in the future no national or racial feelings in the world.' Perhaps the last word can be left to Saitō, who had helped bring him to Japan and was, along with Aurelia and Doi, closer to him than anyone else during his Japanese years:

> It is true that he wrote no poem about Japan, or America, or any country other than England. His world seems, from this point of view, to be nothing but England. And yet he is by no means a narrow-minded patriot. If a patriot, he is an internationally-minded patriot. . . . He was . . . an internationalist in mind, and was able to appreciate what is good, true and beautiful in Japan and elsewhere. His is an extraordinary mind.[30]

27

G.S. Fraser,[1] 1915–80: Poet and Teacher in Japan, 1950–51

EILEEN FRASER

G.S. Fraser

GEORGE FRASER was born in Glasgow and brought up in Aberdeen, where his father was Town Clerk. He graduated from St Andrews University in 1935, with an honours degree in English and History. His early poems reflected his love of Scotland, tempered by dissatisfaction and a restless desire to get away. After graduation he joined *The Aberdeen Press and Journal* as a reporter and acquired writing skills, which were to prove useful to him in later life. In September 1939 he joined the Army, serving mainly in Cairo and Eritrea. Exile and the exoticism of Egypt and Africa inspired some of his most moving poems, which were published in *Home Town Elegy* in 1944. After six years in the Army he settled in London. He married Eileen (Paddy) Andrew in 1946. He earned a living as a free-lance critic and journalist, somewhat precariously, but he did manage to support his family by writing mainly for *The Times Literary Supplement* and the BBC. More poems were published in these years – *The Traveller Has Regrets* in 1948, travel books on Latin America and Scotland and translations of poetry and prose from Italian, Spanish and French. In 1947 he visited Uruguay, Argentina and Chile as a member of a cultural mission designed to foster friendship between Britain and Latin America.

In January 1950 he was invited by the Foreign Office to be Cultural
Adviser to the UK Liaison Mission in Japan. He was to succeed Edmund
Blunden,[2] one of a long line of British poets, who taught in Japan, going
back to Ralph Hodgson, Robert Nichols, William Plomer,[3] Peter
Quennell and William Empson.[4] Japanese professors said of Quennell:
'We didn't understand him, but he was so beautiful.' Later younger poets
like James Kirkup, D.J. Enright[5] and Anthony Thwaite[6] carried on the
tradition. The Japanese have a reverence for poetry and for them writing
poems is a skill acquired by all educated people; at select parties to view
the full moon or the cherry blossom people are expected to write on the
spot *tanka* or *haiku* celebrating the beauties of nature. George became
adept at this and at turning out sonnets at short notice: at Sakurajima[7] in
the winter of 1951 he was asked to write one about the famous volcano:

> Still as a painting now, these austere slopes
> Have seen this beast-god gulp up soil and houses,
> Whose long tongue licks to swallow human hopes
> When drunk with his own anger he carouses.

Perhaps poetry is a necessity for the Japanese. Yoshida Kenichi,[8] son of
Prime Minister Yoshida Shigeru, said once in a drunken moment: 'The
Americans send us corned beef and rice, but the British send us poets!'

George Fraser arrived in Tokyo in March 1950, with his wife, Paddy
and his eight-month-old daughter, Helen. He was also accompanied by
Ronald Dore,[9] a young graduate research student, working on a study of
'City Life in Japan'. His Japanese was excellent and he proved to be an
enormous help, especially in coping with the press, as when immediately
on arrival in Yokohama, George was asked what he thought of Japan. He
helped to make the household run smoothly and sorted out domestic
problems – for example, when two of the house servants were competing
for the affections of the milkman, both threatening to leave.

Our first impressions of Japan on the road from Yokohama were
depressing: ugly, shabby factories, heaps of scrap metal, derelict buildings.
But this was post-war Occupied Japan, hardly recovered from the
devastation of war. American and British Commonwealth forces were
everywhere; the only cars on the roads seem to be large American ones.
Frank Lloyd Wright's Imperial Hotel was used by senior American
officers. The Marunouchi Hotel, a much smaller and less prestigious but
convenient one had become the social centre for the British in Tokyo.

On the day of our arrival we were invited to lunch by the Ambassador,
Sir Alvary Gascoigne,[10] a genial man with a military air. Striving to find
topics of conversation in common, (literature and diplomacy), we found
that Sir Alvary had known Sir Osbert Sitwell at Aldershot. He
commented: 'He had a good seat on a horse' – It later turned out that
Lady Gascoigne ran a rescue centre for abandoned dogs in Tokyo; new

arrivals were expected to adopt one straightaway, which we duly did. On our first evening we encountered grand embassy-style entertaining at a formal dinner given by the Blundens for Prince and Princess Takamatsu.[11] The food and wines were sumptuous and kimono-clad servants glided smoothly round the tables – rather different from the modest spaghetti suppers given by the Frasers in their Bloomsbury flat. With characteristic generosity the Blundens had asked us to stay in their house, even though they were then in the midst of packing to go home. There was no house available in the Embassy compound; instead, we were lodged in a fine house, part Western-style, part Japanese in the country at Seijo-machi, twelve miles outside Tokyo. But the roads were bad and the ancient embassy car, with a sometimes drunken Korean chauffeur, kept breaking down; so a move was made to Shinano-machi, much nearer to the centre. During the Occupation houses and servants were provided for the diplomatic staff by the Japanese Government. The servant problem was not easy at first; our cook had run a hamburger bar in Tokyo and knew very little about European cooking: he found the notion of 'French dressing' strange. We were tempted at first to replace him, but he had eight children and we had not the heart to dismiss him; he gradually became used to our strange ways. Things improved generally when an embassy-trained maid came to supervise the others. Edmund and George were welcomed as teachers. There was a long tradition of English studies in Japanese universities, which produced some fine scholars and translators: the whole of Shakespeare had been translated into Japanese and someone was then engaged on the almost impossible task of translating James Joyce's *Finnegan's Wake*. The severing of ties with Britain during the war years meant that teachers and students had been cut off from contemporary writing in England and were eager for news of current books and ideas. It was George's task to meet this need.

Succeeding Edmund Blunden was a hard task for George. Edmund had taught in Japan in 1936 and was greatly loved by his students, many of whom were by this time distinguished professors. He was said to have 'a genius for being loved' and this was apparent. At a lunch soon after George's arrival, Abe Kōbō,[12] a well-known novelist, said in a speech of welcome: 'Mr Fraser has replaced Mr Blunden at the British Embassy. Ah. But Mr Blunden loved and understood the Japanese people.' The suggestion might be that Mr Fraser would not be the same. Signs of Edmund were everywhere; all over Japan in the visitors' books of Japanese inns could be seen accomplished poems written in his fine hand. George wisely decided that the only way forward was to be himself.

Edmund Blunden had specialized in the Romantic poets; he had also given the Japanese the benefit of his wide learning in a series of books surveying the whole of English literature. George was expected to bring them up to date on the 'Moderns': Yeats, Pound, Eliot, Joyce. He lectured at all the major universities in Tokyo: Tōdai, Keiō and Waseda, and in other parts of Japan: Kobe, Osaka, Kyoto, Kyushu, Nagasaki and Hiroshima. Only five years after the bomb, Hiroshima was still a tragic sight, a shanty town, stirring feelings of guilt and horror among the visitors. What made it even more painful was the eager way the sights were shown to us, as if they were local points of interest: the terrible shadow of a man's body burnt into the steps of a bank was one of the many harrowing experiences.

The audiences at these lectures were large, not always understanding, but enthusiastic. At that time the Japanese were not good linguists. Direct communication was sometimes difficult and conversations meant long pauses to allow meaning to be digested. Lectures had to be typed out and copied beforehand, so that students had the script in front of them as they listened. Free and frank discussion between teachers and students was hard to foster; respect for the *sensei*, the teacher, goes deep: he must be right, so disagreement is not encouraged. Young lecturers were more forthcoming; they were anxious to know about current critical theory: the work, for example of I.A. Richards, William Empson and F.R. Leavis. On one occasion a young man was invited to continue the discussion over a drink at the hotel, but when the time came he did not turn up; his head of department came instead, apologising for his colleague's indisposition. Of course this was a social gaffe; the young man's senior should have been invited; George had forgotten about rank.

After the lecture there would be visits to local beauty spots and dinners with the professors going on far into the night. Sometimes there would be a visit to a tea-master for the tea-ceremony or an evening at a tea-house with a geisha in attendance. On one privileged occasion we were allowed to attend the annual geisha concert in Kyoto, given for their patrons, a feast of music and dancing. Dinners in tea-houses were usually provided by the university, so that the professors could enjoy a little feasting at someone else's expense. They were poorly paid, but extremely generous in entertaining us sometimes in their own homes.

The strains imposed by these tours were immense, but they did give us a wonderful chance to see the country and experience its cultural life. George particularly enjoyed the theatre: the *Bunraku* puppets in Osaka, the Kabuki and especially the Noh, which surprised his hosts, who expected him to be bored. Perhaps it was the slow stylized movements, the hypnotic music, the feeling, as he said, of 'appeasement and serenity' it gave him, almost of 'purification'.

He took to Japanese food with gusto, even enjoying sea-slugs, and developed a taste for sake. Imperial sake was particularly strong and was served in small tumblers instead of the usual tiny cup. Visits to the imperial stock farms for cherry-viewing or duck-netting, arranged by the Grand Master of Ceremonies sometimes ended in disaster, because of the strength of the sake: one Third Secretary was sick in the ambassador's car; another fell in the duck-lake. We failed to join the ambassador's departing procession of cars, because the Korean chauffeur was again drunk.

The fine simplicity of Japanese art and architecture appealed very much to us. George liked what he described as 'the beautiful Japanese sense of order and space'. He was impressed by the artistic skills of ordinary men and women. On one occasion at the house of a famous potter, a circle of professors deftly decorated plain, unglazed plates while we were still biting the ends of our paintbrushes. George came to believe that love of beauty in all its forms was deep in the Japanese psyche. The humblest of homes had its *tokonoma*, with a flower arrangement and *kakemono*, marking the seasons with appropriate trees and flowers. Viewing the cherry blossom, the iris, the azalea was a celebration of the Japanese love of flowers as well as being the occasion for partying and writing poems.

In 1950 Japan was still very much an occupied country. The Occupation seemed to us benign and sensible; the education system was overhauled, medical services and hospitals were improved, and, by allowing the emperor to remain, the country was painlessly and peacefully transformed into a constitutional monarchy. The Americans seemed to us occasionally gung-ho, as when one official asked another: 'How many institutions have you democratized today?' Or 'How many universities have you created?' Sometimes they offended Japanese sensibilities by referring to cultural treasures like ancient court dancing as 'cute'.

The impact of American culture was already evident in popular music, bowling and gambling machines. Industry was beginning to revive and copying of European technology was growing: imitation Leica cameras were already being sold at about a third of the German price.

But defeat in war had badly shaken confidence in the old way of life. The Japanese wanted to learn more from Western countries and adopt a Western way of life. Of course the British felt inadequate, only too aware of the weaknesses of the West. The impact of American culture had a disturbing effect on the younger generation, especially women. George's secretary, Keiko, was torn between the desire to be a 'new woman' with a career and parental pressure to learn flower-arranging and tea-ceremony and find a good husband. The strain was too great: Keiko had a breakdown, from which thankfully she recovered. It seemed then that Japanese men in particular, were leading two lives, using modern technology in offices and factories and returning home to traditional family life, heading the order for the bath, donning the *yukata*, continuing the age-old customs of the country.

Politeness has been instilled in the Japanese from birth. George attributed the refined manners of the people he met to the need for consideration for others in a crowded society, where there is so little privacy. Expressing feelings such as anger or grief might cause embarrassment, so – better to be detached, reserved, except when drunk – a release from repression generally tolerated. Politeness meant an unwillingness to make appointments to see the *sensei*, since this would seem presumptuous. Or refusing to ask a favour point-blank, since this would seem discourteous. George was often asked to write a preface for a book or an article for a newspaper; quite often the request would come through a go-between.

The Japanese dislike of being under an obligation (*on*) led to an embarrassing flow of gifts: lacquer boxes, whisky, flowers. These were so numerous that Vere Redman,[13] Counsellor for Information, called a meeting of editors and publishers urging them to stop the flow. 'Mr Fraser is a gift from the British Government to the Japanese people,' he said. 'He has a salary and does not need extra rewards.' Vere Redman was a great support to us. He had lived in Japan before the war and was very knowledgeable about Japanese life and customs. He was not at all a conventional diplomat and was often blunt and irreverent. When General MacArthur asked that *The Times*[14] correspondent should be sent home because he criticized the Occupation, Vere stamped angrily up and down his veranda, denouncing this attack on the freedom of the press. But then other members of the Embassy were far from the usual stereotypes; they were lively individuals with interests outside their work: Chinese pots, English poetry, the Japanese theatre. Embassy life proved to be a contrast with our modest bohemian life in London. We had to get used to an intensive social life: formal dinners, cocktail parties, ambassadorial receptions and indeed to join in the round ourselves, with the added duty of entertaining Japanese professors and their wives.

George's main function was lecturing at all the major universities in Japan, but in addition there were requests for articles, reviews, obituaries (on Bernard Shaw for example) and advice for Japanese writing in English. The strains were prodigious; George was a willing horse and never said no. But there were great compensations: the chance to see the beauties of the countryside, the splendours of art, of temples and palaces, the delights of staying in Japanese inns, where the grace and charm of the welcome warmed the heart.

A period of quiet came in July with a stay at Lake Chūzenji. Many of the Embassy staff in those days moved there in the hot summer months. We rented a large wooden house on the shores of the lake, complete with sailing boat. Amateurs in this sport, we ventured on the lake, armed with *Ten Easy Lessons in Sailing*, borrowed from the American Forces Library in Tokyo. The sailing was tricky; puffs of wind blew up through gaps in the nearby mountains. One Sunday we were away for several hours; anxious colleagues stood on the shore awaiting our return: a rousing cheer went up when we finally drew into the shore.

Even at Chūzenji there were demands on time and energy: there was a need for a book on modern English Literature. George had already published *Post-War Trends in English Literature*, based on lectures given at Keiō University, brought out by the Hokuseido Press in 1950, but clearly something on a larger scale was needed. So in the summer of 1950 George dictated to me, what became *The Modern Writer and His World* composed without any reference books beside him. This was, in his words, 'a plain and clear account of literature in England from 1880 to the present' (1950), covering ideas, the novel, drama, poetry and criticism; it was rich in illustration and anecdote, told in a personal tone, which made it more than a mere history. This book, modest in its original intention of giving the Japanese a map of modern literature, went into several editions in England, published by Penguin, and proved to be of lasting value to teachers of all kinds.

There had been a build-up of fatigue and stress over several months: overwork, too many parties, and late nights, too much drink. This culminated in a nervous breakdown on a visit to Hokkaido. The causes may have been in the past, in deep-rooted fears and anxieties, triggered by something that may have happened on the journey. George went home by air, followed by his family. He made a remarkable recovery. After six months in hospital he returned to writing books and to journalism. In 1958 he was appointed to a lectureship at Leicester University, later to be appointed to a Readership in Poetry. He was Visiting Professor at Rochester University in the US in 1963-64. He died in January 1980.

It was a sad end to fifteen months in Japan, but the experience had been rich and rewarding. Memories of the beauties of Japan lasted, as did his friendships with Japanese teachers and scholars.

28

Enright's Japan[1]

RUSSELL GREENWOOD[2]

D. J. Enright

'IN THE EARLY FIFTIES we were the only Foreign family in the hamlet of Okamoto', wrote D. J. Enright[3] years later, in *The Terrible Years*. He added that 'the natives were very kind to us'. Deservedly so, for the kindness was reciprocal, and Denise, his French wife, and their diminutive daughter were most welcome strangers in Okamoto / Sumiyoshi, still relatively rural areas on the outer fringes of the city and port of Kobe.

They were lucky to have chosen Kobe as their centre for activity. Whereas Tokyo (the *Dai-Wen*) so dominates its satellite cities, Kobe is simply one of three points in the Kansai triangle. Osaka is pre-eminently the bustling centre of big business and banking. 'Making any money?' is the traditional greeting, 'couldn't be worse!' the standard reply. Kyoto, with delectable Nara nearby an unexpected bonus, is the decorous pillar of culture and learning, almost as arcane now as it was in the Heian period, the days of Sei Shōnagon and Murasaki Shikibu. Kobe, though by no means lacking in a history of its own, is the newcomer of the three, cosmopolitan even in the Fifties, jaunty, and a little given to excess, as if it had heard one too many mariner's tales.

By rail at least, all these cities are so close and accessible that an intrepid traveller – the Enrights were intrepid – may breakfast in Kobe, take lunch in Osaka, and dine in Kyoto. It would just be possible, with a bit of Pelion on Ossa, to include a cucumber-sandwich tea in Nara in the nineteenth-century lounge of the Nara Hotel's old wing, where the ghosts of such British Japanophiles as Sir Ernest Satow or Sir George Sansom may be summoned up without undue alarm.

The speed of modern travel and the sense of antiquity, the solemn dignity of a Kyoto temple garden and the garishness of the advertisement displays immediately surrounding the temple precincts, produce a perpetual sense of contrast in Japan. The country is always a paradox, bewildering to poet and to mute inglorious alike. The medal, like the Queen's Gold Medal for Poetry, awarded to Enright in 1981, displays the remarkable reverse. After nearly four decades of absence, would the Enrights recognize Japan today? The answer, predictably, can only be Yes and No.

No, because Kobe's skyline, always impressive has seen many a change, with vast new buildings, from the admirable, through the merely grandiose, to the distinctly grotty. Okamoto is today a smart and expensive suburb, with blocks of apartments edging their way up the hillsides. In a uniquely Japanese fit of zeal, they even sliced the top off a minor mountain, though the twin peaks of Rokko San and Maya San remain comparatively undisturbed. The surplus earth has been transported to the sea by conveyor-belt and bogie, then redistributed to provide the foundations for a high-tech container port, sports-and-leisure complex, plus a luxury hotel called Portopia. Pelion off Ossa, in this case. Romans will be relieved to note that all this was not accomplished in one day.

Yes, some things would remain recognizable, since Japan is a very mountainous, labyrinthine country, where comic little railways clunk their way up and down the hills. The ruling party needs the farmers' votes, so no one has ever dared to do a Beeching on Japanese railways, and loss-making lines can still shake you past the rice terraces, 'the pasteboard houses and the plywood schools', which Enright saw in 1953 as a Busybody under a Cherry Tree. They may be taking you to a sophisticated terminus like Arima hot springs or, if you are prepared to travel hopefully, you may still in the Nineties find yourself alongside peasants, produce, even poultry and piglets, in a manner and milieu more reminiscent of a stopping train in Southern Thailand.

Distance may lend enchantment to the view, but to view Enright's Japan in 1953, a pair of powerful binoculars is required. Japan was an early stage on a journey which had already taken in Cambridge, extra-mural Birmingham, and, in between, exotic Alexandria with shades of Cavafy. With Berlin, Bangkok, and an epic stint in Singapore ahead, it was to be a lengthy journey, with some bumpy take-offs and landings, with occasional turbulence in the air. It must have been a relief eventually to sink into the swivel-chair at Chatto & Windus vacated by C. Day Lewis. My only object in this biographizing is to wonder how far the Japanese experience coloured the subsequent product, especially the twelve years or so in South-East Asia. There are few echoes of Egypt in the poems of the Japanese period, but there seems to me – with hindsight, perhaps – quite a lot of Japan's influence in the later work. The Japanese experience, except to the insensitive or actively hostile, tends to be a lasting one.

Since the Enright family were the only foreigners in Okamoto, I should perhaps declare my interest, as I was the only long-nosed foreign devil in the adjacent village of Mikage (Honourable Shade), just one stop down the line. We became friends, and since then it has been a pleasure and privilege to dwell in the 'honourable shade' of the Enrights in more countries than one. Kōnan University lies in the neighbourhood of these hamlets, far from Elsinore. Enright was appointed Visiting Professor, a title bestowed somewhat indiscriminately by the Japanese, but infinitely preferable to 'Distinguished Professor' – an Enright abomination.

Kōnan is one of the best private universities in Japan, though Keiō and Waseda, Tokyo's leading (and rival) private universities might be tempted to dispute the claim. This type of university often has many mansions and many manifestations. Kōnan, for example, has a senior boys' high school which it likes to call 'the Eton of Japan'. The rivals for this distinction are so formidably vociferous that the Battle of Waterloo could well have passed unnoticed on their playing fields. Still, Kōnan was ambitious enough to invite D. J. Enright, possibly with outside support, for in those days Japan was poor (newly deserving poor) and we were allegedly prosperous. Extracting the binoculars again, one can see through the mist Austin A40s and Hillman Minxes shipped sectionally to Yokohama for the Japanese to complete a screwdriver operation. They were not too bad on buses and light pick-up trucks (dubbed 'bata bata') but had not yet mastered the art of inventing, producing, much less mass-producing, a serious saloon car.

Accommodation appropriate to a lower-case distinguished professor from Oxbridge was in short supply (it still is today). So the Enrights moved in initially with one of Kōnan's trustees. They were really rich, perhaps one of the reasons for Enright's early awareness of the contrasts of wealth as in 'Happy New Year', when:

. . . I met a banker weeping through his smiles upon that
 hectic morn.
Omedetō, he told me while the saké bubbled on his lips.
His frock-coat trembled in its new and yearly bliss.
'A hard year for Japan' . . .
and walking away from the 'bright new house':
 . . . my head was full of yen, of falling yen.
I saw the others, with their empty pockets,

Merry on the old year's dregs, their mouths distilled a warm amen!

(CP, 19-20)

Enright's host was Takeda Chōbei, the Chairman of Takeda Pharmaceuticals, the Mr Boots of Japan. An orchid-lover, he too had been at Cambridge before the war, and, as the sixth generation of his family firm, had heard the chimes at midnight. If Takeda was Dennis's first Lord High Executioner, then Iwai Yūjirō was Lord High Everything Else. He was Chairman of what is now Nissho-Iwai, one of Japan's Big Six trading companies. He ruled the Japan-British Society with an iron hand in a not so-velvet glove. By a great coincidence, he (too) had been at Emmanuel College, Cambridge, contemporary with the then British Consul-General, a dear, dour man, whom Iwai once described to me as 'a bit of a poet, like Enright'. Iwai took to the Enrights and introduced them to *fugu*, the blow-fish, delicious but lethal if ill-prepared. A number of people die of *fugu* poisoning every year; some are said to play Russian roulette with its poisonous elements. Foreign professors, expensively imported, are not permitted to die thus, company chairmen even less so. A fairly safe way of embarking on *fugu* is through an invitation from the Chairman of a major Japanese company. Roman Emperors took precautionary measures not dissimilar in nature.

If I have elaborated on these tycoons (one of the few English words indisputably derived from the Japanese), it is because I think they were important to Enright. They at least had a modicum of shared educational experience. They were tough, but kindly men. They were helping to resurrect Japan from an abject post-war poverty to a living competence, towards a global respect for their commercial integrity and, after their deaths, to a national GDP beyond their wildest expectations.

On the academic side, though there were always exceptions, there was little to learn from the average *sensei*.[4] They were then ill paid, ill housed, often ill clad and, though they retained their special status, they found it hard to command general respect. Books in foreign languages were in short supply, but were occasionally made available through the ministrations of a benign and Midas-like United States government. I recall one particular occasion when a number of Japanese academics benefited from an unusual concatenation of circumstances. The monstrous Senator McCarthy sent his henchmen, Cohn and Schine, round the USIS libraries of Japan, the consequence of which was the banning of books by authors other than US citizens. Thus quantities of heavily labelled volumes of Shakespeare, Bunyan, Wordsworth, down to Keynes and Orwell, found their way into Japanese university libraries, The USIS officials stopped well short of burning the books – though I encountered one or two of them who would gladly have consigned Messrs Cohn and Schine to the flames.

Enright was encouraged towards Kyoto, to some extent by the British Council who were then keen to expand in that desirable direction. Not that it normally takes much persuasion to move in the direction of Kyoto. (And, the sooner it is said the better, D. J. Enright does not take kindly to being directed by officials. Quite rightly so, but that was later, and in another country.) For a time he kept an eye on the books that later became the basis of the Council's library, and gave a weekly lecture in Kyoto. There were more sensitive teachers to be found in un-bombed Kyoto: to have seen the city, as I did, just after the end of the war, and to have compared it with the devastation elsewhere in Japan was a revelation of a chastening, even chilling, nature. Enright seemed to find it a 'grey city':

> A pallid grace invests the gliding cars.
> The Kamo keeps its decent way, not opulent nor bare.
> The last light waves a fading hand. Now fiercer seasons
> start like neon in the little bars.

> (CP, 30)

Probably the most distinguished of these teachers was the late Jugaku Bunshō,[5] very much a scholar of the old school, but also a person whose pallid grace invested the word *sensei* with greater dignity than the more raucous *shachō* (company chairman) could ever command. He was expert in many fields, but especially on Blake and Dante. When I visited Professor Jugaku, then housebound, in the later Seventies, he recalled Enright with visible pleasure as a good, kind, and generous man. Another jovial influence of a more voluptuous nature was Osaka's Prefectural Librarian, Nakamura, translator of some of Winston Churchill's works. Though Osaka was his home, he gravitated quite naturally to Kyoto and occasionally entertained his favourite foreigners in Ponto-chō or Gion, the original geisha quarters of Heian Japan. These riverside districts, now hideously marred by boutiques or even jazz bars, had a gentle grace of their own. They were, at their best, inaccessible to a foreigner except as the accompanied guest of a Japanese *habitué*. There perhaps 'the Kamo keeps its decent way' in a manner of speaking – or possibly poetic licence is justifiable in the licensed quarters.

Enright's Japan was not confined to the Kansai. Even then Tokyo beckoned. It was, after all, 'that Eastern capital', as an elderly aristocratic lady from Kyoto ('the capital capital') once described it to me disparagingly. The so-called bullet train now takes some three hours from Osaka to Tokyo. In those days the stately express departed from Osaka's Umeda Station at precisely 9 a.m. and reached Tokyo at precisely 5 p.m., the white-gloved station masters being at hand both on departure and arrival. They usually looked at their watches, approvingly.

Enright had friends in Tokyo: for instance, Bill and Helen MacAlpine, a cheerful and curiously ubiquitous couple who were equally at home in Dylan Thomas's Soho as they were in the bar of the Strand Hotel, Rangoon. Another lively soul was the late Yoshida Kenichi, critic, belle-lettrist, saké-lover, who had been an undergraduate briefly but, by his own admission, ingloriously, at King's, Cambridge (again!); one cross that Kenichi managed to bear fairly lightly was that his father throughout that period was Japan's Prime Minister.

Some of the Tokyo experiences emerged in later poems, in *Addictions* (1962), for instance, where the poem 'In Memoriam' simultaneously observes a live elephant on the roof of the Takashimaya deapartment Store and a dying Englishman, who had been Takashimaya's Father Christmas:

'He would have died anywhere.
And he lived his last year in Japan, loved by a
Japanese orphan, teaching her the rudiments of
Happiness, and, (without certificate) teaching
Japanese students.
                                    (CP 49-50)

But Tokyo by stately railway train was a long way from Okamoto. Social life in Kobe was less rarefied, and evening relaxation easily obtained by taking the prestigious Hankyu Line from Okamoto to Kobe's Sannomiya Station. Three railway companies sent their trains on separate tracks, competitive, relentless, and parallel, between Osaka and Kobe, to where, much lower down the scale, indeed under the tracks of the oft-despised National Railway, stood or crouched the Bar Canna, alas no more. A cheerful and understanding Mama San, assisted by three girls (Akiko, Sumiko, Chiyako), entertained from behind their Stand Bar, as they were then called: they stood behind the bar, you sat in front. And chatted and drank a fair amount of bottled beer which might cost the guest £2 or £3 a session (now tenfold for its approximate equivalent). We often went there, virtually the only foreigners, but apparently welcome. Especially Dennis's wife, who often accompanied us, and who personified the security of marriage and to the girls the opportunity to catch a rare glimpse of European womanhood, surely a dream of French luxury (or lingerie) and fine living.

Enright wrote of all this in *The World of Dew*, and concluded that there was less 'viciousness' in Japan than could be found 'in Piccadilly or Place Pigalle'. It was the world of Miss Moth rather than Madam Butterfly. Their names, if not their attributes, appear in their poems: Akiko, 'she shall be glorified, if any are'; and Sumiko:

So pour the small beer, Sumichan. And girls
    permit yourselves a hiccup, the thunder
Of humanity. The helpless alley is held by
    sleeping beggars under

Their stirring beards . . .

(CP, 20-1)

The objects of Enright's compassion, in and out of the Canna were there for all to see. The girls were poor but honest, the beggars still poorer and with fewer hopes. All were a long way (ten minutes by taxi at 11 p.m.) from Takeda Chōbei's orchids and his pharmaceutical products, on which they had to rely to survive. If they could afford to survive was the message of the plaintive poems. Bleak, but not quite so annihilating as 'Hiroshima', whose citizens might have wished for something lasting, 'like a wooden box'.

For Enright as teacher there must have been grounds for frustration as well as compassion. The average Japanese university student, though often endearingly loyal, is not very articulate in any language. Nor is he ('she' more often is) noticeably diligent, since the university tends to be looked upon as a four-year breathing-space (not necessarily an unworthy assumption) between the examination hell which has preceded it and the highly competitive business world which is to follow. So a well-delivered lecture is apt to be received with deafening silence, a plea for cooperative questions with blank dismay; most amiable jokes, except straight banana-skin, drop with a dull thud. Sometimes a similar sense of the dead hand can be felt in relations with academic colleagues, as if the new broom, once swept clean, can now be discarded. The foreign lecturer tends to search his conscience and ask 'where did I go wrong?'

It is alleged
An empty saké bottle in your company was seen . . .

(CP, 27)

But he need not worry, any more than Hokusai's mad poet need worry. The tap turned off will suddenly turn on again, often with some gesture as welcome as it is unexpected. In Enright's case, it seemed to at least one observer that his wit, good humour, and lively sense of the ridiculous was always at hand to provide a more than adequate antidote to frustrations of this kind.

Aside from the academic world, there must have been many problems in maintaining a family home in nether Kansai in the early Fifties. True, a live-in cook, a nanny-cum-maid-of-all-work was an eminently feasible proposition and some combination of this arrangement represented a necessity for the Enrights. The near-prose poem 'A Poor Little Lonely Child' perfectly depicts the domestic scene. The parents gad about, the mother lectures in French, marks examination papers, the father lectures on good literature and takes refuge at home in bad language. It is a nightmare of a Cultural Festival to which the parents are bidden: the description does justice to the inanities that the Japanese are occasionally capable of perpetrating. On their return home, the child greets her parents with the pertinent observations of a 4-year-old on a new and arty Japanese plate:

> That is a good plate. I do not like it now. Because I
> do not like the colours, now. But that is a good plate.
> And I shall like it when I am bigger.
>
> (CP, 24-5)

How right and reassuring. Said with all the aplomb of her four years, with quite a bit of schooling already behind her, including personal attention from the 'Head Monster', as she calls him in 'Blue Umbrellas'.

Verbal sallies have always intrigued Enright, who in his essays has given a measure of praise to the pun, and has mused outrageously on his Swedish typewriter called FACIT. In Japan, there was ample scope for this, dextrously when the Japanese were employing their own language, less so when the medium was the English language. Every self-respecting salaryman in Japan, even the teacher-poet, requires a seal or 'chop' for the transaction of official business. In Japanese *kanji*, Enright acquired an impressive seal, the three characters of which, to his delight, read 'EN-RAI-TO', or 'Monkey comes to town'. Madeleine had to be similarly equipped, for Western wives are often accommodated in areas where most Japanese wives would fear to tread (though they are frequently the real guardians of the family finances). She was rewarded with a seal differing only in the initial character and became 'Swallow comes to town'.

In English the situation is more precarious. As is well known, Japanese has no letter 'l', so the capital city of the United Kingdom is 'Rondon'. It is peculiarly contagious, and I once found myself in temporary agreement with a student who said 'o for orange, R for remon'. But the sagacious Japanese *sensei* who has regaled his students with ponderous jokes about 'Words'worth' over compensates. Aware of his language's consonantal deficiencies and recognizing that 'r' is a sop to Cerberus, he will in all seriousness address his letter to 'Professor D. J, Enlight', with its clear intimations of immortality.

For over a century now, foreign teachers of English have visited Japan. Today there are thousands, varying from the refreshingly youthful and idealistic, to the highly skilled language teachers and not forgetting the unwashed sub-culture ('Come, come, Baby. English lessons' – a notice I once pointed out to Enright, mentioned in *The World of Dew*). But there were some notable characters in the distant past. Lafcadio Hearn can scarcely be included amongst the British contingent, for he was such a mixture from the cradle to the grave, ending his days as Koizumi Yakumo, his wife's maiden name, revered but rootless. Later there were many others. Unlike today when it is highly profitable to come to Japan to teach, it was in pre-war days fashionably eccentric. After all, Part III of Gulliver's Travels was entitled 'A voyage of Laputa, Balnibarbi, Luggnagg,

Glubbdubdrib and Japan'. Writers of the stature of Peter Quennell, William Plomer, and William Empson went out to Japan and made their temporary marks, but scarcely a ripple remains. The exception is the self-effacing Edmund Blunden (later, acknowledged in his *World of Dew*, the 'Honourable Mr Middleman' who introduced him to Kōnan University), Hearn came and stayed forever. Of the others, only Blunden returned. The Professor at Tokyo University, 1924-7, became the the the Cultural Attaché at the UK Liaison Mission (i.e. Embassy) 1948-50. I recall a slightly exasperated American diplomat saying at the time, 'We put USIS officers all over the country. You do it with one Blunden.' He certainly scattered his image through the land in the way of *ad hoc* verses. There seem to be a proliferation of Blunden originals at Senior High Schools and the like in most quarters of Japan. Even the one genuine English pub in Kobe (now completely Japanese-owned, but 'lovingly preserved', as Pevsner would say) is honoured with a Blunden sonnet, ending like a wounded, though non-Alexandrine, snake: 'with the King's Arms proud over it'.

How far, then, did Dennis Joseph Enright enlighten the Japanese scene in the Fifties? Probably far more than he ever imagined. 'The best fruits of a good teacher's work are those he is never likely to see' observed the late scholar-educationalist, Sir Richard Livingstone, a shade sententiously. But his praises are still sung there, by acquaintances ranging from very elderly professor, ex-University of Hiroshima, to ex-student of Kyoto University, now himself a professor in Nara, and visiting professor at Kōnan Women's University. Which is significant for one who left so long ago, and never came back. I have often wanted to ask Dennis whether his motto, unconsciously albeit, might not be:

The Moving Finger writes; and, having writ,
Moves on . . .

29

Nishiwaki Junzaburō, 1894–1982:
A Self-made Englishman

NORIMASA MORITA

Nishiwaki Junzaburō

INTRODUCTION

NISHIWAKI JUNZABURŌ'S first collection of Japanese poems, *Ambavarlia*, published in 1933, opens with a short poem with the mundane title 'Weather'. The poem itself, however, is far from ordinary:

> On a morning like 'upturned gems'
> Someone whispers with somebody in the doorway.
> This is the day a deity was born.[1]

The publication of this brief 'imagist' poem had great symbolic significance. With this poem a new phase of modern Japanese poetry began. Murō Saisei, a highly respected poet of the time, praised it, especially the line '. . . a morning like upturned gems'.[2] Nishiwaki's poems and writings on modernist and surrealist poetry transformed the poetic landscape in Japan.

Nishiwaki was a prolific poet; sixteen major books of poems were published in his lifetime. They were highly acclaimed and some of them were awarded prestigious literary prizes. In 1957 he was officially

nominated to the Swedish Academy as a candidate for the Nobel Prize for
literature through the indirect recommendation of Ezra Pound.[3]
   Although Nishiwaki is remembered as arguably the greatest twentieth-
century poet in Japan, he was also a well-known scholar, teacher and
translator. He became a professor of English at Keiō University in 1926 at
the age of thirty-three, teaching mainly English literature, Old and Middle
English, and linguistics, until he retired from the post in 1962. Nishiwaki
served for three years as dean of the faculty of literature at Keiō and
published scholarly books on English writers from William Langland to
T.S. Eliot as well as literary criticism and essays. His students included
many who were later to become prominent poets, writers, journalists,
scholars and businessmen. When the Japanese Society for English
Literature was founded in 1929, Nishiwaki read a paper at its first
conference entitled 'English Classicism'. His translations include Chaucer's
Canterbury Tales, T.S. Eliot's *The Waste Land* and poems by James Joyce.
In his later years he was honoured by being elected to the Science Council
of Japan, inducted into the Academy of Art, recommended as an honorary
member of the American Academy of Arts and Science, and finally
awarded the Order of the Sacred Treasure.
   Almost all poets and writers in modern Japan have been attracted to the
West in one way or another. However, none was more attracted to
Western literature than Nishiwaki. From a very early age he determined
to read, speak and write English as well as a native English speaker. He
believed that it was not possible to become an international writer if you
wrote in Japanese. When he first started writing poetry, he chose to write
in English and French and it was only years later that he began to write
poems in Japanese, first as translations of his own French poems. Until his
mid-thirties, he had hardly read any Japanese books apart from a small
number of poems, and had rarely published anything in Japanese.

UPBRINGING

Nishiwaki Junzaburō was born on 20 January 1894 as the second son of a
wealthy banker in Ojiya, Niigata Prefecture. The town of Ojiya sprawls
along the Shinano River and used to be known as the centre of
production of thin linen crepe called *Ojiya chijimi*. The Nishiwakis had
been manufacturers and wholesalers of linen crepe and had become
wealthy by rice trading, land speculation and banking. Ojiya, where
Nishiwaki lived until he was eighteen, was a peaceful, provincial town
with considerable natural beauty, but despite material comforts, his
childhood does not seem to have been an entirely happy one. He wrote
little about his parents. His father seems to have been an intelligent,
competent if somewhat colourless banker, who was often ill. He died of
tuberculosis at the age of fifty-one in 1911. His mother, Saki, was 'strong

313

both physically and mentally and a classic example of a hysterical woman being reduced to skin and bones like a sardine since she was young'.[4] As this unkind comment shows, the relationship between him and his mother was tense. Until he was about five he was brought up by a wet-nurse. He was a shy, introverted boy and neither went out of his home often nor made friends with local boys of the same age. The house in which he lived as a child was his whole world and he spent most of his childhood picking flowers, playing house with his two sisters and drawing pictures.

Nishiwaki was sent to a local school. As soon as he entered Ojiya Middle School, he became absorbed in the study of the English language and gained the nickname, half sarcastic and half honorary, of *eigoya* (English freak/specialist). He read hardly any books in Japanese but collected as many English books as possible and bought specialist magazines on the English language. He was said to have taken all his notes at school in English, memorised the entire five volumes of the *National Readers* and taught English grammar to a university student. Nishiwaki's uncle, Saizaburō, had studied at Cambridge and looked after Nishiwaki following his father's death. In his warehouse there was a large collection of English books to which Nishiwaki had free access.

From an early age Nishiwaki developed a passion for Western paintings and claimed that his yearning for things European and dislike of most things Japanese stemmed from this. At middle school Nishiwaki, in addition to his prowess in English, showed a definite talent for drawing and painting. He neglected other subjects and detested mathematics. He showed no interest in Japanese fiction but read many English novels. His ignorance of Japanese literature, apart from some classics and modern poetry, often amazed his literary friends. In one of his essays Nishiwaki recalled: 'When I discovered that I had to have a profession, I cursed life for the first time.'[5]

On the recommendation of his art teacher, Nishiwaki decided to train to be a painter and was accepted as a boarding apprentice by a famous oil painter, Fujishima Takeji, in Tokyo. He also joined the *Hakuba* school on Fujishima's recommendation and visited other leading painters such as Kuroda Seiki and Shirataki Ikunosuke, pioneers in Western-style painting in Japan. Although every door was opened for him, he was never enthusiastic enough to become a professional painter. This involved rigorous training. He did not enjoy the drawing lessons at Fujishima's studio and did not want to be taught how to draw and paint. He thought that teaching which put too much emphasis on mere skill would prevent him from painting freely and believed that art should be self-taught as he had taught himself English. He also objected to drawing nude figures. Naked women in heated studios apparently reminded him of a public bath house; he was never comfortable in an enclosed space with a naked woman. Although he was not keen on becoming a professional painter, he dreamt of going to Paris to study art. In those days it was regarded in Japan as a *sine qua non* for any would-be artist to spend some time in Paris. Instead his guardian wanted him to enter the Tokyo College of Arts. Nishiwaki, however, thought it ridiculous to paint cherry blossoms, or pine trees in oils and, because he was not allowed to go to France, gave up the idea of becoming a painter.

Around this time Nishiwaki started writing poems in English while continuing to study English. His relations persuaded him to take the entrance exam for the University of Tokyo. According to Kagiya Yukinobu, who was a student of Nishiwaki at Keiō, he took only the English exam and spent the rest of the day reading *A Midsummer Night's Dream* in the college yard.[6] Nishiwaki's own version was slightly different.[7] The Nishiwakis had had a close connection with Fukuzawa Yukichi and Keiō University since Teijirō, Nishiwaki's great uncle, had given a large sum of money to the university. He was accordingly admitted to the preparatory course of Keiō university.[8]

After he came to be regarded as a great scholar-poet, he wrote somewhat self-mockingly that he was accepted by the university only on the basis of his fluency in English.

The department at Keiō to which he was admitted after two years in general studies was neither literature nor that political science which he preferred, but economics. This was the choice of his uncle and his mother on whose financial support he was totally dependent, but he had no interest in the subject. Instead he studied intensely languages such as Greek, Latin and German, as well as English. The only 'economics' textbook he read was *Das Kapital*. Nosaka Sanzō, who was to become the chairman of the Japan Communist Party, was his classmate and they read it together.

Nishiwaki submitted his BA thesis in Latin to the Department of Economics at Keiō University. His supervisor and examiner, the famous Christian economist, Koizumi Shinzō, could not read Latin very well and demanded an extended Japanese abstract from Nishiwaki. The submitted abstract was fifteen pages long and it later became a legend at the university that Nishiwaki was awarded his BA degree by writing only a fifteen-page 'thesis'. Nishiwaki explained that he wrote his BA thesis in Latin because he wished to study in England and knowledge of Latin was necessary to enter Oxford.[5]

Although Nishiwaki was an avid reader of books in English, he did not know much about literature in general. Washio Hiroshi, a distant relative and contemporary at Waseda University helped him form his literary taste. Through his influence Nishiwaki became an admirer of Baudelaire and French symbolist poets. He visited Washio's lodgings nearly as often as he went to the university. There, with fellow students such as Naoki Sanjūgo, who was to become a prominent writer of popular fiction, and

Tanizaki Seiji, Jun'ichirō's younger brother, they spent hours discussing literature. His favourite writers in those days were Verlaine, Rimbaud, Flaubert, Maupassant, Shakespeare, Walter Pater, Arthur Symons, Oscar Wilde, W.B. Yeats, Dostoevsky, and Nietzsche. He read Pater's *Renaissance* many times over. Although there were English classes at Keiō, Nishiwaki learnt more from studying on his own. He was determined to learn English pronunciation scientifically and read Henry Sweet's *Phonetic Study of Language* many times so that he almost knew it by heart. By the summer of 1914 he had studied English for three years and could read the complete works of Shakespeare in the original even if with a little difficulty. The goal he set for himself in studying English was a high one: 'I always hoped that one day I could think and feel in foreign languages as native speakers do.'[8]

After graduation in 1917 Nishiwaki found a job at *The Japan Times*, the only English language newspaper at that time. Less than a year after he started work as a staff writer, there was a financial crisis at *The Japan Times* and he had to leave. His relatives then sent him to a job interview at the Bank of Japan. Fortunately or unfortunately, a mild case of amyloidal filtration of the lungs was discovered in a health check at the bank, and he spent the next six months in a warm climate convalescing. Having nothing else to do, he read the complete works of Pater and discovered the pleasures of literary criticism. He returned to work in 1919, this time as a part-time official in the treaty department at the foreign ministry in Tokyo. The Versailles peace negotiations were then being conducted and it was his job to translate the telegraphed drafts into Japanese and to edit other translations.

In 1920 he was appointed to the post of English teacher at the preparatory school of Keiō University. Nishiwaki had for some time been writing English poems but these were essentially exercises in improving his proficiency in English. He wanted to write sonnets in the style of Keats and wrote more than 250 poems in English during his life (including some that remained unpublished), but it was not until 1926 that he began to compose poems in Japanese, some fifteen years after he first began writing poetry. 'Why had I not written poems in Japanese? I had not doubted for a moment that Japanese poetry had to use archaic and flowery poetic diction. I had believed that by writing in English I could do without such diction.'[9] In fact, not all Japanese poems were written in archaic, literary language and there were also artificial and stifling conventions in English poetry. Another reason why Nishiwaki did not write in Japanese was because he hated the excessive sentimentality of Japanese poetry:

> The young men of literary type in my generation shared a tendency to talk precociously about sex, drink sake, and call in geishas. They tended to be of a delicate and effeminate artistic type and under the sway of a vulgar sentimentality.[10]

This was also untrue. His inclination to despise Japanese things and praise Western things grew stronger after he settled in Tokyo at the age of eighteen.

In 1920 his friend, Fukuhara Rosō, who was a haiku poet, recommended to him a book, which led Nishiwaki finally to write poems in Japanese. The book was Hagiwara Sakutarō's *Tsuki ni Hoeru* ('I Howl at the Moon'). It was an immediate success when it was published in 1917 but Nishiwaki did not then know of its existence because he rarely read Japanese books. The impact of the book on Nishiwaki was gradual. Urged by Fukuhara he took it with him to England. He also took with him Baudelaire's *Les Fleurs du mal* and the English translation of Nietzsche's *Also Sprach Zarathustra*. He read many times *I Howl at the Moon*. '. . . Hagiwara Sakutarō was a revelation for me. This wonderful existence suddenly opened my eyes to Japanese poetry. . . However, I did not dare to write poetry in Japanese for the next ten years. . .'[11] If he had not been introduced to Hagiwara's book, Nishiwaki might not have become one of the greatest Japanese poets of the twentieth century and might have been known simply as a scholar and university professor.

LONDON

Only two years after Nishiwaki became a lecturer at Keiō University, with its long tradition of English studies (*eigaku*), he was sent to England. Despite this tradition, the university had a serious shortage of English teachers with an adequate command of the language, especially at a practical level. Some English-language classes were even taught by lecturers in German philosophy who happened to know some English.[12] The university wanted its English department to be more academic and up-to-date and his task was to bring to Japan the most recent academic trends in the study of English literature.

In early July 1922, Nishiwaki left Kobe. He did not keep a diary of the voyage and wrote few letters, but he recorded the journey to England through Singapore, Egypt, Italy and France in his poems and essays (*Ambarvalia* contains many poems referring to this trip). On the ship he met Tokuda Keijirō, a lawyer working in London who later introduced him in London to Kōri Torahiko, a friend of Ezra Pound, whose works are thought to have exerted an important influence on the plays of W.B. Yeats.

Nishiwaki arrived in London on 22 August 1922, having spent some time in the South of France en route. After a few days in London in a rather luxurious hotel, he went to Oxford to be enrolled as a full-time student only to find that it was too late to matriculate. He had to wait for a year and chose to stay in London instead of Oxford. 1922 was a crucial year for the history of English literature because T. S. Eliot's *Waste Land*

and James Joyce's *Ulysses* were both published in that year. In London Nishiwaki met many young writers, artists and journalists and through them was initiated into modernism and then surrealism, of which he had not even heard while in Japan.

Nishiwaki moved to a cheaper hotel near Notting Hill Gate on the recommendation of Nomura Kōichi, whom he had known since his undergraduate day and who later became a well-known music critic. Nomura took Nishiwaki to numerous concerts:

> . . . most evenings we went to a concert and on our way home we discussed music and literature in a coffee shop. I went to second-hand book shops everyday and bought a few books, but I piled them under my bed without reading them. Around this time I might have been mentally lethargic or the system of my thought might have changed. As I could not accept what other people wrote, I did not feel like reading any books at all.[13]

He moved in late autumn to new lodgings in Highgate and lived there for a month or so with an aged English businessman who worked in a small office in Tottenham Court Road. The Englishman left early in the morning and came back late in the evening. In the hotels where he had stayed previously, there were plenty of people to whom he could talk. However, in Highgate he was left alone all day and spent most of the time in the house occasionally looking out of the windows at a large pear tree in the back garden and hitting the keyboard of the piano because he could not play it. More than thirty years later this particular Englishman was mentioned in the poem entitled 'Pear' included in *The Modern Allegory* (1953). One evening, the English businessman gave him a copy of Baudelaire which he had found in a second-hand bookshop.

At this time Nishiwaki was introduced to John Collier by Sherard Vines, who was going to Keiō to teach English and English literature from April, 1923. Collier had started publishing poems in his teens and later came to be widely known as a writer of fantastic stories with the publication of *His Monkey Wife* in 1933. The script for *The African Queen* is his best-known work. When Nishiwaki first met him, he was filing cards at the Admiralty and lived in a dingy attic flat in Lambeth. Though Collier was only twenty-two years old at that time, he would become the greatest literary influence on the twenty-nine-year old Nishiwaki. Through Collier, he met other poets and journalists. They went to pubs almost every night and talked about recent developments in poetry, literature and the arts. Collier admired T. S. Eliot and recommended Pound, Lewis and Joyce. He lent Nishiwaki Eliot's *Waste Land* which had been published in the October issue of *The Criterion*. He also recommended Nishiwaki to buy back-numbers of the magazine, *The Blast*, co-edited by Pound and Lewis.

Collier also introduced him to modern art movements. They visited exhibitions of Cezanne, Van Gogh, Picasso, Matisse, the primitivists, and African sculpture. Together they saw the Russian ballet and listened to the music of Stravinsky. Collier took Nishiwaki to bookshops in Charing Cross Road, and one of these, which stocked a number of poetry books, especially, Surrealist and Dadaist works imported from France, became his favourite shop. It was also patronized by T.S. Eliot.

After he had met Collier, Nishiwaki's literary tastes changed completely. He temporarily abandoned Pater, Symons, Georgian and Edwardian English literature, and concentrated on contemporary avant-garde works. He also transformed himself from a writer of rhymed verse to an imagist and modernist poet. Some time after he first met Collier Nishiwaki plucked up enough courage to show him the poems which he had been writing in Japan and England. They were immediately dismissed and he is said to have thrown all his old poems into the River Thames. Whether this is true or not, they were certainly destroyed and all that survived are some published in magazines like *Mita Bungaku* and *Eigo Bungaku* before he left Japan. The poems he started to write after he met Collier were heavily influenced by Eliot, Pound and H.D. 'A Kensington Idyll' was one such poem and he showed it to Collier one evening in a pub. Collier liked it and immediately recommended him to send it to Harold Monroe, the owner of the famous Poetry Bookshop and the publisher of a historically important magazine called *Chapbook*. Nishiwaki duly sent his poem to Monroe. Although its publication was delayed for nearly a year, it appeared in the 39th volume in 1924 alongside Eliot's 'Doris's Dream Songs', which later became *The Hollow Men*:

Atkinson has a tremendous storm of gloom
   When the lilacs come into bloom.
The waves of languor dash against his breast:
   In his pyjamas he takes a rest.
His tongue is as bitter as a tansy leaf:
   His eyes are cloudy with grief.
His windpipe is deprived of sonorous words;
   His hair makes a nest for the birds.[14]

Atkinson here reminds us of Eliot's Prufrock and the subject of the poem is the disillusion and *ennui* of a modern man, a theme also found in Eliot's early poems. Although his English poems are far better than those of Yone Noguchi, who also wrote poems in English and taught English literature at Keiō, they were by no means his best poetic efforts. Nevertheless, nothing pleased him more during his stay in England than the publication of 'A Kensington Idyll' and the event considerably boosted his morale.

As the title of the poem suggests, Nishiwaki was living in Kensington when he wrote it. Since he started going out with Collier nearly every evening, he had found Highgate too far away. In January 1923, he moved into the Hotel Roland near the Old Brompton Road. In late 1922 or early 1923, he was introduced to Marjorie Biddle, an art student, probably by Kōri Torahiko who had lived in the house in Dulwich owned by her family and who had known her since she was a young girl. According to Dr Marjorie Williams, who was Marjorie's housemate in Hampshire before she died, and Nishiwaki Midori, the poet's daughter-in-law, they fell in love immediately and started seeing each other in London frequently.

OXFORD

In October 1923, Nishiwaki enrolled at New College, Oxford, which was Sherard Vines' old college. John Collier and his friends were allergic to the stuffy and conservative academic atmosphere of Oxford and Cambridge and tried to dissuade him from going to Oxford. It was a tremendous wrench for him to leave Marjorie Biddle, Collier and the free and creative life in London, but he was in England to pursue an academic career and he had a strong sense of duty. He had a room in the college from October 1923 to December 1924, although he did not leave Oxford till the end of the Trinity term in 1925. He specialized in Old and Middle English. The reading list set by his tutor included some Old English texts, the Gothic translation of the Bible, *Beowulf*, Langland and Chaucer and he spent almost every minute available to him reading these texts. The moment term started Nishiwaki felt depressed and missed his London life and friends. He often went to London to see Marjorie and Collier. He also discovered that students of English at Oxford were not as well respected as those studying Greats and he wrote a letter to his colleagues at Keiō asking for permission to switch. However, his request was politely refused.

While keeping his room in college, Nishiwaki rented early in 1924 a room in a house near the Ashmoleum Museum. Marjorie Biddle was a frequent visitor to this address. Her parents were opposed to her relationship with Nishiwaki, not because it was an inter-racial one but because the young couple started cohabiting before engagement or marriage.[15] They lived together in Oxford for about six months but finally on 25 July 1924 they had a civil wedding in London. Nishiwaki's witness was Tokuda Keijirō and the reception was held at the house of Okuyama Giichi, the manager of Kawasaki Line's London branch, whom Nishiwaki had met on the ship to Marseilles. They spent their two-week honeymoon in Sussex. The Sussex landscape was described in one of Nishiwaki's most lyrical poems entitled 'Spiral Clouds':

And then
Yellow corn fields.
Along their top edge

We saw the cobalt blue of the sea.
There was a path of plantains.
In the countryside with windmills
We spent a summer like tortoiseshell.[16]

After the honeymoon he went back to Oxford while Marjorie remained in London. In his poems and essays Nishiwaki wrote a great deal about his Oxford life but he never mentioned his wife and even gave the impression that he had lived a rather solitary life on his own. In *Tsunobue wo Migaku* (Polishing a Horn), for example, he described the new term at Oxford saying that 'it did not seem that anything exciting was going to happen'.[17] Then he wrote about how he saw Robert Bridges, the poet laureate, cashing a cheque at Barclay's Bank as if this were the most exciting thing that had ever happened to him in Oxford. In *Eikoku no Den'en* (About the English Countryside) he describes in detail a short trip he made with Mr Lightfoot, the warden of the college and later professor in theology, to parish churches in Warwickshire and Gloucestershire. Mr Lightfoot was said to have told Nishiwaki what a lichgate was, explaining that it was like a *torii* in a Japanese shrine. In *Eikoku no Shizen* (About Nature in England) he writes about his Oxford days:

> That I lit a fire and read Shakespeare in my dim digs on the second floor remained in me as the strongest impression of the winter in Oxford. I sometimes went for a walk along a stream with willows planted on its banks and saw the sun setting beyond the fields which were often flooded in winter. Then I felt lonely.[18]

In these essays there is no mention of Marjorie. They were written a long time after they had divorced and by the time they were published he was married to a Japanese woman and had had a child by her. His life in Oxford between 1924 and 1925 must have been much happier and fuller than he suggested. He was certainly not a 'prisoner' in the 'concave paradise' as he described in one of his poems. Marjorie concentrated on painting, while Nishiwaki moved from Old and Middle English to Milton and Shakespeare.

Just before they married Nishiwaki submitted a poem to the Newdigate Prize poetry competition in May 1924. The previous prize-winners included Oscar Wilde and T.S. Eliot, (Ruskin twice failed to win the prize); it was the most prestigious prize for students aspiring to become a poet. The subjects for that year were Michelangelo for English poems and Napoleon for Latin poems. Nishiwaki first attempted to submit a Latin poem and, buying a few books on Latin prosody at Blackwells, he spent hours studying the subject. None of his Latin poems satisfied him because he could not get the rhymes right and in the end he submitted an English poem. He later said that he had not expected his poem to succeed but when the results were announced, he was disappointed that his poem had not been chosen. However, Nishiwaki's poem, 'A Kensington Idyll' was published in the latest issue of *Chapbook*. From this moment in November 1924 he went on to accumulate English poems with the intention of publishing them as a book. He left Oxford in December, 1924 and stayed in London until he returned to Japan. His book of English poems, *Spectrum*, was published in August 1925 at his own expense by the Cayme Press.[19] Many years later, he looked back on the publication of *Spectrum* describing it as '. . . a product of a man who had had a nervous breakdown and a miserable book from which even a dog turns away'. His poems in *Spectrum* do not have enough traditional poetic beauty in terms of rhythm, imagery and tone, and at the same time they are not subversive enough to be true modernist and surrealist poems. They often read like self-parodies of the poems of the modernist movement. Nishiwaki cannot be judged as a poet from his English poems alone as his best poems were written in Japanese after he returned to Japan. Explaining why he tried to write poems in English at that time he wrote: 'I could not or did not want to express myself in the traditional style used by most Japanese poems. It was an acrobatic act of my youthful inexperience that I tried to publish French and English poems in France and England and to compete with European poets.'[20] His best friend, John Collier, was kinder about his poems, commenting: '[Nishiwaki's] poems are not as pedantic as those by Eliot and more loose and visionary. His poems were very new and there weren't many people in the general public who could appreciate them.'[21] Short reviews of his book appeared in *TLS* and *The Daily News* in October and November, 1925. The former review was dismissive, quoting one of his verses and criticising it as '[lacking] the art either of sense or nonsense', though the latter was more sympathetic, commenting: 'Mr Nishiwaki seeks a standard manner capable of expressing, without modulation, any really modern thing from a cigarette to a fit of delirium.'[22]

RETURN TO JAPAN

Nishiwaki and Marjorie left London in October 1925 for Japan via Paris. The purpose of visiting Paris was to meet Jean Cocteau, who was one of his favourite living poets, and to ask him to write a preface to his collection of French poems. A meeting could not, however, be arranged. So he took the typed manuscripts to a publisher who had dealt with Cocteau's works and asked about the possibility of publishing the poems at his own expense. The response was lukewarm; they told him to leave it with them and said that he would hear from them shortly. As he could not stay long in Paris and did not want to entrust the only copy of his poems to them, he reluctantly took it with him to Tokyo. The poems in the manuscript, which was entitled *Une mantre sentimentale*, were included in his collected works in 1973. Most of the poems in this book are clearly more surrealist exercises than the Prufrockian *Spectrum*. His first poems published after he returned to Japan were translations of these French poems.

Nishiwaki and Marjorie landed at Kobe on 8 November 1925. They were met only by his cousin, Yokobe Tokusaburō and stayed in an inn in Kobe. Yokobe wrote: 'That night Jun-sama [Junzaburō] excitedly told me about surrealism well into the night as if he had forgotten the weariness of the long journey. Surrealism totally bewildered me.'[23] He said nothing about Marjorie whom he saw for the first time.

They first settled in a house in Shirogane, behind the Sacred Heart Women's University. Their two-storey house was old and humble and was no better than the houses that the students used as their lodgings.

Nishiwaki resumed teaching in April 1926, this time as a full professor in the department of literature. In mid-1920s Japan he stood out even among his colleagues in Keiō. His impeccably Western, not to say eccentric, appearance and his perfect English surprised his colleagues. He turned up on the university campus wearing tweed knickerbockers and pince-nez with pipe in his mouth. Although he quickly gave up the knickerbockers, he continued to dress in a dapper English way; he was seen wearing a well-tailored woollen suit and a trilby hat in the winter and a linen suit and a straw hat in the summer. The fact that his poems had already been published in England attracted the attention of his students. Although he read out English texts with a beautiful English accent, he often could not find an appropriate Japanese word. For instance, while translating an English passage during one lecture, he could not recall the Japanese word for 'stamp' and struggled to explain it by saying, 'something you stick to a letter, you know?' Takiguchi Shūzō, Nishiwaki's favourite student and a future surrealist poet, was attending this lecture and urged his classmates to come and see this professor whose Japanese was so rusty. His lectures in the first few years after he became a professor included Old and Middle English, history of English literature, and general introductions to literature and linguistics. He also taught English at the preparatory course. His lectures on literature were mainly about English literature, but he often discussed his own poems. In the introduction to linguistics, he chiefly lectured on phonology and the historical transformation of pronunciation in English. His lectures were fairly systematic and were based on well-prepared notes. However, in some lectures, he drifted away from the prescribed subject or dreamily looked out of the window forgetting his students. When he taught English, he used Plato's *Republic* as one of the textbooks, but he did not ask his students to translate it into Japanese. Instead, he translated it himself and made them write it down in their notebooks. During the lectures he never looked directly at his students and just talked on. In his English composition class he often made his students write poems. One day he told his class: 'Your English poems are awkward and inaccurate, but they are interesting to me because you try so hard to express the ideas of grown-ups in the language of children.'[24]

Despite his heavy teaching load at the university, Nishiwaki contributed literary criticism and his own French poems to *Mita Bungaku*. His critical essays mainly covered modern English and French poetry and were heavily spiced with his own opinions on literature in general. For him the task of a poet was to make totally dissimilar things meet in the same poetic space. His essays surprised readers of *Mita Bungaku* in many ways. They dealt with themes which were new to most of the Japanese readers and were written in a colloquial and inimitable style. His 'Paradis perdu' was published in *Mita Bungaku* in June 1926 and its translation *Shitsuraku-en* (Paradise Lost) appeared in its July issue.

Undergraduate students taught by Nishiwaki were fascinated by him. Some made it a weekly habit to go out with their professor after his lectures. Satō Saku, who became a professor in French literature at Keiō, remembered his undergraduate days with Nishiwaki:

> . . . after his lectures *Sensei* [maitre] always asked us if we wanted to go for a cup of coffee. Normally six or seven of us went to a café near our university. . . However, our talk did not end there. As he lived in Tengenji, which was close to our school, we followed him to his house. We talked and talked till ten or eleven o'clock at night . . . *Sensei* treated us to his favourite bowl of noodles and then we ran back to our digs.[25]

In 1927, these students published, with Nishiwaki's encouragement, an anthology of surrealist poems, *Fukuikutaru Kafu yo* ('Oh! My Fragrant Fire-feeder'). He chose the title and contributed the preface and a few poems. Marjorie provided the cover design.

Haruyama Yukio discovered Nishiwaki and commissioned from him an article for almost every single issue of his *Shi to Shiron* (Poems and Poetics) which started in September 1928 and became the most influential poetry magazine for some years. He also published Nishiwaki's early collections of literary criticism: *Chōgenjitsushugi Shiron* (Surrealist Poetics) in 1929, *Surrealism Bungakuron* (On Surrealist Literature) in 1930, *Europe no Bungaku* (European Literature) in 1933 and *Wa no Aru Sekai* (The World with a Circle) in 1933. These all contributed to making Nishiwaki one of the outstanding literary critics of his generation. Hyakuta Sōji was a poet and the editor of the literary magazine called *Shii no Ki* and he arranged for Nishiwaki and Hagiwara, whose mutual respect was apparent by this time, to meet for the first time. Nishiwaki contributed poems to the magazine in 1930 and again sent four short poems for the first issue of his little magazine, *Shaku Doku*, which started in January 1933. These four poems were included in his first collection of Japanese poems, *Ambarvalia*, published by Hyakuta in the same year. This was later considered as one of his best works.

The war in China and then in the Pacific forced Nishiwaki to change. He was unable to read or buy English books freely. He was once threatened with arrest by the special political police as a leading 'Surrealist' poet who was a subversive element and tantamount to being an anarchist. He was granted leave from the university to escape from the air raids on Tokyo and spent the war years in the small town where he had been born and brought up. Instead of reading his favourite writers, like Walter Pater, Arthur Symonds, Baudelaire and Flaubert, he immersed himself in classic Japanese literature and books on Japanese folklore by Yanagita Kunio, whom he had known since his London days.

Nishiwaki emerged from World War II as a more complex figure than he had seemed on his return from England. He continued to teach English literature and to write books about it. However, his poetic works were transformed. His *No Traveller Returns* published in 1947 has been regarded as the work which marked the poet's 'return to Japan'. Unlike his earlier modernistic poems, the majority of the poems included in this book have Japanese motifs, are nostalgic in tone and traditional in style expressing such Japanese concepts as *mujō* (transcience), *mononoaware* (pathos) and *sabishisa* (loneliness/desolateness), found in Japanese classical literature and art. In the same year, a new version of *Ambarvalia* was published. The title was now written in *hiragana* instead of the alphabet. The core poems in the original version remained in the revised version but the poems newly added displayed the same characteristics as those in *No Traveller Returns*. From then on, Nishiwaki appeared to be pulled towards two opposite poles by a force of almost equal strength; the poles were the West and the East, the sublime and the banal, the modern and ancient worlds, and sophistication and rusticity. One of the poems clearly demonstrating such complexity is:

> Around that time I was on a boat
> To see cherry blossoms at the upper reaches of the *Arakawa* River.
> I was reading Mauppassant.
> The loneliness is that the sun is setting
> And a clog is floating among reeds.[26]

Since Nishiwaki had started learning English at middle school at the age of thirteen, his interest had been exclusively in the West. In language, literature and art the West had been of paramount importance to him. He had read almost solely Western literature, whenever possible in Western languages, and appreciated only Western art. He had also tried hard to make himself look more Western than Westerners and speak and write their languages better than they did. Nishiwaki had been a perfectionist when it came to learning Western languages. Undeniably he had disliked Japan and the East. On being asked once by Fukuda Rikutarō, a professor of English literature, about his attitude towards Japan in his youth, he spat out: 'I loathed everything in Japan, really everything. I also loathed China as well.'[27] All of this, however, began to change after he came back from Europe in 1925 and he started writing poems and literary criticism in Japanese. Writing in Japanese may have worked as some form of therapy for his identity problem. The moment he began to publish in Japanese, recognition, something which he had never experienced in England, came his way. Whatever he wrote was received with praise and admiration and his students were mesmerized by his erudition and knowledge of European literature. The 1930s, which were dominated by the surge of militarism and fanatical nationalism, was not the best time for a writer and scholar to be involved in Western culture. From then on Nishiwaki began nostalgically to lean towards Japanese literary and cultural traditions.

Nishiwaki's poetic and critical achievements in his maturity would not, however, have been possible without his total immersion in English language and literature and his experiences during his three years in England. Most of his later poems employ Japanese motifs, but their language, diction, and style are original and have no exact precedents in traditional and modern Japanese poetry. These characteristics clearly originated from those twenty years when Nishiwaki tried to make himself into an Englishman and went through a period of both internal and external exile from his country.

30

Richard Storry, 1913-82: A Life-long Affair with Japan[1]

IAN NISH

Richard Storry

GEORGE RICHARD STORRY is widely known for having written in 1960 the Penguin *A History of Modern Japan*, perhaps the most popular scholarly work on the subject. He was well qualified to write such a study by his experiences before the war in Japan, during the war and by strategically timed visits after the war. He was, of course, not unique in having both pre-war and post-war experience. In the United States teachers like Edwin Reischauer, Marius Jansen and Jack Hall carried the message from their life in pre-war Japan into their teaching of Japanese Studies at American universities after the war. In Britain, similarly, there were those whose exposure to Japan had been both before and after the war. What was special about Storry was that he wrote in a vivid, popular style which met the needs of a reading public which was gradually acquiring an appetite for Things Japanese and was increasingly disenchanted with the crop of books which had been published concentrating on the warlike actions of Japan.

A native of Doncaster, Storry was educated at Repton School and went up to Merton College, Oxford, to study History Greats. One of the memorable experiences during his Oxford days was when he attended the meeting of the Oxford University Conservative Association on 23 February 1934 at which Winston Churchill spoke controversially.[2] On graduation he applied for a post in Japan at the suggestion of Edmund Blunden, an English tutor at Merton, and was appointed. In the summer of 1937 he took up his post as a teacher at the Otaru Commercial College (*Kōtō Shōgyō*, generally abbreviated to *Kōshō*). By coincidence he succeeded Frank Daniels, who was later in his career to become Professor of Japanese at the School of Oriental and African Studies, University of London.[3]

Otaru was one of eight commercial colleges set up by the Japanese government: Tokyo, Kobe, Yamaguchi, Nagasaki, Otaru and Nagoya (in that order). They were separate from, and lower in status than, the great imperial universities at Tokyo, Kyoto and Kyūshū. They were designed to prepare students for a commercial life and offered a high level of vocational and practical education. For linguistic reasons, if for no other, they often employed large numbers of foreign staff. Otaru was located in the northern island of Hokkaidō and was still a thriving port in the thirties. Hokkaidō had been a sort of frontier state which had been developed from the 1870s by central government through bodies like the Colonial Board, the *Kaitakushi*. It may have been the intention that Otaru should serve as the capital of that province. From the trading point of view, it was well placed opposite the ports of the Russian Maritime Provinces, including the naval port of Vladivostok. But Japan's relations were traditionally bad with Russia who was seen as a predatory state. Following the Russo-Japanese war of 1904–5, the high expectations for the city had to be reduced. But its port was still used in the thirties by British companies like Shell and the Blue Funnel line.

Within a month of Dick's arrival in Hokkaidō, the North China Incident which proved to be the first step on the path to war with China broke out and inevitably affected his teaching and his thinking. His attitude to his students is shown in the following extract from a letter:

> As I look at my students, either in a lecture room or as they drill and do manoeuvres in the snow, my heart aches at the pity of this war and the wars that will come upon them. But they think it no tragedy; their greatest glory is to die in the service of the Emperor.[4]

From the start of his teaching he faced wartime conditions; and the predicament of his students confronted with the draft at the end of their studies was worrying for him.[5]

Most teachers used the opportunity for travel outside Japan in the long vacations which the college allowed. Storry was no exception, making a memorable journey to Japanese-occupied Korea and China in the summer vacation of 1939. This was adventurous because war was well under way in north China whose cities were in practice under Japanese military occupation and British nationals came under suspicion because of their country's alleged sympathy and support for China. Still only twenty-five years of age, Dick (as we shall now call him) sailed on 2 August from Otaru on the coastal steamer, *Kōkai Maru*, calling at Hakodate, Fukushi, Hagi ('the prettiest spot I have yet seen in Japan', he wrote) and Pusan in Korea. He travelled the next phase of his journey by train to Seoul, the capital of Japanese Korea, thence to Inchon where he rejoined the boat to sail as far as Dairen (Dalien). He then toured Tianjin and Beijing at which point war broke out in Europe. Nonetheless he returned to Otaru to fulfil his contract.

In spite of the adverse international climate of the time, Storry spent three fairly contented years at Otaru *Kōshō*, the college on the steep hill. The following letter testifies to his nostalgia for the place:

> The students, those hundreds of young men who went up and down that long hill [to the college] every morning and afternoon, I came to love. My interest in Japan, my concern for modern Japanese history, was stimulated in the first place by their good nature, their eagerness to learn, and their thoughtfulness for the foreigner in their midst.[6]

There is every reason to believe that this affection was reciprocated. Consider the touching story that, when Dick was due to set off on his journey homeward by way of Montreal and Liverpool in April 1940, one of his students who accompanied him as far as Tokyo asked him to go to the Imperial Palace Plaza to pray to the gods for his safe passage back to England.

WAR YEARS

Britain's war with Japan was fast approaching. Although exempted because of bad eyesight, Dick was ultimately commissioned into the Intelligence Corps in Egypt in October 1941. Told to report to Singapore, he arrived there on 28 January 1942 during an alert and with the knowledge that the Japanese were at the Causeway. Within two weeks, those who were Japanese speakers were ordered to leave and report to General Wavell's headquarters in Batavia. After various adventures he reached Colombo in Ceylon on 5 March and was posted to the Intelligence School (India) located in Old Government House, Karachi. But in June he was transferred to the Combined Services Detailed Interrogation Centre India (CSDIC) (I) at the Red Fort, Delhi, for interrogation duties.

It may seem strange that at a time of military crisis and acute shortage of transport, such a series of rapid moves should have been possible and necessary. But it was vital for Britain to mobilize people like Storry. It is well to remember the dilemma in which Britain found herself because of pre-war governments' short-sightedness. Dick later explained in detail Britain's vulnerability because of its lack of expertise in Things Japanese and the shortage of Japanese linguists in particular:

> Their defeats in South East Asia made the British settle down to an intensive study of everything connected with their enemy, from his tactics and system of supply to his language and psychology. A serious handicap during the campaigns in Malaya and Burma [in 1942] had been the dearth of trained linguists who could properly interpret captured Japanese documents or question the few prisoners who fell into British hands. For example, during the first Burma campaign, in General Slim's Burcorps there was only one officer who could read and speak Japanese reasonably well. The War Office had started to compile a roster of Japanese speakers early in 1941. In the following year an attempt was made to muster all those who had ever lived and worked in Japan. Broadly speaking, these belonged to one of four categories – language officers, missionaries, teachers and businessmen. Of these the first were able to make the most immediate contribution. . . . In 1942 there were in the British and Indian Armies about fifty officers who at some stage in their careers had studied the Japanese language to an interpreter's standard. Their value lay, of course, in the fact that unlike, for example, the Japanese-speaking missionary they were familiar with Japanese military terminology, to some extent a specialized subject in itself. When account is taken of the demands of War Office Intelligence in London, of GHQ India in New Delhi, and of organizations concerned with cryptography, it will be seen that the ideal arrangement – of a linguist with each brigade in the field – could not be achieved. . .
>
> Eventually, a few former missionaries and most of those who had worked in business or in academic life in Japan became involved, in one way or another, with the British military organization in the East. . . Accordingly, this not very numerous category of 'Old Japan Hands' had to be trained in India, by former language officers in the intricacies of the Japanese vocabulary and syntax, military style.[7]

Obviously, there were wide differences between the men available according to their length of stay in Japan and the degree of their language competence. But it is interesting that, with the perceived need for expertise, language officers became hot properties in the services, moving on quickly regardless of transport difficulties at the time. The result was that Storry met up again with people he had known previously in Japan and later Singapore.

Dick was transferred to Assam and thence in February 1943 to Imphal in upper Burma taking part in the battle there in the following year. He was promoted major and went on to command No 1 Mobile Section of CSDIC (I). By early June of the following year Dick's unit, now part of 14 Army, was established in Rangoon. In the following month Dick was recalled to Delhi for repatriation through Bombay. He had seen service in Singapore, India and Burma and in the course of it had come face to face with the Japanese armies, though latterly during the phase when they were mainly in retreat. In later life, however, he preferred not to discuss battles as he had (he admitted) never fired a shot in anger.

POST-WAR ADJUSTMENT

After demobilization Dick's mind turned increasingly in the direction of research and scholarship. He was awarded first a research scholarship – one of the first of these scholars – and later a fellowship by the newly-founded Australian National University in Canberra. Since that institution was in its infancy and had only limited library resources on the Japanese side, he was permitted to study archives in the United States and Britain and allowed generous study leave in order to conduct research in Japan.

Storry embarked on the study of Japanese nationalism between the world wars. The raw material for this research was the comprehensive collection of Transcripts and Exhibits of the International Military Tribunal for the Far East (IMTFE) which had sat in Tokyo, and the Saionji-Harada Memoirs, copies of which he studied in the Library of Congress, Washington DC. He wrote up his material on Japan's fanatical nationalists in Canberra in 1953-4. It was eventually published in 1957 under the title of *The Double Patriots: A study of Japanese nationalism.* It was a description of those Japanese who practised the 'doubly' extreme form of ultra-nationalism in twentieth-century Japan, but especially after 1931. It was a contribution to the scholarly literature on both Japanese history and politics. Underlying it was the question of how nationalism would develop in post-war Japan. During this period of residence in the Australian capital, the Japanese ambassador was Nishi Haruhiko, with whom the Storrys struck up an acquaintance, which was to continue when Nishi was later promoted to become ambassador in London.[8]

In order to cover research materials only available in Japan, Dick visited Tokyo between June and November 1949 when he was attached to the Australian Mission in Tokyo. He was accompanied by Dorothie whom he had married in April of that year. Japan was engaged in painfully re-establishing her economy within the parameters laid down by the Allied Occupation. Being based in the Tokyo area, Dick was able to observe and assess the workings of the Occupation, and especially the dominant personality at GHQ of General Douglas MacArthur, at first hand.

When he next went to Japan between February and September 1953, Japan was an independent sovereign state which had signed the San Francisco treaty of peace with most of her wartime adversaries. Storry contributed to the new English-language cultural journal, entitled *Japan Quarterly*, through his friendship with Aiko Ito (Clark) who was on the editorial staff. It was a house magazine of the *Asahi Shimbun* and was intended to reach an international audience. For half a century it was to be an influential magazine with mainly Japanese contributors but with the occasional feature article by foreigners. Dick contributed an article entitled 'An Englishman looks at Diet Hill' in which he gave his reflections on the new parliamentary institutions and party structures which had arisen in Japan as part of the post-war movement towards democracy. But he did so as one made cynical by the doings of the Mother of Parliaments in Westminster.[9]

Another of his articles at the time included his observations on the end of the political career of Yoshida Shigeru who had dominated Japanese post-war politics. Storry was, like many foreign scholars, deeply distrustful of Japanese politics. In 1954 he wrote:

> The resignation of Mr Yoshida [in December 1954] who has been Premier of Japan continuously since October 1948 cannot be regarded as in any sense a surprise. Three years ago after the San Francisco Peace Treaty had been signed he enjoyed unrivalled prestige and popularity. But since that time events have conspired against him. . . Inside the Diet, and inside his own party, he made plenty of enemies thanks to his somewhat impatient and cantankerous manner. . . I think it is fair to say that, in spite of the fierce attacks made on him by the Opposition and by the press as a whole, he was rather admired by those who form the still largely inarticulate majority of the population of Japan – namely the farmers and the fishermen. Something about Mr Yoshida – perhaps it was the obstinate, irritable temperament that so infuriated politicians in Tokyo – appealed to the vulgar imagination. He seemed to those living outside the cynical, iconoclastic capital – a little larger than life.[10]

Despite this sympathetic portrait of Japan's long-term prime minister, Dick was uncertain about the future. For one who had been studying how Japanese politics in the thirties had broken down, it was hard to be optimistic about how the new Japan was shaping politically. Thus, he wrote in the concluding paragraph of *Double Patriots*:

> Nobody can dare to predict that such insanity [as ultra-nationalism] will not again infect the body politic of Japan. But

if it does, the resistance that can be offered will be more robust and lasting than it was before the Pacific War.[11]

It was, one assumes, a formative time in developing Dick's thinking about post-war Japan. As the fifties passed into the sixties, Storry grew increasingly sceptical about the machinations of the right in the Japanese Diet. He was heard to tell a senior Japanese professor that, while he was right-wing in British politics, he found, when he visited Japan, that he developed left-wing sympathies.

BACK IN OXFORD

In 1955 the Storry family took up residence again in the United Kingdom and Dick was awarded the Roger Heyworth Memorial Fellowship at St Antony's College, which had just been founded in Oxford, and an Official Fellowship in 1960.

Dick had agreed to write *A History of Modern Japan* on the advice of Vere Redman of the British embassy, Tokyo, who was like himself a pre-war teacher in Japan. It was published in the Penguin series in 1960. It was one of the first histories of Japan to appear in Britain after the war and was courageous enough to depart from the propagandistic assessments which had characterized much of wartime and post-war literature. It was reprinted six times, most recently in 1992. While sales figures for the earlier years are not available, Penguin has sold 112,000 copies of the book since 1973. It has also appeared in French, German, Italian and Japanese translations. Professor Tsuzuki Chūshichi, in a recent bibliographical assessment says of it:

> In its own way [it] marked an epoch in the Western historiography on modern Japan. The book is in full sympathy with its subject and reveals a first-hand knowledge of the Japanese mind acquired at a time when the author was an impressionable young teacher in northern Japan in the 1930s.[12]

This was to be the first of several general surveys of Japan which Dick wrote in the 1960s. His account of the doings of the Soviet spy, Richard Sorge, in Japan during the thirties, written in association with F.W. Deakin, appeared in 1969.[13]

In 1970 Dick succeeded Geoffrey Hudson as Director of the Far East Centre. It was at the weekly seminars that he gathered round him a group of regional experts, not all from Japan. But it was the Japanese who studied at St Antony's that formed the core. During his study leaves in Japan Storry had struck up a warm friendship with Maruyama Masao, whom he saluted as 'perhaps the most interesting Japanese writer on [nationalism in Japan]'.[14] By this and other contacts St Antonys had gained a reputation which attracted academic visitors including senior Japanese scholars like

Oka Yoshitake, Seki Yoshihiko, Ishida Takeshi, Ikeda Kiyoshi and Tsuzuki Chūshichi, to name only a few. Younger scholars also came to take Oxford degrees and joined a distinguished group of postgraduates too numerous to mention. Many paid several return journeys and developed a great attachment to the college. The impact made on this influential group of Japanese scholars comes out in a recorded conversation between two Antonians, the late Hagihara Nobutoshi and Yokoyama Toshio about their intellectual and other experiences in the college to which they built up a tremendous loyalty.[15]

If he was a sceptical observer of Japan's political scene, Richard Storry had no doubts about his support for the Japanese monarchy and the historical role of the Shōwa Emperor in particular. In autumn 1971 David Bergamini published a long book, *Japan's Imperial Conspiracy*, which condemned the Emperor for his pre-war and wartime actions in condoning the coming of war. He came to Britain in order to publicize his book which had been published in the United States some months earlier and had created a great controversy. Dick who was upset by the book was interviewed along with Bergamini by Joan Bakewell on 'Late Night Line Up', a BBC discussion programme which went out live in these pioneering days of intellectual television. If Bergamini hoped to get some support from the author of *The Double Patriots*, he was mistaken. Storry had risen from High Table to be driven through darkened suburbs to the BBC studios in London for the late-night encounter. Appearing with sheaves of notes and his gown over his arm, Dick had clearly done his homework and ably defended his corner. But the inevitable clash of historical sources and interpretations took place; and Dick – and I in a lesser capacity – did not dent the armour of the writer, though he had placed his doubts and disagreements on record.

Japanese PEN convened an international conference on Japanese Studies at Kyoto in November 1972. Dick was one of the delegates and, along with Josef Kreiner and Gianni Fodella, made a seminal speech. In the search to promote Japanese studies at university level, the first European conference was held in April 1973. The first – and principal – sessions were held at St Antonys College, Oxford. The second part of the deliberations was held at the School of Oriental and African Studies, London; and it was from there that the first 'European collection of Japanese studies' was published under the title *Modern Japan: Aspects of History, Literature and Society*, edited by Professor W. G. Beasley. The other outcome was the establishment of the European Association for Japanese Studies. Taken together, these factors were an attempt to put Japanese scholarship in Europe on the world map at a time when so much was being done about Japan in the United States. Storry had played his part in launching these endeavours and remained a conscientious attendee at European Association conferences.

In 1979 Dick's last book *Japan and the Decline of the West in Asia, 1894-1945* was published. It was an introduction to the controversial subject of decolonization and its origins. While accepting that Western powers did decline in Asia in the first half of the twentieth century, he is less sure about whether Japan had a genuine mission of liberation and, if she had, whether she realized that her limited strength did not allow her to fulfil it with the result that her actions only led to long-term instability in the Asian region. Again his object was to maintain a fair balance between excessively uncritical enthusiasm about Things Japanese and unwarranted scepticism. By and large the critics did not demur.[16]

LAST YEARS

At the triennial conference of the European Association for Japanese Studies which was held in Florence in September 1979 Storry was honoured by being elected as the convener of the section dealing with History, International Relations and Politics. Under his chairmanship the sessions were lively ones conducted at a brisk pace. It was fitting that he should have had this important role at Florence, which was a city that he clearly loved.

Earlier that summer it was announced that the munificent gift of £1.5 million would be given to Oxford University by the Nissan Motor Company in order to develop an Institute of Japanese Studies. The bequest was the result of a lot of hard work by many people. Dick had been active over the years with former ambassadors to the Court of St James's; and there was hardly a visit to Japan when part of his time was not taken up with fund-raising for scholarly purposes. It was a moment of happiness for him that the Institute when it was opened in late September 1981 should be closely associated with St Antony's College.[17]

In April 1981 Oxford University appointed Storry Professor of Japanese Studies for his last term before retirement. In June he was made a Professor Emeritus. His pleasure is recorded in this characteristic note:

> Thank you indeed for your congratulations, which are much appreciated. I must say that the University has been generous to me beyond my deserts, giving me the professorial title and, by a decree to be published in the Gazette tomorrow, giving me the title of 'Professor Emeritus' from the date of my retirement on 30 September. As the Duke of Wellington remarked in another context, there is 'no damned merit' in it – and also, no effect on either salary or pension. All this is as it should be – the title above is indeed a great honour.[18]

This was followed by the decision of St Antony's College in which he had served as Director of the Far East Centre (1970-81) and as Sub-Warden (1975-7) to make him an Emeritus Fellow of the College, where he had been a Fellow for nearly thirty years.

Dick was further honoured by the Japanese. In 1959 he had been awarded the Order of the Sacred Treasure 4th class. In 1981 within a month of his retirement he was awarded the Japan Foundation prize for 1981 which had previously been given to Professors George Allen and Ronald Dore and travelled to Japan to receive it. But it was a tiring trip and he had a heart attack there from which he hardly recovered. It was typical of him to make the journey to Japan at personal risk to attend the presentation ceremony. That he enjoyed the experience – his farewell journey to Japan – goes without saying.

Professional recognition had come late for Storry; but it had come from all directions. He retired at the age of 68 after a busy life of travelling. On 19 February 1982 he died. On 22 May a memorial service was held at the Church of St Philip and James close to where the old Far East Centre had once been. It was a gathering of numerous friends and colleagues for Dick had a rare capacity for friendship.

Richard Storry was teacher, researcher, writer. As teacher, he had taught initially in Japan and later in Britain. As researcher and writer, he provided a legacy of a large volume of books and papers. As the compiler/editor of his *Collected Writings*, I know that he banged out many scripts on an ancient typewriter and copiously corrected them in a large and not very elegant hand. That is not to say that he did not depend on his secretaries but his essays and articles were generally self-typed. Yet the end-product was that of a personalized voice, the voice of a man of letters. To quote Raymond Carr, he was 'a formidable scholar in his own right and a historical stylist of great distinction'. He was a popular author whose style few professional historians can nowadays match.[19]

Richard Storry was, of course, primarily a historian and a diplomatic historian. History is Broad Church and historians are broad churchmen. He had in *The Double Patriots* written for a scholarly readership; and its reputation still stands high today. But he had also written the Penguin *A History of Modern Japan* and *Japan and the Decline of the West in Asia* that were by their nature a different kind of exercise, an attempt to interpret Japan for the general reader at a time when her rate of growth was regarded as something of an economic miracle. In his interpretations he applied the great knowledge he had accumulated over just short of half-a-century of contact with the Japanese. Professor Tsuzuki writes that Dick's work was always 'enriched as it is with episodes and anecdotes'[20] As in his writing so he punctuated his conversations with little nuggets of Japanese lore which he had picked up from his long experience of the country with which, as he said, he had had a life-long affair.

31

Eric Bertrand Ceadel, 1921-79: Japanese Studies at Cambridge

PETER KORNICKI

Eric B. Ceadel

ERIC CEADEL was the founding father of Japanese studies at Cambridge and it was his energy that established the upstart new subject in the Faculty of Oriental Languages, as it was then called. He taught for twenty years until 1967, when he was appointed University Librarian and immersed himself in the affairs of the University Library and the challenge of computerization, with an inevitable diminution of his focus on Japan.

EDUCATION AND WAR SERVICE

Ceadel was born on 7 February 1921 and won an open scholarship to Christ's College, Cambridge, in 1937 to read classics. He graduated in 1941 with First Class Honours. He was indubitably an exceptionally talented classicist, for by the time he graduated he had already published three articles in the *Classical Quarterly* on questions relating to Aeschylus, Sophocles and Euripides; he described these as 'spare-time research undertaken while working for the Classical Tripos', but they are still consulted today for his insight into metrical problems in Greek tragedy. Although he won a research scholarship to continue his studies, it was, of course, war-time and in September 1941 he joined the Suffolk Regiment.

In February 1942, however, doubtless as a result of his linguistic skills, he was posted as a Lance-Corporal to the Inter-Services Special Intelligence School at Bedford, where he studied Japanese under Captain Tuck, RN. As a result of his rapid mastery of the language he was transferred to the Intelligence Corps, in which he finally attained the rank of Captain; more impressively, by October 1942 he had acquired such a command of the language that he was appointed Instructor in Japanese. He served in this capacity until October 1945 and during those three years taught more than 200 men the elements of the written language in a succession of six-month courses. Although he was teaching some thirty hours a week on these intensive courses, he found the time to undertake 'research on grammatical problems' and to compile a practical grammar of Japanese which was photo-lithographed and used on all the Bedford courses. Tuck's assessment of his contribution was laudatory:

> He has been working under me for three years and is now [29 June 1945] my Chief Assistant. He has acquired a very good knowledge of the Japanese Written Language used in formal documents and reports and also of that form of the Spoken Language in which newspaper articles and lectures are printed. . . . He has compiled on an entirely new principle a grammar which we find here more useful and accurate than any other. He has also produced an Index of the Chinese characters which has been duplicated by the government and is in constant use in the Intelligence Departments. He can read any printed book; and what is much more unusual and difficult he can read the handwriting commonly used by journalists and commercial firms and in ordinary correspondence. He has shown great aptitude for the emendation of corrupt texts, large numbers of which are constantly passing through our hands.

Tuck's reference here to 'corrupt texts' refers probably to captured Japanese documents and decrypts, which he was also engaged in translating.

CAMBRIDGE – JAPANESE STUDIES

In October 1945 Ceadel was demobilized and returned to Christ's College as a research student, as he had originally intended in 1941. There was one difference, however, for his subject was no longer in the field of Classics but 'The structure and syntax of the Japanese literary language with special reference to its historical development'. As he wrote when applying for his lectureship in 1947:

> I have a deep interest in the early texts, especially the

Manyōshū, and wish to be able to study the latter minutely with a view to being able eventually to prepare an edition and translation. The tradition of its text is a subject which largely occupies me, containing as it does textual and philological questions on which both native and European scholars have made comparatively little progress.

It is evident, then, that during his busy war service he had somehow managed to familiarize himself with one of the key texts of early Japanese literature. On this he began working in 1947, while at the same time attending lectures on classical Chinese given by Professor Haloun.

When the Scarbrough Commission on the future of 'Oriental, Slavonic, East European and African Studies' in Britain reported in 1947, there were no teaching posts in Japanese studies outside London, but in Cambridge things were about to change, thanks to a substantial grant made to the university to fulfill some of the recommendations of the Scarborough Report. A university lectureship in Japanese was advertised that summer, and Ceadel naturally applied. Other applicants included Major-General F. S. G. Piggott, whose residence in Japan went back to 1888 and who had taught Japanese at the School of Oriental and African Studies during the War, but who was at 65 too old for serious consideration. Two other applicants were military men who had learned Japanese well before the outbreak of war, and another was a Japanese resident in Zurich, but all were considerably older than Ceadel, and doubtless this was in his favour as well as his impeccable Cambridge credentials at a time when most academic appointments were made to Cambridge graduates.

The Japanese course Ceadel designed was, perhaps intentionally, a mirror of his earlier studies as a classicist, an unremitting and highly demanding initiation into the *Kokinshū*, the *Manyōshū*, *Tale of Genji*, some Nō texts and even some *kanbun*. Indeed, the first Japanese text students cut their teeth on was the Japanese preface to the *Kokinshū*, written around a thousand years previously! In the first year he taught alone, but in 1948 he was joined by J. R. McEwan,[1] an expert on the Tokugawa thinker Ogyū Sorai, who was appointed to an assistant lectureship in Japanese history. In that same year Donald Keene arrived in Cambridge; in view of his glittering subsequent career as a scholar of Japanese literature it is extraordinary to note that, in spite of his war-time studies of Japanese, he was at the time intending to study Arabic and Persian at Cambridge. It was Ceadel who steered him away and back in the direction of the study of Chinese and Japanese, and in 1949 Keene was appointed an assistant lecturer in Japanese; in 1950 he was appointed lecturer in Japanese and Korean, a post he held until 1954. Thus, Donald Keene's first teaching of Japanese was done in Cambridge, under the wing of Ceadel.

In 1947 there was, of course, not a single Japanese in Cambridge, owing to the travel restrictions imposed on occupied Japan. It was only in 1950 that the first Japanese lector, Kamei Takashi, joined the Faculty, adding modern spoken Japanese to an essentially classically-oriented course, although orals in Japanese were not introduced until 1957. However, students were few and far between: between 1947 and 1960, there were only eighteen altogether, and in 1949-51 there were no starters at all. On the other hand, many of these pioneering students went on to have distinguished academic careers, like W. E. Skillend, G. W. Sargent, R. H. P. Mason, I. J. McMullen and D. B. Waterhouse.

CAMBRIDGE UNIVERSITY LIBRARY

Given the paucity of students, Ceadel, like his colleagues, had few demands on his time. Apart from faculty administration and university politics, in both of which he came to play important roles, he devoted himself to his research and to the library. On his arrival in 1947 the University Library had already a superb collection of early Japanese books from the collections of three nineteenth-century Japanologists, W. G. Aston, Ernest Satow and Heinrich von Siebold, but no modern books, not even dictionaries and basic reference works, and Ceadel set out to remedy that deficiency. In doing so he laid the foundations of the superb reference and research collections that Cambridge is blessed with now. In 1949 he and Professor Haloun received the very considerable sum of £6000 from the university for the purchase of Chinese and Japanese books; that same year Haloun travelled to China and Japan, and the following year Ceadel went to Japan for the first time, and between them they bought more than 13,000 volumes, including many complete runs of pre-war serials. Ceadel began cataloguing them with the help of Donald Keene, Ronald Dore and a succession of Japanese lectors. He continued to build up the collection and devised, with Piet van der Loon, later professor of Chinese at Oxford, a classification system which is still in use. In 1962 he published a *Classified catalogue of modern Japanese books in Cambridge University Library*, which, before the convenience of on-line catalogues, made the knowledge of the Library's holdings accessible to all, that is to the small band of Japanologists in Britain at the time.

RESEARCH AND PUBLICATIONS

Ceadel's research focused at first on early Japanese poetry, the subject he had been working on for his PhD, which he never completed. In the 1950s he published several learned articles on the Ōi river poems of Ki no Tsurayuki and on the prefaces of the *Kokinshū*; these were, appropriately enough given his training as a classicist, largely textual and philological, but he also essayed analyses of the poems. Most of his articles, including a number of surveys of recent Japanese academic writing on East Asian subjects, were published in *Asia Major*, a journal which described itself as 'a British journal of Far Eastern studies'; he was a member of the editorial board and a frequent reviewer. He also gave several lectures to the Japan Society of London, which were later printed in the Society's *Bulletin*. One of these, in February 1952, on his four-month visit to Japan in the summer of 1951, drew attention to the intellectual isolation from which he found Japanese academics to be suffering in spite of the end of the Occupation. He also drew attention to the recovery of the infrastructure since 1945, with the customary expression of hope that British Railways would learn from Japan where he found 'trains which start punctually and arrive punctually'.

In 1953 Ceadel put together a little book entitled *Literatures of the East, an appreciation*, which was based on a series of lectures given in Cambridge the previous year by members of the Faculty of Oriental Studies. Ceadel was responsible for the section on Japan, in which most attention was paid to classical literature, with a few lines each on Chikamatsu and Bashō and nothing on modern literature but the names of four writers who 'have attracted much attention', Sōseki, Akutagawa, Ōgai and Tanizaki. He concluded with a general assessment of the literature of Japan. 'Its worst weakness,' he wrote, 'may be said to be its lack of profundity and of deep understanding: as a result some works appear thin and trivial, without real power or purpose. Only a few books, the *Genji monogatari* among them, have enough body and consistent aim, entirely to escape this criticism'. On the other hand, its 'charm and its attractiveness and its wit, satire and humour are all of the highest quality'. Unlike F. V. Dickins, an earlier classicist-turned-Japanologist, then, Ceadel did not find Japanese literature ultimately wanting when judged by the standards he was accustomed to.

In 1960 and 1961 he was at the University of Michigan as a visiting professor, and had evidently attracted enough attention to be offered a full professorship there; he turned this down, as he also did a similar offer in 1964 from the University of Toronto. He was at work at this time on two substantial research projects, either one of which would have made his name as a scholar of Japan. Alas, his move to the University Library and his subsequent early death prevented him from bringing either to fruition, although the materials he gathered remain in the University Library. One of these projects was the preparation of a detailed catalogue of the early Japanese books in the Library from the Aston, Satow and von Siebold collections. Ceadel not only recognized their importance but also taught himself the essentials of pre-modern Japanese bibliography, probably with the assistance of Itasaka Gen, who was a lector from 1957 to 1960 and later taught at Harvard. His numerous draft entries for the catalogue testify to his extraordinary bibliographical acumen and good judgement, and are occasionally quoted in the complete catalogue which was finally published in 1991 and dedicated to his memory. The other project was a study of the

Hyakumantō Darani, the Buddhist invocations printed in Japan in 764-770, of which the Library possesses four examples, together with the miniature pagodas in which they were originally housed. Ceadel used micro-photographic techniques to seek an answer to the problem of the techniques used to print the invocations, and he took part in a number of discussions on the subject with Japanese colleagues at Tenri University, some of which are printed in the university's journal *Biblia*.

ASSESSMENT

Ceadel played a significant role in the administration of the university and of his college, Corpus Christie, of which he was a fellow and at one time senior tutor. He served on all senior committees of the university as well as many of lesser importance, impressing his colleagues with his scrupulous fairness when facing problems. When he had to implement the decisions that had been made he did so irrespective of his own views, but always ensured that scholarly standards did not suffer. The support which he gave to his young colleagues was invaluable. Dr Carmen Blacker who joined him at Cambridge in 1955 as an assistant lecturer in Japanese has recorded that 'There was no problem, whether intellectual, bibliographic, administrative or psychological which lay beyond his powers to solve. Although he never aspired to any chair in Japanese, which did not then exist, he was regarded as an authority by all the existing professors – Hebrew, Sanscrit, Arabic, Egyptology, Persian and Chinese – until 1967 when he took on the tremendous responsibility of the university librarian.'

He was indefatigable as a worker, with a word perfect knowledge of university regulations, and was totally single-minded in his devotion to duty.[2] Dr Michael Loewe, a Chinese specialist, noted that 'those who passed by the library at 10 or 11 o'clock at night, whatever the season, would notice a light from Eric's window in the tower; it shone as a beacon to encourage his colleagues'. Having once arranged for an addition to be built to the library, he discovered that a grant for this purpose would be forfeit unless building had started by the given dead-line. There were delays in beginning the work: so, according to one of his colleagues, at 23.59 on the evening before the day in question Eric Ceadel, spade in hand, turned one sod and put a brick in position where the first trench was to be dug.

Ceadel's achievements testify to the dramatic impact made upon him by his exposure to Japanese in the extraordinary conditions of war-time. Had it not been for the war, he would never have considered studying the language, but having once acquired a command of it he found that it aroused an intellectual curiosity which sustained him for much of his academic life. His scholarly legacy is small, but his role as a pioneering teacher at Cambridge of many of the post-war generation of Japanologists was pivotal.

Sources: 'University Lectureship in Japanese, 1947' (archives of the Faculty of Oriental Studies, Cambridge); bound volume of Ceadel's offprints in the library of the Faculty of Oriental Studies; Richard Bowring, ed., *Fifty years of Japanese at Cambridge 1948-98: a chronicle with reminiscences* (Faculty of Oriental Studies, 1998); Gordon Johnson and Derek Brewer, 'Foreword', in Nozomu Hayashi and Peter Kornicki, *Early Japanese books in Cambridge University Library: a catalogue of the Aston, Satow and von Siebold collections* (Cambridge University Press, 1991), comments from friends and colleagues.

32

Louis Allen (1922-91) and Japan

PHILLIDA PURVIS

Louis Allen

ORIGINS

LOUIS LEVY was born in 1922 in Redcar, the only child of a Lithuanian Jewish father and an Irish Catholic mother, both estranged from their families who opposed their marriage. Louis Levy's father died before young Louis was born. As a single mother Anne Levy struggled in extreme poverty to bring up her son. With her Jewish surname she was conspicuous within the Catholic community of Middlesborough, the home of her own and her husbands' families, and soon reverted to her maiden name, Allen, although she never lost touch with her in-laws. Her son, after the war, also chose to change his name, which did not affect his relationship with his Jewish cousins, with whom he remained in close touch all his life. He also remained interested in Judaism and visited Jersualem with his son Felix not long before his death.[1] 'I took, after living for a quarter of a century with my father's Jewish name, with its irritation and occasional wretchedness, and occasional pride, my mother's Irish name. I realize now that this was a mistake.' 'I was really remote from Ireland and remote from Jewry.' 'The world will not see it as I see it, and from Semitic darkness thrusts me into Celtic twilight.'[2]

344

STUDYING JAPANESE

Allen was an exceptional student and from St Mary's College, Middlesborough, easily gained a place at Manchester University to read French. He was awarded the County Major Scholarship in 1940. Even at that stage he had 'a mania for languages'. 'Within a month of entering university', he recalled, 'I had a go at Spanish, Portuguese, Welsh and Russian and even had a class of Danish.'[3] His Professor of French, Eugene Vinaver, had been charged by the Services with the task of talent-spotting amongst his students. One day he asked Allen if he would be interested in learning Japanese. Allen preferred the idea of Russian but, as he had anyway already volunteered for the RAF and knew that nothing would come of the Russian idea, he replied, 'Why not?' Unexpectedly, shortly afterwards, he failed his important medical. 'I didn't squint fast enough. So I began to learn Japanese.'[4] In December 1942, Allen left Manchester and in February 1943 he entered the Services Translators' Course in Japanese at the School of Oriental and African Studies (SOAS) at London University where 'a motley group of people assembled to be taught Japanese by an even more motley group'. The Services decided that some should be trained to be Interrogators and some Translators. The reality was 'in the end, you had to cope with both'.[5] Allen was put in Translators V, which consisted of only nine students, 'the rowdy class'. Hugh Cortazzi, who was in the concurrent Interpreters course, remembers Allen as the ringleader of this boisterous group. Despite the background to this unusual training, Allen never felt, nor were his later writings ever coloured by, any sense of arrogance towards the Japanese. Rather, from his first Japanese experiences at SOAS, 'every Japanese who had taught us, and every Englishman too, had filled us with liking for the Japanese at a time when it was fashionable to regard them with hatred, distrust or contempt'. 'At no time did prejudice against the Japanese play any part in my attitude.'[6] His fellow students, many of whom were to become significant Japanologists, such as Charles Dunn, Pat O'Neill and Ron Dore, were similarly affected. Oba Sadao, himself a veteran of Java and long-term resident of London, describes in his book on the SOAS war-time teaching of Japanese that what happened there 'was the very opposite of what you might expect from a propaganda exercise – that the people who were taught Japanese in war-time were in the end the people who resurrected knowledge of Japan in a totally non-hostile way'.[7]

WAR SERVICE

For Allen, who had no difficulty picking up European languages, it was 'a chastening experience'. 'I never quite got accustomed to the fact that what I was learning was some day to be put to use.' Allen and comrades very soon found themselves in Delhi seconded to the Intelligence Corps at the South East Asia Translation and Interrogation Centre (SEATIC) at

Mountbatten's Rear Headquarters. Here 'whole sacks of captured Japanese documents were thrown at us and we were told to get on with it'.[8] They were helped enormously by the US Nisei without whom 'the system might well not have functioned at all'. Their first introduction to Japanese prisoners, at Lal Qila, the Red Fort in Old Delhi, was a further major challenge to young Allen's language skills but the atmosphere and their demeanour was at least relaxed if resigned.

When he arrived in Burma the situation was quite different. Many of the prisoners were sick and diseased, suffering from beriberi, dysentery and malaria. From late-1944 their anguish was so acute that Allen felt enormous compassion for them and knew that his position was extraordinary. 'Those of us who knew Japanese were at the cutting edge of knowledge of the enemy in Burma.' 'We were the only ones who could make any sort of contact with the enemy, who could speak to prisoners and read Japanese documents.' 'For months at a time we lived with them (the prisoners) in these camps, shared their daily life, talked to them about war and built up, from conversations with them, the first accounts of what the war in Burma had been like from their side.'[9] In all Allen interrogated about 600 prisoners. Translations had to be delivered swiftly. 'It was vital to be able to translate, at speed, the most important operation orders and maps brought in by the patrols.' At the same time that he was so immersed in Japanese, his passion for languages was such that he was still keeping his other languages up to scratch; he polished up his Portuguese by learning by heart the Luiz Vaz de Camões epic, The Lusiads.[10]

From SEATIC Allen was transferred to No 2 Mobile Section of CSDIC (India) and served as a translator with 1V Corps and 17 Division and saw action at Pegu and Sittang. These actions are fully described in his book Sittang, the Last Battle.[11] Billing it as one of Allen's most significant contributions, Stanley Charles, from whom he took over CSDIC responsibilities at Penwegon, site of the 'Breakout Battle', tells how everyone regarded as of no importance a bag recovered from a dead Japanese soldier, 'covered in mud', except Allen, who quickly realized that it was details of the entire Japanese battle plan. 'It was a peach of a document from an intelligence point of view.'[12] He laboured without rest, barely eating and drinking, for thirty-six hours to complete its translation. The document was captured on 4 July and distributed to all divisions by 7 July. It helped win the day against the Japanese in the Battle of Sittang as their attempts to break out across the Sittang river and regroup with formations in Rangoon and Thailand had, through Allen, become known to the British Army two weeks beforehand. Allen witnessed the entire battle from start to finish from a number of Burmese villages strung out along the Rangoon- Mandalay road. 'The river which had witnessed the greatest defeat of the British army in Burma in the disastrous campaign of early 1942 now actively assisted the final disintegration of an entire Japanese army, only weeks before the Imperial Army surrendered unconditionally.' For this work Allen was mentioned in despatches and promoted.

CONTROVERSY OVER MEMOIR BY PROFESSOR AIDA YUJI

It was certainly a desire to introduce the Japanese viewpoint to a British audience which made Allen receptive to the suggestion to co-translate, with Ishiguro Hide, a Japanese lecturer in philosophy at Leeds University,[13] the work of Professor Aida Yūji of Kyoto University, *Prisoner of the British*. His account of being a Japanese Surrendered Personnel (JSP) held by the British in the Aron camp in Burma at the end of the war 'accuses the British of cold racial contempt against their Japanese prisoners', which he declares to be 'worse than physical brutality'.[14] 'We had glimpsed the unknown soul of the British Army and of the British. We had seen it. To us it was a frightening monster. This monster had ruled Asians for several hundred years and caused untold misery.' 'I felt that their treatment reflected the cruellest attitude a man can have towards his fellow men.'[15] Aida's contention that 'being treated cruelly with detachment is worse than being treated brutally by someone wild with hatred'[16] found a strong response in Japan, and the book became a best-seller when it was serialized in 1962 by the intellectual review *Chūō Kōron*. Writing in January 1965 to Cresset Press, who subsequently agreed to publish the book, approaches to Penguin and other publishers having been unsuccessful, Allen explained 'it is an important and interesting book since it represents an attitude of mind which aroused great sympathy in Japan itself'. Aida himself was glad to agree to the translation: 'British people have not had the opportunity to hear what Japanese people have to say. . . both British and Japanese people need to speak clearly. . . thus I am grateful to you for translating my book.'[17]

The collaboration with Ishiguro Hide (she translated some chapters which Allen checked and vice-versa) involved them in a monumental volume of correspondence with each other, the publishers, Aida and others, the whole exercise lasting from 1964-66. Sadly, the experience was ultimately unhappy. It is worth here examining the reasons for this as it is an example of the difficulties which can intrude into any account of perceptions and evaluations of the British by the Japanese. It was over their intended prefaces that the exchanges became particularly lengthy and heated. Ishiguro refers to her 'indignation' over their differences and Allen to 'the vicissitudes of our collaboration'.[18] Misunderstanding had arisen over loss of an original typescript which clearly caused Ishiguro to believe that Allen had, in an underhand way, 'palmed off on Cresset a preface of which Ishiguro disapproved. She criticzed Allen for 'neutralizing the effect the book might have in prompting British self-reflection' and accused him of trying to use Aida's book 'to defend the British military' and claimed that Aida himself was amazed at the preface '*Oya oya to omotta*' ('Could it really be true?'). Aida had asked if 'Louis Allen wrote these things not to placate his readers, but because he believed them?' 'For a Japanese intellectual who is always cynical about armies it is rather hard to believe someone feeling so involved in defending its decency, justness etc.' Allen was particularly hurt by the accusations of Aida that he was 'a typical Japan-basher masquerading as a Japanophile'. Allen had checked and checked all Aida's claims and wrote that he had found so many of them to have been factually untrue that he felt an explanatory preface to be essential.[19] 'In spite of his (Aida's) culture and sensibility' he displayed 'pathological over-sensitivity', which is the end-product of the 'actual expression of contempt and condescension by Englishmen to countless Japanese over the last 100 years'. Aida's younger colleague at Kyoto University, Professor Yokoyama Toshio (who met Allen while taking a D. Phil at Oxford) explained that Aida's own upbringing, in an elite, highly academic family, allowed him the intellectual space to be this culturally sensitive, in a way so as ultimately to undermine any confidence he may have had in 'Western humanism'.[20]

When Allen met Aida[21] in April 1964, then professor of European history specializing in the Renaissance period, Aida admitted that his memory was rather casual on a number of points. Allen was surprised that, even as a historian, he seemed unable to examine his own experience in a subtler, more complex, more sophisticated way. He felt that what Aida's book lacked was another chapter – 'an assessment by the Aida of today of the Aida of 1945-47'. In a letter to Ron Dore, who was called on to adjudicate, Allen explained: 'I feel that this business of Japanese prisoners is one on which the British do have a moderately clean bill.'[22] 'All my postscript was meant to do was to show that where this seemed to be related to contrived attitude it could well be the result of the misunderstanding inherent in a singularly difficult situation (of Aida as a JSP).' Allen was extremely offended at Ishiguro's accusation that his comments were 'nasty' (whereas she felt her own only ever to be 'critical') and believed her objections resulted from advice she had received that 'if Louis Allen's motive in translating the book is to say that the British always did the best they could to their prisoners and that Aida's suffering is entirely based on illusions and misunderstanding, then it would be a purely negative act' and that if she, Ishiguro, were to be identified in Japan with 'the venture to expose Aida's stupidity' she would 'get into trouble with *Chūō Kōron*, with Aida and, above all, with the Japanese intellectual world'.

Allen wanted British readers to know Aida's account and that this was how some Japanese felt, but he did not like to let factual inaccuracies pass. Allen himself was in the camp described by Aida, 'Yes the food was bad (only a little more so than the British rations. . .) and yes the Japanese soldiers worked extremely hard . . . but I don't think this was at all unfair when one considers the devastation of the Burmese towns and countryside which was a direct consequence of their invasion in 1942,' . . . 'but there were no untoward woundings or killings of the kind Aida refers to'.[23] Ishiguro, and Aida, felt by adding any explanation Allen was guilty of trying to tone down, even whitewash, the cruelty Aida experienced. He rejected Ishiguro's suggestion that Aida should be allowed a riposte on Allen's preface as time had run out and suggested she herself quickly amend her introduction to take account of Aida's views. This she did, writing in her preface: 'There is a lesson in his (Aida's) assertion that both sides can harm each other through vindictiveness, misunderstanding, differences of belief in psychological attitudes, that ignorance or complacency can be as damaging as intentional cruelty.' This was the message Ishiguro was fighting for the right of Aida to express to a British audience.

As the exchanges became more rancorous, Allen expressed his concern that Ishiguro was giving mutual friends 'an impression that I am anti-Japanese, but nothing could be further from the truth'. These painful exchanges highlight the heart of the difficulty of the JSP debate for Allen personally and for many British people, even sixty years on, with recollections of Japanese ill-treatment of POWs. In his review of the book in *Modern Asian Studies*, Charles Fisher of SOAS wrote: 'Professor Aida is entitled to his view that the callousness (displayed by British soldiers, who by then knew of Japanese treatment of POWs, in taking out their hatred of the Japanese in many different ways which remained within the letter of military law), which this measure of self-control implied, was harder to bear than the unpredictable outbursts of berserk fury which had been vented on British prisoners over the preceding three-and-a-half years, but I doubt he will persuade many British people of it.' Certainly, he did not persuade Allen of it.

Throughout a lifetime of sharing strong friendships with Japanese and a sincere desire to transmit to others at home an understanding of the reasons for the profound regard he felt for Japan he was never prepared to be an apologist for the Japanese military over their treatment of prisoners-of-war or, ultimately, to fall in with the desire of the Japanese intellectual community as well as of his Japanese war veteran friends, to brand the British army as politically motivated in the way they knew their own to have been. He did agree with Charles Fisher that 'the Japanese were far more deeply humiliated by captivity than were the British because they were more vulnerable to humiliation. To a considerable extent that vulnerability was the product of the racial arrogance and contempt which, both consciously and unconsciously, innumerable Westerners had long displayed towards all peoples of non-white skins.' He also knew of many instances where JSPs had not been treated appropriately – for instance when they were used in fighting against the Annamese insurgents.

Japanese accusations not only of general cruelty to the JSPs but of specific reprisals against them by the British have emerged from time to time and Allen was always anxious to ascertain if they had any foundations. In an address to the British Association of Japanese Studies in 1980[24] he explores the claims of Ienaga Saburō that treatment of suspected Japanese war criminals by British forces 'appears to have been extremely callous', 'according to *Shijitsu kiroku sensō saiban – Eiryō chiku*'. Allen explained that his 'own experience is of distant relations and hard labour, both of which might be expected in the circumstances'. A further claim, by Shinozaki Mamoru, in *Shokun* in 1974, is that the British 'in revenge and malice aforethought, by certain ways of treating that (Japanese) labour force, killed them off in numbers equivalent to the numbers of British and Australian POWs killed on the Burma-Siam Railway'. 'Between September 1945 and April 1947, more than 10,000 soldiers and civilians met their death without ever treading once more the soil of their homeland'. Since no other sources mention this claim (Allen refers to the official accounts for the evacuation of South-East Asia and Hattori Takushirō's *Dai Tōa Sensō*, as well as the *Ichiokunin no Shōwa-shi*) Allen regarded Shinozaki's account as non-proven. Shinozaki himself later revised the figure down to 2,500 and removed any reference to the deaths being part of a carefully planned atrocity. Allen regretted that his *End of the War in Asia* had not dealt with Malaya and Singapore and committed himself to further investigations of what took place in Singapore.

EFFORTS TO ACHIEVE RECONCILIATION

Perhaps this dual desire to introduce to Western audiences the best of Japan, at the same time as to ascertain factual evidence behind accusations of the worst, on both sides, lay behind Allen's strong belief that mutual understanding and reconciliation was an ideal worth striving for. Another factor was, undoubtedly, his conviction that he had been put in a very special position between Britain and Japan by his on-the-job learning of Japanese, and by his introduction to Japanese thinking which came through his extraordinary early experiences of meeting and listening to the Japanese during the war and that he should not squander its value. 'In the aftermath of the surrender I reckon I got to know one element of Japanese life – the military element – in a way that nobody since has been able to get to know . . . a curious, tiny, unrepeatable moment of time.'[26] This understanding and introducing of Japan was a lifetime mission for Allen.

Without question, Allen's greatest legacy to Anglo-Japanese under-standing of the two countries' wartime encounter was his book *Burma: The Longest War 1941-45*.[27] It was, and still is, highly acclaimed as presenting 'the story from both sides using evidence from private soldiers as well as generals, from correspondence and conversations since 1945, and from personal knowledge of the battlefield itself.[28] When the war ended, 'Allen's immediate duties were to persuade Japanese soldiers on the run that war was over and then assemble them in camps. When this had quietened down, Allen was moved to a POW camp in Rangoon where he interviewed Japanese staff officers from Matsuri (15 Division) and the Saku Army Group (28th Army) on the development of Japanese strategic planning in the different divisions.'[29] Allen compiled information about the life of Japanese in camps all over South-East Asia, Thailand, French Indochina and Singapore as well as Burma and carried out interrogations as preliminaries to war crimes investigations, as part of the historical record being compiled of the campaigns in South-East Asia from Japanese sources. While debriefing senior Japanese officers[30] he recorded and translated the accounts of the operations in which they had been involved.[31] The fact that he was able to keep copies of some of those reports[32] and some of the 77-page debriefing questionnaires must have been a further reason why, so early on, he had clearly resolved to try to match the accounts of the Japanese with those of the British and write a combined and definitive account of the Burma war.

Amongst other information, Allen helped to uncover the work of F. Kikan, (named after its commander Major Fujiwara Iwaichi) of Japanese Army Intelligence, which had been the liaison point with the Indian National Army. This experience gave rise to an interest in colonialism and liberation movements in South-East Asia.[33] Keeping in touch with those with whose debriefing he had been involved 'my contacts remained sporadic or continuous, from the time they sailed back in 1946. I visited them in Japan. They wrote about the war in Burma and put me in touch with others who did.'

> Bit by bit, conversation by conversation, document by document, I was able to piece together the Japanese side of things and make it match, where matching was possible, and sometimes it wasn't, with the accounts of those who wrote about Burma from our point of view. There were endless new facts from both sides to put together in a single volume using experience on the ground, a knowledge of what Burma was like as a place in which to live, a constant study of the literature that has been written about it, and an unbroken contact of 40 years with the Japanese Army, either in the flesh or in print.[34]
>
> I don't want to be on either side. I want to see as close as I can the true story and tell it from both sides. It's quite difficult to do actually. It gets you a lot of enemies.[35]

Allen was to spend considerable time, over the years, examining not only the archives of the Japanese Defence Agency, but also privately printed regimental association bulletins and similar documents. His expertise in military history later caused Allen to be invited to lecture on Japanese strategy and intelligence at conferences of the US Army War College and to contribute papers and reviews to the journal *Intelligence and National Security*.

At the same time as he undertook all this debriefing, Allen was forming deep and enduring friendships which he treasured his whole life. One such friendship was with an officer who had first appeared, when forced to surrender after the war had ended, as a raging 'Robinson Crusoe'; Naval Lt. Cdr. Tsutsumi Shinzō who ended up as Vice President of Mitsui, after a posting in London when he again met Allen. Others included Tsuchiya (a one time 28 Army staff officer who had helped Allen with his research) and *F Kikan*'s Fujiwara Iwaichi, (later Lt. General in the Self-Defence Forces), to whom Allen had been reintroduced by Professor Yokoyama Toshio, when he was back from studying in Oxford in the 1980s).[36] Allen had been posted to French Indo-China twice in 1946, as he could speak French, and had worked closely with Major Fujishima over the repatriation in 1946 of the remaining Japanese units and he was one of the many others with whom he thereafter met when he could in Japan and kept in touch through Christmas cards. Thanks to these contacts, Allen also collected material for later broadcasts, such as a series of radio interviews with leading Japanese scholars on *Nihonjinron* (The nature of the Japanese) and on *Nanshin* (Japan and South-East Asia), and for lectures at Tokyo University, the Australian Defence Academy, and the Department of History in the University of Singapore. His interest in Japan and South-East Asian relations was, much later, to lead to his being awarded an Emeritus Leverhulme Fellowship for research in the Japanese war-time occupation of Singapore.

With the help of all his many friends in Japan and from this range of first-hand sources, diaries, accounts and archives in both Japanese and English, Allen was able, in *The Longest War* to draw an immensely detailed picture of the stages of Japanese engagement in Burma and of the 'variety of different races involved with different motivations and fighting in jungle, mountain, desert, at sea and in vastly differing climates'.[37] His is the accepted view of the Japanese reasons for invading Malaya and the Philippines (to destroy the power of the two nations who dominated the sea-lanes, and the supply of oil from the Dutch East Indies) and of the stages by which it accomplished both this and the move into Burma. 'Mutaguchi's dream of wresting India from the British, thereby completing the collapse of British power in the East', is recognized but little space is given to the part which Russia played in Japanese thinking. Allen gives as the reason on the British side for war in Burma the determination 'to keep open the road to China and to hold down a mass of Japanese divisions that might otherwise have been used against the Allies'. He describes the turn-around in British fortunes from the time when the idea of beating the Japanese overland was unthinkable to eventual victory. At the same time he questions what that victory was for. 'At the very moment when Britain was using the Indian Army at its most courageous and successful, Britain was also on the verge of renouncing its empire in India and Burma forever.'

Burma: The Longest War was translated into Japanese by Hirakubo Masao, a Burma veteran and long-term resident of the UK, who was the main instigator of reconciliation on the Japanese side. Allen was always grateful to Hirakubo for that laborious work and always respectful of Hirakubo's determined efforts, which he himself supported, to bring together former British and Japanese enemies in reconciliation and to honour the war dead through joint memorials. Hirakubo wrote of his belief that the book 'will help Japanese veterans and younger generations to understand the plain truth of the Burma war, because in Japan, as well as in the UK, the veterans used to live in their own records, while Louis Allen's book is based on the record and interviews of both sides on which he has spent 40 years'.[38]

Allen was always conscious of the need for reconciliation and mutual understanding on both sides. When the Crown Prince of Japan visited England in 1953 for the Coronation,[39] he visited Durham, at the suggestion of Allen, who was his guide. So soon after the war Allen accepted that 'feelings ran high . . . the impact of the war was still strong, and hostility to Japan was taken for granted', and was not surprised that 'the University authorities were . . . terrified lest some untoward event occur'.[40] As late as 1988, however, Allen was unhappy to witness the ferocious reactions to the imminent death of the Emperor and to have to acknowledge that 'there still exists in the UK a layer of residual anti-Japanese feeling . . . (which) has lingered in the minds of many, and not necessarily just those old enough to remember the war'.[41] He definitely believed that 'the moral character of the Japanese Army in 1945 was at an all-time low', but he needed to know whether 'the army was a special case, and if it was, what had made it so, and if it had been made so, was it redeemable?'[42] In reaching his conclusion Allen refers to the writings of Field Marshal Hata Shunroku in *Nihon Shūhō*, 1945:

> Modern war takes the form of total war, in which the whole people is mobilized . . . if disgraceful incidents occur in any units of the armed forces, or atrocities of this kind, we must say that it is because of a decline in the moral standards of the people themselves', and to Prince Mikasa's comment: 'the crow stands out among a hundred herons. How could it have happened that, twenty or thirty years after the First World War, the Japanese Army turned into an atrocity army? I think we, the Japanese people, must earnestly reflect on this fact.[43]

In addition to his writings and as another practical part of his mission to promote understanding between the two countries, Allen was one of the earliest on the British side to organize two-way visits of reconciliation. This began with his own contacts from the war and surrender period and a trip to Japan in 1964, as a guest of the Japanese government. He went on to play an important part in conceiving and organizing the first reconciliation exchanges of Burma war veterans. In 1984 a group of Japanese veterans, members of the *Go Hachi Kai*, who fought at Kohima, under their Chairman Nishida Susumu, came to England and Allen was their host in Durham. In June 1989 another party, led by General Ushiyama, who had been a staff officer in North Burma, also visited Britain; Allen arranged a welcome for them at the Imphal Barracks in York. Later that year British Burma veterans, including Stanley Charles and Jack Scollen, visited Japan, with the help of the Japan-British Society's Tamayama Kazuo. Allen was able to participate in much of their programme, as he was on a lecture tour of Japan.

The party toured around Japan, everywhere being met with warm hospitality by the *Zen Biruma Senyūkai* (All Burma Veterans' Association of Japan) amongst many others and a high level of press coverage. The only uncomfortable note arose from Allen's wish to avoid a group visit to the Yasukuni Shrine. Later, there was criticism from some quarters of their making such a tour and, additionally, of having taken Sasakawa Foundation funding for it, which Allen countered in his presentation to the Japan Society the following year.[44] This visit was to pave the way for future similar trips which helped to achieve on both sides much personal reconciliation and peace of mind. It also contributed to the diminution of criticism of the visits. For his part Allen saw that the purpose, and success, of these and later reconciliation exchanges between veterans (which after 1990 were organized by the Burma Campaign Fellowship Group) derived from the encounters of old enemies, and the avoidance of 'trading prejudices' or rather a parallel discussion of historical facts and their interpretation and an attempt at understanding military behaviour and wartime events. He himself was 'exasperated' not to get beyond the absurd apologist explanations of the treatment of Far East Prisoners-of-War. Aida contended that, because the Japanese have not traditionally kept cattle, they simply badly managed the business of 'herding' the prisoners around – and the British could not understand this as they had been 'herding' people in their colonies for decades, 'it is not merely a reflection of the malicious intention of the Japanese, it is a reflection of their inexperience and ignorance'.[45] Others said the prisoners were merely suffering culture shock from being made to eat rice. He was equally critical of the ignorance on the British side. Having himself enjoyed, since the war, the 'encounter' element of reconciliation it was the mutual understanding which he most wanted to see and to this his own work made probably the greatest contribution of any.

THE SCHOLAR

Allen was demobilized at the end of 1946 and returned to Manchester University where he repeated courses in French and Japanese, graduating with a First Class honours degree in French in 1947. He went on to study in London and in Paris, at the Sorbonne, on Manchester University's prestigious Kemsley Prize, where he also took Japanese courses at the École des Langues Orientales in Paris, before arriving at Durham University in 1948, to teach French literature and start his married life with Margaret Wilson, who was the mainstay of his private and family life until her tragic and untimely death in 1979.

To everything he did, from researching, writing and lecturing, to bringing up six children, Allen gave himself wholeheartedly. Colleagues recall: 'He was a dynamic figure, with a strikingly wide range of knowledge and erudition, and his restless, enquiring mind and questing spirit fed into everything he did, to the immense benefit of students and colleagues alike.'[46] He was successively Lecturer, Senior Lecturer and Reader in French until 1988 and was a prolific author on a wide range of French writers, famous and less famous. 'A Chair could easily have been his had he been more ingratiating or more narrowly ambitious.'[47] He inspired generations of students with his dynamic teaching style and his powerful oratory; they remembered with affection 'the intellectual generosity that radiated from his portly, usually bearded presence', even beyond the walls of the French Department. Sebastian Dobson never forgot the impact of Allen's lectures on Japanese history, beginning with the singing of Japanese soldiers' songs, which were influential in directing him into Japanese studies. In the late 1960s Allen had even taught a course in Japanese for both staff and students, with considerable success.

As a major figure in the field of Japanese studies, Allen was an active participant in the British Association of Japanese Studies, and its President in 1980. He applied for the newly-established chair of Japanese at Cambridge in 1984, but his prime academic expertise was in French and he probably did not expect to be selected. He was happy at Durham, but it was sad that his achievements in Japanese did not lead to a university post in Japanese studies. In addition to military history, and the history of the transfer of power in Burma and South-East Asia, Allen wrote extensively about Japanese literature and undertook many translations of classical Japanese fiction:

> In order to know a nation fully you have to go beyond knowing the way it expresses itself in its laws, its military behaviour, and its political systems. You have to know the way it talks about itself unconsciously and through its fiction. In other words, the fiction of a nation is as important as the facts of a nation if we want to know it properly.[48]

He was especially fascinated in and knowledgeable about Lafcadio Hearn and wrote a number of pieces on him.[49] Hearn's connection with Durham and his mixed-religion parentage no doubt echoed with Allen, but, most importantly, he found much to agree with in Hearn's analysis of the conflict between traditional and modern which challenged Japan:

> In Lafcadio Hearn, the material engineering triumphs of nineteenth-century Europe are at war with the spirituality that he saw in Japan. That's the real conflict. And anyone who knows Japan now must see the conflict still there.

Indeed, according to one of his publishers, Paul Norbury,[50] (a view subsequently confirmed by his son Mark), Louis Allen very much saw himself in the mould of Lafcadio Hearn, especially in his role as an interpreter, insisting that Hearn's contributions to Western understanding of Japan were as relevant today as ever they were. Thus, delays in publishing Allen's Hearn anthology,[51] which finally appeared in a much reduced version posthumously in 1992, caused him considerable distress, generating something of an abrasive exchange on the subject of 'why not publish now?'.

One of Allen's visits to Japan, at the invitation of Professor Hirakawa Sukehiro of Tokyo University who became a close personal friend, was for an international symposium on Lafcadio Hearn. Allen also wrote articles and reviews about Japan's connections with the North-East,[52] about Japanese culture[53] and on how the Japanese view themselves.[54] A full bibliography will be published in *Collected Writings of Louis Allen* due to be issued in 2004.[55]

Allen was a member of the Japan Society, the Royal Society for Asian Affairs, the Burma Star Association, the Indian Army Association, the Burma Campaign Fellowship Group and the British Association of Orientalists – as a member of which he attended the 1960 International Congress of Orientalists in 1960, in Moscow, Leningrad and Central Asia. In addition to his writings and translations on Japanese literature, Allen was always interested in the problems raised by technical and scientific translations from Japanese, and translated many Japanese scientific texts, in such fields as naval architecture, chemical engineering and glass technology for the research organizations of such firms as Rolls Royce, Pilkingtons, ICI, the British Shipbuilding Research Association and a number of Ministries. In yet another field, Allen is remembered for his writings on Catholic Theology as well as the Oxford Movement. His erudition on a vast range of subjects was widely recognized by listeners to the BBC's 'Round Britain Quiz' and 'Transatlantic Quiz', which he co-chaired throughout the 1980s with Gordon Clough and for which he devised the majority of the questions. He wrote many theatrical and literary reviews and was a frequent broadcaster as well as serving on the advisory council of the BBC and chairing its north-east advisory council.

FINAL YEARS

The desire to promote understanding and friendship between Britain and Japan was the overriding passion of the last ten years of his life.[56] He was concerned that the boom in Japanese studies in the 1980s was fuelled by a desire to discover the Japanese 'secret' and that the approach continued to be adversarial. He helped welcome to Durham the young students of Teikyo University, when their university opened a campus at Durham. It was perhaps the influence of Allen that lay behind their decision to name their main building after Lafcadio Hearn. Recognition of Allen's untiring efforts in the field of Anglo-Japanese relations was given by the European Association of Japanese Studies, who made him a life member, and later by the Northumbrian Universities East Asian Centre, who made him an Honorary Fellow. According to Ines San Miguel of Teikyo University, who was the first researcher to look at Allen's archive at Durham University, the university was approached by the Japanese Embassy over the award of a Japanese government honour to Allen. Sadly 'he did not live long enough to share with his fellow servicemen any of the awards offered by the Queen and the Emperor of Japan for services to Anglo-Japanese reconciliation'.[57]

Weeks before his death on his sixty-ninth birthday, pushed in a wheelchair and suffering painfully in the advanced stages of his illness, Allen gave a lecture on Burma at the Imperial War Museum's conference to mark the fiftieth anniversary of the start of the Asia-Pacific War. The *Asahi Shimbun* wrote of Allen's lecture, 'even today fifty years after the start of the war, the image of the cruel Japanese is hard to remove from the minds of the Britishers'. As Professor Ian Nish has commented on this unfair report, 'Louis always realized that one of the factors in achieving reconciliation was to break down the assumptions of the media'.[58] Even now, over sixty years since the start of war, just as the whole Aida debate had highlighted forty years ago, real, widespread and mutual understanding of many aspects of the war remains elusive. Allen was the most relentless of all in seeking out the facts and refusing to sidestep the difficult issues. Anglo-Japanese relations, and the record of its history, are indebted to him.

A cherry tree was planted in memory of Louis Allen by Durham University on 16 August 1988 on Palace Green in Durham. The inscription reads: 'This tree was planted as a sign of friendship and reconciliation between the United Kingdom and Japan, and in memory of Louis Allen, who lived at Dun Cow Cottage, a tireless worker for these purposes.'

33

John Corner, 1906-96: Controversial Biologist and Friend of the Shōwa Emperor

CARMEN BLACKER

John Corner

JOHN CORNER (Edred John Henry C.B.E., F.R.S., F.L.S.) has been authoritatively described as one of the most colourful and controversial biologists of the century. His last post was that of Professor of Tropical Botany at Cambridge. He was a Fellow of the Royal Society and of Sidney Sussex College, Cambridge, where he delighted many of the other Fellows by his wit, warmth and easy erudition. (When the college decided to admit women in 1973, however, he walked out, never to return. The true cause of his resignation was never revealed.) His contribution to botany was so noteworthy that no less than thirty-six seed plants and three species of fungi have been named after him.[1] His work on the odd, stinking yet delicious durian fruit is still respected, as is his study of the *clavaria* genus of fungus.

Corner was famous also for his successful training of macaque monkeys to gather specimens of rare flowers from the thick overhead canopy of the Malayan forest.[2] No human being, however good a tree climber, could hope to penetrate the dense tangle of twigs and epiphytes, but the *berok* monkeys naturally enjoyed snatching coconuts and watching them crash to the ground. Corner at once perceived that these monkeys could be trained to gather not only coconuts but also specimens of the rare flowers and fruit that had still defied botanical naming and classification. Enquiries among knowledgeable Malays confirmed that the monkeys could be easily fed on rice and vegetables, together with the caterpillars and stick insects found in the course of their work, and that they could be trained to obey simple words of command. Condign punishment might have to be administered occasionally to prevent 'naughtiness' such as throwing stones and savaging children, but there was no need to make the monkeys cry. Corner successfully trained several monkeys to gather such rare flowers, some of whom could distinguish at least twenty-four Malay words of command. He even took one of them to visit the Singapore Zoo, and was surprised to observe an instant friendship develop between it and a 'demoniacal creature' known as the Black Ape of the Celebes. They shook hands, the ape extending his black arm through the bars of the cage, and crooned together with mounting affection until perforce separated. 'This little scene of friendship at first sight recurred to me when Yamashita's army invaded Singapore,' Corner enigmatically added.

SINGAPORE 1929-45

His relationship with Japan was ambiguous. He lived in Malaya and Singapore from 1929 to 1945, absorbed, until 1942, by the study of tropical plants, the training of his botanical monkeys, and by his responsibilities as Director of the Singapore Botanical Gardens and the Raffles Museum. When the Japanese invasion came in 1942, and the lightning advance of the Japanese army under General Yamashita down the Malay Peninsula ended with the capture of Singapore in February, he found himself in a difficult dilemma. The obvious course was to stick by his countrymen, and with them be herded as a prisoner of war into a horrendous gaol such as Changi prison. But what would then happen to the Botanic Gardens and the Museum, with their unique and priceless collections of flora, seeds, chests and boxes of specimens so carefully catalogued over the years, and for which he was responsible? In all likelihood everything would be destroyed by looters. He had seen an example of the appalling and mindless destruction which looters could perpetrate when he saw what was left of the Fullerton Building in Singapore shortly after the Japanese invasion. Desks and cupboards broken open, their contents trampled on the floor and covered with human filth, clothes, diaries, letters, the pages of a Bible likewise reduced to a urine-sodden mess on the floor; shirts and all coats ripped up with a tin-opener. . . Could he allow this to happen to the gardens and the museum? He, went to sleep 'thinking and thinking. . . .' A dream apparently solved his problem.

At dawn the next day he woke laughing and exclaiming:

> What a fool I am! Of course, of course! In a lucid flash I had
> seen myself go to the Japanese authorities, and be received
> with open arms. There were no details, but a crowd of persons
> where I was happy. I dressed quickly, and went to find the
> Governor, Sir Shenton Thomas, to seek his approval for my
> mission. . .³

In short, the dream told him to give himself up at once to the Japanese
enemy in order to obey the higher loyalty to the gardens and to science.
His surrender was to be conditional, but it was surrender nonetheless.

But Sir Shenton, he wrote, had already had the same idea, and when
Corner presented himself that morning wrote 'a pencilled note in which
he requested the Japanese authorities to preserve the scientific collections,
libraries and matters of historic interest, particularly at the Museum and
the Botanical Gardens'. This note Sir Shenton handed to Corner, charging
him to deliver it. 'I saw no option,' Corner continued. He had not lived
in Singapore for its social round. 'I was a crank in that pleasure-seeking
society.' So he decided in the light of his dream 'to throw in my lot with
the Japanese . . . and to turn from nationality to the neutral, or the
international cause of the conservation of knowledge.'⁴

So he made his way to the Supreme Court, where the Japanese Military
Police gave him a cigarette and made him sit among 'rows of Chinese
ragamuffins', all guilty of looting and roped neck to neck. Eventually, he
made his way to the Municipality Building, where Sir Shenton's note
enabled him to jump the queue and explain himself to a Mr Toyoda, the
former Japanese consul, who politely told him to await a Professor who
was soon to take charge of scientific affairs, and to come back the next
day.

He was soon designated a civilian internee, or paroled enemy civilian.
He had to swear by Almighty God that he would not try to escape, would
do nothing to benefit the enemies of Japan, and would not converse with
any POW. He had to live at a designated address, and wear a designated
mark when going out. A Mr Birtwistle (referred to hereafter as 'Birt'),
formerly Director of Fisheries, was ordered to stay under the same
conditions. But nearly all the rest of the British community were declared
prisoners of war, and herded into appalling jails, many of them to Changi
prison itself.

'Not one of his 'companions', Corner wrote, was prepared to join him
in his stance. They were all possessed of 'the same determination to suffer
in unity, which I would not, and I saw that at heart they were not
scientists.'

In Corner's eyes, therefore, loyalty to the Gardens and the Museum
was a higher moral duty than loyalty to his country. Those who put their

country first were not at heart scientists. But it is not surprising to find that to this day there are still people, not only survivors of the frightful conditions of overcrowding, filth, starvation and disease in camps and prisons, who bitterly resented Corner's conduct. He was a traitor. He had surrendered to the enemy. He had later hobnobbed and dined with Marquis Tokugawa Yoshichika, the Japanese 'Governor' of Singapore. He walked always, until the end of the war, a relatively free man.

Corner's further account of his captivity in Singapore until the Japanese surrender in 1945 is written largely in terms of the two courteous and civilized Japanese gentlemen who were his immediate superiors, and with both of whom he was able to become firm friends. These were 'the Marquis', or Marquis Tokugawa Yoshichika, the 'Governor' of Singapore, and 'the Professor', or Professor Tanakadate Hidezō, appointed Director of the Gardens and Museum.

'The Marquis', at the time the aristocratic head of the Owari branch of the Tokugawa family, had been appointed by General Tōjō, then Japanese Prime Minister, to the post of supreme command of the island of Singapore. It was said that his knowledge of Court Malay and his friendship with more than one Malay Sultan had contributed to his appointment, for General Tōjō had realized that such accomplishments were likely to prove useful to the Japanese occupation. In the 1920s the Marquis had been well known as a big game hunter in Malaya and Borneo, and even given the nickname *toragari no tonosama*, 'Lord Tiger Hunter'. It is not known how far he was concerned to promote the cult of State Shinto, with its supporting myth of Japan's destiny to rule the world, but he is known to have been among the sympathizers with the officers of the *Ni-ni-roku* incident of 1936, and to be an advocate of *Nanshin* or Japan's expansion south. At the same time, however, he was a man of deep culture, with scholarly interests in zoology, botany and Malay history. On the strength of these qualities he received the further appointment of President of the Botanic Gardens and the Raffles Museum.

Thus began a period of friendship and scientific collaboration with Corner. The two got on famously from the start, and although Corner found that he was prohibited by his humble status of 'enemy alien', from dining more than once with so exalted and powerful a figure, the Marquis was always generous with his invitations to join excursions by car or motor launch to visit nearby Sultans, their zoos and collections. This friendship between the Marquis and Corner shows how it is possible, in Louis Allen's words, even in a conflict between nations with very different ideals and objectives, for men who recognize that they have a duty to science as well as to their country, to collaborate in the collection and rescue of scientific evidence. 'The dark history of the times needs such occasional illumination.'[5]

Typical of his kindness, Corner wrote, was the Marquis's concern over the plight of children interned with their parents in Changi jail, whose education might later be found to be deficient. He ordered Corner and 'Birt' to select suitable books for these children from the piles dumped in the Museum. These, plus a good many toys discovered by Corner in a cupboard, were delivered to the jail in time for Christmas 1943, 'with what result I do not know'.

The second sympathetic and generous Japanese scholar whom Corner was lucky enough to have as his immediate superior was Professor Tanakadate Hidezō of Tōhoku University. Usually known as 'the Professor', Tanakadate was at once recognizable by his 'nodding head, thick untidy hair and ugly face' and by the crumpled hat and shabby mufti which he usually wore. When he arrived in Singapore, although he had no more clothes than he stood up in, he came as the express emissary of no less a person than the Emperor. For this illustrious figure was a committed marine biologist and botanist, and deeply concerned that the valuable scientific collections on the island should be preserved and respected. The Professor, therefore, as an imperial messenger no less, carried instant authority with the military, convincing even General Yamashita of his prerogative over his chosen sphere.

He was hence appointed Director not only of the Raffles Museum, but also of the Botanic Gardens and Library. He insisted from the first that the museum's important treasures, such as the letters of Sir Stamford Raffles and the diaries of the botanical explorer Frank Kingdon-Ward, should be kept safe from both looters and Japanese journalists. He and Corner seem to have become firm and instant friends. Corner often stayed in his house in Lermit Road when work so demanded, and was often entrusted with the absent-minded Professor's wallet containing his passport and money. Corner furthermore did the Professor's laundry, arranged his meals, found him a wardrobe of clothes from an empty bombed house, and even retrieved his false tooth which kept falling out as he talked. It was odd, Corner later wrote, to think of an enemy alien acting as valet to this 'simple and sympathetic' yet powerful Professor, who refused the high military rank offered him because in his shabby mufti he could talk more easily to the ordinary people of Singapore, who were often at the time reduced to starvation and to be seen touting cigarette ends.[6]

The Professor likewise did Corner many a good turn. He took effective precautions to stop all rumours that Corner was a collaborator. He told Japanese journalists that Corner's name, after that of General Yamashita, was the most familiar to Japanese in Malaya, for was he not the author of the wonderful book *Wayside Trees of Malaya*, which even the Emperor had read ? He even arranged for a 'British Room' to be set aside in the Museum where 'Birt' and Corner could take an occasional rest, and where the portraits of Queen Victoria and other royal persons could be safely consigned.

Gathering at the Chinsan-so Restaurant, Tokyo, 6 September 1966. (*From left to right*): The Marquis' secretary, Dr Tamada, John Corner, Tadamichi Koga, Yoshichika, Shuichi Asakura, Professor Kazuo Okochi, Yata Handa

And when an appalling housekeeper, Mrs Arbenz, wife of the Swiss Consul, was manoeuvring to get Corner arrested and turned over to the military police, it was the Professor who prevented her wiles in the nick of time. Just when Corner confessed that he was contemplating murder, she was fortunately murdered herself in a contrived car accident.[7]

It was the Professor, furthermore, who first introduced Corner to the Emperor. On a brief visit to Japan in 1942 he presented to the Emperor a copy of Corner's book *Wayside Trees of Malaya*. Apparently the Emperor was delighted, for the Professor reported solemnly on his return to Singapore that 'The Emperor of Japan wishes to thank you for the gift of the book on Malayan trees. It is the only book he has read in bed.' Indeed, it transpired that the Emperor did keep the book on a table in his bedroom, which he had never done before with any other book.[8]

Above all, however, it was the shared devotion to the high loyalty of science that chiefly bound the two men together. Without the Professor's friendship it is arguable that Corner might not have survived to argue his case.

During the three years that Corner spent in captivity as a civilian internee in Singapore, his activities seem to have been many and various. He was able to continue, in collaboration with the Professor, 'Birt' and a few others, his principal work looking after the collections in the Botanic Gardens and the Museum. But he also recalled helping the Marquis, and later an Imperial Prince, to plant monumental trees in the Botanical Gardens, including a sapling of *Dracontomelum*. And he helped to entertain a group of Japanese scientists from Burma, Borneo and the Philippines, who had gathered in Singapore at the behest of the Marquis to report on the state of conservation in Japanese-occupied countries.

He had to cope, too, with a fanatical new Japanese Director of the Museum, sent by the Japanese Ministry of Education (*Mombushō*) early in 1945. This man, who is not named, ordered everything Western to be destroyed and replaced by things Japanese. He would certainly have destroyed the museum and its library had he not after a short period 'lost face' with the museum staff and been directed elsewhere.

In 1944 Corner helped to cope with a bad infestation of worms (*turbellarians*) in the drinking water supply of Singapore. By then Singapore was beginning to succumb to a terrible combination of 'disease, starvation and putrefaction'. Fortunately, however, Corner writes, the atom bomb and the end of the war forestalled this otherwise inevitable collapse. For Singapore, the end of the war came none too soon.

By 1944 food was gravely short, and Corner proved himself an inventive cook with the small supplies available of tapioca-root, bananas and tropical yeasts. Various wild yeasts, he noticed, exudate from broken trees and leaves, their 'slimy and alcoholic clots' being greatly relished by his botanical monkeys, and proving a useful ingredient in home-made curacoa.[9]

Corner and his companions often faced horrendous sights during their years under Japanese occupation in Singapore. He describes the terrible conditions under which Javanese men and women were rounded up for labour, and driven into Singapore before being transferred to Thailand. Many of them were huddled in suffocating conditions, near the house where Corner lived, in conditions so frightful that many died, their bodies eaten by rats and insects. Every night the women were herded into camps for prostitutes. Such sights repelled the native Indonesians, and revived their failing spirit 'against the vainglorious South-East Asia Co-Prosperity Sphere.'[10]

CORNER AND THE EMPEROR

A notable feature of Corner's relations with Japan was his friendship with the Shōwa Emperor. This apparently dated from the time during the war when he had presented the Emperor with a copy of his book *Wayside Trees of Malaya*. After the Emperor's death in 1989 Corner assumed responsibility for writing a long obituary of the Emperor for the *Biographical Memoirs of the Fellows of the Royal Society*.[11] In this memoir Corner described the Emperor's upbringing, his nascent interest in marine biology, his huge collection of shells, his explorations of the marine life of the Sagami Bay area where his Hayama villa was situated, his finding of a large red prawn unknown to science in 1918, later called *Sympasiphaea imperialis*, and the building and equipping in 1925 of the first biological laboratory in the grounds of the Akasaka Palace.[12] He insisted from the outset that the 'Scholar Emperor and Imperial Biologist' should always be distinguished from 'His Majesty the Emperor of Japan'. The Emperor performed two roles, each clear and distinct from the other, and each as important as the other. Most Western biographers had tended to treat the Emperor's interest in biology as a mere hobby, a means of escape from the stifling confines of court etiquette into the wider freedom of the world of nature. It was nothing of the kind. 'No amateur,' Corner wrote, 'could have encompassed and mastered the vast field of nature that he did, and risen to international authority.' The Emperor may certainly have worn two faces, one passive and obedient to the call of duty, the other that of an eager investigator bent on discovering more about the world of animals and plants. The more lowly and humble the creature, moreover, the greater was the Emperor's inspiration in studying its habits. Eventually, he chose to specialize in two of these humble orders – the slime moulds, *nenkin* in Japanese, and the marine organisms known as *hydrozoa* organisms. And, Corner continued, it was this very humility which gave him in the hour of need the strength to rescue his country from 'shattering and abject defeat'. It was due to the Emperor's courage at Japan's dark hour, in short, that led him to insist on delivering the broadcast speech on 15 August 1945, announcing Japan's surrender to the allies.[13]

Corner even referred to the Emperor as one of his 'mentors'. He was full of praise for the thirteen 'splendid monographs' which the Emperor had written on the various marine animals he had collected and studied in the Sagami Bay area. These included a 'great one' on crabs which described no less than 346 species of crab, including three new species. Another monograph was devoted to starfish, in which sixty-three species were recorded, eight of which were new. Others recorded hermit crabs, sea-urchins, and brittlestars. No mere amateur escapist could have accomplished the exacting tasks of collection and identification necessary for such work. And although he certainly kept a 'biological court' about him, the members of which sometimes lent their names to such publications, Corner wrote that it was obvious that the guiding light of scientific enthusiasm and rigour came from the Emperor himself. His research on the slime-moulds of the Nasu district, where another Imperial villa was located, was equally distinguished, with no less than 125 species of this humble creature described. Corner was always impressed by the ease with which the Emperor could turn from affairs of state to matters of intricate biology. When relaxing over matters botanical he would and could 'laugh with puckish humour'; this showed that he was a true scientist at heart.

The varied material which Corner needed to compile his memoir of the Emperor for the Royal Society was apparently gathered by him in 1989 during seven weeks of travel in Japan. He wrote to the present Emperor, whom he had met as Crown Prince in 1985, to request his permission to present the 'biological side' of the old Emperor's life to the scientific world, of which the West knew little or nothing. To this request the present Emperor responded quickly. 'The Palace gates were opened and every facility unostentatiously provided.' Friends old and new among Japanese scientists rallied to the cause. He found himself invited to lunch at the Akasaka Palace, and to dinner to meet senior Japanese scientists. He was escorted to the biological laboratory which the Shōwa Emperor had had specially built for his own use in the Palace grounds.

The climax of Corner's recognition in Japan came in 1985, when, to mark the Jubilee of the Emperor, an International Prize for Biology was created. Corner was selected to be the first recipient. The Prize was a silver vase embossed with the chrysanthemum crest in gold, a medal made of *shibuichi*, a Japanese alloy of gold, silver and copper, and two million yen. In 1983 he had been awarded the Golden Key of the City of Yokohama. He is also credited with the introduction to Japan of the 'important and delicious potato' known as the *danshaku-imo*.[14]

ASSSESSMENT

The moral problem which confronted Corner in 1942 is still an arguable one. I have asked various people in responsible walks of life what they would have done in like circumstances. The scientists, both men and women, unhesitatingly say that Corner was morally right to take the course he did. Loyalty to science is on a morally higher plane than loyalty to one's country, and the agreement of Japanese biologists shows that Corner's attitude transcended vows to country.[15] Others, not scientists, are less sure. They are glad that they never found themselves in the terrible position that Corner did. On one level, yes; on another, no. One scholar of Dutch extraction declared that England had shown great tolerance in giving, after the war, the Chair of Tropical Botany to Corner, together with a fellowship of the Royal Society, and another of the Linnean Society. It was not every country that would have been so magnanimous.

Corner himself never had a moment's doubt that he had made the right decision. He had turned from nationality to the international cause of the conservation of knowledge. His mission had always been 'to understand the surpassing complexity of the Malayan forest', and to find out for himself whether the hypothesis of evolution was true. It was not to indulge in cocktail parties or the expected social round. But there is little doubt that an element of luck, as well as of conscientious judgement, came his way. For he was almost miraculously fortunate to find that the two Japanese men in authority who were most concerned with his work and responsible for his freedom to carry it out, were thoroughly sympathetic, generous, kindly and scientifically knowledgeable scholars. Had this not been the case, and had Corner found himself serving two fanatically convinced supporters of State Shinto, he might well not have survived to tell any tale at all.

It is surely to Corner and to his two sympathetic superiors that the scholarly world owed the preservation of the scientific collections in Singapore when these were threatened with destruction in 1942. Nor should we forget Corner's feeling that 'some direction from on high' had contributed to his good treatment. The Linnean Society were apparently delighted to hear that they had been right during the war not to strike out the Emperor's name from their list of Fellows. At Corner's instance they let it remain.

34

Basil William Robinson, 1912- : the Japanese Sword and the Victoria and Albert Museum

YAHYA ABDELSAMAD

Basil W. Robinson

INTRODUCTION

IN THE MEIJI PERIOD, many thousands of foreigners with skills in fields such as engineering, medicine, education and the military sciences were offered short-term government contracts on generous salaries to work in Japan; they were known as *o-yatoi gaikokujin* – literally 'honoured foreign employees', although the term had rather pejorative undertones. These specialists, like Sir Francis T. Piggott, legal adviser, or the architect Josiah Conder, brought back to their home countries many art objects which were either given to them as departing presents or were items which they had bought while residing in Japan. Some of these objects, such as swords, woodblock prints, netsuke etc., were given or lent to museums. In Britain the Victoria & Albert and the British Museums were the main recipients. The majority of the objects were of medium quality, but a few high-quality items were included.

Former samurai and many of the newly-created nobility sold off their family heirlooms to keep up their status and lost interest in their ancient heritage, whilst trying hard to adopt a neo-Western life-style. Some of these objects were shown to the British public for the first time in exhibitions such as the Japan-British exhibition at Shepherd's Bush in London in 1910 and later at the Red Cross exhibition of 1915.[1] These exhibitions contributed to the interest in Japanese art which had seen its peak in the late nineteenth century.

Basil William Robinson, who became an expert on Japanese swords, was one of those who as a result became fascinated by aspects of Japanese art and who helped to inspire interest in the Japanese sword and its associated arts and crafts. By his diligent scholarship, through his essays in sword journals such as the JSS/US (Japanese Sword Society of the United States), the Journal of the Tōken Society of Great Britain and Tōken Bijutsu of the NBTHK (Nippon Bijutsu Tōken Hozon Kyōkai – the Society For the Preservation of Japanese Swords) and his monumental book *Arts of the Japanese Sword*, Robinson made a signal contribution to promoting knowledge of the art of Japanese sword-making.

Before Robinson's *Arts of the Japanese Sword* appeared in 1961 there were really only two reliable books in English about Japanese swords and both had been published after the end of the Second World War. These were *Nippon-tō* by the Japanese sword dealer and authority Inami Hakusai in 1947 and *The Samurai Sword* by the Japanese-American, John (Masayuki) Yumoto in 1958. They were the first books specifically about Japanese swords to have been written in the English language since Joly's *Sword and Same* had appeared at the end of the nineteenth century. These were basic books and only gave the briefest outline of the history of the craft. They were essentially reference books in the sense that they concentrated on giving a chronological view of the history of Japanese sword-making. They did little to explain to the Western student the complexities of the aesthetics of the Japanese sword, the relationships between various schools of sword-making, or the influence of individual sword-makers.

Robinson in his preface to *Arts of the Japanese Sword* in discussing the situation in 1961 noted:

It is not, perhaps, surprising that little or nothing original has been, or is likely to be, written on the Japanese sword by anyone who is not a Japanese. At best, a non-Japanese writer can only hope to serve up a cold collation of ingredients culled from Japanese authorities with an occasional seasoning from his own necessarily limited observation. European amateurs of the subject are thus through no fault of their own forced to spend the necessary years in patient study and comparison of the finest representative blades of all schools and periods, and so can never acquire that deep knowledge and wide experience that are the marks of the Japanese *kanteisha* (sword appraiser). In writing the section on blades, therefore, I have leaned heavily on the Japanese authorities, especially Hon'ami Kosan, Fujishiro Yoshio and Honma Junji, and have followed to some extent the arrangement of my little handbook *A Primer of Japanese Sword-blades* (1955), now out of print, from which the illustrations of *hamon* (the sword's tempered edge) and the table of characters used in swordsmiths' names have been incorporated.

Publication of Robinson's book inspired the next generation of sword collectors and scholars in the 1980s and 1990s to publish works on the subject. One of these was Han Bing Siong in the Netherlands who is admired by many in the worldwide sword community as one of the pre-eminent non-Japanese sword scholars outside Japan. He publishes frequently in Japanese, English and Dutch and has always acknowledged Robinson's contribution to the study of the Japanese sword. Leon Kapp of San Francisco who published his landmark book *The Craft of the Japanese Sword* in 1987 on sword forging, also acknowledges his debt to Robinson. The forging of swords had not previously been the subject of a study in a European language as sword–makers were most reluctant to explain their methods as they did not wish to reveal their techniques.

Rowland J. Gregory of Bedfordshire and his friend Richard Fuller of Bristol collaborated on a series of books on the Japanese military sword in the 1970s and 1980s, which won worldwide acclaim from collectors around the world. When they set about gathering materials for their first book they were much encouraged by Basil Robinson. Gregory met Robinson in 1946 when he used to deal in Japanese antiques in the Portobello Road and to buy Japanese swords from servicemen who had been in the Far East during the War.

The July/August 1974 issue of *The Journal of the Tōken Society of Great Britain* contained a transcript of a talk by Robinson about his early life and subsequent career with the Victoria and Albert Museum (the V&A) under the title 'Reminiscence' Programme 81. In producing this essay I have drawn on this and on 'Japanese surrendered swords: A Reminiscence of 1945' from Programme 100 of the same society.

EARLY LIFE AT SCHOOL AND EARLY CAREER WITH THE V&A

Basil William Robinson was born in South Kensington, London, on 20 June 1912, within 'five minutes' of his future place of employment. He recalled how his mother and aunts used to take him to the various museums in the area to keep him amused. He was immediately fascinated by the extinct animals at the Natural History Museum. The names of

Triceratops and Megalosaurus 'used to trip off my tongue quite lightly'. As he walked further up the road he quickly graduated to the V&A where 'Oriental things seemed to click with me, why I don't know there is no family reason. My poor parents were mystified by this curious line that I developed.' He recalled how in Crowborough in East Sussex he used to fence with his friends in mock combat with curved branches of pinewood resembling Japanese swords.

At the age of nine he was sent to preparatory school where he recalls that a friend was nearly caned for bringing to school *Tales of Old Japan* by A.B. Mitford because it included tales of adultery. Robinson commented:

> I can still remember that dreadful picture of poor Chōbei in the bath, being speared and all the blood coming out. Very soon the book was confiscated by the Headmaster as he thought it wasn't suitable for us to read.

However, he remained unrepentant fifty-four years later exhorting friends, colleagues and members of the sword society to read the book for it 'is one of the most marvellous books on Japan ever written'.

Later, he went to Winchester where, when he was given leave from school, he spent his time touring the antique shops. He bought his first Japanese sword for four shillings and six pence. It was in very bad condition and stuck in an Indian Tulwar scabbard, but he was very proud of his new acquisition. A little later in the same shop he bought some fine old Japanese pipes which led later to an important meeting with A.J. Koop, then assistant Keeper of the Metalwork Department of the V&A (Koop was Keeper from 1935-37). He recounted how with his mother he knocked on the door of Mr Koop who generously gave him the information he wanted about his pipes. There was one pipe with a signature which Koop had not seen before. He duly recorded the signature which years later, when Basil Robinson assumed Koop's position as head of the Department, he discovered among the records kept by Koop.

After Robinson completed his studies at Corpus Christi College at Oxford he applied for a post with the V&A, but was turned down. On his second attempt the following year he made the shortlist but was not selected. Despondently, he resigned himself 'to head-mastering for the rest of my life' at Bognor Regis. Fortunately, however, he was asked as a matter of some urgency to take over a post at the V&A which had become vacant as the lady occupying it was getting married. In those days when a woman married she had to resign her position. Robinson who had been the runner-up at the last selection board was appointed to the Museum on 2 January 1939 as Assistant Keeper.

He was appointed to the library where he said: 'So now I was in the library which is a very good thing, for the library is the heartbeat of the museum and if you can find your way about the library it's half the battle – you know where to find information and I was very glad for that.' Luckily for him there was shortly afterwards a vacancy in the Metalwork Department. He asked to be transferred to this post as he knew that the department had a large collection of both Japanese and Persian Art in which he was very interested. 'There I found that they had a splendid departmental library of Japanese books on swords. . . I buried myself in those and I think I improved my ability to get information from them.' No doubt this collection of books helped him later to write his celebrated articles and book.

Robinson was scandalized to find out that the year before he entered the department the then head of the department had, for various reasons, disposed of a large number of swords bearing the signatures of (or were attributed to) famous masters:

> I found out that about a year before I entered the Department, there had been a disposals board on Japanese swords. The Keeper at the time was a retired military gentleman (Major Charles Bailey) and very good on European arms and armour, but had absolutely no feelings for the East. He had suffered under A.J. Koop, who was Keeper before him and who had rather hogged the whole field for Japanese stuff and I think he was trying to get his own back. Anyway he put a great number of swords on the disposals board and two other members of the board were the Keeper of the Textiles Department and a young gentleman who had recently entered the Department of Sculpture. They were hardly qualified I think, to pronounce on Japanese swords and we lost a great many Japanese swords, including examples by Senjūin, Sukehiro of Osaka, and Sa Yukihide which were written down as duplicates!! Well I had to swallow this as best as I could for the swords were already sold.

ON ACTIVE SERVICE WITH THE 1ST BATTALION 2ND PUNJAB REGIMENT AT IMPHAL AND MALAYA

Robinson was called up in 1942 and sent to the Depot of the Royal Sussex Regiment with the rank of Corporal. He was then sent to the officer cadet training unit at Wrotham in Kent. Owing to an attack of mumps, he was not put on the original draft for the Italian campaign. Instead he went by troopship to Bangalore in India. There had been heavy casualties among officers during the retreat from Burma in 1942. He was commissioned in the 2nd Punjab Regiment after passing an examination in Urdu, the working language of the Indian Army. After repeated requests he was sent to the Intelligence school in Karachi. He wrote an essay attempting to describe the Japanese character entitled 'Sword and the Fan'. This got quite a good mark and he was soon promoted to the rank of Captain and was then posted as an Intelligence officer to Headquarters 14 Army. This was under the command of Lieutenant General Sir William Slim (later Field Marshal Viscount Slim KG GCB CGMG GCVO GBE DSO MC) who had led the remnants of the army in Burma back into India, and was later responsible for the defeats inflicted on the Japanese at the battles of Imphal and Kohima during their invasion of India in May 1944.

After the Japanese surrender Robinson was sent to Singapore where his knowledge of Japanese swords led to his being given the task of evaluating the quality of surrendered swords. He relates with typical humility:

> I was given the job of sorting out about 1800 Japanese surrendered swords in a large gymnasium in Singapore, deciding which should be given to Brigadiers, which should be given to Colonels, to Majors and so on. That was an instructive experience. I saw this mass of Japanese swords and I really knew very little then, much less than I know now. Conscious of my inadequacy for this task, I sent down to the Japanese Prisoner of War Camp at Rengam nearby to ask if there were any Japanese officer prisoners of war with a good knowledge of swords. In due course there arrived Colonel Yamada Sakae of the 3rd Air Force, who had been a member of the judging committee for the swords attached to the War Office. He was a quiet, cultured and polite man of middle age, and with the help of an excellent young interpreter, a certain Lieutenant Horiuchi, we embarked on a series of sessions. Horiuchi, I remember, was a Roman Catholic and I was able to obtain permission for him to leave the camp from time to time in order to attend Mass. The Colonel would examine the trophies briefly, blade by blade and his findings, faithfully communicated to me by Horiuchi, were duly noted down. This was my first experience of a *kanteisha* (sword appraiser) in action, and I was astounded at the unhesitating confidence with which he assigned each blade to its correct period and school – often to the actual maker – before removing the hilt and looking at the signature.

Robinson was deeply impressed by the effortless way Colonel Yamada went about his *kantei* and duly had Colonel Yamada write him a list of what he considered the best swords were:

> I still have a rather tattered typed list of 60 *Kotō* [old sword] (900-1596) and 80 *Shintō* [new sword] (1596-1750), *Shinshintō* [new-new sword] (1750-1868) and *Gendaitō* [modern swords] (1868-present day) blades which he considered to be the best

of the lot. Of these he starred 4 of the former and 16 of the latter as exceptionally fine and members may perhaps be interested to know what they were. The four *Kotō* were Kanemitsu II of Bizen (mid 14th c.), Ichimonji of Bizen (early 14th c.), Naminohira of Satsuma (early 16c) and Sukesada of Bizen (early 3rd quarter of the 16c.). The later ones were Tadakuni of Hizen (3rd quarter of the 16c. 2 blades) Kunisuke of Osaka (mid 17th c.) . . . it is interesting to note that three *Gendaitō* were also included among these top-class blades, by Yasukiyo, Yasutoshi and Yasunori, all of Tokyo. No doubt some of these fine blades are rusting on the walls of country houses or suburban villas, but it seems likely that quite a few have by now found their way, via the sale rooms, into the hands of appreciative collectors.

Robinson was allowed to keep two swords for himself. Both were sixteenth century *wakizashi* (short sword) in *shirasaya* (white scabbard) which nobody else wanted! These blades were by Tsunahiro of Sagami province and Uda Kunimune of Etchu province. Robinson still has them although as he admits, 'they did not earn one of Colonel Yamada's stars'. What he treasured above all was the pencil-written introduction to the study of Japanese swords by Colonel Yamada, which had been translated by Lieutenant Horiuchi.

Robinson was not impressed with the quality of the victors' justice imposed on the vanquished in the war-crimes trials in Singapore. He agreed that the death penalty was often deserved, although in a less emotionally charged atmosphere a punishment of imprisonment would have been considered sufficient. In the only trial he attended, his friend, as defending counsel did a splendid job in defending a Japanese officer, Colonel Mori Yoshitada who was responsible for keeping order in a large and unruly area during the occupation. Despite his friend's skill in presenting his case the officer was sentenced to death. The charge was apparently that Colonel Mori had had in the compound an exceptionally troublesome prisoner, who had escaped repeatedly and was recaptured twice. Mori warned the prisoner that if he attempted to escape again, he would be shot. Unfortunately for the prisoner he was caught again and was henceforth shot. Mori's conduct made an impression on Robinson:

> His dignity and composure as he faced his judges was in sharp contrast to the sneering and gloating of the Malays and Chinamen who filled the court and hung over the galleries. He had been allowed to write a farewell letter to his wife in Japan, and a translation of it was printed in the Headquarters Intelligence Bulletin, a proceeding which struck me and several others as cruel, macabre, and in the worst of taste. War

is indeed hell.

Robinson finally managed to track down Colonel Yamada after the war. He was living in Tokyo, Koganei, running a radio shop with his sons. One day, Yamada's daughter visited London and called upon Robinson at the museum and gave him a pearl necklace for his wife. In return, Robinson gave Yamada's daughter, 'a strikingly beautiful woman' a sword to give to her father. It was a *wakizashi* (short sword) by the famous Osaka smith Sukehiro. Colonel Yamada died some time in the mid-1960s.

BACK AT THE V&A, AUGUST 1946

Robinson returned to England and to the V&A in August 1946. It was at this time that he started to write about Japanese swords. He worked in close consultation with Dr Honma Junji of the Japanese Ministry of Culture and with the noted Japanese sword expert Hon'ami Kōsan. Robinson's first Japanese sword-related work appeared in 1955 entitled *A Primer of Japanese Sword Blades*. His friend, Captain Craig, an officer from the First World War and noted sword collector in the United Kingdom, gave Robinson a book entitled *Nihontō Jiten Kotō-Hen/Shintō-Hen* written by the Japanese authority Fujishiro Yoshio. In 1996 Fujishiro's younger brother was designated by the Japanese Government as an 'Important Intangible Cultural Asset' (also known as *Ningen Kokuhō* or 'Living National Treasure') in the field of sword-polishing. Fujishiro's book shows charts of Japanese sword *hamon* patterns peculiar to schools or regions of sword-making in Japan. Robinson based his own 'Primer' closely on Fujishiro's and many collectors and enthusiasts bought copies of this accessible book and it quickly sold out. Following this success Faber & Faber, who were doing a series of books on Oriental Art, asked Robinson to enlarge on his earlier primer. This led to the publication in 1961 of his *Arts of the Japanese Sword* with a further edition in 1970.

Having been Deputy keeper since 1954, Basil William Robinson was officially appointed Keeper of Metalwork on 6 June 1966, succeeding Charles Oman. In 1972 he became Keeper Emeritus until his retirement in 1976. In this unique position he set up a new Far Eastern Department at the V&A. His lasting memorial is the legacy of knowledge and appreciation which he leaves to us.

35

Three Great Japanese Translators of Shakespeare

PETER MILWARD

Mr Fukuda Tsuneari   Professor Anzai Tetsuo

INTRODUCTION

THE GRAND OLD MAN of Shakespeare translation in Japan is without doubt Tsubouchi Shōyō (1859–1935),[1] whose name is indelibly associated not only with Waseda University, to which he bequeathed his Shakespeare Museum, but also with the *Bungei Kyōkai*, which he founded for the performance of Shakespeare's plays – needless to say, using his translations. Already before the outbreak of World War II he had completed his life-work of translating the whole corpus of Shakespearian drama into Japanese. Not for that alone, however, does he deserve his fame in the field of Shakespeare studies in Japan, but rather for the high quality of his translation. What ensured that quality, moreover, was the fact that his was not merely an academic translation, with emphasis on textual accuracy, but rather an acting translation, with a view to performance on stage. What he aimed at in his translation was neither literal (*chokuyaku*) nor literary (*iyaku*) Japanese, but a living Japanese in which he strove to do justice at once to the original English of Shakespeare and to the language of contemporary Japanese, while taking into account the dramatic tradition of Japan.

All this was a matter of history when I came to Japan in 1954, and especially when I set out on my career of Shakespearian scholarship at Sophia University in 1962. I shall limit my account of Japanese translators of Shakespeare to the post-war scene, of which I have been both an interested spectator and to some extent an active participant. And from among the many translators who have appeared on that scene, both in the academic and in the theatrical world, I propose to deal with three in whom I recognize the marks of greatness and with whom I have enjoyed varying degrees of acquaintance.

FUKUDA TSUNEARI

The first of these is, again without doubt, Fukuda Tsuneari (also known as Kōson) (1912-94). After graduating from Tokyo University, he devoted himself to the life of a literary critic and translator – not only from Shakespeare but also from Shaw, Chesterton and others – with the idea of using his translations for performance on stage, and so among his many competitors in the field of Shakespeare translation he came to be rightly regarded as the successor to Tsubouchi Shōyō. Again, however, this is not just because his translations were for actors and spectators rather than for university students, but also because of their refined quality in which he paid as much attention to the tradition of Shakespearian acting as to the requirements of his native Japanese. With this in view he set out to translate at least all the major plays of Shakespeare, and he also established a theatrical institute of his own named *Gendai Engeki Kyōkai* connected with the acting group called *Kumo* (Cloud), which began operations with a highly successful production of Fukuda's translation of *A Midsummer Night's Dream* in 1963.

My own connection with Fukuda began about this time with an article I had been commissioned to write by Father Joseph Roggendorf, the respected editor of *Sophia* (a quarterly review published at Sophia University), on 'Shakespeare in Japanese Translation'.[2] I limited my attention to the major speeches in Shakespeare's four great tragedies, as variously translated by Tsubouchi, Fukuda and a number of academic translators. While paying tribute to the past greatness of Tsubouchi, as still recognized by the older generation of Japanese scholars, I laid special emphasis on the outstanding abilities of Fukuda, in contrast to most of the academic translators – although the fact of their being academic did not lessen my esteem for their translations. My own interests in Shakespeare were more academic than theatrical, and I was at the same time rubbing shoulders with not a few of the academic translators in my membership of the Shakespeare Society of Japan (or *Shakespeare Kyōkai*).

It must have been this article which first brought me to the favourable notice of Fukuda, although I forget the precise circumstances of our first acquaintance. From that time onwards I would receive complimentary tickets for his Shakespearian productions. I also shared with him the honorary position of adviser to a student Shakespeare group at Reitaku University. Then I went on to share with another Japanese scholar and translator, Anzai Tetsuo (born 1933 – see below), as adviser to our Sophia *Shakespeare Kenkyūkai*, which produced two plays of Shakespeare in English every year for ten successive years. I even induced Fukuda to take over my Shakespeare class at Sophia University when I suddenly fell ill and was diagnosed as having T.B. Subsequently, on the strength of his introduction I was able to visit one of his leading actors, Akutagawa Hiroshi, son of the famous novelist Akutagawa Ryūnosuke, when he was also in hospital with the same illness. I went in company with Anzai. I wanted in particular to interview him about his experience as a Shakespearian actor, not just for my own sake, but rather on behalf of an American scholar-friend of mine, Marvin Rosenberg, who was then working on a series of books on *The Masks* of each of Shakespeare's great tragedies with emphasis on their stage interpretations, and who wanted to include mention of Japanese performances. Also, on my friend's behalf, I borrowed from Fukuda a video-tape recording (such as were available in those days) of *King Lear*, in which Akutagawa had played the part of the old king. I had not seen the actual production, but from what I saw on the video-tape I found it to be among the most impressive productions of any Shakespearian play I had seen.

At the same time, it occurred to me that what distinguished Fukuda from other Shakespearian translators in Japan was his unwillingness to limit his attention to Shakespeare alone, that perennial temptation to Japanese scholars and translators in the field of Shakespearian drama.[3] So even while presenting Shakespeare's plays through his company of *Kumo*, he also collaborated with a student group from Sophia University for a production of his translation of Shaw's *Saint Joan*. On that occasion I remember his remarking to me that Shaw, for all his typically provocative words on religion, was in fact a deeply religious man. I, too, as a Catholic priest, was coming to look on Fukuda himself in the same light. Not that he ever, like Shaw, uttered provocative words on religion, but that he was, like Shaw, a deeply religious man, even to the extent of publicly describing himself as an unbaptized Catholic. For in the great divide of modern Christianity between Catholic and Protestant, or Scripture and Tradition, he was very much in sympathy – like his good friend Yoshida Ken'ichi[4] – with Catholic tradition.

This traditional, Catholic preference of his came out in his other interest in translating the Father Brown stories of Chesterton into Japanese – not only in published form (in which he came to be regarded as the leading Chesterton translator of the 1950s) but also in dramatized versions of the stories for the radio. Subsequently, when I came to edit a series of Japanese translations of Chesterton's more philosophical writings for Shunjūsha, I obtained the cooperation of Fukuda as co-translator (with Anzai) of *Orthodoxy*, as well as of Yoshida Ken'ichi for the *Autobiography*. It may have been in this connection that I visited Fukuda at his Japanese home in Oiso. In the course of a long conversation on his religious leanings, he said that, while he would like to be a fully baptized Catholic, he was withheld by fear of having to give up his Japanese identity. He wanted to remain fully Japanese, while looking on European tradition and Shakespearian drama from a Catholic viewpoint. Much of our talk also centred on the difference between suicide and martyrdom, a difference that had been blurred for him by a reading of Endō Shūsaku's novel *Silence*.

Another link I had with Fukuda was the fact that his son Hayaru was a student of mine in the department of English Literature at Sophia University, and it was only natural for him to specialize in Shakespeare under my tuition. This was a good preparation for him to follow in his father's footsteps, both as translator and as producer of Shakespeare's plays, mainly for the theatrical company *Subaru* (Zelkova), which had come to replace *Kumo* in the ever-changing forms of Japanese theatrical production.

Akutagawa as King Lear

ANZAI TETSUO

An even more important link was provided for me by Anzai whom I have previously mentioned. He was not only a former graduate student of mine, but also my colleague at Sophia University, in whom I have come to recognize the second of the three great Japanese translators of Shakespeare indicated in my title. Unlike Fukuda, and even more than Tsubouchi, Anzai strikes me as a notable example of one who combines an academic interest with the approach to Shakespeare's plays of both an actor and a producer. It was perhaps as a result of my weekly tutorials during his doctoral course at Sophia University (whither he had come from Ehime University in Shikoku) that he became convinced of the importance of the academic as well as the actor's approach; and this deepened when he followed me in 1966 as a research fellow at the Shakespeare Institute in Birmingham, under the late Professor Terence Spencer. From then onwards he became my valued assistant, whenever I needed a translator or annotator for the various books and articles on Shakespeare I came to write for Japanese readers and students.

Anzai soon began to publish books on Shakespeare both for study and for the stage; and he proceeded to carry on in the field of translation and production from where Fukuda was leaving off. Thus he translated the late romance of *Pericles* and produced it for the first time in Japanese with notable success. In addition, I particularly remember three other excellent productions of his, though I cannot remember their chronological order. One was of *Much Ado About Nothing*, with the customary Shakespearian setting in Renaissance Sicily impressively transposed to Yokohama at the time of the Sino-Japanese War and the return home of the victorious Japanese army. It was all the more successful as it enabled the Japanese actors to be themselves for once, instead of having to imagine themselves in a pseudo-European situation. Another was of *Julius Caesar* at the Tokyo Globe Theatre,[5] although what I chiefly remember was the fact that my complimentary ticket was for the royal box at a matinee performance. The third was a production of *Hamlet* in Anzai's translation of the first or 'bad' quarto, presented in Japan for the first time. I remember especially the performance of Hamlet himself by Hashizume Isao, and the way he tore the hero's non-existent passion in 'To be, or not to be' – contrary to Hamlet's own advice to the players – to 'tatters'. At the time Hashizume was just beginning his stage career, in which he went on to distinguish himself in Shakespeare's comic parts, and later as a detective and a samurai on the TV screen.[6]

The company for which Anzai who had become a professor was now translating and producing plays not only by Shakespeare but also by Ben Jonson bore the name of *En* (Circle). They were a very competent company and I always enjoyed their performances, but I find it difficult to recall them apart from each other. It was, however, in connection with a production of *Measure for Measure* that an English actor professor from Hawaii University, Terence Knapp, was brought in as visiting producer, since he had been a favourite disciple of the great Shakespearian actor Sir Laurence Olivier.[7]

ODAJIMA YŪSHI

A more revolutionary, modernistic translator was Odajima Yūshi (born 1930), whom I cannot claim to have known as intimately as I did Fukuda or Anzai. Like Fukuda, he was a product of Tokyo University, which has been more productive of academic scholars than practising actors or producers. Yet instead of proceeding at once to the theatre, Odajima remained in the academic world, if on the more 'progressive' Komaba campus of Tokyo University than on the more 'traditional' campus of Hongo. I came in contact with him more often at academic meetings of the Shakespeare Society of Japan than in the theatrical world. I was struck by the fact that he invariably preferred to speak in Japanese than in English, as if he wanted to keep his English in storage for his task of translating Shakespeare's English into a modern Japanese idiom.[8]

Odajima who also became a professor, now stands preeminent over all previous Japanese translators of Shakespeare. His golden age began in the 1970s, in the immediate aftermath of the long continued and often violent student struggle, when Tokyo University was one of the most seriously afflicted, in the days when I was a visiting lecturer there. Then it was his ambition, which he subsequently realized, to translate all the plays of Shakespeare into Japanese; and his partner in this enterprise from the complementary viewpoint of production was Deguchi Norio, whose parallel ambition was likewise to produce all those plays with a young Shakespeare company, named Jean-jean, at a small 'underground' or 'avant-garde' theatre in Shibuya. Somehow, Shakespeare, being (like his clown Feste, and like his predecessor Sir Thomas More) a 'man for all seasons', lent himself no less pliably to these revolutionary young actors than to their more conservative counterparts under the direction of Fukuda or Anzai. What Odajima did in translating Shakespeare into a modern idiom, using frequent and effective transpositions of Elizabethan English words and phrases into terms readily appreciable to modern Japanese audiences, Deguchi did with his novel, modernistic interpretations of the plays and their characters. At the time, however, I had little connection, and little sympathy with this new approach, which has in the course of time – as happens with all revolutions – assumed something of a traditional character. But subsequently, when I received an invitation to attend an all-female performance of *Twelfth Night* (with only one male actor, taking the part of Feste), at a new theatre in the same location, with

Deguchi still as producer and Odajima as translator, I was agreeably surprised at the high level of acting and I was happy to meet Deguchi himself and to give him my warm congratulations.

It was not only in the 1970s that Odajima came into his own as translator of every one of Shakespeare's plays. Since then his translations have been almost invariably used for performances of Shakespeare both by professional companies and by amateur student groups – except where the companies in question are committed to the following of Fukuda (as with *Subaru*) or Anzai (as with *En*). Yet with all his knack of appealing to the gallery and adapting the Elizabethan and Jacobean Shakespeare to the minds and ears of modern Japanese audiences, I cannot suppress an uneasy suspicion, on the strength both of his past conversations with me and of the occasions I have heard him airing his ideas about Shakespeare on Japanese TV, that he is more familiar with modern Japanese, both the young people and the language to which they are accustomed, than with the true mind of Shakespeare himself. For in all his plays Shakespeare warns his audiences against the danger of being deceived by outward appearances, urging them rather to seek the reality which is hidden; whereas in Odajima's translations and Deguchi's productions – as also in the famous 'Shakespearian' films by Kurosawa Akira and the more recent productions by Ninagawa Yukio – I fear the main emphasis is on outward show and impressive spectacle, with a striving after theatrical effect by means of 'gimmicks' rather than through the innate power of Shakespeare's language.

In this respect I find the translations and productions of Professor Anzai much more impressive. What is more, behind all his work for the stage, he has developed a well thought out and highly articulate theory of Shakespeare's inner meaning and craftsmanship which raises him to a higher level of greatness than all other Shakespeare scholars in the Japanese academic world today. I may be prejudiced in his favour, after having been his teacher in his early days, and later his colleague at Sophia University; but I am sure that time will bear me out.

36

John Russell Kennedy, 1861-1928: Spokesman for Japan and Media Entrepreneur

PETER O'CONNOR

John Russell Kennedy

FOR NEARLY TWENTY YEARS, John Russell Kennedy worked at the heart of Japan's international relations. During that time, he developed an acute understanding of Japan's international ambitions and took a central role in building a media structure to advance them. Kennedy knew most of the Meiji oligarchy and was especially close to Itō Hirobumi and to power-brokers like Shibusawa Eiichi. These were considerable achievements for an Irishman with no special training for such a life, but Kennedy was reviled by many in the Tokyo foreign community as a toady and a journalistic mercenary, and his professionalism and integrity were frequently questioned by colleagues – Japanese and foreign alike.

It is a curious fact that, of the small group of Irish-born or Irish-connected writers and journalists who became involved with Japan's propaganda programmes in the first half of the twentieth century, almost all were Protestant.[1] Captain Francis Brinkley (1841-1912), Japan's loudest and most indiscriminate champion, was a direct descendant of the notorious Bishop Brinkley, whose statue stands outside Trinity

College, Dublin. George Bronson Rea (1869-1936) and Patrick Gallagher of the *Far Eastern Review*, the *Daily Telegraph*'s George Gorman, 'hand-in-glove with the Japanese' for his work on the *North China Standard* and the *Manchuria Daily News*,[2] and Joseph I. C. Clarke (1846-1925), author of *Japan at first hand* (1918) – Clarke was the only Catholic (and certainly the only member of the Irish Republican Brotherhood).[3]

John Russell Kennedy was born in Bray, Co. Dublin, Ireland, in October 1861, to Elizabeth 'Mabella' Russell of Malahide, Co. Dublin, and the Rev. William Studdert Kennedy (1825-1914), a Church of Ireland cleric. There were five children: John, Mabel, Norah, Eve and Frances. The family was Irish Protestant with roots in Clare and Galway, and strong Anglican connections. Kennedy's paternal grandfather Robert M. Kennedy was Church of Ireland Dean of Clonfert in Co. Galway, and Kennedy's father eventually moved the whole family to Leeds where he became Vicar of St Mary's Church.[4]

Russell Kennedy was educated at Trinity College, Glenalmond, Perthshire, an establishment with a strong military tradition, and, like his friend and mentor Brinkley, joined the British army after graduating from Trinity College, Dublin. As a young officer in the Cameron Highlanders, Kennedy distinguishing himself in two campaigns in Egypt in the early 1880s, winning the Egyptian medal with two clasps and the Khedive Star.

Kennedy then became an army journalist in Canada. His career as a civilian journalist began when he sent samples of his work on an army newsletter to the *Toronto Mail*, which offered him a job in 1885. In 1889, Kennedy moved to newspaper work in Palatka, Florida, USA, where he met and married Emily Cripps Campbell, and from there to a paper in Macon, Georgia. Sometime in the 1890s, he joined the *Washington Post* as editor of the society pages.

In 1901, Kennedy was taken on as a reporter by the Associated Press in New York. AP was then America's premier news agency, with extraordinary power over the news and its dissemination ('380 papers west of the Mississippi alone!'), operating a near-monopoly that would last until a Supreme Court decision in 1945. In 1901 (and for the next twenty-five years), AP was headed by the slightly notorious but legendary Melville E. Stone, who had been its guiding light in its transition from a fractured group of regional news agencies into the unified cooperative established in New York in 1900.

Kennedy initially served four years in AP's London office, then returned to New York for three years, working directly under Stone as night news manager and supervisor in the head office. This brought Kennedy closer to Japan and his life's work, for Stone had already established close contacts with the Meiji élite.

Stone had first met Itō Hirobumi in 1872, in Chicago, when Itō visited as a member of the Iwakura Mission.[5] By the summer of 1905, when Stone went to cover the peace conference between Russia and Japan at Portsmouth, New Hampshire, he looked upon the Japanese delegates as 'personal friends' and shuttled between them and the Russian party in an unofficial attempt to break the deadlock over the question of a Russian indemnity. His reward was to be the first to break the news that Japan would not seek reparations.[6] Stone is also credited with introducing the idea of a Japanese national news agency (*kokka daihyō tsūshinsha*) in an off-the-cuff speech to members of AP's Tokyo office around 1910.

EARLY DAYS IN JAPAN

Posted to the Associated Press office in Tokyo in 1907, Kennedy worked with some of Japan's greatest journalists, Furuno Inosuke (1891-1966), as well as Mori Hachijutarō, Date Genichirō, and perhaps his most trusted aide, his secretary, Higashigawa Kaichi, all of whom would later achieve prominence at the *Japan Times & Mail*, the Kokusai News Agency (*Kokusai Tsūshinsha*), and Kokusai's news agency successors, Rengō and Dōmei.

In 1908, Kennedy became involved in committee work for the International Press Association. From this base, Kennedy cultivated relations with Itō Hirobumi and Hayashi Tadasu, the foreign minister, with Henry W. Davidson, an American adviser to the *Gaimushō*, with Shibusawa Eiichi, Katsura Tarō and other members of the Meiji élite. In time, Kennedy would know some of these people well enough to make appointments with them directly by telephone.[7] Itō Hirobumi, in particular, warmed to Kennedy's creaky charm, and 'made me his confidant' at their first meeting.[8]

In 1909, the proposal in California of a law preventing Japanese from owning land in the state was causing considerable apprehension in Japan. One of Japan's leading informal spokesmen and influence peddlers in the United States, the applied chemist Takamine Jokichi (1854-1922), pointed to the need for Japan to make an effective case on the issue and for Japanese immigrants to be better understood by Americans. Kennedy visited Takamine in New York and discussed the problem, and then spoke to Shibusawa Eiichi about starting a national news agency in Japan.

The following year, Shibusawa Eiichi paid a three-month visit to the USA and Europe. Shibusawa returned deeply impressed by the strength of anti-Japanese sentiment and the dearth of information about Japan in the USA, and convinced of the need for a Japanese news agency. Shibusawa consulted Makino Nobuaki, the Foreign Minister, met again with Kennedy and showed enthusiasm for his news agency plan. In March 1911, Melville E. Stone urged Kennedy to push the news agency idea.

Another enthusiast, possibly encouraged by Stone, was Furuno Inosuke. Yet another enthusiast was Zumoto Motosada, founder of the *Japan Times*. In 1913 the law preventing Japanese from owning land was passed in California, and to Shibusawa, Furuno, Kennedy, Stone and Zumoto this confirmed the urgent need for a news agency which would put a better case for Japan before the American people.[9]

Japanese dissatisfaction with Reuters' reporting of Japanese news was another factor that favoured starting a Japanese news agency. Working along a great stretch of British-owned cable line, Reuters delivered to Japan only the news for which there was a general demand by all the papers along the chain; comparatively little effort was made to collect Japanese news for distribution to the West. Reuters was unwilling to wire to Europe sound informational reports about Japan that were lacking in news value, but did not hesitate to carry unpleasant messages whose publication some Japanese would have preferred to hinder. Not without reason, some Japanese saw Reuters as an adjunct of the British Foreign Office, just as Havas, Wolff and Stefani were held to be partial to the French, German and Italian foreign secretariats, and this perception added to the momentum behind the creation of a semi-official national news agency for Japan.

NEGOTIATIONS WITH REUTERS AND THE SIEMENS INCIDENT

The origins of Kennedy's lasting involvement in Japan's national publicity are bound up in the nature of his contacts with the Meiji élite and with Melville Stone and other media entrepreneurs, in his early negotiations with Reuters and in his successful campaign to discredit the Reuters representative in Japan, Andrew Pooley. After some fairly unprincipled in-fighting among foreign journalists in Japan, Kennedy found himself at the top of the heap and never looked back. Possibly the most notorious of these early rucks was the Siemens Incident.

In 1912, Baron de Reuter and his aides in London had become displeased with the situation of Reuters in Tokyo. Kennedy, then working for AP, was sharing an office with the Reuters' correspondent, Henry Satoh (Satō Kenri), and had somehow made of Satoh a second-in-command, himself writing and sending the most important despatches to both Reuters and the Associated Press.

This situation led to Kennedy's dismissal as AP's Tokyo correspondent and to the replacement of Satoh by Andrew M. Pooley.[10] Pooley was expressly instructed to have nothing to do with the 'pushful' Mr Kennedy who, according to letters from Baron de Reuter read out in the Tokyo District Court in 1913, when Pooley was being tried for blackmail in connection with the Siemens Scandal, was actuated by a 'pure outflow of vanity and the desire to pose before the world as the source of news' and who would, de Reuter maintained, given the chance, 'stretch it to his personal profit and aggrandisement'.[11]

However, when Andrew Pooley began work in Japan, the despatches he sent to Reuters were far from pleasing to Japanese government circles. Kennedy had 'conceived the idea that the duty of a correspondent was, not to send unpleasant news of petty quarrels, nor of trifling corruptions, but to weld together East and West', but Pooley's despatches for Reuters implied that the government was manipulating the gold reserve.[12] Pooley published in Shanghai and London *The Secret Memoirs of Count Hayashi*, and on his expulsion from Japan would publish the highly critical *Japan at the Crossroads* (1917),[13] and *Japan's Foreign Policies* (1919). Pooley did little to make himself likeable in the way that Kennedy did. Indeed, he probably made Kennedy look more attractive to the powers that be.

But still a little push was needed. Hugh Byas (1875-1945) edited the *Japan Advertiser* from 1914-22 and 1926-29. As a frequent target of Kennedy's journalistic venom, he followed his adversary's career with some interest. In draft notes for a 1914 *Japan Advertiser* leader, Byas wrote:

> There is no written evidence in our possession to prove that Mr. Kennedy intended to wrest Reuters from Mr. Pooley, but it was generally talked about that Mr. Kennedy who was relieved of the position as the Tokyo correspondent of the Associated Press was endeavouring to interest the powers that be in a scheme of establishing a purely Japanese news agency, in order to supersede some of the foreign correspondents in Japan. In order to accomplish that it was thought necessary that connections be established with a powerful news agency or news agencies in the west. He was supported in that scheme by men like Baron Shibusawa and others of financial influence in Japan, who at that time were anxious to see that the Japanese-American relations be relieved of the strain caused by the San Francisco school incident, the Land Question, the Japanese immigration question in America, etc., by influencing the public opinion in America. . . But there was Mr. Pooley. . . Mr. Pooley, a young and brilliant journalist, whatever his faults, was perhaps too severe and merciless in his criticism of things Japanese, so that he found himself a non persona grata among some of the leading Japanese, who regarded him as a viper.[14]

Byas continues:

> In 1914 Pooley obtained papers revealing that heavy bribes had passed between the German firm of Siemens Schuckert, Vickers in England and the Japanese admiralty. Pooley was

induced to return the papers to Siemens Schuckert for £5000 and was afterwards tried and convicted of blackmail but was allowed to leave the country. During the trial Kennedy intervened with a letter to the judge incriminating Pooley. Pooley's counsel retorted by reading correspondence with Baron Reuters regarding the sale of the business in Japan to Kokusai. The effect of the correspondence was to show that Kennedy came to London and forced Baron Reuter to sell out by showing that Kokusai had government support. After referring to the Japanese ambassador in London, Reuter decided to sell. The official nature of Kennedy's apparently independent correspondence was thus revealed, and the character of his dispatches, particularly during [sic] the 21 Demands were being enforced on China and when the Japanese government was hedging on its promise to restore Kiaochou, which it took from the Germans, fully bore out the general suspicion under which Kennedy laboured.[15]

Hugh Byas had it about right. Given the low personal esteem in which de Reuter held him, Kennedy met with little success in his initial attempts to get him to hand over the interests of Reuters in Japan to his projected news agency.[16] Kennedy met with similar lack of success in talks with the Havas, Wolff and Stefani agencies in negotiations in Europe. However, in November 1913, a letter from Melville E. Stone, and final checks with the Japanese embassy in London, finally persuaded Baron de Reuter that if the powerful new news agency were to be established in Japan, Reuters' long-term interests would be better represented there by Kennedy's Kokusai Tsūshinsha than by Andrew Pooley's lone correspondence, however valiant and truth-serving (Japan Times, 1966: 60).

When Kennedy returned from London in January 1914, having secured Reuters' Japan interest, the Siemens scandal came up and Pooley was charged with blackmailing Siemens Schuckert. Here is Hugh Byas again:

> There was no better opportunity than that situation afforded in pushing down Mr. Pooley to the ditch, and to the ditch Mr. Pooley was pushed. What has done that work? Who did it? There is no written evidence that any particular person has done, but it was generally believed at that time that the trio composed of Mr. Kennedy, Mr. Henry Sato and Mr. Zumoto, or one of the three, gave evidence to Mr. Shimada [Saburō], a leader of the Doshikwai and known as one of the best political orators of modern Japan, who mentioned the name of Pooley in the diet.[17]

CONFLICTS OF INTEREST AND PERSONALITY

Under Hugh Byas, the *Japan Advertiser* objected vigorously to the handing over of the Reuters interests to Kokusai. In a leader headed, *British Newspapers and Japan News* it pronounced:

> Unless the views of Reuters subscribers have changed to a very extraordinary extent, we doubt whether they approve of the interests of Reuters Agency being entrusted to a Japanese news agency financially supported solely by Japanese businessmen, and which is assured of the undivided moral support of the Japanese Foreign Office.[18]

In 1912, Kennedy created a publishing foundation for Kokusai by buying (for ¥9,000) a half-share in the *Japan Mail* from the estate of his old friend Captain Francis Brinkley then buying the *Japan Times*. Both the *Japan Times* and the *Japan Mail* were operating at a joint loss of ¥10,500 a month when Kennedy bought them on behalf of the new agency. Bringing them together into one organization, it was felt, would enable these losses to be covered.

Kokusai had been established partly in the hope that it would influence the *Japan Chronicle* and *Japan Advertiser* and other English-language newspapers to be more positive in their coverage of Japanese news. Thus, as the official *Japan Times* story has it, 'in order to insure smooth liaison between the news agency and the English-language papers', Kennedy also became President of the *Japan Times* in March 1914, replacing Zumoto Motosada and making a lasting enemy.[19]

It cannot have helped Kennedy's relations with Zumoto that most of the financial interests marshalled behind the Kokusai Tsūshinsha by Shibusawa Eiichi, many of them semi-government institutions, had been associated with Zumoto and Yamada Sueharu's original 1897 consortium, as assembled by Iwasaki Yatarō, of backers for the *Japan Times*. Zumoto was the author of the 1941 *Short History of the Japan Times*. According to the *Short History* Zumoto 'occupied a very important post in the news agency out of his relation to Viscount Shibusawa', and Kennedy's appointment was 'contrary to general expectations'. As for the Presidency of the *Japan Times*, which Kennedy assumed in April 1914, 'The management of the *Japan Times* was left to Mr. Kennedy. Thus, Japan's international propaganda lost a chance to detach itself from Reuters.'[20]

Had Zumoto disappeared from view, his resentment would not have mattered, but by setting up (in 1916) the *Herald of Asia*, and in his numerous other activities, Zumoto established a substantial rival semi-official media and propaganda satellite that would challenge Kokusai and the *Japan Times*, and become a forum for those who resented Kennedy's ever rising star.

KENNEDY AT KOKUSAI AND *THE JAPAN TIMES*

Kokusai was set up in March 1914 with capital of ¥100,000, as a joint stock company, part of the *Japan Times Kabushiki Kaisha*. Company headquarters were in Tokyo at 3, Aoi-cho, Akasaka. Kokusai had two representatives (*daihyō shain*) on the board, both of them directors from other Shibusawa companies. Some members of the Shibusawa family also became directors (*riiji*). Kennedy became General Manager of Kokusai in February or March 1914, and President of the *Japan Times* on July 2nd 1914, when it became part of the *Japan Times Kabushiki Kaisha.*[21]

Shibusawa Eiichi drew heavily on his contacts in government and business, soliciting subscriptions from Inoue Junnosuke, then of the Yokohama Specie Bank, Ōno Eijirō of the Nihon Kōgyō Bank, Dan Takuma, a director of Mitsui, Kabayama Aisuke of Nippon Steelworks (Nihon Seitetsu) and Ishii Kenkichi of the Daiichi Bank.

Kennedy needed all the help he could get. In the *Japan Times Kabushiki Kaisha*'s first year of business ending in July 1915, expenditure on the news agency was ¥18,000, and on the newspaper business, the *Japan Times*, ¥67,000. The cost of buying both the *Japan Times* and the *Mail* had been ¥75,000, and the consortium had to be repaid at ¥5,000 a month. In year two, spending and income almost balanced. By 1916 the *Japan Times Kabushiki Kaisha* was beginning to turn a small profit.

Thus Kennedy's management style was necessarily guided by the need to observe economies. At one point in his second term as President, he cut the editorial staff of the *Japan Times* down to only two: the Anglo-Chinese reporter John Goodrich, and the translator Ueno Mogami, with only Kennedy, Matsuo Kanji and Higashigawa Kiichi as directors, and Doi Tsuneo as company auditor.

As general manager of Kokusai and President of the *Japan Times* Kennedy conducted much of his business as his mentor Brinkley had before him, from his home, which he preferred to his office at Kokusai's first headquarters in Aoi-chō, Akasaka.[22] However, unlike Brinkley, who received and sent a steady stream of messengers to and from his home, Kennedy received information and gave instructions over the telephone.

Not long after its foundation in 1913, Kennedy realized that Kokusai would be open to the charge that it was purely a propaganda agency if it exported news to other countries, and if the English-language press of Japan continued to oppose it. In an attempt to circumvent the bad opinion of his contemporaries, Kennedy devised a plan whereby Kokusai collected news within Japan and then, 'after clarifying and filtering' it, as Kennedy put it, delivered the result to the resident representative of Reuters for transmission to Western newspapers. Thus Kokusai collected and synthesized but Reuter delivered news from Japan.[23]

Soon after arranging the contract with Reuters in November 1913,

Kennedy, negotiating directly with his old mentor, Melville E. Stone, came to a similar arrangement with the Associated Press. Like Reuters, AP was given material collected and written by Kokusai, which was sent to the USA as AP Tokyo news. Similar contracts were negotiated with Havas, Wolff, Stefani and other news agencies.

Whatever the arrangement, the world did not take kindly to the establishment and activities of Kokusai.[24] Strictly speaking, Kokusai was not the Reuters or AP correspondent agency, but as J.R. Kennedy was both the Reuters correspondent and general manager for Kokusai and closely associated with AP, Kokusai was seen to hold, in his person, a near-monopoly over the export of Japanese news to many foreign countries from its establishment in February or March 1914 until the arrival of Malcolm Kennedy as Reuters correspondent in February 1925.

Perhaps the fundamental problem was not so much John Russell Kennedy as Kokusai's perceived closeness to Japanese officialdom. In 1917, reviewing the state of wartime propaganda in China, a senior official at the British Legation in Peking reported:

> The Legation know much more about what is happening in Siberia than Shanghai can possibly do. The latter only know what they see in the papers, which is generally very inaccurate, the bulk of it emanating from that futile Kokusai Agency, which is nothing more nor less than the Japanese F.O. in a thinly disguised form.[25]

When it started up in 1914, the key exceptions to Kokusai's near-monopoly on news from Japan were the foreign correspondents in Tokyo of *The Times*, the *Manchester Guardian* and the *Morning Post*, other Japanese news agencies, notably Nippon Dempō, the oldest Japanese news agency, with its United Press tie-up, Teikoku, and the Tōhō agency, which operated in China, and the English-language press insofar as it was read outside Japan.

Since the *Japan Advertiser* provided, by way of side jobs for its foreign staff, practically all the correspondence for American newspapers not covered by AP or UP, it constituted possibly the main American exception to the Kokusai monopoly.

Of the three British newspapers, only the *Manchester Guardian* correspondent operated without a *Gaimushō* subsidy. The *Japan Chronicle* had taken a government subsidy in the 1880s, when it campaigned for a repeal of the unequal treaties, but thereafter it was stubbornly independent and refused all subsidies. The *Chronicle's* editor, Robert Young, went to great pains to ensure the pristine self-sufficiency of his newspaper, and it enjoyed a foreign circulation and influence out of proportion to its circulation in Japan.

Despite these exceptions and despite widespread reservations as to the quality and reliability of its services, Kokusai enjoyed a privileged position through its command of Japanese news, and Kokusai news items became, if not the predominant perhaps the most broadcast influence affecting foreign views of Japan for over a decade, a period which saw the Twenty-One Demands, the Lansing-Ishii Agreement, the Versailles Treaty, the 1919 Yap and Shantung issues and the risings in Korea and China, the allied intervention in Siberia, the negotiations for the renewal of the Anglo-Japanese Alliance, the Washington Conference, the US Exclusion Act limiting Japanese emigration to California, and many other vital concerns – not to mention a host of domestic upheavals.

Kokusai reported Japan to the world and the world to Japan along thousands of miles of privileged Reuters and AP cable. Abroad, many European, British and American newspapers, and domestically the *Japan Times* (amalgamated with the *Japan Mail* from April 1918) and the vernacular press carried these reports. This gave Kokusai considerable power, which Kennedy did not hesitate to exercise.

Early in 1915, Kennedy's blatant denials, purporting to be issued from the *Gaimushō*, of European news stories about the Twenty-One Demands made by Japan on China, had the effect of critically undermining not only Kokusai's but Japan's credibility. Kennedy conducted an intense campaign against foreign journalists in Japan and elsewhere in the *Japan Times* and in Kokusai reports at the very time that Kokusai was trying to suppress news of Twenty-One Demands made on China by Japan. Kennedy first issued outright denials of the Demands, then sent a heavily watered-down version to the British and other concerned governments. Kokusai might have escaped censure had not the Chinese, in a campaign managed by Yüan Shih-k'ai's Political Adviser, G. E. Morrison, and *The Times* Beijing correspondent (*in loco*) W.H. Donald, leaked details of such authenticity that Kennedy was forced to make considerable revisions to his version of the story and Japan to the Demands themselves.[26]

Kennedy's mismanagement of the news of the Twenty-One Demands marked a new low in Japan's international reputation. It now occurred to his masters that he could not hold down so many posts successfully. On 5 August 1916, Kennedy met with Shibusawa and the *Japan Times Kabushiki Kaisha* board in an emergency meeting. It was decided that Kennedy should resign from the *Japan Times* presidency and from the board of directors and that Kokusai and the *Japan Times* should became separate companies.[27]

Kennedy hung on at Kokusai, but hostile articles in the vernacular press began highlighting his failure, through Kokusai and the *Japan Times*, to win the trust of Anglophone readerships in Japan and abroad. In one of these, published in *Nihon oyobi Nihonjin* in March 1918 and given in translation in the *Japan Advertiser*, Dr Honda Masujirō urged the creation of a successor to both *Kokusai* and the *Japan Times*, both of which he maintained had failed in their mission, in large measure because of Kennedy's management.

Honda's article gave an unusually candid glimpse of the perceived value of the *Japan Times* from an official perspective. As he saw it:

> The only newspaper in a foreign language published in Japan by the Japanese is the *Japan Times*. It now has become a possession of the Kokusai News Agency. This newspaper is considered at home and abroad as an organ of the government, yet the government does not seem to be making full use of it, and it does not win the confidence of foreigners as an organ of expression of the voice of the nation. It is a great mistake to leave such an organ under the direction of foreigners. . . . When conducted by foreign managers, such a newspaper is only overshadowed by its contemporary which is likely to criticize Japan unmercifully. Foreign readers lose their confidence in such an organ and it will be obliged to depend upon the Japanese readers to keep itself alive. An organ of the Japanese nation should be conducted so as to attract the attention of foreigners, even if it may be a financial failure.

Nor could Honda find anything to praise at Kokusai:

> We cannot call the work of the Kokusai News Agency a success. As a branch of Reuters it may be necessary to have English managers for it, but when there is so much incoming stuff and so little news is sent out, and when this little of news sent out as Tokyo dispatches is discredited abroad, the undertaking can only enrich the Reuters agency at the expense of Japan. Although it may be necessary now to get so much incoming stuff because of the war, yet all the news which comes from abroad is government news of foreign countries highly censored. This may be due either to the fact that the foreigners connected with the agency are discredited abroad, or that the contract made with the foreign news agency is one-sided.[28]

Three years later, many of the problems highlighted by Honda's article would be addressed but for now, despite this broadside, Kennedy's friends in high places ensured that he would return for a second term as President (and part-owner) of the *Japan Times* from 1918 until 1921, and continue at Kokusai until November 1923 (although he was kicked upstairs in December 1921), and as the Reuters representative until February 1925.

WASHINGTON, VERSAILLES AND THE *GAIMUSHŌ JŌHŌBU*

John Russell Kennedy's career in Japan was defined and mobilized by his closeness to the powers that be. In March 1911, he received the first of his Japanese decorations, the Order of the Sacred Treasure (Third Class), and (according to Hugh Byas) two other honours.[29] According to the citation, the award was for 'conveying accurate information regarding the Far East through the Associated Press and materially helping to correct false statements in the yellow press', but it came three years before the creation of Kokusai, and it is not clear what Kennedy had done to deserve it.[30]

In November 1917, Kennedy accompanied Japan's special envoy Ishii Kikujirō to negotiations with US Secretary of State Robert Lansing in Washington, returning to Japan with the Lansing-Ishii Agreement, which recognized Japan's 'special interests' in China (without closely defining what these special interests were). The part played by Kennedy in reaching the Agreement, which was seen as a considerable coup for the Terauchi Masatake cabinet, has not been established, although it seems likely that he was in Washington as a spokesman for the delegation. The *Japan Times* trumpeted the centrality of Kennedy's role, while the *Japan Chronicle* paid Kennedy the backhanded compliment of wondering aloud why such a mediocrity should be involved in these high-level discussions, but this was only the beginning.

Late in 1918, Kennedy sailed from Yokohama with Japan's official delegation to the Paris Conference as press manager in Matsuoka Yōsuke's publicity team. Unfortunately, Japan's performance in Paris was characterized by a series of publicity disasters. One problem was the unbending formality of the Japanese delegates, not least Saionji Kinmochi, who holed up in the Hotel Bristol and only conferred with old Parisian acquaintances, avoiding the press at all costs.

Kennedy could do little to change this, but he lost favour by his failure to anticipate the poor impression made on the Conference by reports of Japanese brutality in Korea, which came at the very time that Japan was pushing for a Racial Equality clause to be inserted in the Covenant of the League of Nations. Kennedy organized rebuttals in the *Japan Times* and *Seoul Press*, but these failed to convince other delegates, and the Racial Equality amendment was voted down. At the same time, consultants to the Chinese delegation such as Thomas Millard and George Bronson Rea organized an extremely effective propaganda campaign against Japan's retention of leases in China.[31]

By now, Kennedy had gained a reputation for sailing close to the wind. For the Foreign Office's Far East Department, Frank Ashton-Gwatkin commented:

> He is a tempestuous Irishman, and loves a grievance and a fight. He is, I am sure, a perfectly loyal British subject. . . but at the same time, it is his professional obligation to champion the Japanese cause and to assist Japanese propaganda. The story of Reuters in Japan, including the Pooley episode, the Naval

Bribery scandals, and the Pooley-Kennedy feud has been a very sensational one.

In the same file, Miles Lampson wrote,

> Note that Mr. Kennedy accompanied the Japse delegates to Versailles as their chief propagandist. His name is notorious in the F.E. as being practically in Japanese pay. This statement (though I am sure it is true) cannot easily be substantiated. But his paper (?the Japan Mail, in the editorship of which he succeeded Captain Brinkley) can receive valuable support from the Japse govt in devious and indirect ways. Kokusai stinks in the nostrils of the F.E., & as their manager is also Reuters's correspondent, the position is pretty clear. I know Kennedy personally & do not for a moment doubt his loyalty: but note: he dropped his British nationality years ago & became a U.S. citizen to help him in his career with the associated press. . .[32]

The publicity failures at Versailles called for a radical new approach, and led Japan's new Prime Minister, Hara Kei, in April 1921, to establish the Gaimushō Jōhōbu, Japan's first agency dedicated to the production and management of propaganda. Despite his close association with the Korean and Chinese fiascos, Kennedy was invited to advise those planning the new agency, and for a few years in the early 1920s he was almost wholly occupied with the task of opening branch offices and engaging staff for the Jōhōbu in China, the USA, England, Australia, Russia and elsewhere, and establishing bases for the production and distribution of propaganda. A large proportion of the ¥5 million set aside for the new agency went through Kennedy's hands in this endeavour, as he travelled the globe as master builder of Japan's inter-war propaganda system.[33]

A MAN OF PARTS

In February 1914, the Japan Mail moved to premises in Kanda at Mitoyo-chō, 3-chōme. The Japan Times Monogatari and other sources assert that from 1914 on the Japan Mail existed in name only, until its formal amalgamation in April 1918 with the Japan Times. However, although Hugh Byas described it as being 'in its death agony', the Japan Mail was still being published in 1916-17, functioning largely as a sort of approving chorus for the more vindictive Japan Times campaigns.[34]

Kokusai, the Japan Times, Reuters: even this portfolio of responsibilities was not enough for Kennedy. Yet another interest was the Kokusai Keizai Tsūshinsha, which Kennedy had started up as a financial news service. The new business had its headquarters in Ōsaka and was managed by Kennedy's old secretary from his days with AP Tokyo, Higashigawa Kaichi. Soon the Keizai Tsūshinsha was Kokusai's most successful operation, distributing news of international commodity prices, exchange rates and stock prices directly to banks and brokers throughout Japan in the form of '*aka den*' (red telegrams) and later in its own report, *Kokusai keizai shuppō*.[35]

Finally, there was the J. Roland Kay (Far East) Co., an advertising agency with premises in the Kokusai Building at 5, Uchisaiwai-chō, Hibiya Park, otherwise known as 'the J.R.K. Company', slogan: 'We Make Your Money While You Sleep'.[36]

Thus we have the *Japan Times & Mail*, the Kokusai editorial department, the Reuters correspondence, the *Japan Times*, the Kokusai Keizai Tsūshinsha and the J. Roland Kay Co. In the early 1920s, with the exception of the Osaka-based Kokusai Keizai Tsūshinsha, Kennedy had all his various interests neatly parcelled in one building, and later in one area, Hibiya Park. The *Herald of Asia*, edited by Kennedy's rival, Zumoto Motosada, also occupied an office in Hibiya Park, which became something of a home from home for organs representing the Japanese point of view.

For Kennedy, when he was not doing business over his home telephone, such proximity must have made for convenience. Down to the *Japan Times* office to pen a blistering column on the shenanigans of his contemporaries.[37] Over to Kokusai-Reuters to tell it to the world. Upstairs to the J.R.K. company to pen some sparkling copy for Tanzan Mineral Water and other favoured clients. Then off to his cottage in Karuizawa for a weekend of tennis and picnics.

Thus, in 1921, everything seemed to be going well for John Russell Kennedy. Outside the fourth estate, he was well liked in the foreign community, popular on the tennis court and off, a genial figure in the American Club and an officer of the Tokyo Club, President of the Tokyo British Legion and Master of the Tokyo Lodge of the Freemasons.

Then came the fall. In December 1921, Kennedy was asked to resign from the *Japan Times* and removed from the day-to-day management of Kokusai, though he kept his office and his salary until 1923. Essentially, Kennedy's usefulness had been exhausted, he was no longer young, and the newly established *Gaimushō Johōbu* wanted to put the management of Japan's main organs of international opinion more firmly in the hands of capable Japanese like Kennedy's successors, Sheba Sometarō at the *Japan Times* and Iwanaga Yūkichi at Kokusai.

If the *Johōbu* could not loosen the stranglehold of Reuters on Japanese news, it could at least remove foreigners from positions of influence along the pipeline. One of Iwanaga's first actions on becoming Kokusai's new manager was to remove another eight high-ranking foreigners from the Kokusai administration. Honda Masujirō's 1918 *Nihon oyobi Nihonjin* article not only advocated but anticipated the thinking behind the removal of foreigners like Kennedy from positions of control over Japan's 'ears and voices' as Kokusai had tried to be and Dōmei later would succeed in becoming (the phrase was Furuno Inosuke's).

RETIREMENT POSTPONED

After leaving the *Japan Times* and Kokusai, Kennedy's career became predictably quieter. Hasegawa Shinichi describes him as relaxing and travelling abroad.[38] Kennedy had intended to retire to Palatka, Florida, where he owned property, but in September 1923, at the age of 62, he lost his Tokyo house, a considerable library and other valuables in the Kantō earthquake, making a quiet retirement impossible.[39]

Thus Kennedy continued to work to make up his losses and in September 1924 he was reported in the *Japan Times* as having returned from trips to the USA and England 'with even more work to do than the much he laid down'. With his half-brother, Hugh Studdert Kennedy, formerly of the *Christian Science Monitor* in Boston and author of what is still one of the clearest-sighted biographies of Mary Baker-Eddy, Kennedy established 'the Russell-Kennedys Interpretative News Service', providing 'international interpretative news services from East to West and West to East'. Kennedy also took on the Tokyo correspondence of the *Chicago Daily News* and conference the *Daily Telegraph*, became Japan representative for Wickham Steed's *Review of Reviews* and directed 'Far Eastern activities' for a brace of advertising agencies.[40]

Kennedy died of heart failure on 16 January 1928. His funeral, at Holy Trinity Church, Tokyo, was attended by Ishii Kikujirō, Shidehara Kijūrō, Baron Okura, the British Ambassador Sir John Tilley, and others of the great and good. Hugh Byas wrote a generous obituary with barely a hint of the rancour that had passed between them over the years, even praising Kennedy's achievements in smoothing the relationship between Japan and the West.[41]

Kennedy's place in the pantheon of historical figures associated with the *Japan Times* seems assured. In 1941, the 15,000th commemorative issue of the *Japan Times & Advertiser* pictured him as one of '11 prominent personalities' in the history of the paper, the full caption reading: 'The *Japan Times*, in its long history, has been under the direction of 11 prominent personalities.[42] Starting with the late Mr Sueharu Yamada, first president, up to the present [1941] head, Mr Toshi Go, each has contributed much to the growth of the journal which continues to expand in consonance with its position as the largest English-language paper in the Far East', a rubric that has been repeated, with variations, in most of the *Japan Times* anniversary editions published since.[43]

Kennedy has been described as a 'wheeler-dealer'.[44] Was this all? Was Kennedy a businessman? Was he a journalist? Hugh Byas, who knew Kennedy as well as anyone in Japan, thought he was neither:

A fact which has influenced my judgement on this matter as much as anything is that though Kennedy has lived in Japan for 16 years he has never, so far as I know, written an article showing personal inquiry into, or even personal interest in, any aspect of Japanese life. He has always been a mouthpiece, and as representative of the Associated Press of America and later of Reuters, he has been an effective exponent when one was needed.[45]

It is not an awkward compromise to say that Kennedy was both, and that, at least in the busy decade in which his fortunes were bound up with the Kokusai Tsūshinsha and the *Japan Times*, he combined journalistic and entrepreneurial skills in just the proportions needed to open a vital window of communication for Japan. Before Kokusai, the communications window had always been into or onto Japan, but Kennedy, largely by force of personality but aided by considerable financial muscle, helped open, if only partially, a Japanese window onto the world.

37

Hessell Tiltman (1897-1976) and Japan, 1928-76: On the Road in Asia

ROGER BUCKLEY[1]

Hessell Tiltman

BEFORE THE SECOND WORLD WAR

'I AM THE "DOYEN" of the press corps here, with the longest service in Japan.'[2] Hessell Tiltman's private comments to the editor of *The Manchester Guardian* in May 1954 were indeed an accurate statement of his already lengthy involvement with Japan and the wider Asia-Pacific. A more boastful individual could have been forgiven for rehearsing the details of what had already proved to be a remarkable career that had begun precociously after the First World War and would only end in the mid-1970s.

There were many Hessell Tiltmans. While ever the journalist, he was also a left-wing novelist, current affairs writer on the rise of totalitarianism in Europe[3] and Asia, author of one of the first biographies of Ramsay MacDonald,[4] aircraft designer in partnership with Nevil Shute,[5] futurologist before the word had been coined, three times president of the Foreign Correspondents' Club in Tokyo and a respected adviser to the Japanese Foreign Ministry. Given the range of his interests it is hardly surprising that the British Library catalogue for Tiltman has twenty-seven entries, while

web searches trawl in an extraordinary amount of data. Yet much remains
unknown about a writer, who left no personal papers, revealed little about
himself in print and whose activities possibly overlap with those of his near
namesake the important cryptographer John Hessell Tiltman.[6]

Hugh Hessell Tiltman came from Sussex[7] and his widow,[8] herself a
novelist and journalist, remained in the county until her death at the age of
98. Tiltman became a journalist after the First World War and spent the
next twenty years engaged in the frantic pursuit of a series of ventures. At
an early age Hessell Tiltman set out to write a succession of books. Some,
not unexpectedly, were little more than pot-boilers but others deserve to
be unearthed and re-examined.[9]

It remains unclear when Hessell Tiltman first became interested in Asia
but the publication of *The Pacific: A Forecast* with Colonel P.T. Etherton in
1928 marks a major shift in his endeavours. While he continued to report
and write on European affairs during the early 1930s, it is certain that his
successful collaboration with Etherton prompted greater attention to the
Asia-Pacific; by 1936 he had become a resident correspondent in Tokyo,
ensconced, as he would be again after the Second World War, in the
comforts of the Imperial Hotel. Tiltman probably needed the cooperation
of Etherton to gain a toe-hold in the region. Etherton was very much a
figure from an earlier generation, he listed his recreations as 'motoring,
travel [and] big-game shooting'. He had gained considerable first-hand
experience through pre-war service in the Indian army and consular work
on the Chinese borders. More importantly, Etherton, who had something
of a reputation as an authority on Asian affairs, probably saw Tiltman as an
emerging figure capable of grafting material for possible publication. The
best evidence of their joint efforts was seen in January 1933 when they
collaborated in the authorship of *Manchuria: The Cockpit of Asia.*[10] It was a
good title and even the 'cheaper' edition that followed twelve months
after the original had gone through five impressions remained a hard-back
volume with an arresting cover. The advent of the paperback was a
publishing phenomenon later in the decade.

The book made Tiltman. Through it he demonstrated that he could
write entertainingly and seriously on a highly topical Asian subject. His
intention, expressed in the opening sentences of the Foreword, had been
to explain the Manchurian Crisis. He and his co-author announced:

> Few questions in recent years have excited more interest and
> anxiety in diplomatic and political circles than the future of
> Manchuria, that rich treasure-house of natural wealth forming
> three of the outlying provinces of China, in which Japan, the
> United States, Soviet Russia, and Great Britain have vital
> interests yet which to the public is scarcely more than a
> name.[11]

Etherton and Tiltman's work can be said to have gone some way towards presenting the salient background and political realities of a convoluted issue. It also had some sensible, if depressing, predictions on the future of Japanese-controlled Manchuria. Tiltman was anxious to warn British readers that Imperial Japan would not listen to protests from London, Washington and Geneva. He stated:

> Japan, securely in possession of Manchuria, proceeds to strengthen her armed forces and to ignore the advice of friends and possible antagonists alike. Tokyo, Tiltman and Etherton concluded, never had, and has not now, any intention of leaving Manchuria. To do so would mean the economic extinction of Japan as a World Power.[12]

While they would be proved wrong in rejecting the suggestion that Japan might assume direct control of the three provinces, they were certainly correct to conclude their work with the statement that 'nothing short of a national defeat in war can rob Japan of the fruits awaiting the nation which develops the riches of the Manchurian plains'.[13]

Although fully aware of the commercial and political challenges that Britain must now face from a strengthening Tokyo, Tiltman displayed some general sympathy for Japan's predicament in Manchuria. He shared a fairly common view of Western residents that China, too, could be faulted over what he regarded as its 'misbehaviour and lawlessness'. He felt also that if Japan were able to sponsor the peaceful development of Japanese-dominated Manchuria 'for half a century' there would be enormous consequences for all the great powers in the Asia–Pacific. The result would then be 'profound changes favourable to Japan', although he added the caveat that such strategic and industrial advantage was contingent on domestic solutions to 'the pressure of population, the food problem, and urgent need for some outlet for her surplus millions' that avoided 'social upheaval in Japan itself'.[14]

Tiltman clearly enjoyed making such grand predictions. He continued:

> Knowing the very real dangers which Japanese Governments must face at some time during the next thirty years – dangers which if not averted by wise statesmanship may bring the onward march of Japan to a full stop – one cannot but admire the courage with which the Government seeks, while there is time, to provide 'safety valves' for the future. Of all the possibilities in sight, apart from the setting aside of a portion of Australia for Japanese colonization, Manchuria offers the great hope of relief and the greatest source of future strength.[15]

The unfortunate fact that the area was part of the sovereign territory of Japan's greatest neighbour apparently did not overmuch concern Tiltman. He preferred instead to excuse gross imperialism by explaining that: 'It is, we must repeat, the peculiar tragedy of the Japanese people that they rose to the position of a Great Power too late to join in the carving up of the world's empty places in the interests of the predominant nations.' Tiltman held that Japan was entitled to secure boundary changes in northeast Asia, arguing that international society needed to be fully aware of the unpleasant consequences if it wished to resist strenuously Tokyo's claims.

Evidence of Tiltman's developing sympathies for Japan is apparent in the concluding chapter of the book. He and Etherton, it is impossible unfortunately at this distance from events to distinguish individual opinions, proclaim a robust defence for Japan based on justice and realism. Two of their final paragraphs deserve to be quoted in full:

> Admitting both the breaches of treaty obligations by the Japanese in Manchuria, and the abundant provocation offered to them by successive Chinese Governments, it says much for Japanese patience that she waited until her investments, her property and the lives of her subjects had been rendered insecure by the spread of lawlessness north of the Great Wall before she attempted to secure, by direct action, that position in Manchuria which is vital to her existence, interests which, however just in abstract may be the Chinese case, no Japanese statesman dare permit to go by default.
>
> For good or ill, the future of Manchuria will be fashioned in Tokyo. Other nations may insist upon the 'Open Door'. Susceptibilities may have to be considered. Camouflage may be employed to conceal uncomfortable facts; but the central fact will remain – Manchuria, the Promised Land of Asia, will in the immediate future go forward to a new era of swift development under the guiding hand of Japan, in the interests of the world in general.[16]

Such pro-Japanese sentiments contrast strikingly with the authors' other writings on the threat that Tokyo posed to Western interests in the region. Clearly, Tiltman stands accused of suggesting that Japan deserves to expand in Manchuria but should not be permitted to encroach elsewhere in the Asia–Pacific. This double standard, from a writer who had written favourably of social democracy in Europe and criticized the Soviet Union at length, was unfortunate. While correct to underline the emergence of the Pacific as 'the New World Centre',[17] Tiltman warned that since 'British expansion in the Pacific has ceased', the best it could now hope for was 'a period of consolidation'. He saw the rise of Japan as heralding 'the awakening of Asia' and was quick to identify 'all the problems now looming up for the moment when they will compel world-wide attention'.[18] Problems, it would seem, that might be partly solved through encouraging Tokyo to garrison troops, construct railways and build factories north of the Great Wall, in the hope that this might distract attention from the vulnerability of British investments and territories elsewhere in East Asia.

Tiltman repeatedly drew his readers' attention to the position of Japan in international relations. From the late 1920s he clearly saw his task as one of cautioning a growing audience that there might well be unpleasant and possibly violent days ahead. His writings were intended to prepare the public for an increase in Pacific rivalries where 'Japan is strongly organized whether to fight trade rivals or to conduct a naval and military campaign'.[19] Against the emergence of Imperial Japan, Tiltman displayed only a limited confidence in British power. In his analyses he weaved strategic, military and industrial factors together to form a pessimistic picture for the future. At times, it is true, he could raise the trumpet and declaim that the British Empire was still Number One, but this assumed filial ties between London, Canberra, Wellington and Ottawa and an enhanced naval posture at Singapore. Even then he warned that 'Great Britain's future in the Pacific – essential as it is to Europe and our Empire – will not be assured without sacrifices'.[20] Tiltman also looked at the economic underpinnings behind the pomp and feared that the coming industrialization of Asia, led necessarily by Japan, might seriously weaken British manufacturers. There might be an eventual golden age of universal peace and economic cooperation in the still distant future but, long before mankind reached nirvana, Tiltman prophesied that British industry would be hard hit by new competitors in third markets. Manchester and Birmingham would suffer as '. . . there will inevitably be many changes, possibly more than one armed dispute, before the factory chimneys stretch from Paisley to Chefoo'.[21]

The challenges that Tiltman charted first with Etherton in 1928 grew in the 1930s and necessarily reduced the earlier qualified confidence in a reinvigoration of Britain's position in the Asia–Pacific. When the two authors returned to the charge in the mid-1930s their tone was noticeably less calm. They titled their last collaborative book *Japan: Mistress of the Pacific?*. While they equivocated over providing any direct answer to the question set, it was intended to leave the reader in little doubt that Imperial Japan might well have fresh ambitions in mind after Manchuria had been swallowed. The authors noted:

> Today no [Japanese] statesman who dared to question the wisdom of recent events in Manchuria, or the policy of which the conquest of that region formed a part, could survive the storm of public opprobrium which would ensue. He would be fortunate to escape assassination at the hands some fanatic, drunk with the faith in the future glories awaiting Japan in the mists of time.[22]

There was, therefore, the likelihood of vast Japanese expansion into further parts of China, to which neither the League of Nations nor the West (defined as Britain and the United States) appeared willing to deter. Any solution was held to rest with 'the Japanese militarists who are in control at Tokio', since only if these individuals 'see the danger, and recognize the wisdom of advancing in step with other nations' could eventual conflict be avoided. Japanese public opinion was dismissed as blind and her industrialists, who had the most to gain 'if she chooses the path of peace', were hardly in a position to make state decisions, although Tiltman did hope that financial restrictions, such as 'a foreign embargo on loans' might perhaps make Japan think twice. In the concluding paragraph Etherton and Tiltman argued that Japan, 'while consolidating her position in Manchuria' and extending 'her growing trade in Eastern markets by every means in her power', might be rescued from a position of considerable peril'.[23] Their final argument, however, that '. . . it would need greater resources than even the energetic Japanese command to make their country the Mistress of the Pacific in opposition to the interests and conscience of the civilized world' was turned upside down in December 1941.

Yet long before Pearl Harbor confounded this sentence, Tiltman had warned of the probability of a Japanese-American war and, in company with other respected commentators such as Hector Bywater, already reckoned on the outcome. For Tiltman, never confident in British strength, conflict between Tokyo and Washington would begin with a succession of Japanese victories in capturing Guam, Manila and then Pearl Harbor, through 'a concerted and powerful aerial onslaught by trained pilots'.[24] 'Having swept the Stars and Stripes out of the Pacific', Etherton and Tiltman predicted that 'the immensely superior resources' of the United States would in time produce its 'counter-blow' when 'Japanese aims at the domination of the Pacific would be swept away for generations'[25] and lead to 'the disappearance of Japan from the ranks of world Powers'.

Tiltman warned Japan that 'any fleeting initial triumph of Japanese arms' would be of little worth against the military and industrial might of a fully mobilized and enraged United States. He also predicted any future war in the Pacific 'would be a contest between scientific experts in the production of engines of destruction, rather than one between navies and peoples',[26] which 'would transcend, in physical and material losses, in horror, and in the ferocity with which it would be waged, anything previously known'. Both authors knew what they were talking about.

Tiltman's own first-hand experience with aeroplane design led him to suggest 'torpedoes, poisoned air, and unseen rays, coupled with the power of fire, steel, and explosives' plus the accompanying factors of 'disease and pestilence, famine and drought' would create 'the destruction of all mankind within the area of the war zone and far beyond it'.[27] As an unfortunate description of what would prove to be the wastelands of Hiroshima and Nagasaki and the dire conditions on the Kanto plain between Yokohama and Tokyo in August 1945 this could hardly be bettered.

After co-authoring *Japan: Mistress of the Pacific* Tiltman's career as an author was largely over. He reverted to journalism and would proudly recall later that he had 'travelled 25,000 miles in all parts of Eastern Asia and the Pacific' between 1935 and 1937, before covering the Sino-Japanese War for the *Daily Express*. In semi-retirement Tiltman would enjoy reminiscing over the fact that he had been one of the very few foreign correspondents in Tokyo when the February 1936 attempted military coup occurred. He also delighted in recounting his memories of Victor Sorge, the successful spy from the Soviet Union, whom he used to describe as having completely fooled him with his performance as the perfect Nazi. By 1938 he had returned to Europe and thereafter worked as a senior foreign correspondent in the United States for the *Daily Sketch* and the Kemsley newspapers stable, while contributing also to *The New Statesman*.[28] He would not see Japan again until the start of the Allied Occupation.

Writing in 1934 Etherton and Tiltman noted that 'The possibility of a conflict between Japan and the United States – a clash by which the mastery of the Pacific would be settled for generations – has been predicted so often that many are inclined to consider an Americo-Japanese war inevitable sooner or later.'[29] While wisely suggesting that 'Because an event may happen, however, it does not follow that it *will*', the authors were in little doubt that 'the rising tide of nationalism in Japan itself' left little ground for optimism. Their conclusion was that 'As long as Japan adheres to her present dreams of hegemony in the Pacific, so long must the United States keep an anxious watch and ward over far eastern waters, and wonder what the morning will bring forth.'[30] Yet deterrence did not deter and the Pacific War that followed in December 1941 was not resolved until the late summer of 1945.

AFTER THE SECOND WORLD WAR

Once the Allied occupation began, Hessell Tiltman returned to Tokyo where his reputation was assisted both by pre-war experience of the region and by his familiarity with US journalism and its ways. Tiltman's wartime years in the United States had enabled him to develop important contacts and thereafter he acquired a degree of financial security that would have been impossible if he had worked only for British newspapers and had been obliged to share in the age of austerity. It also altered his prose style by the, at least temporary, introduction of Americanisms that he delighted in putting into his columns. The considerable resources that

Tiltman enjoyed in Japan, through his contributions to papers such as the *Washington Post* and its associated syndicates, enabled him to support the services of various secretaries, interpreters, translators and drivers. Tiltman rather glorified in living up to his image as the established foreign correspondent, ever required to entertain to gain the necessary contacts and to demonstrate to Asian figures that he represented the best newspapers drawn from the Western world.

For post-war British readers, however, Tiltman's greatest fame was not won until he began reporting regularly for *The Manchester Guardian*. Yet this arrangement did not start until January 1951 and coincided with the preparations for the much delayed Japanese peace treaty.[31] Detailed evidence of Tiltman's dealings with the newspaper which would later become known merely as *The Guardian* is now available and would appear to be the only archive that has yet been discovered on his career. Considering that Tiltman wrote several million words for at least a dozen papers and had published a dozen full-length books by 1937 alone, it is to be hoped that a great deal still remains to found.

Tiltman was proud to be associated with *The Manchester Guardian*. In May 1952 he told A.P.Wadsworth, its editor from 1944 to 1956, that 'I feel greatly privileged to be writing for *The Manchester Guardian*', adding, what would appear to be the case, that 'I have recently expended time on that task without much reference to the amount of the financial return'.[32] Tiltman probably saw this as his just reward for decades as a journalist. The evidence from *The Guardian* archives strongly suggests that Tiltman was as eager to be published in the 1950s as he had been when he was a generation younger and far less well known.

Yet there were problems. Tiltman filed frequently and he had the habit of reckoning he should also write something akin to editorials and possess a watching brief for the Asia-Pacific region, while the foreign desk for its part was obliged to delay the printing of some dispatches. Tiltman's enthusiasm led to *The Manchester Guardian* gently suggesting that he might go a little slower, since the foreign editor knew it was unwise to attempt to force-feed too many reports from their Tokyo correspondent on a sometimes indifferent public. Part of the issue was the small size of British newspapers in the 1950s, caused by government restrictions on newsprint, though the fact that the United States had dominated events in post-surrender Tokyo had also contributed to a resistance to closely monitoring what was happening in Japan. The region was assumed to be of lesser importance to readers and even sensitive, textile questions did not warrant quite the attention that Tiltman must have hoped for.

One criterion for judging Tiltman's prowess is the opposition that his writing engendered. Responsible journalism ought to create waves and Tiltman was indeed entitled to cite his battle honours. He informed Wadsworth that during the Occupation General MacArthur had instructed 'Colonel Bunker, his personal aide, to denounce me in writing to Mr. Graham, the proprietor of the [*Washington] Post*, as a liar for suggesting in an article published in the *Post* on the fifth anniversary of Japan's surrender, that may be this country might not have become quite so pure a democracy as some GHQ handouts stated'.[33] Tiltman thus became 'one of ten leading Far Eastern newsmen to be so smeared by order of the Supreme Commander for the Allied Powers during the Occupation. Of the ten, I was the only one with a non-American passport'.[34] In fact, there were other British journalists who also incurred the wrath of MacArthur, including *The Times*' Frank Hawley, but whether Tiltman was aware of such incidents is not clear. Of equal merit was Tiltman's 'medal'[35] earned for standing up to Yoshida Shigeru. This led to a period of enmity among old friends and was created by Yoshida's anger in being termed 'a conservative rather than a "progressive reformer", which he and his feudalists prefer'.[36] According to Tiltman, Yoshida, 'whom I have known for years, refused to receive me for more than eighteen months'. But their personal bridges were repaired and Tiltman tried hard in June 1954 to gain a front-page listing for the premier only to discover at the last moment that Yoshida's proposed visit to Asia had been cancelled. Tiltman feared that 'the prestige alike of Mr Yoshida and myself is most horribly involved' in gaining decent coverage for what was an intended exclusive but by the next week he could joke that 'anything can happen in the Orient – and probably will'.

Tiltman's range when covering post-peace treaty Japan was wide but he clearly held that the domestic political scene had by necessity to be the foundation for his reportage. He based his work on both well-established contacts and his ability to focus intently on the subject at hand. His editors saw immediately that Tiltman was 'indefatigable', though this led them to add that the paper was 'only sorry that we have not been able to get your pieces in promptly'. Similar comments appear frequently in the Tiltman-Wadsworth correspondence and are testimony to his labours. Tiltman would file well before obvious anniversary dates, took to following the activities of the big textile firms in Osaka, and attempted, with no more luck it has to be said than his rivals, to catch the slightest crumbs that might fall accidentally from the palace's table.

Hessell Tiltman lived well and cherished the local fame[37] that came from a near half century of close contact with Japan and the Asia-Pacific. From 1945 to 1952 he had witnessed what he called 'the changing post-war Japanese scene based upon virtually continuous day-to-day observation of events in this country', yet in some ways he was more at home in an earlier Japan. He had been following what would become almost his adopted nation from the 1920s and, though he had few illusions about pre-war Japan, it is clear that he enjoyed living in what he described to his editor in May 1952 'in a manner becoming to a friend of Prime Ministers and ex-Prime Ministers'. Since nearly all Japan's premiers for the first two decades after the surrender were drawn from this pre-war milieu, it is not hard to see why Tiltman looked over his shoulder so often. The fact that in his last years he had semi-formal links to the Ministry of Foreign Affairs can only have strengthened these earlier bonds. Tiltman was sceptical both of Japan's supposed professions of internationalism before 1941 and dubious about the validity of General MacArthur's claims to have revolutionized post-war Japan. What Tiltman's career also sadly demonstrates is that the role of his own nation and the context much of the time for his writings was greatly reduced in the decades of his prime. Tiltman bore witness to the shift in Britain's status from that of established regional power to little more than a European bystander by the time of his death. While Tiltman attempted to get his readers to focus more single-mindedly on Japan and the Pacific throughout these decades, the task was clearly far beyond the resources of his profession and the talents of any single, however talented, practitioner.

38

Frank Hawley, 1906–61: Scholar, Bibliophile and Journalist

MANABU YOKOYAMA

Frank Hawley

FRANK HAWLEY (1906-61) was the first post-war correspondent of *The Times*[1] in Japan. He represented the paper in Tokyo from 1946 to 1952. As the special correspondent of what was then the leading newspaper in Britain he held a privileged position and had eight one-to-one interviews with General Douglas MacArthur between November 1947 and July 1949. His reports were frank and often critical of American policies in Japan. MacArthur did not take kindly to criticism from Hawley which he regarded as 'negative and carping'. On one occasion MacArthur complained with 'characteristic trenchancy' to Sir Alvary Gascoigne, the head of the United Kingdom Liaison Mission in Japan about Hawley.[2] Gascoigne responded that he could not control the press and pointed out that criticism in the press, however unjust or tedious, had to be tolerated in democracies. The General was not mollified and by the end of the occupation Hawley was virtually *persona non grata* with the Americans. The General's complaint to Gascoigne led to questions in the House of Commons where MacArthur's attitude was described as 'unjustified interference' contrary to the principles of freedom of the press. Hawley may not have had long years of experience as a journalist, but he had spent ten years in Japan as a young scholar and was well versed in Japanese culture. As a result the articles which he sent back to London were based on first-hand experience and knowledge.

Hawley was a renowned collector of rare Japanese editions. If a book carries his *ex Libris* stamp (*Hōrei Bunko*, the Hawley Library), its value is guaranteed. For scholars and students of Okinawa culture, he is acknowledged as the original owner of the Loochiu Collection Hawley Library, now housed in the University of Hawaii Hamilton Library. Many historical materials were lost during the Pacific War, and so the value of this collection of books and documents is widely recognized.

Frank Hawley was an accomplished Japanologist who wrote some distinguished books on Japanese culture. Before the war, as a young linguist, he published various studies of Japanese culture in literary magazines. After the war he became known as a scholarly journalist with an immense knowledge of the Japanese language. In his later years he worked assiduously for the Kansai Asiatic Society and promoted cultural exchange between Japanese scholars and foreigners living in Japan.[3] The greater part of his private library contained works dealing with medicine, paper-making, Chinese herbal medicine and animals, botany, fauna and flora, early Christianity in Japan, Japanese cultural history, religions, architecture, art, Noh, whales, special materials about China (mostly linguistics), and also special collections dealing with Mongolia, Manchuria and Okinawa.

YOUTH

Frank Hawley was born in 1906 in Stanley Street, Norton. He went from Norton-on-Tees elementary School to Stockton-on-Tees secondary school for boys. In 1924 he went on to the University of Liverpool where he studied for two years specializing in French and each year winning various scholarships. From the third year, he studied in France at the Sorbonne (Université de Paris) and Germany at the Friedrich Wilhems Universität in Berlin. From 1928 to 1930 he was a research student at Peterhouse, Cambridge, where, presumably, he began to study oriental languages.

JAPAN BEFORE THE SECOND WORLD WAR

At the age of twenty-four, Hawley was teaching Manchu at London University when a Japanese professor of English literature visited him and offered him a position as an English teacher in Japan. Hawley who seems to have taken some lessons in Japanese at the School of Oriental and African Studies (SOAS) under Yoshitake, the only Japanese lecturer there at that time, travelled out to Japan via Siberia, Manchuria and Korea, arriving in the summer of 1931. On 18 September, the day on which the Manchurian Incident began, he was appointed professor at the Tokyo

School of Foreign Languages. He also taught at Tokyo Bunrika Daigaku (School of Pedagogics) in Tokyo. Later, he accepted a post as professor of English in the Third National Gymnasium, and went to live in Kyoto. His eccentric approach there caused some consternation. To the despair of his students he used to write complicated Chinese characters or difficult *senryū* (humorous short poems) on the blackboard. He did not take kindly to those who asked him about English drama. He was regarded as an eccentric teacher, but his personality made a strong impression on his students.

Soon after arriving in Japan in 1931 he met his first wife, Minoda Toshiko, a Japanese of good family. They were married in 1934.Her father who was an expert in railway construction was an intellectual who owned a large oriental library and who helped Hawley financially in the pre-war period. Hawley, with her help, became fluent in spoken and written Japanese.

Two years after his arrival in Japan, Hawley wrote two articles in Japanese for a journal, 'Sketch of a History of Japanese Literary Studies in Europe' and 'The Origin of the Japanese Language'. The editor, impressed by his command of the language, reproduced Hawley's signature in the journal. Noting his linguistic ability, the *Kokusai Bunka Shinkōkai* (Institute for Promoting International Cultural Relations) invited him and Sir George Sansom to take part in a colloquium about the problems of learning and mastering Japanese.[4] Hawley was well aware of Japan's intention to advance into Asia not only politically and militarily but also culturally. The Japanese authorities before the war emphasized the unique nature of Japan's culture, but Hawley's articles, based on a wider study of linguistics, showed that Japanese culture was more complex and international in its origin than the nationalists suggested.[5]

At that time Hawley was interested in compiling a Japanese dictionary for foreigners, especially for scholars of Japanese culture and for the descendants of Japanese emigrants abroad. The work would include not only standard vocabulary but also technical terms for cooking, as well as Japanese-Chinese (*Kango*) words used in the literature of authors such as Kōda Rohan.[6] Hawley completed most of the manuscript by 1937. The *Kokusai Bunka Shinkōkai* was planning to compile a Japanese dictionary for foreigners to commemorate the 2600th anniversary of the founding of the Japanese empire, and Hawley was chosen as the compiler. But Hawley resigned from the project when he received a critical letter from a Japanese scholar of English, who expected a dictionary for practical use by beginners with 'suitable idiomatic instances'. Hawley had planned to produce the sort of dictionary that he would himself have wanted when he learned Japanese. The work should, he thought, provide accurate information about delicate nuances of words and expressions, self-evident for native speakers but not generally apparent to foreigners. He was convinced that the dictionary should provide connotation, not denotation. In a sense he was introducing a new approach, although the anonymous critic probably did not have the opportunity of reading Hawley's refutation.[7]

In 1937, the well-known publisher Kenkyūsha invited Hawley to be one of the compilers of Kenkyūsha's *Simplified English Dictionary*. Hawley devoted himself wholeheartedly to this project, and asserted proudly that he had written nearly all of the entries. But the publisher did not evaluate his work very highly and a conflict arose between Hawley and the company. After some negotiations, however, the parties reached an understanding and Hawley's name was listed in the preface as a collaborator in the compilation. In Hawley's opinion, the negotiations with the publisher about this matter had been a complete waste of time.[8]

Hawley was then offered a post in the recently-established Oriental Institute at the University of Hawaii. Personally, he wanted a career entirely devoted to scholarship, but he had to abandon this dream for two reasons; he needed a regular income and he faced a problem of transporting his bulky library. Meanwhile, Hawley received an invitation to join the School of Oriental and African Studies at London University as an assistant professor of Japanese. Hawley accepted the offer. The university wanted him to return to Britain as soon as possible, but he was forced to postpone his return to England for a year so that he could obtain all the books he needed. While he was preparing to move, World War II broke out. Under the auspices of the newly-established British Ministry of Information, the British Library of Information and Culture was opened in Tokyo. Vere Redman, a former teacher and newspaper correspondent in Japan[9] 'was appointed to conduct official British propaganda in Japan' and Hawley was appointed director of the institution. This had a cultural atmosphere and was frequented by pro-Japanese scholars, such as Robert van Gulik of the Netherlands Embassy, E. H. Norman of the Canadian mission, and the journalist John Morris. While occupying this post, Hawley was able to enjoy himself reading books, book-hunting, and meeting with friends.[10]

SECOND WORLD WAR

Hawley was arrested on 8 December 1941 the day war broke out between Japan and the US. He was repatriated to Britain in 1942 after seven months confinement. His wife Toshiko remained in Japan both to look after her parents but also to do what she could to preserve his library. His library of 16,000 volumes was, however, confiscated by the Japanese government along with those of the British Library of Information and Culture, and was purchased by Keio University. Having foreseen this, Hawley had asked his secretary to compile a catalogue of his library, and wrote to her from the Lourenço Marques in Africa, where the British and Japanese internees were exchanged, that he spent all the time looking through the catalogue. Despite his distressing experience in detention he did not bear ill-will against the Japanese, remarking that as a foreigner he was treated no differently from the others. Japanese in Sugamo prison camp, he noted, were treated far worse than Europeans there. But Hawley criticized the Japanese judiciary as a whole, and in John Morris' *Traveller from Tokyo*, Hawley's experiences and observations are recorded.[11]

When Hawley returned to England there were various positions where his ability in Japanese and his knowledge of Japanese culture could-be of value. He taught Japanese for six months at the School of Oriental and African Studies where service language students were studying Japanese. This was the post to which he had been previously appointed. He then joined the Japanese service of the BBC as an adviser and worked as a censor. Later, he joined the staff of the Foreign Office and until one month before the end of the war he was on the staff of G2 in Washington where he was engaged in translating the diaries of Japanese prisoners. During his stay in Washington Hawley met Gwynneth Laura Tambure, a Canadian, who was a graduate of Toronto University and who later became his second wife.

Hawley wanted to return to Japan as soon as possible, for the loss of his confiscated library deeply worried him. A week before the end of the war he returned to London and sought a post which would allow him to do so. He sent a long report to the British Council recommending the reopening of the British Library of Information and Culture in Tokyo. He also approached the Foreign Office to see whether he could obtain through them a suitable post in Tokyo. But these efforts were unsuccessful and he was despondent. However, Major General Francis S.G. Piggott, one of his old acquaintances in Tokyo, recommended him to the editor of *The Times*. On 21 February 1946, Hawley was accepted by the newspaper, and after three months' training, which confirmed his ability as a journalist, he was sent to Tokyo as *The Times* correspondent. In his letter of recommendation Piggott said that he expected Hawley to be an outstanding correspondent on account of his 'scholarship in the language', and that in this respect he would follow in the footsteps of Frank Brinkley and Hugh Byas.[12]

CORRESPONDENT IN JAPAN

Hawley arrived back in Tokyo on 28 July 1946, having travelled via Cairo, Basra, Karachi, Calcutta, Rangoon, Saigon, Hong Kong and Shanghai. He found the centre of the city destroyed by air-raids, and the few remaining buildings had been requisitioned by GHQ. He lived at first in the Tokyo Correspondents Club and opened the 'Tokyo Branch Office of *The Times'* on the seventh floor of the *Asahi Shimbun* building. Gwynneth Tambure, who had come to Japan after the war as a secretary in the British mission to SCAP, in the evenings helped Hawley in his capacity as correspondent of *The Times*. This led to Hawley's marriage to Toshiko being dissolved in February 1948.He then married Gwynneth. They had a son, John, in 1949 and a daughter, Felicity, in 1951.

Hawley had to work hard as he was the only staff member of his paper in Tokyo, while *The New York Times* had no less than ten. He reported that he sent back almost three thousand articles to London between 1946 and 1952. He not only provided information about Japan in its post-war rehabilitation, but also interviewed many Japanese of different classes. He received requests from all over the country to deliver lectures or to take note of local news. *The Times* correspondent, so proficient in Japanese, was widely held in high esteem. The Korean War began in 1950 and increased Hawley's workload. His paper sent out an additional member of staff, Ian Morrison, to help him, but he was soon transferred to Korea as war correspondent. Morrison died there on duty, and Hawley contributed a lengthy and sympathetic obituary in *The Times*.[13]

In 1952 the new management of *The Times* asked Hawley if he would go to Rhodesia, but he refused to transfer to Africa and resigned from the paper. With the ending of the Occupation, the situation in Tokyo greatly changed. For a short while he worked for *The Daily Telegraph* and *The Christian Science Monitor* as special correspondent, but soon gave up both these jobs.

While busily working as a newspaper correspondent, Hawley did everything he could to recover his requisitioned library. He successfully appealed to the British Embassy and to GHQ to oblige Keiō University to return his books. When he received back any of the volumes he examined their condition closely. He submitted to the Japanese government a list of unreturned items and demanded, and received, compensation.

Hawley's status as a well-paid correspondent of the most prestigious newspaper of one of the victorious powers helped him greatly to find and purchase many valuable old books in keeping with his interests as an expert collector and philologist. The Hawley Collection grew day by day with the acquisition of rare classical books and precious cultural documents such as the *Hyakumanto Darani*, or the printed prayers belonging to the *Million Miniature Pagodas*, dating back probably to the seventh century. He planned to use the abundant source material he had collected to begin a full-scale study of Japanese culture as a specialized philologist. In this context he began writing, *A Bibliographical Introduction to Special Collections Dealing with the Loochiu Islands* and *The Secret Skill in Paper-Making*, projects which had been impossible for him to complete while he was still a busy correspondent.

PUBLICATION OF *MISCELLANEA JAPONICA*

In the autumn of 1952 and after his retirement from *The Times*, Hawley moved to Yamashina, a suburb of Kyoto, and as he had for so long desired began a new academic life. He took up the study of the language of the Ryukyu Islands with Shimabukuro Hisa, who came from the islands and who lived with Hawley and his son John in Yamashina. He sought a divorce from Gwynneth but a long drawn out law-suit over custody of the children and liquidation of debts was still continuing when he died.

He had the principal role in running the Kansai Asiatic Society which had been established in Kyoto in 1949 by R. A. Egon Hessel as a branch of the Asiatic Society of Japan. Together with his friends P. E. Perkins and Suzuki Hidesaburo, he organized the society's activities, and under his direction eighty-five monthly meetings were held and ten volumes containing twenty-one papers were published. The number of Society members, both Japanese and foreigners living in the Kansai region, increased to 253. Although *The Transactions of the Kansai Asiatic Society* regularly published articles, Hawley himself did not write for *The Transactions* and preferred to publish the results of his studies in a different way.[14] He decided to initiate his own academic series in which to publish his work, which he called *Miscellanea Japonica*, aiming to present his work in an ideal format. The series was to appear in folio size measuring 30.5 x 23.2 cm, using handmade paper from Shiroishi in Miyagi prefecture. The newly-invented '*Tsubaki* (camellia)-finishing' technique made it possible to print on both sides of fine Japanese paper. The cover was red ochre in colour with the title printed on a smaller piece of paper. The cover wrapping was treated with an astringent made from persimmon. The spine of the second volume of the series was made from sheepskin with the title added in gold foil. The volume was enclosed in a case covered with 'mulberry paper', made from the rough fibre of Japanese mulberry and having a distinctive delicacy. The title pages and illustrations were completed by expert craftsmen of the day and were printed on Japanese paper of the highest quality.

An English Surgeon in Japan in 1863-1865 was published in 1954 as the first volume of *Miscellanea Japonica*. It consisted of the diary of a British naval surgeon who took part in the bombardment of the Shimonoseki batteries in 1864 by the combined fleet of Britain, France, Holland and the US.[15] The text was based on the handwritten original and annotated by Hawley. He had found the diary in London just after the war and had transcribed its text while still a correspondent.

The next volume consisted of three parts, the first of which was *Whales and Whaling in Japan*. Hawley had gathered and translated documents on the subject, supplying a full explanation because he felt 'keenly the need to let Japanese and other people know the history and the record of the

415

business of catching whales, in which the Japanese have excelled from of old.[16] In 1955, the manuscript of the first part of this work was sent to Kawakita Printing Press, which provided numerous proofs but Hawley was never satisfied. Four years later he sent out a subscription prospectus to potential purchasers. Off-prints were distributed in the following year to provide readers with a sample of the printing; these were produced in the same luxurious fashion as the real edition, printed on the same type of Japanese paper and illustrated with woodblock prints. Many acquaintances, who reviewed the off-prints, praised the splendid production and esteemed the work highly.[17] Proof-reading was repeated again and again, but Hawley found it impossible to stop making corrections. Soon after the final proof-reading, however, an illness from which he had been suffering since the previous year took a sudden turn for the worse, and Hawley died of liver trouble at the age of 54 on 10 January 1961.

After his death Shimabukuro Hisa completed the first part of the second volume of the series, *Whales and Whaling in Japan*. The second part, *A Full and Particular Account of the Use of the Various Parts of the Whale in Old Japanese Medicine*, had been completed but remained unpublished. *Choumei Benran* (*Handbook of Names of Birds*) compiled at the request of Shimazu Shigehide was to be published by Hawley in 1960, but Hawley's death brought to an end the publication of *Miscellanea Japonica*.

HAWLEY THE BIBLIOPHILE

Teruyama Etsuko, Hawley's secretary at the British Library of Information and Culture, who had also worked for him as a secretary in the Tokyo office of *The Times* described him as follows:

> He was indifferent to his clothes and was always brushing away cigarette ash from his jacket, and as a result they always showed white spots. . . He used to lumber along the streets, always looking into the windows of antique bookshops and carrying a big parcel of old books under his arm. His appearance reminded us of a hermit scholar.[18]

Hawley's house was always overflowing with books; they were in fact the master of the house and he was obliged to live in the narrow spaces between the shelves. The books in his library were for him the tools for his studies. He had many interesting ideas and every time he obtained more books he thought up new plans for research. As a result he was always on the look-out for new books, even if it meant giving away some of his old ones. When he managed to enlarge his library space, he bought more books, and so his collection grew ever bigger. It was his library that decided the direction of his life. He had hesitated to take up the post which he had been offered at the University of Hawaii because of the problem of moving his books. He did not return immediately to the UK as London University wanted him to do, because he wished to obtain more books for his library. As a result he was interned and his library was requisitioned by the Japanese government. In prison he used to look at the list of his collection every day, and after the war he made every effort to find a suitable position which would enable him to return to Japan and to his books. Indeed, he only accepted the post of correspondent in Tokyo for this reason.

Sakamaki Shunzō, dean of the Summer Session of the University of Hawaii, happened to read Hawley's obituary while staying in Tokyo, and determined to obtain for the university all of his materials dealing with Okinawa. Sakamaki had been planning to establish a research centre for the history and culture of Okinawa, as many people from those islands, or their descendants, lived and worked in Hawaii. On condition that they would be called The Hawley Collection, the University obtained all of the 2000 or so volumes of material relating to Ryukyu-Okinawa, which are today preserved in the University's Hamilton Library as the Sakamaki-Hawley Collection.[19] The rest of his collection was sold by auction in the Tokyo Art Club. Tenri Library in Nara bought 433 volumes on Japanese paper; the catalogue of these books was compiled by Sorimachi Shigeo, the director of the well-known bookstore Kobunso.[20]

Robert van Gulik, one of Hawley's best and most sympathetic friends, wrote an obituary, 'lest an outstanding scholar who greatly contributed to Japanese studies be forgotten through lack of documentary evidence'. He continued: 'It was Hawley's cherished ideal to publish some day a Japanese classic in a "final edition", and for that purpose he had assembled a fine collection of rare old editions and manuscripts.'[21] Hawley gathered as many variant texts and different manuscripts as possible to obtain the very best versions. He wanted to bring out a critical edition of Japanese classics with scholarly editing and annotation. For this purpose he had to collect many texts of the highest quality; this was the root of many of his problems, for despite his many plans and ideas, Hawley left behind him only two volumes of *Miscellanea Japonica*.

Van Gulik deplored this and wrote: 'Hawley himself had often expressed the hope that even if it were not to be given him to publish larger works, his library would remain as such a lasting monument.'[22] Unfortunately, Hawley's collection was scattered and lost. Many volumes bearing his *ex libris* seal were dispersed to libraries and collectors throughout the world. However, in Hawaii and Tenri (Nara prefecture) all the materials which he collected relating to Okinawa and Japanese paper-making are preserved in their original form just as Hawley so painstakingly collected them.

39

Hasegawa Nyozekan, 1875-1969: Journalist and Philosopher

AYAKO HOTTA-LISTER

Hasegawa Nyozekan and daughter

HASEGAWA NYOZEKAN[1] (1875-1969) was well known in Japan for his enthusiasm for Britain. Yet, his periods of residence in Britain were short, covering four months in 1910 at the time of the Japan-British Exhibition and a short return visit in 1956. He wrote about these visits extensively in the popular press and also published a book which linked his name with Britain.

He graduated in 1898 from Tokyo Hōgakuin (Tokyo Law School), formerly until 1899 called the Igirisu Hōritsu Gakkō (English Law College), which finally became Chuō University in 1905. Under the influence of liberal thinkers in early Meiji, he developed an admiration for British law and institutions. He lived through the turbulent Meiji, Taishō and Shōwa eras and witnessed enormous changes in Japan. He was greatly influenced throughout his life by British liberal and democratic ideas and became known as a thinker and liberal journalist of 'the English school'. He was one of the leaders of the so-called Taishō democracy movement and influenced many others including the late Maruyama Masao.

During his long and active career spanning at least seventy years, he wrote more than three thousand articles in various quality journals and newspapers, and published many books in which he firmly advocated the importance of democracy, freedom of speech, equality and democratically-elected government. He abhorred any form of fascism or military government and any government propaganda. Ohya Sōichi, a prominent critic, wrote of him in 1952: 'If you try to enter into his head, you will find everything there. It is as if you are in a jungle without daylight, yet you can find a unique ultra-modern highway running through it.'[2] It is not, therefore, surprising to find that many scholars in Japan and overseas became interested in him and wrote about him analysing his philosophical views, particularly on his main theme, the roles of the state and society.

EARLY YEARS

Nyozekan (his original first name was Manjirō and Nyozekan was his pen name) was born in 1875 the 8th year of Meiji, when profound changes were taking place in Japan. Kenneth B. Pyle, who interviewed him in 1964, explained how youths like Nyozekan were influenced by the ferment of ideas in Meiji Japan. Although they benefited from the cultural revolution, Pyle argues, they also became its victims in that they experienced a crisis of identity: while they embraced the traditions and values of Western culture, 'the corresponding negative image of their own heritage involved them in painful inner conflicts'.[3] Nyozekan suffered in childhood from a severe illness of the digestive organs and throughout his life he was prone to illness in varying degrees at different times. This often confined him to his room, although he took advantage of this by studying, reading and writing. He was sent to various private *Juku* (small private schools), such as those run by Tsubouchi Shōyō, where from the age of ten he was nurtured in English literature. He learnt English at a school run by Sugiura Jyūgo. His studies provided a firm basis for the ideas of liberal thinkers.

Around the age of fourteen he was excited by the writings of prominent writers and journalists such as Fukuzawa Yukichi, Tokutomi Sōhō and many members of *Seikyōsha* such as Kuga Katsunan, Miyake Setsurei and Shiga Shigetaka. He was profoundly influenced by the philosophy of Kuga and determined to become a journalist. He was also much influenced by Japanese traditions: Andrew E. Barshay[4] calls him, an 'Edo urbanite'. Born the son of a timber merchant in Fukagawa, Tokyo, he was immersed in the old Edo culture of craftsmen and artisans, whose skills and customs he much admired throughout his life. He also attended private lessons given by scholars of Chinese and Japanese literature. His interest in philosophy began in his mid-twenties. Over many years he studied classical philosophers. He was particularly influenced by British philosophers such as Hobbes, Spencer, Bentham, Mill, Smiles, Hobhouse and Russell, as well as by the Russian Kropotkin. From the age of twelve or thirteen he had read books written in English. He learnt English law and after graduating from Tokyo Hōgakuin, he continued to study criminology. He was also interested in various social movements such as socialism, anarchism and nihilism. In 1903, his wish to become a journalist was finally achieved and he was employed by the newspaper, *Nihon*. However, following a change of management at *Nihon* in 1906 as a result of Kuga's illness he, Miyake Setsurei and other *Seikyōsha* members resigned and joined the newly-established journal *Nihon Oyobi Nihonjin*. In 1908, he was employed by the *Osaka Asahi Shimbun*.

FIRST VISIT TO BRITAIN

He was sent to Britain for the first time by the *Osaka Asahi Shimbun* to report on the Japan-British Exhibition held in London between 14 May and 29 October 1910. Although his knowledge of England was, as he himself modestly admitted in his writing, mainly derived from his reading, his background knowledge of Britain enabled him to give an interesting insight into the country at the time. In addition to his reports on the exhibition in the *Osaka Asahi*, his book, *London* was published in 1912. This was very popular at the time. Some of the points he made in the book are still valid today. During his stay in London, he quickly noticed something which he had often seen in Japan, 'the inequality', that was also prevalent in British society. He noted that the area to the north of Hyde Park near Cumberland Gate was frequented by unemployed and homeless men, while the area to the south from Hyde Park Corner as far as Kensington Gardens and along Rotten Row was filled with upper-class men and women immaculately dressed, riding in carriages pulled by well-groomed horses, showing off their wealth. Along the Victoria Embankment, which had been built at vast expense, he noted destitute and depressed-looking men without any money sitting on benches.

He did not find the House of Commons, despite its reputation as the most democratic parliament in the world, as democratic as he had expected. He noticed that the entrance for the general public was not the same as for Members of Parliament and he reported that they were not given as much freedom of speech as they wanted. He was surprised to find that the House of Lords was more liberal than the Commons, as he was able to use the same entrance door as the Lords and he was not asked to print his name and sign in a book, as he had had to do in entering the House of Commons. Nyozekan, who had been a great admirer of British liberalism and democracy with its long history, was puzzled by some of the inequalities which he saw in London. In his first published novel written at the age of twenty-two in 1898 in the magazine, *Futasuji Michi*, he had drawn attention to the inequality existing in Japan. He could not understand why such conditions had developed and this became one of the main concerns of his life.[5]

Other subjects which attracted Nyozekan while he was in London were railways, newspapers, Speakers' Corner, the prime minister's residence and a small factory in Suffolk. He perceived British 'liberalism' at railway stations, where virtually anyone could get on and off platforms without buying tickets or without being questioned by the police, unlike at most stations on the continent. He also noted that the prime minister's residence was not so different from his own lodgings. It was very modest for the chief minister of a great state such as Britain and he saw this as a healthy sign of liberalism. To Nyozekan, the journalist, British newspapers were the least provocative and sensational in the world at a time when the commercialism of the press had become more prominent. He was concerned that Japanese newspapers seemed to follow the American example and were becoming increasingly sensational. He thought that the British press would not become sensational because of British conservatism, the education of the general public and the high moral standards in society. He was greatly impressed by the activities at Speakers' Corner: he saw this as a way for the British general public to learn about politics and religion and become more aware of the world in general. It also helped members of the public to become articulate and learn to speak in public.

He was particularly impressed by a visit which he made to a small factory in Suffolk. He had wanted to learn if good relationships existed between employer and employees in this most developed and advanced country. He was overjoyed to find that this was the case in this factory. He found that the company provided its employees with help for their general well-being, both physical and mental; he noted the provision of medical assistance, social welfare, housing and leisure facilities. The company had formed a whole village as a single 'company community'. It also provided some aged, long-serving employees with jobs, which were no longer relevant to the company, but which enabled them to remain in work. The employees seemed happy with their conditions and by the equal distribution of wealth in the company. The owner proudly claimed there was not a single socialist among his employees. He was almost in tears, he wrote, to have found in Suffolk conditions which had been common in the Edo period but had long since disappeared in Japan. He noted that the employers treated their employees and families with respect and courtesy. He attached the greatest importance to this visit and regarded it as his most worthwhile activity while staying in London.[6]

Apart from the ongoing Japan–British Exhibition, the year 1910 in London was an eventful one for visitors to Britain, and Nyozekan was fortunate enough to witness some important events. In May one month after his arrival in London, King Edward VII died. He was officially invited to attend the funeral and wrote extensively about the event. He went out in the streets to observe the general public's reaction. Although it was a sad occasion, he felt privileged to see members of the Royal family, and prominent representatives from Britain and abroad, attending the funeral, including Lord Kitchener, the Kaiser and former US President Theodore Roosevelt. Witnessing the whole funeral ceremony and procession brought home to him Britain's long history and traditions. Another event which he observed was quite different. He watched one of the biggest suffragette marches in London that June. Although he wrote apologetically that his motive had been mere curiosity, he was impressed by the orderly march of over 10,000 enthusiasts and by the convincing speeches eloquently given by the leaders. He remarked that even the police were ordered around by the organizers, something that never happened in Japan. He was utterly overwhelmed by seeing a group of lively suffragettes drinking pints of beer out of large glasses, a scene which he had never witnessed in Japan.[7]

NYOZEKAN'S CAREER IN JOURNALISM AND AS A CRITIC

In 1909, Nyozekan published his first book, *The Man With A Forehead*, though initially its title was just '*?*', a question mark. His colleague on the *Tokyo Asahi*, Natsume Sōseki, in reviewing it in that paper wrote: 'its interest owes much to the stimulation that derived from the strange and curious views given by the fictitious men of opinions'. After the so-called *Hakkō* Incident, relating to the Rice Riots in 1918, the *Osaka Asahi* was forced by the Terauchi government to change its liberal stance. This incident was a turning point for many liberal journalists, including Nyozekan, and they resigned *en masse*. This bitter experience seems to have prompted him to use the journalist's pen to fight fiercely against the power of the state. As an independent writer, he needed an outlet and in 1919 he set up his own journal *Warera* ('We, ourselves') with the help of former *Asahi* fellow journalists.

The fifteen years between 1919 and 1934 which followed were a golden period for Nyozekan who was then in his prime. He reached the firm conviction that the state should be part of society, not above it. Through his journal, *Warera*, renamed *Hihan* ('criticism') in 1930, his reputation as a critic became firmly established and many prominent writers, philosophers and academics were induced to contribute to his journal, which became a major organ for the exchange of ideas as well as a symbol of democracy. Tsurumi Shunsuke noted that Nyozekan differed from other critics in that his criticism always included himself and that, whatever era he wrote about, the pre-Meiji period was brought into the discussion.[8] Nyozekan also wrote his most celebrated major works in this period. *The Critique of the Modern State* appeared in 1921; its sister book,

The Critique of Modern Society in 1922; *Rekishi Wo Nejiru* ('History Twisted') in 1930 and *The Critique of Japanese Fascism* in 1932. He was in much demand to give talks on various topics at the invitation of numerous groups and organizations, and to travel as an observer. He made three trips to China and Manchuria, and one to Korea. He contributed many articles to high-quality journals such as *Chūō Kōron* and *Kaizō*.

His independence and education helped Nyozekan to pursue his long career as an independent liberal critic. He only worked for someone else for a total of fourteen years, whereas his independent career spanned half a century. In a radio interview in his late eighties, he spoke proudly of how American journalists had been impressed by his long freelance career without any affiliations; it was very difficult in America, as in Japan, to maintain such an independent career.[9] Barshay compared two of Maruyama Masao's mentors, Nanbara Shigeru and Nyozekan: the former was tied to the narrow and rigid academic world based on his Kantian political philosophy, while the latter was a free man, anti-metaphysical, with an Anglo-Saxon empirical approach.[10]

Despite the fact that Nyozekan constantly criticized government policies and the repressive measures taken to control 'dangerous thoughts', he seems to have been left alone by the authorities, while many other journalists were subjected to harsh treatment from them. He was nevertheless always one of the targets of the 'Thought Police' although his articles were only rarely officially proscribed. The *Hihan*'s December 1931 issue on the Manchurian Incident and its May 1932 issue on the establishment of Manchukuo, which were regarded by the authorities as disturbing public order and fuelling anti-war sentiment, were banned and *The Critique of Japanese Fascism* in 1932 was immediately suppressed. Ohya Sōichi, who was often a co-speaker with Nyozekan at conferences, describes him as 'the philosopher whose life-line is a curve'. He explains that one of the things in which Nyozekan excelled was the oblique way that he used to describe things. This meant that, even if what he was trying to say would have been harsh and uncompromising if said directly, it would not have struck the reader as so dogmatic and radical. Nyozekan compared his tactics with the more direct approach of Bertrand Russell.[11] This is well illustrated by a caricature of Nyozekan entitled 'The target that has never been hit: *Nyozekan Odori* ('dance')'. This showed him dodging copies of his books and journals being thrown at him by men, apparently from the 'Thought Police', equipped with some elaborate tools to scrutinize his work closely.

Another turning point in his life came on 22 November 1933 when an incident profoundly affected him and changed his tactics for the rest of his life. He was for the first time taken into custody at the local police station and interrogated by the 'Thought Police', who questioned his relationship with a former communist party member. Although he was released on the same day it must have been a severe blow. He had hitherto stuck to his practice of never getting physically involved. After his release he openly declared that he was totally against communism and that he had always been, and would remain, a law-abiding citizen. Soon afterwards, in February 1934, he shut down his journal *Hihan*. After fifteen years of doing battle even if indirectly against censorship, the 'Thought Police' and successive governments, he was exhausted and wanted some peace and quiet.

Nevertheless, he continued his campaign, though in a much less energetic way, by concentrating on examining the roots of Japanese culture. He wanted to prove that in ancient times Japan had been democratic like Britain. The current undemocratic fascist system in Japan was, he argued, derived from German ideology, particularly that of Hegel, and followed the German model. This was the main theme which dominated the rest of his life. He concentrated on studying Japanese culture and in 1938 his book *Nihon-teki Seikaku* (Japanese character) was published. His study of *Spencer* which appeared in 1939 was a biography of this liberal thinker. He contributed regularly from 1934 until 1940 to the *Yomiuri Shimbun*'s column, 'One topic a day'. In these articles and in articles in other newspapers and journals he still criticized the state, although mildly and indirectly,

SECOND VISIT TO BRITAIN

Nyozekan was now an established scholar of Japanese culture and it was in this capacity that his second golden age began in the 1950s. Some Western scholars, including Arnold J. Toynbee, interviewed him. In March 1956, when he was eighty he was invited to America to give a lecture tour lasting three months; after this he travelled to Europe for the second time after an interval of forty-six years, visiting London, at his specific request. His admiration for Britain was just as firm as in 1910. In the series of articles which he wrote upon his return to Japan in July that year, his overall impression of Britain was of a country that in every sphere maintained its traditions. He[12] was encouraged to find that most things were just as they had been five decades earlier. After having visited America he was pleased to see that Britain had not become Americanized. He had found everything in America tasteless, informal, divorced from tradition and without history, whereas in Britain he thought everything tasteful, traditional and historical. He wondered how these two Anglo-Saxon peoples could be so different. His assumption was that the Americans knew that they could not possibly compete with the long-established European civilization, and so deliberately tried to break away from such old traditions in order to seek their own identity. He expressed great uneasiness and concern about Japan, where he thought people were pushing everything through in a tasteless American way, as for instance in the reconstruction of Tokyo. There could not be as ugly a city as Tokyo anywhere in the world; it was a jumble of American styles, totally disregarding Japan's long traditions, history, climate and environment. In London, instead of repairing bombed office buildings, the authorities were giving priority to new public housing in the suburbs in order to cope with the desperate housing shortage. Tokyo, on the other hand, which had been flattened during the war, had no city planning, and opportunists were trying to exploit the situation for their own benefit. Commenting on the tall glass buildings in New York, he pointed out that the idea of using glass buildings had originated in Britain as early as 1851. He thus praised Britain as a country which retained the best of the old but was also innovative. [13]

In this period, Nyozekan was invited to take part in numerous dialogues with other prominent scholars and particularly in the last decade of his life he was frequently interviewed by NHK radio and television. He seems to have attracted many followers and admirers who clubbed together, and to his great satisfaction presented to him in 1956 his houses in 1939 and 1954. He continued to work until his death in Odawara in 1969 a few weeks before his ninety-fourth birthday. In these final years he finished a number of books on a variety of subjects, including his autobiography (1950) and *Ushinawareta Nihon* ('The Lost Japan') (1952). He also continued to contribute to various quality journals and newspapers. In 1948 he was awarded the Order of Cultural Merit (*Bunka Kunshō*) and in 1953 he was made an honorary citizen of Tokyo (*Tokyo Meiyō Tōmin*).

THE INFLUENCE OF BRITISH IDEAS ON NYOZEKAN

In his writings he gave much prominence to his views of Britain, the British and their characteristics as well as to the roles of the state and society and the importance of equality. His image of Britain as a model society and the British as model people, which he constantly compared with other countries and peoples, was an idealized one. He was for ever comparing English ideas with German thinking which he could not abide. The Japanese adoption of German systems in almost all spheres in the mid-Meiji period was the target of his fiercest attacks throughout his life. He blamed this tendency for the major disasters and aggressive policies of the Meiji, Taishō and Shōwa eras. He urged Japan to return from German to British systems. Writing in 1918 on his favourite topic, the role of the state, he said that the British regarded the state as 'a necessary evil' and 'a private company' for profit-making for shareholders. Thus, while there were times when the state behaved brutally towards other countries or people, such actions were done for the shareholders, i.e. the general public; as a result the state would never ignore individuals. He was convinced that Britain would never become an ultra-nationalist country like Germany and Japan, totally ignoring individuals. He was opposed to the Japanese government's repressive policies, to the German concept of the state and to Hegel's philosophy.[14]

After Japan's defeat in the Second World War he found that his convictions had been correct and he seemed as a result to have gained more confidence in his beliefs. In 1948, writing an article almost identical to the one he had written in 1918, he strongly recommended the Japanese to emulate such commendable British characteristics. He regretted that, after the mid-Meiji period, nobody had listened to what he had said about Britain, and he felt that, had the Japanese taken his advice at that time, there would not have been such a period of disaster.[15] Soon after the end of the war, he suggested that, just as the would-be leaders of socialist parties were sent to the Soviet Union to be trained, potential liberal leaders of democracy in Japan should be sent to either America or Britain to study true democracy and liberalism, of which most Japanese did not have enough knowledge and experience. This was a good opportunity for Japan to start again from scratch: the Japanese should emulate the leaders at the beginning of the Meiji period and travel to the West to study anew, just as the young Tōgo Heihachirō had been sent to Britain in early Meiji to undertake naval studies: 'The Japanese should shed their pride and be humble enough to emulate the spirit of early Meiji and start all over again for the sake of the new nation and become a true liberal democratic country.'[16]

His main theme before and after the war, 'Return from German to British ways', was repeated over and over again. His draft manuscript dated 11 November 1950 entitled, 'From German to British Study', prepared for a speech given at an occasion for Chūō University, lists the topics in historical order which he wanted to cover. He wrote an almost identical article in April 1969, about six months before his death: even then he thought it necessary to repeat the same message. Indeed, he said 'Even as early as the Taishō period, I used to advocate the idea of "returning from the German to the British system", but, it is sad that, even now, 50 years on, I still have to repeat the same message.' As usual keeping Hegel's philosophy in mind, he said: 'To maintain independence and individualism, it is important not to worship philosophy and treat it like a religion. The British kept religion separate from empirical, proof-oriented philosophy. Studying must be done scientifically and not treated as a religion.'[17]

He even took the opportunity to express similar views at dinners to which he was invited. Ienaga Saburō made a note of such an occasion in March 1951, when Nyozekan said that he had wished British sociology had been more popular in Japan. When scholars of German philosophy had tried to explain the concepts of sociology they could do no more than write shallow introductions without any substance. They should start from first principles by studying the origin of British sociology.[18] In 1967, when he was asked by a specialist, who compared him with Bentham and Russell, what was his message to young Japanese people currently studying English thought, his reply was the same: 'Since these students have been educated under the German system, they must first discard what they have learnt which revolves solely around ideology and theory, and then study totally anew, from ABC, English thought based on experience, practice and empiricism.'[19]

Nyozekan also liked to emphasize similarities between Japan and Britain, as though trying to justify his conviction that the aggressive conduct of the undemocratic Japanese military government was totally out of character. He repeatedly pointed out that, just as Japan had adopted Confucianism rather than Taoism, Japan in early Meiji adopted English utilitarianism rather than continental philosophy. To him, this was a natural choice for Japan, as it was merely a continuation of Japanese tradition, based on realism, not ideology.[20] Nyozekan is often compared with Bertrand Russell and seems to have been proud of the comparison. He admitted in 1951 that, when he had read Russell's books some thirty years earlier, he had been struck by the fact that the philosopher had said exactly what he had wanted to say himself, but had written in a much better way than he could have done. He thought that both of them might have used the same sources to reach similar conclusions. He was proud to admit that he had often been regarded as an eccentric like Russell, but he had stubbornly determined not to change his stance. Russell's writings often pleased him: he thought some of Russell's amusing remarks were similar to *Rakugo* (Japanese comic story-telling). He noted that his views and some of Russell's such as those on the roles of the state and on Greek and German philosophy were very similar.[21] His anglophile sentiments led him to note similarities when after the war Japanese scholars produced ideas similar to those of British writers. One example was Nakaya Ukichirō, a scientist, whose arguments were always based either on substantial evidence or on common sense derived from experience and realistic assessments. He was so impressed by Nakaya that he commented on the latter's book in an article in a journal.[22]

CONCLUSION

These are only a few examples of Nyozekan's views and impressions of Britain, the British and their characteristics, but they are a fairly accurate portrayal of what he believed. When he came to Britain for the first time in 1910 at the age of thirty-four, he was yet to establish himself as a writer and had had little experience. However, on the basis of his wide-ranging education and his discerning mind and curiosity, together with an ability to see things objectively in the widest context, he was a remarkable observer. When he came to London for the second time in 1956 at the age of eighty, he was regarded, if not as a sage, at least as a significant and experienced journalist and philosopher. His beliefs and observations on Britain were based on his two short stays in London and on the writings about Britain in which he had immersed himself over several decades. His image of Britain was an idealized one. His tendency to exaggerate British good points and overlook British failings was partly due to his reaction against the German system and post-war Americanization which he abhorred. He was a die-hard anglophile and one of the most distinguished liberal philosophers and journalists that Japan has ever produced.

PART VI

Long-term Residents in Japan, Judo Pioneers and a Philanthropist

40

Dr Thomas Baty, 1869-1954: Legal Adviser to the Japanese Foreign Ministry, 1916-41

MARTIN GORNALL

Dr Thomas Baty

INTRODUCTION

REVERED IN JAPAN, reviled in Britain, Dr Thomas Baty, Legal Adviser to the Japanese Foreign Ministry from 1916 to 1941, was a complex figure of contradictions and extremes. A pacifist fascinated by war, a male lawyer and female writer, he was combative in argument yet gentle and kind, passionate yet mischievously cerebral, cynical yet unworldly, prosaic and poetic, radical and reactionary, homely yet erudite, with a deep love of music. An archetypal post-modern figure of oppositions, he carefully constructed the persona of the élitist, anti-utilitarian, Tory sage, 'Dr Baty', who believed in law as a numinous revelation of organic society and the Absolute; and that of Irene Clyde, feminist polemicist and author, who held a utilitarian position on the infinite malleability of the individual nature by nurture, and espoused a universal gender as relative psycho-cultural construct independent of biological sex. His was a protean, self-referential linguistic style, which, ranging from the perfunctorily anecdotal to rigorously analytic, from the fervidly lyrical to dryly ironical, mirrored a mode of perception in which the literal moved in and out of phase with the implied, evincing the relationship between identity and gender.

YOUTH AND EDUCATION

Thomas Baty was born in 1869, into an established cabinet-making family, at Stanwix, a genteel suburb of Carlisle. Indeed, he still owned business premises and some houses in Fisher Street there until his death in 1954. His father William, died at Christmas, 1876. Thereafter, his maternal uncles, Joseph and William Matthews, together with his mother, Mary, were significant influences in the upbringing which he shared with his sister, Anne. Baty regarded his home as a microcosm of enlightened society. A common ideal of gender informed diversity of function, each mixing freely with his or her own circle. The family is notable for strong-minded, independent women.

Baty's own account of his life is to be found in the posthumous *Alone in Japan*,[1] which appears to have been thrown together in 1946, when his identity and integrity were threatened. By his own exacting literary standards, the book is uneven, being an eclectic mix of opinions on Japanese militarism and culture, gender, aesthetic idealism, law, and personal reminiscences. Since Baty self-consciously deployed the gamut of rhetorical strategies, his writings, including the published oeuvre of Dr Baty the lawyer, and Irene Clyde, the novelist and 'extreme feminist', must be interpreted with critical circumspection and not treated as 'privileged discourses'.

Baty paints a picture of a boy precocious in reading, reasoning and aesthetic experience, but virtually innumerate. However, after studying with a Mr Williamson, he spent eight years at Carlisle Grammar School (1880-88),[2] from which he obtained a Hastings exhibition in mathematics to Queens College, Oxford. Having transferred to law, he graduated in 1892. He then spent a year at Trinity, Cambridge, as Whewell scholar, and was temperamentally attracted to the Idealism which was soon to be supplanted in academic philosophy by the mathematical logic of his contemporary, Bertrand Russell. Back at Oxford, this time at University College, he received a BCL degree in 1895 and became Stowell Fellow, a position which lapsed in 1901.[3] He was admitted to the Inner Temple in January 1896, and was called to the Bar, not, as he claimed, in 1895, but in November, 1898.[4] In addition to the 'day job' in Lord Romer's chambers, Baty then promoted his academic career through books, and articles in the British and American legal press, receiving doctorates from both universities.

LAWYER AND FEMINIST

He set out his stall in *International Law in South Africa*[5] (1900), based on his Oxford lectures. His view, echoing Common Law concepts, and supported by close analysis of cases, was that *public* international law emerges as precedent from negotiation between equal states, and must be based on observable facts rather than 'intentions'. The jurist's role is to *describe* established practice. He rejected Austinian theory that law is the command of a sovereign authority, backed by coercion, as but utilitarian tyranny clothed in proletarian democratic forms. Internationally, he held that there can be no power higher than the sovereign state. Strong nations will adopt such ploys as 'continuous voyage' or 'pacific blockade' to override the rights of neutral states and their ships. He regarded such bodies as The League of Nations or the UN as doomed to failure when they cross the interests of powerful belligerents. Analogously, he objected, in *War and Its Conduct and Legal Results*[6] to extensions of state power over the individual in war, or, in *Vicarious Liability*,[7] to employers being held liable for their employee's torts. He explored the relations between *private* international jurisdictions in *Polarized Law*[8] (posited on a mathematical metaphor!).

From 1905 to 1916, numerous letters of his were published in *The Times*. In 1913, a prolific year, his letter was the only one published in a South American Supplement, supporting *The Times* case against extension of the Monroe Doctrine in Mexico. From 1905 to 1915, he served as Secretary to the International Law Association, arranging its international conferences, and reorganizing its library at his own expense. He was a lifetime Member, and his services were recognized by a large silver 'loving cup'.

In the pre-war period, Baty played an active role as an anti-socialist feminist, and advocate of female emancipation. He founded the *Aethnic Union*,[9] a feminist organization loosely associated with Theosophical beliefs (although Baty was not a member of the Theosophical Society until the 1930s[10]), and an offshoot of *The Freewoman*. Advancing the feminine as an aesthetic ideal for a common gender irrespective of biological sexuality, in 1909 he published, as Irene Clyde, *Beatrice the Sixteenth*,[11] a very modern novel in which a doctor meets with an accident in a desert and finds herself on an oblique plane of existence in a Grecian dreamscape, peopled almost exclusively by women. In a conflation of the Utopian/ Swiftean tradition with the exoticism of Rider Haggard, the heroine finds herself in a country uncannily like Japan advising potentates on the conduct of war. There is a sub-plot of lesbian 'love interest'. Barbarian children are bartered for carpets, and nurtured into conformity with Clyde's rather masculine feminine gender ideal.

LEGAL ADVISER TO JAPANESE FOREIGN MINISTRY

In the autumn of 1915, already an established authority on international law, Baty was recruited, on Shidehara's[12] recommendation, to succeed the American, Denison, as adviser to the Japanese Foreign Ministry. A member of the Japan Society, Baty had always been an aficionado of Japanese culture. He regarded the Heian period as congenially aristocratic, but doomed, as men and women, without distinction of gender, luxuriated in a sybaritic life of elegance, charm and aesthetic cultivation, exchanging poems and partaking of artistic delights. Since England had surrendered itself to utilitarian tyranny, in his late forties, he no longer felt at home there.

Although unworldly, he drove a hard bargain, demanding a salary of 20,000 yen, and settling at 15,000,[13] a figure later doubled, and agreed a five-year contract. Accompanied by his aged mother, his sister Anne, and his cousin Esther Matthews, Baty sailed on the *Katori Maru* and arrived in Japan on 29 May 1916. On the journey he had found that not all Japanese were elegant and charming. While his official residence at Kasumigaseki was being prepared, he and his entourage travelled in Japan, but his mother died in August. Easing himself into his duties, in 1917, Baty, a loyal Englishman, provided Lord Bryce[14] with an assessment of Japanese attitudes to Germany, reporting that, despite German influence in Japanese law, the army and medical profession, Germans were disliked, but not persecuted as they were in England.

At the time of Denison's death, Japan had been at loggerheads with America over immigration into California,[15] and sought an English adviser who would help consolidate her post-war international position on a sound legal footing. From the Versailles Peace Conferences of 1919 onwards, Baty provided theoretical support, whilst the day-to-day business was handled by Professor Tachi.[16] Baty described his duties as 'nominal' and 'light', but will have assisted Shidehara's moderate, internationalist agenda in China, particularly when the Anglo–Japanese Alliance was superseded, under American pressure, by the Nine Power Treaty after the Washington Naval negotiations of 1922. The Batys went on home leave in 1923, fortuitously missing the Kanto Earthquake.

In Japan, Baty was free to pursue his feminist convictions, and had the means to publish a periodical, *Urania*,[17] unknown to his Japanese friends, and family. He covered his tracks, 'laundering' his identity through Bombay. In association with cronies from the *Aethnic Union* days, Baty promoted through the magazine his ideal of a common, feminized, gender, irrespective of biological sex. It reproduced accounts of women's achievements, and of cross-dressing, and spontaneous sex-changes. Upper-class lesbians who had come 'out' were of particular interest, for Baty advocated a mutual adjustment of psycho–cultural gender-stereotypes and sexuality. He declared that he had always passionately desired to be a 'lady', but out of love for, and admiration for, an inclusive ideal of the feminine. Opposing entrenched militant feminism, however, Baty insists, '. . . the essential basis of women's rights is the removal of all artificial obstacles to the attainment of a perfect character' rather than 'women's coteries' based on a 'mere selfishness – or a desire for more power and greater amenities'.[18]

Through the Twenties, he built a wide international acquaintance, and bought his own summer house on the shore of Lake Chūzenji. He published *Supreme Court Practice*,[19] and contributed to American legal journals articles on such topics as the obligations of extinct states and sovereignty, which were relevant to Manchuria. In addition to *Urania*, in 1926 he issued a Swiftean open letter on *Love and Marriage*, in which he argued that sex thwarts individual fulfilment, and that parthenogenesis would be a more satisfactory alternative. He personally preferred contemplating heraldic arms.

It was in 1927 in Geneva that Baty took a 'hands-on' role, advising the Japanese delegation,[20] which tried to intercede between wrangling British and Americans.[21] His claim that he was a mere 'fly on the coach wheel' is perhaps modest to the point of disingenuousness. However, with Shidehara's internationalist agenda under increasing pressure from military hot-heads,[22] it was over Manchuria, the League of Nations and Lytton, that Baty played the kind of active role usually undertaken by Professor Tachi. Following the Mukden Incident of 18 September 1931, Baty, believing the official Kwantung Army account that the railway had been attacked by Chinese bandits (which Lytton regarded as plausible[23]), drafted the Five Points (October 1931), by which Japan sought a bilateral settlement with the Nationalist government, and scripted Yoshizawa's[24] thwarted speech to the League in November.

Following the publication of the Lytton Report, Baty drafted *Japan's Observations*,[25] in which it was claimed that China was not an 'organized state', was not continuous with the defunct Chinese empire, and had never exercised authority in Manchuria. In the *IMTFE* transcript,[26] Shiratori[27] testified that Baty wrote it, and that he himself merely translated it into Japanese. The authorship is evident on stylistic grounds: 'But all these observations and conclusions are enveloped in a mist of optimism the glamour of which is certain to be misleading to anyone who does not know the true facts.'[28] Malcolm Kennedy,[29] who spent three hours reading the draft, suspected, from an obscure quotation from Deuteronomy, that Baty or Medley[30] was responsible. This was subsequently confirmed when Medley denied that it had been him.

The *IMTFE* transcript suggests that General Araki[31] suffered amnesia over Baty and his advice. It is put to Araki, on Kido's evidence,[32] that Baty went further than Tachi by advising the cabinet privately that

Japanese military action in establishing Manchukuo was against both treaty and customary international law, and that Araki knew this. However, in circumstances in which the internationalist grouping within the Foreign Ministry was called upon repeatedly to defend *post facto* the actions of the Kwantung Army, Baty provided a very professional public apologia, through influential press articles, *Japan's Observations* and elsewhere. The British never forgave him.

By 1930, the Batys were part of an extensive international social round, of diplomats, ministers, journalists and Japanese colleagues. The Kennedys and Byases[33] were close friends. Baty entertained at the Tokyo Club, or, with Anne, at home, which gained the reputation of being an international salon. To promote informal international cultural contact, Baty established the *Kōhakubaikai Society*, which was commended by General Piggott.[34] Malcolm Kennedy gives an account of a jaunt in the country, which included Shiratori, Makino,[35] the Kennedys and assorted diplomats. At the same time, Baty's less orthodox friendships included Richard Ponsonby-Fane,[36] to whose death-bed he went on a last pilgrimage in 1937.

The *Kennedy Diaries*[37] portray a close international community in Tokyo, with an understanding of the China situation 'on the ground', as against remote, ill-informed home governments. For instance, Baty's view that China was anarchic appears to have been universally shared, by the British Ambassador, Sir Francis Lindley[38] and others, Kennedy regarding it as shameful that home governments (notably the Dutch) insisted on regarding China as an organized state for mercenary reasons to underwrite their treaty rights.

Kennedy provides a snapshot of the Manchuria period in Tokyo, describing a dinner party at the Batys on 4 February 1932, at which guests included Sir Francis and Lady Lindley, Shidehara (Foreign Minister to 31 December, 1931), Baron Hayashi,[39] and Baron Bassompierre, Belgian Ambassador, among others. Lindley was delayed by work on the Three Power proposals, and Vice Minister Nagai[40] had to withdraw due to pressure of work. On other occasions, Baty was summoned during dinner to advise on international crises as they unfolded.

In summer, the Batys would transfer their entire domestic establishment, presided over by *major domo* Mitamura, to their lakeside retreat at Chūzenji.[41] This Westernized Japanese house had its own private beach and jetties. The guests would dine formally downstairs, and retire to upstairs rooms giving onto a covered veranda overlooking the lake. Marjorie, Baty's cousin's daughter, has vivid memories of these 'magical' summers, at which the family, including the now-married Esther Lewis, would gather. She recalls Baty as a very kind man with a gentle manner and voice, who would lie prone on his jetty while fish fed from his hand. He had a rowing-boat made for her, and would chat to her over tea while nursing his favourite cats, the ginger Kinkan, or Tatsu. Although a strict vegetarian, he would insist that his guests enjoyed the best cuts of veal. Idyllic days would be spent on picnics and walks, or else sailing. Dmitrii Abrikossov,[42] ex-White Russian diplomat, recalls in his memoirs[43] this annual refuge from the pressures of life, the sun-sets, solitaire, and Baty's cats. Marjorie remembers 'Dmitrii A' at his desk on the veranda writing letters, and still has one of the silver cats which he presented to Baty in token of thanks each year. 'Sendo-San' would sail Baty's yacht, *The Ark*, while the two men luxuriated in the atmospherics. Abrikossov maintained a secret box in which there was always a round Nestlé's chocolate to be found, even in his absence. The Batys entertained a number of notabilities at Chuzenji, including Sir Charles Eliot,[44] and Sir John Latham.[45]

During the 1930s, neighbours among the British community included the Craigies[46] and the Morlands.[47] Esther was a skilled sailor, and a leading light at the Nantai Yacht Club. Marjorie took part in the yacht club regatta, winning the novice's event in 1940. In 1941, as the situation in Shanghai worsened, and the Lewises were transferred to Singapore, Anne wrote to Marjorie that the Batys had lent her personal boat, *Mercury*, to the Morlands, and mentioned that its name-board would need repainting before Marjorie's return. There was no hint of imminent war, or that the family had spent its last summer at Chūzenji, never to meet together again.

The Batys spent 1934 in England, and Baty says that he did what little he could to explain Japan's position, presumably to members of the International Law Association. Members included Sir John Simon, whom Baty claimed had been a friend since their Oxford days. A number of his books had been dedicated to Simon with permission. However, the papers of possible contacts have proved unyielding.

During the Thirties, in addition to his official duties, Baty kept up a prodigious work rate. *Canons of International Law*[48] came out in 1930, and Irene Clyde's major feminist polemic, *Eve's Sour Apples*[49] in 1934. *Urania* appeared throughout the decade. Through the American legal literature, he influenced Edwin Borchard, Professor of International Law at Yale. In 1936, at a meeting of American jurists[50] chaired by Henry L. Stimson[51] (who had condemned Manchukuo), the discussion contrasted America's political isolationism with its economic internationalism, in the light of American proposals to impose equal embargoes on belligerents in conflict. Borchard cited Thomas Baty, who needed no introduction to the meeting, on the futility of coercing nations into virtue.

Towards the end of the 1930s, when militarism took hold, and the international community fragmented, all began to change. Baty's official position complicated his British friendships, as the Foreign Office in London came to learn about him from afar and he was suspected of 'anti-British activities'.

In 1938, Katayama Sakai sent a letter to Downing Street[52] suggesting that Baty should receive Seventieth Birthday congratulations for his contribution to Anglo-Japanese understanding. The Foreign Office condescendingly found the style of this supposed nonentity amusing. W. Davies,[53] a young man Baty mentions as 'quietly taking things in', reported that Baty was the most eminent Englishman in Japan, after the Ambassador and George Sansom,[54] and that, an honourable man, he had been conscientious in discharging his duties. Davies suggested, however, that Robert Craigie did not entirely 'approve' of him, and indicated that some of his guests, including Araki, were prominent militarists. Hoyer-Millar[55] in London advised Downing Street:

> He has, however, become more Japanese than the Japanese and he obtained certain notoriety by the defence of Japan's aggression in Manchuria and by an attack on the Lytton Commission. In fact, any services he has rendered have been to Japan and to Japan alone, and to us he may be regarded as having done disservice rather than otherwise.

SECOND WORLD WAR AND AFTER

In 1942, soon after the outbreak of the War in the Pacific, Robert Craigie and his staff, having been confined at the embassy, were marched unceremoniously with the remnants of the British community onto a ship bound for Lorenzo Marques.[56] The Batys were old, and had lived in Japan since 1916. Baty wrote that he never lost faith in peace, and did not hear of the ugly side of Japanese militarism until it was too late. Their nearest family, the Lewises, were chased out of Singapore by the Japanese and lost everything. Esther and Marjorie were fortunate to get on the last refugee ship, whilst Esther's husband escaped on a junk, bargained for his life with Chinese pirates, and made it to Bombay, where he later became English Electric manager.

The Foreign Office case against Baty appears to have been given impetus, in 1942, by Sir Robert Craigie in a despatch hot from his arrival at Lorenzo Marques,[57] alleging that the Batys had refused repatriation. In 1943, hoping to contact the Lewises, Anne sent a letter via the Turkish Ambassador and British Embassy in Ankara, to English Electric in London. The letter, dutifully intercepted, was taken as evidence that Baty used his office at the Foreign Ministry. A Japanese article in the *Yomiuri*, in which Baty purports to express confidence in the Japanese fighting spirit, was translated by Arthur Waley, who advised that Baty might mean no more than that Japan was in a mess, but would recover. Nevertheless, W.E. Beckett,[58] whose slim monograph on private international law[59] echoes Baty's earlier *Polarized Law*, concludes 'there is no doubt that Dr Baty has committed treason', and that the sworn testimony of 'British diplomats in

Japan' would be sufficient proof.

By 1945, there was uncertainty within the Foreign Office[60] as to which department was dealing with Baty. Craigie's information was crucial, yet evidence that Baty had acquired Japanese nationality, that his passport had been impounded, and that he had refused repatriation had gone astray. Ground now shifted to articles in *Contemporary Japan*. MacDermot[61] (who was investigating civilian 'undesirables') remarked casually, 'I suppose that old Dr Baty is a traitor'. Baty was dismissed as 'old and senile', or else 'not normal', it being alleged that he dressed as a geisha in public. This hints at an underlying cause of Foreign Office animosity towards him. His guilt being presumed: 'It is now for consideration whether action should be taken against him.'

A key file of 1946[62] shows the way in which the Foreign Office consensus is established through the bureaucratic process, Baty's articles in *Contemporary Japan* being regarded as a 'sustained and insidious attack on British and American policy'. H. Sawbridge[63] questions the MI5 view that Baty is 'senile and eccentric', and favours his removal to India. L.H. Foulds[64] asserts that Baty's 'high treason seems to be clearly established', but Esler Dening,[65] lamenting this impossible dilemma, regards the hanging of a seventy-seven-year-old 'abnormal type' as 'sound law but bad politics'. Beckett points out that Baty merely 'served the Japanese' and adds: 'As far as I know, Dr Baty did not at any time actually try and acquire Japanese nationality.' He tries to concur with Dening, who slaps him down. Dening's recommendation is that Baty should NOT be allowed to remain in Japan, that SCAP (in apparent contradiction) should be informed that his 'facilities as a British subject' have been withdrawn, and Bevin (Foreign Secretary) informed that Baty is a traitor. At this time, Beckett removed documents to assist a 'purge' of the Institute of International Law.

By now, the Batys' old neighbour, Morland, reported from the British liaison mission in Tokyo that 'it has been difficult to obtain evidence against Baty'. Of the incriminating articles, he says: 'Baty has been at pains to convey the impression of an objective historian and international lawyer and to avoid outright vilification or unmistakably treasonable statements. He presents his arguments with great subtlety and with much learning.' The Japanese conceded that Baty had enjoyed the use of his office, and 3000 yen a month, but that his title had been merely nominal. Morland claimed that he had been a paid propagandist on a par with William Joyce. He reported that Baty was under 'loose control' at Atami and recommended that he should be shipped home to stand trial.

Under interrogation by Lt Colonel Figgess[66] for MI5, Baty admitted having written the articles and having received his salary, but said that he spent the war working on 'private papers'. He then detailed his movements, ending at the Kanaya Hotel in Nikko, where his sister died in 1945. He wished to join his family in Bombay, where he expected to practise law. Figgess remarked genially: 'This seems pretty spry for an old boy of 77.'

In defiance of Baty's wishes, the Indian solution was resisted, in September 1946, by Alvary Gascoigne,[67] who regarded Baty as 'deranged mentally' but dangerously persuasive.[68] Bevin was informed that Baty was a traitor, but should be allowed to stay in Japan, and SCAP was informed that Baty's passport would be withheld.

By October 1946,[69] Beckett had been replaced by Mr Vallat,[70] who exercised a moderating influence. He was against plans, advanced by Esler Dening, to use unattributed, off-the-record press briefings to smear Baty. His view was, and is to this day,[71] 'If Dr Baty is not going to be tried for treason, he ought not to be held out to public hatred and contempt as a traitor.' He added, 'The principle that a man who has not been convicted of a criminal offence, may nevertheless be punished by administrative action is, to my mind, unsound.' Indeed, he thought that Baty might have a case for libel. MacDermot concurred with Vallat's opinion, and Sawbridge followed suit. On the other hand, there was pressure from Tokyo to use Baty as an example to the Japanese, and to satisfy American and Australian critics that the British had not gone soft on 'Eton and Balliol'.

In late 1946, the International Law Association tried to intercede on Baty's behalf,[72] so that he could join his family in India, but was informed that he was a traitor, and that his passport had been withdrawn. So was its loyalty to its past Secretary.

When Baty's situation was conveyed by SCAPHQ to the Japanese Foreign Ministry, Mr Kishi[73] described the British decision as 'stupid, foolish and harsh'[74] and conveyed the support of Yoshida[75] and Shidehara. Yoshida wrote:[76]

> While the measures seem uncalled for, yet you are, I hope, maintaining the usual serenity of mind which we all so deeply admire in you. We know that you have only upheld the cause of truth from a dispassionate scholarly point of view. Servant of light, as you are, it is indeed seldom, I regret to say, that such a servant receives a deserving reward.

In 1948, Yoshida raised Baty's case with Gascoigne,[77] who regarded Yoshida as 'likeable enough', but 'an intriguer and trouble-maker' trying to split Britain and America. Dening found Yoshida 'silly', and thundered of Baty: '. . . this foolish old man should consider himself very lucky to have got off so lightly'.

For the rest of his life, Baty corresponded with his family, with old friends like Dmitrii Abrikossov, and latterly with Edmund Blunden,[78] a fellow Queen's man, who knew Baty through Baty's wartime work on early Western attitudes to Japan, published in *Monumenta Nipponica*. Baty informed Blunden[79] that he had been cut by Morland and George Sansom, but seemed genuinely perplexed about the cause of this ostracism, speculating that it was because of anti-Soviet articles in *Contemporary Japan*, in which he had accused Churchill and Roosevelt of helping Stalin to establish the Soviet Empire. In exchanges with his old friend Tsutsui Kiyoshi,[80] he was genuinely mystified as to how the militarists had come to power, and the Pacific War had come about.[81] Dmitrii Abrikossov, like others who actually knew the man, regarded the British charges as unjust and vindictive:

> . . . there was nothing of a traitor in him, his only fault having been in living in an artificial world created by his own idealism and kindness of heart, where there was no room for hate and hostility.[82]

Many other old friends, such as John Latham[83] or Hugh Macmillan,[84] gave Baty the polite brush-off.[85] Others expunged him completely. A letter from the ILA of 16 July 1952[86] states:

> . . . when on December 9th 1946 we sought, in response to a cable sent by you, to assist your desire to get to India, we received information which led us to think that in the circumstances existing at that time it would be best if the publications of this Association (having its seat in London) did not continue to carry your name.

The ILA archive has no record of this.

During his later years, Baty came under increasing financial pressure. The thirteen codicils to his will map his declining fortunes, through diminishing provision for his loyal servants, and the mortgaging, then sale, of his house at Chuzenji. During this period, the American diplomat, Cabot Coville[87] tried to help Baty secure the position of Chancellor of 'New Zealand University', and provided Baty with financial help and advice.[88]

Baty died on 9 February 1954, in a cottage at Ichinomiya, where he took a keen interest in the local community. At eighty-five, he had just corrected the proofs of *International Law In Twilight*,[89] in which he recapitulated the principal legal themes which he had developed consistently over a lifetime, and, presciently, related them to the post-war world order. It is in this context that his denial that he collaborated should be read. He was, he claimed, merely enjoying the private sphere of personal action allowed to individuals during war, which he had expounded in print for half a century. The views expressed are, in style and content, consistent with those which were regarded as incriminating in *Contemporary Japan*,[90] occasional jarring rhetoric suggesting 'sexing up' by another hand. To present arguments with 'great subtlety and with much learning' was, to anyone familiar with his work, his habitual method, and not a ploy to conceal some treasonous purpose. Baty was opposed to totalitarianism of all complexions, and foresaw the danger of the Cold War. The British popular press[91] vilified him in terms familiar from Foreign Office files, as a traitor and broken man; yet *The Times* obituary, evidently by an old friend, gave a more measured view of his life and achievement. He never lost his serenity of mind or mischievous humour.

ASSESSMENT

Despite his strictures on American political action, he made a significant contribution to American legal debate. Even in modern American legal literature, he is cited on discrimination in the workplace (Vicarious Liability), the status of ABM treaties between America and the defunct Soviet Union, and in interpretations of sovereignty under the Montevideo Convention.

The complexity of Baty's life, illustrious career and ignominious demise, illustrates the problematic nature of such apparently straightforward notions as loyalty and betrayal, and the scope allowed to individual thought and expression in maintaining the intellectual vigour of a free society. Pertinently, Baty's case turned upon interpretations of international law which are still, in the age of globalization, highly contentious. In so many areas, ranging through feminism, to theories of Law, and the fate of collective security, Baty, with his roots in Victorian England, anticipated the issues which were to dominate our own times with greater urgency than ever. He is, warts and all, a pre-eminently prophetic figure.

41

Samuel Heaslett, 1875-1947: Missionary and Bishop

A. HAMISH ION

Samuel Heaslett

INTRODUCTION

P R O V I D E N C E or fate could have hardly handed Samuel Heaslett[1] a worse time to be a missionary bishop in Japan than the twenty years that stretched from 1922 to 1942. During these two halcyon decades the placid world of the mission compound was rent apart by a succession of crises of great magnitude that evoke the Biblical images of wind, earthquake and fire of 1 Kings,[2] or, transferred to the Japanese setting, typhoon and flood, earthquake and fire.[3] Heaslett has been described 'an example of steadfastness in service'[4] who faithfully served in Japan through all perils, both actual and metaphorical, for forty-two years. While Heaslett's steadfastness might well be a characteristic that Britons admire in their fellow countrymen during wartime, his experiences and struggles as a bishop during the inter-war years not only reveal the weakness of the British missionary movement but also can be taken as emblematic of a more general decline of British influence in Japan.

Born in Belfast in 1875 into a clerical family and educated at Durham University, Heaslett served as a missionary belonging to the Church

Missionary Society (CMS) from 1900 in Osaka, Tokushima and Tokyo before seeing war service in France as an officer in the Chinese Labour Corps in the latter part of the Great War. Returning to Japan, Heaslett was elevated in 1922 to the bishopric of South Tokyo in succession to Cecil Boutflower, and subsequently went on to serve as presiding bishop of the Nippon Seikōkai[5] (NSKK, the Anglican Church in Japan) between 1935 and 1940.[6] Most of his earlier career had been spent teaching at the Central Theological College in Tokyo. He was fluent in Japanese (something that Boutflower had not been), and his linguistic ability was a key factor in his appointment as bishop of South Tokyo, a diocese largely supported by the other major Church of England missionary society, the Society for the Propagation of the Gospel in Foreign Parts (SPG) and not the CMS. Happily, Heaslett was known for his witty after-dinner speeches and his Irish good humour.[7] He also wrote well and some of his letters contain perceptive comments on the religious and political situation in Japan. Throughout all his trials and difficulties, he maintained a genuine fondness for the Japanese.

In December 1942 William Temple, then archbishop of Canterbury, in his introduction to Heaslett's *From a Japanese Prison*, wrote that the last thing Heaslett wanted in writing about his imprisonment was to intensify ill-will between Britons and Japanese for 'it is among the Japanese Christians . . . that we see persisting through all the stress of war the spirit which will from that side make possible the renewal of happy relationships, despite all cruelties, when the war is over, and the hope of good-will and of the peace which is its consequence'.[8] According to Major-General F. S. G. Piggott,[9] Heaslett maintained to the end an 'unshaken faith in the eventual advent of happier days and reconciliation' between the two former enemies.[10] It was reconciliation between British and Japanese Christians that led Heaslett in 1946 to make, at the behest of both archbishop Fisher of Canterbury and the NSKK,[11] his last visit to Japan in order to assist the restoration of the NSKK and to help heal the wounds caused by schism and persecution during the war.

This essay concentrates on two challenges in Heaslett's career as a bishop in Japan. These two challenges serve not only to show the steadfastness in his character but also the flint in the personality of this kindly and talented man when called upon to protect those Christian values that he held dear when they were threatened with destruction both from without and within. He faced the first challenge at the start of his episcopate and this was the daunting task of revitalizing the British Anglican missionary movement after a long period of decline. Despite the natural disaster of the Great Kantō Earthquake of 1923, he was largely successful in increasing British influence in the NSKK. The second challenge, and the major focus of this essay, occurred in October 1937 when Heaslett was presiding bishop of the NSKK. It was created by the archbishop Cosmo Gordon Lang of Canterbury as a result of his chairing a protest meeting held at the Royal Albert Hall in London.

Organized by the *News Chronicle* newspaper,[12] this protest was an event of little or passing significance in Britain itself, but it had not only profound consequences for Japanese Anglicans and British missionaries, including Heaslett himself, but also an important impact on the deterioration of Anglo-Japanese relations in general. Writing in 1940, Heaslett detailed a litany of events since 1931 that had fuelled anti-British feelings in Japan and which had 'swelled up into an ugly chorus in 1937 when the Archbishop of Canterbury took the chair at an anti-bombing-of-open-towns meeting,' before eventually reaching fever heat over Tientsin and the *Asama Maru* affair.[13] The archbishop's actions at the Albert Hall meeting proved to be an old grudge that Japanese Anglicans did not swiftly forget.[14] This incident intensified the desire of some Japanese Anglicans for the complete independence of the NSKK. It also drew the attention of the military police to the Church and, ultimately, led to the arrest of Heaslett and later to that of Japanese Anglican priests on spy charges.[15]

BISHOP OF SOUTH TOKYO

Yet twenty years earlier, there was seemingly no previous time when the malaise of the British Anglican endeavour in Japan was more evident than just before Heaslett was appointed bishop of South Tokyo. This was largely owing to the failure of the British missionary movement to attract new and young missionaries, and had led to the very continued existence of a British Anglican presence in Japan being questioned. In June 1921 there were only four European priests supported by the SPG in the South Tokyo diocese, two of whom were going home, where ten years before there had been ten missionary priests.[16] Indeed, no new SPG clerical missionary had been appointed since 1908.[17] The CMS faired little better for its last clerical missionary had arrived in 1916, but, by 1923, financial retrenchment and new regulations regarding the retirement of missionaries threatened to reduce the combined number of its male and female missionaries throughout Japan from sixty to forty.[18]

If the SPG was to continue its Japan work, there was a pressing need for new missionaries. In 1922, in looking at missionary problems and policies in Japan, it was argued that 'without any deliberate intention to Westernize, Christianity is yet the one subject in which foreign influence, guidance and control are still supreme. . . Japanese Christians and missionaries recognize foreign control as a necessity'.[19] While all looked forward to a day when the Japanese Church would be self-maintaining, it was felt that this could be achieved only in the hypothetical future.

Other factors were also at play. There was a widespread fear among

British missionaries that the American bishop, John McKim,[20] wanted to do away with the English bishop of South Tokyo.[21] In 1923 two Japanese, Motoda Sakunoshin[22] and Naide Yasutarō[23] were elected to become bishops of Tokyo and Osaka respectively. Heaslett did not entirely approve. In his objections to the two Japanese bishops, his own theological views become clear. He argued that both Japanese were theologically liberal and 'both are men of American Church ideals. I believe in definiteness and fear vagueness. I prefer a sound High Churchman to an easy-going Liberal. I prefer a modern up-to-date Evangelical to both. Japan's great need is men who can humbly but definitely say "I know".'[24] British missionary disdain for the influence of the American Church mission on the NSKK was echoed in March 1925 by Audrey Henty[25] who thought that American missionaries had a tendency 'to shallowness, to over-emphasize the secular side, to reliance on a perfected organization backed by American money, rather than on patient teaching backed by prayer,' and she believed that the mission field had need of 'both the tortoise and the hare, the English plodder and the brilliant American runner. There is too a tendency to Americanize rather than to merely Christianize.'[26] For his part, Heaslett saw that future Japanese bishops would also come from the American side of the NSKK because the Americans had a large number of Japanese clergy trained in the United States and that 'CMS & SPG failure in the past to send men to England for training has put us very definitely in a secondary position in the Church councils. We have to do something.'[27] This was particularly true in the dioceses of Kobe and Hokkaidō which had been held by SPG and CMS men respectively and were now vacant.

Heaslett wanted these posts filled by Englishmen. (In fact, he was doing triple duty as bishop for he was taking care of the ecclesiastical duties in the vacant dioceses as well as his own.)[28] A replacement for the aged bishop Hugh James Foss[29] of Kobe was found in Basil Simpson, a Japanese-speaking SPG missionary who was, according to Herbert Kelly, 'a thoroughly sensible Catholic' [that is, High Anglican].[30] Bishop Basil was Heaslett's sound High Churchman drawn from the SPG. The question of Hokkaidō diocese proved to be more difficult. Initially, there was a genuine fear that the CMS headquarters in London wanted to stop supporting the Hokkaidō diocese and its evangelistic work.[31] In February 1924 John Batchelor, the long-time CMS missionary in Sapporo, after hearing the rumour that the American Church mission was going to take over the CMS work in Hokkaidō warned that 'many of their clergy are practically Roman'.[32] It remained the desire of the diocesan Synod of Hokkaidō, however, that the CMS should continue to support the diocese as it moved forward to being self-supporting.[33] Heaslett who had been acting as bishop in charge of the Hokkaidō diocese must be given credit for keeping this northern diocese within the CMS fold. In 1927,

Gordon Walsh was consecrated bishop of Hokkaidō,[34] and Heaslett had his modern up-to-date Evangelical. In advocating the consecration of new British bishops, instead of Japanese ones, Heaslett was, in fact, sowing the seeds for future problems.

Such Episcopal concerns, however, paled in comparison to the devastation caused by the Great Kantō Earthquake on 1 September 1923. Fortunately, as most missionaries were still away on their summer holidays in Karuizawa, there were no British missionaries killed in the earthquake. Heaslett himself was in Hokkaidō and returned to Tokyo to find that the diocese of South Tokyo had not suffered any loss of life but churches and parsonages had been totally destroyed in Yokohama, Odawara and Hadano. The losses amounted to an estimated £45,000 which was small in relation to the £200,000 that the American Church mission suffered in Tokyo where only three or four of its pre-earthquake twenty-three churches continued to stand.[35] As all the churches in metropolitan Tokyo had been earmarked for the diocese of the new Japanese bishop of Tokyo, the American losses were particularly devastating to immediate financial viability of that diocese. While the American Episcopal Church was quickly able to raise £100,000 pounds in relief funds, and the SPG some £12,000 by February 1924, the CMS had disappointingly only raise £3,000.[36] It was, however, the spiritual reconstruction of the NSSK after the earthquake (that is getting churchgoers back into regular habits of worship), which was considered by one senior SPG missionary as being more important than the material reconstruction.[37]

In light of the difficulties that the British missionary movement and the NSKK were confronting and his own need for information about Japan, Archbishop Davidson of Canterbury in 1924 decided to send out to Japan a special emissary, Bishop Arthur Knight, warden of St Augustine's College, Canterbury, to inquire how best the Church in England could help the Anglican Church in Japan.[38] Happily, Bishop Knight was able to report that there was a need for the continued existence of the British missionary movement in Japan. It was vindication of Heaslett's efforts in trying to maintain a British presence in the Anglican Church in Japan. Difficult though the 1920s might have been, the 1930s proved to be even more challenging.

PRESIDING BISHOP

In 1935 Heaslett succeeded the American McKim as presiding bishop of the NSKK, and problems soon reared their heads. As early as 1936, Heaslett had informed the British Ambassador that it was becoming increasingly difficult for missionaries to work off the beaten track.[39] While the Foreign Office recognized that the Japanese authorities wanted foreign missionaries out of Japan,[40] there was little that it was prepared to do except to advise missions 'to hang on in the places where they are tolerated & wait for the national temper to change'.[41] Hang on British missionaries did, but there was little change in the national temper.

In October 1937 the Japanese national temper flared over the Albert Hall meeting. As he was responsible for the subsequent crisis that engulfed Heaslett and the NSKK, it is useful to look at Archbishop Lang's motives in participating in this meeting. Lang[42] was well-known for protesting against atrocities. In March 1937, for instance, he had urged the British government to protest against the use of poison gas by the Italians in Ethiopia.[43] Before the Albert Hall meeting took place, Lang had been annoyed by 'so much fuss' being created by the announcement that he would chair it but he was also concerned about the wording of the resolution that the meeting was going to endorse.[44] He took the precaution of speaking to Neville Chamberlain, and been warned by the Prime Minister about the possible adverse impact of his chairing the meeting. However, Chamberlain did not expressly forbid him from taking part in the protest.[45] Lang could use this to justify his actions, and to ensure that he would not be blamed for any British political consequences of his action.

However, it did not go unnoticed in Japan that the government was critical of the archbishop taking part in the protest meeting at the Albert Hall for the *Japan Advertiser* reported that both the government and the Foreign Office were 'bitterly critical of the participation of the clergy in such political demonstrations' as well as 'surprised that they should indulge in international polemics in a public meeting'.[46] Part of the Japanese concern was that the meeting, which brought labour, clergy and leftist leaders together on the same platform, might produce an anti-Japanese boycott resolution.[47] Lang had made it clear to Barry of the *News Chronicle* that he would not participate if such a resolution was put forward, and ultimately the resolution finally adopted simply urged the British government 'to take the lead in securing with concerted action – by economic measures or otherwise – the stopping of the indiscriminate attacks upon civilian non-combatants by the Japanese forces in China'.[48] The *Japan Advertiser* reported that the resolution was directed towards halting Japan's military campaign and 'was passed by a bristling crowd of 10,000 Labour, Leftist and church group followers during an anti-Japanese boycott demonstration in the Albert Hall'.[49] It was clear that the attempt to moderate the call for a boycott got lost along the telegraph lines between London and Tokyo. The fact that Lang emphasized 'the indignation of the world against Japanese acts is justified and added that the protest is more or less a direct appeal to the Government and the people of Japan'[50] obviously did not help.

In explaining to Yoshida Shigeru, the Japanese Ambassador, his decision to consent (which he did with considerable reluctance, he assured

Yoshida) to chair the meeting, Lang pointed out that it was scarcely possible for him 'as a representative of moral and especially Christian opinion in this country to refuse to give some expression to those feelings, though I hope I shall do with fitting moderation'.[51] In case his actions were misunderstood in Tokyo, Lang asked Yoshida to make it clear to the Japanese government that 'the Archbishop of Canterbury is not a high State official in the sense that he represents or speaks for the Government of the country'.[52] Such subtlety was lost on most Japanese who assumed that an archbishop of the Church of England would speak for the government. For its part, the *Japan Advertiser* was not above suggesting that 'the archbishop's action in regards to Japan was prompted by considerations of British Far Eastern policy'.[53] The Japanese government found an apologist in Sir Francis Lindley, the former British Ambassador, who was ready to blame the Chinese for the then current difficulties around Shanghai.[54] It was also suggested that the *News Chronicle*, which was viewed as an enthusiastic supporter of the League of Nations, had never forgiven Japan for delivering the ideals of the League such a serious blow over its stand on Manchuria.[55] Lines were seemingly drawn between those who supported the League and those who did not.

Further support for the Japanese came from the Vatican which announced that it was instructing its missions in East Asia to cooperate with the Japanese Army in China 'whenever the Bolshevist danger appears active'.[56] This sparked criticism in the *Japan Advertiser* that prelates should stay out of politics.[57] However, the archbishop was not hazed by opposition. In any case, he was buoyed by the many telegrams and letters of support for his speech at the Albert Hall from Chinese Christians, the Honan diocese of the Canadian Church Mission, and the Relief Fund in Shanghai. Despite the furor afterwards, Lang did not regret taking part in the meeting.[58]

Writing to Heaslett at the end of October, Lang firmly maintained his view that a leading spokesman of the British conscience it was impossible for him 'to be silent on a matter which on the basis of the facts as we saw them affected the principles of Christianity and of humanity'.[59] However, his views did not prevent him from leading a joint service in Westminster Abbey on 29 October to celebrate the Golden Jubilee of the NSKK and the Silver Jubilee of the Anglican Church in China. Naïvely, Lang hoped that this service would strengthen the ties between those Churches and the Church of England.[60] He later stressed that he never uttered or implied a single word of criticism of Japan in his sermon or elsewhere in the celebratory service for everything was directed towards the maintenance 'even in the midst of the present tension the Christian fellowship of the Churches of China and Japan'.[61] Lang congratulated himself on being scrupulously fair to the Japanese. Yet, it is hard to see that Japanese Christians who were described by one senior British missionary as being 'very nervy and touchy, and in the desire to prove that they are patriotic are inclined almost to out-do other people in their nationalism,'[62] would not be offended by a joint service celebrating the different jubilees of the Japanese and Chinese Churches. Whether the archbishop liked it or not, the hostilities between Japan and China had divided the two Anglican Churches along national lines and no joint service could bridge the chasm between them which the Albert Hall meeting had only served to widen.

Heaslett was with Bishop John Mann of Kyūshū when he learnt from Bishop Matsui of Tokyo on 1 October about the archbishop's intention to take the chair at a meeting of protest against indiscriminate bombing, and 'knowing something of the Japanese mind and of its sensitiveness to criticism we realized that we were up against a problem that might even involve the withdrawal of all Church of England help from Japan'.[63] Thus began for Heaslett an amazing two weeks in which he had to deal with a procession of people including the Ambassador, General Piggott, the British Association,[64] newspapers, police, gendarmes, officials, private persons, clergy, bishops, and the Executive Committee of the NSKK. Heaslett thought that the archbishop's action in taking the chair at the Albert Hall affected work in Japan in three ways. The first was the Japanese public did not understand that the connection between the Church of England and the NSKK was a spiritual one, for they believed that the NSKK was under the control of the English Church. For that reason, the public reaction in Japan to the NSKK was most unpleasant. Second, as far as the British community in Japan was concerned, it was felt that Lang's action put all movements to improve the relations between the two countries in an impossible position. Thirdly, Heaslett held that 'it focused attention on the mission work of other nations in Japan and gave ammunition to the party that wishes for isolation and the elimination of the Christian religion and the triumph of pure Japanism, viz. Shinto'.[65]

In Japan, the Albert Hall meeting was trumpeted as an anti-Japanese meeting. Because of the presence and speech of a Chinese professor at the meeting, Heaslett had difficulty in arguing successfully that the meeting was not against Japan but a protest against the bombing of non-combatants in keeping with the archbishop's earlier protest against Italian actions in Ethiopia.[66] Heaslett believed that he was eventually able to convince the Japanese official class that British missionaries were in Japan to help the NSKK and not to control it. Yet, he also felt that the Japanese public still considered that the NSKK was a foreign-controlled body of Japanese. The main cause of this was the preponderance of foreign bishops in the House of Bishops.[67] Something that Heaslett in promoting new English bishops was much responsible for. Heaslett's solution was either to have more dioceses and more Japanese bishops or have fewer dioceses and fewer foreign bishops. This had the support of three other English bishops of the NSKK, Walsh of Hokkaidō, Simpson of Kobe, and Mann of Kyūshū who were also of the opinion that the Japanese would ask for drastic changes in the future which would affect all the British work in Japan.

Kenneth Sansbury, the Chaplain at the British Embassy who had been on furlough when the Incident took place, later saw the difficulties in the NSKK stemming from a generational gap in the ranks of the Japanese clergy. He regarded the older people in authority in the NSKK as men of low social background and narrow culture who 'swallow the official view of everything and are only anxious that the Church should conform to government requirements in every respect. The younger clergy are better educated and more broad-minded. They know they are being kept in the dark and they realise how critical is the time for the Christian Church.'[68] Clearly, Sansbury had in mind, the two senior Japanese bishops, Naide of Osaka and Matsui of Tokyo both American trained and very eager to rid the NSKK of its British connection. Indeed, at the Executive Committee meeting of the NSKK on 1 October unpleasant things were said about the archbishop. A heated discussion led to the bishops of Osaka and Tokyo openly agreeing with the view that 'the work of the English Mission in Japan has come to an end'.[69] Happily, Heaslett was able to prevent this, and thwart the very considerable opposition in the diocese of Tokyo to continued British missionary presence. In November Heaslett's eyesight temporarily started to fail with the result that he could only read with the greatest difficulty. As a consequence, he was prepared to give up two of his five offices that of being chairman of the General Synod and president of the Executive Committee of the NSKK. These passed to Bishop Naide of Osaka. This was sufficient both to stop the Japanese clergy's demand for his complete resignation and to satisfy the demand of the Education Department for a Japanese to be head of the Church and to represent the Church to the government. Heaslett remained for the time being presiding bishop.[70]

This arrangement meant that Bishop Naide presided over the sessions of the 19th General Synod of the NSKK which took place in Kyoto at the end of April 1938.[71] Heaslett described Naide as 'an ultra-nationalist and the leader of that section of the Church which almost puts Country before God'.[72] The Synod under the presidency of Naide was seen as posing some danger to the Church. Apart from seven foreign bishops (four Britons and three Americans), there was only one foreign missionary delegate elected to the Convention, the redoubtable Canon A. C. Hutchinson of Fukuoka, who was the CMS Japan mission secretary.[73] The two most serious issues for Heaslett and the foreign missionaries were the proposals that the Synod en masse should visit the tomb of the Meiji Emperor where all would make an orchestrated deep obeisance to the tomb and the memory of the Emperor, and that the Synod should also issue a resolution of loyalty to the nation which expressed sympathy to the people of China. Fortunately, at a meeting of the NSKK House of Bishops in late March, the proposal for the *sampai* (worship) at the tomb was scotched, and the resolution watered down so that it was acceptable to British and Japanese bishops alike.[74] Heaslett and the foreign bishops still could exert influence in the bishops' meetings but Heaslett realized that if Bishop Naide told his friends what happened in the meetings there could be trouble.

Fortunately, at this juncture, Naide and his friends did not cause trouble. Happily also the archbishop of Canterbury began to realize that he had caused problems for the NSKK. At the end of May 1938 he was asked by the Earl of Listowel to take part in a protest meeting over the bombing of Canton. Lang's response was that he did not want to take part in any public protest because when he had done so in previous October 'the results were to create considerable anxiety among Japanese Christians particularly members of the Nippon Sei Ko Kwai – the Anglican Church there which is largely composed of Japanese Bishops and clergy as well as laity,' but most importantly, Lang also added 'in any case a few words from His Majesty's Government would be more effective than any renewed public agitation'.[75] If he had only left the protest to the British government in October, a great deal of trouble for Heaslett and the NSKK would have undoubtedly been avoided.

CONCLUSION

Archbishop Lang acted on Christian and humanitarian grounds. It is clear, however, that he gave little thought to the consequences of his actions on the NSKK and the British position in Japan. He believed that all people – Britons and Japanese – would understand that he was not attacking Japan but protesting against the indiscriminate bombing of non-combatants. The clear demonstration of his scrupulously fair treatment of the Japanese was demonstrated in his sermon at the joint celebratory service of the golden and silver jubilees of the Japanese and Chinese Anglican Churches held in Westminster Abbey. Lang assumed that everybody thought in the same subtle and clever way that he did. Unfortunately, subtlety was lost along the telegraph lines, and less clever men saw his actions as politically motivated and anti-Japanese. In light of his latter actions, they were not far off. While Lang did not publicly protest against the Japanese bombing of Canton in May 1938, he privately became increasingly active in his support of China in her struggle against Japan. In hindsight, the archbishop's chairing of the Albert Hall meeting can be seen to mark symbolically the point when Japan lost and China gained the support of British Christians.

It was Heaslett who had the task of dealing with the consequences in Japan of the archbishop's participation in the Albert Hall meeting. Lang precipitated a major crisis for the British missionary movement and the

NSKK. Heaslett was successfully able to minimize the immediate damage to the missionary movement by the time of the 19th Synod in April 1938. Yet, Heaslett could not stop forever Japanese demands for complete control of the NSKK. In the wake of the persecution of the Salvation Army in August 1940, Bishops Naide and Matsui demanded that all foreign bishops resigned which they did, with the exception of Bishop Basil Simpson of Kobe, by October 1940. Heaslett remained in Japan to look after the needs of the British community in Tokyo and Yokohama and was able to attend the 20th General Synod of the NSKK held in April 1941.

Heaslett reported then that 'the Church is facing the facts and has a good solid foundation. The N.S.K.K. is now a self-governing, self-supporting, self-expanding branch of the Anglican Communion.'[76] That was true for the moment but soon the NSKK would suffer schism when Bishop Naide decided in late 1941 that the Church should join the Nihon Kirisutokyōdan (Kyōdan), the union church which the government wanted all Protestant denominations to join. A rump of the NSKK resisted amalgamation into the Kyōdan and struggled through the war to remain an Anglican Communion in Japan. Heaslett was most opposed to any Anglican union with the Kyōdan. The fact that so many Anglicans from the British and Canadian missionary side of the Church remained outside the Kyōdan was in itself a testament to the influence of Heaslett and other British missionaries like the Anglo-Catholic Herbert Kelly of Kelham on the younger Japanese Anglican clergy. After the end of the war, those Anglicans who had joined the union Protestant Church and wished to return to the Anglican fold were welcomed back without any acrimony.

However, during the late 1930s the Japanese government was putting enormous pressure on all Christian organizations in Japan to rid themselves of foreign control and influences. Changes in regulations for schools made it very difficult for missionary teachers to continue to work. All Protestant denominations, not only the NSKK, were confronted with demands to join in the national spiritual mobilization campaign in support of the war effort in China. Likewise, the passing of the Religious Bodies Law in 1940 gave the government increased control over religious organizations and affected all Churches. The NSKK was not alone in finding that informal government pressure was being applied to cause it to join the Kyōdan. To a greater or lesser extent, all missionaries were watched by the police, their movements monitored and their mail opened. Yet what Lang had done was to draw attention to the British missionary movement and to the NSKK. The Albert Hall Incident saw Christian principle and humanitarian impulse collide with Japanese sensitivity and nationalism. For the Japanese authorities, it offered an excuse to use the British missionary movement as a whipping boy to excite anti-British feeling, and to free Japanese Christianity from foreign control and influence. Of all the foreign Church leaders in Japan on 8 December 1941, it was aged Heaslett alone who was cast into prison like a common criminal.

During his time in prison, Heaslett's Japanese friends successfully lobbied for his release and eventually he was repatriated. Without his connections to the outside and without his knowledge of Japanese, Heaslett's imprisonment would have been far worse. The loyalty and kindness of Japanese friends also undoubtedly influenced his view that Japanese Christians could play an important role in the reconciliation of Japan and Britain after the war. Yet nothing can change the fact that Heaslett had the misfortune of being a missionary bishop in Japan during a very difficult period. The presence of foreign bishops in a Catholic Church like the NSKK depended on the absence of racial discrimination. Unfortunately, the late 1930s were not times when this principle was highly prized in Japan. Yet, ultimately, the legacy of this last British presiding bishop was that the NSKK was able to survive the perils of the war and continues to exist to the present day.

42

Pioneers in Bringing Jūjutsu (Jūdō) to Britain: Edward William Barton Wright, Tani Yukio and Ernest John Harrison

RICHARD BOWEN

E. W. Barton Wright

THE EARLIEST KNOWN lecture on jūjutsu in Britain, indeed in Europe, was that delivered by Takashima Shidachi as the inaugural lecture of the Japan Society of London on 29 April 1892. Takashima Shidachi, Secretary of the London Branch of the Bank of Japan, was assisted by Goh Daigoro of the Consulate General. The lecture, entitled *Ju-Jutsu – The Ancient Art of Self-Defence by Sleight*, went into the history of the art, a description of its methods, some anecdotes, and ended with some throws and strangles. Takashima Shidachi spoke of the aims of his teacher, Kanō Jigoro, and his particular school of jūjutsu, the Kanō *Riu* (*Ryū*), now better known as jūdō, or more correctly Kōdōkan Jūdō.[1] The *Saturday Review* commented on the lecture, confusing jūjutsu with displays of sumo which had taken place earlier at the Japanese Village in Knightsbridge.[2]

EDWARD WILLIAM BARTON WRIGHT

While it is possible that there were occasional reports in the press of jūjutsu by travellers returning from Japan, it was not until 1898 before another exhibition took place in London. This was given by Edward William Barton Wright at the St James's Hall, Piccadilly. He wrote of the event: 'I challenged anyone to attack me in any form he care to choose. I overcame seven in succession in three minutes, all of whom were over fourteen stones.'[3] At this time he was calling his system Bartitsu, later explaining its derivation as partly taken from his name Barton and partly from jujutsu which, as he wrote, 'Means fighting to the end'.

Journalists had trouble with the spelling of Bartitsu, writing about Bartisu, Barstitut and other variations. In 1893 City gents and many others were wearing black armbands and ties out of respect for Sherlock Holmes, who had fallen to his death clutched in the arms of his arch-enemy, Professor Moriarty. Persistent public pressure forced Sir Arthur Conan Doyle to resuscitate Sherlock Holmes, and in doing so he must have picked up one of the variant spellings. In 1903, in the *Return of Sherlock Holmes – The Adventure of the Empty House*, Holmes tells Watson how he saved himself from going over the falls: 'We tottered on the brink of the falls. I have some knowledge, however, of baritsu, or the Japanese system of wrestling, which has more than once been useful to me. I slipped through his grip, and he with a horrible scream kicked madly for a few seconds, and clawed the air with both his hands. But for all his efforts he could not get his balance, and over he went.'[4]

One outcome of the St James's Hall performance was that Wright received a Royal Command from Edward, Prince of Wales, for a demonstration. He was also elected a member of the Bath Club without entrance fee and free of subscriptions for three years. It was at the Bath Club that he gave an exhibition on Ladies' Night on 9 March 1899.[5] However *The Times* for 18 October 1900 reported that the Royal Command performance at the Gallery Club had to be cancelled as Barton Wright had cracked a bone in his hand while cycling to Margate. In fact, there had not been a bicycle accident. Two louts had picked a fight with him, and in knocking both out he damaged his hand.[6] *The Times* continued with a long report on a private viewing at the Alhambra Music Hall by Barton Wright who gave a short lecture on jūjutsu helped by two Japanese (see below). While the two were not pleased at having to perform in front of a paying audience, Barton Wright managed to persuade them to give a demonstration.

Barton Wright was born in Madras on 10 October 1860.[7] His father, William, an engineer, was Superintendent of Locomotives of Madras Railways, an important position placing him in the top three of the local executives of the company, the head office of which was in London. His mother, Janet, was a Scot. With such parents he was bound to have a first class education. His schooling started off with an English tutor, then he went to a German college, and finished at a French university. He described himself as a Civil Engineer and it appears this qualification came from the French university.[8]

From his earliest days he was obsessed with self-defence, learning boxing, wrestling, fencing, *savate*, the use of the stiletto, under masters of these arts, and also by employing 'roughs' for training purposes. He also mentioned that, while he earned his living as a mining consultant in different parts of the world, he often had to defend himself against various forms of attack, always successfully. It is likely that reading about the Takashima Shidachi lecture prompted him to set off in 1894 for Japan, where he spent three years in Kobe working for E.H. Hunter and Company and studying jūjutsu under a local master.[9]

By 1898 he was back in London where he formed Bartitsu Limited,[10] which was incorporated on the 26 November. The company occupied a 'huge subterranean hall'[11] at 67A Shaftesbury Avenue. While he referred to the premises as a School of Arms, and had collected a number of top athletes to teach their specialities, he had also set up an electro therapy clinic in the same premises. The directors of the company were inefficient as they failed to make the required Annual Returns to Company House despite frequent reminders. In July 1901 the Registrar dissolved Bartitsu Limited, although this did not seem to make any difference to the operation.[12]

In 1899, a two-part article running to seventeen pages, appeared in the March and April issues of *Pearson's Magazine* under the heading 'The New Art of Self Defence'. This was a description of Bartitsu, well illustrated with photographs. In the text Barton Wright states that in foreign countries people never fight for amusement or diversion, as is often the case in England or the United States. 'In this country we are brought up with the idea that there is no more reasonable way of settling a dispute than resorting to Nature's weapons, the fists, and to scorn taking advantage of a man while he is down. A foreigner, however, will not hesitate to use a chair, or beer bottle, or a knife, or anything to come to hand'. The concept of a fair fight existed in Britain, probably encouraged by the public schools, but there was plenty of violence reported in the Victorian press, not only in the slum rookeries.

In 1900 Barton Wright sponsored three Japanese jūjutsu experts. Tani Yukio and his brother Tani K. arrived in September, followed in October by Yamamoto S., the three were the first genuine jūjutsu experts to reach Europe.[13] While ostensibly they were to augment the teaching staff in Shaftesbury Avenue, there is no doubt that Barton Wright had, at the back of his mind, an ambition to introduce jūjutsu to the public by means of the music halls. At the time, wrestling and strongman acts were of intense public interest, and no doubt this influenced Barton Wright's decision.

On 13 February 1901, Barton Wright gave a lecture and practical demonstration for the Japan Society,[14] assisted by Tani K. (8 stone) and Yamamoto (14 stone). During the lecture Barton Wright mentioned that he was expecting the arrival of another expert. Tani K. and Yamamoto were not too happy with their lot, particularly with the idea of doing stage-work and opted to return to Japan. It is unknown when they left Britain, but it was probably shortly after the Japan Society demonstration. Tani K. perished in the Great Kanto Earthquake of 1923.[15] It is not known what became of Yamamoto.

In the September 1901 programme for the Tivoli Music Hall,[16] item eighteen reads: 'Real Self-Defence: Demonstration by the Japanese Instructors of the Bartitsu School of Arms and Physical Culture.' The programme also contained an open challenge to the audience for anyone who would like to chance their arm with the Japanese. Barton Wright had persuaded, it is suspected without difficulty, Tani Yukio and the newly-arrived Uyenishi Sadakazu to take to the stage. Jujutsu had arrived on the music halls. At first, there was some disbelief in its effectiveness, with suggestions that it was nothing more than acrobatic feats. But with the defeat of many challengers it became obvious that jūjutsu was a complete system of fighting, new to Europeans. All the leading newspapers carried lengthy reports on the incredible feat of these small men literally toying with opponents of, at times, twice their weight. They, and Bartitsu, became famous overnight.

Apart from the press (and Conan Doyle), others mentioned the Japanese. For instance, Bernard Shaw, who lived around the corner from the Tivoli, must have seen Bartitsu as in his play *Major Barbara* there is: 'Todget Fairmile o' Balls Pond. Him that won £20 off the Japanese wrestler at the music hall by standing out seventeen minutes four seconds agen him.' In Douglas Sladen's book *Queer Things about Japan*, published in 1903, he has five pages describing what he saw, both at Shaftesbury Avenue and the demonstration for the Japan Society. Sladen writes that he had not seen jūjutsu during his visits to Japan (by now the name 'jūjutsu' was gradually replacing Bartitsu).

However, all was not well as a rift had developed between Barton Wright and his two Japanese employees (for that was what they were). The most likely cause was money. Barton Wright was paying the two a wage while pocketing the very considerable income from their stage appearances. While this is speculation, the split probably occurred sometime between late 1902 and early 1903. With the two Japanese gone, Barton Wright concentrated on his electro-therapy clinic, closing down the school of arms.

On 3 March 1906 the 'Bartitsu Light Cure Institute'[17] was incorporated as a Joint Stock Company with a share capital of £10,000, increased within a few months to £22,500. Barton Wright had outgrown the Shaftesbury Avenue premises. He sold the equipment and goodwill of his existing enterprise for £9,000, £1,500 in cash and the balance in shares. The new premises were on the first floor at 1 Albemarle Street[18] (formerly the Hotel Albemarle), on the corner with Piccadilly, a prestigious address nearly opposite the Ritz Hotel. The accountant, who drew up a financial report in the Prospectus, wrote that the new premises, '. . . occupy absolutely the most central and fashionable position in the whole of London'. The yearly rental was £1,120.

The Prospectus[19] was accompanied by an eighteen-page booklet, which opened with a list of the names and titles of patients who had agreed to be used as references, these being: Countesses, Ladies, Baronesses, HIH the Grand Duke Michael of Russia, Lords, Judges, Barons, Baronets, Generals, Colonels, Clerics, Doctors, and others. At the time the use of electricity in medical treatments was entirely new, it was popular and there were more than twenty 'Galvanises' operating clinics in London, all in good central positions. The fees at the new Institute were ten shillings and sixpence (half a guinea) for a twenty-minute treatment, or one guinea per hour. There were thirteen types of electrical procedures available, and the afflictions that could be treated numbered fifty-nine, including Golfer's Elbow, Hunter's Sprain, Loss of Hair, and that awful complaint known as 'Liver'. A cure was guaranteed in some cases. Tucked away at the back was a coy statement that Piles can be totally cured by a course of eight to fourteen visits. There was also a note in the booklet that English, French, German, Dutch, Portuguese and Japanese were spoken, giving an indication of Barton Wright's education and travel.

The new venture was not apparently successful as on 7 December 1908, two creditors filed a petition to wind up the company.[20] The court appointed a Receiver and a Manager (Administrator) on 20 January 1909. This suggests that it was thought possible to either revive the company or run it for a while to clear the debts. In the event, the company was finally dissolved on 6 June 1913. From that time there is no trace of Barton Wright until 1939 when he was listed in the electoral roll for Kingston upon Thames.[21] In 1950 Koizumi Gunji interviewed him in his rooms above a grocer's shop in Surbiton Road, still surrounded by his electrical treatment equipment.[22] In March 1951 he was invited to attend the 34th Annual Display[23] of the Budokwai at the Royal Albert Hall, where he was introduced to the audience as the man responsible for the introduction of jūjutsu to Britain, indeed to Europe. A few months later, on 13 September 1951, he died at home. It seems that he had either distanced himself from friends and relatives, or he had outlived them, or he had none. There was nobody to take care of the interment and consequently he rests in an unmarked grave in Kingston-upon-Thames Cemetery. The enterprising and colourful Barton Wright cannot be ignored, nor should he be. He has by far the strongest claim for the introduction of jūjutsu to Europe.

Tani Yukio

TANI YUKIO

Following their break with Barton Wright, Tani Yukio and Uyenishi came under the managerial skills of the Scot, William Bankier,[24] a flamboyant but honest showman who used the stage name of Apollo for his strongman act. Soon Uyenishi set up his own academy in Golden Square, Soho,[25] the first jūjutsu school in Europe, and spent most of his time teaching with occasional stage appearances, using the name Raku. He left Britain in about 1908, and after spending time on the Continent probably returned to Osaka where he was born. No further trace of him can be found. Tani Yukio, under the guidance of Apollo, set about the defeat of most of the champion wrestlers of the day, both here and on the Continent. The usual system was to give a demonstration of jujutsu followed by an open challenge from the stage. The bait, which varied, was a pound for lasting every minute over five, twenty pounds for lasting ten minutes, or a hundred pounds if Tani was beaten. Challengers were required to wear a jūdō jacket and throws did not count, the opponent had to submit from an arm-lock, or a strangle, or sheer exhaustion.[26] In 1905, over a typical six-day week at the London Lyceum, he defeated twenty-six wrestlers, one trying four times in the course of the week.[27] By now ordinary members of the audience realized that they stood little chance, but amateur and professional wrestlers were keen to try. To have defeated Tani would have enhanced their reputation. At that time the professional wrestlers were genuine, in the sense that matches were not pre-arranged as most came to be years later.

To select reports on a few of Tani's matches: Fournier, the French fourteen-stone heavy-weight champion, one night jumped on the stage at the Oxford Music Hall after Tani had already beaten four men. He lasted exactly forty seconds, 'and was so badly beaten that it was quite two minutes before he revived sufficiently to be able to understand that the Japanese had beaten him by the collar hold'. Tani had strangled him.[28]

Chemiakin, a Russian heavy-weight wrestler, lost to Tani after being thrown into the orchestra.[29] In his match with Marc Gaucher, the heavy-weight amateur boxing champion of France, the Frenchman managed to get in some blows but then Tani brought him down and choked him.[30] Another 'mixed' bout took place between Tani and the boxer Young Josephs, each using his own style. Josephs, a stone heavier, 'could not get a blow in edge-ways, Tani side-stepping all his advances in wonderful style; the bout ended in five minutes and thirty-four seconds with the boxer in an armlock'.[31]

James Mellor of Stalybridge, Lancashire, the light-weight Catch-As-Catch-Can (now known as Free Style) Champion of the World, a professional at the very top of the sport, was famous and much respected. He met Tani at the Tivoli, the advertised purse of a thousand pounds turned out to be nothing more than a 'come on' to attract an audience. The match was under Free Style rules where both shoulders had to be pinned to the mat for a win. Both men weighted nine stone four pounds. The bout started a few minutes after three in the afternoon in a temperature of nearly eighty degrees. In the first round Mellor managed to pin Tani's shoulders to the mat after fifty-nine minutes. In the second round Tani equalized after nineteen minutes and thirty-three seconds. In the final round Tani pinned down the Stalybridge man after fourteen minutes and twelve seconds. The rules at that time allowed for long bouts. This was the first time that Tani had ventured into Free Style wrestling.[32] 'To accomplish what he (Tani) did with Mellor – defeat the best man in the country at his weight – without any preliminary training of familiarity with a style of wrestling foreign to him cannot be easily be forgotten.' The match was widely reported in the major newspapers: *The Daily Telegraph*, *The Post*, *Mirror*, *Mail*, *Sportsman*, and *Chronicle*, the last writing: 'The cleverness displayed approached near to necromancy.' The audience became so excited that the police had to be called. Many years later Apollo wrote: 'It was, of course, well known that Tani had no idea of Catch wrestling. The result of the match broke poor Mellor up. He died not long after.' Immediately after his defeat of Mellor, Tani then went down to the Hippodrome Brighton for his twice-nightly performance.

Apollo wrote about his first meeting with Tani:[33] 'I myself candidly confess that I pooh-poohed the idea that a nine-stone man, no matter how skilfully, could defeat a man twice his own weight.' He went to Barton Wright's club where Tani Yukio was produced: 'and wrestled me a bout. To my astonishment, however, he had me at his mercy in less than two minutes. How it was accomplished I did not know, but there I lay at the end of the bout, completely tied up, with the Japanese lying alongside, grinning from ear to ear and laughingly asking me if I had had enough.'

The South African amateur wrestler and strongman, Tromp van Diggelen,[34] described his first meeting with Tani at a gymnasium, during

461

which they had a friendly bout. 'Seventeen seconds later I was not smiling, but choking.' And, in a second try: 'This time only fifteen seconds had elapsed before I was choking and tapping the mat with both hands as fast as I could (the sign of submission).' Tromp asked him if he was really the Japanese champion: 'No, no,' came the immediate reply, 'that is only publicity talk. In Japan, I am only third rate, the great champions are amateurs and they never give public shows of our art. To the masters of jūjutsu our science is almost a religion.' On other occasions when asked the same question, Tani gave the same answer, but adding that he was unequalled when dealing with wrestlers, boxers, and street fighters.

The inevitable happened, in December 1904 a real Japanese champion turned up. Apollo gave a detailed account of the arrival of Miyake Taro, and years later a further account. The two differ substantially. But the outcome of the match remained the same. Tani, performing at the Tivoli, issued his usual challenge, and Miyake appeared from the audience. It was agreed that the match should not last longer than fifteen minutes. Almost immediately Tani was thrown, landing on the back of his neck. He arose and it seemed obvious to all that he had been stunned by the hard fall. A few seconds later Miyake threw him again, even harder. Tani managed to get up only to be thrown once more. A fourth throw caused Tani to mutter something in Japanese whereon Miyake stepped back. Apollo announced to the audience that Tani had given Miyake the victory after six minutes and ten seconds. Such was Tani's popularity that someone shouted: 'Three cheers for Tani,' and, 'Like one man the huge audience spontaneously burst into applause, rising the while and shouting themselves hoarse.'[35] Apollo wrote of Tani's reaction: 'No questioning of the decision, no wailing of bad luck. Just the same stoic acceptance of the fact. A good job it is a Japanese.' Apollo wrote that Tani's defeat caused many theatre bookings to be cancelled with the subsequent loss of earnings, and it may be that this caused the eventual break between the two which appears to have happened about that time.

Tani, having acquired another manager, continued to tour the country and, being famous, packed theatres wherever he went. Miyake also toured, trading on his reputation of having defeated Tani. There was no ill feeling between Tani and Miyake, indeed in February 1905, a few weeks after their match, both took part in a display of jūjutsu at Chelsea Barracks,[36] and later at the Regent Street Polytechnic.[37] While mostly they performed separately, they certainly appeared occasionally on the stage together. About this time they opened a school in Oxford Street, quite a large establishment, staffed by two Japanese, three Englishmen, and a Welsh girl, all adequate enough for beginners but not for the experienced fighters Miyake and Tani were used to meeting. The school lasted for just over two years, failing because the two principals were always absent on tour. In 1906 the two co-authored the best book of the early years, *The Game of Jujutsu*,[38] a volume highly praised in the press.

Tani and Uyenishi, the first to take jūjutsu to Paris and then beyond to Portugal and Spain, were later to be followed by newcomers such as Miyake and others, such as Maeda Mitsuyo and Ohno Akitaro, both of whom were exponents of champion grade. Two Frenchmen, Ernest Régnier and Edmond Desbonnet,[39] also helped the spread of jūjutsu to the Continent by opening a school in Paris. Desbonnet, world famous creator of French physical culture, had attended the Bartitsu School; Régnier was a pupil of Uyenishi's Golden Square school. In October 1905, Régnier had an intensely and widely publicized jūjutsu versus *savate* match with Dubois, a past-master of *la savate* and a good boxer and fencer. One report said the contest lasted twenty-six seconds, ending with Dubois caught in an arm-lock. The Prefect of Police, who was present, was so impressed that he decided his men should be trained in jujutsu.[40]

In November 1905, Higashi Katsukuma turned up in Paris calling himself 'Champion of the World'. Higashi was based in America where he attained some fame, probably by the claims of the journalist who had sponsored him. One night Higashi threw out his usual open challenge from the stage of the Paris Hippodrome, and Tani popped up from the audience. There were many reports of the encounter. One lengthy account had this: 'For in two minutes and a half the London champion had incapacitated the Paris champion – had apparently come close to killing him – and Paris didn't like it.'[41] These are the words of Arnold Bennett who saw the fight. Higashi had to be taken off to hospital.

By about 1910 only Tani, of the professional exponents, was left in Britain although both Miyake and Maeda made occasional visits. The era of the music halls was drawing to a close and the public interest in wrestling, strongman, and jūjutsu acts had dwindled. Even so, Tani was famous enough to attract large audiences wherever he went. But the start of the first World War reduced his activities. In 1918 the London Budokwai[42] opened and Tani was appointed chief instructor, a position he held, on a free-lance basis, until stricken by a stroke in February 1937.

Little is known about Tani's early days in Japan, it has been reported that he was one of the jūjutsu stars of the then Dichasia College but they have no record of him graduating. His birth-place is unknown, but his daughter is certain her father came from Tokyo. His father and grandfather were both teachers of jūjutsu. There is a story related by Tani, that his grandfather to show that pain can be controlled ordered his pupils to kick him unconscious in a demonstration before the shogun of the time. Tani was not a gentle teacher, his principle was that one learnt by suffering. If he thought a senior pupil held back out of fear, he would denounce the unfortunate as a coward and not speak to him for, at times, weeks. He was a fighter through and through, his style was to attack unremittingly and he had scant regard for those who caved in easily.

Tani's earnings over the early years of his career were spectacular, Apollo put them at £250,000,[43] this at a time when the weekly wage was about thirty shillings. But when it came to money Tani was naïve and much of it went on gambling and living the life of an Edwardian man about town. For instance, he would invite the entire chorus line or indeed the whole company for a trip on the Thames, complete with supper and drinks.[44] Away from the jūjutsu training hall, he was a kindly and generous man; too generous as in his hallway there was a tray with sovereigns so that friends and, no doubt, scroungers could help themselves to a few.[45] He was not against telling stories about himself. At a dog track he was asked for a light and while he fumbled in his pocket for a match he was knocked out and robbed, proving the accuracy of the Japanese proverb 'Even monkeys can fall'. His wife was English, and they had one daughter. He died in January 1950, aged 69. Many years later a journalist wrote: 'Big fellows, one after the other, he used to take on in quick succession, to dispose of all as nonchalantly as one would please. Over they would go, all in their turn, each in attitudes of distress. At inflicting terrible bone-breaking punishment Yukio Tani was a veritable holy terror.'[46] His height? Five feet three inches!

Ernest John Harrison

ERNEST JOHN HARRISON

Ernest John Harrison was born in Manchester in 1873.[47] He had no memories of his mother as she died when he was three. A sister, the oldest, died at the age of thirteen, while his elder brother went on to become a professional pianist, but he, too, died early at the age of twenty-nine. Following a family rift, his father emigrated to America within a year of his wife's death, leaving the brothers to be brought up with a cousin by two uncles, one of whom, John Serles Ragland Phillips, was a one-time editor of the *York Herald* and later editor of *The Yorkshire Post*. A further distant relative was John Edward Taylor, the founder and first editor of *The Manchester Guardian*.[48] Although the young Harrison attended three schools, part of his education was by private tuition. At the age of fifteen he started work at the Manchester Reference Library where he became an avid admirer of Shakespeare and Macaulay. He continued his education at evening classes, studying French and becoming an expert stenographer and typist, and also joining the YMCA where he became a proficient gymnast and learnt to skate and swim and the elements of wrestling (Catch).[49]

In his nineteenth year, with the permission of his uncles, he set off for Canada with the intention of becoming a fruit farmer. He arrived in Vancouver where the clean air evidently drove all thoughts of farming from his mind. Instead, he was taken on as a cub reporter on *The Vancouver News Advertiser*, and it was here that he wrote about his interview with Mark Twain, a report which was telegraphed throughout the USA. He moved to a mining community on Vancouver Island, becoming the news editor and reporter on *The Naniamo Free Press*. It was in Naniamo that he became a skilled Catch wrestler at the local miner's club.[50]

He moved to San Francisco, hoping to find work as a freelance journalist. In the event he was employed by the *San Francisco Call*, a post which, in common with other journalists, called for him to carry a pistol as there was gang warfare and professional killers abroad. In the spring of 1897, having been engaged to work on *The Japan Daily Mail*, he set off for Yokohama. On arrival he found that he was the only foreigner on the staff, apart from the proprietor, J.H. Brookes, who was then seventy. On the death of Brookes, Harrison became the editor.[51]

Occasional traces of Harrison can be found in the local press at this time. For instance, in 1899 he is listed as a guest at Wright's Hotel,[52] and in 1902 *The Japan Daily Advertiser* reporting on a boxing and jūjutsu exhibition in Yokohama recorded: 'And the skill displayed by Mr Harrison at once evoked the admiration and applause of the entire audience.'[53] He was well known in Yokohama: 'Oh, that's jūjutsu Harrison, but what the hell does he do for a living?' As at this time the foreign population of Yokohama was comparatively small, they tended to make their own entertainments. Harrison wrote of turning up at a fancy-dress party dressed as a coolie, and on another occasion as a samurai, complete with a genuine Masamune blade! It was in Yokohama that he started on his lifelong passion for jūjutsu. He was introduced to a local *dōjō* (training hall) of the Tenshin Shinyō Ryū, where the practice consisted of *atemi, ne-waza, kata*, and *kiai* (striking methods, ground grappling, formal sets of techniques, and a type of shout).

In 1904 he moved to Tokyo to cover the Russo-Japanese War as foreign correspondent for the *Daily Mail* of London, and as a staff member of *The Japan Times*. Here he enrolled at the Kōdōkan, the headquarters of jūdō, and met all the early famed exponents including the founder of

Kōdōkan Jūdō, Kanō Jigoro, an eminent educationist and the first Japanese member of the International Olympic Committee. It was about now that Francis McCullagh, foreign editor of *The Japan Times*, advised Harrison to take up Russian, which he did, in time becoming adept enough to translate twenty-four of Chekov's short stories for publication in the Sunday editions of the *Japan Chronicle* of Kobe.[54]

Shortly after the Russo-Japanese War, he travelled to England, staying briefly in Moscow and St Petersburg, the then capital. Not forgetting his jūdō, he placed an advertisement in the *Novoe Vremyas* offering free lessons in jūdō.[55] Once back in Japan he studied under a qualified teacher of Russian for the first time, continuing his studies by sharing lodgings with Silinski, a giant Cossack, who was learning English (Harrison's height was five feet six inches).The house rule was that conversation was in Russian one day and the following day in English.[56] Later, when once more back in Tokyo, he shared lodgings with the American, David L.T. Weed, who taught English at Keio University. Weed, who shared Harrison's obsession with judo, holds the unique honour of being the first Westerner to gain a *shodan* (first degree black belt)[57] in 1910 at the Kodokan (followed by Harrison in 1911, and then by another Englishman, William E. Steers in 1912, and the Russian Vasili S. Oshchepkov in 1913).[58] Harrison writes that the Russian mission was headed by Archbishop Nikolai, adding: 'With whom I was on very friendly terms. This truly great and devout man was profoundly venerated by his Japanese followers and respected by all who knew him.'

In 1907 he went to Korea to cover a trial and then continued north, visiting South and North Manchuria, Peking, and Eastern Siberia. He was accompanied by a Russian writer and a British Military Attaché with an official Japanese escort for part of the way. The escort turned out to be one of the assassins responsible for the murder of the Queen of Korea [Queen Min Bi was assassinated on 14 October 1895]: 'He proved a most agreeable companion and guide.'[59] During this journey he collected material for a book, *Peace or War East of Baikal*,[60] on the political dilemmas facing China, Russia and Japan in the Far East.

A year later, in May 1912, he married for the first time. His bride, Cecily Muriel, was the sister of a friend, A.J.Ross. Ross, obsessed by jūdō after Harrison introduced him to the Kōdōkan, returned to England and qualified as a doctor before settling in Australia where, apart from his medical practice, he set up a jūdō club. The marriage ended in an affable divorce in 1923, a break probably caused by Harrison's frequent absences in Siberia and European Russia.[61] In 1913 he was invited to join the staff of a newspaper, *Dalykaya Okraina*, in Vladivostok, a city he had visited a number of times. There he split his time between his duties on the paper and teaching English, with plenty of time left over for various sports including jūdō at the club run by his old friend, the Russian

Oshchepkov.[62] While Harrison was in Vladivostok he interviewed Fridtjof Nansen, then collecting material for his book on Siberia. In May 1914 *The Japan Times* carried a report that Harrison had returned to Japan for an operation on his ear, caused by jūdō. A few weeks later the same paper commented that he was recovering and shortly expected to return to Vladivostok. By the time he was back in Russia the Great War had started, and responding to a message from Robert Wilson, correspondent for *The Times* in Petrograd (formerly St Petersburg), for Harrison to join him there as an Assistant Correspondent, he cleared up his affairs in Japan and started off for the Russian capital, a journey normally taking about ten days, but because of troop movements it stretched to near three weeks.

He was present at the Duma when the Tsar came to open the session in 1915. 'The display of enthusiasm and loyalty was spontaneous and universal. . . had Nicholas II possessed a spark of political imagination. . . nothing would have been easier for him to retain a place in the affections of his subjects.'[63] His jūdō continued in the form of teaching a family of girls in one of the palaces. He was also present in the capital when Grigori Rasputin was assassinated in the early morning of 20 December 1916, and drafted a three-thousand word communiqué culled from the local police and other sources. Because of the strict censorship he was not able to get it out of European Russia. He decided rightly that the censorship might not be so efficient in Vladivostok and that is where he managed to smuggle the report out of Russia. Once back in Japan the report was published, incurring the wrath of the Russian and British Embassies.[64]

Feeling that he should contribute to the war effort, he enlisted as a second lieutenant in the Chinese Labour Corps, a body designed for labouring tasks behind the lines in France, releasing soldiers for the actual fighting. As ever, jūdō was not forgotten, the Chinese put on a show for the Chinese New Year which included wrestling in which Harrison joined in. He also put on a forty-minute display of jūdō for the local European Club assisted by a couple of Japanese.

The Corps came under an attenuated form of discipline necessary to control the many thousands of volunteers under contract, particularly as they had to be transported to France. Following several weeks of training in China, Harrison's company set off on the monumental journey to France.[65] Once in France Harrison put in for a transfer to a unit where his languages could be put to use. This came through with orders to join the North Russian Expeditionary Force in Murmansk and Archangel, composed of soldiers from six nations to strengthen the White Russians in their fight against the Bolsheviks. His task was to set up a newspaper for the British forces, but confounded at every turn by military red tape he gave up the unequal battle, and took over responsibility for a daily communiqué.[66] The Americans, uncluttered by red tape, soon had their paper, *The American Sentinel*, up and running. Among Harrison's contributions to that publication was a poem about Shackleton Boots. This special footwear for artic conditions designed by the explorer and issued to British troops in Northern Russia, proved to be extremely slippery, to the annoyance of all who had to wear them. Shackleton himself turned up in Northern Russia and hearing about the poem, asked Harrison for a signed copy.[67]

He left the army in February 1919 and once back in London joined the Budokwai.[68] His jūdō training was interrupted when he was appointed Secretary to the British Mission to the Baltic States in the same year. Later, as acting British Vice-Consul in Lithuania, he saw considerable fighting when Poland, having signed a treaty with Lithuania, invaded the country. Harrison managed to escape on the last train, carrying the confidential papers of the Consulate.[69] Back in London his wandering days were over; with his strong connections with Lithuania he became Press Attaché to that country's Legation in London, a post he held for many years until it was ended by the Russian invasion of Lithuania in 1940. With the Legation cut off from funds, not only was he out of a job but he lost his Lithuanian pension, a serious matter for a man in his sixties, in particular as he had remarried and had a daughter of thirteen or fourteen.[70] To eke out a living he took various jobs and eventually the family took in lodgers.

During these years he continued his jūdō at the Budokwai, also serving as a Budokwai Committee Member. Finally, after advice on medical grounds his jūdō came to a halt. He applied for and was employed in the Government's Post and Telegraph Censorship as a Grade One Examiner in Russian, Lithuanian, Polish, German and French, a position which lasted until the end of the war (his other languages were Japanese, and to a lesser extent Chinese, Spanish and Italian). By now he was in his early seventies and his finances were as shaky as ever. At the time there were few books available on jūdō and other martial arts; this led him to translate works on these subjects from French and Japanese and this became an important source of income for him.

Never one to back down before a threat, he was once involved in a brawl with several sailors – he won in a spectacular fashion, clearing the bar of sailors. But as he neither smoked nor drank why was he in a bar – to test his judo?[72] He was a lover of cats and indeed all animals, making small contributions to the various societies for their protection. He loathed the then Russian administration, but loved the ordinary Russians. He thought little of authority, addressing his local council as the 'Bumbledom of Hammersmith' and always referred to the Inland Revenue as 'Blood Suckers.'[73] He had a list of people who would serve humanity greatly if only they would do away with themselves. In his eighties he was still rising at seven, doing his exercises, having a cold bath, and then starting on the household chores. This remarkable man, who is described as a 'colourful character',[74] died on 23 April 1961, aged 88.

43

Yoshimoto Tadasu, 1878–1973: 'Father of the Blind in Japan'

NOBORU KOYAMA

Yoshimoto Tadasu

BRITAIN AND THE WELFARE OF THE BLIND IN JAPAN

YOSHIMOTO TADASU (1878-1973) has been called 'the father of the blind' in Japan. Honma Kazuo (1915–2003), the founder of the Braille Library of Japan, when asked to name the pioneers of welfare for the blind in Japan, mentioned Iwahashi Takeo (1898-1954), the founder of the Nippon Lighthouse Welfare Centre for The Blind, and Nakamura Kyōtarō (1880-1964), the first editor of the Braille Mainichi (the Braille edition of the Mainichi daily newspaper), but declared that Yoshimoto Tadasu had made a unique and outstanding contribution.[1]

It was due to the pioneering efforts of Yoshimoto that the British example was so important for the development of welfare for the blind in Japan. As a result of his work the blind in Japan learnt about the advanced level of welfare provided for their counterparts in Britain. This encouraged them to seek improvements in their conditions.

Nakamura Kyōtarō, who was encouraged and given financial help by Yoshimoto, was the first completely blind Japanese to study abroad. He stayed in Britain for about two years from 1912. Following him, Iwahashi

Takeo studied at the University of Edinburgh in 1925-27 and received his M.A in 1927. He was the first blind Japanese to receive a degree from a foreign university. Honma Kazuo's Braille Library, founded in 1940, was modelled on Britain's National Library for the Blind. When Honma visited the National Library for the Blind in London in 1964, he was moved to tears.[2] He told the young member of staff, who showed him around, that he had decided the direction of his life as a result of the existence of the library.

The direct impact of the British example and of its advanced welfare provisions for the blind stemmed from the publication of a Japanese book, entitled *Shin no Eikoku* – or 'True Britain', by Yoshimoto Tadasu.[3] It appeared in 1902, the year in which the Anglo-Japanese Alliance was concluded. By explaining the provisions available in Britain and illustrating what could be done to improve conditions for the blind in Japan, Yoshimoto's book has been regarded as sounding 'the trumpet call' for the reform of arrangements for the treatment of the blind in Japan.[4]

Yoshimoto lived both in Britain and Japan and although he had weak eyesight, he travelled between the two countries more than a dozen times before the Second World War, initially for business purposes, but also for what he regarded as his life's mission. This mission, inspired in part by his Christian faith, was to improve the welfare provisions for the blind in Japan; his business enterprises existed in order to provide funds for this mission. Yoshimoto described the purpose of his business to the associates of the 'Oxford House', which he had established in the context of his business, in the following terms:[5]

> Our Oxford House was set up to serve the blind and other handicapped people in accordance with God's will. The fundamental principles are that we should worship God and love our neighbours. We should not strive always for money but must try our best to help others even while we are working in business. Although our house exists to earn funds for the blind, money must not be our main purpose. We must not confuse means and ends.

YOSHIMOTO'S EARLY LIFE

Yoshimoto Tadasu was born in Osaka on 23 January 1878, the first son of Yoshimoto Tadaakira (1846-1919), a retired army surgeon and a wealthy medical practitioner. He studied at the Higher Commercial School in Tokyo, now Hitotsubashi University, and graduated in 1900.[6] He was born with weak eyesight, but later became completely blind. He was the first Japanese with weak eyesight to receive higher education in Japan. While studying at the Higher Commercial School in Tokyo, he became interested in Christianity and in the works of Uchimura Kanzō. He was introduced to Uchimura through Yamagata Isō (1864-1959).[7] Yamagata, who was a relative of Yoshimoto and a well-known scholar of English as well as the chief editor of an English language newspaper in Seoul became his mentor.

Uchimura Kanzō (1861-1930), the most important Christian thinker in Japan at that time, wrote the preface to Yoshimoto's book, *Shin no Eikoku* ('True Britain'). The high esteem, in which Uchimura held him, is evident from his diary entry for 29 April 1921:[8]

> I was glad to know from his letter that Yoshimoto Tadasu who was staying in Britain would be coming back to Japan soon. He is a Japanese who can discuss with us the nature of God and His love for humanity and who can forget about making money while working to improve the lot of blind people in Japan. He is regarded as a British gentleman because he behaves so differently from a Japanese. It is an honour for Britain, but a great disgrace for Japan.

After graduating from the Higher Commercial School in Tokyo, Yoshimoto, with funds provided by his father, travelled to Europe to visit the International Exposition in Paris in 1900 and then came to Oxford where he matriculated at the University in January 1901. However, for health reasons, he had to return to Japan prematurely in the autumn of 1901. *Shin no Eikoku* was published in 1902, and copies were donated to schools for the blind in Japan.

After medical treatment, Yoshimoto in 1906 took up the post of lecturer at Waseda University where he taught English for a couple of years. He returned to England to start a new business in 1908.[9] He was then thirty years old. With his father's financial help, he proposed to start a trading business which could provide financial support for his activities for the blind. Experience had taught him that without money he could do nothing: as a teacher at Waseda University, he had set up an organization for the blind, but 'he could not do one per cent of what he wanted to do because of a shortage of funds'.[10]

YOSHIMOTO'S TRADING BUSINESS

Yoshimoto set up three offices or shops in Kobe, London and Oxford some years after he had returned to England in 1908.[11] The details of these arrangements are not clear. Some sources suggest that Yoshimoto had set up the Oxford Shōkai (Oxford Trading Firm) or the Oxford House in 1908, but this name seems to belong to a slightly later period.[12] Originally, Yoshimoto intended to import Japanese goods into Britain and sell them in Oxford and London while at the same time exporting British goods, such as woollen cloth to Japan, but over time the latter became the main activity of his business. This aspect of his business stemmed from his marriage. His father-in-law helped him in the exporting of woollen cloth to Japan. Yoshimoto Tadasu's brother, Yoshimoto Misao (1882-1973) describes this situation as follows:[13]

> This English lady's father [Yoshimoto's father-in-law] was living in retirement after having worked for a woollen cloth company in England. Probably in this context, my brother [Yoshimoto Tadasu] started a business to export English woollen cloth to Japan and also to import some Japanese sundry goods into England. Although my brother was not suited to such business, his wife possessed business ability and was also attentive and careful. His business progressed smoothly and its profits were used for the welfare of the blind.

Kelly's directory for Oxford (1911 edition), listed Yoshimoto Tadasu as a fancy goods importer at 12 Ship Street, Oxford.[14] This must have been the location for his Japanese shop Fujiya, which he set up in Oxford. Yoshimoto was listed as a fancy goods importer in the 1915,[15] 1920[16] and 1924[17] editions of Kelly's directory, but the location of his business moved from 12 Ship Street to 5 Ship Street. Takakura Tokutarō (1885-1934), a Christian priest and theologian, lived in the attic (on the second floor) of Fujiya in 1922 and 1923. He mentioned his experience there in his book, *Jidenteki bunshō, kikō, sonota* (Autobiography, accounts of travel and other matters).[18]

HIS MARRIAGE AND BUSINESS

In 1912, Yoshimoto's book *A peasant sage of Japan: the life and work of Sontoku Ninomiya: translated from the Hōtokuki* was published by Longmans in London. Ninomiya Sontoku (1787-1856) was an agricultural administrator during the Edo period esteemed for his virtuous behaviour. In the preface, Yoshimoto thanked two people for revising his English, one of whom was Miss E. M. Pauling, his future wife.[19] Yoshimoto Tadasu and Elsie Margaret Pauling (1887-1976) married in 1912. According to their marriage certificate, Yoshimoto was then thirty-two years old and Margaret was twenty-four. Yoshimoto was registered as a student. The residence of both was given as 18 Warnborough Road, Oxford. Margaret's Father, Asaph Pauling's profession was described as 'fancy goods dealer'. In fact he was a tailor or a retired tailor who lived at 18 Warnborough Road, Oxford.

Yoshimoto Tadasu and Margaret had three children, David Tadasu born in 1916,[20] John Misao in 1917[21] and Mary Eva in 1920.[22] According to a letter from Mary Yoshimoto:[23]

> Mother's Father [Asaph Pauling] was well acquainted with Mr and Mrs Alfred Hewlett who attended the same Strict Baptist

Chapel in Oxford where he also worshipped. Their daughter Miss Priscilla Hewlett was the Welfare Worker over the Weavers at Cawthra Woollen Mills, Bradford, Yorkshire, and she would have been most willing, at Mr. Pauling's request, having knowledge of my Father, to recommend him to the Mill Owners, for his business desires of exporting woollen cloth (excellent quality) to Japan.

Woollen exports became Yoshimoto's main business; importing fancy goods from Japan appears to have been less profitable, and consequently declined in importance. According to his brother, Yoshimoto Misao, his wife Margaret played a significant role in Yoshimoto's business. Yoshimoto's daughter, Mary, mentioned another helper:[24]

My parents employed a young girl, Ethel Burden, who had just left school at 14 years of age, having, I believe, just lost both parents. She proved to be a most trustworthy and also capable helper; first at the Fujiya shop, and later continuing with them for many years, helping with some of the typing, etc

CRISIS AND ACHIEVEMENT

In December 1913, Yoshimoto's business faced a sudden crisis.[25] Yoshimoto received a telegram from Japan at the end of 1913 which informed him that the manager of his business in Kobe had lost a large amount of money in speculative ventures. The manager had been cheated by a swindler and this had led to the bankruptcy of his business and also the loss of his father's fortune. As a result his father had become seriously ill and Yoshimoto had to return to Kobe at short notice.

He left London on 31 December 1913 to return to Japan via the Trans-Siberian railway. Yoshimoto had a series of misfortunes on this journey. In London, he unwittingly bought the wrong ticket. In Warsaw, the conductor declared his ticket invalid. Fortunately, he managed to beg a place in a third-class carriage. However, he immediately lost his money and passport to pickpockets on the platform and had to travel through Russia without passport and money. This was probably the most serious crisis in his life and he ascribed to his faith his ability to endure it with fortitude. In Moscow, he was unexpectedly greeted by an old friend of his from the Japanese Consulate, who had received a telegram from him. He reached Japan safely on 13 January 1914 and managed to solve the debt problems by dealing with the creditors. He returned to England in the spring of 1915. This experience further strengthened his Christian faith.

In 1919, Yoshomoto set up the Association of Blind Christians (Mōjin Kirisuto Shinkōkai) and Nakamura Kyōtarō devoted himself to the work of the association.[26] In 1922, the Mainichi Newspaper Publishing Company (Osaka) started to publish the Braille Mainichi (the Braille edition of the Mainichi Daily Newspaper) with Nakamura Kyōtarō as the editor. The idea of the Braille Mainichi had been thought up by Yoshimoto Tadasu while Nakamura Kyōtarō was in Britain in 1912. Yoshimoto and Nakamura met Kōno Mitoshi, London Correspondent of the Mainichi Daily Newspaper in Oxford and Yoshimoto had strongly recommended Kōno to issue a Braille newspaper.[27] Ten years later, the Mainichi Newspaper Publishing Company started the Braille Mainichi on the suggestion of Kōno Mitoshi in commemoration of its new premises in Osaka.

In 1924, the entire Bible was published in Japanese Braille (New Testament: 11 volumes, and Old Testament: 23 volumes) by the Association of Blind Christians (*Mōjin Kirisuto Shinkōkai* in Japanese).[28] It was only the second full translation into Braille after the English Braille edition. Yoshimoto's financial contribution was indispensable for this achievement.

In 1931, Yoshimoto published *Sokoku ni kisu: Eikoku no tamashii* which was the revised and enlarged edition of *Shin no Eikoku* ('True Britain').[29] The title translates as *Contribute to Fatherland: the spirit of Britain*. He also published *Jūjika o tate ni shite: Kyūritsubō kaikoroku* (in English, 'The Cross as a shield: the memoirs of Kyūritsubō') in 1934.[30] Kyūritsubō literally meant people standing at Kudan Hill, but referred to Yoshimoto himself. In Tokyo, there were humble people who pushed carts up and over Kudan Hill, and Yoshimoto compared his role in pushing the people who were climbing up the hill of faith to the humble people on Kudan Hill.

The deteriorating relations between Britain and Japan directly affected both Yoshimoto's business and himself. He left Britain and returned to Japan in April 1940 leaving his family in Oxford.[31] He was only allowed to take £20 with him. During the Second World War, he stayed in Japan where, because of malnutrition, he completely lost his eyesight. He was not able to return to England until 1947.

AFTER THE SECOND WORLD WAR

Yoshimoto's book *Eikokujin to Kirisutokyō* ('The British and Christian-ity')[32] was published in 1948. In 1949, he attended the International Conference on the Blind at Oxford. In 1950 he was elected as the chairman of the committee for establishing the Japan Council of Evangelism for the Blind (*Nihon Mōjin Kirisutokyō Dendō Kyōgikai*), which was established in the following year.[33] He participated in the first Asian Conference for the Welfare of the Blind at Tokyo in 1955. Iwahashi Takeo had been the main promoter of the conference, but he had died in the previous year. Public acknowledgement of Yoshimoto's contribution for the welfare of the blind came in due course. In 1965 he received the first Braille Mainichi Award of Cultural Merit (*Tenji Mainichi Bunkashō*) and in 1967 he was awarded the Order of the Rising Sun (third class) (*Kun Santō Kyokujitsu Chūjushō*) by the Japanese Government. In the same year, he published the autobiographical *Who is my neighbour?*[34] and its Japanese translation, *Waga rinjin towa dare ka.*[35] Yoshimoto Tadasu died in 1973 at the age of ninety-four.[36]

Yoshimoto frequently referred in his books to his parents, but he wrote almost nothing about his family in England. As he stayed in Japan for many years leaving his family at Oxford, his friends often asked him if he felt lonely. He answered that although one of the greatest pleasures in life was living together with one's family, one may have to desert one's wife and children and give up happiness in order to devote oneself to the service of the Lord but that he did not feel lonely in such a situation because God accompanied him.[37]

Yoshimoto's wife, Margaret, died in 1976, three years after her husband's death.[38] Their first son, David, studied at University College, Oxford, and became the head master of a private school in Einsley, Colchester; he later became a schoolmaster at Bishop Stortford College School.[39] He died in 1994 aged seventy-eight years. The second son, John, was an undergraduate at Pembroke College, Oxford, and studied medicine in London and Oxford, becoming a surgeon.[40] During the war he served in Africa as a medical officer; after the war he worked as a general practitioner in Dartford. Mary served as a nurse during the war, and afterwards, took a Froebel Teacher's training course.[41] She then taught in the East End of London until 1967 when she returned to live with her parents in Oxford, teaching locally. She now lives in Buckinghamshire.

Acknowledgement
I am grateful to Mary Eva Yoshimoto who kindly provided me with much helpful information.

The British Commonwealth War Cemetery at Yokohama[1]

LEN HARROP[2]

Commonwealth war graves cemetery, Hodogaya, Yokohama

BRITISH COMMONWEALTH WAR DEAD IN JAPAN – THE PRISONERS OF WAR

THE FIRST OF THE MANY Allied prisoners captured by Japanese Forces in South East Asia during the Pacific War landed at Yokohama in August 1942 for forced labour. The Japanese War Ministry in March 1942 had set out its policy towards prisoners of war making it clear that all prisoners were to take part in forced labour to relieve the labour shortage and that prisoner-of-war camps were to be established, not only in the southern regions of the Japanese Empire, but also in Japan itself, as well as in Taiwan, Korea, Manchuria and China. A secondary purpose was to create in the peoples of East Asia, who had long resigned themselves as being no match for the white races, a feeling of trust towards Japan and a demonstration of the power of the Empire. A network of POW camps was established within Japan, and at the time of surrender the Japanese Government reported to the Supreme Commander Allied Powers

(SCAP) that there had been ninety-four camps, which held 32,407 Allied POWs.

October 1943 marked the completion of the Burma-Thailand Railway when the fitter of the surviving POWs made the long and dangerous journey to Japan by rail and sea. Of the 2,218 Australian and British prisoners assembled in Singapore for 'Convoy College' on 4 September 1944, to run the gauntlet of US submarines and aircraft in unmarked troopships in the China Sea, less than 300 were to reach Japan's shores alive. The 'troop ships' ranged from ancient cargo steamers to modern ocean liners such as the *Kachidoki Maru* and the ex-*President Harrison*, USA, which had been captured near Shanghai in 1941. One, the *Lisbon Maru* sailing from Hong Kong and heading for Japan, was sunk en route with 900 POWs who were either drowned or died; a few survivors who were rescued reached Yokohama on 10 October 1942.

For many POWs these journeys were a terrible ordeal, battened down in cargo holds, or travelling on open decks. Accommodation was primitive at best, hellish at worst, medical supplies were scarce or non-existent, and food inadequate and generally inedible. The overcrowded conditions and the lack of water and fresh air in the hot latitudes added to the horrors of these long voyages in frequently stormy seas.

Nevertheless, in spite of these heavy losses, Japan continued its policy of transporting Allied soldiers, Merchant Navy and civilians of all Allied nationalities as slave-labourers into the homeland. The change of climate, after the POWs' earlier sojourns in the tropics, and still wearing the rags of tropical clothing were to be traumatic, especially if the prisoners were landed in mid-winter as frequently happened. To go from the extremes of equatorial heat to the freezing cold, and to be housed in sub-standard accommodation, lacking clothing, heating and nourishment proved fatal for many of the exhausted travellers.

Death[4] was common among the prisoners, and funeral services were arranged by camp commandants, after which bearers would deliver the coffin to a local civilian crematorium or burial ground. Small urns containing the ashes of deceased prisoners were stored in camp offices or deposited in temples for safe custody. These remains were eventually collected by the Red Cross and the Graves Registration units of the Australian Army War Graves Group for re-interment in their final resting place in the reflective and tranquil atmosphere of the Yokohama British Commonwealth War Cemetery. A few remains found elsewhere than in Japan were also brought here to Yokohama for similar treatment.

THE END OF THE WAR

By mid-August 1945 the war was beginning to wind down, and the *Indefatigable* was the only British Commonwealth aircraft carrier operating off the east coast of Honshu. The group was fuelled by American tankers on 14 August and returned the next morning to fly eighteen aircraft against targets in the vicinity of Tokyo. These were engaged by Japanese aircraft in an air battle over the Chiba peninsula, a *Seafire* was shot down, the pilot Sub-Lieutenant (A) Fred Hockley RNVR baling out and landing unhurt: he was captured and executed that evening and secretly buried. The observer of an *Avenger*, Sub-Lieutenant (A) John Francis Joseph Andrew Bonass RNVR fell to his death in what villagers described as a 'human bomb' and propped his dead body against a utility pole at a road junction along which his fellow pilot would travel later that morning. Their graves are in a section of the cemetery facing the entrance of the British section (see below).

At 07.00hrs on 25 August 1945 Admiral Nimitz ordered the cancellation of all strikes against Japan; this was followed by a further signal at 11.00 hrs that the Japanese had accepted the Allied peace terms.[4]

THE ARMY GRAVES SERVICE (DGRE) AND THE CWGC

The Commonwealth War Graves Commission (CWGC) is a maintenance organization dealing with the upkeep of graves, cemeteries and memorials of those servicemen and women who died during the two World Wars. It is also concerned with the task of keeping and maintaining the records of the fallen. However, the Commission does not have a historical function in connection with its work, nor does it have access to records of the actions which resulted in the deaths of those it commemorates. The Army Graves Service is responsible for searches for the individual grave-sites based on information provided by chaplains, burial officers, and other sources: it also scans battle areas for some tell-tale rifle or steel helmet which might betray the location of a forgotten grave.[5]

It is the Army's responsibility to identify and register the war dead, and to convey the remains to marked graves in prepared permanent war cemeteries and to hand these over, along with their verified details supplied by regimental record offices, to the CWGC for their horticultural and architectural development and their care in perpetuity. The cost of the work of the Commission is borne by the partner Governments – Australia, Canada, India, New Zealand, the Union of South Africa and the United Kingdom and Northern Ireland, – based on the proportion of their graves. Other Commonwealth nations contribute by paying for the maintenance cost within their territories.

THE QUESTION OF REPATRIATION OF THE WAR DEAD

The Commission, since its establishment by Royal Charter of 21 May 1917, has maintained its principles, which have remained unchanged over the years, that each of the dead should be commemorated individually by grave marker or memorial, that such inscriptions should be uniform and permanent, and that there would be no distinction made on account of military or civil rank, race or creed, and that 'those who died together should be buried together'. This effectively ruled out individual exhumation and repatriation. This was a brave decision. The Americans, when they came into the war had promised to return the dead to all relatives who wished to bury them near their homes, but their casualties had been relatively few; the British had not made a similar commitment. Moreover, the Commissioners felt that to allow a few remains (of necessity only those relatives who could afford the cost) would be contrary to the principle of equality of treatment.

In 1945 strong feeling was building up in both Australia and New Zealand against leaving graves in Japan. New Zealand wanted them moved out to the nearest British, or at least Allied territory, but this was resisted by the Commission. Nevertheless, Sydney (Australia) War Cemetery contains the ashes of a few members of British Forces that died as POWs in Japan, their ashes apparently having been carried by their returning POW comrades. The Far East was new territory to the Commission, and already the responsibility for graves in some areas had been transferred to a new ANZAC Agency for Australia and the south-east Pacific, formally headed by the Australian Minister of the Interior. During the war the Australians had wanted to break away from the Commission and create a purely Australian war graves commission, but this arrangement has worked well over the years.

THE WAR GRAVES AGREEMENT WITH JAPAN

The Geneva Convention – an agreement made by European powers at Geneva in 1864 – established humane regulations regarding the treatment of the sick and wounded in times of war, as well as the burial of the dead.[6]

The area for a British Commonwealth cemetery in line with the provisions of the Geneva Convention was provided by the Japanese Government under the terms of the Treaty of Peace signed at San Francisco on 8 September 1951. It was confirmed by an agreement drawn up between the Commonwealth governments and Japan signed on 21 September 1955.[7] The agreement came into force one month after the date of acceptance by the Australian government and was ratified on 22 May 1956. The Agreement covered the war graves, cemeteries and memorials of Indian servicemen and women in Japan, notwithstanding the fact that India was not a signatory to the Treaty of Peace.

Commonwealth war graves cemetery, Hodogaya, Yokohama

THE BRITISH COMMONWEALTH WAR CEMETERY AT YOKOHAMA

A proposed burial site in Hodogaya Ward, Yokohama, had been reconnoitred, soon after the occupation began, by Lieutenant-General Sir Horace Robertson, Commander-in-Chief, British Commonwealth Occupation Forces (BCOF). By late 1945 preparatory work on the site by the Australian Army War Graves Group was well advanced. Unlike in Europe, the CWGC had no existing war cemetery in Japan. The only grave in Japan of a soldier still in service at the time of his death was that of a British Military Attaché, who had been the Commandant of a German POW camp during the First World War and had been buried in a temple burial ground in Dogo Spa, Matsuyama, Shikoku.

Plans for the cemetery were drawn up between the Anzac Agency of the War Graves Commission in Melbourne, and the Head Office in London. An experienced Australian War Graves officer, who had seen service on the Burma-Thai railway, was installed as Supervisor at the cemetery, and the work of preparing the site, laying out the different sections, the reburial and marking of the graves got under way. By the summer of 1948 the Australian Army Graves Service had satisfactorily completed its responsibilities and obligations, and on 6 September 1948 the war cemetery, which includes the adjacent post-war section, was handed over to the Imperial (later Commonwealth) War Graves Commission, for its maintenance and development – to preserve in perpetuity the memory of those who died, by caring for the most tangible

481

reminders of their sacrifice – the graves and memorials.[8]

The area was previously a juvenile recreation-ground, set up to mark the ascension to the throne by the Shōwa Emperor in 1926. During the war years the area was used as an ammunition storage area and transport workshops by the Japanese Navy. The municipality was compensated for the loss of this facility by the provision of new public parks and gardens, a children's botanical garden, and other recreational facilities, and the whole area has been nominated 'a green zone'.

The British Commonwealth War Cemetery is about nine kilometres southwest of Yokohama Station, alongside the Tōkaidō highway, and is easily reached by public transportation from Yokohama, and by expressways from Tokyo. Buses and taxis are also available from Hodogaya Station on the JR Yokosuka Line for the four-kilometre journey to the bus terminal near the cemetery entrance.

The war cemetery, beautifully situated in woodlands at the head of a valley, is approached by a minor road lined with evergreen oaks and cherry trees, and entered by wrought iron gates flanked by beds of flowering shrubs. The cemetery is divided into five national plots; the British section, the Australian section, the combined Canadian and New Zealand section, the Indian Forces section, and the Post-war section.

On the left descending the cobblestone slope is the handsome records building which houses the register box and a marble desk for the visitors' book. The walls of this building are constructed of *Oya-ishi*, a Green Tuff material composed of fine kinds of volcanic detritus fused together by heat. The American architect, Frank Lloyd Wright who employed it for the façade of the original Imperial Hotel in Tokyo in 1916, used this material with pleasing effect. This stone 'breathes', because of its porous nature and requires treatment with water-repellent chemicals, and has to be protected from rising damp from the ground. In some situations in the cemetery the Oya-stone walls have been capped by limestone copings, and over the years these have suffered from deterioration from frost damage and atmospheric pollution. It has been noted that in many places Oya-stone features have been replaced by granite which weathers extremely well. The granite for the Crosses of Sacrifice came from a quarry in Kasama, Ibaragi Prefecture, on the northern slopes of Mount Tsubaki, while the obelisk in the Indian Forces section came from a smaller quarry in the same area with a finer grain.

Local construction was carried out by Seki Kōmuten, a company also responsible for rebuilding the British Embassy after the Great Kanto Earthquake of 1923.

The marble used in the cemetery is a local stone, coming from Kakogawa, a small town on the Inland Sea coast about 35 kms west of Kobe, and it has long been used in Japan for indoor decoration. The site was visited by Philipp Franz van Siebold, the Bavarian naturalist and traveller during his stay with the Dutch mission in Japan (1823–30) and is widely used as an architectural polished stone in the country.

On the left-hand side an iron gateway leads to the manager's house and office; there stands a fine specimen of a *Magnolia obovata*, which flowers early in spring. On the other side of the driveway are the stores and machinery workshops, masked by dense evergreen shrubbery.

Ever since its inception the cemetery was lucky to have a skilled head gardener named Mori, who served his apprenticeship in the temple gardens of Osaka; small and wiry, he was drafted as a fireman in Tokyo during the war years. He came to Hodogaya as foreman of the Tokyo Nursery Company, which provided the manual labour in digging the graves in the early days of the cemetery. He then joined the cemetery staff as head gardener, serving until his retirement some forty-five years later.

THE BRITISH SECTION

Stone pillars each with a bronze panel support the bronze entrance gates of the war cemetery. One is inscribed with the years '1939-1945' and the other records that the government of Japan generously provided the cemetery area. The curving stone walls either side of the gateway, the two small flower boxes let into the wall on either side, all tend to focus the eye on the point of interest – the Cross of Sacrifice in the British section.

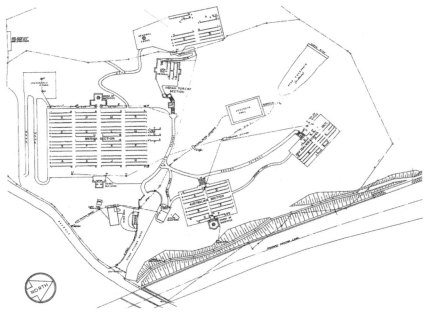

Plan of Commonwealth war graves cemetery, Hodogaya

The pathway leads directly into the British section, and continues on to the steps leading into the Indian Forces section and on to the Post-war section.

The winding pathway to the right leads past the Australian section on the right and terminates at the Canadian and New Zealand section.

The British section has 1,010 graves, including that of the single casualty of the First World War (see above), and four whose names are not known.

A bronze plaque resting on an inclined pedestal marks each grave in the cemetery. This arrangement is regarded as being more likely to withstand the frequent earth tremors than the upright headstones used in war cemeteries elsewhere. The horticultural treatment applied is basically the same in all countries in which the Commission operates. The lawn cemetery with fine, level turf covering all the graves and an absence of paths is universal, with narrow flower borders between the recumbent grave markers. The aim is to produce the effect of a garden rather than a cemetery, and the plentiful use of roses, cottage garden plants, flowering shrubs, and colourful flowering trees is the way in which this is achieved.

A large Cross of Sacrifice stands before a background of pine and evergreens; facing it across the expanse of lawn is the Ashes Shrine.

THE CREMATION MEMORIAL

This beautifully designed structure houses an urn on a marble altar containing the ashes of some 335 Commonwealth soldiers, sailors and airmen, commingled with the ashes of 48 United States and 21 Royal Netherlands military casualties. Their names, except for 51 who were never identified, are inscribed on the walls of the shrine.

The remains were recovered from a mass grave located in Moji, a port city of Kyushu, Southern Japan, which stands at the entrance of the Inland Sea. A similar urn, containing the ashes of mostly American prisoners, but also those of a lesser number of other Allied nationalities, was handed over to the American authorities at the Jefferson Barracks National Cemetery, in St Louis, Missouri, USA, for burial there.

The inscription on the rear of the wall above the urn is taken from the Book of Ecclesiasticus and reads:

> *There be of them, that have left a name behind them, that their praises might be reported. And some that be, which hath no memorial; but their righteousness hath not been forgotten and their glory shall not be blotted out.*

THE AUSTRALIAN SECTION

The Australian section is reached by a low flight of stone steps, and contains six plots holding a total of 277 graves. One is that of Stewardess Lorraine Elizabeth Gleeson, Australian Merchant Navy, of S.S. *Nankin*, a ship that was captured by the German raider *Thor* in the Indian Ocean on 10 May 1942. A prize crew took the *Nankin* to Yokohama where it was renamed the *Leuthen*; it was destroyed there in an explosion on 30 November 1942 that threatened to destroy the city. Mrs Gleeson died in captivity in the Fukushima civilian internment camp on 7 April 1945.

The Cross of Sacrifice overlooking the plots is backed by a screen of varied eucalyptus trees grown from seed collected from each State of the Australian Commonwealth in 1952. Snow gums from Tasmania thrived under Yokohama's climatic conditions. A magnificent Taiwanese Liquidambar stands beside the service road to the left; it is conspicuous at all times, especially in autumn, when its maple-like leaves assume a rich crimson colour. There are displays of flowering plants and trees on the banks between the pathway and the plots. Here are Japanese apricot *Prunus mume*, both white, followed by pink, first to blossom in the New Year, and which require a calm evening to enjoy their delicate fragrance.

Mori, the Japanese head gardener, was responsible for the range of delicate Japanese maples (*Acer palmatum*) throughout this section, clusters of soft green feathery leaves in spring, a beautiful form and brilliant colouring in the autumn, and for the production of many types of azaleas that adorn every section in spring.

The Australian and New Zealand sections also benefited from plants donated to the cemetery at the conclusion of Expo 70 held in Osaka. There is also a fine specimen of the Paper Bush (*Edgeworthia papyrifera-Mitsumata*), the fibres of which furnish the strong paper used to print ten thousand yen notes.

Most pathways are bordered by beds of flowering plants and banks with ground cover, separated or supported where necessary with outcrops of rock. This is tufa collected from the slopes of Mount Fuji, and skilfully built up with a mixture of cement and lampblack to provide pockets of soil for typical rock garden plants.

THE CANADIAN AND NEW ZEALAND SECTION

Further on, the pathway terminates at the stone steps leading to the platform where the Cross of Sacrifice stands before the row of New Zealand graves of men who died during the occupation of Japan. Behind these graves are two plots of Canadian graves, including that of Lance-Sergeant Murray T. Goodenough, M.M., of Cookshire, Province of Quebec, captured in the battle for Hong Kong, who died in Japan of illness on 22 December 1943 at the age of 18, which makes him the youngest soldier buried in the cemetery. This grave caught the attention of Canada's Prime Minister Diefenbaker while on an official visit to Japan. On his return to Canada he gave a moving account of the cemetery and the sacrifice of so young a soldier.

Here European and Canadian deciduous trees contrast with the conifers and evergreens of Japan, and there is a fine example of *keyaki* (*Zelkova serrata*), a large tree of graceful, wide-spreading habit. In autumn the leaves turn to bronze or flaming red in sharp contrast with the green stands of bamboo in the valley below. A small stream wends its way along the valley floor, past a living relic of a fossil genus, a *Metasequoia glyptostroboides* finally to flow into a fish pond in the adjacent public park. The 'Dawn Redwood' is reported to be the best example of this tree growing in Kanagawa Prefecture. The first specimen of this genus was discovered in Hupeh province in China in 1941. In 1944 further trees were located, and the news created a sensation. The ease with which it can be propagated, its rapid growth in an urban environment and its ornamental value have made it the most popular conifer worldwide. The tree in the cemetery was provided by the Forestry Agency in an exchange of plant material in 1956. Its leaves are bright larch green in spring, and turn to old gold in autumn and finally the litter the floor with a carpet of mulch in the winter months.

THE INDIAN FORCES SECTION

The Indian Forces section is an example of how advantage can be taken of a natural disaster. The approach used to be a narrow pathway through the United Kingdom section which then entered the rear part of the section by the side of the Yokohama Memorial. Heavy typhoon rains caused a massive landslide that extended well into the British section below. This permitted a more stable hillside profile, and the construction of a new stone access stairway leading directly into the section and onward to the Post-war section above.

The Indian Forces section is provided with an obelisk mounted on a low square base which has the words 'India' and 'Pakistan' inscribed on two of its faces. A panel set in the north wall, on the opposite side of the plot, records those members of the Occupation Forces from India and Pakistan whose final resting-place is not known. Other men from the Commonwealth Forces, who died in Japan and have no known graves, are commemorated elsewhere on memorials designed for the campaigns in which they took part. Among the larger of these are the Rangoon Memorial, Taukkyan War Cemetery, Myanmar (26,875 names), the Singapore Memorial (24,327 names) and the China, Hong Kong Memorials (4,579 names).

THE BRITISH MILITARY (POST-WAR) CEMETERY

The pathway continues up to the post-war section, which contains the grave of one of the two holders of the Victoria Cross who died in Japan. Warrant Officer (II) Rayene Stewart Simpson, VC, DCM, was serving as a Commander of 232nd Mobile Strike Force Company of the 5th Special Forces Group operating near the Laotian border. Here he won the Commonwealth's highest awards for bravery in Vietnam. The other was Lieutenant (A) Robert Hampton Gray, VC, DSC, Royal Canadian Navy (VR), a pilot and the only member of the Fleet Air Arm and the Royal Canadian Navy to receive it in World War II. He was engaged in attacking enemy vessels in Onogawa Bay, Miyagi Prefecture on the morning of 9 August 1945. Despite fire from shore batteries and heavy concentrated fire from five warships Lieutenant Gray lead the attack flying low to ensure success. Although in flames he scored a direct hit on the 1,000 ton Japanese escort destroyer *Amakusa* which exploded and sank. His body was never recovered from the depths of the bay, although several searches have been carried out. He is officially commemorated on the Naval Memorial to the Missing in Halifax, Nova Scotia, a great Cross of Sacrifice over 12 metres high and clearly visible to all ships approaching Halifax. This memorial bears the names of more than 3,000 Canadian men and women who lost their lives at sea. However, in recent years local people and the Canadian community dedicated a small garden of remembrance on a hillside overlooking the scene of action.[9]

HORTICULTURAL NOTES

The horticultural range of Japan is unique. The island chain extends over many degrees of latitude, and consequently there is a wide range of temperature and climate. Owing to its location in the Pacific Ocean it has a relatively higher humidity and heavier rainfall than continental regions. Northern Japan is covered with snow for two or three months of the year, while a rainy season, which is welcomed by rice farmers in early June, lasts for three or four weeks. This gives the country a range of plant species perhaps double that of other countries. January begins the annual parade of flowering plants with the white and pink blossoms of Japanese flowering apricot. Japan is a land of flowers, and can boast that it has provided the gardens of the world with more flowering shrubs and trees than any other country.

One the important features of a war cemetery is an overall carpet of green turf, and strains of *Zoysia matrella*, Manila or Korean grass were selected for both Kranji cemetery in Singapore and Hodogaya. This low, gregarious grass is normally planted out rather than sown. It is grown from rigid, wiry rootstocks, and it favours open exposure close to the sea. The finer type provides a good covering at the entrance to the United

Kingdom section, and a coarser, leafed variety has been chosen to stand up to the areas of heavier traffic. The turf makes a very solid cover, which chokes out weed competition. One minor disadvantage of this grass is that in the colder months it looses its colour. It has a natural life-cycle of about thirty years, when it is best replaced with new material from the established turf nurseries.

Kariba-chō was once a 'hunting reservation' and it well describes the area over fifty years ago when the nearest habitation was some distance away. Over the years suburban sprawl crept up to the cemetery boundaries and changed the nature of the surrounding countryside. Sometimes this worked to the advantage of the cemetery. Spoil from levelling operations at a new housing estate, was trucked in to produce terraces at the steep slopes at the southern end of the British section. This brought sunshine to an area where previously snow could linger for several months during the winter months. These terraces provided additional space for tree nurseries, which form windbreaks against cold Siberian winds.

The construction of a new expressway running along the cemetery boundaries led to massive earth movements. The deep valley on the other side of the cemetery entrance was filled in to accommodate a toll-booth and an interchange. Part of the land at the rear of the Australian section was handed over to the Expressway Corporation and boundaries adjusted. Luckily, the loss of this land had no visual effect on the appearance of the Australian section, and most visitors to this area are unaware of the heavy traffic running nearby.

Yokohama Foreign General Cemetery

GERALDINE WILCOX

Foreign general cemetery, Yokohama

THE YOKOHAMA Foreign General Cemetery lies on the slope straddling the Yamate Bluff at Yokohama and overlooking the harbour. It is more than just a cemetery. It is a tangible record of the history of foreign residency in Yokohama, and of the role that those residents played in shaping both the city and modern Japan itself.

The cemetery, which covers over 20,000 square metres, is the last resting place for more than 4500 people. It has been in use by the foreign community since 1854. Over the years, people from 40 different nations and many religions have been buried there. It has survived earthquakes, typhoons and wars to become one of the most important historical sites of the Kanto area, and is a part of the history of Yokohama.

The Yokohama Foreign Cemetery tells a fascinating story. A walk through the grounds and the tombstones is like reading a book spanning the last 150 years of Japanese history. Many of the tombstones tell of each person's part in bringing Japan out of its two hundred years of isolation. Collectively they spell out some of the trials and tribulations that the individuals buried there went through and the changes that have occurred in Japan since it was established.

In 1853 Commodore Mathew C. Perry, with his four *kurofune* (black ships) appeared off Uraga in Edo Bay (Tokyo Bay). Perry landed at Kurihama, south of Yokohama, to deliver a letter from President Fillmore and demanded that the *Bakufu* (the Tokugawa shogunate) open their ports to American vessels. The next year, when Perry returned with a squadron of seven battleships for the negotiations, a 24-year-old marine, Robert Williams died aboard the USS *Mississippi*. Perry requested that a piece of land be given as a cemetery for Americans and in which to bury Williams.

After negotiations, the *Bakufu* offered a place within the Zōtokuin Temple of Yokohama village and that was where Williams was buried, with a view overlooking the sea (a condition asked for by Perry). This was how the cemetery began on the Bluff, although three months later the grave of Williams was moved to Gyokusenji Temple in Shimoda.

In 1859, soon after the opening of the port of Yokohama, extreme nationalists killed two Russian marines named Roman Mophet and Ivan Sokoloff. The *Bakufu* bought the adjoining farmland of the Zōtokuin for their graves. This Russian tomb is the oldest recorded in the cemetery and, although it was once a magnificent stone monument, now only the pedestal remains. At that time the shogunate considered collecting land rent for the cemetery but finally decided against doing so. As the number of foreigners increased with the opening of the country, inevitably there was an increase in the deaths of foreigners in Japan and it became difficult to find space for burials of Japanese and foreigners. In 1861, therefore, the Japanese graves were moved to a new resting place.

The cemetery area defined at that time is now the area near the Motomachi Gate, where the oldest tombs can be found. One of these tombs is that of Charles Lennox Richardson, a British merchant who was killed on the Tōkaidō near Namamugi on 14 September 1862 by retainers of the Satsuma daimyo. His death led to the bombardment of Kagoshima by a British fleet in 1863 and the stationing of British and French troops in Yokohama to protect the foreign community.

Almost all the graves of members of the British armed services who died in Japan are in the Commonwealth War Graves cemetery at Hodogaya on the outskirts of Yokohama (see Appendix I(a)) but the cemetery contains the graves of Major G.W. Baldwin and Lt R.N. Bird who were murdered at Kamakura in 1864. Some members of the British forces, who were stationed in Yokohama in the latter part of the nineteenth century and who died in Japan were buried in the cemetery, some in a mass grave. A number of these deaths were due to smallpox.

Many foreigners died on 1 September 1923, when the great Kanto earthquake struck Yokohama, and are buried in the cemetery.

Happily, not everyone died in violent circumstances, many of those buried in the cemetery brought with them to Japan talents that would enrich Yokohama. One, to whom many foreigners owe a dept of gratitude, was J.P. Mollison who in 1868 founded the Yokohama Cricket Club, now the Yokohama Country and Athletic Club, where generations of people have been able to relax and play sport. Others buried there include John Reddy Black, who introduced newspapers into Japan, teachers like Mere Sister Mathilde Raclot, who founded St Maur International School, William Copeland, a Norwegian born American, who was a pioneer brewer in Japan, and Edmund Morel, who came to build the railway between Yokohama and Shimbashi, and who sadly died from tuberculosis at the age of thirty.

In 1864, the *Bakufu*, with the Legations of the United States, Britain, France, and Holland, signed the memorandum for the Foreign Settlement at Yokohama. The enlargement of the cemetery area to the top of the Bluff was acknowledged by Article Three and was further extended almost to its present area by the convention for the Improvement of the Settlement of Yokohama in 1866. In 1868, the new Ministry of Foreign Affairs sent a letter to each consulate stating that although the land would be lent without charge, the consulates should pay the maintenance costs.

In 1890, it was decided to form a committee for the management of the cemetery; this committee was incorporated as a *Zaidanhōjin* (Foundation) on 13 April 1900 and remains in existence to this day. The Executive Committee oversees the running of the foundation while the day-to-day care of the cemetery is in the capable hands of the manager Higuchi Shisei and his staff. The principal work of the Committee is funding the upkeep as 80% of the graves have nobody to care for them. Many have become run down; so finding the funds to care for the grounds and the building is very important.

The cemetery had been closed to the public for 130 years, but, in response to growing interest, it was decided that it should be opened to visitors at regular intervals. Before this was achieved, a great deal of work had to be done; embankments had to be strengthened, drainage improved, paths widened and repaved, trees and shrubs planted. In 1992 the committee proposed a new project to improve and beautify the cemetery. There was a small rather rundown house close to the entrance. It was decided to replace this with a more suitable building to be used for various purposes, but principally to provide a small museum or archive to introduce to the general public some of the more interesting historical facts about the cemetery. A fine new building was opened on 20 October by the British Ambassador, Sir John Boyd. Representatives of the American, Dutch, French and Russian Embassies attended. This major project was only made possible with the help of the Prefecture of Kanagawa, the City of Yokohama, corporate sponsors, the Yokohama

Lions Clubs, and many Japanese and foreign residents.

Since 4 July 1998 the committee have instituted an 'Open House' policy. On weekends and national holidays, from noon to 4 pm, the cemetery is open to members of the public, who can take part in a guided walk through the cemetery and a visit to the museum. Visitors are asked for a donation of Yen 200, and up to 2003, some 51 million yen had been raised for the upkeep of the cemetery. These arrangements are run entirely by volunteers from the Japanese public, persons who own burial plots and students from St Maur International School and the Yokohama International School. Ozawa Seiji, the world famous conductor, has twice performed benefit concerts for the cemetery. The funds raised from his most recent concert were used to renovate a portion of the grounds, which has made it possible to have 60 more plots for future use.

British graves in other parts of Japan

PHILLIDA PURVIS

Kobe cemetery

DURING THE *SAKOKU* ERA when Japan was largely closed to the outside world Christianity was banned and Christian burials forbidden. Churches were destroyed and the graves of the few Christians who had been buried in Japan since the early sixteenth century were dug up. In Hirado, 'all the dead men's bones were taken out and cast forth'. The foreign dead during this time had to be buried at sea. Christopher Fryke, in 1683, describes a burial in Nagasaki: 'In this Port dyed three of our men and a Carpenter's Boy. Some Japanese carried them out of the Harbour in a small boat into open sea, where they threw them over; for they are so far from suffering any Foreigners to be Buried among them.'[1] The only Europeans buried in Japan during that time were Dutch men, who were allowed to trade from Dejima in Nagasaki harbour. They were allotted a burial ground at Goshinji Temple, at the foot of Mt Inasa.

KOBE

In May 1867, preceding the opening of Japan, an agreement was signed between the British Minister in Japan and the Japanese government. It included the following clause: 'The Japanese Government will form a Cemetery for the use of all nations at Hiogo, on the hill in the rear of the foreign settlement, and another at Osaka at Zuikenzan.'[2]

The Japanese, however, had made no arrangement for such a cemetery in advance of the arrival of the foreign officials, sailors and merchants on 1 January 1868. The deaths of four seamen on board the ships bringing the foreigners precipitated urgent action. The Consuls were obliged to accept the unsuitable site which the Japanese proposed – Ono, at the mouth of the River Ikuta, on its west bank. An officer, Lieutenant Archibald Henry Turnor RN of HMS *Rodney*, was buried there on Christmas Day, 1867, shortly followed by seaman William Collins. Time has worn away the lettering on their headstones. The oldest now legible is that of Francis Gerhard Myburgh, 'Her Britannic Majesty's Consul for Hiogo and Osaka who died on 19 January 1868, aged 30'. This unfortunate cemetery at Onohama was so close to the sea that the sea water seeped into the graves which then had to be dug so shallow 'that at times foxes came down from the hills at night time, scraped the earth away and gnawed at newly buried coffins'.[3] Nearby were rubbish dumps, slaughter houses and piggeries making it 'the dreariest plot of ground surrounded by a rotten fence of wooden palings which are of no avail to keep out intruders who steal the shrubs and marble crosses.'[4]

Eventually, in 1899, the Ono Cemetery was closed and a new cemetery opened at Kasugano. By the 1930s the site of Ono Cemetery lay in the way of development of the city of Kobe and the consular corps, and such families as could be contacted, together with local representatives of their various religions, agreed to the suggestion that the entire cemetery be moved to a site in the mountains, Shugohara behind Futatabi. Flooding and the war delayed the move but it was finally completed in May 1952. In May 1954 Kasugano Cemetery was closed and Shugohara became the site of all new foreign burials. In 1960 and 1961 the Kasugano graves were also moved to Shugohara. Of the total of 1,404 graves from Kasugano, 471 were British. At the request of the next of kin, or the institutions to which they were attached, four British graves were transferred to the Tama Cemetery in Tokyo and three to Yokohama.

Today, Shugohara is a beautifully landscaped and spacious hilltop spot which is wonderfully restful, because of the continuing policy by the City not to permit entry except to families and others with a particular purpose. All the plots are carefully tended which adds to the sense of order and peace. The cemetery is divided into sections including those for Protestants, Catholics, Greek Orthodox, Jews, Muslims and Hindus.

The Onohama cemetery and the graves removed from the Kasugano site stand separate.

There are about 600 British buried at the Cemetery,[5] which is still in use. Of the 671 in total 289 were removed from the Ono Cemetery. Headstones make the usual record of children's and other untimely deaths. Japan, in those early days was not a healthy place to live and deaths from various sicknesses were commonplace. 'Kobe (Hyogo), Nagasaki, Niigata and Yokohama were all counted (by Britain's Japan Consular Service) as unhealthy posts, and attracted added years for superannuation purposes.'[6] Others record unfortunate stories – Mr Crofts of Shanghai, for example, died while on a visit to Kobe as did, in 1906, James Smyth of the China Maritime Customs, while on his way home; Robert Paton 'died at the Gas Works' in 1899. As far as it is recorded on the headstones, a number of the British in this cemetery 'died at sea' or were connected with it, such as Robert Slorford at age 22, whose headstone was erected by 'the crew of the Steamship *Galley of Lowrie*' in 1884; James How Pyne, Commander of the SS *Hiroshima Maru* in 1892; Captain John Tonkin, Captain of the *Pride of the Thames*; Captain W.M. Houghton, Pilot; Henry Webster of the SS *Falcon*, in 1905; Lowry, Chief Officer of the SS *Indrani*; and John Wynn, Master Mariner, in 1899 'who commanded the troopship *Bravo* in the Crimea War and was for many years Commander of the Mitsubishi and Nippon Yusen Kaisha's mail steamers. Some records indicate profession – Emma Ruth Cribb in 1940, Missionary, and others give indications about the person buried by recording who erected the headstone – that of Mr Hughes was 'erected by the Masonic brotherhood' and that of Mr Haselwood in 1888 by the Hong Kong and Shanghai Banking Corporation. John Fowler Mitchell, Master Shipbuilder, who died in 1903, is recorded as being 'formerly of Nagasaki and 44 years resident of Japan'. He was one of four brothers from Aberdeen who all went to sea. James, who erected a memorial in Nagasaki to his three brothers, William, who died in Abyssinia in 1868, George who died in Nagasaki in 1871 and Andrew who was drowned in a shipwreck off the Goto islands in 1874, was one of the earliest residents of the foreign settlement in Nagasaki where he established the Aberdeen Yard and built Japan's first yacht, the *Phantom*.

Two government servants are placed in the best position in the Onohama section at Shugohara, Myburgh, mentioned above, one of the earliest graves, and that of 'HBM's Consul for Hiogo and Osaka, James Joseph Enslie, who died in 1896 and was formerly Vice-Consul in Hakodate in 1882 and Consul in Nagasaki in 1886.

The Scots of which there are many, such as Graham, Dick, Robertson, Ritchie, Urquhart, Grigor, Morrison, Anderson seemed keen to record their origins in Scotland and the Welsh, such as Thomas of Pembrokeshire and Williams of Carmarthen, the area they were from. Most headstones however do not record birthplace or nationality at all but since an effort has been made to keep nationalities together, (based on knowledge, records and advice at the time of religious leaders and others in the community) where the name does not quickly contradict it, one can assume that many of the unnamed headstones in certain areas of the Protestant, Catholic and old graveyards are British. These small, low headstones only have the names and dates of birth. Some in those areas are now totally illegible.

Those buried in Kobe may have lived anywhere in the west of Japan – one British grave was even of a victim of the 1923 earthquake in Yokohama. One monument records the removal of the 64 unnamed graves removed from Onohama, many of which may have been British. In his account of 1978, Harold Williams of the International Committee of Kansai urges us not to be sentimental about them:

> Some are those of seamen whose names have not survived, but many were the graves of beachcombers, tramps, derelicts from China ports, or men who had deserted their ships and had no right to be here. In those early days such men often importuned the Japanese, disgraced the foreign community in the eyes of the Japanese, and embarrassed the foreign consuls by their presence. From time to time the Consuls gathered up such unwelcome persons and deported them. Some, however, died here and had to be buried in the local foreign cemetery.[7]

OSAKA

In the case of Osaka a similar agreement to Kobe was reached with the Japanese authorities, in May 1867, for the provision of a cemetery at Zuikenzan (now in Minato-ku). Again, it was not a well-favoured spot. 'The cemetery is a dismal sand-patch close to two small hills. Had those hills been included in the cemetery reservation we should have had nothing to complain of. . .'[8] 'A neglected and dismal sandpatch does duty for the Foreign Cemetery of Osaka. . . a dismal swamp which is our God's acre'.[9] Not only were the graves at risk from local wildlife but also from grave-robbers; one newspaper account describes the desecration of an infant child whose funeral had taken place a month earlier, 'motives of the perpetrators . . . seem to have been that they thought some valuables may have been buried with the body. . .'[10]

Osaka, like Kobe, also began to expand rapidly and in 1904 the controversial decision was taken to move the nine graves to a new site at Abeno.[11] This was as inauspicious a site as its predecessor and only half the size of the Kobe cemetery,[12] and Harold Williams, resident of Kansai since 1919, began a campaign for a new cemetery:

Monuments that stood there for over half a century are now being overturned. Stone crosses erected within the last two years have not survived even that short period. The place is not unlike those dismal cemeteries in the slum areas of European cities of more than a century ago. . .'[13]

Finally, in 1960, the Abeno cemetery was closed and a new site at the Municipal Hattori Sacred Gardens was opened at Hirota, near Toyonaka City. Of the 49 graves, 43 were moved to this new cemetery, of which 13 were British.

NAGASAKI

The largest community of foreign nationals in the earliest days resided in Nagasaki. The Dutch cemetery at Goshinji Temple is the site of the oldest European grave in Japan, that of the director of Dejima, Hendrik Duurkoop, who died in 1778. This cemetery was in use until 1870 and contains 41 Dutch graves as well as three British and a handful of other nationalities. It is alongside the Chinese cemetery, which has 230 graves, the earliest dating from 1627; the Chinese obtained permission to trade and came to settle in Nagasaki from 1600. Trade agreements were signed with Russia, Britain, France and the US in 1858 and the Nagasaki authorities therefore made available land at nearby Inasa for an International Cemetery which was briefly used from 1859 to 1869, and contains 31 foreign graves of which nine are British.

At the time of the opening of Japan the Nagasaki authorities made available a plot of land at Oura, close to the foreign settlement, and this became the main graveyard for foreigners from 1861 until 1888, by which time it contained 282 graves, of which 133 are British, mostly of seamen from ships anchored in Nagasaki harbour. Two new cemeteries succeeded Oura, one at Urakami Yamazato (now Sakamoto-machi) and the other at Urakami Fuchi, for those who died of contagious diseases. The latter with 166 graves was closed in 1920, The original Sakamoto International Cemetery, which contained 377 graves, including 103 British, was extended across the road and is divided according to religion. It is now closed, with 70 tombstones of which 31 are British. The foreign community looked after the international cemeteries at Nagasaki, even if they did not do much else.[14]

Most of the tombstones in the international cemeteries of Nagasaki offer little information about the lives of the individuals buried there. The earliest legible gravestone, from 1861, marks the burial place of Charles Collins, a 27-year-old coal-stoker on HMS *Odin*.[15] He was mysteriously murdered while out on a drinking binge as his ship lay anchored in the harbour. Two other British sailors, Robert Foad and John Hutchings, both 23 years old, on shore leave from the British ship *Icarus* in August

1867, were hacked to death as they slept by a Chikuzen (Fukuoka) samurai 'for his amusement'. The incident became highly political; the British Minister and Consul General Sir Harry Parkes sent Ernest Satow to investigate and, eventually, the culprit was discovered and obliged to commit *seppuku* (ritual suicide).

Amongst the most well-visited graves at Sakamoto is that of Thomas Blake Glover, of Fraserburgh. He arrived in Nagasaki in 1859, setting up his trading business, Glover and Co., two years later. He introduced into Japan the first slip dock, railway and telephone line as well as the first coal mine. He also introduced 'everything from the first ironclad warship to equipment for the mint which produced the first yen'.[16] Additionally, he played a major role in the establishment of the Kirin Brewery. Glover died in 1911 in Tokyo but his ashes were brought back to Nagasaki. Glover's sister, Martha, who died in 1903, his brother, Alfred, who died in 1904 and a nephew, Thomas Berry Glover, who died in Yokohama on leave from India in 1906, are also buried in Nagasaki. So also is at least one of his children, Kuraba Tomisaburō, who committed suicide after the atomic bombing of Nagasaki.

Nagasaki's cemeteries are full of the graves of foreigners whose lives were unusual and, where information can be found, they reveal fascinating life stories. Many have been researched and are fully described in *International Cemeteries of Nagasaki*.[17] Some brief examples drawn from that research illustrate the sort of British people who lived and died in the international ports of Japan in the early days of Meiji.

A large cross, erected by the Japanese government at Oura, marks the burial place of George B. Newton, a Royal Navy physician who established hospitals for contagious diseases in Yokohama and Nagasaki. One of his achievements was the testing for venereal diseases of all prostitutes in Nagasaki. He died in 1871, his services to medicine being recognized by both the British and Japanese governments. Bonham Ward Bax of the Royal Navy, died of dysentery in 1877 while on his fourth visit to Japan en route to survey the coast of Korea. He is remembered for his detailed written account of his impressions of Nagasaki which were very favourable. Matthew Adams came to Japan in 1862 and worked as a ships chandler, general store keeper and naval contractor, until his death in 1881 on the way from Vladivostock to Hakodate. He is buried at Oura with his son, Matthew who died in Hokkaido in 1937. The grave of Rebecca Wetherell is to be found at Sakamoto Cemetery. She was drowned in 1891 when the *Cape City* from Shanghai, captained by her husband, capsized and sank in the harbour while briefly without ballast. Wetherell had his mariner's licence revoked for negligence following this tragedy. John Meldrum Stoddart, who ran the coal mines at Takashima, died of influenza in 1891. Charles Sutton, stevedore, ballast and water contractor, who arrived in Nagasaki in about 1860, and was the victim of a vicious attack in 1864 by another sword-wielding samurai, was buried in 1892 at Sakamoto after 'the most numerously attended funeral ever witnessed in Nagasaki'.[18] The grave of his younger brother, George, who died the following year, lies adjacent. Ship's engineer, John Calder of Midlothian, died in 1892 while manager of the Mitsubishi Dockyard and Engine Works. He helped found the Masonic Lodge of Nagasaki and served as its first Master. Eliza Goodall stopped off in Nagasaki on her return to England from India, in 1876, after the death of her husband. Here she died in 1893 after 17 years as a missionary and dedicated service to girls' education, mainly through her Girls Training Home where she taught English and sewing. Charles Arnold worked for eight years in Nagasaki, as the physician for foreign residents and medical lecturer at the Nagasaki Government Hospital before his death at 36 years of age in 1894. James Williams came to Nagasaki in the mid 1880s. He and his Japanese wife ran 'The Land We Live In' restaurant. Their daughter Rita died at the age of 16 in 1898 and is buried in Sakamoto, followed by James two years later. Henry Snell, a sailor, and Leander Brooks, a stoker, on HMS *Bonfleur* were killed by French assassins, in street fights, four days apart in 1901, during a visit to Nagasaki. From 1862-63 Simeon Lawrence was sergeant in charge of the British Legation in Tokyo before becoming constable to the British Consulate in Hakodate for 13 years. He transferred to Nagasaki in 1879 where he was constable to the British Consulate until 1898. He died in 1902 and is buried at Sakamoto.

An example of the few foreigners who were not buried in the main cemeteries of Nagasaki is Scotsman John S. Massie, a childhood friend of Thomas Blake Glover, who came to Nagasaki in 1864 and established the International Hotel. He lived and was buried, in 1917, in the Japanese neighbourhood of Junin-machi.

HAKODATE

At Hakodate on the island of Hokkaido there are other British graves from the earliest days, when there was a British Consulate at the port. The Protestant cemetery at Irifune-chō dates from 1870, when the foreign consuls requested a plot of land. There are also separate Russian and Chinese cemeteries. Earlier burials of foreigners were at temples, alongside the Japanese, but they were reburied when the foreign cemeteries were opened. The earliest legible headstone at Irifune is of a US seaman, from 1854, while the earliest British grave dates from 1855. It is a joint grave of John Madden, Ordinary Seaman of HMS *Winchester* 'who departed this life at Hakodadi', aged 22, and of Dane Courtney, of the same ship who was drowned a month later at the same age. In October 1859 James Prince, a stoker on HMS *Highflyer*, died at the age of 26, and in 1862 Captain John Newton of the *Barque Egean* of London buried his 25-year-old wife 'F. L. S. Pith', who died at sea. She was the first foreign woman to be buried at Hakodate. In 1891, James Marr's death was 'regretted by many friends'. Edmund Bulst, who died in 1865 in the Russian Hospital aged 17 years, might have been British as also the baby daughter of Walter and Victoria Den, in 1870, Baby Bellows in 1874, little Minnie Violet in 1882, and two month old Florence Squire in 1885. Most of the headstones, like these, do not name birthplaces, although the Scots, again, were fond of naming their origins, such as James Scott of Kincardineshire, in 1925. The many seamen of RN Ships who met their ends in the seas around Hokkaido are likely to have been British; for those who were responsible for the burial of their comrades it seems sometimes to have been a matter of importance to make their provenance clear; for instance George Wilson Todd, A Native of England, Late Chief Engineer of the SS *Mary Tatham* 'suffocated on board' at Cape Yerimo in 1882. There are records of some sort about two thirds of the graves in the Protestant Cemetery at Hakodate.

In Hokkaido most British burials took place in Hakodate, although Louisa Batchelor, wife of the pioneering scholar of the Ainu language, John Batchelor, died in 1936, at the age of 93, and is buried in Sapporo.[19]

OTHER GRAVES

Of all the well known Britons for whom Japan was their final resting place the most famous is Elizabethan seaman and adventurer William Adams – Miura Anjin – who died in May 1620, in Hirado, Nagasaki, at the age of 56. His grave, which survived the desecration of the *sakoku* period, is now claimed to be in Tsukayama Prefectural Park in Yokosuka.[20] He arrived in Japan in April 1600, as Pilot Major for a Dutch fleet. Shogun Tokugawa Ieyasu took a liking to him and made him his trade adviser and rewarded him with a fiefdom and the rank of samurai. His life has been made famous by the novel, *Shogun*, by James Clavell, later made into a film.

In Tokyo there are a number of different burial grounds containing the graves of British nationals. Gokoku-ji Temple, for example, is the burial place of architect Josiah Conder, who was invited to Japan in 1877 to teach architecture. He trained most of the major Japanese architects of the Meiji era and designed buildings that included the Tokyo Imperial Museum, the Rokumeikan and the St Nikolai Cathedral.

Hugh Fraser, the British Minister from 1889-94, died at his post and was buried in the Aoyama cemetery.[21] So also was Thomas Baty, the extraordinary progressive intellectual lawyer who, in 1916, was invited to Japan by the Ministry of Foreign Affairs, to be a legal adviser on international treaties.[22] His mother was buried in Aoyama cemetery in 1916, and his sister, Anne, in 1945.[23]

English scholar, John Lawrence was buried in 1916 at Soshigaya

Cemetery in Tokyo (the burial place also of Lafcadio Hearn). Alan Owston, who founded the Yokohama Yacht Club, a native of Surrey, was buried at Negishi, Yokohama, in 1915. In Tama Cemetery, George Gauntlett was buried in 1956. He came to Japan in 1891 and worked as an English teacher at schools all around the country, later teaching Esperanto. He founded the Esperanto association in 1906.

Minna Tapson, who died in 1940, is also buried in the Tama Cemetery. She came to Japan in 1888, as the first woman CMS missionary, and worked in Osaka, Hakodate, Shounan and Chiba. In 1924 she established a women's hospital, the 'Garden Home' in Nakano, Tokyo in 1924.[24] The second CMS woman missionary was Hannah Riddell, who arrived in 1890. In 1895, together with another Englishwoman, Grace Nott, she opened a Leper Colony in Kumamoto, where they were teaching English. They were joined in 1896 by Hannah's half-niece, Ada Wright. Hannah was obliged to resign from the CMS and independently continued her work for the lepers until her death in 1932. Ada had rejoined her in 1923 and continued the work Hannah had begun until the leper hospital was closed in 1941 and she was forced to go to Australia. Eventually, in 1948, she was allowed to return to Japan and died there in 1950. Both Hannah Riddell and Ada Wright are buried in Kumamoto.[25]

In Okinawa there are two individual graves worthy of mention. The first, dating from 1816 is of a young seaman who died while his ship was experiencing the legendary hospitality of the Okinawan people as they waited for Lord Amherst's embassy to the Chinese court to return. His headstone reads: 'Here lies buried, Aged Twenty-One Years, William Hares, Seaman, Of His Britannic Majesty's ship *Alceste*, Died Oct. 15, 1816. This Monument was erected By the King And Inhabitants of this most hospitable Island'. The second grave is marked by a large headstone which reads: 'Henry E. Amoore, Teacher in the Okinawa Prefectural Middle School, Died on 16 February 1908 at the age of 68.' He was a single man who had taught English for many years in Okinawa and the headstone was erected by his former students. Finally, a more recent memorial remembers the loss of British lives in the Second World War. The names of 82 British Military Personnel are listed on the Memorial in the Peace Park at Naha, the capital of Okinawa

Outside the Christian cemeteries, from as early as the Meiji days, are the graves of other British-born spouses of Japanese, whose families chose that they be buried as Buddhists. One of the most interesting examples, for the romantic story of her life, is that of Countess Iso Mutsu. Born Ethel Passingham, she met Count Hirokichi Mutsu in 1888, when he was 20 and a student at Cambridge University.[26] She died in 1930, before experiencing the horrors of her native and adoptive countries at war with each other. Hirokichi died in 1942 and, after the war, their son, Younosuke (Ian), had their remains reburied in the Mutsu tomb with

Hirokichi's father, Munemitsu Mutsu, Foreign Minister in the 1890s. They lie side by side in Jufukuji Temple in the Kamakura they loved.[27]

Loss of HMS *Rattler*
Extracts from Ernest Satow's Diary of 1868

Sept. 7 [?].   Embarked on board the Rattler commanded by Stephenson, nephew of Admiral. Keppel, with Adams for a political trip northwards. . . It appears probable that the Russians have taken possession of two of the Kurile group, namely Kunashiri and Itōrup [Etorofu] and we are to go up there to find the truth of this report and to look for a port in that neighbourhood which may be opened to foreign trade and Yezo thereby.

Sat. Sept. 12.   Arrived at Hakodate in the evening after about 84 hours steaming . . . and went with Adams to call on (?) little Eusden who of course was perfectly ignorant of everything and could give us no information about Yezo. In fact we had already got out of Inouye [Iwami no Kami who had accompanied them on the ship] all we wanted to know about. the principal places on the coast.

Sund. Sept. 13. Went to call on the governor, a *Kuge* [court noble] named Shimizudani with Stephenson and Adams. There has been some difficulty about this individual refusing to see the consuls, but that is being got over as far as Eusden is concerned through the influence of negotiations conducted by Sir Harry Parkes at Yokohama with Komatsu Tatewaki the *Sanyō* [councillor]. We have therefore had no trouble in arranging that we shld. be properly received. We walked out to Kamieda [Governor's residence] and arrived there at half past two. Chairs had been placed in a circle in the interview-room used by the former governors. . .Adams was placed in the seat of honour and after the ordinary compliments had passed we had some conversation about our expedition to Kunashiri and Itorup. Inouye is to start on the 16th [?] at latest and to go round by the east coast; we on the same day by the west coast to call at Iwanai and other places. Shimizudani is a rather good looking young *Kuge* of about 25 with a well-shaped nose but heavy jaw and open mouth, and his teeth being lacquered made this a bad feature. He is evidently intelligent and not stuck up as we should have imagined from his proposal to receive the Consuls three rooms off. That was doubtless a dodge of his leery subordinates.

Sept. 14.   Shimizudani came off to make a call with Inouye. . .Very friendly and cordial. It was settled that we should start on the morning of the 16th, the *Rover* [a merchant ship] also . . . coming up to Iwanai. . .

Sept. 15.   Spent last night at Howells *à la Japonaise*. A lot of machinery has to be put on board the *Rover* for the mines at Iwanai and departure consequently delayed. My advice is to throw over the Japanese altogether and to go up to Etorofu and make inquiries on our own look.

Sept. 16.   We were to have started this morning at daylight but put it off on account of the *Rover* not having left. . .

Sept. 17.   Left Hakodate at about 9 a.m. Fine weather but contrary breeze. Passed close in front of Matsumae about 5 p.m. Large town situated on seashore with Daimio's castle in centre towering up above the other houses. Hills covered with wood to east and north. Grassy downs on the west.

Sept. 19.   Reached Kayanoma near Iwanai in Yezo at 6.50 p.m. Distance from Hakodate 170 miles. Much head wind all the way had kept us back. The *Rover* which left at noon on the 17th arrived on the evening of the 18th having crept up inshore. The Bay is enormous. . .

Kayanoma lies on the seashore some 5 miles from Iwanai. It is a purely Japanese settlement of fishermen. Gower's coalmine lies abut two miles up a winding valley and is not visible from the anchorage. The *Rover* brought up some trucks, iron rails etc. for the tramway which is intended to connect the mine with the beach and other machinery under the superintendence of a man named Scott brought out here for the purpose. The climate of this place is very cool even in summer, the thermometer falling to 20 deg. Fahrenheit at night. In winter the cold is intense, to -8 degrees and the ground is covered with snow. Bears abound in the neighbouring hills. Salmon, salmon trout are taken in the river Ishibetsu halfway between Iwanai and Kayanoma, and cod. . . *iwashi* [sardines] and other fish abound in the bay . . . awabi [abalone] and fish manure are exported in large quantities from Iwanai.

Sun Sept. 20.   Horrid bad weather, raining and blowing, so had to give up the idea of going to Iwanai: but as there are only about 30 or 40 Ainos there [it did not matter very much]. The word Aino is the name those people give to themselves and is said to mean man. Japanese are called *shamo*.

A party of us visited the coalmine in the afternoon under Gower's guidance. Sleepers and longitudinal wooden rails have been laid down from the seashore for a distance of about two miles up the valley, and now that the iron rails have arrived in the *Rover* the tramway will soon be completed. Half a mile from the seashore on the side of the railway stands Gower's house, built of wood and furnished in European fashion. The entrance to the mine is halfway up a very steep hill, up which the tramway cannot be conducted.

From the bottom of the hill therefore several (three) gradients have been cut of very steep grade, especially the middle one, and smaller cars are to be run down there by a rope round a drum. The main gallery of the mine – 12 ft high by 7 wide – already extends some seventy yards into the hill, and a good deal of coal has been taken out already in making this tunnel; but the beds, of which there are four, seven feet thick each, have not yet been commenced.

Gower talks of supplying the whole of China and Japan with coal at $4 a ton. When the works in progress are finished, will be able to extract 200 or 500 tons a day. Very sanguine man. Talks of bringing the coal down in sledges over the snow in winter time. The sides of the valley are gentle inclines, covered with tall impenetrable grass bound together with the lacquer vine so poisonous to the blood. No Japanese has ever been five miles from the sea coast, so dense is the jungle. But the soil is rich and easily brought under cultivation: population alone is wanted.

Sept. 21.   Left Iwanai at seven in the morning for Otarunai, distant by the charts only 75 miles. The weather was bad, rainy and easterly breeze, so that when we got abreast of Cape Novosiltrof [sic] it became impossible to continue our course: so ran into Shakotan a little bay on the west side of this cape. Seven Ainos, whom little Harris, a middy [i.e. midshipman], called Indians, came off to the ship. A party of us went on shore about one o'clock. Very rocky place. Situated at the mouth of a very narrow valley, with a path up it by the stream leading over the hills. The village contained a big house called an *unjōya*, and some dozen or two of Aino huts, besides a small temple on an island some few yards from the shore. Population not exceeding 150, of whom Ainos 60. Is the centre of a district which is estimated to contain about 2500 souls altogether. In the evening weighed anchor and stood out to sea under a light breeze, with the hope of seeing Otarunai, of which we have heard so much, tomorrow morning.

Sept. 22.   Vain hope. Violent wind has sprung up during the night which drives us westward or north westward across the Gulf of Tartary. Otarunai thereby becomes an impossibility. Very rough sea, and sickness as a consequence.

Sept. 23.   Weather moderated this morning and we steam towards Soya, at about 2.30 p.m. Come in right of Rishiri, island on the west of Soya, close to entrance of La Perouse straits.

Sept. 24   Going into Soya bay at six in the morning, fine and water smooth, the ship ran aground about two miles off the village of Soya. Various attempts were made to get her off by laying out anchors at the stern, but one having broken its shaft under the strain and another having dragged further experiments were abandoned as futile, especially as the sea began to get up, preventing the pinnace from taking out the best bower anchor.

Highwater being about three o'clock violent efforts were made to drive her off by reversing the engines but all proved of no avail. In the hopes of getting the ship off four of the 32 pr [pounder guns] were thrown overboard and 5 more guns landed in the pinnace and a shore boat, but the approach of night put an end to this very soon. I went on shore to endeavour to get some pilots (2), to assist us in landing the ship's stores and to hire a godown in the village.

Before I left the ship Stephenson confided to me his belief that the ship would never be got off, and that we should all have to sleep ashore the next night. With some difficulty I obtained an interview with an official who happened to be delayed here in his voyage to Sakhalin named Hotta Gorozaemon; and tho' he appeared at first inclined to be impudent and refer me to the local officials, I gained the victory over him and he did all that was asked. Rain becoming very violent, I returned to the ship where I found everybody apparently prepared for the worst, and after dinner everybody began packing up his goods.

With the wreck of the *Racehorse* near Chefoo fresh in my memory, I hardly thought it worthwhile to make any such preparation, but Noguchi [Satow's servant] did for me. About 9 o'clock a petty official of Soya, accompanied by two Japanese sailors and an Aino, came off. Their opinion as inhabitants was worth listening to, and was certainly not encouraging. The chief boatman declared that he doubted whether the vessel could possibly hold together during the night, and that if the N.W. wind should spring up her existence would be speedily terminated.

As this differed slightly from our own view of the case, and moreover no boats could be procured to land our baggage, we determined to make the best of it, and try to get off everything early in the morning. The ship bumped heavily all night, breaking both arms of the rudders yoke and springing the jib-boom, and still she made very little water, not more than a foot per hour, but towards five o'clock in the morning the bottom began to give way under the engine room and speedily split the whole length of that part of the ship.

As early as three o'clock the biscuit was all passed up from the headroom and deposited under tarpaulin in a Japanese lighter which had been brought off about 8 o'clock the previous evening, but as the heavy rain obscured the sky it was judged more prudent to put off the start till daylight. In the meantime the cutter which was to have towed this boat in got loose and drifted away from the ship to our great anxiety, but luckily she was recovered again before seven o'clock. At six o'clock the engine room was quite full of water, nearly over the cylinders. I went on shore with my own baggage, Noguchi and Adams' teacher about seven.

The officials had allotted to us a large house to live in and keep all our stores etc. in, but as it was too small for all of us, I obtained the loan of the barracks situated in a little gully at the back of the village, at 5 minutes walk from the shore. It rained fearfully all day, and we had to remain huddled up in the *Unjōya* on the wood floor round a great fire of logs over which the Aino cook was constantly cooking rice and soup for the natives.

Everybody was landed by the early part of the afternoon with bag and baggage. On inspecting the barrack which I had borrowed, Stephenson found it too far off to be convenient, and we therefore applied for other quarters and had the satisfaction of getting a capital building close to that in which the men were lodged. The paper slides were in very bad condition and could not be mended before the evening, so that most of the officers remained in the *Unjōya* lying where they had spread their mattresses round the fire.

Whilst we were smoking round the fire in the afternoon there came in the young damsel whom we saw yesterday morning. Without the least shyness she sat down by me and commenced to talk. Her father's name is Nozaki and the family has been stationed at Tonnai in Aniwa bay for 8 years, having been previously four years at Hakodate. They are now on their way back to Yedo, and the daughter with her mother and younger brother are awaiting here the arrival of their father, who is still at Tonnai.

Last night few of us had even a wink of sleep but we all sat up in the wardroom and cabin smoking and feeling not quite at ease in our minds at every bump on the rocks, and I never waited for the dawn with so much impatience or welcomed it so gladly before.

By the first boat which went ashore Stephenson despatched a letter to Eusden informing him of the wreck and that all hands were saved: this is to reach Hakodate about the 2nd October; and in the afternoon we sent off a messenger to Shibetsu with letters to Du Petit Thouars of the

Dupleix, and Inouye Iwami to inform them of our disaster: these letters should reach their destination about the 3rd or 4th October.

Sept. 26.   This morning I climbed the down at the back of the village and walked some distance northwards towards Cape Soya: the ground is covered with broad leaved bamboo grass (Sasa) [笹] and dwarf oak with here and there a juniper tree. Paths concealed almost by the grass lead in various directions, evidently little frequented, the seashore being used here as in most other parts of Yezo as the ordinary route for travelling. The sea was too rough to allow of any boats putting off to the ship, and the day was spent chiefly in arranging our quarters and pasting up the windows.

The centre room of about thirty two mats, formed by throwing three into one, is occupied by the wardroom officers as sleeping room and mess quarters, the mats being taken up in the middle for the table at which nine of us can sit and eat. To the left as you enter the house are the store room and stewards' quarters then two rooms of eight mats each occupied by Stephenson, Adams and myself for sleeping quarters. The remainder of the house to the right of the entrance is occupied by the gunroom and engineers' messes, with a kitchen in the Japanese style at the end. A verandah enclosed with papered slides runs along the whole of the front and at the back of the rooms are numerous little cupboards and washing places.

In the afternoon little Harris, the middy, went out round the north point and shot three teal, and Adams, who went westwards along the beach before breakfast, killed some uneatable animal between a rabbit and a weasel. Salmon are scarce in consequence of the wind. After dinner, as we were sitting smoking, the steward rushed in and reported the robbery of a cask of beer which had been left in the *unjōya* by a bluejacket. The executive turned out and arrested the man accused of being the culprit and the whole ship's company was mustered in the moonlight before the *unjōya*, to the great astonishment of the Ainos, who collected in a crowd and squatted on the ground opposite. There was small inducement for sitting up late, and I went to bed before ten like the rest.

Sept. 27.   This morning the thief of beer had three dozen [lashes] administered to him on the parade ground in the presence of the ship's company and the assembled population. [illegible phrase]

After breakfast we went along the beach in the direction of Sannai towards Cape Soya, Adams with his gun, the produce of which was one solitary gull. The weather was fine and bright, but too windy for any operation on board the wreck. A reef runs along the seashore inside of which the water is extremely shallow. The downs come quite down to the edge of the water in some places, in others receding a few hundred yards and leaving the path room to run along on solid ground. Off Cape Soya is a large rock about a mile from the shore. Shaped like a lion couchant [resting]. A few Aino huts in one or two places along the shore.

Sept. 28 & 29. First day bright and fine. Landing gear from the ship all day long, great excitement on the part of the boatmen etc. because our people had just taken possession of the junk in which Hotta was going over to Sakhalin. Following day confoundedly cold with violent rain, nevertheless landing gear went on at a great rate. Begin to feel anxious about provisions and relief: unless we make arrangements at once for a supply of rice, we shall have nothing to eat during the winter.

Sept. 30.   Walked along the beach eastward with Adams in pursuit of game this afternoon, with bad success. Seeing some ducks on the water a good way from shore beckoned to an Aino who was sculling a canoe along to take us out in order that Adams might have a shot, but as soon as we got on board the wretched craft it began to fill, and the poor Aino was put to a great deal of trouble to plug up the holes in the sides through which the water was rushing in. The canoe was made of very light planks fastened together with iron rails at the stern, but along the sides with string passed through an infinite number of holes bored at the edge of the planks. So we judged it safer to get out and proceed on foot again to the point, where we lay down in the grass, and Adams told stories of diplomatic life in Paris and Washington.

Oct. 2.   This morning I met the damsel and saluted her as usual. I had just passed her train when a little boy rushed after me and said he was brother to her, that she was slightly out of her mind and begged me not to take any more notice of her. I said very sorry for you, and promised to say no more to her. At first I thought this only a dodge to prevent our becoming intimate, but a Japanese, who came to talk to me while I was basking on the steps of the temple of Benten, in the afternoon confirmed the story of her insanity, which he said had commenced about a year previously. Probably nymphomania. My resolution was tested very strongly a few hours later, when she came to the temple and sat down by my side, but I answered her as shortly as I could and continued to read. She made a bow as she moved away, with a look as if she did not comprehend my silence.

After that was over I went into the *unjōya* and talked to a fellow there about the Ainos. He said that they are very docile and that the number of bad characteristics is but small. Nearly all the full grown males work willingly at the fishery for the sake of the allowance of rice, the tobacco, pipes and pipe cases, and clothing which they get. The quantity of rice exceeds what a man can consume, being 7½ *go* per diem of hulled rice, the old and infirm are fed gratis, but the women and children have to be supported on the surplus of the men's allowances. Snow lies to the depth of four feet in winter here on the seashore, and sledges are then put in requisition as a means of carrying. Leather shoes and snow shoes are worn, the former over hard snow, the latter over soft.

Oct. 8.   The weather during the last week has been splendid. Hot suns and little wind, and calm seas, which facilitated much the landing of ship's gear etc. Snipe and plover have been shot in sufficient numbers to give us a dish of game at dinner two nights out of three. The seine [net] has been drawn every day at the mouth of the little stream which runs into the sea on the west side of Sōya, supplying the table with abundance of flatfish and other varieties.

But all these resources have been quite eclipsed by the discovery of the salmon fishing at Koëtoi ten miles across the bay. A visit was paid to this place about the 5th [October] by the cutter and dingy, and these boats returned late at night with about 150 large salmon, weighing up to 20 lb. according to the account of the Sub-Lieutenant accompanying the boats. About half of these fish were caught in our seine and the rest obtained from the Ainos by the payment of three boos [*bu*]. But the truth seems to have been that only 24 were caught by our people, and those even were taken inside Ainos' nets. But as the Japanese at the factor's house here had concealed the existence of this fishery and refused to supply us though we offered to pay for the fish, no great wrong was done. The Ainos were no losers, as they were only fishing for their master the factor.

Yesterday morning the cutter and dingy started before dawn and Stephenson, Adams and myself followed at about a quarter to ten in the whale boat. It took us an hour and three quarters to get across, with five men pulling. We steered in a direct line from Sōya with the point where the southern limb of Rishiri comes down to the hills of Cape Nosshap. On our arrival at Koetoi, the wreck was no longer visible, her hull being entirely hid by the dip, and the lower masts, all that remains still standing, invisible against the hills of Sōya.

There is a factor's house at Koetoi and over a dozen Aino huts. A river some 30 yards broad issues into the sea from behind a sort of sandy spit; it is navigable for five miles in boats, to where it issues from a large marsh, which is also said to be navigable for about four miles in a direct line. Two fishing boats lay about five hundred yards of the mouth, busily engaged in hauling in the salmon, of which large quantities were being salted in stacks in a warehouse or hanging out to dry in the sun on frames.

From information obtained on the spot we found that the fishing season has already lasted for ten days, and that 10,000 fish have been already taken, and as the fishery still continues for about ten days, at least 15,000 will be the entire product. Most of them are cleaned and salted for the Yedo market, and the kippered salmon finds its way to Hakodate and Matsumae. There are two other places this side of Cape Nosshap called Yamawakannai (or Yamakannai) and Tōbennai at which the fishery is stated to be equally productive.

Round the headland is a herring fishery. Our seine was dragged in the river, and brought in a large quantity of flatfish and a fish called *ugoi* by the Japanese, besides a few of the ugly animals called toadfish, which of a truth are like toads with a tail. They have the power of inflating their bellies enormously, and bite like sharks. We provided ourselves with salmon in the same manner as on the previous occasion, and left a little before two. The return voyage was about three hours, owing to an abortive attempt at sailing and a headwind.

Oct. 9.   We had just finished breakfast this morning, when a shout was heard outside that the smoke of a steamer was visible. Everybody ran out to look in great excitement and we perceived with gr. difficulty a little puff of smoke on the horizon, now showing itself and then dying away. Gradually it came closer and closer. Someone from the wreck had seen from the maintop a large steamer rounding the point. Various conjectures.

Adams and Stephenson set off in a boat to meet it as soon as it was made out for certain to be the *Dupleix*. She came nearer and anchored about two and a half miles off the shore as I should judge. Du Petit Thouars came ashore with Stephenson, and it was arranged after a little discussion that we should all embark by night and start next morning. Which we did, to my great joy and relief, for I had resolved to offer to remain if only a part of us went. Du Petit Thouars' kindness extreme. He gave up his stern cabin to Stephenson and ourselves: four wardroom officers accommodated in the wardroom etc. etc. More than any English captain could or would.

Oct 12.   Arrived at Hakodate at 7 a.m. Stephenson, Adams and I going to visit the *Chifuji* [governor] met him on the road coming to us on board; so we all turned into the Consulate and took possession thereof for the space of an hour. . .

Oct 17   Returned Yokohama. Arrived at 2 pm. *Ocean* already sailed for Hakodate with letters and clothes on board for us.

NOTES

Chapter 1 JOHN RAWLINS **William Anderson, 1842–1900: Surgeon, Teacher and Art Collector**

1.   Surgeon Vice Admiral Sir John Rawlins, KBE FRCP FRAeS. My interest in William Anderson stemmed from an invitation made to me in August 1993 to take part in a memorial ceremony at Anderson's grave at the cemetery in Kensal Green. In 1996 I was invited to give an illustrated memorial lecture about William Anderson at the 43rd reunion of the OH-YI-KAI in Tokyo. This portrait in so far as it deals with Anderson as an anatomist and surgeon is based on my lecture on this occasion.

2.   I studied anatomy under Professor Wilfred Le Gros Clerk, grandson of Anderson's teacher, 75 years later.

3.   According to a lecture by Dr Takaki Kanehiro (see Note 6) at St Thomas's Hospital in London on 7 May 1906 (*The Lancet*, 19 May 1906) a Naval Medical Bureau had been established in 1872 and Dr Wheeler, attached to the British Legation, was invited by the Naval Hospital to give lectures, both theoretical and practical. William Anderson was then specially invited from England to teach junior medical officers and students.

4.   *The Lancet*, 10 November 1900.

5.   See Hugh Cortazzi's *Dr William Willis in Japan, British Medical Pioneer, 1863–1877*, Athlone, London 1985.

6.   Takaki Kanehiro later studied at St Thomas's and was very proud of his qualification as an F.R.C.S. which he always added after his name. According to the biography of Takaki by Matsuda Makoto, published in 1990 in Tokyo, Takaki one night after he had gone out drinking with his friends called on Anderson much the worse for wear. Anderson rather reluctantly invited him in and Takaki gulped whisky straight from the bottle and became fighting drunk. When on the following day Takaki called on Anderson on another matter the latter fiercely upbraided him for his behaviour unbecoming to a gentleman.

7.   According to *The Lancet* 'His lectures, judging from the reports of some students who afterwards came over to England, were highly valued by his pupils, some of whom became deeply attached to him.'

8.   *The Lancet*.

9.   According to Takaki's lecture at St Thomas's Hospital in London on 7 May 1906 (reported in *The Lancet* for 19 May 1906) sixteen graduated from the school in 1877. These included in addition to himself Surgeons General Yamamoto, Totsuka, Suzuki and Kimura. Surgeon General Suzuki was the chief medical officer of Admiral Togo's fleets. Takaki recorded that while he was away studying in England 'the levying of medical students was stopped and Mr Anderson's duties came to an end. It was then found that as the newly adopted medical

511

officers could not understand a foreign language nor could they follow the progress of medical science in general.' Takaki declared that on his return to Japan he 'insisted on reestablishing the Naval Medical school and enlisted some students... English was taught as an extra subject and by 1894 80 students passed out as officers.' Takaki said that he had joined the navy in 1872 and began to treat the sick and wounded.

10.   This site later was occupied by the residence of members of the imperial family. In 2003 it was the residence of Princess Takamatsu.

11.   *When the Twain Meet: The Rise of Western Medicine in Japan* by John Z. Bowers, MD, The John Hopkins University Press, Baltimore and London, 1980 page 170.

12.   According to the FO lists for these years he was the official medical adviser to the British Legation from 1875-1880. Ministering to the medical needs of the Diplomatic community in Tokyo was a task which later fell to the eminent German physician Erwin Baelz (1849-1913) who was called in by foreign diplomats and senior Japanese to advise and treat eminent individuals in Tokyo. Baelz wrote a memoir about his life in Japan which was published in English in the USA in 1932. In 1876 he had been appointed Professor of Physiology and Internal Medicine at the Imperial Medical Academy in Tokyo. He spent most of his working life in Japan. Anderson and he must have met in Japan.

13.   *The Lancet.*

14.   Sir Harry Parkes (1828-1885), a biographical portrait of whom by Hugh Cortazzi was contained in *Biographical Portraits*, Volume I, Japan Library, 1994.

15.   See Hugh Cortazzi's *Dr Willis in Japan 1862-1877*, London, 1985.

16.   Obituary in *The Times* of Wednesday 31 October 1900.

17.   According to *The Lancet* he was given charge of the Department for the Diseases of the Skin at St Thomas's.

18.   *The Lancet.*

19.   *The Lancet.*

20.   The sources of his collection are not known.

21.   Information from Endō Nozomi to Tim Clark, March 1992.

22.   Edward Morse (1838-1925), archaeologist, collector and scholar.

23.   Ernest Fenollosa (1853-1908) was invited to Japan by Morse in 1878 and taught philosophy and political economy at Tokyo Imperial University. In 1886 he resigned his teaching post and accepted a contract with the Ministry of Education and the Imperial Household which enabled him to concentrate on Japanese art. He was instrumental in the movement which eventually led to the founding of the Tokyo University of Fine Arts. In 1890 he returned to the USA to head the Oriental Department of the Boston Museum of Fine Arts. His major work *Epochs of Chinese and Japanese Art* was published in 1912 after his death.

24.   Emile Guimet published, with illustrations by Felix Regamey, *Promenades Japonaises* in 1878 and 1880. Established the Musée Guimet in Paris.

25.   Louis Gonse: *L'Art Japonais*, 2 volumes, Paris, 1883.

26.   S. Bing: *Artistic Japan*, 6 volumes, 1891.

27.   Josiah Conder (1852-1920).

28.   The Rokumeikan was built in 1883.

29. *Landscape Gardening in Japan*, 1893
30. *Flowers of Japan and the Art of Floral Arrangement*, 1891.
31. Kawanabe Kyōsai (1831–89).
32. Galen or Claudius Galen (c 130–201) Greek physician gathered together all the medical knowledge available at that time. He was regarded as the authority on medicine for centuries.
33. From Hippocrates came the idea that the 'animal spirit' was infused from the spinal cord; so Leonardo introduced a channel passing from the lumbar spine through the upper part of the penis which had two channels, one for urine and one for semen. Another channel from the testes 'the source of ardour', led straight to the heart, the source of the emotions. There was also a connection between the uterus and the spinal cord and another from the uterus to the breasts. Anderson drew attention to this extraordinary anomaly amongst Leonardo's brilliant anatomical studies. This cartoon had been drawn before Leonardo embarked on his series of dissections.
34. Versalius, Andreas (1514–64), Flemish anatomist.
35. Charles Estienne (also known as Charles Stephens) (1504–64), after studying medicine, became in 1552 Royal Printer in Paris. His classical drawings of subjects displaying their anatomy appeared in his *De dissectione partium corporis*, Paris, 1545, Fol. min., which was contemporaneous with Andreas Vasel's *De humani corporis fabrica*, Basle, 1543, Fol.max.
36. John Hunter (1728–93), physiologist and surgeon, born in Scotland, is considered to be the founder of scientific surgery.
37. Sir Ernest Satow, who was Minister to Japan from 1895–1900, consulted Anderson in his professional capacity in 1897 about a finger which had 'for a long time been contracted'. Anderson operated successfully on the finger.
38. Article on Anderson in the *Dictionary of National Biography* (DNB).
39. Obituary in *The Times* for 31 October 1900.
40. I am indebted to Tim Clark of the Department of Japanese antiquities for this section. See British museum *Magazine*, No 13 (spring 1993).
41. Olive Checkland in her book *Japan and Britain after 1859 – Creating Cultural Bridges*, RoutledgeCurzon, 2003, notes (page 126) 'Curiously for a man supposedly so involved with Japan, he himself apparently had no collection of Japanese art to be disposed of at his death. In his will his only reference was to his "large bronze dragon". The gross value of his estate was over £11,000, the net value £9,473, a considerable sum in 1900.'
42. *The Lancet* obituary and DNB entry on Anderson.
43. Japan Society *Proceedings*, Volume V.
44. The Japan Society's obituary of Anderson (*Proceedings*, Volume V) commented that: 'Although a man of many engagements, whose life had few spare moments, he never failed to discharge the self-imposed and honorary duties of the chairmanship – duties which commencement were numerous, and requiring unfailing tact.'
45. In their article on 'The British Discovery of Japanese Art' in *The History of Anglo-Japanese Relations, 1600-2000, Volume V Social and Cultural Perspectives* edited by Gordon Daniels and Chushichi Tsuzuki Yuko Kikuchi and Toshio

Watanabe (page 159) note that Anderson took a negative view of Rimpa artists, criticizing their 'delineation of the human figure and quadrupeds'. He thought that the paintings of Kōrin and Hōitsu had 'too much mannerism and too little resemblance to nature to please the European eye.' This view would not be endorsed by students of Japanese art in England today.
46.   DNB entry on Anderson.
47.   From Mr R Clement Lucas.

Chapter 2 HIDEKO NUMATA **Marcus Huish (1843-1921) and Japan**

This paper is based on my research on The Fine Art Society and Japan with a subsidy from the Kajima Art Foundation in 2001. I am grateful for the help of the Fine Art Society, Mr Payton Skipwith and Mr Max Donnelly, the Japan Society, Mr Patrick Knill, The Victoria and Albert Museum, Mr Gregory Irvine. I am also grateful to Sir Hugh Cortazzi for giving me the opportunity to contribute this paper and for help in my research.

1.   Joseph Foster, *Man at the bar, a biographical hand list of the members of the various Inns of Court*, London 1885.
Joseph H. Longford, 'Obituary, Marcus Bourne Huish,' *Transactions and Proceedings of the Japan Society*, vol. 18, 1920-21, px, pp. x-xi.
Hilarie Faberman, 'The Best shop in London' The Fine Art Society and the Victorian Art Scene, in *The Grosvenor Gallery*, Yale University Press, 1996 p.148
The Fine Art Society Story, Part 1, 201, The Fine Art Society, London, p.5.
2.   FAS Minute Book, April 25, 1876.
3.   For the history of the FAS, see Faberman, pp.147-148; The Fine Art Society Story, p.4.
4.   Philippe Burty: *Charles Meryon, Sailor, Engraver and Etcher. A Memoir and Complete Descriptive Catalogue of His Works*, Translated from the French by Marcus B. Huish, London, 1879.
5.   *The Fine Art Society Story, Part 1*, 2001.
About exhibitions at the FAS, see 'Complete List of Exhibitions', *125 Years of Exhibitions at the Fine Art Society*, the Fine Art Society, London, 2001.
6.   Whistler and the FAS, see *The Fine Art Society Story Part 1*, pp.7,8, Farbernan p.154.
7.   Ruskin and the FAS, see *The Fine Art Society Story Part 1*, p.6, Farbermen pp.152-153.
8.   *The Fine Art Society Story*, p.5.
9.   For a biographical portrait of Sir Rutherford Alcock see Hugh Cortazzi's essay in *Biographical Portraits*, Volume II, Japan Library, 1997.
10.   For a biographical portrait of Lasenby Liberty see essay by Sonia Ashmore in *Biographical Portraits*, Volume IV, Japan Library, 2002.
11.   *The Fine Art Society Story Part 1*, p. 5.
12.   About the exterior of the Building of the FAS see Farberman pp. 149, 150
13.   The Fine Art Society Minute Book 294.
14.   *Catalogue of/and Notes upon the Loan Exhibition of Japanese Art*, The Fine Art Society, London 1888.

15. *Catalogue of a collection of Drawings and Engravings by Hokusai*, The Fine Art Society, London, 1890.
16. See Sir Hugh Cortazzi (ed.) *A British Artist in Meiji Japan, Sir Alfred East*, London, 1991; Kenneth McConkey, 'Haunt to Ancient Peace, the Landscape of Sir Alfred East' in *Haunt of Ancient Peace, Landscape by Sir Alfred East R.A.*, The Alfred East Gallery 75th Anniversary Exhibition, 1988.
17. *Catalogue of a Collection of Pictures and Drawings of the Landscape of Japan by Alfred East, R. I.* with an introduction and notes by Dr. F. A. Junker, the FAS, 1890.
18. *Catalogue of a Collection of Water-Colour Drawings by Alfred Persons, R. I. Illustrating Landscapes & Flowers in Japan*, with a prefatory Note by the Artist, The Fine Art Society, 1893.
19. Miyake Kokki: *Omoi-izuru mama* [As I remembered], Kodaisha, Japan, 1938, pp.56-60.
See *Japan and Britain: An Aesthetic Dialogue 1850-1930*, Exhibition catalogue, Setagaya Art Museum, Tokyo, 1991; Hiroto Kannno, 'Three British Water-colourists in Meiji Japan', in *Ruskin and Japan 1890-1940, Nature for Art, Art for Life*, Exhibition Catalogue, Koriyama City Museum of Art, et al., 1997, pp.339-343; Hideko Numata, 'Alfred East and Japan', in *Bulletin of Yokohama Museum of Art No.1*, Yokohama Museum of Art, 1998.
20. Marcus B. Huish, *Japan and its Art*, The Fine Art Society, London, 1888, preface.
21. Huish, 1888, preface. The name Kataoka Masayuki is sometimes given as Kataoku Masayuke; Kataoka seems to have had a shop dealing in Japanese and Chinese art at 8 Hanover Square, London. The Victoria and Albert Museum bought some *ukiyo-e* prints from him and employed him to make a list of its collection of Japanese books and prints. The record of the purchase of *ukiyo-e* prints is in V&A Storekeeper's Office Report no. 15130, 1895 and his employment is recorded in V&A Minute Paper No. 937a, Registered No. 1435, 1887.
22. Marcus Huish, 'Is Japanese Art Extinct?', *Nineteen Century; A Monthly Review*, March, 1888, pp.354-369.
23. About the report of the Commission, see Akiko Sugimura ed. 'Archives of E. F. Fenollosa in the Horton Library of Harvard University', Tokyo, 1892, pp.67-98.
24. Huish, Is Japanese Art Extinct?, p.356.
25. Sir Hugh Cortazzi, *The Japan Society, A History, 1891 to 2000*, The Japan Society, London, 2001.
26. Officers and Councils 1892-93, General List of Members 31 December 1892, Sir Hugh Cortazzi and Gordon Daniels, *Britain and Japan, Themes and Personalities*, Routledge 1991, Japanese version Shibunkaku, Kyoto, 1998, pp. 38-45.
27. Bing was elected at the meeting of 31 March 1892. T. Hayashi was elected at the meeting of 26 April 1892. Japan Society Minute Book Vol.I1 (1891-1893), pp.38, 42.
28. Joseph H. Longford, Obituary; Marcus Bourne Huish, The Japan Society

Transactions vol.18, 1920–21, p.X.
29. Japan Society Minutes, January 1909–March 1919, p.54.
30. Akiko Mabuchi, 'Japonisme and Texts' Preface for *Japanese Art and Japonisme, part 1: Early English texts*, Edition Synapse, 1999, p. 10.
31. V&A inv. no. 20-1919 – 31-1919, Victoria and Albert Museum, Objects submitted on approval for gift record, 16 April 1919.

Chapter 3 DOROTHY BRITTON **Prince and Princess Chichibu**

1. His full name and title in English was His Imperial Highness Yasuhito, Prince Chichibu (*Chichibu no miya Yasuhito shinnō denka*). For some reason, it is the custom in Japan regarding their royalty to say for instance, 'Prince Chichibu' in English, although 'Chichibu no miya' literally means 'the Prince of Chichibu'. At his birth on 25 June 1902, (the same day and month, incidentally, as that of his mother), he was given the title Prince Atsu, which was changed to Prince Chichibu when he came of age.
2. Princess Chichibu: *The Silver Drum, A Japanese Imperial Memoir*, Folkestone, Global Oriental, 1996, pp.192-3 (translation by Dorothy Britton of '*Gin no bonboniēru*'), Tokyo, Shufunotomo-sha, 1991).
3. This was the study which had been occupied by the Prince of Wales later Edward VIII.
4. *The Silver Drum*, p.116.
5. A translation of a paper by Prince Chichibu entitled A Climb in the Japanese Alps was printed in *The Transactions of The Japan Society of London* volume XXVI for 1928-1929.
6. *The Silver Drum* p.116.
7. According to Princess Chichibu the only stadium in Japan named after an individual.
8. *The Silver Drum* p.192.
9. Kanroji Osanaga: *Hirohito: An Intimate Portrait of the Japanese Emperor*, Gateway, Los Angeles, 1975, p.18 (translation by Stanley Rader and Osamu Gotoh of *Tennō sama*, Tokyo, Kodansha, 1975).
10. Hosaka Masayasu, *Chichibu no Miya: Shōwa Tennō otōto miya no shōgai*, Tokyo, Chuō Kōronsha, in Chuō Bunko series, 2000, page 51 (first published as *Chichibu no miya to Shōwa Tennō*, Tokyo, Bungei Shunjū).
11. Leonard Mosley, *Hirohito: Emperor of Japan*, New Jersey, Prentice Hall, 1966, pp.57, 61, 63.
12. Prince Chichibu, *Gotemba Tales* (*Seiwa*), Sekai no Nihonsha, Tokyo, 1948) quoted in Kanroji Osanaga, *Hirohito*, p.91.
13. Mosley, *Hirohito*, p.52.
14. Ibid. pp.70-71.
15. Princess Chichibu, *The Silver Drum*, p.91.
16. Ibid. p.92.
17. Ibid. p.98.
18. Ibid. p.101.
19. Ibid. pp. 112-113.
20. Hosaka, *Chichibu no miya*, p.258.

21. Ben-Ami Shillony, *Collected Writings*, Folkestone, Global Books, p.112.
22. Hosaka, *Chichibu no miya*, p. 342.
23. Hosaka, *Chichibu no miya*, p.340. *Michinoku no/Tsumoru shirayuki/Kakiwa-kete/Ima hi no ōji wa/Noborimasu nari.* This poem was written by Hiraizumi Kiyoshi, Prince Chichibu's history professor, who was a reformist sympathiser, and who joined the Prince part way along his train journey to Tokyo on 26 February, 1936, ostensibly 'to prevent the Prince from getting the wrong idea from people he might meet en route'.
24. Ben Ami-Shillony, *Collected Writings*, p.111.
25. Honjō Shigeru, *Honjō Nikki*, quoted in Hosaka, *Chichibu no miya*, p.260.
26. Hosaka, *Chichibu no miya*, p.268.
27. Ibid. p.269.
28. Princess Chichibu, *The Silver Drum*, p.123.
29. Hosaka, *Chichibu no miya*, p.309.
30. Kanroji, *Hirohito*, p.126.
31. Hosaka, *Chichibu no miya*, p.342.
32. Ibid. p.343.
33. Princess Chichibu, *The Silver Drum*, p. 127.
34. Hosaka, *Chichibu no miya*, p. 268.
35. Matsumoto Tōru, *Ni-ni-roku jiken goshinnen no hitokoma*. Quoted in Ben Ami-Shillony, *Collected Writings*, p.119-120.
36. Sir Hugh Cortazzi, *The Japanese Achievement*, London, Sidgwick and Jackson, 1990, p. 230.
37. Kōno Tsukasa, *Shichigatsu jūninichi no kiroku*, quoted in Ben Ami-Shillony, *Collected Writings*, p.122.
38. On the morning of 26 February 1936 the Emperor Shōwa is quoted as having received the news of the rebellion with the dejected comment, 'So they've finally done it.' Then he muttered to himself, sadly, 'It's all because of my lack of moral fibre.' (Kanroji Osanaga *Tennō sama*, Tokyo, Kodansha, 1975, quoted in Hosaka, *Chichibu no miya*, p. 310) As time went on, the Emperor's feeling of guilt seems to have become almost unbearable – first fuelled, perhaps, by his younger brother's many harangues. What might he have done to help his people then, and later when things built up to World War II? In his indirect Japanese way, when his war council was waiting for him to sign the declaration, he had tried to convey his unwillingness to do so, and his hatred of war, in a Heian-period fashion by quoting his grandfather Emperor Meiji's poem:

> All the world's seas
> And oceans are one,
> Like brothers;
> Oh why does wind and wave
> So belligerently rave?

(*Yomo no umi/Mina harakara to/omou yō ni/Nado nami-kaze no/Tachisawaruramu*) Should he have done what his brother, Prince Chichibu, wanted him to do in 1932? Should he have refused to sign in 1941? He had felt it was his duty to uphold his role under the Meiji Constitution as he understood it. The weight of it all was so great, that a few years after the war ended, sometime around 1948, the Emperor had his chief chamberlain, Grand Steward Tajima Michiji, draft an apology for him to make for the enormous devastation and suffering caused by the tragic war for which he felt a deep responsibility. Using the imperial pronoun *chin*, the document included the solemn words, '*Chin no futoku naru, fukaku tenka ni hazu*' (It was because of our lack of moral fibre, and we apologise with profound shame to all beneath heaven). *Tenka* (All beneath heaven) can either mean 'the whole nation' or 'the world'. Because of doubts expressed in various quarters about the wisdom at that time of allowing the Emperor to make such a declaration, the apology never saw the light of day, and was discovered by chance among Tajima's papers by his biographer, Katō Kyōko, in May, 2003. (Katō Kyōko, *Shōwa Tennō 'shazai shōchoku sōkō no hakken* (The discovery of the Emperor Shōwa's Imperial Apology Proclamation draft), Tokyo Bungei Shunjū, 2003.

39. Princess Chichibu, *The Silver Drum*, pp. 133-134.
40. Ibid. pp.140-141.
41. Ibid. p.198.

Chapter 4 HUGH CORTAZZI Crown Prince Akihito in Britain

1. Unfortunately, the report which was surely written by David Symon who accompanied the Crown Prince on his tour cannot be found. Through the good offices of the Japanese Embassy I was given a copy of the report on the Crown Prince's tour made by Matsui Akira, a member of the suite, who later became private secretary to Prime Minister Yoshida Shigeru, Ambassador to France and finally to the United Nations. His father was a pre-war Japanese Ambassador to the Court of St James. A detailed account of the visit is also given in Japan Society's Bulletins Numbers 10 and 11 of 1953.
2. Minute by John Pilcher to Rob Scott, Assistant Under-Secretary on TR72/ 14 (FO 372/7161.
3. Dening to Rob Scott of 26 August 1952 (TR72/19) reporting a conversation between Vere Redman and Matsudaira Yasumasa. Dening was concerned about an AP report suggesting that the invitation to Japan might be dropped because of ill feeling over the case of two sailors arrested by the Japanese police in Kobe. He was also anxious that no list of those to be invited should be issued without Japan being on the list. Dening wrote: 'Unless there is a serious deterioration in our relations my personal view is that it would be a very good thing for the Crown Prince to attend the Coronation.' In fact I can find nothing in the official papers to suggest that there were any doubts on the part of the British Government about the invitation to the Emperor to be represented at the Coronation. They determined from the outset that the Crown Prince should be treated 'on the grounds of absolute equality with that of other foreign royalties.' Dening also recorded on 11 October 1952 that when he 'suggested to Yoshida that 'it might be a good thing for the Crown Prince to get out and about more in order to prepare himself for the occasion the Prime Minister agreed and said that he hoped I would constitute myself His Highness's tutor. I do not think this should be interpreted too literally.'
4. Prime Minister Yoshida wanted the Crown Prince to be accompanied by

Dr Koizumi Shinzo, his tutor who had been President of Keio University, and by Mrs Matsudaira Nobuko, widow of Matsudaira Tsuneo, a former Japanese Ambassador in London. The Imperial Household rejected these suggestions. Perhaps in the case of Mrs Matsudaira this may have been wise. Yoshida had told Dening that Mrs Matsudaira 'was something of a despot and was liable to order the Crown Prince about'.

5.   The Crown Prince was also accompanied by Dr Sato, his medical adviser, and by two other chamberlains Toda and Kuroki.

6.   David Symon sadly died in Tokyo from an embolism as a result of a skiing accident in 1964.

7.   The Crown Prince had been taught English by an American Quaker Elizabeth Vining who later wrote a book about her experiences entitled *Windows for the Crown Prince*. In a note on Embassy files in March 1953 David Symon recorded that he had given eleven lessons in English to the Crown Prince between 8 January and 21 February 1953. David noted that 'the Crown Prince was rather silent to begin with, but he seemed much more at ease and willing to express himself in English when Marquis Matsudaira [Matsudaira Yasumasa] left us to ourselves. . . His favourite topics are the sports which he practises himself such as riding and tennis; and he shares the Emperor's taste for natural history. Yet he is dutifully anxious to be interested in all the right subjects . . . the hours passed easily and the Prince proved himself capable not only of discussing a wide variety of topics interestingly and intelligently but also of introducing new ones.' After his final lesson David Symon had a tête-à-tête lunch with the Crown Prince. The Marchioness Matsudaira had asked David to 'note whether His Imperial Highness used his knife and fork correctly. In the event the Prince was at his best and proved himself to the hilt that day. . . It is my impression that the Prince is well equipped in character, training and language for his forthcoming tour.'

8.   Dening in a letter to John Pilcher dated 14 January 1953 urged that 'the idea will be dropped of dressing him like Pooh Bah'. Dening thought the British public would burst out laughing if they saw the Prince in the costume he had worn at his coming-of-age ceremony. Nevertheless it seems that some on the Japanese side were reluctant to give up the idea. On 17 March 1953 Dening reported that Shirasu Jiro, an eminence grise of Prime Minister Yoshida Shigeru, had reverted to this idea.

9.   Dening added: 'Though I would not exaggerate the importance of the Monarchy in present day Japan, the Crown Prince has, as I have said, a special niche in the hearts of the Japanese people, who will react favourably to every evidence they receive of his friendly reception in the United Kingdom'.

10.   John Pilcher said that Piggott was the only Englishman he knew who really believed that the Japanese Emperor was a living god! Frank Ashton Gwatkin (see Ian Nish's Biographical Portrait in Volume I) and Richard Ponsonby Fane (see Dorothy Britton's Biographica; Portrait in Volume II) also viewed the Emperor as divine.

11.   Mitani Takanobu in his memoir published in Tokyo in 1980 and republished by Chuokoronshinsha in 1999 used the phrase '*yorokobanai kiji*'.

12.   Ambassador Matsumoto was the first post-war Japanese Ambassador. His

English was limited and perhaps in view of his service in Indo-China during the war was cordially disliked by Sir Esler Dening.

13. Mitani Takanobu in his memoirs (see v above) used the phrase '*fuyukai na kiji wa issō sareta*'.

14. Quaintly referred to in the Japan Society's bulletin as 'Colony'.

15. See 'Crown Prince Hirohito in Britain' by Ian Nish in *Biographical Portraits*, Volume II (1997).

16. *The Daily Express* controlled by Lord Beaverbrook had carried an article on 30 March 1953 by Russell Spurr in Tokyo under the headline 'The Co-ed Prince – divine no longer – is on his way'. This was a supercilious and silly article which contained the absurd statement that 'Sometimes he slips off for a private film show at the British Embassy with his friend Sir Esler Dening, the Ambassador.' He was critical of 'Pompous courtiers [who] interfere in all his activities.' On 22 April the paper carried a piece headlined 'Should Akihito of Japan see our Queen crowned' in which the author and former prisoner of war Russell Bradon argued that he should not and Russell Spurr quoting Vere Redman, the Information Counsellor in the Embassy, who had been badly treated by the *Kempeitai* in 1942, argued that we should welcome the Crown Prince: 'Surely we've not forgotten how to forget and forgive'. Following the lunch the Beaverbrook press found other more sensational topics for their journalists.

17. Arthur Waley, translator of *The Tale of Genji, Japanese No Plays* and other Japanese classical works had never visited Japan. See Philip Harries' biographical portrait in *Themes and Personalities*, Routledge 1991.

18. See for instance Gordon Daniels essay in *Themes and Personalities*, 1991

19. PRO, PREM.11/468.

20. Mitani Takanobu in his Memoirs (see v above) records that Churchill had asked his private secretary to bring down and place on the table two brass horses. The Prime Minister said that his mother had brought these back from Japan as a souvenir when he was still a boy and these reminiscences provided the introduction to his impromptu speech in which he said that these horses showed that Japan was a country which produced superb art objects (*kono uma ga shimesu yō ni bijutsu no men ni oite me subarashii mono wo motsu kuni de aru*).

21. Lady Randolph Churchill, née Jennie Jerome, daughter of Leonard Jerome, described by Roy Jenkins in *The Chancellors*, 1998 as 'a New York financier of verve and considerable but fluctuating fortune.' After Lord Randolph Churchill died she had two subsequent marriages.

22. In his minute to the Prime Minister covering Sir George Sansom's draft Montague Brown wrote enigmatically that apart from Sir Winston's advice to the Prince on leaving 'the only addition I can think of is your remark about 'Sex in bronze'. What I wonder was this?!

23. Matsui Akira in his confidential report on the tour recorded Sir Winston's words as 'The British people hope that you will have a happy stay in Britain. If you hear anything different ignore it.' [*Eikokujin wa denka no taiei ga happi de aru koto wo kibō shite iru. Sore to kotonaru ȳ na koto ga o-mimi ni haite mo ki ni nasaru na.*]

24. Matsui wrote: *Eikoku wa ōshitsu wo hajime seifu mo tsutomete kōtaishi denka wo go-kangei mōshi-ageru taidō wo totta.*

NOTES

25. PREM.11/468.
26. *Denka no go-ryokō ga yukai de aru koto wo inoru. Watakushi wa Tennō heika wo zonji-agenai ga kikoku seraretara dōka denka wo taikanshiki ni o-sashi-asobase ni natta koto ni tsuki atsuku on-rei wo mōshiagete kudasai.*
27. In a brief speech at the dinner on 11 May the Prince declared: 'I will not say how much it weighed. I think this should be something for my diary and not for public consumption.'
28. See Marie Conte-Helm *Japan and the North East of England*, 1989, pp.131.
29. Matsui's report on the tour.
30. The word used by Matsui *inbō* is very strong and could be translated as 'conspiracy'. The Lord Mayor's words as recorded in Japanese translation by Matsui were; *POW no mondai wa ichibu shōsū no mono no inbō ni sugizu makoto ni ikan de aru. Kubi ni kakete iru kono kane no kusari wa Newcastle no shōchō de ari, denka ni kore wo o-me in kakeru koto wa sunawachi Newcastle ni kite itadaita koto ni naru.*
31. See separate essay about Louis Allen by Phillida Purvis in this volume.
32. Shimanouchi told Redman (Redman's letter to Pilcher of 8 July 1953 that 'the manager of a certain inn [in Cambridge], himself an ex-prisoner of war of the Japanese, had refused accommodation to a Japanese journalist, but never, of course, was there any question of Prince Akihito staying at a hotel.'
33. *The People's Emperor, Democracy and the Japanese Monarchy, 1945-1995* by Kenneth J. Ruoff, Harvard, 2001 p. 213.
34. Redman to Pilcher of 8 July 1953.
35. *The Times* index for the period of the visit records 27 references to the Crown Prince in Britain.
36. The *Illustrated London News*, which gave impressive coverage to the coronation, only carried two photographs of the Crown Prince. One showed him viewing the Elgin Marbles at the British Museum, the other was a formal portrait among others of foreign dignitaries attending the coronation.
37. Matsui wrote: '*Mochiron Newcastle no furyōkai no ketsugi no gotoki jakkan no fuyukai na jikken mo atta.*'
38. See note 12.
39. FO Despatch to Tokyo of 18 June 1953.
40. The despatch was only released in 2003 having been held back for 50 years instead of the usual 30 years.
41. Ibid.
42. The Japanese Ambassador Katō Tadao, who was a big man, suffered more.
43. The Crown Prince expressed a wish to see rabbits in the wild. Fortunately, we managed to show him some in Hyde Park!

Chapter 5 ANDREW COBBING **Terashima Munenori, 1832-93: Master of Early Meiji Diplomacy**

1. Ozaki Saburō, *Ozaki Saburō jijo ryakuden* [Short Autobiography of Ozaki Saburō], vol.1 (Tokyo: Chūōkōronsha, 1976), p.118
2. Terashima often appears in English spelled Terajima, the preferred pronunciation of many Meiji government colleagues. The island in Satsuma from which he took his name, however, is Terashima, he was addressed as such in

Foreign Office correspondence, and in the letter of credentials he presented to Queen Victoria, his sovereign, the Emperor Meiji, declared: 'We have determined to invest with the character of our Envoy Extraordinary and Minister Plenipotentiary our trusty and well-beloved Shoshie Terashima Munenori, whose zeal, ability and discretion have been well approved in his service as one of our Ministers for Foreign Affairs . . . Mutsuhito, Emperor'. FO 46/160.
3.   Isabella Bird, *Unbeaten Tracks in Japan* (San Francisco: Travelers' Tales Inc., 2000), p.9. Parkes had a reputation for driving a hard bargain but he could be 'a careful and attentive host', notably during the Iwakura Embassy's visit to Britain. James Hoare, 'The Era of Unequal Treaties', in Ian Nish and Yoichi Kibata (ed.), *The History of Anglo-Japanese Relations*, vol.1 (London: Macmillan, 2000), p.112.
4.   Inuzuka, *Terashima Munenori* (Tokyo: Yoshikawa Kōbunkan, 1990), pp.8-11.
5.   Ibid., p.14. My thanks to Sebastian Dobson for pointing out that, contrary to a longstanding tradition in Japan, it is highly unlikely that Ueno Shunnojō took a camera with him to Kagoshima on this occasion and photographed Shimazu Nariakira, then the daimyo's 32-year-old heir.
6.   As Terashima pointed out, in the 1840s there had been only two or three previous cases of Satsuma sending officers to train outside the domain, and these were young men in their twenties. Terashima Munenori, 'Jijo nenpu' [Autobiographical Chronology], vol.3. Kokkai Toshokan (National Diet Library)
7.   Terashima to Kawamoto. *Ihi nyukō roku* [Record of Ports of Call in Barbarian Lands], vol.1 (Tokyo: Nihon Shiseki Kyōkai, 1930), p.250.
8.   Japan's first reverberating furnace was built in 1850 by the Hizen domain in the castle-town of Saga. The second was built by the Tokugawa *Bakufu* at Nirayama in the Izu Peninsula.
9.   Under Shimazu Nariakira's leadership Satsuma made rapid progress in developing its own navy. It was a Satsuma ship that in 1854 first flew the 'Hinomaru' flag, a red sun on a white background, more familiar today as the national flag of Japan.
10.   Willem van Kattendyke, *Uittreksel uit het dagboek van W.J.C. Ridder H. v. Kattendyke gedurende zijn verblijf in Japan in 1857, 1858 en 1859* ('sGravenhage, 1860), p.97.
11.   J.L.C. Pompe van Meerdervort, *Vijf Jaren in Japan* (Leiden, 1867): Numata Jirō, Arase Shinkyō (trans.), *Pompe nihon taizai kenbun ki* (Omatsudō Shoten: Tokyo, 1968), pp.259-61, 298.
12.   Ernest Satow, *A Diplomat in Japan* (Tokyo: ICG Muse Inc, 2000), pp.185-6
13.   Terashima was the first Satsuma officer to be officially sent, but there were notable precedents of others reaching Europe. Bernardo, the first known example from Japan, was a poor Satsuma samurai who arrived in Lisbon in 1553 and became a Jesuit priest. In 1724 two fishermen, Gonzō and Sōzō were the only survivors of a crew killed when their vessel ran aground in Kamchatka. Taken to St Petersburg to teach at a Japanese language school, Gonzō compiled the first Russian-Japanese dictionary, translating 12,000 words into his native Kagoshima dialect.

14. Terashima recalled: 'Mitsukuri Shūhei and I investigated the treatment in hospitals and education in schools . . . we shared responsibility between our fields, recording it all when we returned to our hotels so that we ended up compiling a large volume'. '*Yōkō ni kan-suru Terashima Munenori jiki rireki shō*' [Extract from Terashima Munenori's Own Account of His Overseas Travels], *Sappan kaigun shi* [History of the Satsuma Navy], vol.2 (Tokyo: Sappan kaigun shi kankō kai, 1928), p.935. In Paris he exchanged letters with the japanologist Léon de Rosny, and became the first Japanese member of Rosny's Société d'Ethnographie. Inuzuka, *Terashima Munenori*, pp.67-9. In 1865 they met again when Rosny visited London on behalf of the Comte de Montblanc to establish commercial ties with Satsuma. Cobbing, *The Satsuma Students in Britain* (Folkestone: Japan Library, 2000), pp.78-81, 86-8.

15. Letter to Kawamoto Kōmin, 10 June 1862. *Ihi nyūkō roku*, vol.1, pp.237-40.

16. Satow, *A Diplomat in Japan*, p.82.

17. For an account of the Namamugi Incident and the subsequent bombardment of Kagoshima see Hugh Cortazzi's biographical portrait of Lt Colonel Neale and Appendix I in *British Envoys in Japan 1859-1972* (Folkestone: Japan Library, 2004).

18. There is some evidence that Terashima, perhaps in order to keep informed of developments, undertook translation work for the *Bansho Shirabesho* during his months in hiding in Musashi. Cobbing, 'The Nagasaki Information War', *Kyūshū daigaku ryūgakusei kiyō* [Kyūshū University International Student Centre Bulletin], *no.10, October 1999*, pp.57-76. This may have been why Satow later questioned his loyalty after hearing that he had worked for the *Bakufu* even after the bombardment of Kagoshima. Satow, *A Diplomat in Japan*, pp.185-6.

19. Laurence Oliphant had served as secretary to the mission by the Earl of Elgin to China and Japan in 1858 and had been first secretary to Rutherford Alcock at the British Legation in Edo where he had been injured in the first Tōzenji incident in 1861 in which a band of *rōnin* attacked the temple then being used as the legation building.

20. Russell to Parkes, 23 August 1865, FO 262/88. Apart from Terashima himself, it is unclear exactly whom Russell was referring to when he mentioned Satsuma and Chōshū officers sent to negotiate with the British government. He may have been thinking of Yamao Yōzō, a Chōshū student in London, whose views had been reported in detail to the Foreign Office the previous year. Yamao vigorously defended his domain's policy and, much like Terashima, protested against the *Bakufu*'s monopoly on trade. Memorandum by Reginald Russell, 1 July 1864, FO 46/49.

21. Glover's introduction to Oliphant was recorded by one of the Satsuma students. 'Kaigun Chūshō Matsumura Junzō yōkō dan' [Matsumura Junzō's Account of His Overseas Travels] *Sappan kaigun shi* [History of the Satsuma Navy], vol.2, p.903. Cobbing, *The Satsuma Students in Britain*, pp.70-1, 94. There was no conscious British policy to 'sabotage the shogun' despite some collusion by merchants and diplomats with domains like Satsuma and Chōshū, notably over mutual commercial interests. Even Ernest Satow's ingenious articles in the *Japan Times*, read in translation as 'Eikoku sakuron', had no effect on official

policy. James Hoare, 'The Era of Unequal Treaties', in Ian Nish and Yoichi Kibata (ed.), *The History of Anglo-Japanese Relations*, vol.1 (London: Macmillan, 2000), pp.110, 112. In this context it is nevertheless worth noting that Terashima's strategy on Satsuma's behalf, conveyed with help from Glover and Oliphant, did exert some influence on the political outlook of the Foreign Office.
22. Parkes's initial scepticism towards reports of Terashima's overtures reflected his unfamiliarity with Japanese politics in his first year as Minister, apparent in his suggestion that Satsuma had been forced to seek outside help from Britain due only to political isolation at home. Gordon Daniels, *Sir Harry Parkes: British representative in Japan, 1865-1883* (Folkestone: Japan Library, 1996), p.57.
23. '*Yōkō ni kan-suru Terashima Munenori jiki rireki shō*', p.943.
24. Cobbing, *The Satsuma Students in Britain*, p.129. Inuzuka, *Terashima Munenori*, p.134. Terashima's document was based on a text drawn up by the Comte de Montblanc and also reflected suggestions made by Satow. This received imperial approval on 13 January 1868, as Terashima reported to Parkes the same day. He was again present at Kōbe Customs House on 8 February when Higashikuze Michitome of the Board for Foreign Affairs presented an adjusted imperial proclamation to the assembled envoys of the treaty powers.
25. Hoare, 'The Era of Unequal Treaties', p.112. See also J.E.Hoare: *Japan's Treaty Ports and Foreign Settlements*, Japan Library, 1994.
26. Ibid, p.125.
27. Letters from Lachlan Fletcher, British consul in Kanagawa, to Terashima Tōzō and Eseki Saiemon, '*Bakumatsu yori meiji shoki made no kakkoku tono ōrai shokan eikoku raiō kan*' [Correspondence with foreign countries at the end of *Bakufu* rule and early years of Meiji – letters from Britain], vol.2, Gaikō Shiryōkan (Foreign Ministry Archives).
28. Inuzuka, *Terashima Munenori*, p.153.
29. Of the official correspondence from the British Legation to the Ministry of Foreign Affairs in the early Meiji years, 60 out of 94 dispatches to Sawa, 33 out of 35 to Iwakura, and 42 out of 50 to Soejima, were also addressed to Terashima in his position as vice-minister. During Terashima's own term as minister, however, such letters were never addressed to the vice-minister as well. '*Bakumatsu yori meiji shoki made no kakkoku tono ōrai shokan mokuroku – eikoku kōshi yori raikan mokuroku*' [List of correspondence with foreign countries at the end of *Bakufu* rule and early years of Meiji – list of correspondence from the British minister], Gaikō Shiryōkan (Foreign Ministry Archives).
30. Ozaki, *Ozaki Saburō jijo ryakuden*, vol.1, p.117. Inuzuka, *Terashima Munenori*, p.179
31. Parkes to Granville, 3 December 1870, FO 46/127.
32. Ozaki Saburō, *Ozaki Saburō jijo ryakuden*, vol.1, p.113.
33. It was from the South Kensington Hotel at 19 Queen's Gate Terrace that the first correspondence on the headed notepaper of 'the Legation of Japan' was sent to the Foreign Office. Terashima to Granville, 5 September 1872. FO 46/160. Cobbing, *The Japanese Discovery of Victorian Britain* (Folkestone: Japan Library, 1998), p.112.
34. For details of the Bowles Brothers' financial scandal see Cobbing, *The*

Japanese Discovery of Victorian Britain, pp.127-8. Also Cobbing, 'Early Meiji Cultural Encounters' in Ian Nish (ed.), *The Iwakura Mission to America and Europe: a new assessment* (Folkestone: Japan Library, 1998), pp.40-1 48-9 and 'Three Meiji Marriages' by Noboru Koyama p.387 in *Britain and Japan: Biographical Portraits Volume IV*. Terashima's role in resolving the financial plight of Japanese students is related in Ozaki, *Ozaki Saburō jijo ryakuden*, vol.1, pp.119-27.
35. Cobbing, *The Japanese Discovery of Victorian Britain*, pp.148-9.
36. Records by W.G. Aston of interviews between Granville and Iwakura held at the Foreign Office on 22 November, 27 November and 6 December 1872, FO 46/160 reproduced in full in Hugh Cortazzi's paper in the Transaction sof the Asiatic Society 2002. The Japanese records of these interviews appear in *Jōyaku kaisei kankei nihon gaikō monjo* [*Japanese Diplomatic Documents on Treaty Revision*], vol.1 (Tokyo: Nihon Kokusai Kyōkai, 1941), pp.223-33. Although broadly similar in content, the Japanese account records, unlike Aston's, that much of the dialogue, particularly in the second interview, was conducted between Terashima and Parkes.
37. For details on Iwakura's stance on freedom of religion see John Breen, 'Public Statements and Private Thoughts: the Iwakura Embassy in London and the religious question', *The Iwakura Mission in Britain, 1872, Sticerd International Studies* IS/98/349, London School of Economics, pp.53-67.
38. In Aston's account this statement is attributed to Iwakura, in the Japanese version to Terashima. FO 46/160. *Jōyaku kaisei kankei nihon gaikō monjo*, vol.1, p. 226.
39. Inuzuka, *Terashima Munenori*, pp.193-6. As Isabella Bird pointed out in 1878, passports for travel on specific routes in the interior were obtainable for reasons of 'health, botanical research, or scientific investigation'. In her case, thanks to Parkes's efforts, she had 'practically unrestricted' access 'to travel through all Japan north of Tōkiō and in Yezo without specifying a route'. The bearer of the passport had to 'conduct himself in an orderly and conciliatory manner', could not 'light fires in woods, attend fires on horseback, trespass on fields, enclosures, or game-preserves, scribble on temples, shrines, or walls, drive fast on a narrow road, or disregard notices of "No thorough-fare"'. He was also 'forbidden to shoot, trade, to conclude mercantile contacts with Japanese, or to rent houses or rooms for a longer period than his journey requires.' Bird, *Unbeaten Tracks in Japan*, p.38.
40. Hoare, 'The Era of Unequal Treaties', p.112. R.G. Watson, acting chargé d'affaires during Parkes's absence in 1872-3, argued that the presence of the British garrison was no longer justified and deeply resented by the Japanese population. R.G. Watson to Granville, 19 December 1872, FO 262/225.
41. Parkes refused to accept that Japanese game laws should apply to British subjects. In one dispatch he was scathing of Bingham's response to a communication from Terashima to the foreign envoys canvassing their opinion over hunting laws: 'Mr Bingham is evidently at a loss to know how unlicensed shooting in Japan by an American citizen is to be punished by American law, but as he holds the theory that Japanese law can be enforced in the United States Consular Courts, he suggests that the insufficient means provided by Congress for

the control of American citizens in Japan should be remedied by Japanese legislation.' Parkes to the Earl of Derby, 22 January 1877, FO 262/302.

42. 'The present convention shall take effect when Japan shall have concluded such conventions or revisions of existing treaties with all the other treaty powers holding relations with Japan as shall be similar in effect to the present convention, and such new conventions or revisions shall also go into effect.' Article X of Yoshida-Evarts Convention, signed 25 July 1878, ratified 8 April 1879. *Jōyaku kaisei kankei nihon gaikō monjo*, vol. 1, pp.467-73, 532.

43. The actual wording of this message reads 'if you refuses [sic] firm with S. Parkes'. Telegram from Ueno Kagenori to Terashima Munenori, 9 April 1879. Ibid., p.642.

44. Ibid., p.543.

45. Soon after the Iwakura Embassy's departure from Britain, Parkes had made an impassioned appeal on behalf of British merchants claiming that 'liberty in the hands of the Japanese to alter the Tariff as they like could soon ruin the Trade'. Criticizing US Secretary of State Hamilton Fish who was 'inclined to think that the Japanese Government had a right to claim this power', he warned that this 'would tell chiefly against British Trade, as we are the principal importers. The United States have no import trade in Japan, but would like to become the Emporium of produce of that country and China.' Parkes to Granville, 24 December 1872, FO 46/156.

46. *Jōyaku kaisei kankei nihon gaikō monjo*, vol.1, p.658.

47. Inoyue Yuichi, 'From Unequal Treaty to the Anglo-Japanese Alliance', in Ian Nish and Yoichi Kibata (ed.), *The History of Anglo-Japanese Relations*, vol.1, p.139.

48. James Hoare, 'The Bankoku Shimbun Affair: foreigners, the foreign press and extraterritoriality in Japan', *Modern Asian Studies*, vol.9, no.3 (1975), pp.289-302.

49. See Janet Hunter, 'The Abolition of Extraterritoriality in the Japanese Post Office, 1873-1880', *Proceedings of the British Association for Japanese Studies*, vol.1 (1976), Part 1: History and International Relations, edited by Peter Lowe, pp.17-37.

50. In 1881 the *Japan Mail* reported: 'We cannot pretend that Sir Harry Parkes's policy has kept pace with the changes among which his lot has been cast'. Hoare, 'The Age of Unequal Treaties', p.126. The same year, in a letter to F.V. Dickins, Satow even likened Parkes to Napoleon in the eyes of his enemies, describing him as 'the bugbear of the Japanese public; in the popular estimation he occupies much the same position as "Boney" with us fifty years ago'. Daniels, *Sir Harry Parkes*, pp.178, 188.

51. Inuzuka, *Terashima Munenori*, pp.228, 300.

52. Cobbing, 'Mori Arinori: from diplomat to statesman' in Sir Hugh Cortazzi (ed.), *Britain and Japan – Biographical Portraits*, vol.4 (Folkestone: Japan Library, 2002), pp.3-13.

53. Inuzuka, *Terashima Munenori*, pp.259-60, 273-4.

Chapter 6 IAN RUXTON **Suematsu Kenchō, 1855-1920: Statesman, Bureaucrat, Diplomat, Journalist, Poet and Scholar**

1. Richard H. P. Mason, 'Suematsu Kenchō and patterns of Japanese cultural and political change in the 1880s', Papers on Far Eastern History, Australian National University, Dept. of Far Eastern History, 1979, pp. 1-55. (Hereafter 'Mason').

2. The former Hizen province is now absorbed into Saga and Nagasaki prefectures.

3. *Pōtsumasu e no michi: Kōkaron to Yōroppa no Suematsu Kenchō*, by Matsumura Masayoshi, published by Hara Shobō, 1987. p. 2. (Hereafter *Portsmouth*).

4. *Wakaki hi no Suematsu Kenchō: Zaiei Tsūshin*, [Suematso Kenchō in his youth: Correspondence from Britain] by Tamae Hikotarō, published by Kaichōsha, 1992, pp. 65-6. (Hereafter *Wakaki hi*). He was also given the pen name (*gō*) of Seihyō.

5. *Wakaki hi* p. 73.

6. The rift is described in *Wakaki hi*, pp. 186-7.

7. *Hatenkō: 'Meiji Ryugakusei' Retsuden*, by Noboru Koyama, published by Kodansha Metier, 1999, p. 135. (Hereafter *Hatenkō*). Allegedly Suematsu wrote the letter from Yamagata to Saigō Takamori recommending that he surrender (*Wakaki hi* p. 178).

8. Suematsu commissioned a Hungarian scholar G.G. Zerffi to write a modern, general survey of European historiography. Suematsu met Zerffi in 1878 or 1879 in London. Suematsu's letter with 'instructions' attached was included in Zerffi's *The Science of History*, published in 1879. Suematsu spent a lot of money on the royalty and printing expenses, (later reimbursed by the Historiographical Institute led by Shigeno Yasutsugu) and recommended the book's translation to Itō Hirobumi. (See *From Habsburg Agent to Victorian Scholar: G.G. Zerffi, 1820-1892* by Tibor Frank, Atlantic Research and Publications Inc., New Jersey, 2000. With thanks to Noboru Koyama for this information.)

9. Margaret Mehl, 'Suematsu Kenchō in Britain, 1878-86', *Japan Forum* (BAJS), Vol. 5, No. 2, October 1993, pp. 173-193, at p. 180. (Hereafter 'Mehl'). Sixteen letters from Suematsu to his family were discovered in 1980 (*Wakaki hi*, p. 3).

10. A collection of the letters from Suematsu to Itō spanning the years Meiji 9-37 (1876-1904) is contained in *Itō Hirobumi Kankei Bunsho (Monjo)*, Vol. V, pp.288-457 (Hanawa Shobō, 1977). Some of the letters which bear no year have been chronologically misplaced, or not placed at all. (Hereafter *Itō*).

11. Mehl, p. 174.

12. See *Wakaki hi* p. 17. The illustrations were downloaded from the internet.

13. See 'Mori Arinori, 1847-89: from Diplomat to Statesman' by Andrew Cobbing, Ch. 1, *Britain and Japan: Biographical Portraits*, Vol. IV.

14. *Itō*, Vol. V, p. 367.

15. *Eagle* (college magazine), Vol. 13, p. 123.

16. The lecture by Mr Edwards was published in *Transactions and Proceedings of the Japan Society, London*, Vol. 7 (1905-07), London, 1908, pp. 45-58.

17. Ibid. p. 48.

18. Arthur David Waley (1889-1966) attended Rugby School and King's College, Cambridge (1907-10). Self-educated in Chinese and Japanese, he began translating while employed as an assistant at the British Museum. He never accepted a university appointment, and steadfastly refused to visit Asia!

19. Edward George Seidensticker (1921-). Professor emeritus of Japanese at Columbia University. Has translated many Japanese works, including Tanizaki Jun'ichirō's *Sasameyuki* ('The Makioka Sisters') and Kawabata Yasunari's *Yukiguni* ('Snow Country').

20. *Wakaki hi*, pp. 126-7. *Itō*, Vol. V, p. 361.

21. *Itō*, Vol. IV, pp. 366-7.

22. *Itō*, Vol. V, pp. 379-80.

23. Mason, p. 7. On *Kagaku-ron* in detail see Mason, pp. 6-20.

24. Mehl, p. 189.

25. *Wakaki hi*, p. 194.

26. Brian Powell, pp. 107-110 in 'Theatre Cultures in Contact: Britain and Japan in the Meiji Period', Part II, Ch. 6, *The History of Anglo-Japanese Relations 1600-2000, Vol. V, Social and Cultural Perspectives*, ed. Daniels and Tsuzuki (Palgrave, 2000). (Hereafter 'Powell').

27. Mason, p. 20. On the Theatre Reform Movement, see Mason pp. 20-40.

28. See in particular the *Jiji Shinpō* of 12 October 1886.

29. Powell, p. 106.

30. The *Rokumeikan* ('Hall of the Baying Stag') designed by Josiah Conder was a pleasure pavilion built to entertain foreign diplomats and persuade them that Japan was as civilized and Western as their own countries, and therefore deserved equal treaties.

31. The doctorate in literature (*Bungaku Hakushi*, D. Litt.) has been said to be awarded in 1888 by Keiō University (*Portsmouth*, p. 40), but see *Wakaki hi*, p. 207 citing *Who Was Who* (*Alumni Cantabrigienses*, Part II, 1752-1900) which states D. Litt. Tokyo Imperial University. In fact it could not have been awarded by Keiō, because the university did not receive accreditation by the government until 1920 under the *Daigaku-rei* (Imperial Ordinance regarding Universities) of 1918, and the first doctorate of that university was only awarded in 1921 according to Keiō's centenary history (*Keiō Gijuku Hyakunen Shi*). But equally it could not have been awarded by Tokyo Imperial University, because between 1888 and 1920 all doctoral degrees were issued by the Minister of Education according to the *Gakui-rei* (Imperial Ordinance regarding Degrees) of 1887 without being related to any university, a notion which may seem strange to Western thinking but is understandable as the system was only just being established. In 1918 Suematsu was awarded a second doctorate in law (LL.D.) for his translations into Japanese of Roman Law texts which he had first studied at Cambridge (*Portsmouth*, p. 285). Suggestions that this was a doctorate of Tokyo Imperial University should, however, be discounted. It was not until 1920 that a new *Gakui-rei* allowed universities to issue doctorates subject to the approval of the Minister of Education, and from 1947 without the Minister's approval. (With thanks to Noboru Koyama for clarifying this by e-mail in April, 2004.)

32. *Wakaki hi*, p. 193.

33. Mason, p. 42 quoting Yoshino Sakuzō (ed.), *Meiji Bunka Zenshū*, III, pp. 202-03.
34. *Emperor of Japan: Meiji and his world 1852-1912*, by Donald Keene, Columbia University Press, 2002, p. 685. (Hereafter 'Keene'.)
35. *Itō*, V, p. 450. Letter no. 158, 11 January 1904, Suematsu to Itō and Yamagata.
36. See *Nihon Gaikō Bunsho*, Nichi-Rō sensō V, nos. 459, 441 for detailed instructions from prime minister Katsura and foreign minister Komura.
37. This letter has been incorrectly dated in *Itō*, V, p. 301 as 9 February <u>1878</u> which is impossible because it refers to Ikuko sending her good wishes. Suematsu did not marry her until 1889. Also the content suggests a grave political crisis, i.e. 1904. (*Hatenkō*, p. 137)
38. Itō to Lansdowne, 9 February 1904, FO 800/134. (*Portsmouth*, pp. 31-36) The letter may have been written by Suematsu himself, or a third party, as it was unusual for Itō to write in English. Lansdowne's cordial response dated 18 March spoke of his regret that war had become necessary and the 'intense interest' in the war in Britain. (*Portsmouth*, pp. 291-2)
39. Keene, pp. 611, 612.
40. Dr. Waraker was a member of Lincoln's Inn. Just after graduating from Cambridge Suematsu may have introduced Waraker to Mutsu Munemitsu, whom he advised on constitutional government. (See p. 87, 'Mutsu Munemitsu in Europe, 1884-85: The Intellectual in Search of an Ideology' by Hagihara Nobutoshi in *Mutsu Munemitsu and Identity Formation of the Individual and the State in Modern Japan*, Louis G. Perez (ed.), Edwin Mellen Press, 2001.)
41. *The Risen Sun*, Archibald Constable, London, 1905, p. 15.
42. Keene, pp. 491-95.
43. Keene, p. 605.
44. Like Donald Keene, Suematsu focuses on Emperor Meiji's poetry to introduce his elusive personality.
45. Nitobe Inazō's book *Bushido: The Soul of Japan* first published in 1900 became internationally popular during the Russo-Japanese War and appeared in a tenth revised edition in July, 1905.
46. Mitford referred to it as the 'Cambridge Society of Japan' but from 1905 it was the Cambridge & Oxford Society. The Cambridge Club was probably founded at a dinner attended by Sir Ernest Satow according to his diary on 24 January 1896. (*Hatenkō*, pp. 214-19) Only in Japan does Cambridge precede Oxford!
47. Austin Chamberlain was Suematsu's Cambridge contemporary and later Chancellor in Balfour's cabinet, 1903-05. He and his father Joseph the former Colonial Secretary supported Suematsu when he revisited England in 1904-06. (*Portsmouth*, pp. 113-16).

Chapter 7 NOBORU KOYAMA **Kikuchi Dairoku, 1855-1917: Educational Administrator and Pioneer of Modern Mathematical Education in Japan**

1. *Sūmitsuin kōtōkan rireki*, vol. 3, Tokyo, Tōkyō Daigaku Shuppankai, 1996. p.302.

2.   Jiromaru, Kenzō, *Mitsukuri Shūhei to sono shūhen*, Kumenan-cho (Okayama-ken), Mitsukuri Shūhei Denki Kankōkai, 1970. pp.34-5.
3.   FO 262/120.
4.   FO 46/72.
5.   Ishizuki, Minoru, *Kindai Nihon no kaigai ryūgaku shi*, Tokyo, Chūō Kōronsha, 1992. pp.203-06.
6.   *Kokusaijin jiten*, Tokyo, Mainichi Komyunikçshonzu, 1991. p.163.
7.   Orme, Temple, *University College School, London alphabetical and chronological register for 1831-1891*, London, H. Walton Lawrence, 1919. pp.30-1.
8.   Kikuchi, Dairoku, 'Toeidan 3', *Taiyō*, vol.14 no.1, 1908.
9.   'Japanese Success at University College', *London and China Telegraph*, 11 August 1873.
10. University of London, *The calendar for the year 1874*, London, Taylor and Francis, 1874. pp.322-23.
11. *The Japanese Club at Cambridge*, [no.1], [1890].
12. Venn, J. A., *Alumni Cantabrigienses; a biographical list of all known students, graduates and holders of office at the University of Cambridge, from the earliest times to 1900*, Cambridge, Cambridge University Press, 1940-54. 6 vols.
13. Edwards, H. J., 'Japanese undergraduates at Cambridge University', *Transactions and Proceedings of the Japan Society, London*, vol.7 (1905-1907), London, Japan Society, 1908. p.47.
14. Douglas, James, *Rowing on the Cam*, Barton, Cambs, Bird's Farm, 1977. p.28. Sedbergh School is a public school amid the bleak hills of what is now Cumbria. The school motto says it all: '*dura virum nutrix*' meaning 'hard nurse of men'.
15. Edwards, H. J., 'Japanese undergraduates at Cambridge University', *Transactions and Proceedings of the Japan Society, London*, vol.7 (1905-07), London, Japan Society, 1908. p.47.
16. *Sūmitsuin kōtōkan rireki*, vol. 3, Tokyo, Tōkyō Daigaku Shuppankai, 1996. p.304.
17. *Ibid.*, p.306.
18. *Ibid.*, p.309.
19. *Ibid.*, p.310.
20. Ogura, Kinnosuke, *Sūgaku kyōiku shi*, Tokyo, Iwanami Shoten, 1973. p.338.
21. *Sūmitsuin kōtōkan rireki*, vol. 3, Tokyo, Tōkyō Daigaku Shuppankai, 1996. p.315.
22. *Ibid.*, p.317.
23. *Ibid.*, pp.320-21.
24. Japan, Ministry of Foreign Affairs, Archives (JFMA), file 3.8.4.34 (*Rondon Daigaku ni oite Nihon yori kōshi shōhei mōshikomi ikken*).
25. Kikuchi, Dairoku, *Japanese education: lectures delivered in the University of London*, London, Murray, 1909. pp.1-2.
26. Satō, Hideo, 'Tetsugakukan Jiken shinsetsu', *enryo website Kikanshi satia 47* (http://www.toyo.ac.jp/enryo/htmls/f-html/f-08.5.htm), 14 December 2003.
27. Felkin, F. W., *From Gower Street to Frognal: a short history of University College*

School from 1830 to 1907, London, Arnold Fairbairns & Co., 1909. pp.36–38.
28.   *Sūmitsuin kōtōkan rireki*, vol. 3, Tokyo, Tōkyō Daigaku Shuppankai, 1996. pp.323–324.
29.   Kikuchi, Dairoku, *Shin Nihon*, Tokyo, Fuzanbō, 1910.
30.   *Ibid.*, p.326.
31.   Fujisawa, Rikitarō, 'Obituary notice', *Taiyō*, vol.23 no.12, 1917.
32.   *Asahi shinbun* [Tokyo], 20 August 1917 and 23 August 1917.
33.   *Asahi shinbun* [Tokyo], 7 March 1921.

Chapter 8 FUJIKO HARA **Ozaki Yukio (1858–1954) and Britain**

In preparing this essay on Ozaki and Britain I am indebted to my husband, Martin Blakeway, for his invaluable collaboration and support, to Nagaoka Shōzō for sharing his scholarship and to Shinagawa Mitsue for her painstaking research.
1.   *Hōchi Shimbun*. Daily newspaper started in 1872. After 1882 became a paper affiliated to the Progressive Party. In 1942 it was merged with *Yomiuri Shimbun*. Since 1950 it has been a sports paper.
2.   Ozaki, Yukio, *Ozaki Gakudō Zenshū* Volume 1, Ozaki Yukio Memorial Foundation, 1 February 1958, pp.263–69.
3.   Ibid.
4.   Ibid.
5.   Ibid. The origin of the concept Ozaki used in his famous impeachment against Prime Minister General Katsura Taro in 1913 is found here.
6.   Ibid.
7.   Ozaki, Yukio, *Ozaki Yukio Zenshu* Volume II, pp. 310–311, 346–79.
8.   Ozaki's Autobiography translated by Fujiko Hara (2001) stated that 'Ozaki was born on 20 November 1858. For unknown reasons the entry on the family register records his birth as being in the following year. . .'
9.   Private school run by Hirata Kanetan a disciple and adopted son of Hirata Atsutane(1776–1843), Japanese scholar who was in turn a disciple of Motoori Norinaga.
10.   Sohma Yukika, Ozaki's daughter, has commented that Ozaki was struck by the submissiveness of a condemned man at Ise compared with the cheeky remark to the executioner of the victim in Takasaki: 'My neck is tougher than your sword, you'll see!'
11.   *Ozaki Gakudō Zenshū* Volume XI.
12.   Published by Maruya Zenshichi (now Maruzen) in November 1877 and September 1879.
13.   Social Statics was translated later in full by Matsushima Tsuyoshi and published in six volumes between 1881 and 1884 as *Thesis on Social Equal Rights*. It became a best-seller.
14.   *Gakudō Ozaki Yukio*, ed. Sohma Yukika, Tomita Nobuo, Aoki Kazuyoshi, Keiō Gijuku University Press, 2000, p.12.
15.   Born in St. Helen's near Liverpool in 1811 and emigrated to the United States in 1832. Died 1882.
16.   First published by Harper and Brothers, and in Japanese by Shuseisha Books, January 1880.

17. Published in three volumes in 1886 by Shūseisha Shōten. Japanese title may be translated as 'Advice and Achievements'.

18. It was published in 1882 and 1883 by Jiyū Shuppan Kaisha.

19. A biographical portrait of Henry Dyer by Olive Checkland was included in *Britain and Japan Biographical Portraits Volume III*, Japan Library, 1999.

20. A biographical portrait of Rev Alexander Croft Shaw by Hamish Ion was also included in *Biographical Portraits III*.

21. Published by Kelly and Walsh Ltd, Yokohama, 1917.

22. Isa Hideo, *Biography of Ozaki Yukio (Ozaki Yukio Den)* pp.406–408, 28 April 1951 by Ozaki Yukio Biography Publishing Committee (Ozaki Yukio Den Kanko-kai.

23. Published by Kelly and Walsh Ltd, Yokohama, 1917.

24. Isa Hideo, *Biography of Ozaki Yukio (Ozaki Yukio Den)* pp.406–408, 28 April 1951 by Ozaki Yukio Biography Publishing Committee (Ozaki Yukio Den Kanko-kai).

25. *The Times*, Court Circular, Marlborough House, 5 July.

26. IPU Record p.105.

27. Hosoya Chiharu, *Japan's View of the Anglo-American World and East Asia in Inter-war years*, p.1.

28. Yukika and her elder sister attended a Buckingham Place Garden party on 21 July 1932.

29. According to Sohma Yukika, Ozaki was also impressed by the way in which some British Ministers declined their pensions if they were well enough off to do without them. It was in emulation of this spirit of public service that Ozaki quit the office of Mayor of Tokyo just short of completing his second term, thus denying himself the benefits he would have acquired if he had served out the full term.

30. *The Times*, 'The Japanese and Manchuria', 28 July 1932.

31. *The Times*, 14 April 1932.

32. Ozaki Yukio, *Japan at the Crossroads; An Outspoken Warning to the Peoples of the World*, P.S. King & Son, Ltd., London.

33. See 'Three Meiji Marriages between Japanese Men and English Women' by Noboru Koyama in *Britain and Japan: Biographical Portraits, Volume IV*, Japan Library. 2002.

34. His father John Robert Morrison b. 1805 was not related to Robert Morrison (1782–1834), a sinologist who translated the Bible into Chinese or to his sons John Robert Morrison (1814–1843) and George Staunton Morrison who was consul in Nagasaki. (Noboru Koyama's letter addressed to Professor R. Bowring, Faculty of Oriental Studies, Cambridge, 26 January 1992).

35. The other daughters were Kimiko Maude Mary Harriet, born January 1872, who married Alfred James Hewitt in 1906, and Muriel who married the actor Sir Ralph Richardson. The third daughter, Masako Florence Bathia Alexandra, was born in October 1873 and married a Swede, Henrik Ouchterlony in Japan in 1909.

36. Letter to Sohma Yukika from Nagaoka Shōzō.

37. C.f. *A Diplomat's Wife in Japan, Sketches at the Turn of the Century* by Mary

Crawford Fraser, edited by Hugh Cortazzi, Weatherhill, Tokyo, 1982, also biographical portrait of Hugh Fraser by Hugh Cortazzi in *Britain and Japan: Biographical Portraits Volume IV,* Japan Library 2002.

38. Mary Crawford Fraser was born in Italy in 1851 of American parents. Her father was the sculptor Thomas Crawford who designed the Washington Monument. Mary was sent to England to be educated where she met and married Hugh Fraser, a British diplomat, in 1874. She had two real homes, she was to say, Japan and South Italy, 'where beauty lives'.

39. She need not have feared. The complete e-book of her *Japanese Fairy Tales* is available on the Internet.

40. Baroness Albert d'Anethan, *Fourteen Years of Diplomatic Life in Japan—Leaves from the Diary of Baroness Albert d'Anethan,* New York, McBride, Nast and Company, 1912, p.354.

41. Fraser, Mary Crawford, a rather lengthy (3,500 words) biographical sketch of Yei Theodora Ozaki as a Foreword to Yei's *The Japanese Fairy Book.*

42. Baroness d'Anethan, p.456.

43. *Op. cit.* p.468.

44. *Op. cit.* Fraser, Foreword to the *Japanese Fairy Book.*

45. Ibid.

46. Ibid.

47. Ibid.

48. One such was Mme Van Royen, the wife of the Dutch Ambassador at the time of Yukika's birth. She became Yukika's godmother and gave her the name Alexandra.

49. Tennyson, Alfred Lord, *Locksley Hall.*

Chapter 9 IAN NISH **Lord Curzon and Japan**

1. Major biographies of Curzon include (Lord) Ronaldshay, *The Life of Lord Curzon,* 3 vols, London: Benn, 1928; Kenneth Rose, *Superior Person,* London: Weidenfeld, 1969; and David Gilmour, *Curzon,* London: Murray, 1994.

2. The most detailed account of this journey is to be found in Stephen Gwynn (ed.), *The Letters and Friendships of Sir Cecil Spring Rice,* 2 vols, London: Constable, 1929, I, 125.

3. Ronaldshay, I, 190-1.

4. Spring-Rice, I, 125-40.

5. An alternative view of the book is to be found in G. Daniels and Tsuzuki Chushichi (eds), *The History of Anglo-Japanese Relations: Social and Cultural Perspectives,* Basingstoke: Palgrave, 2002, pp. 7-8. *Problems of the Far East* (1896 edition) was reprinted by Palgrave-Macmillan in 2002.

6. Curzon, *Problems* (1896), Introduction and p. 366.

7. Curzon, *Problems* (1896), pp. 363-4.

8. Clearly a reference to the *Dreibund* (Russia, Germany, France) of 1895. Curzon, *Problems* (1896), p. 387.

9. Salisbury to Curzon, 27 June 1895 in Ronaldshay, I, 234-5.

10. The information comes from the Satow diaries through the kindness of Mr Ian Ruxton. Curzon to Salisbury, 29 December 1897 in Ronaldshay, I, 277f. For

details of the 1897-8 crisis, see Ian Nish, *The Anglo-Japanese Alliance*, London: Athlone, 1966, pp.47-57.
11. For the British-Indian troops present according to British War Office estimates, see Ian Nish (ed.), *British Documents on Foreign Affairs*, series E (Asia, 1860-1914), vol. 13, doc. 34. Following this, the Indian army began sending officers for the study of the Japanese language in Tokyo.
12. Curzon to Selborne, 9 Nov. 1900 in D.G. Boyce (ed.), *The Crisis of British Power, 1895-1910*, London: TH Press, 1990, p.104.
13. Selborne to Curzon, 19 April 1901 in Boyce, p.113.
14. Curzon to Edward VII, 24 Feb. 1902 in the Royal Archives, W1/18, quoted in Nish, *Alliance*, p. 369.
15. Ian Nish, 'Alliance and Empire' in *Collected Writings*, Part I, 'The Anglo-Japanese Alliance', Richmond : Japan Library, 2001, pp. 100-9. Andrew Roberts, *Salisbury: Victorian Titan*, London: Weidenfeld, 1999, p. 779.
16. Ian Hamilton, *A Staff Officer's Scrap-book during the Russo-Japanese War*, 2 vols, London: Edward Arnold, vol. I, 1905.
17. G.P. Gooch and H.W.V. Temperley (eds), *British Documents on the Origins of the War, 1898-1914*, London: HMSO, 1929, vol. IV, no. 155.
18. CAB 1/16, 6 Sept. 1905. The quotation is interesting for the Committee of Imperial Defence's interpretation that the Russo-Japanese War came about because of independent action by Russian officials in the East.
19. *Documents on British Foreign Policy, 1919-39*, series I, vol. xiv, no. 167 fn. (hereafter cited as *DBFP*).
20. Curzon was critical of Balfour politically and even more critical of Balfour as Foreign Secretary. On 8 March 1918, Curzon called on Hankey before the start of a cabinet and attacked Balfour, suggesting himself as Foreign Secretary. Salisbury had trained him, he alleged, and had always designated him as his successor. While Hankey told the Prime Minister of this, nothing happened for a year. Stephen Roskill, *Hankey: Man of Secrets*, 3 vv., London: Collins, 1972, II, 506.
21. *DBFP*, I (vi), no. 436 and p. 562.
22. *DBFP*, I (vi), no. 484. Ku Daeyeol, *Korea under Colonialism: The March First Movement and Anglo-Japanese Relations*, Seoul : Royal Asiatic Society, 1985, chs 2 and 3.
23. *DBFP*, I (vi), nos 761, 789.
24. *DBFP*, I (xiv), no. 97.
25. *DBFP*, I (xiv), no. 405.
26. *DBFP*, I (xiv), no. 328.
27. *DBFP*, I (xiv), nos 335, 340.
28. *Hara Kei Nikki*, vol. 9.
29. Curzon to Geddes, 25 Sept. 1921 in *DBFP*, I (xiv), no. 384.
30. Curzon to Hankey, 17 Oct. 1921 in Roskill, *Hankey*, II, 236.
31. GNC, 'The palaestra of Japan' in *Tales of Travel*, London: Hodder & Stoughton, 1923, p. 174.

NOTES

Chapter 10 ANTONY BEST **Lord Hankey (1877–1963), R.A. Butler (1902–82) and the 'Appeasement of Japan, 1939–41'**

1. Sir Maurice Pascal Aiers, First Baron Hankey (1877–1963). He was commissioned into the Royal Marines and served in naval intelligence from 1902–06. He became Secretary to the Committee of Imperial Defence in 1912, and later Secretary to the Imperial War Cabinet until its dissolution in 1919, when he became Secretary to the Cabinet. He also became Clerk of the Privy Council. He retired in 1938. At the outbreak of the Second World War he became Minister without portfolio in the War Cabinet. In 1940 he was appointed Chancellor of the Duchy of Lancaster and from 1941–42 Paymaster General.

2. Richard Austen Butler, Baron (1902–82). He was elected as Member of Parliament for Saffron Walden in Essex in 1929. He held various junior ministerial offices, including at the Foreign Office. He was Minister of Education from 1941–45. In post-war Conservative party governments he was Chancellor of the Exchequer, Lord Privy Seal, Leader of the House of Commons, Deputy Prime Minister and finally Secretary of State for Foreign Affairs 1962–3. As Foreign Secretary he made an official visit to Japan. In 1965 he was appointed Master of Trinity College, Cambridge. 'Once described as "both irreproachable and unapproachable" he will go down as one of the most progressive, thoughtful and dedicated of Tory leaders.' *Chambers Biographical Dictionary*, 1990.

3. S. Roskill, *Hankey: Man of Secrets*, vol.III, 1931–1963 (Collins, London, 1974) pp.649–50.

4. A. Howard, *R.A.B: The Life of R.A. Butler* (Jonathan Cape, London, 1987) pp.70–87, and P. Stafford, 'Political Autobiography and the Art of the Plausible: R.A. Butler at the Foreign Office 1938–39', *Historical Journal*, 1985, 28/4, pp.901–72.

5. Brabourne papers, IOLR, Mss.Eur.F97/20A/Butler to Brabourne, 12 December 1935.

6. R.A. Butler, *The Art of Memory: Friends in Perspective* (Hodder & Stoughton, London, 1982) p.40.

7. PRO FO371/23483 F3368/372/10/Sale to Butler, 30 March 1939.

8. PRO FO371/23571 F3144/2691/23/Butler minute, 7 April 1939.

9. See A. Best, '"That Loyal British Subject"?: Arthur Edwardes and Anglo-Japanese Relations, 1932–41' in J.E. Hoare (ed.,) *Britain and Japan: Biographical Portraits*, Vol.III (Japan Library, Richmond, 1999) pp. 227–39.

10. PRO FO371/23532 F9583/6457/10 Butler minute, 26 August 1939 and F9638/6457/10 Edwardes to Butler, 26 August 1939.

11. PRO FO371/23556 F10295/176/23 Butler minute, 18 September 1939, and F10459/176/23 Edwardes to Butler, 22 September 1939.

12. Ibid., F10710/176/23 Butler memorandum, 22 September 1939.

13. PRO CAB66/2 WP(39)56 'Sino-Japanese Hostilities' COS memorandum, 28 September 1939.

14. PRO FO371/24650 F1638/5/10 Butler minute, 8 March 1940.

15. See A. Best, *Britain, Japan and Pearl Harbor: Avoiding War in East Asia, 1936–41* (Routledge, London, 1995) pp.92–95 and 102–7.

16. FO371/25077 W6205/8/49 Butler to Cross, 5 April 1940.
17. FO371/24724 F2169/23/23 Butler minute, 1 April 1940.
18. FO371/24667 F3597/43/10 Butler/Shigemitsu conversation, 11 July 1940 and F3590/43/10 Butler/Shigemitsu conversation, 19 July 1940.
19. PRO FO371/24708 F3633/193/61 Butler minute, 23 July 1940.
20. Ibid., Butler minute, 26 July 1940.
21. Butler papers, Trinity College Library Cambridge, E3/19[1] Sale to Butler, 15 August 1940, E3/19[66] Sempill to Butler, 19 August 1940 and E3/5[42], Edwardes to Butler, 2 September 1940.
22. PRO FO371/24725 F3592/23/23 Butler minute, 12 August 1940, and Butler papers, E3/5[46] Butler minute, 6 September 1940.
23. PRO FO371/24710 F4770/193/61 Butler minute, 18 September 1940.
24. PRO CAB96/1 FE(40) 10th meeting, 28 November 1940.
25. PRO CAB21/1008 Hankey-Yoshida conversation, 18 February 1938.
26. Hankey papers, Churchill College Cambridge, HNKY4/31 Sandberg to Hankey, 1 March 1939, and HNKY8/35 Hankey to Wilson, 31 August 1939, and Roskill, op.cit. pp.410-11.
27. Piggott papers, Imperial War Museum, Edwardes to Piggott, 17 June 1940.
28. Hankey papers, PRO, CAB63/177 Hankey to Piggott, 8 October 1940. See also Hankey affidavit for Shigemitsu, defence exhibit 3457, in R.J. Pritchard & S.M. Zaide (eds), *The Tokyo War Crimes Trial*, vol.xiv, (Garland, New York, 1981) pp.34512-13.
29. Hankey papers, PRO, CAB63/177 Hankey to Piggott, 10 December 1940.
30. PRO FO371/27901 F234/27/23 Lloyd to Halifax, 4 December 1940, and Halifax to Lloyd, 17 December 1940.
31. R.J. Pritchard & S.M. Zaide (eds), op.cit. pp.34512-13.
32. PRO FO371/27889 F2303/17/23 Hankey to Butler, 24 March 1941.
33. PRO FO371/27886 F648/17/23 Butler minute, 5 February 1941.
34. PRO PREM3/252/6A Butler to Churchill, 28 March 1941.
35. Hankey papers, Churchill College Cambridge, HNKY1/7, 9 June 1941.
36. Roskill, op.cit., p.519.
37. Hankey papers, PRO, CAB63/177 Hankey to Sempill, 8 August 1941.
38. Eden papers, PRO, FO954/6 466 FE/41/35 Eden minute, 5 October 1941.
39. Hankey papers, PRO, CAB63/177 Hankey to Piggott, 14 November 1941.
40. Hankey affidavit for Shigemitsu, defence exhibit 3457, in R.J. Pritchard & S.M. Zaide (eds), op.cit., p.34521.
41. Lord Hankey, *Politics, Trials and Errors*, (Pen-in-Hand, Oxford, 1950).
42. Roskill, op.cit., p.652-3.

Chapter 11 IAN NISH Komura Jūtarō (1855-1911) and Britain

1. An earlier version of this paper was presented at the conference held on the occasion of the 80th anniversary of Komura's death at Nichinan city, Kyushu in November 1991. This is reproduced from *Florilegium Japonicum* 'Studies Presented to Olof G. Lidin on the occasion of his 70th birthday, Akademsisk Forlag, 1996.
2. See biographical portrait in this volume by Noboru Koyama.

3. Nish, Ian H. *Anglo-Japanese Alliance, 1894-1907*, London, 1966, Athlone Press, 1985, p.132.
4. Nish, *op.cit.*, pp.170-2.
5. Akashi Motojiro. 1988. *Rakka ryūsui*, ed. by Inaba Chiharu, Helsinki: SHS, p. 56ff.
6. Okamoto Shumpei. 1970. *The Japanese Oligarchy and the Russo-Japanese War*, New York: Columbia University Press, pp. 150-5.
7. C.M. MacDonald, 'Annual Report for Tokyo Embassy for 1907 in K. Bourne and D.C. Watt, (eds.). 1990, *British Documents on Foreign Affairs*, Maryland: University Publications of America, Part IE, vol 9, p. 74.
8. *Komura gaikōshi*, 2 vols, Tokyo: Foreign Ministry, ii, 242-3; Okamoto Shumpei, 'A phase of Meiji Japan's attitude toward China: The case of Komura Jūtarō' in *Modern Asian Studies*, 13(1979), 431-57.
9. MacDonald to Grey, 29 June 1906 in Archives of the British Foreign Office, Public Record Office, Kew, FO 371/86.
10. Pooley, Andrew M.(ed.). 1915. *The Secret Memoirs of Count Tadasu Hayashi*, London: Nash, pp. 14-15.
11. MacDonald to Grey, 23 May 1906 in FO 371/86.
12. MacDonald to Grey, 13 July 1908, in Papers of Sir Edward Grey (Public Record Office, Kew), vol. 68; *Nihon gaikō bunshō*, Meiji 40, Tokyo: Foreign Ministry, vol. 1, pp. 140-4.
13. MacDonald to Grey, 19 February 1907, in Grey papers, vol. 29.
14. Tsunoda Jun. 1967. *Manshū mondai to kokubō hōshin*, Tokyo: Hara Shobo, chs. 4-9.
15. Matsumura Masayoshi. 1987. *Nichi Ro sensō to Kaneko Kentarō*, Tokyo: Shinyudo, pp. 430.
16. V. Chirol to G.E. Morrison, 19 July 1907 in Lo Hui-min. 1976. *Correspondence of G. E. Morrison*, Cambridge: University Press, i, 423 [Hayashi was foreign minister at the time of this letter].
17. MacDonald (in London) to Hardinge, 11 Jan. 1907 in FO 371/270.
18. Nish, Ian H. 1966. *The Anglo-Japanese Alliance*, London, Athlone Press, pp. 346, 353-4; Shimojo Akiko. 1994. *Junai: Ethel to Mutsu Hirokichi*, Tokyo: Kodansha, p. 207. 18.
19. Nish, Ian H. 1972. *Alliance in Decline*, London: Athlone Press, pp. 11-13.
20. Hotta-Lister, Ayako, 'The Japan-British Exhibition of 1910' in Nish, Ian H. 1994. *Britain and Japan: Biographical Portraits*, Folkestone: Japan Library, pp. 146-58; Nish, *Alliance in Decline*, pp. 28-9.
21. Minute by Campbell on MacDonald to Grey, 8 June 1908 in FO 371/474.
22. *Komura gaikōshi*, ii, 282-4.
23. *Nihon gaikō nempyō narabini shuyō bunsho*, 2 vols., Tokyo: Foreign Ministry, i, 305-12; *Nihon gaikō bunshō*, Meiji 41, no. 1.
24. V. Chirol to Komura, 19 July 1909 in Lo Hui-min, *op. cit.*, i, 497-501.
25. C. M. MacDonald, Annual Report for Tokyo Embassy for 1911, in *British Documents on Foreign Affairs*, Part IE, vol. 9, p. 243.
26. V .Chirol (in Japanese waters) to Morrison, 7 July 1909, in Lo Hui-min, *op.cit.*, I, 490-1.

27. Macdonald, annual report for Tokyo Embassy for 1911, in *British Documents on Foreign Affairs*, Part IE, vol 9.
28. *Komura gaikōshi*, ii, 242-3.
29. Yoshizawa Kenkichi. 1958. *Gaikō 60-nen*, Tokyo: Jiyu Ajia, pp. 40-1.
30. MacDonald to Grey, 19 Feb. 1908 in Grey papers 68.
31. Nish, Ian H., 'Hayashi Tadasu' in Cortazzi, Hugh and Daniels, Gordon (eds.). 1991. *Britain and Japan, 1859-1991: Themes and Personalities*. London: Routledge, pp. 151-7.

Chapter 12 IAN NISH **Inouye Katsunosuke, 1861-1929**

1. C.G. Thorne, *Allies of a Kind*, London: Hamish Hamilton, 1978. P.C. Lowe, *Great Britain and Japan, 1911-15*, Macmillan 1969, is the most thorough account of the general history of this period.
2. Segai *Inouye-ko den*, Tokyo, 1934, vol.5, contains an appendix dealing with the life of his adopted son and heir, *Kōshaku Katsunosuke kun ryaku-den*, pp. 1-285. (hereafter cited as '*Katsunosuke-den*'.) I am unable to reconcile this evidence about his marriage with British Embassy reports that Inouye Kaoru had two daughters and the elder one married Katsunosuke who thereafter took on the adopted family name of Inouye. *British Documents on Foreign Affairs*, Part I, Series E, vol. 9 (Maryland: University Publications of America, 1989), p. 71 (Hereafter cited as '*BDOFA*').
3. Ian Nish, *Anglo-Japanese Alliance*, London: Athlone, 1966, chs 4 and 9.
4. *Katsunosuke-den*, pp. 117-19.
5. *Katsunosuke-den*, pp. 128-33; *The Times* (London), 7 July 1913 (at the time of Arisugawa's death).
6. *BDOFA*, vol. 9, p. 126.
7. Ian Nish, 'Katō Takaaki' in Hugh Cortazzi (ed.), *Britain and Japan: Biographical Portraits*, vol. 4, London: Japan Library, 2002, pp. 14-27.
8. Inouye's speech engagements included American Independence Day at Savoy Hotel (14/7); Trafalgar Day (21/10); Launch and Visit of IJN ship *Kongo* to British ports; Guildhall (9/11); Shipbuilders' Association dinner (30/3/14); Colchester City. Details in *Katsunosuke-den*, pp. 178-84.
9. *BDOFA*, vol. 9, p. 363.
10. *Shidehara Kijūrō*, pp. 72-8.
11. PC Lowe, 'Sir William Conyngham Greene' in Cortazzi (ed.), *Biographical Portraits*, Vol. 4, pp. 64-77.
12. Lowe, ch. 6 and Ian Nish, *Alliance in Decline*, London: Athlone, 1972, ch. 7.
13. Nish, *Alliance in Decline*, pp. 128-9.
14. *Nihon Gaikō Bunshō*, Taishō 3-nen, vol. 2, docs 595-606, pp. 865-953. (Hereafter cited as '<u>NGB</u>').
15. *NGB*, Taisho 4-nen, vol. 2, doc. 488; *Katsunosuke-den*, pp. 215-23.
16. FR Dickinson, *War and National Reinvention: Japan in the Great War, 1914-19*, Cambridge, Mass.: Harvard UP, 1999, p. 115.
17. Putnam Weale, *An Indiscreet Chronicle from the Pacific*, Basingstoke: Palgrave, 2002, p. 308. I have carried out a limited search to try to trace this in the Japanese and British press and through Japanese official sources but without success.

Katsunosuke-den, p. 224. Inouye was in touch privately with Tokyo affairs through correspondence with his brother-in-law, Tsuzuki Keiroku.
18. *NGB*, Taishō 4-nen, vol. 2, docs 609 and 635.
19. Dickinson, pp. 111-12; *Katsunosuke-den*, pp. 224-7.
20. *Katsunosuke-den*, pp. 229-30.
21. (British) Foreign Office papers, 410/65 [222589], Greene to Grey, 26 September 1916.
22. *Katsunosuke-den*, pp. 247-9; *The Times* (London).
23. *The Times* (London).
24. *Katsunosuke-den*, pp. 253-5.
25. *Katsunosuke-den*, pp.255-7; P. Ziegler (ed.) *The Diaries of Lord Louis Mountbatten*, Glasgow: Collins, 1987.
26. *Katsunosuke-den*, pp. 262-4.

Chapter 13 IAN NISH Chinda Sutemi, 1857-1929: Ambassador in Peace and War

1. The best general treatments of the subject are R.H. Fifield, *Woodrow Wilson and the Far East*, New York: Crowell, 1952; and Bruce Elleman, *Wilson and China: A revised history of the Shantung question*, Armunk, NY: M.E. Sharpe, 1984.
2. Kikuchi Takenori (ed.), *Hakushaku Chinda Sutemi-den, 1857-1929*, Tokyo: Kyōmeikaku, 1938.
3. *British Documents on Foreign Affairs*, Part I, Series E, vol. 8, Maryland: University Publications of America, 1989, p. 69.
4. Honda Kumataro on 'Chinda and Spring Rice' in Kikuchi, p. 288.
5. Kajima Morinosuke, *Diplomacy of Japan*, Tokyo: Kajima, 1980, vol. 3, p. 203 (my parenthesis). See also *Nihon gaikō bunshō*, Taishō 6/3, doc. 667 [hereafter cited as 'NGB'].
6. Professor Seki Eiji in his book *Nichi-Ei dōmei*, Tokyo: Gakushū Kenkyū, 2003, devotes chapters 2 and 3, pp. 71-179, to Japan's Mediterranean expedition and Malta experiences.
7. There are new studies of this topic by Yoichi Hirama and Ian Gow with John Chapman, *History of Anglo-Japanese Relations*, vol. 3, 'The Military Dimension', Basingstoke: Palgrave, 2003, while the older study by G. Nakashima, 'Japanese Navy in the Great War, 1918-20' in *Proceedings of the Japan Society of London*, 31(1917) is still useful.
8. See C. Andrews and D.N. Dilks, *The Missing Dimension*, London: Macmillan, 1984, pp. 144 and 147. Barbara Tuchman, *The Zimmermann Telegram*, London: Macmillan, 1983.
9. NGB Taishō 6/3, docs 106 and 110.
10. Margaret Macmillan gives a good pen portrait of Saionji and how his role puzzled foreigners. *Peacemakers*, London: John Murray, 2001, pp. 316-19.
11. Kimura Eiichi as quoted in Kikuchi, pp. 220-2. This view is generally supported by Naoko Shimazu, *Japan, Race and Equality*, London: Routledge, 1998.
12. Japan's claim for mandates over the Pacific islands which is sometimes depicted as a failure was eventually settled in her favour. The allocation, initially

made at the Paris conference, was confirmed at the San Remo conference of 1920 and later by the League-Japan agreement in 1922.

13. Fifield, pp. 546-7 contains only the shortened version passed to the Americans. For the full version, *Documents on British Foreign Policy, 1919-39*, London: HMSO, 1(vi), doc. 429. [here-after cited as 'DBFP'].

14. George Scott, *Rise and Fall of the League of Nations*, London: Hutchinson, 1973, p.56.

15. NGB Taishō 9, vol. 3/2, doc. 882.

16. NGB Taishō 9, vol. 3/2, doc. 884.

17. Kikuchi, pp. 214-5.

18. NGB Taishō 9, vol 3/2, nos 888-9; Kajima, vol. 3, p. 427.

19. NGB Taishō 9, vol. 3/2, doc. 986. George Shaw was an Anglo-Chinese merchant with business interests on the Yalu river. He was arrested by Japanese police in Korea on what seemed to Britain to be flimsy charges.

20. *The Times*, 7 Sept. 1920.

21. Ogata Sadako in Dorothy Borg and Shumpei Okamoto (eds), *Pearl Harbor as History*, New York: Columbia UP, 1973, pp. 462-3. Japan League of Nations Association was formed on 23 April 1920 and grew rapidly.

22. *DBFP*, 1(xiv), docs. 277 and 287. Ian Nish, 'Crown Prince Hirohito in Britain' in Ian Nish (ed.), *Biographical Portraits*, vol. I, Richmond: Japan Library, 1997. Dealt with also in F.S.G. Piggott, *Broken Thread*, Aldershot: Gale and Polden, 1950, pp. 123-31 and Philip Ziegler (ed.), *Diaries of Lord Louis Mountbatten*, London: Collins, 1987.

23. *The Times*, 18 August 1920.

24. Kikuchi, p. 222-5.

25. *The Times*, 18 August 1920.

Chapter 14 HARUMI GOTO-SHIBATA **Hayashi Gonsuke (1860-1939) and the Path to the Washington Conference**

1. This was seven years after Commodore Matthew Perry of the US navy had come to Japan to demand the country to open its doors to outsiders; an incident that had thrown the country into economic and political chaos.

2. Hayashi Gonsuke, *Waga 70 nen wo kataru* [On my 70 years] (Tokyo: Dai ichi shobō, 1935), pp. 2-39. The last daimyo of Aizu was the father of Matsudaira Tsuneo, the Japanese Ambassador to Britain from 1929 to 1935.

3. *Ibid.*, pp. 70-72.

4. *Ibid.*, pp. 419-421; Ian Nish, *Alliance in Decline* (London: Athlone Press, 1972), p. 309.

5. *Chū Ei taishi no kōtetsu to Nichi Ei dōmei no shōrai* [The change of the Ambassador to Britain and the future of the Anglo-Japanese Alliance], *Gaikō Jihō* [Revue Diplomatique], no. 374, 1 June 1920, p. 1011.

6. Daniel Varé, *Laughing Diplomat* (London: J. Murray, 1938), p. 175; Hayashi, *Waga 70 nen*, pp. 352, 356-7.

7. PRO, FO 371/10329, F 3834/20/87, letter from Waterlow to Anderson (Home Office), 18 Nov. 1924.

8. PRO, FO371/12525, F8585/8585/23, 13 Oct. 1927, from Tilley, no. 541.

9.   See also Antony Best, *British Intelligence and the Japanese Challenge in Asia, 1914-1941* (Basingstoke: Palgrave Macmillan, 2002), pp. 45-8.

10.   *Nippon Gaikō Bunsho* [Documents on Japanese Foreign Policy] (hereafter, NGB), Taisho 9 nen, vol.3, ge (hereafter, T9-3-2), no. 894, Hayashi to Uchida, 29 Sept. 1920.

11.   NGB, T9-3-2, no. 899, 9 Nov. 1920; T10-3-2, no. 799, 19 Jan. 1921.

12.   Kobayashi Tatsuo (ed.), *Suiusō Nikki* [Diary of Itō Miyoji] (Hara shobō, 1966), p. 333, 8 Dec. 1918. *Gaikō Chōsakai* was constituted in June 1917 to unify discussion of foreign policy, and worked until September 1922.

13.   *Ibid.*, pp. 334-42.

14.   NGB, T10-3-2, no. 799, 19 Jan. 1921, Rangai chūki.

15.   Nish, *Alliance in Decline*, p. 302.

16.   *Ibid.*, p. 303.

17.   *Ibid.*, pp. 324-5.

18.   NGB, T10-3-2, no. 868, 25 May 1921.

19.   *Hara Takashi Nikki* [Diary of Hara Takashi] (Tokyo: Kangensha, 1950), entries for 27 and 28 May 1921.

20.   NGB, T10-3-2, no. 875, 3 June 1921.

21.   NGB, T10-3-2, no. 876, 6 June 1921.

22.   NGB, T10-3-2, no. 877, 9 June 1921; Nish, *Alliance in Decline*, p. 327.

23.   Nish, *Alliance in Decline*, p. 331.

24.   NGB, T10-3-2, no. 901, 28 June 1921; no. 903, 30 June 1921.

25.   Hayashi, *Waga 70 nen*, p. 374; *Hara Takashi Nikki*, entry for 1 July 1921.

26.   Hayashi, *Waga 70 nen*, pp. 374-5; Nish, *Alliance in Decline*, pp. 335-7.

27.   *Hara Takashi Nikki*, entries for 2 and 7 July 1921.

28.   NGB, T10-3-2, no. 910, 4 July 1921; Nish, *Alliance in Decline*, p. 340-1.

29.   NGB, T10-3-2, no. 915, 4 July 1921; Nish, *Alliance in Decline*, p. 339.

30.   Asada Sadao, *Ryō taisen kan no Nichi Bei kankei* [Japanese-American Relations Between the Wars] (Tokyo Daigaku Shuppankai, 1993), pp.104, 114.

31.   Nish, *Alliance in Decline*, pp. 341-2.

32.   *Ibid.*, pp. 348-9.

33.   Hayashi, *Waga 70 nen*, p. 376.

34.   *Hara Takashi Nikki*, entries for 25 and 26 August 1921.

35.   See for example the following articles in *Gaikō Jihō*. 'Editorial', no. 9 of 1915, 1 May 1915, p. 930; article by Ninagawa Arata, no. 5 of 1915, 1 Sept. 1915, pp. 459-460; article by Tanaka Suiichirō, no. 376, 1 July 1920, p. 7; and 'Jiron' by Hanzawa Tamaki, no. 389, 15 Jan. 1921, p. 132.

36.   Ian Nish, *The History of Anglo-Japanese Relations*, Vol. 1 (Basingstoke and London: Macmillan, 2000), p. 257.

37.   F. S. G. Piggott, *Broken Thread* (Aldershot: Gale & Polden Ltd., 1950), p. 147.

Chapter 15 TADASHI KURAMATSU **Matsui Keishirō, 1868-1946: An Efficient Public Servant**

1.   *Matsui Keishirō Jijo-den* (Tokyo, 1983) [hereafter cited as *Matsui*]. A week before his death Matsui instructed his son that the publication of his

autobiography had to wait until all the people mentioned in it had passed away. His son, Akira, became Ambassador to the United Nations (1963-67) and France (1967-70).

2. It was set up in 1880 by then Foreign Minister Inoue Kaoru to investigate legal issues relating to the Treaty revision issues.

3. See portrait of Katō Takaaki by Ian Nish in *Biographical Portraits*, Volume IV, 2002.

4. *Matsui*, pp.7-12.

5. See portrait of Aoki Shūzō by Ian Nish in *Biographical Portraits*, Volume III, 1999.

6. See biographical portrait of Hugh Fraser by Hugh Cortazzi in *Biographical Portraits*, Volume IV, 2002 and in *British Envoys in Japan 1859-1972*, 2004.

7. See Ian Nish, 'Aoki Shūzō (1844-1914)' in *Britain and Japan: Biographical Portraits*, Volume III, 1999, p.133.

8. *Matsui*, pp.13-14.

9. See separate portrait in this volume.

10. Katō Takaaki *haku den hensan iinkai* (ed.), *Katō Takaaki*, Vol.1 (Tokyo, 1970), p.678.

11. Yokohama Species Bank, Parrs' Bank, Hongkong Shanghai Bank and Chartered Bank of India, Australia and China.

12. *Matsui*, pp.39-42. Also see Toshio Suzuki, *Japanese Government Loan Issues on the London Capital Market, 1870-1913* (London: Athlone Press, 1994), pp.69-74.

13. Matsui to Aoki, 16 & 27 Nov. 1899, *Nihon Gaikō Bunsho* [hereafter *NGB*] Vol.32, Doc.76, 78, 82, pp.205-9, 213-14. Also see a draft reply from Salisbury to Matsui, 21 Nov. 1899, FO 46/521.

14. For this issue see Ian Nish, *The Anglo-Japanese Alliance* 2nd Ed. (London: Athlone Press, 1985), pp.80-95. See also Ian Nish's portrait of Hayashi Tadasu in *Britain and Japan: Themes and Personalities*, Routledge, 1991.

15. Aoki to Matsui, 9 June 1900, *NGB* Vol.33 Supplement 1, Doc.329, p.341.

16. Matsui to Aoki, 11 June, *NGB* Vol.33 Supplement 1, Doc. 336, p.345.

17. Matsui to Aoki, 13 June, *NGB* Vol.33 Supplement 1, Doc. 343 & 361, pp.352-53 & 361-63.

18. Matsui to Aoki, 6 July 1900, *NGB* Vol.33 Supplement 1, Doc.589, pp.570-71. For Memoranda of Matsui's conversation with Salisbury on 25 June and 5 July, see *NGB* Vol.33 Supplement 1, Doc. 584, pp.556-63.

19. Cabinet Decisions, *NGB* Vol.33 Supplement 1, Doc. 592, pp.572-73.

20. The offer was later defined as a million pounds for additional twenty thousand troops. Memorandum from British Chargé to Aoki, 8 & 14 July 1900, *NGB* Vol.33 Supplement 1, Doc.605 & 618, pp.579-80, 589. In the end the Japanese government did not want to appear that they were sending more troops because of the British request with an offer of financial assistance and tried in vain to prevent the offer being included in the bluebook. *NGB* Vol.33 Supplement 1, Docs. 638, 640 & 641, pp.610-12.

21. Ian Nish, *The Anglo-Japanese Alliance*.

22. *Nihon gaikō hiroku* (Tokyo, 1934), pp.65-7; *Matsui*, pp.47-8.

23. Hayashi to Komura, 3 Dec. 1901, *NGB* Vol.34, Doc. 53, p.62.

24. For the official version of Matsui's conversation with Itō, see *NGB* Vol.35, no.25, pp.41-3. Also see *Matsui*, pp.50-1.
25. *Jiji shimpō*, 12-17 July & 21 Aug. 1913; Yui Masaomi (ed.), *Nochi wa mukashi no ki hoka* (Memoirs of Hayashi Tadasu) (Tokyo, 1970), pp.295-383; A. Pooley (ed.), *The Secret Memoirs of Count Tadasu Hayashi* Reprint Ed. (Basingstoke: Palgrave Macmillan, 2002).
26. See separate portrait in this volume.
27. See portrait of Sir Claude MacDonald in *Biographical Portraits*, Volume I, 1994 and in *British Envoys in Japan 1859-1972*, 2004.
28. *British Documents on Foreign Affairs*, Asia, 1860-1914, Vol.8, Doc. 338, p.305. The author is indebted to Professor Nish for this reference.
29. The year before Matsui married Imamura Teru, following a *miai* at *Genrō* Inoue Kaoru's place. The *nakōdo* (go-between) was Mr & Mrs Kurino.
30. According to a magazine reporting on the Japanese diplomats at the time, Matsui was described as someone well-versed in diplomatic business, but lacking flare. *Taiyō* 17(9)(15 June 1911), cited in *Gaimushō no hyaku-nen* (Tokyo, 1969), pp.569-70.
31. However, Matsui first had to go to Peking (Beijing), then on to Shanghai during the 1911 Revolution in China.
32. See portrait of Sir William Conyngham Greene by Peter Lowe in *Biographical Portraits*, Volume IV, 2002 and *British Envoys in Japan, 1859-1972*, 2004.
33. *Matsui*, pp.78-80.
34. See separate portrait in this volume.
35. *The Times*, 25 Aug. 1920.
36. See biographical portrait of Sir Charles Eliot by Dennis Smith in *Themes and Personalities*, Routledge 1991.
37. F473/14/23, Eliot to Curzon, 14 Jan. 1924, F473/14/23, FO 371/10303. There was an enclosure which said: 'For his services during the war he was created a baron. He has the reputation of being an extremely efficient civil servant, and as Vice-Minister for Foreign Affairs is said to have earned the encomiums of his chief, Viscount Kato. But doubts are expressed as to his suitability for so responsible a post as that of Minister for Foreign Affairs.'
38. Ashton-Gwatkin of the Far Eastern Department wrote: 'I gather from people who knew him in Paris that he is a typical Japanese official, and not a man of outstanding characters.' Note by Ashton-Gwatkin, 8 Jan. 1924, F55/14/23, FO 371/10303. For Comment on Matsui's speech in the Diet see Eliot to FO 23 Jan. 1924 & Minute by Ashton-Gwatkin, 24 Jan. 1924, F236/14/23, FO 371/10303.
39. For Matsui's statement issued to the American journalists at the time, see *The Times*, 16 Apr. 1924.
40. Eliot to MacDonald, 19 June 1924, F2432/14/23, FO 371/10303.
41. Chamberlain to Eliot, 19 Nov. 1925, F5627/3755/23, FO 371/10965.
42. *Bulletin of Japan Society*, No.2 (Oct. 1950), pp.10-11.
43. 'The Future of Japan' by Matsui, *Morning Post*, 15 Feb. 1926, F694/694/23, FO 371/11707.

44.   Matsui to Shidehara, 1 Dec. 1926 *NGB* 1926 Vol.II Part 2, Doc.962, pp.1125-6; *Matsui*, pp.142-3.

45.   See portrait of Sir John Tilley by Harumi Goto-Shibata in *Biographical Portraits*, Volume IV, 2002 and in *British Envoys in Japan, 1859-1972*, 2004.

46.   Chamberlain to Tilley, 2 June 1927, F5202/201/23, FO 371/12518. For Matsui's version of the record of this conversation see Matsui to Tanaka, 2 June 1927, *NGB* Shōwa Era, Ser.I (1927-31) Part 2, Vol.IV, Doc.4, pp.9-10.

47.   As early as in May 1925 Chamberlain thought that 'close & sympathetic cooperation with Japan which, of course, must be with & not against the U.S.A.' Note by Chamberlain, 22 May 1925, F1713/19/23, FO 371/10961.

48.   See portrait of Frank Ashton-Gwatkin by Ian Nish in *Biographical Portraits*, Volume I, 1994.

49.   Note by F. Ashton-Gwatkin, 3 June 1927, F5202/201/23, FO 371/12518.

50.   Minute by Kenneth Johnstone, Notes by Philip Nichols and Frank Ashton-Gwatkin, 28 Mar. & 19 Apr., F2779/2779/23, FO 371/12524.

51.   T. Kuramatsu, 'Viscount Cecil, Winston Churchill and the Geneva Naval Conference of 1927' in T. Otte & C. Pagedas (eds), *Personalities, War and Diplomacy* (London: Frank Cass, 1997), p.115.

52.   Bridgeman to Chamberlain, 7 Aug. 1927, FO 800/261.

53.   Minutes of CID 228th Meeting, 7 July 1927, CAB 2/5.

54.   A. Best, *British Intelligence and the Japanese Challenge in Asia, 1914-1941* (Basingstoke: Palgrave Macmillan, 2002), p.90.

55.   Memorandum on the desirability, from a Military Point of View, of reviving the Alliance with Japan, MO1(a) memorandum, Feb. 1928, WO 106/129. It states that on military considerations the revival of the Alliance 'would seem to be not only desirable but essential'.

56.   Tilley to Chamberlain, 28 June 1927, F 6510/2779/23, FO 371/12524. Wellesley commented: 'Sir J. Tilley is quite right. You cannot base a policy of co-operation on diversity of interests. What you get in practice is alternate co-operation & opposition according to the circes [circumstances] of the case and the moment. That is precisely what makes our difficulties so great.' Note by Wellesley, 5 Aug. 1927, Ibid.

57.   Matsui suspected that Debuchi, being a relative of Tanaka, wanted to secure an ambassadorship while the latter was in power. Debuchi succeeded Matsudaira and became the Ambassador to the United States.

58.   See portrait of Matsudaira Tsuneo by Ian Nish in *Biographical Portraits*, Volume I, 1994. On this appointment Tilley commented that 'From what I hear of Mr. Matsudaira, I think he would be an improvement on Baron Matsui'. Tilley to Wellesley, 3 Nov. 1927, F9000/9000/23, FO 371/12525. Ashton-Gwatkin agreed: 'Mr. Matsudaira will certainly be an improvement.' Note by Ashton-Gwatkin, 5 Dec. 1927, Ibid.

59.   Chamberlain to Dormer, 3 Apr. 1928, F1594/186/23, FO 371/13246.

60.   Harumi Goto-Shibata, 'Anglo-Japanese Co-operation in China in the 1920s' in I. Nish & Y. Kibata (eds), *History of Anglo-Japanese Relations, 1600-2000* Vol.I: The Political-Diplomatic Dimension, 1600-1930 (London: Macmillan, 2000), pp.244-46.

61. For example, see the letters to the Editor of *The Times* at the time of the Shanghai Crisis and the breakout of Japan-Chinese War. *The Times*, 27 Feb. 1932, 6 & 28 Oct. 1937; Keishiro Matsui, 'Anglo-Japanese Relations', *Fortnightly*, Vol.138 (Nov. 1935), pp.513-23.
62. *Matsui*, p.147.

Chapter 16 HUGH CORTAZZI The Loss of HMS *Rattler* off Cape Soya (Hokkaido) in September 1868 and Commander (later Admiral Sir) Henry Stephenson

I am indebted to Ian Ruxton for transcribing and sending me the relevant section of Ernest Satow's diary which forms Appendix II to this volume. Satow's diary has been preserved in the PRO 30/33 15/2. Adam's report to Parkes is in the PRO, FO 46.
1. See Appendixes I and II to *British Envoys in Japan 1859-1972*, Folkestone, 2004.
2. Later Sir Francis Ottiwell Adams, KCMG, CB. He was appointed an attaché at Stockholm in 1854 and served at Paris and Washington before being appointed Secretary of Legation in Japan on 6 January 1868. He was Chargé d'Affaires there from May 1871–May 1872 when he was appointed Secretary of Embassy at Berlin. His book *The History of Japan*, in two volumes, was published in 1875 in London. In the introduction he paid tribute to Ernest Satow's scholarship. He also served at Paris before being appointed Minister to Switzerland in 1879. He retired on a pension in 1888 and died in Switzerland in 1889.

Chapter 17 JOHN W.M. CHAPMAN Admiral Sir John Fisher (1841-1920) and Japan, 1894-1904

1. The author wishes to acknowledge the support received from the British Academy, London and the *Nihon Shinkōkai*, Tokyo in the winter of 2001 which made it possible to examine records in the *Gaikō Shiryōkan* (GST) and the *Bōei-chō Kenkyūjō Senshi-shitsu*, Tokyo (BKST). Official histories were produced in both countries, but in limited editions for internal circulation only.
2. John Arbuthnot Fisher, first Baron Fisher of Kilverstone (1841-1920), Admiral of the Fleet and First Sea Lord from 1904 to 1910 and again from 1914–15. According to the author of his entry in the DNB 'Fisher was one of the most remarkable personalities of his time, and one of the greatest administrators of the Royal Navy. . . . He possessed a daemonic energy combined with a gaiety and charm which few of his associates could resist'. Fisher was born in Ceylon and his father was a captain in the 78th Highland Regiment of Foot. The location of his birth would appear to have been partly responsible for him being dubbed 'the Asiatic' as early as 1901 by Lord Charles Beresford, one of the principals among his numerous enemies: see the diaries of Admiral George King-Hall, Royal Navy Museum, Portsmouth (RNMP), entry for 22.10.1901. Some of Fisher's correspondence from his first visit to the Far East was employed in the biography by R.F. Mackay, *Fisher of Kilverstone*. (Oxford: Clarendon, 1973).
3. Admiral of the Fleet Sir Edward Charles Seymour (1840-1929) was C-in-C

China Station, 1897-1901. In 1906 he accompanied Prince Arthur of Connaught on the 'Garter Mission' to Japan. Seymour's diaries and letters from the early period may be found in the National Library of Scotland, Edinburgh (NLS), MSS.9486-8.

4.   There is a detailed breakdown of the duties of members of the Board of Admiralty in 1895 at: National Archive, Kew (NAK): ADM1/7255.I

5.   Palmer, William Waldegrave, second Earl of Selborne 1859-1942, First Lord of the Admiralty, 1900-1905.

6.   Admiral of the Fleet Sir Frederick William Richards (1833-1912).

7.   Buller (C-in-C China) Report No.29 of 17.6.95 to Admiralty: NAK, Case S146/95, ADM1/7248, seen by Fisher on 3.8.95. HMS *Edgar* had been transferred to China from the Mediterranean.

8.   Buller Report No.13 of 7.6.1895: Case S155/95, ADM1/7249. Arbuthnot was later chosen by Fisher as his flag-captain when C-in-C, Portsmouth.

9.   Noel's correspondence with Fisher prior to his arrival at Malta provides information about the delays to Fisher completing his previous assignment as naval expert attached to the 1st Hague Conference, when his fellow-delegates had been Lord Pauncefote (later ambassador in Washington) and Major-General Sir John Ardagh, DMI at the War Office. National Maritime Museum, London (NMM), Noel Papers; Fisher Secret Report No.69 of 24.9.1899 at: NAK: ADM121/70; FO97/1694 ff.

10.   The range of radio transmissions increased from 10 miles in 1897 to 25 miles in 1898 and 60 miles in 1899. A report on the 1901 manoeuvres stated that 'the usefulness of wireless telegraphy has been again practically demonstrated, but it has been shown that it should be used in conjunction with some very secret code, as all open signals can be taken in with equal ease by an enemy who is within range.' Fawkes to Selborne, 3.9.1901 at: M.S.Selborne, Vol.28, ff.250-1: Bodleian Library, Oxford (BLO).

11.   Sir John Ardagh had visited Sevastopol in 1894 and had concluded that the Russians were in a position to carry out a *coup de main* in the Bosphorus before any of the Great Powers could intervene. When consular reports were received from agents at Batum in July 1896 about suspicious Russian naval movements and a claim was made by the Russian vice-consul at Colombo that Volunteer Fleet vessels (based on Odessa) were entitled to be treated as warships, Lord Salisbury called for the Admiralty's views. This claim was denied on the ground that such ships had always been treated as merchantmen entitled to pass through the Bosphorus. NAK: ADM1/7261.

12.   ADM121/70.

13.   See the author's 'British Use of "Dirty Tricks" in External Policy prior to 1914,' *War in History* 9/1(2002),pp.60-81. The honorary British Consul at Syra had been recruited in early 1900 and was particularly useful for following French activities, but his work was also relevant to the role of the War Office and Indian Army decryption teams concerned about Boer and Russian activities. He was provided with a quarterly payment from Secret Service funds until 1909.

14.   M.S.Selborne, Vol.26, ff.119-20, 27.2.1901: BLO.

15.   Lansdowne comment to Sir Thomas Sanderson on being informed by Sir

John Ardagh of a discussion with Grenfell, reported by Major Altham from Malta on 27.1.1901:NAK: HD3/111. Fisher Report No.1517 of 8.9.1900 to Admiralty: ADM121/70. The Naval Intelligence Department (NID) was actively involved in gathering intelligence about the Russian naval build-up in the Pacific from March 1895 but apparently only after it was realised what the intention of the relocation of the Russian Fleet to Chefoo was. Before the outbreak of the Boxer Uprising in June 1900 and pressure from Japan to confront Russian expansion in North China, Captain Charles Ottley had been transferred from Washington to Tokyo to report on Japanese naval developments and to supplement what was known in London about Japanese naval expansion since 1895. On 25 May 1900, Ottley reported on visits to Japanese naval bases and on Japanese fleet manoeuvres at which torpedo boats had been his employed to repel invaders: ADM1/7261. Japan had been outfaced by the strength of Russia's Pacific Squadron under Admiral Tyrtov as it had no warship larger than 4,000 tons until orders were placed for the construction of six first-class battleships in British shipyards between 1894 and 1902. See CB611 at ADM231/606; ADM1/7248 & 7260-1.

16. See D. Schimmelpenninck v.d. Oye, *Toward the Rising Sun*. (N.Illinois UP, 2001)

17. General Alexsei Nicolaevich Kuropatkin (1845-1925) C-in-C of the Russian Armed Forces in the Far East during the Russo-Japanese War.

18. Kerr letter of 13.8.1901 in: M.S. Selborne, Vol.27, ff.113-4: BLO.

19. Lord Lansdowne, fifth Marquis (1845-1927) Secretary of State for Foreign affairs 1900-1905. He had been Governor-General of Canada and Viceroy of India.

20. See copies of correspondence in 1900-1 in: Lockhart Papers, Acc.4138, Items 1d and 1e: NLS.

21. See Thursfield and White Papers: NMM and King-Hall Diaries, entries for 19.3.1900, 9.6. & 27.6.1901: RNMP.

22. *Ibid.*,entries for 1.5.01 giving Fisher's account of their discussions and 21.7.01 for statements by Custance.

23. See Battenberg memoranda of 11.2. & 25.2.1902 to Fisher in: Battenberg Papers, Hartley Library, University of Southampton, MB/T3, Items 17-18 and Fisher to Battenberg, 10.2.1902 in: Fisher Papers, Churchill College, Cambridge (CCC): FISR5/9,f.4203 & 1/3, f.88.

24. *Ibid.*, Fisher to Wilson (C-in-C, Channel Fleet): FISR1/3, f.89.

25. Selborne had written to Seymour on 28.2.01 passing on his views about the Manchurian situation. Seymour's reply of 24.3.01 is at: M.S. Selborne, Vol.19, ff.109-113: BLO.

26. Kerr letter of 2.9.1901: *ibid.*, Vol.27, ff.135-6. Selborne secret memorandum of 4.9.01 to the Cabinet: MSS 252, Papers of John Fisher, 1900-1917: Selborne Memoranda Issued to the Cabinet, 1900-1905, Vol.2, Item IXb: RNMP.

27. Admiral Sir Reginald Neville Custance (1847-1935) had been present at the British bombardment of Kagoshima in 1863. He was Director of Naval Intelligence from 1899-1902.

28. An exchange of notes among Kerr, Selborne and Lansdowne of 2.12.01

indicated worries about what the purpose of the mission to Russia was: M.S.Selborne, Vol.27, ff.242-5: BLO. From the Secret Service budget controlled by the Foreign Office, Sanderson had authorized Scott to pay whatever it took to learn what Itō was up to in St Petersburg but his telegram of 27 November 1901 was intercepted and decrypted by the Russian Foreign Ministry's cryptographic bureau, which was likewise reading the contents of German and other cables. See D. Schimmelpenninck v.d.Oye, 'Tsarist Codebreaking-Some Background and Examples,' *Cryptologia* 22/4 (October 1998), pp.342-353. Subsequently, Sanderson revealed that Count Witte's conversations with Sir Nicholas Ofner in early 1898 had been compromised by the unintended revelation of Britain's best available diplomatic cipher. He firmly believed that no code was unbreakable and advised that if any information had to be withheld from the Russians, the only reliable method of communication was by messenger, a solution independently recommended by Japanese Minister Kurino to his government in January 1902. Hardinge Papers, Vol.7, f.76: Cambridge University Library (CUL); Kurino (St Petersburg) Tel.No.17 of 19.2.1902 in: *Raiden Meiji 34-nen*, GST. Lansdowne asked Selborne for his advice on the drafting of a flexible naval agreement on 8.1.1902 after Itō left London: M.S.Selborne, Vol.26, ff.110-1: BLO; see I. Nish, 'The First Anglo-Japanese Alliance Treaty', *International Studies*, Discussion Paper IS/02/432 (London: STICERD, April 2002), pp.1-16.

29.   King-Hall Diaries, entries for 3 & 21.1.1902: RNMP.

30.   Admiral of the Fleet Lord Walter Kerr (1839-1927), First Sea Lord 1899-1904.

31.   This was Captain Charles Ottley, Fisher's first DNI and later Secretary of the CID, who had been sent from Washington in 1900 and found so much new to report on the Japanese Navy that Minister Satow successfully pressed for him to be allowed to stay a further year in Tokyo. MacDonald to Sanderson, 26 & 28.11.1901 at: NAK: FO83/2096; ADM1/7590.

32.   Admiral of the Fleet Prince Louis Alexander of Battenberg (1854-1921), first Marquis of Milford Haven, First Sea Lord, 1912-14.

33.   NAK: ADM116/1231B-C.

34.   Fisher to Selborne, 25.2.02: FISR1/4, f.90: CCC.

35.   Bridge letter of 22.4.1902: M.S.Selborne, Vol.19, ff.174-183: BLO.

36.   Fisher Report No.1025 of 2.6.1902 at: NAK: ADM1/7586.

37.   Brodrick (William) St John (Fremantle, Ninth Viscount Middleton and first Earl of Middleton (1856-1942).

38.   *Meiji 35-nen ken-Ei kantai kankei shorui, hōkoku 1: 10 ken-Ei, ken-Bei*, M35-1: BKST.

39.   'An account of the battle prepared by NID, entitled 'China-Japan War: Narrative of Naval Engagement off the Yalu River with Remarks Thereon (March 1895)' may be found at: NAK: ADM1/7254. This indicated that several smaller Chinese vessels were sunk by Armstrong quick- firing guns and 200 hits were achieved on the Chinese flagship *Ting Yuen*. The Japanese vessel *Naniwa* had already fired a torpedo at *Kowshing* on 25 July 1894, but had missed; off Hai Yang Island on 17 September 1894, the Chinese torpedo-boat *Foo Lung* had fired three torpedoes at the Japanese transport *Saikyo-maru*, two from 4-500 yards and one

from 30-50 yards, but all missed. The Japanese had not attempted to fire any torpedoes in return, apparently because they were heavily outranged by the two principal Chinese warships of 7,000 tons.
40. See Battenberg Papers, MB1/4 (25) for a copy of an undated memo on 'Scouting Squares'; Fisher Report Nos. 503 of 20.3.02 and 981 of 26.5.02 to Admiralty: NAK: ADM1/7587.
41. MacDonald (Tokyo) to Noel (Hong Kong), 25.8.1904 enclosing a report from Captain Pakenham on the lavish employment of radio by the Combined Fleet: Noel Papers: NMM; Noel Report No.966 of 15.12.1905 at: *ibid.*: ADM1/7804.
42. Admiral Sir Cyprian Arthur George Bridge (1839-1924), C-in-C China Station, 1901-04.
43. Sir Claude MacDonald, Minister, later ambassador to Japan (1852-1915). See biographical portrait by Professor Ian Nish in *Biographical Portraits*, Volume I.
44. Fisher (Portsmouth) letter of 31.7.04: M.S.Selborne, Vol.24, ff.136-7: BLO.
45. FISR1/4, f.165: Fisher Papers, CCC.

Chapter 18 JOHN W.M. CHAPMAN **Captain (later Admiral Sir) W.C. Pakenham RN (1861-1933) and the Russo-Japanese War**

1.   Admiral Sir William Christopher Pakenham (1861-1933). Until 1902, British naval attachés were organized on a peripatetic basis. Ottley had been initially accredited to Washington, but the crisis ensuing from the Boxer Uprising and the threat of Russian expansionism in northern China made it necessary to send an individual with technical expertise to obtain the most up-to-date information on the capabilities of the Japanese Navy. Normally, attachés spent weeks or months at one capital before moving on, but Ottley, with the support of Sir Ernest Satow, argued successfully that the special circumstances in Japan made it necessary to spend at least a year there. However, after a number of lengthy reports, Ottley moved on to Russia in the summer of 1901 and was reporting direct to Lord Selborne on the warship construction programme of the Russian fleet following the favourable reaction of the Cabinet to his paper on the balance of power in the Far East.
2.   Rear-Admiral Sir Charles Langdale Ottley (1858-1932) was Director of Naval Intelligence (DNI) from 1905 to 1907, then Secretary of the Committee of Imperial Defence (CID) until 1912.
3.   Admiral Sir Ernest Charles Thomas Troubridge (1862-1926) was the first chief of naval operations in the naval staff from 1912 to 1914.
4.   Admiral Sir Cyprian Arthur George Bridge (1839-1924) was DNI from 1888 to 1891 and C-in-C, China from 1901 to 1904.
5.   See the Strickland-Constable Papers, East Yorkshire County Archive, Beverley (ERCA). Many of Pakenham's surviving letters to members of his family are located in this collection as he never married and there is a group of letters to his sister, Margaret Elizabeth Strickland-Constable.
6.   Admiral of the Fleet Prince Louis of Battenberg (1854-1921), first Marquis of Milford Haven, was First Sea Lord from 1912 to 1914.
7.   Commodore Hugh Tyrwhitt (1856-1907) had commanded HMS *Surprise*

before being appointed Fisher's flag captain at Malta in 1901. Fisher recommended him as private secretary to Lords Selborne and Cawdor.

8.   King-Hall Diaries, entry for 19.6.1903: 'Lord Selborne is entirely in the hands of Sir John'. Royal Navy Museum, Portsmouth (RNMP).

9.   Selborne to Goschen on the New Scheme, 20.12.1902: 'At any rate my mind was made up as to the principles a year ago & my main object in getting Fisher to the Admiralty was to bring there a man whom I knew would sympathize with my views and had exactly the qualities required to give effect to them.' MS.Selborne, Vol.32, ff.179-82: Bodleian Library, Oxford (BLO).

10.   Charles Robert Spencer (1857-1922), 6th Earl Spencer, First Lord of the Admiralty from 1892 to 1895. Fisher to Selborne, 27.6.1902: *ibid.*, ff.10-11 stated how Spencer had backed him up when he wanted to 're-pot some of the big-wigs!'.

11.   Admiral Charles William de la Poer Beresford MP (1846-1919), Baron Beresford, was second-in-command in the Mediterranean from 1900 to 1902 and when C-in-C, Channel was Fisher's most important public antagonist.

12.   Arnold Henry White (1848-1925), journalist and author.

13.   Admiral Sir Reginald Neville Custance (1847-1935) was DNI from 1899 to 1902.

14.   Selborne to Battenberg, 13.9.1902: *ibid.*, Vol.33, ff.49-50. Custance and Kerr had been opposed to the appointment of Battenberg, just as they had been hostile to Selborne's choice of Fisher as 2nd Sea Lord. They opposed Seymour, Fisher's friend, as his successor at Malta and had previously chosen Bridge to head an Admiralty committee on Gibraltar in preference to Fisher.

15.   Both Balfour and Selborne were related to Salisbury and Viscount Cranborne was chosen by Lansdowne as a minister in the Foreign Office. Selborne and Brodrick, the War Minister, both were scandalized by the way that the Duke of Devonshire (selected by Salisbury) conducted matters as chairman of the Defence Committee and were the prime movers in its replacement by the CID. The occasion for change was intimately affected by the Duke's mishandling of the ratification of the secret military and naval agreements with Japan in the autumn of 1902. *Ibid.*, Vol.30, ff.122-7 & 45-50.

16.   Balfour was of the view that it was highly unlikely that Japan would provide support to Britain should the Netherlands be invaded by France or Germany or even if Russia attacked the north-west frontier of India and saw it as 'absurdly one-sided' if the alliance were interpreted as requiring British intervention in a Russo-Japanese conflict. Selborne's view was that Britain should not permit Japan to be crushed by Russia and should be prepared to intervene in such an eventuality, but he went along with Battenberg's argument (already suggested by Seymour and incorporated in the Anglo-Japanese secret naval agreement) that Britain and Japan combined would readily outgun Russia and France combined. To reinforce this position, Vice-Admiral Sir Gerard Noel was named as successor to Bridge on the China Station at this date and informed that his forces would be reinforced substantially. Neither Bridge nor Noel appears to have worked out plans for any combined Anglo-Japanese naval operations against Russia, but Battenberg had drawn up plans in July 1903 for the formation of the Eastern Fleet

and amendments to the standing orders for the East Indies, Australia, Pacific and China Stations: National Archive, Kew (NAK): ADM1/7255 & 7265.

17. Troubridge had served as 5th Naval Attaché under the Custance regime and was due for transfer to a seagoing command, but in late December 1903 he had already been apprised by Admiral Saitō Makoto, the Vice-Minister of the Navy, that he would be allowed to accompany the Combined Fleet and he had had his bags packed in anticipation of war. See Troubridge to Bridge, 13.2.1904: Bridge Papers, BRI/19, National Maritime Museum, Greenwich (NMM).

18. The Japanese naval attaché was Captain Kaburagi Makoto. Pakenham (Admiralty) to M.E. Strickland-Constable, 7.1.1904: ECRA.

19. Troubridge to Bridge, 5.1.1904: BRI/19, NMM.

20. Pakenham to M.E. Strickland-Constable, 9.2.1904: ECRA.

21. MS.82/131: NMM.

22. Bridge apparently decided that he would haul down his flag in Japan as the war had caused difficulties in obtaining steamship passages from Shanghai and it was a convenient location for allowing a more rapid homeward journey via the USA. Noel, his successor, had already reached Hong Kong and Pakenham had observed that Noel would have to put his best foot forward to earn as good a reputation as Bridge.

23. General Sir Ian Standish Monteith Hamilton (1853-1947) was Kitchener's chief of staff at the end of the Boer War and served as Quastermaster-General of the Army from 1902 to 1904.

24. Minister of the Navy, 1898-1906 and Prime Minister, 1913-14 and 1923-24.

25. The circumstances in which Troubridge was replaced in Japan were muddied by various developments which led even Selborne to considering the matter mysterious. One of the problems seems have been caused by Admiral Bridge pressing for the temporary loan of an officer, Captain Ricardo, who was returning home via Japan and the USA and appears to have been compounded by the fact that Pakenham had actually already been selected as successor and the nominal appointment to the staff of the China Station was merely a convenient ruse. It seems, however, that Troubridge had already received informal complaints from Minister MacDonald that he had not been sufficiently discreet so far as relations with the Japanese Navy were concerned. On his return to Tokyo, the charge of indiscretion had been reinforced by the fact that Troubridge had been interviewed by the correspondent of the *Daily Chronicle* and the fact that he had been attached to the battleship *Asahi* at sea was published in London, much to the alarm and consternation of the Japanese Navy. MacDonald reassured everyone that this was contrary to service discipline and Pakenham was warned by MacDonald to avoid repeating such a mistake, as it would jeopardize not only naval relations, but especially his efforts to persuade the Japanese Army to concede similar privileges to the many British and Indian Army officers awaiting secondment to the Manchurian front. Pakenham to Lady Jessica Sykes urged her under no circumstances to pass on any information 'particularly to press men such as Arnold White': NMM.

26. NAK: HH7: Hamilton to Kitchener, 6.4.1904: PRO 30/57.

27.   Thomas Henry Sanderson (1841-1923), first Baron Sanderson, Permanent Under-Secretary at the Foreign Office until March 1906.

28.   Errington, who had been involved in fending off the attentions of the *Okhrana* in the St Petersburg Embassy, dealt with military, naval and secret service questions in Sanderson's office.

29.   NAK: FO83/2096.

30.   Field-Marshal Sir William Gustavus Nicholson (1845-1918), first Baron Nicholson, was Director of Military Intelligence (DMI) at the War Office from 1901 to 1904 and later Chief of the Imperial General Staff.

31.   Hamilton was effectively sacked as Quartermaster-General, but in less brutal fashion than Earl Roberts (1832-1914), the Army C-in-C, and General Nicholson (DMI), who were told to vacate their offices forthwith. The War Reconstruction or Esher Committee, consisting of Lord Esher, Sir John Fisher, then C-in-C at Portsmouth, and Sir George Sydenham Clarke (1848-1933), the Secretary of the CID, which was apparently demanded by King Edward VII and appointed by Balfour, pursued a generally ruthless policy which was characteristic of Fisher's interpretation of his briefs and was explicitly intended by him to make the War Office sit up and take notice. It claimed to have damaging evidence against Nicholson, who was packed off to Japan as the chief observer of the British Army.

32.   Seki Shigetada, *Asahi no hikari: Nichi-Ro sensō Kaigun Shashin.* (Tokyo: Hakubunkan, 1905). Some copies of these shots were presented to Pakenham and there is also a photograph of the British China Squadron at anchor in Yokohama Bay prior to the victory review. Pakenham sent large numbers of his photographic negatives home to his sister, who also was a keen amateur photographer, to be printed with the idea of selling them to the press. Sadly, most of these negatives were of very poor quality and the news value of developments in Japan quickly evaporated after the focus shifted to the USA and all the newsmen returned home. Seki remained on friendly terms with Pakenham for many years afterward and his albums include numerous portraits of Seki and his family right up until the 1920s: NMM and ECRA.

33.   Reginald Baliol Brett (1852-1930), second Viscount Esher.

34.   Gerard to Hamilton, 1.6.1904. Hamilton had informed Kitchener on 30.3.1904 that he was worried about his letters reaching him because only mail dispatched via the diplomatic bag reached London. 'But no bag goes west,' he added, 'and I fear my little Jap friends are too fond of reading letters to an important address.' NAK: HH/6 &16 at: PRO30/57/37.

35.   Pakenham later appears to imply that Troubridge had responded to a request from Minister Yamamoto to supply him with a critique of the Combined Fleet's operations and that Troubridge had supplied a liberal dose of critical comments which did not go down well on the Japanese side with the result that Pakenham judiciously refrained from taking up a similar suggestion from the same quarter – something that had gone down well with Togo and his staff. Hamilton had taken the same line, arguing the need never to be seen to waver in the support for the alliance, but guardedly reserving any doubts or disagreements for strictly private communications securely passed on.

36.   There is a photograph of Pakenham nonchalantly resting on the wheel of an artillery piece on a hill in Manchuria in the company of foreign naval attachés when meeting General Nogi, who had apologized for the fact that naval attachés had been subjected to riding unaccustomedly on horseback to meet him. Pakenham as an accomplished horseman could perhaps afford to be nonchalant.
37.   Consul-General Iwasaki was following up a circular originating in October 1904 with an agent of Minister Makino in Vienna who had originally been a highly recommended agent of the British military attaché there. *Gaikō Shiryōkan*, Tokyo (GST): File 5.2.2.20-2.
38.   Pakenham to Ottley (DNI), 17.4.1905: FISR1/4, f.148 (CCC). The document was annotated by Fisher: 'Pakenham was in the Battle and Togo specially presented him to the Mikado for his marvellous sang-froid and help to the Japanese.'
39.   Pakenham to Lady Sykes, 19.5.1905: NMM.
40.   Admiral Takarabe Takeshi was the son-in-law of Admiral Yamamoto Gonbei, whom he accompanied on his visit to London in 1927 and subsequently was Minister of the Navy from 1926 to 1930.
41.   Admiral Saitō Makoto (1858-1936) was Vice-Minister of the Navy from 1898 to 1906, Minister from 1906 to 1913 and subsequently Prime Minister from 1932 to 1934. As Lord Keeper of the Privy Seal, he was assassinated in the *ni-ni-roku jihen* in February 1936.
42.   See fn.24 above.

Chapter 19 SUE JARVIS **Captain Oswald Tuck RN (1876-1950) and the Bedford Japanese School**

Acknowledgements
I am much obliged to Mrs Sylvia Crotty, Captain Tuck's daughter, for much biographical information, loan of documents and references. Mr Alan Stripp has been most helpful in describing the Bedford Japanese School, and lending me R. Stamp's thesis. Dr John Chapman kindly referred me to documents in the PRO. I am grateful to the staffs of the Japan Society, the Churchill Archives, Cambridge and the Public Record Office, Kew.
Select bibliography:
The Japan Society, *Transactions* and *Bulletins*.
Sadao Oba *The 'Japanese' War* Tokyo, 1988, trans. Kaneko, Japan Library, 1995
Public Record Office, ADM1/7728.
Smith, M. *The Emperor's Codes*, Bantam Press, 2000.
Stripp, A. *Code Breaker in the Far East*, OUP, 1989.
Tuck, O. T. *Far Eastern Diaries*, Churchill Archives, Cambridge, TUCK 1/2 to 1/7
1.   Sue Jarvis took her B.A. in European History at Liverpool University and her M.A. in Oriental History at the School of Oriental & African Studies at London University
2.   Now in the Churchill archives in Cambridge.
3.   Tuck, Diary, 16 December 1902.
4.   Mrs Sylvia Crotty, personal communication.

5.   Tuck, 1903 Diary.
6.   Tuck, Diary, 27 May 1903.
7.   PRO, ADM1/7728. I am indebted to Dr John Chapman of Glasgow University for this reference.
8.   ADM 1/7728 Letter from Capt. Hutchison to Capt. Ottley, 24 April 1905: 'both Jones and Tuck have had to go to hospital . . . on account of trying to cut down expenses and living *à la japonaise* – it bears out entirely what I said that officers with limited means cannot get by in Japan and if they try to live economically they are sure to get ill. . .'
9.   Japan Soc., *Transactions*, Vol.XXIX, 26 November 1931.
10. Admiral Togo's visiting card with Tuck's name on it was inside his diary for 1908.
11. In 1994 a facsimile edition was produced by the United States Naval Institute, so for the first time this work became available to the public. A copy is in the British Library.
12. Copy of letter in the possession of Mrs S. Crotty
13. The School of Oriental Studies was eventually founded in 1917.
14. *The Fighting Forces* Vol I no.2, Sept. 1924, courtesy Mrs S. Crotty. This was a magazine for the armed forces.
15. Japan Soc. *Transactions* Vol.XXI, 28 Nov.1923.
16. ibid., Vol.XXIII, 29 April 1926.
17. ibid., Vol.XXXV, 1938.
18. ibid., Vol.XXXVI, 1938.
19. quoted in Sadao Oba, *The 'Japanese' War*, p.6, Tokyo 1988, trans. Kaneko, Japan Library, 1995.
20. Smith, M., *The Emperor's Codes*, p.122.
21. A biographical portrait of Eric Ceadel by Peter Kornicki is included in this volume
22. Stamp,R, unpublished thesis *Japanese Language Courses at Bedford 1942-5*, p.24, c.1980.
23. Michael Loewe became an eminent Chinese scholar and lecturer in Chinese at Cambridge.
24. J.O.Lloyd after the war was Consul General in Osaka and later Ambassador to Laos.
25. Smith M., *The Emperor's Codes* p.122.
26. Birch F., letter dated 7 December 1945 from DDNS in the possession of Mrs S. Crotty
27. Japan Soc., *Bulletin*, 1950., No. 2.
28. ibid., 1952, No.6.

Chapter 20 JERRY K. MATSUMURA **Takaki Kanehiro, 1849–1920: British-trained Medical Pioneer who became Surgeon General to the Imperial Japanese Navy**

1.   'Vitamins and Vitamin Deficiencies' by Dr Leslie J. Harris, Sc. D. (Cantab) wrote 'This disease (beriberi), known in China as early as 2,600 B.C. , was first completely shown to have a dietary origin in 1882 by Takaki, the Japanese

Director-General of the Medical Department of the Navy. By simply increasing slightly the allowance of vegetables, fish, meat and barley in a diet still consisting predominantly of rice he was able to reduce the incidence of the disease to virtually vanishing point. . .'.

2.   In the same book Takaki is named as one of the eight early pioneers of vitamins.

3.   'Takaki Promontory' (65° 33'S., 64° 14'W., the NE side of Leroux Bay on the West Coast Graham Land).

4.   Four other prominent scholars of vitamins (Eijkmann, Funk, Hopkins and McCallum) were also commemorated in a similar way.

5.   Foreign Minister Inoue Kaoru, proud of Takaki's achievements circulated a notice to all foreign legations in Japan, announcing that any member of the legations and of their families who wished to consult him could request an appointment through the Ministry.

6.   In Mukasa at that time there was a scholarly and widely respected doctor, Kuroki Ryōsuke, to whom the young Kanehiro was drawn. When Takaki decided at the age of twelve that he wanted to be a doctor, his father had been enlisted in the Satsuma forces and sent to Kyoto where he fell ill. After his return to Mukasa and until his recovery Takaki had to support his family. This was the main reason why he could not leave for Kagoshima until he was seventeen.

7.   Mori was killed in action at an early stage of the Bōshin Civil War of 1868. Takaki, when he learnt about Mori's death rushed to Kagoshima to call on Mori's widow. In later life he sent her money every month over many years to help her.

8.   Although he had had to study largely on his own as there was no qualified Dutch teacher there during that period. In 1849 Dr Otto G.J. Mohnike, a Dutch doctor for the Dutch factory (trading post) at Dejima, had a small quantity of smallpox vaccine. Ishigami managed to acquire a small portion for use in Kagoshima, This was very beneficial to Satsuma in preventing the spread of smallpox which was prevalent at the time, although the use of the vaccine was strongly opposed by the practitioners of Chinese style medicine. During his seven years in Nagasaki Ishigami had become proficient in English. This was of great help to him when he was appointed director of the army hospital in Yokohama in 1868, where the principal doctors were Dr Willis and Dr Siddall, the two British Legation doctors, and when he assisted Dr Willis at the Kagoshima medical school and hospital in 1870.

9.   Father of the well-known writers and artists Arishima Takeo, Satomi Ton and Arishima Ikuma.

10.   See Hugh Cortazzi's *Dr Willis in Japan, British Medical Pioneer 1862-1877*, Athlone, London, 1985.

11.   Takaki visited Ishigami in Yokohama on his way back to Kagoshima when the civil war came to an end. Dr Willis also treated patients at this hospital during and after the war where again Ishigami was greatly impressed by Dr Willis's skill and knowledge.

12.   *Dr Willis in Japan*, pages 104, 120-121.

13.   The subjects he taught were English (reading, conversation, grammar, writing), geometry, geography, arithmetic on top of materia medica ('two

subjects of medicine'), anatomy, bandaging, and minor surgery.

14. Under the Tokugawa regime he had been a professor of Dutch and English when anti-foreign sentiment was running high. He was attacked by Chōshū samurai led by Itō Hirobumi and Inoue Kaoru for the simple reason that he was a scholar of foreign learning. He narrowly escaped death by flinging himself into the freezing cold moat near Sakuradamon gate to Edo castle. Itō and Inoue as a result felt particular sympathy towards Takaki and proved to be of enormous help to him in his undertakings in later years. Sewaki also founded the *Yomiuri Shimbun* with two of his foreign ministry colleagues. Sewaki, Ishigami and Terajima Munenori (who became Foreign Minister) had first met when they were studying in Nagasaki a decade earlier.

15. See separate biographical portrait of William Anderson in this volume (Ch. 1).

16. Takaki adopted Ishigami's bereaved six-year old daughter and assumed responsibility for her until he arranged for her to marry a naval surgeon.

17. Internal Medicine: Dr Peacock, Dr Murchison. Pathology: Dr Bristowe. Surgery: Dr L.G. Clark, Mr S. Jones. Surgical Operation: Mr Croft, Mr MacCormac. Anatomy: Mr Barnes. Obsterics: Mr Barnes. Ophthalmologic Surgery: Mr Liebreich. Physiology: Dr Ord, Dr J. Harley. Medicinal Chemistry: Dr Bernays. Pharmacology: Mr Clapton. Forensic Medicine, Hygienics: Dr Stone, Mr H. Arnott. Science, Philosophy: Dr Stone. Post-mortem Examination: Dr Paynes, Mr H. Arnott. Botany: Dr J.W. Hicks. Comparative Anatomy: Mr C. Stewart. Psychopathy: Dr W. R. Williams. Geographical Distribution of Diseases: Mr A. Haviland.

18. Dr Simon had served as a professor at St Thomas's for twenty-five years until shortly before Takaki arrived. He was the author of a book on the history of British hygiene, published in 1885.

19. According to Emeritus Professor Matsuda Makoto of Jikei University School of Medicine.

20. Listed under the title of 'The Takaki Family' read:
(1) Came to S.T.H. in October 1875
(2) Won First to Third College Prize each year from 1875-78
(3) 1878: Cheselden Medal (Surgery and Surgical Anatomy – founded by George Vaughan, Esq.); and Treasurer's Gold Medal – for most meritorious 4 years
(4) 1878-9: Assistant House Physician and House Surgeon (Certificates of honour, 3 months)
(5) 1879-80: Resident Accoucheur (Certificate of honour)
(6) F.R.C.S. Eng. (1880), D.C.L.Durham (1906) (M.R.C.S. (1878), L.R.C.P.(1878))
(7) Extract from Plarr's 'Lives of Fellows of the Royal College of Surgeons': Became acquainted with William Anderson, Surgeon to St Thomas's Hospital. 'A most successful and distinguished student'.

21. A humorous story about the medical world circulating in Tokyo at that time was: 'German wind does not blow south of Nihonbashi'. It meant that the south of Nihonbashi (called the Shiba-Takanawa area where the Ministry of the Navy,

Naval Hospital, Naval Medical School and the above hospitals and schools founded by Takaki were located) was not subject to the predominant German influence.

22. Sales proceeds from these events came to a combined total of ¥15,000.

23. She had been one of the young girls sent to the United States to study who had accompanied the Iwakura Mission and who learnt some nursing at Vassar College and the New Haven Hospital.

24. In particular Professor Parke's book which gave the recognized comparative ratio of nitrogen to carbon discharged daily by a fair-sized adult at 1 to 15 as compared with the food taken by the Japanese sailor at N1 to C17-28. Takaki discovered that beriberi occurred invariably when the latter value exceeded C23.

25. Takaki was accompanied by the Minister of the Navy; Prince Arisugawa and Itō were also present.

26. While waiting for news from the *Tsukuba* Takaki carried out some experiments on dogs: six dogs were fed the regulation naval food provisions comprising mostly polished rice; another group of six dogs were fed beef, barley and soybean. Of the six dogs to whom rice was given as the principal food, in spite of an increase in weight, all but one died before the end of the experiment. The increase in weight of the six dogs to whom barley, beef and beans were given as their principal food was not so conspicuous as that of the other group, but every one of them was healthy and active both mentally and physically until the end of the experiment.

27. In August 1885 he proposed that because of the difficulties of cooking in rough weather bread and biscuits should be supplied instead of equal proportions of barley and rice.

28. Takaki's work was published in the *Sei-I-Kai* Transactions (1885, 1887) and in *The Lancet* (1887).

29. Surgeon Vice-Admiral Sir John Rawlins has commented: 'Takaki's solution to the problem of beriberi was equivalent to that of James Lind in 1794 when he persuaded the Royal Navy to provide lemon juice as a prophylactic against scurvy.' *The Journal of Nutrition Volume 106*, 1976, pages 581-586 states: 'Although Takai had not gone as far as the discovery of vitamins, he was the first person to produce actual evidence suggesting their existence.' Professor Emeritus Matsuda Makoto has pointed out that Drummond, a prominent scholar of vitamins, referring to Lind's discovery in 1794, argued in 1919, with reference to the discovery/naming of vitamin B by Eijkman and Funk in 1890/1912, based on research stemming from Takaki's evidence, that some element in orange and lemon might also be called a vitamin and named it vitamin C.

30. The priest ritually purifies the participants and invites the intercession of the deities while the couple sits before the altar with the go-between and his or her spouse.

31. Weddings were later held in shrines, temples, and since World War II, hotels, restaurants, or special wedding halls, often furnished with special wedding chambers with Shinto architecture.

32. The invitation came from the Cartwright's Lecture Committee of its Alumni Association of the College of Physicians and Surgeons.

33. He delivered his lecture 1,388 times; his total audience amounted to 676,052 people.
34. A programme to which he made a handsome personal contribution.
35. The initial plans were modest involving a total cost of ¥20,000 to be subscribed by local residents.. In 1898 Takaki, who was born in Miyazaki prefecture and who thought it important to arouse national awareness and enthusiasm for the occasion, undertook to support the project (which took ten years for completion) as chairman of the committee. The scale of the project and its cost grew to 475,000. He succeeded in winning national support from Emperor Meiji down to ordinary citizens from Hokkaido to Taiwan. According to the ancient chronicle *Kojiki* (712) and Nihon *Shoki* (720) the Emperor Jimmu, after growing up in the Takachiho palace in Hyūga (Miyazaki prefecture), resolved at the age of forty-five to conquer the Yamato region (Nara area). In an expedition that lasted several years he made his way along the Inland Sea and landed his forces northwest of Yamato. At first defeated by local chieftains, he ultimately subdued the area with the aid of a golden bird and was enthroned as Japan's first Emperor
36. His widow, Tomi, died in 1931. Their eldest son, Yoshihiro, returned to Japan in 1902 after studying at St Thomas's Hospital Medical School and was appointed professor of the Jikei Medical School where from 1942 to 1947 he served as head of the school. He died in 1953. Their second son, Kanetsugu, also studied at St Thomas's where he received many awards. At the age of thirty he was appointed professor in charge of internal medicine at Jikei Medical School, but he died suddenly of typhoid fever in 1919. Takaki's second daughter, Hiroko, married Shigeji Higuchi in 1903 who was a professor of obstetrics at Jikei Medical School. Their only child, Kazushige, became President of the Jikei University School of Medicine.

Chapter 21 SADAO OBA **Mitsui in London**

1. *Kohon Mitsui Bussan Kabushiki-Kaisha 100nen si(jou)* (Manuscript of Centenary History of Mitsui & Co., 1st Volume), Mitsui & Co. Ltd. 1976 p.106.
2. *'Frankurin no Kajitu'* (Fruits of Franklin), by Irwin Yukiko, Bungei Shunju-Sha 1988, p.13.
3. *Kohon Mitsui Bussan Kabushiki-kaisha 100nen si(ditto)* p. 58.
4. Sonoda Kokichi(1848-1923) After having stayed in London for 15 years, he became President of the Yokohama Specie Bank. Knighted as Baron in 1918.
5. *Sonoda Kokichi Den*, by Ogino Nakasaburo, Shuei-sha, 1926.
6. Certified copy of an entry of marriage, General Registration Office, 10 March 1992.
7. According to *The Development of Anglo-Japanese Trade*, Mitsui & Co., Ltd. Ca 1930 these were:
    Joseph Sykes Brothers, Huddersfield (card clothing and cotton card clothing machinery)
    Babcock & Wilcox, Ltd (Water tube boiler-makers, Engineers and Contractors). Later, a joint venture Tōyō Babcock was launched in Japan by Babcock and Mitsui.

Clarke Chapman & Co. Ltd., Gateshead (winches and windlasses manufacturer)
John Hastie & Co. Ltd., Greenock (Electric hydraulic steering gear)
Mactaggart, Scott & Co., Ltd., Loanhead, Scotland (Catapult for launching aircraft)
Mather & Platt, Ltd, Manchester (horizontal steam engines etc)
Samuel Law & Sons, Cleckheaton (Card maker)
Dronsfield Brothers Ltd., Oldham (Card grinding machine)
J. Meredith-Jones & Sons, Ltd., Wrexam, North Wales (Welsh roller leather)
Joseph Stubbs, Ltd, Manchester (Textile machinery)
John Ormerods & Sons Ltd., Castleton, Manchester (Tanning equipments)
Robert Hyde & Co., Ltd, Cheshire (Woolen cloth manufacturer)
Greenwood & Batley ltd., Leeds (Spinning machinery of waste silk)
Barber & Colman Ltd, Manchester (Tying machinery)
Sigma Instrument Co., Letchworth, North of London (Gas calorimeters)
Hulse & Company, Ltd., Manchester (Heavy machine tools)
Thos. Utley & Co., Ltd., Liverpool (Hull panes and deck house windows)
Siebe, Gorman & Co., Ltd (Diving apparatus and submarine appliances)
Morris Motors Ltd, Oxford (Motor cars)
The British Thomson-Houston Co., Ltd, Rugby (Large electrical plants)
Laurence, Scott & Electromotors Ltd, Manchester (Electrical machinery)
'Ben' Line (Shipping)
The Gloster Aircraft Co., Hucclecote, Gloster(Steel aircraft)
A.G. Spalding & Bros. (British) Ltd., London (Golf ball)
Eadie Bros & Co Ltd., Manchester (Rings and Travelers for producing yarn)
8.   *Kohon Mitsui Bussan Kabushiki-Kaisha 100nen si(ditto).*
9.   *'Dai Ei-koku Man'yu Jikki'* (Looking around in Great Britain), by Mizuta Hideo, Hakubun-kan, 1900.
10.   *Kohon Mitsui Bussan Kabushiki-Kaisha 100nen si(ditto)* p.75.
11.   (ditto) p.347.

Chapter 22 KEIKO ITOH **The Yokohama Specie Bank in London**

1.   Omura Tetsutarō, in *Yokohama Shōkin Ginkō Shi, Vol.6*, p.543.
2.   See Keiko Itoh: *The Japanese Community in Pre-War Britain: From Integration to Disintegration*, Curzon Press, 2001.
3.   Norio Tamaki, 'Japan's Adoption of the Gold Standard' and the London Money Market 1881-1903: Matsukata, Nakai and Takahashi', in *Britain and Japan: Biographical Portaits (Vol.1)*, ed. Ian Nish, Japan Library, 1994, pp.126-7.
4.   Chō Sakio, in *Yokohama Shōkin Ginkō Shi, Vol.6*, p.448.
5.   Minakata Kumagusu, 'Rondon Nikki yori' in Nakazawa Shinichi, *Dō to Fudō no Kosumorojii*, Kawade Bunkō, 1991.
6.   Nakai Chōsaburō, in *Yokohama Shōkin Ginkō Shi, Vol.6*, p.532.
7.   Tamaki, 'Japan's Adoption of the Gold Standard', p.130.
8.   Toshio Suzuki, *Japanese Government Loan Issues on the London Capital Market 1870-1913*, The Athlone Press, London 1994, p.99.

9.　David Kranzler, *Japanese, Nazis & Jews: the Jewish Refugee Community of Shanghai, 1938-1945*, Yeshiva University Press, New York, 1976.
10.　Matsumura Masayoshi, 'Nichirosensōgo no Takahashi Korekiyo to Yakobu Shifu', *Kokusai Kankei Kenkyu, Vol.23.No.3*, Nihon Daigaku Kokusai Kankei-gakubu Kokusai Kankei Kenkyūsho, 25 December 2002.
11.　*Yokohama Shōkin Ginkō Shi, Vol.2*, p.115.
12.　Nishiyama Tsutomu, in *Yokohama Shōkin Ginkō Shi, Vol.6*, p.470.
13.　Yano Kanji, in *Yokohama Shōkin Ginkō Shi, Vol.6*, p.536.
14.　Okada Jūkichi, in *Yokohama Shōkin Ginkō Shi, Vol.6*, p.571.
15.　Kanō Hisaakira, 'Rondon Seikatsu Dangi' in *Shōkin-jin*, last edition 1947.
16.　Telephone interview with Yasuda Hiroshi, grandson of Okubo Toshikata and Wakiko, April 2003.
17.　Yano Kanji, in *Yokohama Shokin Ginko Shi, Vol.6*, p.536.
18.　*Yokohama Shōkin Ginkō Shi, Vol.1*, p.489.
19.　Correspondence with Nohara Katsuya, 6 July 2003.
20.　Keiko Itoh, 'Hisaakira Kanō (1886-1963): International Banker from a Daimyo Family', in *Britain & Japan, Biographical Portraits*, Vol.III, ed. J.E. Hoare, Japan Library, 1999.
21.　Hisaakira Kanō, *My London Records*, private print, Tokyo 1956.

Chapter 23 H.TAKENO **The Nippon Yūsen Kaisha (NYK): Two important British Managers, Albert Brown and Thomas James**

1.　Curator of NYK Maritime Museum in Yokohama. In preparing this account the author has drawn on *The Life and Times of the Illustrious Captain Brown* by Lewis Bush, Tokyo, 1969, and *Mitsubishi and NYK 1870-1914* by William Wray, 1984.
2.　For a detailed account of Brunton and his work in Japan see *Richard Henry Brunton: Building Japan 1868-1876*, with an introduction and notes by Hugh Cortazzi, Japan Library, Folkestone, 1991.
3.　Iwasaki Yatarō (1835-85), the founder of the Mitsubishi *zaibatsu*, stemmed from Tosa in Shikoku.
4.　Henry F.Woods: *Spunyarn: Strands from a Sailor's Life*, London (Hutchinson) 1924. The editor is grateful to Sebastian Dobson for drawing attention to this rare book.
5.　Woods (see note 4 above, page 248) thought that James had a special status in Japan. Writing about the Japanese he said: 'I have heard them charged with ingratitude to their Foreign teachers – that once they had all that was to be gotten out of them they were promptly set aside and forgotten. I do not know enough to express any decided opinion on the matter – but there is a grave near Oxted to which many visits are paid by Japanese in a sort of pilgrimage. It is that of the Great English Friend of Japan who rendered such good service to them and was a model of probity – Captain James who sailed with Tōgo all over the Pacific as instructor to Japanese Naval Officers and subsequently reared their Maritime Shipping Companies into prosperity.'

NOTES

Chapter 24 EDWIN GREEN **HSBC: A Fellowship in Banking. Pioneers in Japan, 1866–1900**

1.   The abbreviation H.S.B.C. and variations such as H.S.B. & C. have been used throughout the bank's history. Today's HSBC Group takes its name from this abbreviation for the founding company of the Group. I am most grateful to my colleagues Sara Kinsey, Tina Staples and Helen Swinnerton for their suggestions and comments on this paper.
2.   Muirhead, S., *Crisis Banking in the East. The History of the Chartered Mercantile Bank of India, London and China, 1853-93* (Aldershot: Scolar Press, 1996), pp. 74–75.
3.   King, F., *The History of The Hongkong and Shanghai Banking Corporation*, vol. 2, *The Hongkong Bank in the Period of Imperialism and War: Wayfoong, the Focus of Wealth* (Cambridge: Cambridge University Press, 1988), p.146.
4.   The Mercantile returned to Japan when it opened offices in Tokyo, Osaka (1949) and Nagoya (1963). The business of these branches was gradually merged with HSBC after the Mercantile was acquired by HSBC in 1959. Green, E., and Kinsey, S., *The Paradise Bank. The Mercantile Bank of India, 1893-1984* (Aldershot: Ashgate, 1999), pp. 115, 144-45, 162-63.
5.   Jones, G., *British Multinational Banking, 1830-1990* (Oxford: Oxford University Press, 1993), pp. 21, 23.
6.   The following paragraphs rely heavily on the Japanese branches classified files, HSBC Group Archives, London, H180.2, and King, F., *The History of The Hongkong and Shanghai Banking Corporation*, vol. 1, *The Hongkong Bank in Late Imperial China, 1864-1902: On an Even Keel* (Cambridge: Cambridge University Press, 1987), pp. 94-98.
7.   King, vol. 1, p. 97.
8.   HSBC directors' minutes, 9 November 1876, HSBC Group Archives.
9.   King, vol. 1, p. 224.
10.   Green, E., and Kinsey, S., 'Completing the picture: Records of the national staff of international banks since the 1850s', in de Graaf, T., Jonker, J., and Mobron, J.-J, *European Banking Overseas, 19th-20th Century*, (Amsterdam: ABN AMRO, 2002), pp. 165-77.
11.   *Japan Gazette Directory*, 1887, pp. 73, 105.
12.   Between 1866 and 1900 the mean average length of 30 appointments as manager or agent, amounting to a total of 84 years of service, was 2.80 years. The calculation of years served includes the post-1900 service of D. Jackson at Yokohama (until his death in 1903), R. H. Cook at Kobe (Hyogo) (until 1903) and J. Maclean at Nagasaki (until 1903).
13.   Green, E., 'Export bankers: The migration of British bank personnel to the Pacific region, 1850-1914', in Checkland. O, Nishimura, S., and Tamaki, N. (eds), *Pacific Banking, 1859-1959, East Meets West* (Basingstoke: Macmillan, 1994), pp. 75-99.
14.   Inspection reports on Yokohama and Hyogo by D. McLean, 1875, HSBC Group Archives, K8.2.
15.   Townsend, A.M., *Early Days of the Hongkong and Shanghai Bank* (privately printed, London, 1937), pp. 6-7, HSBC Group Archives, J11.3.2

16. H. D. Sharpin to J. R. Jones, 22 March 1955, HSBC Group Archives, S16.1.
17. Townsend, pp. 3-4. The Yorkshire Banking Company was acquired in 1900 by the London and Midland Bank (later Midland Bank, now HSBC Bank plc).
18. Townsend, p.15.
19. Ibid.
20. Between 1901 and 1905, the London manager was Sir Ewen Cameron, Townsend's own brother-in-law, who was another key figure in the negotiation of the Japanese loans.
    Cameron had never served in HSBC's branches in Japan but Townsend notes that the Camerons visited Japan in 1879 'when we spent a few happy days at Enoshima'. Townsend, p. 16.
21. Suzuki, T. *Japanese Government Loan Issues on the London Capital Market, 1870-1913* (London: Athlone Press, 1994), *passim*. The principal Japanese negotiator in London for these loans was Takahashi Korekiyo, who had served with A.A. Shand at the Mercantile Bank's branch in Yokohama in the 1860s.
22. King, vol. 1, p. 247.
23. Ibid., pp. 614-15.
24. Quoted in King, vol. 2, p.17.
25. King, vol. 1, p.328.

Chapter 25 GEORGE HUGHES **Robert Nichols, 1893-1944: Poet in Japan, 1921-24**

1. I am indebted for much of the biographical information in this essay to Anne Charlton. The biography of Nichols by Anne and William Charlton, *Putting Poetry First: A Life of Robert Nichols* (Norfolk: Michael Russell, 2003) is now the standard work on his life. Anne Charlton is Nichols's niece, and there are obvious differences of emphasis and interpretation in our view of Nichols, but I should like to record my thanks for her generous and patient responses to my many enquiries. I was particularly grateful to be allowed to see the manuscript of *Komuso*, her notes on the huge Nichols-Head correspondence and Nichols's correspondence with Japanese colleagues. I should like also to acknowledge the assistance of the following libraries, whose collections of letters and manuscripts I have consulted: Bodleian Library, Oxford; Brotherton Library, University of Leeds; John Rylands Library, Manchester University; Reading University Library (Chatto and Windus archive), State University of New York, University at Buffalo. I am grateful to Lord Bridges for permission to consult the Bridges-Nichols correspondence.

2. Other poets included Edmund Blunden, Sherard Vines, Ralph Hodgson, William Empson, Peter Quennell, William Plomer, George Barker, D. J. Enright, James Kirkup, Anthony Thwaite and Jon Silkin. Poems and translations by Ernest Edward Speight, who was working at Tokyo University of Foreign Languages at the same time as Nichols, appear in the *Japan Advertiser*, so perhaps he and Nichols are the first of their kind. Lafcadio Hearn was a famous predecessor, but was not a poet.

3. 'Kimono and Bowler Hat', *Listener*, 1942, Charlton papers.

4. *Invocation: War Poems and Others* (London: Elkin Mathews, 1915) 12; 'A Sonnet', 15.

5. *Ardours and Endurances* (London: Chatto and Windus, 1917) 'Noon', 18.

6. Professor Ichikawa Sanki (1886-1970) was assistant Professor at Tokyo Imperial university in 1916 and promoted to full Professor in 1920. He retired in 1946.

7. Letter from Ichikawa Sanki 18 March 1921, Charlton papers.

8. 15 April 1922 to Gilbert Murray, Bodleian.

9. Charlton, 85.

10. *Eigo Seinen* Vol. 48, No. 7, Jan. 1923.

11. *Letters*, ed. Grover Smith (London: Chatto and Windus, 1969) 154.

12. Charlton, 258.

13. Quoted Ann Thwaite, *Edmund Gosse: A Literary Landscape, 1849-1928.* (Chicago: University of Chicago Press, 1984) 471.

14. *Letters*, 91.

15. Charlton, 97.

16. In letters to Wilfred Owen's mother he claimed that this was a terrible loss. Nichols's mother survived until 1942-although none of her family went to visit her during the last twenty years of her life.

17. 23 Oct. 1917. Robert Graves maliciously claimed that Nichols had not seen action, but Anne and William Charlton show in their recent biography that this is not true. Charlton 43-53.

18. Nichols caught syphilis long before penicillin was available to treat it. His history of mood shifts, gastrointestinal pain and convulsive sobbing, and his constant trail round doctors with complaints like 'nervous dyspepsia', point to the pattern by which latent syphilis develops after a primary infection and comes to ape other diseases. His early death from cardiovascular disease would very likely have been a result of late syphilis.

19. 24 June 1922 to Edmund Gosse, Brotherton Library.

20. Charlton, 118.

21. Charlton, 120.

22. 19 Feb. 1922 to Whitworth at Chatto and Windus, Reading University.

23. Charlton, 120.

24. 29 July 1921 to Edmund Gosse, Brotherton Library.

25. Charlton, 120.

26. 15 April 1922 to Gilbert Murray, Bodleian.

27. 7 Aug. 1927 to Henry Head, Charlton papers.

28. Yamato Moto, 'Nichols' in *Nihon no Eigaku Hyakunen: Taishohen.* (Tokyo: Kenkyusha, 1968) 103.

29. Charlton, 119.

30. Yamato Moto, 101.

31. Webb, 148.

32. Charlton, 124.

33. Charlton, 115-6.

34. Charlton papers.

35. *Ardours and Endurances*, 28.

36. Charlton, 119.

37. 29 July 1921 to Edmund Gosse, Brotherton Library.

38. Gosse suggested to him he might be eligible for the Hawthornden prize for these works, and he seems to have believed it likely. He was competing, however, with David Garnett's Lady into Fox and Virginia Woolf's *Night and Day* and, to his annoyance, did not receive the prize.

39. *Japan Advertiser*, 20 Nov. 1921; *Guilty Souls* (London: Chatto and Windus, 1922) lxxi.

40. Charlton, 134.

41. *Fantastica: Being the Smile of the Sphinx and Other Tales of Imagination* (London: Chatto and Windus, 1923) 28.

42. *Fantastica*, 178.

43. Review by J. C. Squire, reprinted in *Japan Advertiser*, 1 July 1923.

44. Charlton, 138.

45. *Japan Advertiser*, 11 Dec. 1921.

46. 11 Dec. 1921.

47. 25 Dec. 1921.

48. Charlton, 125.

49. 15 Sep. 1923 to Chatto & Windus, Reading University.

50. 20 Sep. 1923 to his father, Charlton papers.

51. See A. M. Young, *Imperial Japan: 1926-1938* (London: George Allen and Unwin, 1938) 241, cited in Peter O'Connor 'Home Thoughts, Foreign Bodies', *Tokyo Rika Daigaku Kiyo*, 29. 1997.

52. 5 Nov. 1923 to Gilbert Murray, Bodleian.

53. 30 March 1924.

54. *Masterpieces of Chikamatsu: The Japanese Shakespeare*. Translated by Miyamori, Asataro Revised by Robert Nichols, Formerly Professor of English Literature in the Imperial University (Tokyo, London: Kegan Paul, 1926).

55. 'The House of Mr Nichols', Ichikawa Sanki, *Eigo Seinen*, Vol. 67 No. 7, June 1932.

56. 'Kimono and Bowler Hat', *Listener*, ?1942. Charlton papers; 13 Oct. 1929 to Henry Head.

57. March 14 1942. Charlton papers.

58. 18 Aug. 1935 to Henry Head, Charlton papers.

59. Charlton, 224.

60. 24 Oct. 1936 to Eddie Marsh, Charlton papers.

61. 5 June 1921 to Henry Head, Charlton papers.

62. 25 Nov. 1931 to Edward Thompson, Bodleian.

63. *Ardours and Endurances*, 39.

64. 8 Aug. 1925 to Chatto, Reading University; March 1922 to Eddie Marsh, Charlton papers.

65. 25 Nov. 1931 letter to Edward Thompson, Bodleian.

66. 18 Nov. 1924, Bodleian.

67. Charlton, 222.

68. Chunks of Japanese culture (about household ghosts, fans and insects in

cages) are introduced and explained, but memories of Japan were wearing a little thin: the Japanese words included from time to time are not exactly accurate. Nichols seems to think the phrase '*Ocha dozo*' means 'Bring some tea please'.
69.   29 July 1921 to Edmund Gosse, Brotherton Library.
70.   Uchiyama, 28 May 1925. Matsumoto, 4 March 1924. Charlton papers.

Chapter 26 JOHN HATCHER Ralph Hodgson, 1871–1962: Poet and Artist

1.   Ralph and Aurelia Hodgson Papers, Seymour Adelman Collection, Bryn Mawr College Library. Reproduced by permission of Bryn Mawr College.
2.   'Robert Richards, 'Ralph Hodgson, Poet and Person,' in Wesley D. Sweetser, *Ralph Hodgson: A Bibliography* (New York: Garland, 1980), p. xxviii.
3.   Saitō Takeshi, 'Ralph Hodgson in Japan,' *Japan Quarterly* 9.2 (April–June 1962), p. 154.
4.   Doi, quoted in George Kershner, *Ralph Hodgson: A Biographical and Critical Study*, Ph.D. dissertation, University of Pennsylvania, 1952, p.50.
5.   Saitō 154. For the more prestigious Tokyo Imperial University, however, Saitō made the safer choice of the public school and Oxford educated Edmund Blunden. See Okada Sumie, *Edmund Blunden and Japan: The History of a Relationship* (London: Macmillan, 1988), pp. 198-9 and *Western Writers in Japan* (London: Macmillan, 1999), p. 24.
6.   From a taped 1963 discussion between Blunden, Doi and Fukuhara Rintarō, translated into Japanese and published in *Kokoro* in April 1964. I have quoted from the English transcript, preserved in the Ralph Hodgson Papers at the Beinecke Library, Yale University. This and other unpublished Blunden manuscript materials are reproduced by permission of PFD on behalf of the Estate of Mrs Claire Blunden.
7.   Blunden to Hodgson, ALs, 3 December 1924, Hodgson Papers, Yale. This and other unpublished Hodgson manuscript materials are reproduced by permission of Bryn Mawr College.
8.   Kershner, pp. 49, 50.
9.   Kershner, p. 49.
10.   Kershner, pp. 54-55, 53.
11.   ALs, n.d. [late January-early February 1925], Blunden Papers, Harry Ransom Humanities Research Center, The University of Texas at Austin.
12.   Hodgson to Blunden, ALs, n.d. [early February 1925], Blunden Papers, Texas; Saitō, p. 157.
13.   1963 interview transcript, p.12.
14.   Bush, quoted in Kershner, p. 55. See Doi, 'Ralph Hodgson,' *Nihon no Eigaku Hyakunen*, vol. 2 (Tokyo: Kenkyusha, 1968), p. 134; Yamoto Teikan, 'Hodgson no shi,' *Eigo Bungaku Sekai* 6.6 (September 1971), p. 42.
15.   ALs, n.d. [early February 1925], Blunden Papers, Texas.
16.   Kershner, p. 49.
17.   Richards, p. xxvii.
18.   ALs, 13 April 1928, Ralph and Aurelia Hodgson Papers, Seymour Adelman Collection, Bryn Mawr College Library.
19.   Kershner, p. 51.

20. Barry Webb, *Edmund Blunden* (New Haven: Yale UP, 1990), p. 169.
21. Lewis Bush, 'Edmund Blunden – Man and Friend', *Edmund Blunden: A Tribute from Japan*, ed. Hirai Masao and Peter Milward (Tokyo: Kenkyusha, 1974), p. 71.
22. Saitō 155; Spender, *Journals 1939-1983* (London: Faber, 1985), p. 193, quoted in Okada, *Western Writers in Japan*, p. 100.
23. Kershner, p. 49.
24. Saitō, pp. 156-57; Kershner, p. 51.
25. See Stanford S. Apseloff, 'T.S. Eliot and Ralph Hodgson Esqre.', *Journal of Modern Literature* 10.2 (1983), pp. 342-46.
26. *Collected Poems 1909-1962* (London: Faber, 1974), pp. 150-51.
27. Doi to Aurelia Hodgson, ALs, 5 March [1961], Hodgson Papers, Yale.
28. ALs, 29 August 1935, Bryn Mawr. In *The Skylark and Other Poems* (1958) Hodgson published the second part of this poem, 'The Muse and the Mastiff', but this first part of the poem was neither published nor completed.
29. 'Sons of the North,' *Eigo Seinen* 117.10 (January 1972), p. 37.
30. Saitō, p. 157.

Chapter 27 EILEEN FRASER **G.S. Fraser, 1915-1980: Poet and Teacher in Japan, 1950-51**

1. Quotations from George Fraser's writings about Japan were included on pages 75-77 in *Japan Experiences: Fifty Years, One Hundred Views: post-War Japan Through British Eyes* edited by Hugh Cortazzi, Japan Library, 2001 (hereafter referred to as *Japan Experiences*).
2. Edmund Blunden. See pages 73-75 of *Japan Experiences*.
3. William Plomer. See 'William Plomer (1905-1974) and Japan' by Louis Allen in *Britain and Japan 1859-1991, Themes and Personalities*, edited by Hugh Cortazzi and Gordon Daniels, Routledge 1991.
4. William Empson. See biographic Portrait by John Haffenden in *Biographical Portraits*, Volume IV. Japan Library, 2002.
5. D.J. Enright. See pages 77-79 of *Japan Experiences*.
6. Anthony Thwaite. See pages 103-107 of *Japan Experiences*.
7. Sakurajima is a volcano opposite Kagoshima in Kyushu.
8. Yoshida Kenichi. See pages 207-209 of *Japan Experiences*.
9. Ronald Dore. Professor, Japanese scholar and sociologist.
10. Sir Alvary Gascoigne. See essay by Peter Lowe in *Biographical Portraits*, Volume I, Japan Library, 1994.
11. Prince Takamatsu was a younger brother of the Showa Emperor (Hirohito).
12. Abe Kōbō. Famous novelist and playwright. *The Woman in the Dunes* is the title given to the English version of his *Suno no Onna* (1962).
13. Vere Redman. See 'Sir Vere Redman, (1901-1975)' by Hugh Cortazzi in *Biographical Portraits*, Volume II. Japan Library 1997.
14. *The Times* Correspondent was Frank Hawley.

Chapter 28 RUSSELL GREENWOOD Enright's Japan

1.   Editor: This essay was published in *Life By Other Means, Essays on D.J. Enright* edited by Jacqueline Sims and published in 1990 by Oxford University Press, Oxford. It is reproduced here with the permission of Oxford University Press.

2.   Editor: James Russell Greenwood LVO (1924-93) was Counsellor (Information) in the British Embassy Tokyo from 1968-73 and Consul-General at Osaka/Kobe 1973-77. He had served in the Consulate General at Osaka/Kobe when Enright was in Japan.

3.   Editor: D.J. Enright (1920-2002) whose Obituary appeared in *The Times* of 1 January 2003 was headed 'Poet, novelist and critic whose writing concealed deep, humane feeling beneath its casual wit.' It began: 'One of the outstanding writers of the postwar years.' Born in Leamington of Anglo-Irish parents (his father was a postman) he was educated at Leamington College and Downing College, Cambridge to which he won an exhibition. At Cambridge he read English. From 1947-50 he was lecturer in English at Alexandria University in Egypt. In 1956 and 1957 he lectured at the Free University of Berlin. He was Professor of English at Chulalongkorn University in Bangkok and in 1960 became Professor of English at Singapore University where he stayed for ten years. In Singapore 'he kept up a steady battle against the Government's attempts to put political pressure on the university'. In later years in London 'Enright had a wide circle of friends. Puffing at his pipe, with a look of comic glumness, he delighted them with his witty asperities and the tenderness of his heart.' Extracts from *The World of Dew* were included in *Japan Experiences; Fifty Years, One Hundred Views, Post-war Japan through British Eyes 1945-2000*, Chapter 4. Japan Library, 2001.

4.   Note by Russell Greenwood: '*Sensei*'. A magic word, and yet very equivocal. *Sensei* means 'teacher' plus 'Scholar' plus 'beloved master', it means intellect, learning, culture, taste . . . Yet it also means 'those who can't do, teach', a reciter of old lecture notes . . .' (DJE *The World of Dew*, 24).

5.   Editor: Professor Jugaku was a friend of John Pilcher when he was studying Japanese in Kyoto before the war. See biographical portrait of Sir John Pilcher by Hugh Cortazzi in *Britain and Japan, Biographical Portraits*, Volume III, Japan Library, 1999.

Chapter 29 NORIMASU MORITA Nishiwaki Junzaburo, 1894-1982: A Self-made Englishman

1.   *Nishiwaki Junzaburō Zenshū* hereafter *NJZ*, Vol I, Tokyo, Chikuma Shobō.

2.   '*Hōseki to asa: Atarashiki mono ni furui nioi*,' *NJZ*, Extra Volume, 1983, p. 150.

3.   For the details concerning how Nishiwaki was nominated as a Nobel Prize candidate, see Iwasaki Ryōz's 'Iyaku "Kyoto no Ichigatsu"', Geppō, *NJZ*, vol. 10, p. 7 and Hosea Hirata's *Poetry and Poetics of Nishiwaki Junzaburō*, Princeton University Press, Princeton, NJ, 1993, pp. xv-xviii.

4.   'Shinshun,' *NJZ*, vol. 10, p. 411.

5.   'Nōzui no Nikki,' *NJZ*, vol. 5, p. 331.
6.   'Hiruinaki Shiteki Sonzai: Nishiwaki Junzaburō Tsuitō Zadankai,' *Gendaishi Techō*, July, 1982, p. 25.
7.   'Nōzui no Nikki,' *op. cit.*, p. 331.
8.   'Memory and Vision', *op. cit.* p. 27
9.   'Nōzui no Nikki', *op. cit.*, p. 325.
10. *Ibid*, p. 324.
11. 'Hagiwara Sakutarō', *NJZ*, vol 5, p. 551.
12. 'Shoka no Ichiyō: Nishiwaki Junzaburō Sensei ni Kinku', *Mita Hyōron*,August/September, 1980, p. 68.
13. Quated by Kudō Miyoko, *Sabisii Koe: Nishiwaki Junzaburō no Shōgai*, Tokyo, Chikuma Shobō, 1994, pp. 138-9.
14. 'A Kensington Idyll', in Niikura Shun'ichi, *Nishiwaki Junzaburō: Henyō no Dentō*, Tokyo, Tōhō Shobō, 1994, p. 41.
15. This speculation is based on Kudō Miyoko's interview ith Dr Williams, *Sabishii Koe, op. cit.*, p. 159.
16. *Anbaruwaria*, *NJZ*, vol. 1, p. 189.
17. 'Tsunobue wo Fuku', *NJZ*, vol. 10, p. 237.
18. 'Eikoku no Shizen', *NJZ*, vol. 10, 149.
19. The Cayme press which was at 21, Stanhope Mews was run by Hester Sainsbury's brother, Philip. By the time Nishiwaki approached Philip Sainsbury about publication of his book Hester's husband, Kōri Torahiko, had died of consumption in Switzerland.
20. '*Spectrum* to *Ambarwaria*', *NJZ*, vol. 10, p. 546.
21. Niikura Shun'ichi, *Shijin-tachi no Seikii*, Tokyo, Misuzu Shobō, 2003, p. 182.
22. Both reviews are quoted by Hosea Hirata, *The Poetry and Poetics of Nishiwaki Junzaburō, op. cit.*, pp. xxii-xxiii.
23. Yokobe Tokusaburō, 'Zangeroku no Ichibu dewa Naku', *Mugen*, no. 29, 1972, p. 265.
24. Yamamoto Kenkichi, *Gen'ei no Hito, op. cit.*, p. 63.
25. Satō Saku, 'Nishiwaki Sensei no Omoide', *Gen'ei no Hito, op. cit.*, p. 83.
26. *No Traveller Returns*, *NJZ*, vol. 1, p. 221.
27. 'Wa no Aru Sekai', *Nishiwaki Junzaburō Taidanshū, op. cit.*, p. 318.

Chapter 30 IAN NISH **Richard Storry, 1913-82: A Life-long Affair with Japan**

1.   This title is taken from his article in *Japan Quarterly*, vol. 13, no.3 (1966), pp. 366-71. The most detailed biography is to be found in Dorothie Storry, *Second Country*, Woodchurch: Paul Norbury Publications, 1986. Also relevant is the Introduction to *The Collected Writings of Richard Storry*, London: Japan Library, 2002.
2.   Martin Gilbert, *W.S. Churchill*, vol. 5, Companion, London: Heinemann, 1981, pp. 726-8.
3.   R.P. Dore, 'Otome and Frank Daniels' in Ian Nish (ed.), *Biographical Portraits*, vol. 1, Richmond: Japan Library, 1994, pp. 269-70.

4.   *Second Country*, p. 43.

5.   G.R. Storry, '*Otaru no Hikari*' in *Japan Quarterly*, vol.13, no. 1(1966), pp. 79-81. [Author hereafter cited as 'GRS'].

6.   *Second Country*, pp. 62-3.

7.   GRS, 'War between Britain and Japan' in *Collected Writings*, pp.182-3.

8.   Nishi Haruhiko, *Kaisō no Nihon gaikō*, Tokyo: Iwanami, 1965; GRS, *The Double Patriots: A study of Japanese nationalism*, London: Chatto and Windus, 1957.

9.   GRS, 'An Englishman looks at Diet Hill' in *Japan Quarterly*, vol.2, no.1(1954), p. 66ff. Aiko Clark is thought to have been the inspiration for the heroine in the popular novel of the time: Richard Mason, *The Wind Cannot Read*, published in 1947.

10.   GRS, 'Japan in 1954' in *Collected Writings*, p. 204.

11.   GRS, *Double Patriots*, p.301.

12.   Chūshichi Tsuzuki, *The Pursuit of Power in Japan*, Oxford: University Press, 2000, p. 470.

13.   GRS with F.W. Deakin, *The case of Richard Sorge*, London: Chatto and Windus, 1966.

14.   GRS, *Double Patriots*, p. 304.

15.   *Kokusai Kōryū*, vol. 77 (1997), pp. 4-24. A tribute to Storry's work at the Far East Centre is to be found in Louis Allen, *The End of the War in Asia*, London, Hart-Davis, 1976, p. x.
'Like so many writers on modern Japanese history, I owe [Richard Storry] much for his constant and untiring encouragement, selflessly given, and for the opportunity to test out some of the findings of the chapters on Burma and Indo-China in seminars at St Antony's College Oxford where I was lucky enough to have the late Geoffrey Hudson in my audience to comment on them. If Richard Storry finds any of these pages of interest to him, then this book will have been worth writing.'

16.   GRS, *Japan and the Decline of the West in Asia*, Basingstoke: Macmillan, 1979

17.   The best account of this is to be found in Christine Nicholls, *History of St Antony's College, Oxford, 1950-2000*, Oxford: University Press, 2000, p. 88ff.

18.   GRS, letter to the author, 25 June 1981.

19.   Nicholls, *op. cit.*, 91-2. *The Collected Writings of Richard Storry*, London: Japan Library, 2002.

20.   Tsuzuki, *op. cit.*, p. 472.

Chapter 31 PETER KORNICKI Eric Bertrand Ceadel, 1921-79: Japanese Studies at Cambridge

1.   Dr J.R.McEwan, known to his friends as Mac, had learnt Japanese while serving in the Royal Air Force. He was a considerable scholar, who was deeply read in the Neo-Confucian schools of Chu Hsi and Wang Yang-ming, and also in the views of the *kokugakusha*. Dr Carmen Blacker who joined the department in 1955 said of him that he could talk in the language and manner of Motoori Norinaga when sufficiently stimulated, and his study of Ogyū Sōrai was a major contribution to scholarship in English on this subject. Unfortunately, he became

increasingly eccentric and unbalanced. Living in a flat above the Oriental Institute he began to refuse to pay his rent and would come down from the flat during the night and write elegant poems in Chinese about death on all the blackboards. Two undergraduates complained that he would appear for his 'lectures' but would sit in silence reading a book with his back to his students. If asked for guidance he would reply briefly 'it means what it says' and return to his reading. Eric Ceadel eventually had the locks on the flat changed, and in due course the university authorities persuaded McEwan to resign. He went to Hong Kong where he died.

2.   Dr Blacker illustrates this by a a story which she heard from Pam, Ceadel's wife. When he returned from a visit to Japan early in the 1950s after an absence of many months, the first thing he said to his wife was: 'I hope you've remembered to pump up my bicycle tyres, because I must be off to the library as soon as possible.'

Chapter 32 PHILLIDA PURVIS Louis Allen (1922-91) and Japan

1.   Comment in an interview in October 2003 by Jean Wilson, Allen's colleague and partner, after the death of his wife, Margaret.

2.   *Envoy, A Review of Literature and Art*, Vol. 4. No 13, December 1950, Republic of Ireland, essay by Louis Allen, 'A Change of Name'.

3.   Note to Peter Stollard about *Burma: the Longest War* in the Durham University Louis Allen archive.

4.   Ibid.

5.   Ibid.

6.   Ibid.

7.   Oba Sadao, *Senchū Rondon Nihongogakkō* Chūō Kōronsha 1988 and *The Japanese' War.* London University's WWII secret programme and the experts sent to help beat Japan, translation by Anne Kaneko, Japan Library, Folkestone, 1997.

8.   Note to Peter Stollard in the Durham University Louis Allen archive.

9.   Ibid.

10.   Comment by Mark Allen.

11.   *Sittang, the end of the Japanese in Burma*, Macdonald, 1973.

12.   *Burma: the Longest War.*

13.   Currently Professor and Chair of the Centre of Philosophy at Tokyo University.

14.   *Aron Shūyōjō*, Aida Yūji, Chūō Kōron Sha, 1959.

15.   Ibid.

16.   Preface by Ishiguro Hide to *Prisoner of the British* by Aida Yūji.

17.   Letter from Aida to Allen, Durham University Louis Allen archive.

18.   These and further comments about the translation are all drawn from correspondence between Ishiguro and Allen in the Durham University Louis Allen archive.

19.   In the end Allen's explanation became a postface.

20.   Interview in Oxford with Professor Toshio Yokoyama, 9 November 2003.

21.   Allen and Aida met on three separate occasions.

22.   Letter to Ron Dore in Durham University Louis Allen archive.

23. Postcript by Louis Allen to *Prisoner of the British* by Aida Yūji.

24. 'Not so Piacular' – a Footnote to Ienaga on Malaya, *Proceedings of BAJS 1980 Vol 5*, pp. 111–126.

25. *Shōnan Tokubetsu-shi, Shokun,* July – December 1974.

26. From Interrogator to Interpreter, *Japan Digest* Interview October 1990.

27. *Burma: The Longest War,* Dent, 1984.

28. Cover of paperback edition of *Burma, the Longest War.*

29. Oba Sadao The *The Japanese War* trans. Anne Kaneko, Japan Library, Folkestone, 1995.

30. Examples are:- Lt. Gen. T. Hanaya, Ex–Commander 55 Division and Lt. Gen. S. Katamura, Commander 15th Army.

31. Examples are:- Outline of Ha-Go Operation by 55 Division; Outline of Mai Operation, Shimbu Corps; Outline of Koku Operation; Outline of NO 31 Operation, 55 Division; Outline of the Quelling Operation in Burma 55 Division, Phnom Penh November 1945.

32. Originals of reports mentioned above, and others, are in the Durham University Louis Allen archive.

33. Allen gave lectures on these themes at LSE, Tokyo University, St Anthony's College, Oxford, the Britain-Burma Society and the Association of South-East Asian Studies.

34. Note to Peter Stollard about *Burma: the Longest War* in Durham University Louis Allen archive.

35. 'From Interrogator to Interpreter', *Japan Digest* Interview, October 1990.

36. Allen was to write a 'postface' for the translation of Fujiwara's autobiography, published in English translation in Hong Kong.

37. *Burma: the Longest War,* Preface, p. xx.

38. Hirakubo Masao in a letter to Major McGregor-Cheers, June 1988, in Durham University Louis Allen archive.

39. For an account of the Crown Prince's visit to Britain in 1953 see Hugh Cortazzi's essay in this volume on 'Crown Prince Akihito in Britain'.

40. 'Japan: The Reconciliation, Old Soldiers Never Die', a lecture to the Japan Society, 26 April 1990.

41. Ibid.

42. Ibid.

43. Ibid.

44. Ibid.

45. *Prisoner of the British* by Aida Yūji, Cresset Press, 1966.

46. Obituary by Dr Barry Garnham in *Password,* Feb–March 1992.

47. Obituary by Ken Gardner, *The Guardian,* 13 January 1992.

48. From Interrogator to Interpreter, *Japan Digest* Interview, October 1990.

49. Lafcadio Hearn and Ushaw College in *Rediscovering Lafcadio Hearn,* Folkestone, Global Oriental, 1997.

50. Norbury published Allen in *Japan Digest, Japan Education Journal,* and under the Japan Library and Global Oriental imprints.

51. Louis Allen & Jean Wilson (eds), *Lafcadio Hearn: Japan's Great Interpreter. A new anthology of his writings, 1894-1904.* Folkestone: Japan Library, 1992.

52. 'Japan and Northeast England' in J. Chapman (ed.) *European Association of Japanese Studies, 1973-88.*
53. 'Japan: Standing the Image on its Head' in *Perspectives on Japan Vol 1* (1977).
54. '*Nihonjinron* or What the Japanese Think about Themselves' in *Bulletin of the Japan Society of London*, vol 100 (1983).
55. Louis Allen: *Collected Writings*, (Ian Nish, ed.) Japan Library, 2004, drawing on bibliographies compiled by Beth Rainey, of Durham University Library, and Mark Allen.
56. Comment in an interview in October 2003 by Jean Wilson, Allen's colleague and partner, after the death of his wife, Margaret.
57. 'After the Burma Railway: Louis Allen's contribution to reconciliation with Japan', Ines San Miguel, Durham East Asian Papers, 16, 2002.
58. Professor Ian Nish in his introduction to *Collected Writings of Louis Allen* to be published in 2004.

Chapter 33 CARMEN BLACKER **John Corner, 1906-96: Controversial Biologist and Friend of the Shōwa Emperor**

1. Examples are *Calamus corneri* Furtado, *Globba corneri A. Weber.* Among fungi there is *Corneromyces J. Ginns.* The complete list may be found at the end of the obituary in *Biographical Memoirs of the Fellows of the Royal Society*, vol. 45, 1999, pp. 90-91, by David Mabberley.
2. See Corner's *Botanical Monkeys*, Pentland Press, 1992.
3. In 1981 Corner published a book entitled *The Marquis*, Heineman Asia Singapore. Here he gave an account of his captivity in Singapore 1942-45, and of his friendship with the Marquis, and the 'Professor'.
4. *The Marquis*, p. 25.
5. Louis Allen, in his chapter 'Japan as occupying power; the revision of history,' in *Rethinking Japan*, volume 2, 1990, edited by Adriana Boscaro, Franco Gatti and Massimo Raveri, states that Corner himself was briefly sent to prison. In *The Marquis*, which I follow here, there is no mention of any such incident; see also *ibid.*, p. 25. See also Brian Montgomery: *Shenton of Singapore*, 1984, Chapters 6, 7, and 8
6. See the long chapter in *The Marquis* entitled 'The Professor'.
7. Ibid., pp. 83-6.
8. Ibid., p. 49.
9. Ibid., pp. 129, 134-5, 138.
10. Ibid., p. 126.
11. *Biographical Memoirs*, vol. 36, 1990, pp. 243-72, 'His Majesty Emperor Hirohito of Japan, KG, 1901-89'.
12. Ibid., p. 243.
13. Ibid., p. 252.
14. I am indebted to Mr N. Koyama, University Library, Cambridge, for this information.
15. The mycologist Hongō Tsugio, for example, in his recent book *Kinoko no Hosomichi*, 2003, recalls that for the last thirty years never a Christmas went by without a card from Corner, until 1996 when he heard that this 'genius of a

scientist' had died at the age of ninety. In the three years before 1945 he, together with Marquis Tokugawa, achieved a co-operation on a deep level which lay beyond any temporary sense of 'us and them'. The writer often accompanied Corner on fungus forays and recalls vividly his kindly face, pipe in mouth. It is largely to him, he writes, that the scholarly world owes the preservation of the unrivalled collections in Singapore when these were threatened with destruction in 1942.

Professor Rodney Needham, for example, recalls that when working in the Raffles Museum Library he was struck by the fact that every book and pamphlet was neatly in its proper place. He was told that those in charge of the library had punctiliously maintained everything there as though they were responsible directly to the Emperor for the preservation of all.

Chapter 34 YAHYA ABDELSAMAD **Basil Robinson, 1912- : the Japanese Sword and the Victoria and Albert Museum**

I want to record my thanks to Mrs Alicia Cropley, daughter of B. W. Robinson, who has given me welcome advice particularly about her father's early life, Mr Gregory Irvine, Curator of the Far Eastern Department at the V&A, Mr Eric Alberts, lecturer at the Art Students League in New York City, sword collector and friend for some twenty years. Lastly, but certainly not least, I thank Mr Robinson for encouraging me some five years ago when I was at university to develop my interest in Japanese swords.

Apart from personal correspondence from Robinson and/or from Mrs A. Cropley to myself I have used the following sources:

1. July/August 1974 Programme 81 'Reminiscence', Token Society of Great Britain.
2. July/August 1976 Programme 100 'Japanese surrendered swords: 'A Reminiscence of 1945', Token Society of Great Britain.
3. Basil William Robinson, *Arts of the Japanese Sword*, Faber, London, 1961.
4. Basil William Robinson, *A Primer of Japanese Sword Blades*, Privately printed, London, 1955.
5. Fujishiro, Yoshio, *Nihon-to Jiten*, 2 Vols. 2nd Ed., Tokyo, 1963.

1. Catalogue by Henri Joly and K.Tomita.

Chapter 35 PETER MILWARD **Three Great Japanese Translators of Shakespeare**

1. See biographical portrait by Brian Powell in *Britain and Japan, 1859-1991: Themes and Personalities*, edited by Sir Hugh Cortazzi and Gordon Daniels, Routledge, London, 1991 pp. 223-34.
2. This appeared both in *Sophia* (in Japanese translation) and in a special volume commemorating the fiftieth anniversary of the university entitled, *Studies in Japanese Culture – Tradition and Experiment*, in 1963.
3. Concerning his attitude, one might well adapt the well-known words of Kipling concerning England, 'What do they know of Shakespeare, who only

Shakespeare know?'
4. Yoshida Ken'ichi was the son of Yoshida Shigeru, Prime Minister of Japan, 1946-47 and 1948-54.
5. My ticket was for the Royal Box which was to be used that evening by the then Crown Prince and Princess
6. He has become quite a celebrity, exemplifying (to my mind) the Japanese saying, '*Shippai wa seikō no moto*', or as we would say in English, 'To snatch success out of the jaws of failure'.
7. What I remember of the occasion, however, was not so much the actual production of Shakespeare's play as a by-product; since on my first introduction to Knapp, knowing he was a Catholic, I asked him if he had ever done a one-man performance of one of the Gospels on stage, as another English actor had been doing with notable success, using the Gospel of St Mark, in both London and New York. He replied that he had not actually done so, but he would very much like to give it a try, though he had no time to memorize the text. Accordingly, when the time came, he put our house chapel to good use, attired in cassock and surplice, standing before a lectern and reading the text of St Mark without appearing to be doing so. He recited, or rather acted, the whole Gospel through from beginning to end, with only one intermission before the account of the Passion; and he had the whole audience, or congregation, spell-bound – an audience consisting of some 90 privileged students of the English Literature department, which was all the chapel could conveniently contain. It was then borne in upon me how well the Gospel story lent itself to acting, especially by such an actor who betrayed with almost every word he uttered the lingering influence of Olivier, and also how close Shakespearian drama, especially the four great tragedies, came in spirit to the story of the Gospel, especially of the Passion.
8. It even occurred to me to doubt if he could speak with any fluency in modern English, though that may have been an advantage to him as a Shakespeare translator, considering how many English words have altered their meanings from then to now.

Chapter 36 PETER O'CONNOR John Russell Kennedy, 1861-1928: Spokesman for Japan and Media Entrepreneur

Acknowledgement
I am most grateful to Professor Michael Studdert-Kennedy of Yale University and to his cousin, the historian Gerald Studdert-Kennedy, for their generous provision of family information for this article.

References
Japan Times, The, (1941) *A Short History of the Japan Times* (Tokyo: The Japan Times Ltd.
Japan Times, The, (1966) *Japan Times Monogatari* [the Japan Times story] (Tokyo: The Japan Times Ltd.).
Lo, Hui-min (1978) (ed.) *The Correspondence of G.E. Morrison*, Volume II: 1912-1920 (Cambridge: Cambridge University Press).
Matsumura Masayoshi (1971) 'Gaimushō Jōhōbu no sōsetsu to Ijūin shōdai

buchō' [The foundation of the Foreign Office Information Department and its first head, Ijūin [Hikokichi], in *Kokusai hō gaikō zasshi*, vol.70, no.2.

Matsumura Masayoshi (2001) 'Japan Calling: The origins of the Ministry of Foreign Affairs Information Department in the early 1920s' (trans. Matsumura Masayoshi and Peter O'Connor). In *The Transactions of the Asiatic Society of Japan*, series 4, vol. 16.

Pooley, Andrew M. (1917) *Japan at the Crossroads* (London: Allen & Unwin).

Purdy, Roger, W. (1987) 'The Ears and Voice of the Nation: The Dōmei News Agency and Japan's News Network, 1936-1945', Ph.D. dissertation, University of California at Santa Barbara.

Stone, Melville E. (1921) *Fifty Years a Journalist* (Freeport, New York: Books for Libraries Press).

Tsūshinsha-shi Kankokai (1958) (ed.) *Tsūshinsha-shi* (Tokyo: Taihei Insatsusha).

Wildes, H. E. (1927) *Social Currents in Japan, with Special Reference to the Press* (Chicago: University of Chicago Press).

Archives

Hugh Byas Papers, Manuscripts and Archives, Yale University Library, Conn., U.S.A.

All Foreign Office documents quoted here are in the Public Record Office at Kew, Richmond, UK.

Newspapers: references to the *Japan Chronicle* and the *Japan Times* are to the weekly edition. References to the *Japan Advertiser* are to the daily edition.

Notes

1. In September 1920 the *Far Eastern Review* of Shanghai carried and the *Seoul Press* reprinted 'Asiatic Sinn Fein', a polemic supporting the arrest by Japanese police of Mr G. L. Shaw, an Ulster-born businessman, at his home in Antung on the Korean border with China. The author of the article was Patrick Gallagher, and it led to a libel action by Shaw. In putting this 'Fenian' slant on Shaw's crimes (he was suspected of terrorism by the Japanese police), the *Far Eastern Review* was at one with the Kokusai Tsūshinsha and with the *China Advertiser* of Tientsin which in August had both imputed 'Fenian' motives and background to Shaw in his dealings with Korean 'malcontents'. As the *Chronicle* remarked, this slant was all the odder for the fact that both Kokusai's manager, John Russell Kennedy, and Patrick Gallagher, were Irish ('The Arrest of Mr. Geo. L. Shaw': *Japan Chronicle*: August 26 1920, pp.282-283).

2. FO 395/458 [P1113/2/150], M. E. Dening to Chancery, 2 April 1932; Miles Lampson to Arthur Willert, 15 April 1932. FO 371/21001 [F8927/1043/10], Young telegram to FO, 1 November 1937.

3. For more on Clarke and his work for Japan, see O'Connor, Peter (2004) *Introduction*: Joseph I. C. Clarke (1918) *Japan at first hand: her islands, their people, the picturesque, the real, with latest facts and figures on their war-time trade expansion and commercial outreach*, (New York: Dodd, Mead and Co). (1918). In O'Connor, Peter (ed.) (2004) *Japanese propaganda: Selected Readings, Series I: Books 1873-1942*, Volume 5 (Folkestone, UK: Global Oriental), pp.1-14.

4.   One of Russell Kennedy's half-brothers, by William Studdert Kennedy's marriage to Joan Anketell of Co. Clare, was the Rev. Geoffrey Studdert Kennedy (1883-1929), who became well known as 'Woodbine Willie' for his habit of handing out cigarettes and comfort to soldiers in the First World War. For more on Studdert Kennedy, see Purcell, William (1962) *Woodbine Willie: An Anglican Incident* (London: Hodder & Stoughton) and more recently, Studdert Kennedy, Gerald (1982) *Dog-Collar Democracy: The Industrial Christian Fellowship, 1919-1929* (London: Macmillan).

5.   Stone 1921: 37.

6.   Stone 1921: 284-96.

7.   *Japan Times* 1966: 60.

8.   Wildes 1927: 169.

9.   *Japan Times* 1966: 179; *Japan Times*: 1 July 1956, 12 May 1956.

10.   Another version is that Kennedy had to choose between being posted elsewhere for AP and staying in Japan. He chose to resign from AP.

11.   Wildes 1927: 170.

12.   Wildes 1927: 170.

13.   Where he wrote of Kennedy: 'This gentleman is now the head of the International News Agency of Japan, [Kokusai] a semi-official concern, which controls the Reuters service, the semi-official Japan Times and Japan Mail, and the correspondence of the New York Herald, Christian Science Monitor, and other American papers, besides having alliances with the Havas, Associated Press, and Stefani Agencies' (Pooley 1917: 17).

14.   Byas c.1914.

15.   Byas c.1924.

16.   For example, the Baron described Kennedy as being motivated by a 'pure outflow of vanity and the desire to pose before the world as the source of news', who would 'stretch it to his own personal profit and aggrandizement' (Wildes 1927: 170).

17.   Byas 1914. Both the *Japan Times* official histories (1941 and 1966) take pride in the part played by the *Japan Times* in exposing the naval scandal: '*The Japan Times* played a key role in the exposure of the major scandal involving top Navy officials and foreign manufacturers of munitions. A Reuters dispatch carried in the journal touched off the probe. . .' (*Japan Times* 1966: 273). There is no indication that the Reuters dispatch originated with Andrew Pooley, then Reuters correspondent in Tokyo, and that the scandal nearly resulted in Pooley's imprisonment on evidence given against him by the President of the *Japan Times*, John Russell Kennedy.

18.   *Japan Advertiser*: 4 July 1914.

19.   *Japan Times* 1966: 179.

20.   *Japan Times* 1941: 36.

21.   *Japan Times* 1966: 179.

22.   Wildes 1927:177.

23.   Outside Japan, one of the few welcomes given to Kokusai came in the *Bulletin* of the Japan Society of London, which gilded the event with historical allusions to Japan's great and good: 'Japan has suffered much from an inadequate

news service and misinterpretations sent out to the world from various sources. The news from the outside world transmitted to Japan has been inadequate, while much of it has been sensational and prejudicial to foreign relations. It made a profound impression upon the late Prince Katsura, thrice Premier of Japan. It is said that shortly before his death he sent for Baron Shibusawa, the leading financier of Japan, and urged him to see whether some sort of news association, national in its scope, could not be organised by the business interests of Japan...'
(London, UK: *Japan Society Bulletin*, June 4 1914).

24. FO 395/170 [F122541/-/23], Miles Lampson to Stephen Gasalee, May 1917.

25. Lo 1978: 352-399.

26. *Japan Times* 1966: 62

27. *Nihon oyobi Nihonjinron*: March 1918; *Japan Advertiser*: May 1918.

28. Byas c.1924.

29. *Tsūshinsha-shi*, 1958: 369; Purdy 1987: 75.

30. Kennedy subsequently persuaded Rea to abandon the Chinese and turn his talents to the promotion of Japanese interests. Rea's *Far Eastern Review* steadfastly followed the Japanese line until his death in 1936.

31. FO 395/334 [F1242/730/150], 1920. Minutes: Frank Ashton-Gwatkin, Miles Lampson.

32. Matsumura 2001.

33. *Contemporary Japan*: June 1937, p.49.

34. For a while the editorial department of Kokusai was in Sojura-chō, Ginza 6-chōme, (which eventually became the *Japan Times* premises and was still occupied by the *Japan Times* in the late 1960s), but by 1919 the Kokusai editorial department had moved into the *Japan Times* premises in the Kokusai Building at 5 Uchisaiwai-chō (now the home of the Nihon Kisha Club), and these would remain the *Japan Times* premises until November 1924 when it moved to new offices nearby at 22, 2-chome, Uchisaiwai-chō. No.5, Uchisaiwai-chō then became known as the Kokusai Building.

35. Purdy 1987: 82; *Tsūshinsha-shi* Kankōkai 1958: 116-117.

36. *Japan Times & Mail Weekly*: 11 January 1919.

37. For more on Kennedy's editorial style, see O'Connor, Peter 'Japan's English-language press during the 1914-18 War (I): *The Skibbereen Eagle* bites back' and 'Japan's English-language press in the 1914-18 war (II): Peace scares and pro-German sentiment' in Musashino University, Faculty of Contemporary Society, *Bulletin* No.2, March 2001, and *Bulletin* No.3, March 2002.

38. *Japan Times* 1966: 64.

39. *Japan Advertiser*: 17 January 1928, pp.1-3.

40. *Japan Chronicle*: 11 September 1924.

41. *Japan Advertiser*: 17 January 1928.

42. All presidents of the *Japan Times*, the 11 'prominent personalities' were: Yamada Sueharu (March 1897-1911); Zumoto Motosada (1911-March 1914); J.R. Kennedy (April 1914-August 1916 and March 1918-December 1921); Vice-Admiral Baron Miyabara Jirō (September 1916-March 1918); Hattori Bunshiro (January 1922-March 1924); Tanaka Tokichi (March 1924-April 1925); Itō

Yonejiro (April 1925–December 1931); Date Genichiro (December 1931–January 1933); Sheba Sometarō (acting president, December 1931–January 1933); Dr Ashida Hitoshi (January 1933–January 1940); Gō Satoshi (December 1940–1945).
43.   *Japan Times & Advertiser*: 14 October 1941.
44.   Purdy 1987: 76.
45.   Byas papers, c.1924.

Chapter 37 ROGER BUCKLEY Hessell Tiltman (1897–1976) and Japan, 1928–1976: On the Road in Asia

Editor's note: A selection of comments on post-war Japan from a lecture by Tiltman to the Japan Society on 27 September 1955 was included in Chapter 16 'The Penetrating Eyes of British Journalists' in *Japan Experiences, Fifty Years, One Hundred Views: Post-War Japan through British Eyes, 1945-2000*, Japan Library, 2001.

1.   I am most grateful for the assistance of the staff of International Christian University, Keiō University, and the British Library for unearthing published material relating to Hessell Tiltman and to the John Rylands University Library of Manchester for access to the Guardian Archives' record of Tiltman's correspondence with the paper in the 1950s. I have been unable to discover any previously published assessments of Tiltman's career beyond fragmentary items in *Who's Who*, random items on the internet and pieces in *No.1 Shimbun*, the monthly in–house journal of the Foreign Correspondents' Club of Japan. My preliminary remarks are therefore based on the above sources and private conversations with past and present journalists in Tokyo. Tiltman's widow informed me a decade ago that she had no knowledge of the existence of any personal papers relating to her late husband who had died at sea.

2.   Tiltman to A.P. Wadsworth, editor of the *Manchester Guardian*, 27 May 1954. The archives of letters to and from Tiltman are presently catalogued under B/T119/1–175. No records would appear to have survived within the *Guardian*'s Tokyo bureau referring to the early post-war years.

3.   His work *The Terror in Europe* was published in 1930. His book entitled *Peasant Europe* appeared in 1934.

4.   James Ramsay MacDonald, *An Authentic Life*, London, 1929.

5.   Nevil Shute pseudonym of Nevil Shute Norway (1899-1960) was a writer born in London who first became an aeronautical engineer and designer and took up novel writing in 1926. After the Second World War, he emigrated to Australia. Two of his famous novels were *A Town Like Alice*, 1949 and *On the Beach*, 1957.

6.   John Hessell Tiltman and (Hugh) Hessell Tiltman were not related.

7.   He was born at Rye on 2 February 1897.

8.   He married Marjorie Hand in 1925. Among the novels she wrote were *Quality Chase*, 1940, *A Little Place in the Country*, 1944, and *Born a Woman*, 1951. During the war she worked on keeping the *Times Literary Supplement* going.

9.   See, for example, collaborative efforts with T.C.Bridges, such as *Kings of Commerce* and *Heroes of Modern Adventure*. Bridges was over thirty years older than

Tiltman.
10. *Manchuria; The Cockpit of Asia* was published in 1933 by Jarrolds who also published the other works co-authored with Etherton who was nearly twenty years older than Tiltman.
11. *The Cockpit of Asia*, page 5.
12. Ibid., page 250.
13. Ibid., page 256.
14. Ibid., page 255.
15. Ibid. Tiltman would continue to place considerable store on the role of Australia as a potential, although still developing, power in the region. In other publications he and Etherton spoke out robustly for the continuation of anti-immigration policies 'to stem the Asiatic tide should events cause it to flow southward. She must people her own lands with those of her own kith and kin, and so be ready to challenge the issue'.
16. Ibid., page 256.
17. See Etherton and Tiltman: *The Pacific: A Forecast*, London 1928 page vi.
18. Ibid., page 113.
19. The authors suggested that although 'the Japanese are good organizers' they 'have achieved little as colonizers'. They added that 'the weakness of their position is that, to initiate an idea of 'Asia for the Asiatic', they must rely upon races and tribes lacking the requisite qualities and ideals'. Ibid., page 250.
20. Ibid., page 256.
21. Ibid., page 257. Tiltman warned that 'The industrialization of the Pacific, even now being enacted, will be an acid test for British industries'. His readers were unlikely to have rejoiced in his economic liberalism and the arguments that the eventual 'cessation of the monopoly hitherto enjoyed by Western nations will enrich and benefit the world'.
22. Etherton and Tiltman: *Japan: Mistress of the Pacific?*, London 1934, pages 292-3.
23. Ibid., page 298.
24. Ibid., page 246.
25. Ibid., page 248.
26. Ibid., page 248.
27. Ibid., page 249.
28. According to *Who Was Who, 1971-80* Tiltman was a war correspondent in Nationalist Spain, 1938-9.
29. The co-authors went a stage further and also suggested that if there were a Pacific War, it would still be possible for Japan to survive its inevitable defeat, albeit in reduced circumstances as 'a fourth class Power'.
30. *Japan: Mistress of the Pacific*, page 253.
31. On earlier British coverage see Buckley 'Gambling on Japan: the British Press and the San Francisco Peace Settlements, 1950-1952', *Bulletin of the Graduate School of International Relations*, International University of Japan, no. 2, December 1984. *The Manchester Guardian* cost two pence in 1945 and consisted merely of eight pages. The front page then carried nothing but personal ads. The paper was reincarnated as *The Guardian* on 24 August 1959; news had appeared

on the front page from September 1952. See David Ayerst *The Manchester Guardian: Biography of a Newspaper*, Ithaca. New York, 1971, p. 627.

To date no British historian examining either the Manchurian Crisis or post-surrender Japan appears to have cited Tiltman in the course of their researches.

32.   Tiltman to Wadsworth, private and confidential, 9 May 1952, VCA/T119/41, Guardian Archive, Manchester.

33.   ibid.

34.   ibid.

35.   Tiltman to Wadsworth, 23 March 1952.

36.   Tiltman's opinions on post-war Japan could be highly critical, though he was shrewd enough to keep them well hidden. He informed his paper after a visit by Lord Alexander to Tokyo that the Field Marshal had got Japan upside down and that it was absurd for innocents abroad to remark 'to the effect that it was amazing how Japan had changed'. Warming to his theme, Tiltman let Alexander have both barrels : 'I had about four minutes, before the general talk began – just time to point out that so long as the Japanese conform to the tenets of Emperor worship, the Family system and the Confucian concept of obedience to authority, no fundamental change in thought processes could occur here'. The Imperial Household Office remains one of the most conservative and reticent public offices in Japan.

37.   In 1959 Tiltman was awarded an OBE by the British and the Order of the Sacred Treasure (Fourth Class) by the Japanese.

Chapter 38 MANABU YOKOYAMA **Frank Hawley, 1906–61: Scholar, Bibliophile and Journalist**

1.   Captain Brinkley and Hugh Byas in pre-war days had represented *The Times* but they also represented other papers.

2.   Peter Lowe: 'Sir Alvary Gascoigne in Japan 1946–1951' in *Britain and Japan: Biographical Portraits Volume I*, Japan Library, 1994, and Roger Buckley: 'Split Images: Occupied Japan through the Eyes of British Journalists and Authors' in the same volume, and Manabu Yokoyama, 'Frank Hawley as a correspondent of the London *Times* (1): Hawley incident', *Annual Report of the Research Institute for Culture and Cultural History*, Notre Dame Seishin University, volume 15, 2002.

3.   Manabu Yokoyama: 'A Study of Frank Hawley and the Kansai Asiatic Society', *Annual Report of the Research Institute for culture and Cultural History*, Notre Dame Seishin University, volume 7, 1993, pp 23-76.

4.   See 'Outline of The 3rd meeting about overseas spread Japanese Language', held on 18 March 1938, at the Tokyo Club, by *Kokusai Bunka Shinkōkai*. Meeting Members; Ichimura Hikotarō, Ooka Yasuzō, Katsumoto Seiichirō, Sir George Sansom, Tanigawa Tetsuzō, Doi Kōchi, Nogami Toyoichirō, Harold Henderson, Frank Hawley, Kuroda (trustee), Dan (trustee), Ishida Mikinosuke.

5.   Frank Hawley: 'Sketch of a History of Japanese Literary Studies in Europe', *Bungei*, March 1933, 1-22pp.

Frank Hawley: 'The Origin of the Japanese Language', *Kaizō*, February 1934, 146-160pp.

6.   Kōda Rohan (1867-1947), idealist novelist and poet, was descended from a

minor samurai family which served the Tokugawa shogun in Edo. One of his brothers was Gunji Shigetada, the Chishima-Islands explorer, and another was Kōda Seiyū, a historian, while a younger sister Kōda Nobu was a musician. He became absorbed in Chinese classics and read widely before studying at the government telegraphy school from which he graduated in 1884 He worked for a time in Hokkaidō, but soon abandoned his post to devote himself full time to writing.

7.   Manabu Yokoyama: 'Frank Hawley and His Editing of Kenkyusha's *Simplified English Dictionary*', *Annual Report of the Research Institute for culture and Cultural History*, Notre Dame Seishin University, Vol.16, 1996, 63-84pp.

8.   Manabu Yokoyama: 'Frank Hawley and His Editing of Kenkyusha's *Simplified English Dictionary*', *Annual Report of the Research Institute for culture and Cultural History*, Notre Dame Seishin University, Vol.16, 1996, 63-84pp.

9.   Hugh Cortazzi: biographical portrait of Sir Vere Redman (1901-1975) in *Britain and Japan: Biographical Portraits*, Volume II, Japan Library, 1997.

10.   Manabu Yokoyama: 'Frank Hawley and the British Council (The British Library of Information and Culture) in 1939/42s Japan', *Annual Report of the Research Institute for culture and Cultural History*, Notre Dame Seishin University, Vol.16, 2001, 47-86pp.

11.   John Morris: *Traveller from Tokyo*, The Cresset Press, London, 1943, 110pp. 'But it is important to note that judged by Japanese standards the conditions imposed were good, for there is no doubt whatsoever that the treatment accorded to Japanese prisoners is considerably more harsh.'

12.   Manabu Yokoyama: Frank Hawley as a Correspondent of the London *Times* (1), *Annual Report of the Research Institute for culture and Cultural History*, Notre Dame Seishin University, Vol.15, 2002, 59-86pp.

13.   Obituary Mr. Ian Morrison: 'Far East Dispatches to *The Times*', *The Times*, Monday 14 August 1950.

14.   Manabu Yokoyama: A Study of Frank Hawley and the Kansai Asiatic Society, *Annual Report of the Research Institute for culture and Cultural History*, Notre Dame Seishin University, Vol.7, 1993, 23-76pp.

15.   Frank Hawley: *An English Surgeon in Japan in 1863-1865, Miscellanea Japonica*: being occasional contributions to Japanese studies', I. Printed for the author by the Kawakita Printing Co., 1954, 33p. Extract from the private journal of John T. Comerford, an English surgeon in Japan, 1864-1865. Privately printed, hand-made Japanese paper by Endō Tadao of Shiroishi in Miyagi prefecture. Limited print of 100 copies. Kawakita Printing Company, Kyoto, October 1954. For an account of the bombardment see Appendix II to *British Envoys in Japan 1859-1972* edited by Hugh Cortazzi, Global Oriental, 2004.

16.   Frank Hawley: *Whales and Whaling in Japan I [Part 1 (all published)]*, *Miscellanea Japonica II*, 30.5*23.2cm, 18 plates, including a folding coloured woodblock frontispiece. Pp.354, x, undyed Indian goat and paper boards, original handmade slip-case. Printed on Japanese handmade paper by Endō Tadao of Shiroishi in Miyagi prefecture. The frontispiece is from chromoxylography and was three solid blocks of *sakura*, or cherry and twelve solid blocks of Magnolia *obovata*; there were 13 printing stages. The 18 illustrations are printed on a

handmade *kyokushi* fabricated of *mitsumata* (*Edgeworthia papyrifera*). Kawakita Printing Co. Kyoto: printed for the author, 1961. 125 numbered copies.
17. Frank Hawley: [Offprint of] *Whales and Whaling in Japan I'*, *Miscellanea Japonica*, II. Pp [51]-102, 1958. Limited print of 51 copies. Frank Hawley [prospectus] *Whales and Whaling in Japan I*, *Miscellanea Japonica*, II. October 1958. Publisher's prospectus to vol. 1, which was all that was issued of an intended three-vol. set. Limited print 300 copies. Cover title, self wraps, sewn, as issued. [12]pp. Kawakita Printing Co. Kyoto, Illustrated with folding plate.
18. Teruyama Etsuko: 'Random Memory of Mr. Frank Hawley', *Annual Report of the Research Institute for culture and Cultural History*, Notre Dame Seishin University, Vol.12, 1999, 25-50pp.
19. Manabu Yokoyama: 'History of Establishment of Hawley Collection in the Library of University of Hawaii', *Annual Report of the Research Institute for culture and Cultural History*, Notre Dame Seishin University, Vol.5, 1991, 37-65pp.
20. Manabu Yokoyama: 'Frank Hawley and his Study of Japanese Papermaking', *Annual Report of the Research Institute for culture and Cultural History*, Notre Dame Seishin University, Vol.8, 1994, 27-74pp. See *Bibliographical Catalogue of Hand Made Paper of Hawley's Collection with Comments* edited and published by Sorimachi Shigeo. June 1961, pp.[3]+40, Limited print of 500 copies.
21. See Robert van Gulik: 'In Memoriam: Frank Hawley', *Monumenta Nipponica*, 16 (1960-1961), pp. 434-227.
22. Manabu Yokoyama: *Shomotsu ni miserareta Eikokujin: Frank Hawley to Nihon-bunka*, Yoshikawa Kobunkan, Sep. 2003.

Yokoyama, Manabu, (Dr) Professor of Japanese History, Notre Dame Seishin University, author of *Shomotsu ni miserareta Eikokujin: Frank Hawley to Nihon-bunka*, Yoshikawa Kobunkan, Sep. 2003, is working on a biography of Hawley.

Chapter 39 AYAKO HOTTA-LISTER **Hasegawa Nyozekan, 1875-1969: Journalist and Philosopher**

1. For this research, apart from his numerous published writings, I was fortunate enough to find at the library of Chuo University a vast amount of information and papers relating to Nyozekan, including his manuscripts and photographs donated by Yamamoto Sachiko, his niece, after his death. The staff of the library, particularly, Ms Ohta Sumiko, the chief librarian, were extremely helpful. Furthermore, I am deeply indebted to Professor Yamaryō Kenji of the Kanda University of International Studies, who has been studying Nyozekan for almost fifty years.
2. Ohya Sōichi, 'Hasegawa Nyozekan Ron' in *Kamen to Sugao: Nihon o ugogasu hitobito* ('Discourse on Hasegawa Nyozekan' in 'Mask and unmasked: the movers and shakers in Japan'), (Tokyo,1952).
3. Pyle, Kenneth B., *The New Generation in Meiji Japan: Problems of Cultural Identity, 1885-1895*, (Calif. 1969), p.79.
4. Barshay, Andew, E., *State and Intellectual in Imperial Japan: The Public Man in Crisis*, (Calif. 1988), p. 128.
5. Nyozekan, *London! London?*, (Tokyo 1997), pp.53-67, 101-2, 262-271.

6.   Nyozekan, Ibid., pp.127-8, 257-8, 69, 391-9.

7.   Nyozekan, Ibid, pp.338-378; 379-390.

8.   Tsurumi Shunsuke, 'Nyozekan no mikata' (How to understand Nyoze-kan'views), in *Hasegawa Nyozekan-Shū*, Vol.1, (Tokyo, 1989), p.376.

9.   Nyozekan, Recorded cassette, 'My autobiography: A life without history', a radio interview on 7 March 1963 for NHK Radio No.2.

10.   Barshay, Andrew, E., *State and Intellectual*, op.cit. p.128-9.

11.   Nyozekan, 'The English way of thinking', a discussion with Seki Yoshihiko in *Sekai no Meichō* ('Distinguished books in the world: Bentham and Mill'), Vol.38, Appendix 18, Feb.1967.

12.   Katherine Sansom in her *Sir George Sansom and Japan: A Memoir*, Tallahassee, 1972, recorded a visit by Nyozekan to the Sansoms in Suffolk. She refers to this as having taken place at the time of the Queen's coronation in 1953, but Nyozekan did not come to England for the Coronation in 1953. When he came in 1956 Sansom was in the USA. Nyozekan may well have met the Sansoms at Stanford University as there is evidence to suggest that a meeting between them had been arranged by Dr Kaji Shinzō whose letter to Matsumoto Shigeharu of International House reveals that, as Sansom had been misunderstanding Nyozekan, Kaji wanted to arrange a series of meetings between them to reach mutual understanding. Katherine Sansom (page 168) certainly seems to have recalled a visit to Suffolk as she wrote: 'He walked about the small town, talking with various inhabitants, one of whom particularly delighted him. This was a lad of about 12: he enquired of him, "Do you speak good English?" "No", said the urchin, elaborating the reply in his native Doric, the true unspoiled Suffolk dialect.'

13.   Nyozekan, 'Seeing England', series 1-5, August 1956, *Nishinihon Shimbun*; 'Upon my return from the West: after half a century's return to London', series 1-3, August 1956, *Kobe Shimbun*.

14.   Nyozekan, '*Eikoku-ga*' ('self-interest of England') in *Nihon oyobi Nihonjin*, (Tokyo,1918) p.234.

15.   Nyozekan, 'My view of England', in *Gendai Zuisō Zenshū* ('modern philosophy'), Vol.2, (Tokyo 11.28. 1949), p168.

16.   Nyozekan, 'Make ni Jyojiru' ('To avail oneself of being defeated') in *Bungei Shunjū*, (Tokyo 12.1.1945), later compiled in *Hasegawa Nyozekan Shū*, Vol.1, (Tokyo 1989) p.353.

17.   Nyozekan, 'From German Study to English Study', in *Nichijyōsei no naka naru Nihon* ('Japan in Ordinary Life'), (Tokyo, June 1969), p.55.

18.   Ienaga Saburō, 'Listening to the Okina, Hasegawa Nyozekan', from a note that was made soon after the meeting on 30 March 1951.

19.   Nyozekan, 'The English way of thinking', op.cit. p.12.

20.   Nyozekan, *Watashi no Rirekishō* ('My personal history'), (Tokyo 1962), p.208.

21.   Nyozekan, 'About Bertrand Russell' in *Albion*, June 1951, p.55. 57,62.

22.   Nyozekan, 'The English style Japanese mind' in 'About myself and someone else', in *Albion*, Sept. 1951. pp.18-20.

Chapter 40 MARTIN GORNALL **Dr Thomas Baty, 1869-1954: Legal Adviser to the Japanese Foreign Ministry, 1916-41**

1. Maruzen, Tokyo, 1959.
2. Queens College archive.
3. University College archive.
4. Inner Temple archive.
5. Stevens and Haynes, London, 1900.
6. With J. H. Morgan, pub. J. Murray, London, 1915.
7. Oxford, Clarendon, 1916.
8. Stevens and Haynes, London, 1914.
9. Joy Dixon: *Divine Feminine – Theosophy and Feminism in England*, Johns Hopkins University Press, 2001, especially pp 191-194.
10. Information from Conrad Jamieson of the Theosophical Society, Adyar.
11. George Bell & Sons, 1909.
12. Shidehara Kijūrō (1872-1951), career diplomat, was Councillor in London 1914, served as Vice Foreign Minister, 1915, Ambassador to US, 1912-22, and as Foreign Minister, 1924-27, and 1929-31. He became Prime Minister briefly from October 1945 to May 1946.
13. *Gaimushō 100 nen*, for which thanks to Ian Nish.
14. Letter to Bryce in the Bryce Papers at the Bodleian.
15. *Gaimushō 100 nen*.
16. Tachi Sakutarō – Professor of International Law, Tokyo Imperial University, 1904-32.
17. Apart from Dixon, sources include *Fantasy & Identity: The Double Life of a Victorian Sexual Radical*: Patai & Ingram, in *Rediscovering Forgotten Radicals: British Women Writers, 1889-1939*, Chapel Hill: University of North Carolina Press, 1993. Also *Sex is an Accident: Feminism, Science and the Radical Theory of Urania, 1915-40* by Alison Oram, in *Sexology in culture: labelling bodies and desires*, ed. Bland & Doan, Cambridge Polity Press, 1998.
18. *Alone*, p. 60.
19. E. Wilson, London, 1924.
20. For a Japanese perspective on Baty's role, see Shinya Murase, articles in *Gaikō Forum*, April-June, 2003 (Japanese editions). Also: *Thomas Baty in Japan: Seeing through the Twilight*, Shinya Murase, *British Yearbook of International Law*, 2003. I am grateful to Professor Murase for discussion and correspondence.
21. Robert Craigie: *Behind the Japanese Mask*, Hutchinson, 1945.
22. Ian Nish plots the power struggle between the *Gaimusho* and War Ministry in *Japanese foreign policy, 1869-1942: Kasumigaseki to Miyakezaka*, Routledge & Kegan Paul, 1977.
23. Ian Nish, *Japan's Struggle with Internationalism: Japan, China and the League of Nations, 1931-33*, Kegan Paul International, 1993, Chapter 10.
24. Yoshizawa Kenkichi (1874-1965), a career diplomat, who served in London, Peking and, as Ambassador, in Paris. He was Foreign Minister in the Inukai cabinet, 1932, and was elevated to the House of Peers.
25. Substantial quotations from *Draft Observations on the Lytton Report, October 12, 1932*, by Dr Thomas Baty, are given in 'Dr. Baty's Contributions

Reconsidered', p. (510) 44, by Masakuma Uchiyama, *Journal of International Law*, 1967 (My thanks to Izumi Tytler of the Bodleian Japanese Library for this and other Japanese articles). Identical text is to be found in the League of Nations version. Series VII. Political 1932. VII. 15 (Kindly supplied by Mr H. Takeuchi.)
26.   International Military Tribunal Far East transcript, Vol. 88, p. 35, p. 144, Bodleian Japanese Library.
27.   Shiratori Toshio (b. 1887), Chief of Information Bureau, Japanese Foreign Ministry, 1930-33. Ambassador to Italy 1939.
28.   *Japan's Observations*, Series VII. Political 1932. VII. 15, p. 157.
29.   Malcolm Kennedy (1895-1984), Reuters Correspondent in Japan, 1925-34, and author, among other books, of the controversial *The Problem of Japan*, 1935. Foreign Office (research, then intelligence) 1935-45. See portrait by Jon Pardoe in *Britain and Japan, 1859-1991: Themes and Personalities*, edited by Hugh Cortazzi and Gordon Daniels, Routledge, 1991.
30.   Referred to by Baty in *Alone in Japan* as 'Professor Medley'.
31.   Araki Sadao (1877-1966), a veteran of the Russo-Japanese War (1904) and Siberia (1918), was promoted to Lt. General in 1927. Leader of extreme nationalist *Kōdō-ha* (Imperial Way) faction and idolized by restless young officers. War Minister in Inukai Government, 1932.
32.   *International Military Tribunal Far East* transcript, Vol. 77, p. 13, p. 761, Bodleian Japanese Library.
33.   The Batys gave a farewell dinner party for Hugh and Joan Byas in 1941. Hugh Byas, correspondent for *The Times* (London) and *New York Times* in the 1930s, provided, in the title of his book *Government by Assassination* (1942), a catchphrase for the rise of militarism. Baty criticized this book for failing to distinguish the Japanese from their unpleasant leaders.
34.   F.S.G. Piggott, *Broken Thread: an autobiography*, Gale & Polden, 1950, p. 158.
35.   Probably Makino Nobuaki (b.1861), Foreign Minister 1913-14, who became Lord Keeper of the Privy Seal, and close adviser to Hirohito.
36.   Richard Ponsonby-Fane (1878-1937), scholar and Japanophile eccentric, was a close friend of Baty, with whom he shared an interest in Japanese culture and enlightened Aristocracy. See the portrait by Dorothy Britton, *Biographical Portraits*, vol. II, pp 190-204.
37.   My thanks to Lawrence Aspden, Curator of Special Collections and Library Archives, Sheffield University, for making these available to me.
38.   Sir Francis Lindley (1872-1950), British Ambassador, 1930-34. See Ian Nish's portraits in *Biographical Portraits*, vol. IV, pp. 89-100, and *British Envoys in Japan 1859-1972* (hereafter *'Envoys'*).
39.   Hayashi Gonsuke (b. 1861), lawyer, career diplomat, Ambassador to London 1920. Grand Master of Ceremonies, see biographical portrait by Harumi Goto-Shibata in this volume.
40.   Nagai Ryōtarō (b.1881), Vice Minister of Foreign Affairs. Later elected Minseitō Member of Parliament for Ishikawa-ken many times.
41.   Private Conversations with Marjorie Hué.
42.   Dmitrii Ivanovich Abrikossov (1876-1951) tried to coordinate disparate

White Russian forces in Vladivostok, and remained at the Russian Embassy until 15 February 1925, when Japan finally recognized the Bolshevik government.
43. *Revelations of a Russian Diplomat*; the memoirs of Dmitrii I. Abrikossow, ed. George Alexander Lensen, University of Washington Press, 1964.
44. Sir Charles Eliot (1862-1931), cigar-smoking scholar, diplomat and authority on Buddhism. British Ambassador to Japan 1919-26. See portrait by Dennis Smith in *Themes and Personalities* reproduced in *Envoys*.
45. Sir John Latham (1877-1964), Australian Deputy Prime Minister and Attorney General 1932-34. Leader of Australian Eastern Mission to Dutch East Indies, China & Japan, 1934. Chief Justice of Australia, 1935-52.
46. Sir Robert Craigie (1883-1959), British Ambassador to Japan, 1937-41. See portrait by Anthony Best, *Biographical Portraits* vol. I, ed. Nish, pp 238-251, reproduced in *Envoys*.
47. Oscar (later Sir Oscar) Morland (1904-80), a member of the Consular Service in pre-war Japan, was later appointed to the UK Liaison Mission to SCAP, and became Ambassador in Tokyo, 1959-63. See portrait by Sir John Whitehead in *Envoys*.
48. J. Murray.
49. Eric Partridge Ltd. at the Scholartis Press, 1934.
50. *American Society of International Law* Volume 30, 1936, pp 138-162.
51. Henry L. Stimson (1867-1950), American Secretary of State under Hoover, (1929-33), informed China and Japan that the US would not accept infringements of US treaty rights, or action contrary to the Pact of Paris – the 'Stimson Doctrine'.
52. Public Record Office: FO 371/22193.
53. W.J. Davies (1891-1975), 2nd Secretary, British Embassy, 1918-34, Consul Tokyo, 1934-7. Consul-General, Harbin 1939-41. Japanese Language Supervisor at the BBC 1946-50, and external examiner in Japanese, London University 1948-1951.
54. Sir George Sansom (1883-1965), scholar and diplomat, head of the Commercial Department, British Embassy in Tokyo 1923-40. During his post-war academic career in America, he wrote a three volume *History of Japan*, 1958-64. See portrait of Sansom by Gordon Daniels in *Themes and Personalities*, reproduced in *Envoys*.
55. Later British Ambassador in Bonn.
56. Sir Robert Craigie, *Behind the Japanese Mask*, Hutchinson & Co., 1945.
57. PRO: FO 371/35966.
58. W.E. (later Sir Eric) Beckett (1896-1966). 2nd Legal adviser to FO, 1929-45, Legal Adviser, 1945-53.
59. *The Question of Classification: 'Qualification' in Private International Law*, London, 1934
60. PRO: FO 369/3175. Thanks to Edgar Flacker for help in the early stages of my research.
61. Dermot MacDermot (1906-1989), after extensive Far Eastern experience in the Consular Service, was appointed to the UK Liaison Mission to SCAP. As Sir Dermot MacDermot, he later became Ambassador to Indonesia (1956-59), then

Thailand (1961-65). He succeeded his brother as 'The MacDermot' 1979.

62. PRO: FO 369/3549.

63. Henry Sawbridge (1907-90) saw consular service in Japan (2nd Secretary 1938), Korea and London. After serving as Consul-General Yokohama, 1949, and Geneva, 1953, he became Deputy Director, Centre of Japanese Studies, University of Sheffield, 1964-66.

64. Linton Harry Foulds (1897-1952), member of the Japan consular service before the Second World War, had occupied many Consular Service posts in the Far East in the Inter-War period. He became Minister Plenipotentiary to Manila (1946-51), but his life and career were cut short by illness.

65. Esler (later Sir Esler) Dening (1897-1977), was a pre-war member of the Japan consular service, became political adviser to Lord Mountbatten during the Second World War, was Assistant Under-Secretary of State, Foreign Office, 1946-50, appointed UK Representative to SCAP, 1950-51, and then, following the Treaty of San Francisco, Ambassador 1952-57. See portrait by Roger Buckley in *Themes and Personalities*, and *Envoys*.

66. John (later Sir John) Figgess (1909-77) was appointed to the Liaison Mission to SCAP in 1945, and served with the rank of Lt. Colonel as its Assistant Military Adviser from 1947-52. He was later Military Attaché to British Embassy, 1956-61, and Information Counsellor 1961-68. An expert on oriental ceramics, he became a director of Christie's. See portrait by Hugh Cortazzi, *Biographical Portraits*, vol. III.

67. Sir Alvary Gascoigne (1893-1970), UK Political Representative in UK Liaison Mission to SCAP, with rank of Ambassador, 1946-51. See portrait by Peter Lowe in *Biographical Portraits*, vol. I, and in *Envoys*.

68. PRO: FO 369/3550.

69. PRO: FO 369/3551.

70. Francis (later Sir Francis) Vallat (b. 1912), international jurist, Assistant Legal Adviser to the Foreign Office, 1945-50. He became legal adviser to the UK Delegation to the UN, 1950-54, Legal Adviser to the Foreign Office, 1960-68, and Professor of International Law at London University, 1970-76.

71. Telephone conversation with Sir Francis Vallat, 6 September 2003.

72. PRO: FO 369/3552.

73. Kishi Kuramatsu (b. 1878), career diplomat, was Consul General London, 1916, and served as private secretary to numerous figures, including Foreign Minister (1923), Prime Minister (1936), and Foreign Minister Ugaki (1938). He features in passing in Joseph Grew's *Ten Years in Japan*.

74. Family Archive.

75. Yoshida Shigeru (1878-1967), Japanese Prime Minister. Anglophile Ambassador to London (1936-1939), imprisoned by the Japanese in 1945, was Prime Minister for most of the period from May 1946 to 1954. See Ian Nish's portrait in *Biographical Portraits*, vol. II, pp. 233-244.

76. Ibid. 18 October, 1946.

77. PRO: FO 371/69827.

78. Edmund Blunden (1896-1974), poet and academic. During his second, post-war, stint in Japan (1948-50), Blunden was fêted as a charismatic figure in

austere times. He was Professor of Poetry at Oxford, 1966–68.
79.   Baty letters to Blunden, Harry Ransom Humanities Research Center, University of Texas, Austin.
80.   Tsutsui Kiyoshi (b. 1896) joined the Japanese Foreign Ministry in 1921. He served in a number of diplomatic roles in Belgium, Geneva, and Manchukuo, and became First Secretary in the Paris Embassy in 1938.
81.   Family Archive, and article from *Kasumigaseki-kai-kaiho*, supplied by Mr H. Takeuchi, Minister and Consul-General, Embassy of Japan, London.
82.   *Revelations of a Russian Diplomat*, p. 303.
83.   Information from John Chapman. Latham Papers MSS1009/Series 1/5865–72 of spring 1947 [Nat. Lib. in Canberra].
84.   Hugh Macmillan (1873–1952), jurist and officer of the International Law Association. His work as Lord of Appeal (1930–39 and 1941–47) included the case of William Joyce (Lord Haw- Haw).
85.   Family Archive.
86.   Ibid.
87.   Cabot Coville, Second Secretary under Ambassador Joseph Grew in the late 1930s, was an influential member, from 1942 to 1944, of the State Department 'think tank' on post-war Japan, to which he returned with SCAP, until 1950, when he became Consul General in Nova Scotia.
88.   Family Archive.
89.   Maruzen, 1954.
90.   Kindly supplied by Shinya Murase, Professor of International Law, Sophia University, Tokyo.
91.   *Evening Standard, Daily Mail.*

Chapter 41 A. HAMISH ION **Samuel Heaslett, 1875–1947: Missionary and Bishop**

1.   For a brief biographical note on Samuel Heaslett see *Nihon Kirisutokyō rekishi dai jiten henshū iinkai, Nihon Kirisutokyō rekishi dai jiten* (Tokyo: Kyōbunkan, 1988) [hereafter cited *NKRDJ*], 1260; *Nippon Seikōkai rekishi henshū iinkai hen, Akashibitotachi: Nippon Seikōkai jinbutsu shi* (Tokyo: Nippon Seikōkai Shuppan Jigyōbu, 1975), 130–132. The standard historical survey of the Nippon Seikōkai remains *Nippon Seikōkai rekishi hensan iinkai, Nippon Seikōkai hyakunen shi* (Tokyo: Nippon Seikōkai Kyōmuin Bunsho Kenkyūjo, 1959); a useful short survey is Ōe Shindō, 'Nippon Seikōkai shi', in *Dōshisha Daigaku Jinbun Kagaku Kenkyūjo hen, Nihon Purotesutanto sho kyōkai no kenkyū* (Tokyo: Kyōbunkan, 1997), 17–73. For a survey of British missionary work in Japan, Korea and Taiwan, see A. Hamish Ion, *The Cross and the Rising Sun, Volume 2: The British Missionary Movement in Japan, Korea and Taiwan, 1865-1945* (Waterloo: Wilfrid Laurier University Press, 1993). For a brief survey of Japanese Christianity during the first part of the 20th century, see A. Hamish Ion, 'The Cross Under an Imperial Sun: Imperialism, Nationalism, and Japanese Christianity, 1895-1945,' in Mark R. Mullins, ed., *Handbook of Christianity in Japan* (Leiden: Brill, 2003), 69–100.
2.   See *Holy Bible*, King James version, 1 Kings, chapter 19, verses 11–12.
3.   The Japanese litany prayed for deliverance from those four things. See

Samuel Heaslett, *From a Japanese Prison* (London: Student Christian Molvement Press, 1943), biographical note on Bishop Heaslett, 6.

4. Ibid.

5. The NSKK was formed in 1887 and supported by the American Church Mission (the Japan Mission of the Protestant Episcopal Church of the United States), and the two British Anglican missionary societies, the SPG and CMS, and later by the Japan Mission of the Anglican Church in Canada. In 1937 the NSKK had approximately 46,000 Japanese members on its rolls, 255 ordained clergy and 262 churches. See Church Missionary Society Archive, Section I: East Asia Missions, Part 3: Japan Mission covering 1916-1934; The Japan Mission, 1935-1949; East Asia General – Japan and China, 1935-1949 microfilm (hereafter cited CMSA), reel 52: 4 May 1938, news release 19th General Synod of the Nippon Seikokwai (Holy Catholic Church of Japan).

6. During these years Heaslett faced personal tragedy and difficulties for his wife died in 1936. At the same time, his own health was not good for he had begun to suffer from heart problems in the form of twinges of angina pectoris and also to have trouble with his eyes.

7. Piggott made the observation about Heaslett's after-dinner speaking skills, and C. K. Sansbury, who had been chaplain at the British Embassy, Tokyo in the late 1930s made mention of Heaslett's humour in his tribute to Heaslett, *Times*, 21 October 1947.

8. Introduction by The Archbishop of Canterbury in *From a Japanese Prison*, 7-8.

9. Piggott had been the Chairman of the Church Council of the English Congregation of St Andrew's Church, Shiba between 1936 and 1939. Sir Robert Craigie, the British Ambassador, and E. D'Arcy McGreer, the Canadian Chargé d'Affaires, served as trustees. St Andrew's was the church of the British community in Tokyo, and was situated in St Andrew's mission compound where Heaslett had his residence. See C. Kenneth Sansbury, *St. Andrew's Church, Tokyo (English Congregation) 1879-1939* (Tokyo: St. Andrew's Church, 1939), 58.

10. *Times*, 27 October 1947.

11. The NSKK had been established as an independent church in 1887 by the Japan missions of two British Anglican missionary societies, the CMS and SPG and the American Church Mission (the Protestant Episcopal Church of the United States). Later, these three missions were joined by the Canadian Anglican Church in supporting and developing the NSKK.

12. LPL, Lang Papers, vol. 6: China: flyer, 'Japan's War on Civilians National Protest Meeting'.

13. S. Heaslett , 'A Personal Note' (appended to 'The Crisis in the Churches in Japan: notes on the Seikokwai: August 1940') quoted in Gordon Hewitt, *The Problems of Success: A History of the Church Missionary Society, 1910-1942* (London: SCM Press Ltd., 1977), 2 vols., Volume 2: *Asia: Overseas Partners*, 325-326.

14. Lambeth Palace Library (hereafter cited LPL), Archbishop Cosmo Gordon Lang Papers, vol. 183, Heaslett to Lang, 7 October 1940.

15. Tsukada Osamu, *Nippon Seikōkai no keisei to kadai*.

16. United Society for the Propagation of the Gospel in Foreign Parts Archives (hereafter cited as USPGA), USPGA Series E Annual Reports Japan Individual

1921, W. F. France, Tokyo, June 1921. When the USPGA Archives were consulted they were located in Tufton Street, Westminster, subsequently they have been moved to the Rhodes Library, Oxford.
17. USPGA Series E Annual Reports Japan Individual 1922, W. F. France, Tokyo, August 1922.
18. *C.M.S. Japan Christian Quarterly*, March 1922, 1.
19. 'The Contribution of the Home Church to Missionary Problems and Policies in Japan,' in *Guild of St. Paul Magazine*, July 1922, 6-28, 22. The Guild of St Paul in England was a support group for the diocese of South Tokyo.
20. For a brief biographical note on John McKim (1852-1936), see *NKFDJ*, 1311. McKim was the bishop of North Tokyo, and was the Presiding Bishop of the NSKK from 1896-1935.
21. USPGA Series E Annual Reports Japan Individual 1922, L.B. Cholmondeley to bishop King, 25 October 1922.
22. For a brief biographical note on Motoda Sakunoshin (1862-1928), see *NKRDJ*, 1403.
23. For a brief biographical note on Naide Yasutarō (1866-1945), see *NKRDJ*, 970.
24. CMSA, reel 46: Heaslett to Manley, 8 June 1923.
25. Audrey Henty was niece of the famous author and a long-time CMS evangelistic and educational missionary.
26. *C.M.S. Japan Christian Quarterly*, March 1925, 6.
27. Ibid.
28. Ibid.
29. For a short biographical note on Hugh James Foss (1848-1932) see *NKRDJ*, 1194. Foss had first come to Japan in 1876 and only retired in 1922.
30. LPL, Archbishop Randall Thomas Davidson Papers, vol. 393, Japan 1910-1924. Kelly to Davidson, 4 August 1923.
31. CMSA, reel 46: Painter to Lankester, n.d., received 10 September 1923.
32. Ibid., Batchelor to Lankester, 10 February 1924.
33. Ibid., Heaslett to Archbishop of Canterbury, 20 March 1924.
34. For a short biographical note on Gordon Walsh (1880-1972), see *NKRDJ*, 168.
35. CMSA, reel 46: Heaslett, 'Preliminary Report of the losses and damages to the Church in the diocese of South Tokyo by the earthquake and fires of Sept 1st to 3rd September 1923.
36. Ibid., Moule to Hayward, 16 February 1924.
37. LPL, Davidson Papers, vol. 394, Japan 1924-1926. R.D. M. Shaw Memorandum on Japan, June 1924.
38. Ibid., Davidson to Knight, 19 November 1924; clipping from *Morning Post*, 24 November 1924.
39. Heaslett to Clive, 2 August 1936, enclosed in Clive to Orde, 7 August 1936, FO 371/20291.
40. Ibid., Clive to Orde.
41. J. Thyne Henderson minute on Clive to Orde, 7 August 1936, FO 371/20291.

42. Cosmo Gordon Lang was educated at Glasgow University and Balliol College, Oxford. Before deciding to take Holy Orders, he had read for the Bar. Lang became bishop of Stepney in 1901, archbishop of York in 1908, and archbishop of Canterbury in 1928.

43. See Hamish Ion, 'For the Truimph of the Cross: A Survey of the British Missionary Movement in Japan, 1869-1945,' in Gordon Daniels and Chushichi Tsuzuki, *The History of Anglo-Japanese Relations 1600-2000: Volume 5 Social and Cultural Perspectives* (Houndmills, Basingstoke, Hampshire: Palgrave Macmillan, 2002), 77-102, 91.

44. LPL, Lang Papers, vol. 6: China, Lang to Dawson, 5 October 1937.

45. Ibid., Memorandum of Meeting with the Prime Minister, October 1937.

46. *Japan Advertiser*, 6 October 1937.

47. The speakers included Lord Lytton, Herbert Morrison, Lady Violet Bonham-Carter, Rev. Sidney Berry who was the secretary of the Congregational Union of England and Professor Chang Peng-Chun, a professor of Philosophy and Education at Nankai University, Tientsin who was reputedly the first Chinaman to reach England from the War area.

48. Ibid. flyer, 'Japan's War on Civilians National Protest Meeting'.

49. *Japan Advertiser*, 7 October 1937.

50. Ibid.

51. LPL, Lang Papers, vol. 6: China, Lang to Yoshida, 4 October 1937.

52. Ibid.

53. *Japan Advertiser*, 19 October 1937.

54. Ibid., 13 October 1937.

55. Ibid., 17 October 1937.

56. Ibid., 16 October 1937.

57. Ibid., 19 October 1937.

58. Ibid., Lang to Barry, 16 October 1937. as Lang made it clear to Gerald Barry, the editor of the *News Chronicle*, which sponsored the protest meeting, that he believed the meeting 'was a most impressive gathering and I was very glad to have the opportunity of being present'.

59. LPL, Lang Papers, vol. 6: China, Lang to Heaslett, 27 October 1937.

60. Ibid.

61. Ibid., Lang to Heaslett, 4 November 1937.

62. CMSA, reel 52, Hutchinson to Barclay, 10 November 1937.

63. CMSA., reel 52, Mann to Barclay, 15 October 1937.

64. See LPL, Lang Papers, vol. 6: China, Chapman (The British Association of Japan) to Lang, 27 October 1937. The British Association was concerned that protests and condemnations of Japan would have the opposite effect to what Lang and other condemners wanted. Needless to say, such protest would damage trade.

65. LPL, Lang Papers, vol. 6: China, Heaslett to Lang, 14 1937, enclosure: Note from Pres. Bhp. N.S.K.K. on agitation in Japan over Archbishop's action in taking the Chair at an Albert Hall meeting.

66. Ibid.

67. USPGA, Letters Received 1937, Heaslett to France, 15 October 1937.

68. USPGA, Letters Received 1938, Sansbury Circular Letter no. 1, 7 October

1938.
69.   LPL, Lang Papers, vol. 6: China, Heaslett to Lang, 14 1937, enclosure: Note from Pres. Bhp. N.S.K.K. on agitation in Japan over Archbishop's action in taking the Chair at an Albert Hall meeting.
70.   CMSA, reel 52, Heaslett to Barclay, 14 March 1938.
71.   CMSA, reel 52, Paul Rusch, 4 May 1938, news release: 19th General Synod of the Nippon Seikokwai (Holy Catholic Church of Japan).
72.   USPGA, Letters Received 1938, Bishop's Meeting 24, 25 March 1938.
73.   Archibald Hutchinson and his brother Ernest also a CMS missionary in Japan were born in Nagasaki and Fukuoka respectively and were sons of Arthur Blockey Hutchinson, a CMS missionary in Kyūshū from 1882 to 1918. Canon Hutchinson did not relish the fact that he was going to be the only foreigner in the Synod besides the bishops. See CMSA, reel 52: Extract from Letter from Canon Hutchinson, dated 12th April.
74.   CMSA, reel 52, Heaslett to Barclay, 24 April 1938, enclosure: The Bishop's meeting of March 24th and 25th.
75.   LPL, Lang Papers, vol. 6: China, Lang to Edward (Earl of Listowel) 31 May 1938.
76.   CMSA, reel 52, France to Barclay, 25 June 1941, enclosure: Report on 20th General Synod of the Nippon Seikokwai.

Chapter 42 RICHARD BOWEN **Pioneers in bringing Jūjutsu (Jūdō) to Britain: Edward William Barton Wright, Tani Yukio and Ernest John Harrison**

1.   *Transactions and Proceedings of the Japan Society of London*: 29 April 1892.
2.   *Annual Register*: 1885: The Japanese Village, Knightsbridge. *Illustrated London News*: 21 February 1885: The Japanese Village, Knightsbridge. *The Referee*: 15 February 1885: Advertisement for the Japanese Village, Knightsbridge. *The Times*: 10 January 1885: The Japanese Village, Knightsbridge.
3.   *Health and Strength Magazine*: December 1901: volume 3, number 6.
4.   *The Complete Sherlock Holmes*: Penguin Books (and many others): the Reichenbach Falls.
5.   *Illustrated Sporting and Dramatic News*: 18 March 1899: display at the Bath Club.
6.   *The Times*: 18 October 1900: Barton Wright's bicycle accident. *Health and Strength Magazine*: December 1901: volume 3, number 6: his fight.
7.   *Quarterly Ecclesiastical and Lay Records of Baptisms, Marriages, and Burials under the Archdeaconry of Madras*: British Library: Oriental and Indian Collection: Barton Wright's baptism. *Madras Almanac*: Asylum Press Almanac: 1860: Barton Wright's birth: years 1866 and 1874 contains further information on his father.
8.   *Health and Strength Magazine*: December 1901: volume 3, number 6: education.
9.   *The Japan Directory*: 1895,1896,1897: Yokohama Kaikō Shiryōkan Library: Barton Wright at E.H. Hunter and Company: information from Oba Sadao, and Laszlo Abel (Australian Embassy, Tokyo). *Tales of the Foreign Settlements in Japan*: 1958: Williams, Harold Stennett: E.H. Hunter and Company:

10. Public Record Office: *Index of Registered Companies*: (PRO) BT 37. 8230/ 59684: Barton Wright's first company – 'Bartitsu Limited'

11. *Health and Strength Magazine*: December 1901: volume 3, number 6: description of the premises at Shaftesbury Avenue.

12. Public Record Office: *Index of Companies Registered*: (PRO) BT 37. 8230/ 59684: dissolution of Barton Wright's first company – 'Bartitsu Limited'.

13. Public Record Office: (PRO) BT 26. 163: Incoming passenger lists, noting the arrival of Yukio Tani and K.Tani on 26 September 1900: what the 'K' stands for is unknown. Ibid: the arrival of S. Yamamoto in October 1900.

14. *Transactions and Proceedings of the Japan Society of London*: volume 5: 1898– 1901: Barton Wright's lecture on 13 February 1901: page 99.

15. Conversation with Tani's daughter, Mrs Moya Ward: death of K. Tani in the Great Earthquake.

16. Theatre Museum, Covent Gardens: programme for the Tivoli Music Hall: Bartitsu on stage, September 1901.

17. Public Record Office: *Index of Companies Registered*: (PRO) BT 31. 11427/ 87817: Barton Wright's second company – 'Bartitsu Light Cure Institute Limited'. Incorporated 3 March 1906.

18. 1 Albemarle Street (corner with Piccadilly): formerly the Hotel Albemarle, a top hotel: and before that Gordon's Hotel where Nelson used to stay.

19. Public Record Office: *Index of Companies Registered*: (PRO) BT 31. 11427/ 87817: Prospectus for Barton Wright's second company.

20. Ibid: winding up proceedings for Barton Wright's second company.

21. *Electoral Rolls for Kingston*: 1939: Local History Records, Kingston.

22. *Budokwai Bulletin*: July 1950: Published by the Budokwai: Koizumi's interview of Barton Wright.

23. Ibid: April 1951 issue: Barton Wright at the Royal Albert Hall. Ibid: October 1951 issue: Barton Wright's death. *Evening Standard*: 13-14 September 1951: Barton Wright's death. General Register Office: *Certified Copy of an Entry of Death – Edward William Barton Wright on 13th September 1951*. Records of Interment: Kingston upon Thames Cemetery, Bonner Hill Road, Kingston, Surrey: under Wright, E.W.

24. *Apollo's Magazine of Strength, Skill and Sport: edited by R.P. Watson, London, 1903-c.1908. Jujitsu – What It Really Is*: Bankier (also Banquier), William: published by *Apollo's Magazine of Strength, Skill and Sport*: 1905. *The Era*: 16 November 1901: Apollo's performance at the Oxford Music Hall. *History of the Grand Order of Water Rats 1889-1947*: Russell, Fred: Bankier was King Rat (Chairman) twice.

25. *Sandow's Magazine of Physical Culture and British Sport*: 16 March 1905: volume 14: Uyenishi's Golden Square School. *Apollo's Magazine of Strength, Skill and Sport*: February 1904: a visit to Uyenishi's Golden Square School (opened circa October 1903). *Chamber's Journal of Popular Literature, Science and Arts*: volume 10: 19 October 1906: Chambers, Wm and Rob: 'The Gentle Art of Ju-Ju-tsu': description of Golden Square School.

26. Tani's methods used to finish off his challengers: culled from many reports of the time.

27. *Sandow's Magazine of Physical Culture and British Sport*: 8 June 1905: list of Tani's opponents over a typical week.

28. *Jujitsu – What It Really Is*: Bankier (also Banquier), William: published by *Apollo's Magazine of Strength, Skill and Sport*: 1905. the Fournier match.

29. *The Athlete*: March 1906: the Chemiakin match.

30. Ibid: the Marc Gaucher match.

31. *Health and Strength Magazine*: 26 December 1908: the match with Young Joseph, the boxer.

32. *Sandow's Magazine of Physical Culture and British Sport*: 1904: the Tani versus Mellor match under Catch rules. *Health and Strength Magazine*: 5 May 1904: the Tani versus Mellor match under Catch rules. There are many other accounts of this match.

33. *Jujitsu – What It Really Is*: Bankier (also Banquier), William: published by *Apollo's Magazine of Strength, Skill and Sport*: 1905: Apollo's first contact and bout with Tani.

34. *Worthwhile Journey*: Diggellen, Tromp van: Heinemann 1955: his bout with Tani.

35. *Jujitsu – What It Really Is*: Bankier (also Banquier), William: published by *Apollo's Magazine of Strength, Skill and Sport*: 1905: February 1905 'The Defeat of Yukio Tani' which took place on 23 December 1904. Graham Noble letter of 6 June 1997 containing then unpublished article on Tani and Miyake and others. There are many accounts of this match.

36. *Sandow's Magazine of Physical Culture and British Sport*: 16 February 1905: display at Chelsea Barracks: general display by Miyake, Tani, Eida, and Kanaya: then Tani and Miyake took on the largest Guardsmen available, 'The Guardsmen seemed as little children in the hands of the professors, who threw them about the stage almost at will, but taken care to soften the falls.' Note that it was Tani and Miyake who took on the Guardsmen, they had the ability unlike the other two Japanese.

37. *The Athlete*: November 1905: display at Regent's Street Polytechnic.

38. *The Game of Ju-Jitsu – For the Use of Schools and Colleges*: Miyake, Taro, and Tani, Yukio: edited by M.A. Grainger and L.F. Giblin: published by Hazell Watson and Viney Limited, 1906.

39. *Health and Strength*: 3 September 1953: on E. Desbonnet 1868-1953 who died at the age of 85: Chevalier of the Legion of Honour, Grand Medaille d'Or de Hygiene. *Les Secrets du Jiu Jitsu*: Regnier (Re-Nie), Ernest, and de Montgailhard, Guy: Paul Peclot and Cie, Paris, 1906. *Le Judo: Son Histoire ses Succes*: Brousse, Michel: Editions Liber, Suisse, 1996: early days in France. *Judo – A Sport and a Way of Life*: Brousse, Michel, and Matsumoto, David: International Judo Federation, 1999. early days. *Le Defense dans la Rue*: Renaud, Jean Joseph: 1912: he writes that he studied at the Miyake and Tani school in Oxford Street for two summers running, for three months each summer, every day and sometime twice a day.

40. *Sandow's Magazine of Physical Culture and British Sport*: 9 and 30 November 1905: jujutsu versus la savate in Paris: Regnier (Re-Nie) and Dubois.

41. Ibid: 7 December 1905: the Higashi Tani fight in Paris on 30 November

1905. *T.P's Weekly Magazine*: 15 December 1905: the Higashi Tani fight in Paris: reported in the 'Savior-Faire Papers: Getting Out of the Groove' by Arnold Bennett. *Health and Strength Magazine*: January 1905: the Higashi Tani fight in Paris *The Athlete Magazine*: January 1906: the Higashi Tani fight in Paris.
42. *Britain and Japan: Biographical Portraits*: volume 4: chapter on Koizumi, Gunji, founder of the Budokwai: information on that organization.
43. Tani's earnings: Apollo, who had joined the Budokwai, told T.P. Leggett, who in turn told the writer.
44. Boat trips with supper: in conversation with Leggett.
45. Tray with sovereigns: conversation with Moya Ward, Tani's daughter, in 1995.
46. *Health and Strength Magazine*: 4 September 1926: article by W.A. Pullum. *Certified Copy of Death Certificate*: Yukio Tani died 24 January 1950, in St. Charles Hospital, aged 69, of 37 Clarendon Road, Kensington.
47. *Certified Copy of an Entry of Birth*: 22 August 1873: Ernest John: Father John Harrison, Post Office Clerk: Mother Mary Ann Harrison, formerly Phillips, of 13 Grenville Street, Moss Side: Registration District – Chorlton, Sub-District – Hulme, County of Lancashire.
48. *Harrison Family Tree*: in the possession of his daughter, Mrs Aldona Collins.
49. *Aikido Journal*: volume 26, No.1, 1999: 'A Resume of My Checkered Career' by E.J.Harrison. Autobiographical Notes by E.J. Harrison: in the possession of his daughter.
50. Ibid: Vancouver: Naniamo, etc.
51. Ibid: arrival in Japan.
52. *The Eastern World, A Weekly Journal for Law, Commerce, Politics, Literature and Useful Information*: volume 7, No.314: 4 February 1899: Wright's Hotel.
53. *Daily Province (British Columbia)*: 6 February 1902: citing *Japan Daily Advertiser*.
54. *Aikido Journal*: volume 26, No.1, 1999: 'A Resume of My Checkered Career' by E.J.Harrison. Autobiographical Notes by E.J. Harrison: in the possession of his daughter
55. Ibid: free jūdō lessons.
56. Ibid: the Cossack Silinski.
57. Jūdō Grades: the lower grades are known as *Kyū* grades; the upper grades, who wear a black belt, start at 1st *Dan* (*Shodan*), 2nd *Dan* (*Nidan*), 3rd *Dan* (*Sandan*), and so on up to 10th *Dan*: currently there are no 10th *Dan*: the fighting grades cease at 5th or 6th *dan*, thereafter promotions are on teaching ability and experience.
58. Jūdō Grades of Weed, Harrison, Steers, and the Russian Oshchepkov, are from Kodokan records. Both Harrison and Steers were later members of the Budokwai.
59. *Aikido Journal*: volume 26, No.1, 1999: 'A Resume of My Checkered Career' by E.J.Harrison: in Korea. Autobiographical Notes by E.J. Harrison: in the possession of his daughter: in Korea.
60. *Peace or War East of Baikal*: Harrison, E.J: Kelly and Walsh of Yokohama, 1910.

61. Various documents concerned with the marriage and divorce in the possession of his daughter: mostly in Japanese, with certified translations, as the marriage and divorce were under Japanese law.

62. *The Journal of Asian Martial Arts*: volume 8, No.2, 1999: published by Via Media Publishers, USA: 'The Development of Sambo in Europe and America.' much information about Oshchepkov.

63. *The Passing of the Romanovs*: Harrison, E.J: a very large unpublished manuscript, dated August 1917, Tokyo: in the possession of his daughter: the Imperial War Museum, Department of Documents, possess another copy manuscript, laminated and bound into a handsome volume, running to four hundred pages. *Muscovite Trails*: Harrison, E.J: an unpublished manuscript of about three hundred pages: in his daughter's possession.

64. Ibid: Rasputin, etc.

65. A handwritten one hundred and thirty-two page diary of his time in the Chinese Labour Corps: from China to France: Harrison was in a camp which contained five thousand: the total number of Chinese was about a hundred thousand: the diary is in the possession of his daughter.

66. *The Passing of the Romanovs*: Harrison, E.J: his experiences in Archangel.

67. Ibid: the poem about the Shackleton Boots: the Imperial War Museum's branch at Duxford, Cambridgeshire, possess actual boots.

68. *Britain and Japan: Biographical Portraits*: volume 4: chapter on Koizumi, Gunji, founder of the Budokwai: information on that organization.

69. *Muscovite Trails*: Harrison, E.J: an unpublished manuscript of about three hundred pages: in his daughter's possession.

70. Harrison's second marriage to Irene Scott Oldfield, a classical singer: their daughter has the Lithuanian name of Aldona.

71. Books: the catalogue of the British Library list thirty-seven work by Harrison: some would be re-issues: his earliest books were *Peace or War East of Baikal*, 1910, and the classic *The Fighting Spirit of Japan*, 1913: he produced several in the 1920s: and in the period 1950 to 1960 some thirteen mostly on jūdō, some being translations from Japanese and French.

72. *The Wandering Years*: Martyn, Weston: Blackwood 1940: Harrison's brawl with several sailors in Blood Town, Yokohama, in April 1911.

73. A collection of his letters in the possession of his daughter.

74. *Social Currents in Japan: With Special Reference to the Press*: Wildes, Professor H.E: 1927: footnote referring to Harrison.

The statistics of the Japanese in their most active years were:

	Height:	Weight:
Tani:	five feet three inches	nine stone three pounds (129 lbs)
Uyenishi:	five feet five inches	nine stone six pounds (132 lbs)
Miyake:	five feet seven inches	eleven stone seven pounds (161 lbs)

Barton Wright is described as slimly built and five feet seven or eight inches in height.

Chapter 43 NOBORU KOYAMA Yoshimoto Tadasu, 1878–1973: 'Father of the Blind in Japan'

1. Yoshimoto Tadasu, *Shu wa waga hikari*, Tokyo, Ōzorasha, 1997. p.5

2. Honma Kazuo, *Waga jinsei 'Nihon Tenji Toshokan'*, Tokyo, Nihon Tosho Sentā, 2001, pp.82–83.

3. Yoshimoto Tadasu, *Shin no Eikoku*, Tokyo, Genbunsha, 1902.

4. Kumagai Tetsutarō, *Hakumei no kioku : mōjin bokushi no hansei*, Tokyo, Ōzorasha, 1997. p.172. Kumagai was probably the first blind priest in Japan. With Yoshimoto's financial help, he was able to study at Kansei Gakuin University between 1913 and 1916.

5. Yoshimoto Tadasu, *Jūjika o tate ni shite: Kyūritsubō kaikoroku*, Osaka, Nichiyō Sekaisha, 1934. p.109.

6. Suzuki Rikiji, *Nakamura Kyōtarō den: Nihon mōjin no chichi*, Tokyo, Nakamura Kyōtarō Denki Kankōkai, 1969. pp.83–84.

7. Yoshimoto Tadasu, *Eikokujin to Kirisutokyō*, Tokyo, Shinkyō Shuppansha, 1948. p.147.

8. Uchimura Kanzō, *Uchimura Kanzō chosakushū*, vol. 20, Tokyo, Iwanami Shoten, 1955. p.256.

9. Suzuki Rikiji, *Nakamura Kyōtarō den: Nihon mōjin no chichi*, Tokyo, Nakamura Kyōtarō Denki Kankōkai, 1969. pp.83; Yoshimoto Tadasu, *Eikokujin to Kirisutokyō*, Tokyo, Shinkyō Shuppansha, 1948. p.147.

10. Yoshimoto Tadasu, *Jūjika o tate ni shite: Kyūritsubō kaikoroku*, Osaka, Nichiyō Sekaisha, 1934. p.3.

11. Ibid., p.3.

12. Yoshimoto Tadasu, *Shu wa waga hikari*, Tokyo, Ōzorasha, 1997. p.176.

13. Suzuki Rikiji, *Nakamura Kyōtarō den: Nihon mōjin no chichi*, Tokyo, Nakamura Kyōtarō Denki Kankōkai, 1969. p.83.

14. *Kelly's directory of Berkshire, Bucks and Oxon*, London, Kelly's Directories, 1911. p.255.

15. *Kelly's directory of Berkshire, Bucks and Oxon*, London, Kelly's Directories, 1915. p.252.

16. *Kelly's directory of Berkshire, Buckinghamshire and Oxfordshire*, London, Kelly's Directories, 1920. p.247.

17. *Kelly's directory of Berkshire, Buckinghamshire and Oxfordshire*, London, Kelly's Directories, 1924. p.255.

18. Takakura Tokutarō, *Jidenteki bunshō, kikō, sonota*, Tokyo, Takakura Zenshū Kankōkai, 1936. pp.23–36.

19. Tadasu Yoshimoto, *A peasant sage of Japan: the life and work of Sontoku Ninomiya; translated from the Hōtokuki*, London, Longmans, Greens and Co., 1912. preface.

20. Birth certificate (David Tadasu Yoshimoto).

21. Birth certificate (John Misao Yoshimoto).

22. Birth certificate (Mary Eva Yoshimoto).

23. Mary Eva Yoshimoto's letter of 24 January 2003 to the author.

24. Ibid.

25. Tadasu Yoshimoto, *Who is my neighbour?*, [n.a], [Tadasu Yoshimoto],

[1967], pp.3-16.; Yoshimoto Tadasu, *Jūjika o tate ni shite: Kyūritsubō kaikoroku*, Osaka, Nichiyō Sekaisha, 1934. pp.1-18; Yoshimoto Tadasu, *Shu wa waga hikari*, Tokyo, Ōzorasha, 1997. pp21-39.

26. Yoshimoto Tadasu, *Shu wa waga hikari*, Tokyo, Ōzorasha, 1997. pp.190-192.

27. Suzuki Rikiji, *Nakamura Kyōtarō den: Nihon mōjin no chichi*, Tokyo, Nakamura Kyōtarō Denki Kankōkai, 1969. pp.101-111.

28. *The hundred and twenty-fourth report of the British and Foreign Bible Society for the year ending March 1928*, London, British and Foreign Bible Society, 1929. pp.148-149; Yoshimoto Tadasu, *Shu wa waga hikari*, Tokyo, Ōzorasha, 1997. p.197-200.

29. Yoshimoto Tadasu, *Sokoku ni kisu: Eikoku no tamashii*, Tokyo, Chuō Kyōka Dantai Rengōkai, 1931.

30. Yoshimoto Tadasu, *Jūjika o tate ni shite: Kyūritsubō kaikoroku*, Osaka, Nichiyō Sekaisha, 1934.

31. Yoshimoto Tadasu, *Eikokujin to Kirisutokyō*, Tokyo, Shinkyō Shuppansha, 1948. p.145.

32. Yoshimoto Tadasu, *Eikokujin to Kirisutokyō*, Tokyo, Shinkyō Shuppansha, 1948.

33. Suzuki Rikiji, *Nakamura Kyōtarō den: Nihon mōjin no chichi*, Tokyo, Nakamura Kyōtarō Denki Kankōkai, 1969. pp.217-219.

34. Tadasu Yoshimoto, *Who is my neighbour?*, [n.a], [Tadasu Yoshimoto], [1967].

35. Yoshimoto Tadasu, *Waga rinjin towa dare ka*, Tokyo, Taishindō, 1967.

36. Death certificate (Tadasu Yoshimoto).

37. Yoshimoto Tadasu, *Shu wa waga hikari*, Tokyo, Ōzorasha, 1997. pp.208-209.

38. Death certificate (Elsie Margaret Yoshimoto).

39. Mary Eva Yoshimoto's letter of 14 January 2003 to the author.

40. Ibid.

41. Ibid.

Appendix 1(a) LEN HARROP **The British Commonwealth War Cemetery at Yokohama**

1. In Japanese *Eirenpō Senshisha Bochi*.

2. Editor's note: Lt Colonel Len Harrop MBE joined the Territorial Army in 1938 and served with the 51st Highland Division in Normandy in the battle for Caen in July 1944. He returned to France in September that year to join the Army Graves Service and became an Assistant Director of Graves (ADGRRAE) Western Europe when he was transferred to a similar post at HQ Far East Land Forces (FARELF) in Singapore. He left the army to join the ANZAC agaency of the Commonwealth War Graves Commission as a District Inspector for the Pacific Area, becoming a supervisor for Japan after the signing of the Peace Treaty. Since he became supervisor for the Hodogaya cemetery he has devoted himself to the building and upkeep of the cemetery. Its beauty, with its landscaped gardens and wealth of plants, is largely due to his energy and skill.

3. The United Kingdom POW death rates for 1939-1945 war provide some interesting comparisons. The numbers reported captured by Germany and Italy

came to 142,319, of which 7,310 were killed or died in captivity, giving a death rate of 5%. The number of 'missing', those casualties whose remains were never recovered, was also very low. The treatment of prisoners was very reasonable, no doubt because just under a million German and Italian POWs were in Allied hands. Similar figures for the Far East tell quite a different story. The total number of UK forces captured by Japan was 50,016. Of these 12,433 were either killed or died in captivity, and 17,535 were killed or died elsewhere, 6,252 were 'missing', and 16,529 wounded; thus giving the UK a death rate of 25%.

4.   However, a solitary Japanese aircraft bombed the group flagship *King George V* at 11.20 hrs and was shot down. Later, a radar picket reported a large number of unidentified aircraft offshore, which, on investigation turned out to be Japanese aircraft circling without any obvious offensive intent. One by one they peeled off, diving into the sea. It was learned later that these were *kamikaze* pilots, who, having had funeral services read over them, believed themselves to be officially dead and so could not surrender. The *kamikaze* sorties were the brainchild of Vice Admiral Onishi Takijirō, who commanded the Navy's air arm in the Philippines. He, too, ceremoniously killed himself at midnight, taking long to die.

5.   As Shakespeare has it after Agincourt:
    may wander o'er this bloody field to book our dead, and then to bury them . . . And give them burial as becomes their worth.

6.   It said in part: 'Parties to the conflict shall record as soon as possible, in regard of each wounded, sick or dead person of the adverse Party falling into their hands, and particulars which may assist in their identification and furnish through the same bureau certificates of death or duly authenticated lists of the dead. One half of a double identity disc, last wills and other documents of importance to the next-of-kin, money, and in general all articles of intrinsic or sentimental value shall be sent in sealed packets – and the dead be honourably interred, if possible, according to the rites of the religion to which they belonged.

7.   The signatories were:

For the Government of Japan: Mamoru Shigemitsu
                    (Japanese Foreign Minister)
For the Government of the United Kingdom of Great Britain and Northern
    Ireland: Esler Dening (British Ambassador)
For the Government of Canada: T. C. Davis
For the Government of Australia: A. B. Jamieson
For the Government of New Zealand: R. L. G. Challis
For the Government of the Union of South Africa:
                    Esler Dening
For the Government of India: B. R. Sen
For the Government of Pakistan: O. H. Malik

8.   Recently a pair of volunteers, Mrs Yoshiko Tamura and Mrs Taeko Sasamoto, with the support of the newly formed Prisoner of War Research Network in Japan, have committed themselves to the enormous task of researching the records of all 123 war-time prisoner of war camps and prison hospitals in Japan to try to discover information about the places and causes of death of all those buried at Hodogaya. Nearly all the deaths were preventable and

were caused by malnutrition, vitamin deficiency, dysentery, tuberculosis, colitis, pneumonia, blood poisoning, septicaemia and tropical diseases such as beriberi and malaria. The records and all the reports of the Tokyo War Crimes Tribunals are held at the National Diet Library in Tokyo. Additionally, these researchers have tried, where possible, to interview survivors of those camps to find more information about the lives, families and homes of the war dead.

9.   The Japanese inscription on the memorial plate may be translated:

Now former enemies have become friends and the people of Onogawa Bay with great kindness have supported the establishment of this memorial. It is hoped that it will contribute to the repose of the souls of those who died on both sides and be a lasting symbol of peace and friendship between our two nations.

Appendix 1(c) PHILLIDA PURVIS British graves in other parts of Japan

1.   *The Foreign Cemeteries of Kobe and Osaka*, Harold S. Williams OBE, printed and distributed by the International Committee of Kansai, 1967.

2.   Ibid.

3.   Ibid.

4.   *Kobe Chronicle*, 1897

5.   Information from Tamura Yasufumi, of the Kobe Municipal Foreign Cemetery, in an interview in September 2003.

6.   Britain's Japan Consular Service 1859-1941, Jim Hoare in *Britain and Japan: Biographical Portraits* Vol. II, Chap.7.

7.   *The Foreign Cemeteries of Kobe and Osaka* by Harold S. Williams OBE, printed and distributed by the International Committee of Kansai in 1978

8.   *The Hiogo News*, 29 April 1870.

9.   *The Hiogo News*, 7 February 1872.

10.   *The Japan Daily Herald*, 30 April, 1874.

11.   *In a Foreign Graveyard, Tales of the Foreign Settlements in Japan*, Tokyo, Tuttle, 1958

12.   *Kobe Chronicle*, 11 July 1900.

13.   Open letter in the *Asahi Evening News*, 23 April 1957, to the Governor of Osaka from Harold S. Williams.

14.   *Japan's Treaty Ports and Foreign Settlements: The Uninvited Guests*, 1858-1899, Jim Hoare, Folkestone: Japan Library, 1994.

15.   Information on this and all the following Nagasaki graves is drawn from *Across the Gulf of Time: The International Cemeteries of Nagasaki*, by Lane R. Earns and Brian Burke-Gaffney, Nagasaki Bunkensha, 1991.

16.   *Secret Tales of the Nagasaki International Cemeteries*, by Brian Burke-Gaffney at www.uwosh.edu/home__pages/faculty__staff/earns/tales.html.

17.   *Across the Gulf of Time The International Cemeteries of Nagasaki*, by Lane R. Earns and Brian Burke-Gaffney, Nagasaki Bunkensha, 1991.

18.   According to newspaper accounts of the time, as described in *International Cemeteries of Nagasaki*.

19.   John Batchelor, Missionary and Friend of the Ainu by Sir Hugh Cortazzi, *Britain and Japan: Biographical Portraits Vol. II*, Ch. 16

20. Hirado also claims to have Adams' grave.
21. See biographical portrait of Hugh Fraser in *Britain and Japan Biographical Portraits* Volume IV, 2002.
22. See biographical portrait in this volume by Martin Gornall.
23. This information has been obtained through correspondence and a meeting with, and an article by Professor Murase Shinya, Professor of International Law at Sophia University and Secretary General of ILA Japan Branch in the *Year Book of International Law*, 2002.
24. The above information supplied by Komatsu Akira, September 2003.
25. See biographical portrait by Julia Boyd in *Britain and Japan: Biographical Portraits*, Volume II, 1997, also *An Englishwoman in Japan* by Julia Boyd, Tuttle, Tokyo 1996.
26. See the Mutsu Family by Ian Mutsu in *Britain and Japan: Biographical Portraits, Volume II*, 1997.
27. *Junai Eseru to Mutsu Hirokichi* (True Love Ethel and Hirokichi Mutsu) by Shimoju Akiko, Kodansha 1994.

Index of Names Mentioned in this Volume

INDEX